Games, Rhymes, and ...
Ch...

"Children's lore is a fascinating mixtu[re ...] and change. They will draw readily on t[...] ... day, and in the next minute sing a tune hundreds [...] ...They will play a game that is known the world over, but make a small change and claim it as their own. They can be sticklers for the rules, but willing to change them at a moment's notice, if circumstances dictate. And all the time they are picking up, and passing on, the language and lore of their little community. Nigel Kelsey's is without doubt the most comprehensive collection made in London in the later twentieth century, and it is especially valuable because he succeeded in capturing the children's traditional world in all its wonderful chaos, colour, and irreverence. And he was experienced enough to provide an insightful commentary on the material he found. The editors of this book have done an excellent job organising the material and providing notes and references to other collections. The result is both a scholarly reference work for generations to come, and a joy to read in the present. I defy anyone who was a child between the 1960s and 1980s to read it without being transported back in time, and without exclaiming 'We did that!', or 'That's not how it goes, our version was ...'"

—Steve Roud, author of *Folk Song in England* (2016), *The Lore of the Playground* (2011), and co-author of *A Dictionary of English Folklore* (2000) amongst other works. He is the creator of the Folk Song Index and served as Honorary Librarian of the *Folklore Society*, UK

"It is really exciting that Nigel Kelsey's collection of more than 2000 games, songs, wordplay, beliefs and practices, and other kinds of folklore from children in inner-city London is about to be published. Between 1966 and 1984, as a primary school teacher, Kelsey gathered this material from preadolescents. The quality of his scholarship is outstanding; there are many significant analyses of the historical, cultural, developmental, and social dimensions of children's folklore. With meticulous annotations, this collection constitutes a treasure trove of information and insights for scholars. It will also be of great interest to general readers who are interested in the dynamic transmission of children's traditions."

—Elizabeth Tucker, Distinguished Service Professor of English, *Binghamton University*, USA

"This book coheres with a long and honourable tradition of folkloric research and analysis. Its focus is the folklore of children – still a neglected field of academic study. The authors have built on the fieldwork of an earlier scholar to produce a learned historical, sociological and linguistic study of the playlore of children in inner London in the latter part of the twentieth century. They have connected their source material with relevant research undertaken in other countries, particularly English-speaking societies. It will interest all who seek to remember and explore the lore and language of children at play."
—June Factor, Honorary Senior Fellow, *University of Melbourne, Australia*

N. G. N. Kelsey
Author

Janet E. Alton • J. D. A. Widdowson
Editors and Annotators

Games, Rhymes, and Wordplay of London Children

palgrave
macmillan

Editors
Janet E. Alton
Centre for English Traditional Heritage
Edale, Hope Valley, UK

J. D. A. Widdowson
Centre for English Traditional Heritage
Edale, Hope Valley, UK

ISBN 978-3-030-02909-8   ISBN 978-3-030-02910-4 (eBook)
https://doi.org/10.1007/978-3-030-02910-4

Library of Congress Control Number: 2018963550

© The Editor(s) (if applicable) and The Author(s) 2019
This work is subject to copyright. All rights are solely and exclusively licensed by the Publisher, whether the whole or part of the material is concerned, specifically the rights of translation, reprinting, reuse of illustrations, recitation, broadcasting, reproduction on microfilms or in any other physical way, and transmission or information storage and retrieval, electronic adaptation, computer software, or by similar or dissimilar methodology now known or hereafter developed.
The use of general descriptive names, registered names, trademarks, service marks, etc. in this publication does not imply, even in the absence of a specific statement, that such names are exempt from the relevant protective laws and regulations and therefore free for general use.
The publisher, the authors and the editors are safe to assume that the advice and information in this book are believed to be true and accurate at the date of publication. Neither the publisher nor the authors or the editors give a warranty, express or implied, with respect to the material contained herein or for any errors or omissions that may have been made. The publisher remains neutral with regard to jurisdictional claims in published maps and institutional affiliations.

Cover illustration: © Sonja Belle / EyeEm / Getty Images

This Palgrave Macmillan imprint is published by the registered company Springer Nature Switzerland AG
The registered company address is: Gewerbestrasse 11, 6330 Cham, Switzerland

FOREWORD

Nigel Kelsey's opening line of the Introduction should stick with you. Or at least it has with me. He calls children's lore "the most real and vigorous" of London's contemporary oral traditions, and the ideas in the deceivingly simple phrase are worth thinking about. He likely meant to pin this tag on any contemporary city, raising a question about preconceptions concerning the vitality of traditional knowledge and practice, not only in the workaday city, but in the modern age always accelerating into the future. Because adults are wont to be embarrassed about acting "childish" and probably forgetting use of folklore in their own human development, Kelsey invites them to listen more closely to children's voices and watch their actions so as to appreciate what a lively, "vigorous" world they create for themselves, and often hide from adults. Grownups might presume that media and urban centrality of society have displaced passing down traditions, and Kelsey further reminds them of children's needs for social and psychological connection through folk expression. "Vigorous" is one of his favourite adjectives to describe children's activities, probably to draw out a distinction often made between the rapidity of kids compared with the "settling down" process that comes with maturity and often is accompanied by a certain fatalistic longing for a past freedom of movement. Observers often describe the playground as chaotic, even dangerous, but Kelsey discerns a reassuring cultural order from a child's eye view. What he saw, as well as heard, was not a rote reproduction of games, rhymes, and stories that elders once experienced as children, but rather imaginative variations on old themes and vibrant new expressions using familiar formulas to comment on the world of the here and now as well as in their life journeys ahead. In light of some current debates about institutional restrictions, and even banishment, of recess (Beresin 2010), he finds a predictable commotion that instead of being condemned should be lauded for representing the exciting bloom of youth and studied for what children can teach adults rather than the other way around. Using the metaphor from physics of colliding particles, writers might call the sights and sounds of childhood "dynamic" and note the paradoxical fidelity to tradition at the same time that there is an urge to create anew. Looking from the vantage of the twenty-first century, we realise that the dynamic process he described is hardly a relic of the twentieth century; it continues with ever new trajectories into the digital age.

Why is this news? At least the part about the expressive culture of youth undoubtedly was hardly novel to the students he recorded. I know from my own collecting experience that they might have been guarded about spilling the beans on their cultural world with its distinctive, even secret, language, conduct, and codes, but at the same time appreciative that adults cared to listen rather than telling them what to do, and more often than not, what not to do (Bronner 1988). They are typically unaware of the vintage of their lore or the significance of their invented traditions. Yet they do often know that this lore matters, and can comment on its meaning and function. Indeed a newsworthy aspect of Kelsey's collection is that he recorded what has been called "oral literary criticism" as well as the texts and contexts of the lore (Dundes 1966). These comments allow not just folklorists to dig deeper into the workings of tradition, but also parents, teachers, neighbours, counsellors—and adults who were once children—to grasp what kids are trying to tell about themselves, and us. Adults probably forgot the use of lore in childhood to organise and legislate themselves. They might recall with hurt the taunts, teases, and threats that separated as well as united them. They possibly remember the anxieties about the future expressed in divinations, rituals, and inscriptions, but lest they appear to affect their present, they might dismiss the lore too readily. Kelsey's collection is a chance to identify continuities, and discrepancies, of memory and an opportunity to conduct a life review or prepare to guide the next generation culturally and psychologically.

Kelsey is fairly transparent about his thinking behind "vigorous" in his opening line, but what about the "real"? Is he implying the existence of a "fake" folk culture in London and elsewhere? Kelsey certainly was not looking for children untouched by popular culture and he was not likely to find them even if he had. He did not shy away from lore informed by television and other media, and indeed his documentation of parodies and responses to popular shows is significant. He should be credited, too, with folk expressions among children generated by commercial sports. He was not, in other words, erecting a wall between folklore and modernity, but rather viewing folklore as part and parcel of contemporary society. He did not limit folklore to oral tradition, either, as his delineation of "pen and pencil games" and written inscriptions indicates. He was acutely aware, especially in the 1960s during a "folk revival", that folklore was open to exploitation in tourist and sentimental literature, and Kelsey contrasted what he heard generated by children with literary productions imposed upon children. He garnered trust among his informants to give him risqué material, although he apparently buried some items he considered too offensive, which probably meant he was worried that since his informants were minors he could potentially have been in hot water with their parents. Sure, many collectors, including the famous husband-wife team of Iona and Peter Opie (1959, 1969), gave attention to indelicate games and rhymes, but what I find especially valuable is genres such as jokes, pranks, and parodies that are part of everyday discourse among youth, but are often overlooked or underestimated. I might nonetheless hold Kelsey to task for labelling some of them "just for fun" when in their use of humour and a "play frame", they often broach a serious message. In sum, by "real" Kelsey asks us to look at the integration of folklore in everyday life rather than apart from it.

One indication of this integration is the ages of the youth from whom he collected. He notes that they mostly are between the ages of nine and eleven. Often anthologies of childlore associate any rhymes and games with a broad swath of childhood, and in the process render childhood in often romanticised terms as life before adulthood rather than in terms of human development. Indeed, some parents as well as scholars might imagine that folklore arises early in life from a lack of literacy and formal education. Kelsey was impressed with the amount of material when the children were not only literate but well along in their schooling. Their education, reliant as it was on book culture, was not a reason to abandon reliance on oral tradition. Certainly there was more that he could have done with adolescents, but he implied that the tenor of the lore changed during the teen years away from games and rhymes, and more to social customs, probably owing to post-pubertal interests. He offers evidence to a theory I proposed in *Explaining Traditions* (2011) that youth in middle childhood in modern culture use folklore more so than other times in their lives to provide adjustment to the significant, if often overlooked, emotional, social, and physical changes associated with the pre-pubescent years. Social scientists as well as humanists have been slow to recognise the distinctiveness of this age, although in popular culture, it is sometimes referred to as the "tween" years. Indeed, the betwixt and between nature of the age between toddler and teen status lends a liminal status to the age that impels folkloric functions of dealing with anxiety and paradox in the symbolic realm of folklore. Folklore, with its ritual passages, symbolic tools of expression and persuasion, and lessons for social relations and roles, takes on an extraparental role. With change as the one constant of modern life, folklore provides a familiar, reassuring type of learning, a cultural register in which children can anticipate the future and express concerns about the present. In London, as in other places representing the specially modern, children want to declare their own identity, and lore is their protected expression of cultural connection to one another. Increasingly independent at younger ages, children fiercely hang on to their cultural property to express their distinct personality and social separation from other ages. Increasingly left to themselves, and in fact separating from parents earlier, children use folklore to help them grow and cope.

Toward the admirable goal of interpreting the significance of folklore in youth culture as it affects human development and societal "dynamics", Janet Alton and J.D.A. Widdowson provide an exemplary model for identification and annotation, the first critical step in a folkloristic methodology (Bronner 2017). Annotation is a laborious and challenging task, but nonetheless essential, to establish the traditionality and context of expressions. The notes establish the historic lineage of folklore and identify those items that have arisen in contemporary settings. Their command of the literature is exceptional and they bring a world-renowned linguistic expertise to the study of children's folklore in addition to an intimate knowledge of the settings in which Kelsey collected. Alton and Widdowson are especially good at elucidating the many popular allusions contained in children's folklore that respond to media and advertisements. Indeed, they have made annotation an art form that assuredly illuminates the central significance of play in the lives of children from generation to generation, and from locality to locality. To their credit, they retained multiple versions of folkloric items, and thereby show that there is not a "correct" version but instead various expressions that children freely use and adapt. With their masterful help, Kelsey the teacher has let the students instruct us about the vigorous and real traditions of youth. They will remind us of what it means to grow up in this city, and this world, and how it affects us as grownups.

Simon J. Bronner,
Pennsylvania State University
State College, PA, USA

REFERENCES

Beresin, A. R. (2010). *Recess battles: Playing, fighting, and storytelling.* Jackson, MS: University Press of Mississippi.
Bronner, S. J. (1988). *American children's folklore.* Little Rock, AR: August House.
Bronner, S. J. (2011). *Explaining traditions: Folk behavior in modern culture.* Lexington, KY: University Press of Kentucky.
Bronner, S. J. (2017). *Folklore: The basics.* London: Routledge.
Dundes, A. (1966). "Metafolklore and oral literary criticism". *Monist, 50,* 505–516.
Opie, I, and Opie, P. (1959). *The lore and language of schoolchildren.* Oxford: Clarendon Press.
Opie, I, and Opie, P. (1969). *Children's games in street and playground.* Oxford: Clarendon Press.

PREFACE

This collection of some 2000 games, rhymes, songs, and wordplay of London children has its roots in Nigel Kelsey's work as a primary school teacher in the city. In a career spanning some thirty years, first as a class teacher in Stepney, and later as a deputy head in West Norwood and headteacher in Walworth, his interest in children's traditional lore continued to develop. It was undoubtedly boosted during fieldwork in 1966–68 for his thesis on *Speech and Creative Writing of Fourth Year Junior School Children*, submitted for the University of London Diploma in the Education of Children in Junior School, which was awarded to him in 1969. To smooth the way towards recording the essential information for this research, he first encouraged children to talk freely about their traditional activities, rhymes, and linguistic play. This early foray obviously fired his enthusiasm for the subject, and after his retirement in 1982 he embarked on an ambitious project to investigate the traditional lore and the speech of children in twenty-one Inner London schools in the period 1982–84, partially underpinned by material he had collected in the 1960s. However, it soon became clear that this dual approach would not be practicable, especially in view of the overall aim to publish the material. Consequently, he decided to focus on the traditional lore rather than combining this with a detailed analytical study of the spoken language.[1] Even so, the fieldwork proved so successful, and the material so rich and varied, that the collection offers a revealing snapshot of children's speech and language play in London in the second half of the twentieth century.

Once the fieldwork was over, the daunting task of transcribing the taperecordings and collating the data began. Nigel Kelsey not only completed this work in record time, but also produced the original typewritten manuscript of the collection in 1986. He offered to make the collected material available to students and other researchers by depositing a copy of the typescript in the archives of the National Centre for English Cultural Tradition at the University of Sheffield in 1989. This prompted an offer to work with him in editing the material for publication. Discussions on his views and intentions for the manuscript were conducted by correspondence and the occasional meeting. However, by the time the typescript was received, Nigel Kelsey had become seriously ill, and collaborative efforts were cut short by his death in 1990, at which point only preliminary editing had been undertaken. He bequeathed to the Centre the whole of the material on children's traditional lore which he had collected in the field, together with his manuscript notes and additional information.[2] This was later transferred to the Special Collections Department of the University Library.

The editing of the manuscript continued throughout the 1990s, with the aim of preserving the original as completely as possible. The guiding principle here was respect for the author's work, and for his intentions and expectations regarding publication, many of which are outlined in his Introduction. Consequently, at this point editorial intervention in the main body of the work was minimal, being confined to essential corrections and clarifications. In these early stages a succession of voluntary researchers and students at the Centre assisted with checking and proofreading the manuscript and the necessary revisions. The manuscript was then retyped, retaining the content, arrangement, and overall conception of the original, including the collector's grouping together of examples which have similar characteristics and functions. The whole work was also reformatted in a consistent style of presentation to aid accessibility.

At first sight, the editorial process appeared to be relatively straightforward. However, it was soon realised that there were various ways in which the work as it stood – already a substantial body of data – could be enhanced to provide a unique resource for the researcher and the interested general reader alike. Nigel Kelsey had consulted many of the reference works on children's play then extant, and had noted, beneath each of his own collected items, the authors and abbreviated titles of any printed sources in which he had found parallels, but he had not included page numbers. Readers trying to pinpoint these precedents and similarities in the printed sources would therefore have had to search for them, using only the author and title of the relevant publication as a starting point. The long and challenging process of identifying each reference as precisely as possible then began. During this process, careful checking of each printed source revealed many more parallels and a few additional publications which had not been noted in the first round of editing. Fortunately, by this stage the revised typescript had been digitally captured, which facilitated the complex task of identifying and adding the essential page references. Numerous additional parallels were also found at a late stage by close examination of the Rowland Kellett manuscript deposited in the Vaughan Williams Memorial Library of the English Folk Dance and Song Society. Nigel Kelsey had made tantalising reference to only two parallels in Kellett's work, so may not have had full access to the manuscript during his research. The checking process inevitably proved extremely time-consuming, and was exacerbated by the fact that some of the more obscure references were not traceable in the extensive material bequeathed to the Centre, and not easily identifiable in library holdings or media records.

It was then decided to trace and present only those selective references to publications already accessible to Nigel Kelsey at the time the original manuscript was completed in 1986. This reflected his preliminary annotation of the material in the context of works published up to that date, and we therefore resisted the temptation to trace parallels in works published subsequently. The decision was also prompted by the difficulties already experienced in checking and verifying the thousands of specific references in the wide range of sources published before that date. A period of more intensive work on the references in 2000–02 generated the bulk of this information. It then remained to track down those in the more obscure and elusive printed sources. As a result, it has been possible to reference the most significant of the relevant printed sources published before 1986, and also a number of the lesser known works – over 160 publications in total. Consequently, many of the references to numerous variants and similarities in children's traditional lore from the early nineteenth century onwards have been gathered together in this collection, providing a unique reference resource and a useful starting point for further investigation. The references set the London examples in the wider context of the British Isles and other parts of the English-speaking world, and demonstrate the wide distribution both of genres and individual items of play over time and space. The parallels identified are of course not exhaustive, but nevertheless represent a substantial cross-section of illustrative examples. Readers may wish to consult the Selected Further Reading section (p. 803), which lists both pre-1986 works not consulted by Nigel Kelsey and works published after the present collection was completed in 1986, for pointers in extending the search for parallels.

Nigel Kelsey aimed to offer a representative range of material from a specific age-group (nine to eleven years) in a way that would clearly indicate the geographical spread of children's traditional lore across the area then covered by the Inner London Education Authority, as well as the broad social grouping in the catchment area of each school, and the gender of many individual contributors. In marked contrast to most previous collections, this not only provides important contextual information, but also offers pathways for further exploration and analysis of the data. The dating of examples tells us when each was in current usage, and illustrates development over a period of some twenty years, reflecting the author's awareness that these traditional forms change with the social world around them. It also facilitates direct comparison with the only other extensive collection of London childlore (Norman Douglas's *London Street Games*, 1916) and with other more recent publications.[3]

Unusually in collections of childlore, Nigel Kelsey provides essential information on the scope of the taperecorded data and the methodology he adopted during fieldwork, and he comments revealingly on the reaction to his work by the schoolchildren and their teachers. He worked systematically with small groups of ten to twelve children in each school. Drawing on his long experience as a primary school teacher, he was extraordinarily successful in establishing rapport with the children and gaining their trust. His self-effacing account of the collecting process makes it sound easy, whereas anyone who has attempted it knows how difficult it is. It requires special skills, and a genuine and sympathetic interest in children and their traditional play, to encourage them to share their games, rhymes, and wordplay, especially the more risqué examples, with an adult. Nigel Kelsey's personality, skills, approachability, tact, and knowledge of children enabled him not only to collect a wide range of material but also rhymes and wordplay from parts of the child's world which are normally hidden from adults, reflecting his liberal and broadminded approach. He was even able to record some of the children's own attitudes to such material, and he presents it verbatim and uncensored, while drawing attention to the comparative lack of "unrespectable" examples in most previous collections. The terminology and social attitudes evident in these examples of course reflect those of the period in which they were recorded. However, he omitted some items which "seemed to offend the general consensus of children's extremely liberal conceptions of good taste" (p. xxxiv). The collection also omits examples "which seemed to lack any pattern or shape in meaning or structure" (p. xxxiii), and those apparently made up on the spur of the moment, again demonstrating the author's proficiency and sophistication as a collector. He adds that the collection is not representative of the traditional lore of younger children in the area.

Differing from Douglas's work in many respects, notably in its breadth, depth, and verbatim quotations of data taperecorded during the fieldwork, this collection ranges widely over the whole field of Inner London children's traditional lore in this age-group, including superstitions and seasonal customs, providing copious and detailed examples and variants. These are presented in a sequence of categories based partly on function and partly on subject matter, although distinctions between categories are inevitably blurred. For example, a given rhyme may serve several different functions. These and other similarities between various games and rhymes are signalled by cross-references. The work therefore constitutes a major new resource, not only for the study of childlore in the capital but also for comparison with other collections, especially those from Britain and Ireland, and other predominantly English-speaking countries.

In many ways, this book is a celebration of what the author describes as "the great wealth of traditional and newly created material to be found in almost every school playground" (p. xxiii) in Inner London at the time he was collecting. The evidence amply demonstrates the resilience, creativity, and adaptability of childlore in a rapidly changing world where many adults wrongly believe that such traditional activities are in terminal decline or have disappeared altogether. Such misconceptions[4] are not only proved unfounded by the extensive material presented here, but also by studies undertaken in Britain in more recent years.[5] Comparison with these accounts will indicate the changes which have taken place in children's traditions over the past three decades, not least the effects of the increasingly multicultural mix in London schools and those of many other urban communities in Britain.

In addition to the discussion of the collected material in the Introduction, Nigel Kelsey prefaces each section and subsection of the publication with an introductory commentary foregrounding the characteristic features of the genre concerned. The Introduction and the commentaries, which reflect the situational context of the fieldwork in the early 1980s, offer valuable insights into a range of topics arising from the author's experiences in collecting and scrutinising the material. These topics include the differences in repertoire from one school to another; gender roles; generational traditions; pre-game elimination rituals; the history, provenance, and current representation of individual games and rhymes; games and rhymes learned in the classroom or in Scout and Guide groups and modified in the playground; skipping as a solo and group activity; the interaction between traditional and popular culture; variation and terminology in ball games; references in rhymes to well-known figures; sources of inspiration for new or adapted material; hybrid rhymes; formulaic structures in rhymes; adaptability and mutation of rhymes; linguistic creativity and enjoyment; effects of social change; inevitability of change in children's traditional play; similarities and differences between the traditional beliefs and practices of children and adults; and optimism about the resilience and future of traditional play.

Nigel Kelsey not only presents condensed and informative comments on these wideranging topics, but also discusses children's attitudes towards risqué and scatological material, offering insights into the well-known preoccupation with bodily functions and sex in this age group.[6] This aspect of the child's world, usually hidden from and strongly disapproved of by adults, is seen as part of the experimental process of self-assertion and of challenging authority, which children normally grow out of as they mature. Children's awareness of language "unacceptable" to adults is illustrated by their occasional censorship of their own material during the fieldwork, as noted in the Introduction (p. xliii). While the subject matter of some of the material may be uncomfortable for adults, the language used is for the most part surprisingly unexceptionable. It would be interesting to discover whether this still holds true in playgrounds today.[7]

A particular strength of the book is the wealth of evidence of children's spoken language, amply displayed in their descriptions of games and rhymes, transcribed verbatim from the field recordings, and preserving both the immediacy and the flavour of speech. These descriptions are often both graphic and concise, and add an important dimension to the data which is frequently absent from other collections. It also gives the children a voice, and the freedom to speak for themselves.

After the Introduction, the collection is presented in six sections, each with a number of subsections. Following the introductory overview of each section and subsection, the collected material relevant to the section or subsection is set out, together with a range of significant variants. The annotation includes information on locality, distribution, printed versions, early notings, audio recordings, cross-references and, where necessary, brief elucidatory notes. The typical order of presentation is displayed on pp. xxi–xxii.

The extraordinary wealth of material collected mainly over a period of just two years testifies not only to the vigour and variety of local children's traditions but also to Nigel Kelsey's decision to undertake such a challenging project and to analyse and present the results of his findings. Surprisingly little systematic and extensive fieldwork has been carried out on children's traditions in England in recent years.[8] Nigel Kelsey's collection is unique in its focus on a carefully defined geographical area over a comparatively short period of time, and in the sheer volume of data recorded – the only such substantial collection in the city since that of Douglas seventy years earlier. It fills a major gap in our knowledge of childlore, especially in a specific urban area, and provides incontrovertible evidence of the richness and vibrancy of children's traditional play in the heart of London in the late twentieth century.

Over the years during which this collection has been prepared for publication, the editors have appreciated the assistance and support of the many people who have been involved with the project, whether directly or indirectly. The fieldwork would not have been possible without the agreement of the Inner London Education Authority and of the headteachers and staff of the schools concerned. During the writing up of the collection, Nigel Kelsey greatly valued the advice, help, and encouragement of Marilyn Jorgensen, Iona Opie, Cecilia Riddell, Dave Rogers, Steve Roud, and Jacqueline Simpson. Preliminary checking of the original manuscript was undertaken by Tony Pike and other voluntary staff and students in the National Centre for English Cultural Tradition at the University of Sheffield. The retyped and successive typeset drafts of the emerging final version of the work were proofread and pre-edited by Celia Robinson. The editors are grateful to Paul Smith and Steve Roud for their assistance, especially in identifying a number of the more elusive references, to Joy Fraser who tracked down other problematical references in various London libraries and elsewhere, to Malcolm Taylor for making a copy of the Rowland Kellett manuscript available to us, to June Factor for advice on published Australian childlore collections, to Country Publications and Linda McFadzean for providing a copy of D. Dennison's article on singing games published in *The Dalesman*, to Laura Smyth for supplying copies of two articles by Muriel Searle, to Helen Lewis and Philip Maughan for identifying material published in the *New Statesman*, to Sarah McDonnell for information on the *Woodcraft Folk Song Book*, to Herbert Halpert for his encouragement and his assistance with bibliographical references and proofreading, and to Steve Dumpleton for drafting diagrams of hopscotch markings and for ongoing technical expertise and advice. We especially thank Eileen Collins, Publications Assistant in the Department of Folklore at the Memorial University of Newfoundland, whose exemplary typesetting skills transformed a complex, partially edited typescript into an accessible format for its final editing. We are indebted to successive Deans of Arts and Heads of the Department of Folklore at Memorial University for their support of the editorial work. We are grateful to the Leverhulme Trust for the award of an Emeritus Fellowship, providing the essential financial infrastructure for the preparation of the work for publication, and to the Division of Adult Continuing Education at the University of Sheffield for a grant towards the costs of research assistance. We also thank Cathy Scott and Beth Farrow, our editors at Palgrave Macmillan, for their guidance and support. We particularly wish to thank Mrs V. E. Kelsey-Jansen and Mrs P. J. Roberts for facilitating a generous bequest from Nigel Kelsey's estate as a contribution towards the editing of the collection, and for their patience and forbearance over the long period leading up to its publication. Our greatest debt of gratitude, of course, is to all the children who shared their wealth of traditional lore during the fieldwork, and to Nigel Kelsey himself for his foresight in undertaking this remarkable project, and his courage and determination, despite increasing ill health, to bring it to a successful conclusion.

Edale, Hope Valley, UK   The Editors

NOTES

1. See Wiltshire, R. (2001). *The Nigel Kelsey Collection of children's folklore, 1962–1990. Repository and Media Guide, Archives of Cultural Tradition.* Sheffield: National Centre for English Cultural Tradition, p. 34.
2. See Wiltshire, 2001, pp. 28–34; Wiltshire, R. (2001, April). The Nigel Kelsey Collection of children's folklore, 1962–1990. *Folklore, 112*(1), 82–87; and Wiltshire, R. (2002). The Nigel Kelsey Collection of children's folklore, 1962–1990. *Folk Life, 40,* 72–79. Robin Wiltshire also created a comprehensive catalogue of the Kelsey Collection during his work as Archivist at the National Centre for English Cultural Tradition at the University of Sheffield.
3. The most immediately relevant of these works, an illustrated book aimed at children, is *Inky Pinky Ponky* (Rosen and Steele, 1982), the games and rhymes in which were collected in Inner London at the same time as Nigel Kelsey was working, and which contains many striking parallels.
4. As noted, for example, in Roud (2010, pp. xi–xv). See Selected Further Reading.
5. See, for example, Bishop and Curtis (2001); Green and Widdowson (2003); Marsh (2008); Marsh and Bishop (2013); Opie (1993); Opies (1997); and Roud (2010). See Bibliography and Selected Further Reading.

6. See Introduction, pp. xlii–xliii. See also, for example, Knapps (1976, pp. 61–63, 82–94, 179–190, 211–216); Lowenstein (1974, 1986, 1988, 1989); Opies (1969, pp. 93–97); Opie (1993, pp. 9–10, 14–15, 26, 39–41, 86–87, 160, and passim); Turner (1969, p. 2, and passim); and Wolfenstein (1978, pp. 168–181, and passim). See Bibliography and Selected Further Reading.
7. An indication of recent trends can be found, for example, in Lowenstein (1974), Green and Widdowson (2003, pp. 361–509), and Roud (2010, pp. 413–437). See Bibliography and Selected Further Reading.
8. See, however, Bishop and Curtis (2001); Green and Widdowson (2003); Marsh (2008); Roud (2010); and Marsh and Bishop (2013). See Selected Further Reading.

THE COLLECTION: KEY TO PRESENTATION OF ENTRIES

SECTION NAME, Table of Contents where applicable, and introductory notes
SUBSECTION NAME and introductory notes

Reference number (and title if a rhyme or song, etc.)	Reference numbers run consecutively through each subsection In the case of games with rhymes, the title is usually the first line of the primary example
Illustrative examples and variants, with places and dates of collection	The occasional emendation, clarification, or alternative wording of the transcripts by the author is indicated by brackets. Where similar versions were collected at more than one school, the place and year where the quoted example was collected are underlined, e.g.: Walworth 1979; <u>Dalston, Borough 1983</u> The localities are listed alphabetically within the entries for each year
Child's description of example(s)	Given where possible in the child's own words
Cross-references and/or notes where applicable	These draw attention to other examples in the collection which have a similar form and/or function. Individual genres, sections, and subsections can be located by reference to the Table of Contents, and in the case of rhymes to the Index, p. 811
Tune name, where applicable	
Printed versions	References here are from all works consulted (see Bibliography). Page numbers are given for works cited which were published after the end of the Second World War. References are listed alphabetically by authors' names. Where more than one work by the same author(s) is cited, or where several authors share the same surname, each publication has been given an identifying acronym or abbreviation (for a list of these, see p. 795; full details of all publications referenced can be found in the Bibliography, p. 779)
Early notings	References from works published prior to 1945 are given here in full. They are listed in date order and quote the earliest printed version identified, plus any interesting versions intermediate between this and later examples
Commercially available recordings	See Discography, p. 801

INTRODUCTION

It is probably not an overstatement to claim that children's lore is the most real and vigorous of the oral folklore still alive in London. While my experience does not cover the central areas of large cities in the United Kingdom in general, the two books by Ritchie on Edinburgh children's lore (*SS*, 1964; *GC*, 1965), and Shaw's books about Liverpool (1969, 1970), seem to indicate that city folklore has a wider relevance than what is to be found in the school playground. As someone who has lived and worked through more than six decades in Inner London, apart from children's lore I have encountered the changing aspects of dialects and slang, a few ephemeral parodies, large numbers of risqué jokes, a few urban legends, some obscene songs and verses, but not much more. Most books on Cockney lore tend to dwell considerably on the past. Certainly the rich humour which tends to be associated with this lore seems to be very much on the decline.

All in all I think that what is still left does not add up to very much, in comparison with the great wealth of traditional and newly created material to be found in almost every school playground. I have been fortunate enough in a career of thirty-two years in primary teaching to have spent long periods in three separate and different Inner London school environments and to have been able to observe and note some of the traditional processes at work. These observations have been supplemented by briefer experiences in a number of other schools. Towards the end of

1982 I embarked on a study of all the aspects of children's lore that are generally covered by that term. It involved visiting and recording in twenty-one schools in the area of what was then the Inner London Education Authority and covering a wide social spectrum in all the Authority's ten divisions. The study took two years and included the transcription of about thirty hours of audiotape. Because of the limited timescale, and its coverage of the whole of an inner city area, the study is unique.

Many collections of children's lore, especially of the rhymes and songs used to accompany games activities, have been compiled and published in the English-speaking world over the last century and a half. They have tended to concentrate on singing games, action rhymes, and songs and rhymes used to accompany skipping, ball bouncing and hand clapping routines. Sometimes the collector has restricted the material to a particular region or city, or has covered a specific country. Rarely has the collection of versions of rhymes and other material been restricted to a specific period of time. London has not been well served by such collectors. The only fairly large collection is contained in *London Street Games,* compiled by Norman Douglas. It was first published in 1916 and a further edition appeared in 1931. Both contained ninety-three rhymes, the beginnings of a further forty-six and the titles of twenty-four others. Douglas also listed the names of nearly 800 different games, and gave rudimentary descriptions of sixty-six of them, though he did not attempt to analyse them or explain how they were played. He did not set out to compile a scholarly collection. In fact he made fun of the attempts to explain the origins of courtship rhymes etc., by reference to ancient rituals. He did not include any examples of wordplay, repartee, taunts and the like, for this was not his aim. His intention was that no interpolations or explanations should come between his readers and the vigour and flow of children's rhymes and songs used in play, where one will follow another, often without any interruption or discussion among the children at play.

Examples of London's children's lore appear in writings about childhood memories of London streets and playgrounds. In their book on Cockney lore, *The Muvver Tongue* (1980), Barltrop and Wolveridge give several, as does Charles Keeping in his song book *Cockney Ding Dong* (1975). Grace Foakes remembers some rhymes from her childhood in *My Part of the River*

(1974). Dan Jones, an East London artist, reproduced the words used in play, alongside the groups of children performing them, in a picture of an East London playground painted in 1975. He also included play rhymes in several of his illustrations for the picture book *Inky Pinky Ponky* (Rosen and Steele, 1982). I have received many details of rhymes and games from older citizens, now living all over the country, who remember the games they played in their London childhood, from twenty to as long as seventy years before the present collection was completed. It is frustrating to anyone interested in this lore that so little information is available in print about the circumstances in which the games were played, or about the age or gender of the children taking part. In the case of Norman Douglas's collection we are not told how he noted or recorded his material, over how long a period the collecting took place, or whether he used adult memories of informants to supplement the information from children.

If we look at collectors in other regions of the British Isles, there are two little books of street games from North Shields, dating from 1926 and 1930, compiled by Madge and Robert King. Alfred Gaskell remembers the rhymes of Salford in *Those Were the Days* (1963). A very informative little work published at the University of Durham, and entitled *All the Way to Pennywell* (Rutherford, 1971), contains a large number of rhymes used for various purposes, in many cases with their tunes. It covers the North East area and includes some valuable information from its compiler. Frank Shaw does a rather different job for the rhymes of Liverpool in his two compilations entitled *You Know me Anty Nelly?* from 1969 and 1970 which, like Norman Douglas's book, are intended to be read straight through to appreciate the oral flow. It certainly brings the children's street culture of that fascinating city to life. Many rhymes and fragments are included in the text. A book about singing games and other traditional games in a Nottingham primary school, with clear details of how these are played, was compiled by its headmaster, R. A. Smith, and published, together with a video, in 1982.

When we turn to Scotland there are the two invaluable books noted above about Edinburgh's rich oral lore by James T. R. Ritchie: *The Singing Street* (SS, 1964) and *Golden City* (GC, 1965). A booklet with some of the play rhymes of a school in Ayrshire was compiled at Cumnock Academy in 1961 and entitled *Bluebells my Cockle Shells*. Norah and

William Montgomerie included much play material in their four volumes of Scottish nursery rhymes (*SNR*, 1946; *SC*, 1948; *HBSNR*, 1964; 1966), and there is also a valuable little booklet by Jean Rodger based on personal memory (1958). Ireland is served by Leslie Daiken, who covers the children's calendar in his *Children's Games Throughout the Year* (*CGTY*, 1949) and includes a number of play rhymes (mainly from Ireland) in his *Teaching Through Play* (*TTP*, 1954). He also compiled a little book of Dublin rhymes: *Out Goes She* (*OGS*, 1963). Another Dublin collection is *All In! All In!* by Eilís Brady (1975).

Over the years almost the whole field of children's culture has been covered by Iona and Peter Opie. Their first book to comprehensively cover children's rhymes, superstitions, sayings, epithets etc. was their great work *The Lore and Language of Schoolchildren* (*LL*, 1959), but it has been well complemented by their later publications, *Children's Games in Street and Playground* (*CGSP*, 1969) and *The Singing Game* (*SG*, 1985), and their earlier little book *I Saw Esau* (*ISE*, 1947). Invaluable collections of the lore pertaining to younger children are Gullen's *Traditional Number Rhymes and Games* (1950), and *Number Rhymes and Finger Plays* by Boyce and Bartlett (1941). Typical settings of singing games to music are those of Kidson (1916), Gillington (*OHSG*, *OIWSG*, *OSSG*, 1909; *ODSG*, 1913), and Thornhill (1911), while Ewan MacColl and Dominic Behan recorded children's songs from their childhoods in Glasgow, Salford and Dublin on an LP record entitled *Streets of Song* (1959).

Moving on to important overseas collections covering similar material, there are Brian Sutton-Smith's outstanding book *The Games of New Zealand Children* (1959), Edith Fowke's *Sally Go Round the Sun* from Canada (1969), and Ian Turner's important Australian collection *Cinderella Dressed in Yella* (1969). Caribbean rhymes and games can be found in the works of Beckwith and Roberts (*FGJ*, 1922), Beckwith (*JFL*, 1928), Elder (1965), and Robertson (1971). There are many American collections, of which only a few can be mentioned here. The wide field of American folklore is covered by Botkin's *A Treasury of American Folklore* (*TAF*, 1944) and *Folklore in America* by Coffin and Cohen (1966). Both have sections dealing with children's lore. Some works dealing with specific aspects of children's rhymes are those by Abrahams (1969), Abrahams and Rankin (1980), Evans

(*JRR*, 1954; *WI*, 1956), Morrison (1958), the Petershams (1945), Withers (*CO*, 1946, 1970; *RIMP*, 1948), and Worstell (1961). Talley's *Negro Folk Rhymes* (1922) and *The Book of Negro Folklore* by Hughes and Bontemps (1958) are concerned with African American culture, including that of children.

Turning to some of the early collectors of the nineteenth century, Chambers's *The Popular Rhymes of Scotland* (first published 1826), Halliwell's *The Nursery Rhymes of England* (*NRE*, first published 1842) and *Popular Rhymes and Nursery Tales* (*PRNT*, first published 1849), Northall's *English Folk-Rhymes* (first published 1892), and Nicholson's *Golspie* (1897) all contain some traditional rhymes as well as much material mainly transmitted by adults. It was probably Henry Bolton's *The Counting-out Rhymes of Children*, published in London in 1888, containing hundreds of rhymes and variations used to decide who was to be "he" or the equivalent, which was the first significant collection of genuine children's folklore. Most of the material for Bolton's volume was collected in the USA and the first important collection of children's singing (and other) games was also American. This was William Wells Newell's *Games and Songs of American Children*, first published in New York in 1883. It contains nearly two hundred games, including the words and tunes of many singing games. Versions and rhymes noted in both these sources were still to be found in Inner London school playgrounds at the time of writing.

The first really extensive collection of children's games in these islands was made by Alice Bertha Gomme in her great two volume work entitled *The Traditional Games of England, Scotland and Ireland* published in 1894 and 1898, and reprinted in 1984 in a one volume edition. The original two thick volumes contained the names of, and information on, more than 800 games, some 600 being described in detail. Many variants of the singing games are given, but counting-out rhymes and the vast field of wordplay were obviously outside the scope of the work. Her collection of games, as the title denotes, was drawn from most parts of Britain and Ireland. They were not limited to those in contemporary use and several may have been extinct by the time the volumes were published. She relied on correspondents, on her own collecting, and on printed sources, although many of the citations from printed sources are not followed by a description. It is not clear what age the children were who played particular games, and as some games appear to be of an indoor "party" type, there may have been a certain amount of adult organisation and direction involved. It is still a great work, however, and invaluable for anyone interested in children's play.

Almost all the books cited above are either, on the one hand, specifically limited to a particular category of children's lore, or in some cases to a particular school or area, or on the other hand, cover large areas. In no case were they limited to a particular period. I had a different aim in my study. I wished to cover a specific area, namely Inner London, and to restrict myself basically to the years of my research, 1982–84, supplemented by material I had collected from 1960 to 1982, either as a class teacher or headmaster, using this earlier material to fill gaps or throw light on the tradition. Furthermore, the material was collected from children roughly between the ages of nine and eleven, who are full of their currently used repertoire but can look back to their younger years very easily and without embarrassment. At the same time they pick up a lot of material from elder siblings and friends and from young and old adults.

I aimed to present a representative collection of children's lore, which would however have the limitations of not being fully representative of infant and younger junior children (five to eight), nor of secondary age children (twelve plus). All the examples in each section were collected by me within the bounds of the Inner London Education Authority which in 1963 replaced the old London County Council, set up in 1888. The material is drawn from all of the ten divisions of the Authority (pp. xlv–xlvi).

The overwhelming majority of the examples reproduced were collected from schools visited between 1982 and 1984. In certain cases some material is included from schools in which I taught from 1960 to 1982, and a few items collected from an earlier small study in 1968. These earlier examples sometimes give fuller versions of, or represent, rhymes which were still current at the time of the present study, in the early 1980s, though not collected for one reason or another. They also help to illustrate the development of the tradition over a period of up to twenty years, each example being dated.

The schools visited in the two year period were selected with the help of the Authority in order to cover the widest possible social range. In most of the ten divisions it was possible for me to visit on the one hand a school mainly limited to children whose parents were unskilled or semi-skilled, and on the other hand a school with a fair number of children whose parents were from professional or managerial occupations, or one with a balanced make-up right across the social spectrum. There were some difficulties in always obtaining an accurate breakdown of the social composition in several of the schools visited or of the actual classes or groups who were my informants. However, it became clear that the twenty-one schools visited fell roughly into three categories:

1. Schools where the majority of the children came from professional, managerial and "white collar" families.
2. Schools where the overwhelming majority of the children came from semi-skilled, unskilled and unwaged families.
3. Schools where there was a fairly balanced social composition.

In the two-year survey there were eight schools in category a., nine in category b., and four in category c. Of the three schools in which I taught for a fairly long period, two were in category b., and one in category c. In those three schools I was able to observe the processes of change and innovation over a number of years, nine years in the case of the first school (1960–69), four years in the second (1969–73), and eight years in the third (1974–82). In the case of the first school, which was in Mile End, East London, I visited it as one of the schools included in the survey in 1983. In the schools surveyed a number of other variables affected the extent and the composition of the collected material: gender balance, size of groups, numbers of visits made, and other miscellaneous factors. It can be deduced that children in category a. schools would tend not to play so much in public playgrounds and probably not at all in the courtyards of blocks of flats and in the streets. They would have less practice in acquiring and passing on the skills in ball bouncing etc., or in learning new material from children attending other schools. It was noticeable that most of the examples of inter-school chauvinism came from schools in this category.

The rhymes to accompany skipping, ball bouncing, and hand clapping routines, and the songs for games, mime, and dance were mainly (but not entirely) contributed by girls. A majority of the entertainment rhymes, wordplay, teases etc. were contributed by boys. Counting-out rhymes were provided equally by boys and girls. The question of the integration of boys' and girls' play appears to be a controversial one among folklorists specialising in children's play and customs. Father Damian Webb, for whose work I have a very great respect, expressed himself in his introduction to the 1984 edition of Gomme's *Traditional Games* as being concerned at the effects of the integration of play spaces in schools. He writes (p. 15):

> I am convinced that nothing in this century has done more to destroy our ancient and precious heritage of the singing game tradition than to force boys and girls to play together on the very limited area most junior schools possess.

He considers that "the imposition of mixed sex schooling has dealt a terrible blow to traditional children's games." (p. 15).

When I first became interested in collecting children's play rhymes etc. in the 1960s, many junior schools in Inner London had separate playgrounds or play areas for boys and girls. Now integration is almost universal. I do not share Damian Webb's pessimism, nor do I believe that integrated playgrounds *force* boys and girls to play together, though it obviously makes it much easier. The tendency to break down the old gender differences, whether in playgrounds, lining up, seating arrangements, curriculum or organised games activities, has been encouraged by the Inner London Education Authority as well as the Equal Rights Commission. In my opinion it has only dented the stereotype images of how pre-pubescents are expected to behave. Social changes in the community as a whole have probably played a bigger part in bringing about changes in children's play.

Sluckin tends to emphasise the gender differences, pointing out that in boys' games the emphasis is more on physical strength, achievement, and competitiveness, while in girls' games there is less competitiveness, a greater equality between roles, and an interest in family life. He says (1981, pp. 102–103):

… in public boys and girls will pour scorn on each other. The attraction of teasing, and games like 'kiss-chase', is that they allow children to give vent to a growing interest in the opposite sex. But in both activities, they still have to be wary not to be seen to enjoy themselves. A boy will only let himself be kissed by the girl who catches him after a symbolic struggle. But, as children pass through puberty, the attitudes that can be seen in teasing and 'kiss chase' become more and more a part of everyday life.

In many junior schools, **3.D.7** KISS CHASE was once almost the only playground game shared equally by boys and girls. My researches however indicate that both the more physical games like **3.A.28** BULLDOG, and the gentler ones like **3.B.6** PEEP BEHIND THE CURTAIN and **3.D.2** FORTY-FORTY, are played by boys and girls together, as well as separately, in many playgrounds. I think a lot of assumptions about gender roles may have to be revised. While I would not like to draw firm conclusions from my experiences in the three types of school referred to above, it was noticeable that in schools in category a. there were apparently fewer singing games, skipping rhymes etc., and more games played by boys and girls together, which obviously left less time for activities generally considered to belong to girls. There appeared to be much more wordplay; at least more of this was volunteered, which may not be the same thing. In the schools in category b. there was a richer repertoire of singing games as well as skipping, ball bouncing, and hand clapping rhymes. The boys tended to play more games on their own and there were fewer riddles and examples of wordplay. The schools in category c. varied widely in their traditional play, not only from those in categories a. and b., but also from each other.

I do not know how children's rhymes and games will develop in the future. What is certain is that they are bound to change, to develop, and some to disappear. Some traditions will remain and others vanish. New traditions will be established and they will tend to reflect the wider society of which children form a part. Some delightful things (or what many of us now consider to be delightful) will be found no longer. We cannot expect society to stand still in order to preserve any particular physical or language activity, whatever value judgments are put on this by some folklorists.

My personal belief is that a healthier gender relationship depends in part on changes in gender imprinting. While certain roles which have become hallowed by time continue to be expected from boys and from girls, the process of change will be slowed down but it cannot be halted. Fortunately we have come a long way since those days more than half a century ago when as a lad of thirteen years I had to go into the girls' playground at playtime for the first time to deliver a message and was embarrassed to see a row of girls with their dresses tucked into their knickers, doing handstands against the school wall. *All* the children's lore which I can remember from my childhood (apart from nursery material) came from boys. Boys and girls even sat on different sides of the classroom and stood on different sides of the hall for assembly. My headmaster was considered to be a daringly progressive innovator!

Turning now to the methods used to collect the data for the present study, all the material presented here was initially recorded on cassettes and then transcribed. Most of it was recorded during group sessions in classroom, school library or spare room. Though much of the material was contributed by individual children, it was sometimes amended or supplemented by other members of the group. Many of the singing games and the like could only be satisfactorily recorded by a group singing or reciting together. A version volunteered by one child might stimulate others to provide a different version. Thus there was not always a single definitive version from a particular school.

The groups of ten to twelve children (and sometimes much larger) were representative of their school class but not necessarily of the age group within a particular school. Sometimes, though rarely, I was able to record parallel classes within the same school. The repertoire and the versions might both differ from those of the parallel class. It does not follow that every rhyme or saying I was given was in current use within the school, but material not generally known would usually be in the category of entertainment and wordplay. On the other hand I did not record every rhyme or game then in use by children in the group or among their peers. However, as I covered the whole Inner London area, I do not think that much material in widespread use escaped being recorded somewhere during the fieldwork.

No two schools, or even groups within a school, have the same repertoire. Every school I visited yielded a number of unique items that I did not encounter anywhere else. Many are of an ephemeral nature because they lack the ingredients that would ensure their survival even within the same play group, let alone the school, or the wider dispersal outside. I decided on the method of recording group sessions mainly because of difficulties encountered in using other methods which require more time and yield less material. Most of the rhymes and games were given to me in response to suggestions, questions or actual first lines. In dealing with counting-out rhymes I might start a fairly well-known example and ask the children to complete it or give me their alternative version. I would then ask them for other examples of "dips" and of various ways of starting a game and determining who was to be "he" or "it".

In order to cover the number of schools and to avoid upsetting school arrangements too much, I limited myself to a maximum of four visits of an hour's duration, preferably with a group of ten to twelve children, made up equally of both boys and girls, but sometimes the groups were larger than this and occasionally smaller. Usually I was able to have the same group on each visit and this cut down wasted time in duplicating examples. Sometimes the groups varied and I even had groups from different classes in one or two schools. Occasionally I might have just girls in a group, as I found they were sometimes diffident in the presence of boys and were loath to give me some of their action rhymes and other items.

Of the twenty-one schools visited, I was able to achieve only three visits in the case of four schools and only two visits in the case of one school. I would usually transcribe the recording between visits. This helped to avoid repetition, to complete fragmented offerings or clear up doubts in the case of a poor recording. I have not been able to present every single example and every different version collected, but I have included the maximum possible. Only those which seemed to lack any pattern or shape in meaning or structure have been excluded, along with those which give the appearance of having been made up by the child more or less on the spur of the moment without much thought. A child may do this in trying to hold his/her own with children who have extensive repertoires.

I have included, however, a fair number of ephemeral rhymes and examples of wordplay which, like so many mutants in the natural world, will die and leave behind no trace that they ever existed. Several of the rhymes which are credited to only one school and have no known recorded, noted or printed variants, might be so regarded. Some, however, might be considered as being of more interest than those which have a wider dispersal. I have not bowdlerised or censored rhymes, although in the case of the ephemera referred to above, I have left out some of those which seemed to offend the general consensus of children's extremely liberal conceptions of good taste. In dealing with variants, it has been necessary to select from a very large number in some cases. I have attempted to select those which seem to be typical of a number of very similar examples. Where there are marked differences, two, three, four or even more variants are given. In a few cases where more than one variant has been collected from the same group, and the differences are small, I have composited, but I have not done so with rhymes which have differing versions from more than one source. Where a number of sources are listed, I have underlined the source of the version selected as being the representative one. The others may perhaps differ only in word or line, but are basically similar.

Where printed sources are listed, I have included all those which seem to stem from a common root. Because many rhymes are hybrids, however, I have cross-referenced where this might be helpful. Up to the time when the fieldwork was completed I have tried to include as many collections as possible where variants may be found, but have not included all the sources in North America, Australia etc., and may have missed some British ones. Manuscripts etc. which are not available to the student are also omitted, though a few examples of "early notings" have come from private sources. In such cases the version is reproduced in full and the informant and collector are cited. Where "early notings" are indicated, I have in an arbitrary way interpreted "early" as referring to pre-1945. In the United Kingdom the Second World War involved the dispersal of children all over the country and the consequent widest possible diffusion of children's lore. Postwar developments led to widespread social changes involving housing, leisure, and entertainment. The reorganisation of education into primary and secondary stages at about the age of eleven was also completed. Furthermore, no attempt has been made to provide tunes, but where the tune is likely to be known I have given the name which usually refers to it, and a brief summary of its origins, where available.

The categories into which the collected material is divided may appear strange to some because they are partly based on function and partly on subject matter. Distinctions between functions are blurred of course. Most hand clapping routines include mimed actions, and thus there is no clear distinction between them and other action rhymes which I have included in the section on singing games. Any sung skipping or ball bouncing routine is strictly speaking a singing game anyway. Several ball bouncing rhymes are used for skipping and vice versa. Of course the rhyme has to be adaptable to a change in rhythm and pace. Many are unsuitable for both purposes. Usually the rhyme undergoes a change when it is used for a different purpose and so in such cases different versions may be included in different sections, cross-referenced as appropriate.

Several of the old traditional singing games, such as **6.A.59** ON A MOUNTAIN STANDS A LADY and **6.A.54** ALL THE GIRLS IN OUR TOWN, have had a new lease of life as skipping rhymes. Versions of EACH, PEACH, PEAR, PLUM (**2.44** and **7.9**) have done service as dips, and others as ball bouncing routines. I have been unable to determine which came first. Versions of **2.45** MICKEY MOUSE IN HIS HOUSE have been used for ball bouncing and skipping as well as counting out. Similar versatility has been extracted from D'YOU WANT A CIGARETTE SIR? (**7.7**), COWBOY JOE FROM MEXICO (**2.48** and **6.A.29**) and others.

School rhymes, expressive of both open and concealed attitudes to school authority, and the love-hate relationships with teachers, are important enough, in my opinion, to be considered as a separate genre, although some are seasonal and many are designed to be "just for fun". I have coupled parodies with school rhymes because a number of them express an attitude to aspects of the school curriculum, though probably most are also "just for fun". Many football rhymes contained in the final section are, of course, parodies. Football cries from the terraces are also adapted for school partisanship. Several skipping rhymes are divinatory in nature and could be included in the section on divination. The Opies (*LL*, 1959) got round these problems of classification by including different versions of a particular rhyme under different subject chapter headings, and allowing the index to do the rest. I have given cross-references where necessary. For example, variants of the ROSES ARE RED rhymes will be found under Clapping (**5.21**), School rhymes and parodies (**8.D.44**), Teasing and taunting (**9.C.1c**, **9.C.13**, **9.C.21**, **9.C.31d**), and Miscellany (**12.C.1**). Though there is some consensus on the part of folklorists about categories of children's lore, there are many ways in which one can categorise particular examples.

One might consider a primary school "generation" as six years. As far as acquiring and passing on children's lore are concerned, the four years spent in the junior school or department are the most important. The time during which the process of passing on traditions can be studied even year by year as the children develop is very short. This process of accepting, amending, rejecting, and forgetting can be noticed year by year, as well as that of the mutation, creation, modification, and possible incorporation of new material into the tradition. Obviously I am referring to the group here, not the individual child. Occasionally I have noticed that a rhyme or song from a classroom experience, in music, poetry, drama or movement, will be taken into the playground, to be trimmed, expanded or altered to fit the needs of game activity or action routine. Sometimes a new singing game is taken up with enthusiasm, like the latest commercial craze, only to be abandoned after a few weeks, leaving hardly a trace behind, except in the memory of one or two children who seem to be living repositories of past and present children's lore.

Rhymes and other items appear to die when they cannot be adapted in content, language or rhythm to meet new needs, new habits, and changing taste. This process is akin to that of natural selection in biological evolution: mutations arising, to be followed by selection, resulting in slow modification, rapid radical change, or obliteration. The old forms may continue in an almost unaltered shape. To continue the analogy: old forms may remain, in whole or part, when they no longer appear to have any relevance, like the vestigial appendix or coccyx. Children simultaneously display both conservative and creative aspects of their subculture. I suppose the conservative element will tend to predominate, otherwise there would be little tradition left.

There may be good reason to think that the much greater emphasis on the creative aspects of language work in schools is reflected in the quantity of rhymes and wordplay produced by the children. In most schools there is unique material. When the collective process gets to work on it, most of it will prove to be ephemeral unless it has an appeal, fulfils a need, or is superior to existing examples. If the newly created item has some link with established or at least with familiar examples, it will obviously stand a better chance of being incorporated into the body of orally transmitted material. A joke or riddle which uses a familiar formula of punning or other wordplay is more likely to be passed on than one that strikes an original note. Once, however, a new formula does get taken up and become established, perhaps due to influences from the adult world, many new examples can be expected to follow that pattern. A parody obviously depends upon the familiarity of the original that is parodied; if couched in a familiar form, a taunt will have more effect than a would-be cutting remark, however witty, which has to be thought about.

There are many sources of inspiration for new or newly adapted material. These seem to be some of the principal ones:

- Current popular music
- Popular songs and rhymes of the past
- Television programmes and advertisements, and popular films
- Adult-introduced songs learned when in Cub Scouts, Brownies etc.
- Songs, rhymes, and other items learned at school
- Adult songs of a risqué or obscene type, of non-commercial origin
- Songs from current musical shows or revivals
- Rhymes to fit well-known tunes (the rhyme made up to fit the tune, or a tune sought for a particular rhyme)
- Rhymes or songs introduced by immigrant children and re-adapted (rare)
- Songs and rhymes of the past learned from older relatives

It is often impossible to hazard a guess as to why a particular rhyme or song has "caught on", even if the source is clearly indicated. During the

Second World War, for example, a song was current in adult circles (armed forces etc.) which was an account of sexual foreplay, intercourse, arrival of a baby and then an indication of a repetition of the cycle. It began: "This is number one, and we've only just begun, roll me over, lay me down and do it again". I thought it had died out. However, I first encountered children's versions of it as "Tea for one …" (Brixton 1982), "This is number one …" (Kentish Town 1983) and "Number one …" (Greenwich 1982 and Mile End 1983), presented together under **11.J.18** THIS IS NUMBER ONE. By what process did this song get taken up, changed and disseminated in the 1980s? How did the First World War song **11.J.15** VICTORIOUS appear in a new guise in an Earlsfield school in 1982? As far as I know, it may have now disappeared without trace, still be restricted to that school, or it may be sung in other schools.

As so much of this material is not considered "respectable", much may have been collected which would indicate continuity of tradition, but has been dismissed or suppressed by collectors and/or publishers. We are able to compare the manuscripts of some of the folksong collectors of the past with what was published. If earlier original "field" collections of those interested in children's lore were available, we would have a better picture of the processes of innovation and tradition involved. Nevertheless, it is sometimes possible to note the ways in which traditional material is modified by changes in social conditions, lifestyles and other influences. However, this can only be done in cases where adult reinforcement of the tradition is weak or nonexistent.

No. **4.20** ORANGES AND LEMONS is one of the few old traditional singing games which were still being played by children in the nine to eleven age group during the period in which I was collecting material. In most of the versions I encountered, "You owe me five thousand" had replaced "You owe me five farthings" which was meaningless to them. **10.C.10b** FIND A PENNY, PICK IT UP was replacing **10.C.10a** SEE A PIN AND PICK IT UP, since small coins are more likely to be encountered than pins nowadays. The pre-decimalisation rhyme: **8.A.8** POUNDS, SHILLINGS AND PENCE turned up only in Stoke Newington in 1983 but no doubt it was on its way to obliteration. **6.A.4** EGGS A PENNY EACH, which certainly goes back at least to the early 1930s, I noted in Brixton (1982) and The Borough (1983). This rhyme does not seem to have been influenced by the inflationary changes in the purchasing power of money. These modifications sometimes take a long time.

There are obviously changes in food, work, and entertainment which, often belatedly, find a reflection in the words of rhymes and songs. In Douglas you will find rhymes and games mentioning apple pie, blackcurrant, redcurrant and raspberry tarts, bread and butter, hot boiled beans with melted butter, making bread from flour and milk, mutton chops, mutton pies, plum pudding, pork and greens, roast beef, seedy cake, and treacle pudding.[1] In contemporary rhymes there are many more references to confectionery in the form of caramels, chewing gum, cola, ginger pop, lemonade, and lollies. Foods mentioned include apple crumble, beans, cookies, custard, fish and chips, jam and marmalade tarts, jelly, and sausages.

In Douglas there are five references to laundry or washing clothes.[2] Washing clothes in the old manner survives in the singing game **4.14 DOWN IN THE VALLEY**, originally a courtship game. A reference to "bleaching clothes" in some of the nineteenth century versions (which also included references to making a pudding) apparently became the principal element, and that of courtship disappeared. A version given by Douglas (1916, p. 93; 1931, p. 53) begins: "Down by the river where the green grass grows,/There little Sally was washing her clothes—". The mimed actions in the game included a "little old woman/big fat woman" rubbing or scrubbing clothes. In these days of launderettes and washing machines, this seems to be an interesting survival which will wither away in the course of time. However, in the Douglas rhymes the girl performers would no doubt identify with little Sally who does the washing, though the washing is not taken very seriously and the little old woman has no connection with the girls' families. In version **4.14E**, a little dog, cat, and chicken also wash clothes! In version **4.14B** the "big fat woman" also picks her nose and scrubs her toes.

I discuss at greater length the ONE, TWO, THREE A-LAIRY versions (**7.26**) in that section, but should mention here that I continued to find references to "My ball's down the airy" versions as late as 1983 (Barnsbury and Dalston) where, although basement areas may still exist here and there, it is unlikely that ball bouncers would be inconvenienced by them. In Mile End, however, where all these old buildings with basements had been replaced by modern council blocks of flats and maisonettes, I still came across the rhyme in the late 1960s. When I revisited the Mile End School (1983) in which I had noted this version, I found that the children were unaware of this rhyme in any version. It is interesting to note that I have only encountered rhyme **7.11** FUDGE, FUDGE, CALL THE JUDGE, an American importation probably, which refers to different floors and to an "escalator" (echoing the American "elevator") in parts of Inner London where there are blocks of flats with lifts. In areas made up of terraced housing or prefabs, it did not appear to be used, or even known. It would appear that although versions of rhymes which contain references to social conditions and living styles of the past often continue in the tradition long after these have disappeared, sooner or later the tradition seems to catch up with social change. The only way in which the old versions will continue indefinitely is when they are kept alive by adult reinforcement, as in the case of the nursery rhymes and some of the old traditional singing games with their set ways of performance and often charming piano accompaniments.

The children may learn in the classroom or school hall: "Green gravel, green gravel, your grass is so green/The fairest young lady that ever was seen/We washed her, we dried her, we rolled her in silk/And wrote down her name with a gold pen and ink …". Later, in the playground, they may play a game which involves picking a girl from a ring, turning her round and smacking her bottom, accompanied by a verse: "Green gravel, you are a naughty girl/You told me you loved me, but now it is not true/So turn around you naughty girl and say no more to me",[3] or skip to another version (**6.A.56**). The teacher in the classroom and the children in the playground are both "maintaining a tradition" but in very different ways. Both of these are valuable, but they should not be confused. Without adult reinforcement, singing games can be very drastically pared down from their old versions. Examples of this are the current **4.9** QUEENIE, QUEENIE which is a barely recognisable descendant of the "Lady Queen Anne, she sits in the sun" verses of a century ago; or **4.21** ARE YOU READY FOR A FIGHT? the surviving remnant of "Have you any bread and wine?"

Traditions involving figures in the public eye, or performers or characters from mass entertainment, are not likely to be established as a general rule. The Opies (*LL*, 1959, pp. 118–120) draw attention to the rapid rise, wide dispersal, and equally speedy virtual disappearance of the Davy Crockett rhymes which swept through schools in the 1950s. In the 1960s the Beatles inspired parodies, love rhymes, riddles etc., but left no tradition behind. They might as well have never existed for all the average primary school child of the 1980s knows or cares. I have included in this collection two rhymes collected during the time when the group as such was famous, to illustrate their place (**11.I.56** and **11.I.57**).

Charlie Chaplin is an exception to the general rule. At the time of my survey he had been sung about to accompany action rhymes, skipping rhymes, and ball bouncing routines for nigh on seventy years. I thought I had heard the very last survivals of Charlie Chaplin rhymes in the 1960s, but in 1983 (The Borough) he had still gone "to France/To teach the ladies how to dance" (**6.A.52**) and featured in a ONE, TWO, THREE A-LAIRY rhyme (**7.26**) in Dalston and Barnsbury.

It is difficult to know why two Shirley Temple rhymes were going strong fifty years after this particular "infant phenomenon" entertained cinema-goers. They are: **4.56** I'M SHIRLEY TEMPLE and **7.42** SHIRLEY TEMPLE IS A STAR. I collected a number of versions of the former in the years 1982–84, and a version of the latter in Cubitt Town in 1983. Versions of the former rhyme often include vestigial references to stars no longer known by name to contemporary children. These references can just be recognised by adults with good memories. Betty Grable, the pin-up girl of the 1940s, is encountered variously as "Betsy Gable" (**4.56B**), "sexy cable" (**4.56A**), and even "six times table" (**4.56D**). Marilyn Monroe has become, in at least one version, "Marimin Rowe" (**4.56C**), and Sabrina has become "Semina" (**4.57D**). Others mentioned (in their original form) are Henry Hall, Ginger Rogers, and Rin-tin-tin (there have been several dog filmstars of this name). The more recent entertainment scene is represented by Shirley Bassey and Cliff Richard; the latter and Diana Dors both appear in two rhymes. Cartoon characters who have by now become traditional are Mickey Mouse, Donald Duck, and Popeye. Betty Boop has changed into Patsy Boop (**11.I.43A**). Characters from the field of film, shows, and television include Batman and Robin; Jesus Christ, Superstar; the Smurfs; E.T.; and characters from the *Dallas* series. History provides Nelson, Casanova, Queen Caroline, and Josephine, while folklore and literature are represented by Robin Hood, Cinderella, Tom Thumb, Alice, and Oliver Twist.

Contemporary politics and politicians do not seem to figure very much in the playground lore of Inner London schools. Apart from a crude attempt at a rhyme about Mrs. Thatcher, the only contemporary reference

I have encountered is a version of **11.I.58** BUILD A BONFIRE which replaces the normal "teachers" and "prefects" by "Galtieri" and "the Argies" (Blackheath 1983), a reference to the Falklands War in 1982. Quite unexpectedly I came across two of the many Hitler rhymes once in general circulation: **8.D.13** WHISTLE WHILE YOU WORK/Hitler is a twerp, and **11.I.32** HITLER HAS ONLY GOT ONE BALL. Both of these were found in Finsbury in 1983 and Kensington in 1984.

Any honest review of children's folklore has to recognise the important place that bodily functions of all kinds: urination, defecation, breaking wind, vomiting, copulation, and reproduction, have within it. Aspects of eroticism including nudity, underclothes, courtship, and sexual play have a particular fascination. Major printed collections, with the notable exception of Turner's Australian compilation (1969), seem to have been carefully edited to play down these factors, and in some cases actual bowdlerisation has been practised. As Cray (1970, p. xx) observes:

> Trusting the collectanea in print—the exceptions are very few—one could only conclude that the youngsters are quite as sexless as their elders. But as much as parents may wish this were the case, the fact is that children learn a good deal about sex and excretion quite early in life.

The bold inclusion of collectanea of a scatological and sexual nature in Turner's collection led to its earning a certain notoriety, and a rumour spread that it had been declared unacceptable for the Australian mail. This misconception was due to the work's initially being regarded as ineligible by the Australian Post Office for a discount on the cost of postage. However, the publishers of the second edition (1978) included the words "Not recommended for children" on the dustjacket – a decision which they defended as a sensible warning to prospective purchasers.[4] The folklorist Kenneth Goldstein perceptively stated that "children have a whole world of private beliefs, rhymes, and erotica which only a few sensitive and understanding adults are ever allowed to penetrate."[5] I do not know whether I come into the latter category, but I was given many examples of this material without embarrassment, along with much more "acceptable" examples when I asked for counting-out rhymes, games, action rhymes, and songs. The proportion of what the children called "rude" was greater when I asked them to give me examples of their humour in the form of songs, limericks, riddles, and jokes. If I had told them that such matter was unacceptable, I would have inhibited them and they would no longer have been open and trusting with me. Actually the children would censor each other when really unpleasant material was introduced by a child desiring to "show off".

I had to be aware when collecting children's lore in many schools that I was an ex-teacher, and that if I showed too much familiarity and permissiveness it would not be helpful to discipline. At the same time I was a guest on sufferance in schools totally unfamiliar to me before my initial visits. I had to steer a careful course while gaining the confidence of the children and making it clear to them that what they told me or what they gave me from their repertoires would under no circumstances be told to any adults without their permission. Most of the children seemed to understand, and only a few tried to take advantage of the situation. In most schools the teachers also appreciated what I was trying to do, but in one or two cases I encountered some disapproval.

Some children were prepared to give me their ideas about the "rude" part of their repertoire. They expressed either real or mock disapproval on the one hand, or rationalised it on the other. Of the disapprovals this is typical:

"Well I think some of these things are absolutely repulsive and silly, but some of them are just funny. You just do them for a laugh. Some of them get too silly like the diarrhoea one." girl, 11, Hampstead 1984

Of those who tried to come to terms with the question, there were various approaches:

"Some of us don't know what some words mean and probably we hear our parents say them. We think, 'Oh, this is good,' and we just say it ourselves." girl, 10, Kentish Town 1983

"Children are very interested in different parts of the body and like making rhymes about them, especially rude parts and things like farts. They find it very funny when somebody does a fart in the class, and they all burst out laughing." boy, 11, Finsbury 1983

> "We might as well learn now 'cause when we get older it might happen."
> girl, 10, Kentish Town 1983

When children express an opinion on a particular situation they may have contrasting views. Two ten year old boys (Hampstead 1984) took up a particular theme but did not agree:

> "Well you see to make up a silly rhyme with people urinating against a wall is funny. Well you wouldn't think it funny unless it was a stupid rhyme."

> "When you see someone pissing against the wall you wouldn't say that it's stupid. You just roar out laughing."

The school areas investigated in this survey of children's lore are listed on pp. xlv–xlvi.

NOTES

1. Douglas (1916), p. 59, (1931), p. 32 (apple-pie); (1916), p. 44, pp. 86–87, (1931), p. 23, pp. 49–50 (bread and butter); (1916), p. 57, (1931), p. 30 (bread from flour and milk); (1916), p. 89, (1931), p. 51 (hot boiled beans and melted butter), (1916), pp. 71–72, (1931), p. 40 (mutton pies/chops); (1916), p. 47, (1931), p. 25 (pork and greens); (1916), p. 86, (1931), p. 49 (roast beef and plum pudding); (1916), p. 91, (1931), p. 52 (seedy cake); (1916), p. 51, (1931), p. 27 (tarts); (1916), p. 45, (1931), p. 24 (treacle pudding).
2. Douglas (1916), pp. 54, 65–66, 78, 82, 93; (1931), pp. 28–29, 36, 43, 46, 53.
3. A version from Andover, Hampshire, 1980 (Steve Roud, personal communication).
4. The editors are grateful to June Factor, one of the editors of the second edition of Turner's collection, for clarification of this sequence of events (personal communication, 2012, May 8).
5. Goldstein, K. (1964). *A guide for field workers in folklore*. Hatboro, PA: Folklore Associates, for the American Folklore Society, pp. 150–151.

INNER LONDON EDUCATION AUTHORITY SCHOOLS WHERE DATA WAS COLLECTED

DIVISION	INNER LONDON BOROUGHS	SCHOOL AREAS	SOCIAL MAKE-UP
1	London Borough of Hammersmith and Fulham	Shepherds Bush WI4 (1983)	c
	Royal Borough of Kensington and Chelsea	Kensington W8 (1984)	a
2	City of Westminster, also covering pre-1963 borough	St. Marylebone NW1 (1967)	c
	London Borough of Camden, covering pre-1963 boroughs of Holborn, St. Pancras and Hampstead	Kentish Town NW5 (1983) Hampstead NW3 (1984)	c a
3	London Borough of Islington, also covering pre-1963 borough of Finsbury	Barnsbury N7 (1983) Finsbury EC1 (1983)	b a
4	London Borough of Hackney, also covering pre-1963 boroughs of Shoreditch and Stoke Newington	Dalston E8 (1983) Stoke Newington N16 (1983)	b a
5	City of London		
	London Borough of Tower Hamlets, covering pre-1963 boroughs of Stepney, Bethnal Green and Poplar	Mile End E1 (1960/ 1979/ 1983) Cubitt Town E14 (1983)	b c
6	London Borough of Greenwich, also covering pre-1963 borough of Woolwich	Greenwich SE10 (1982) Blackheath SE3 (1983)	b a
7	London Borough of Lewisham, also covering pre-1963 borough of Deptford	Brockley SE4 (1967) Brockley SE4 (1983) (different school) Deptford SE8 (1983)	b c b
8	London Borough of Southwark, also covering pre-1963 boroughs of Bermondsey and Camberwell	Walworth SE17 (1974/1982) The Borough SE1 (1983) Dulwich SE5 (1983)	b b a
9	London Borough of Lambeth, also covering parts of pre-1963 borough of Wandsworth	West Norwood SE27 (1970/1973) Brixton SW9 (1982) Streatham SW16 (1982)	c b a
10	London Borough of Wandsworth, covering most of pre-1963 borough of Wandsworth and borough of Battersea	Putney SW15 (1966) Clapham SW4 (1973/1974) Earlsfield SW18 (1982) Battersea SW8 (1982)	c c a b

Key to Social Make-Up Categories

a. majority of children from professional, managerial and white collar families.
b. majority of children from semi-skilled, unskilled and unwaged families.
c. fairly balanced intake.

Contents

PREFACE xi

THE COLLECTION: KEY TO PRESENTATION OF ENTRIES xxi

INTRODUCTION xxiii
    INNER LONDON EDUCATION AUTHORITY SCHOOLS WHERE DATA WAS COLLECTED xlv

PART I   GAMES AND GAME RHYMES, CHANTS, AND SONGS 1

SECTION 1   STARTING A GAME 3

SECTION 2 COUNTING-OUT RHYMES   11

Introduction   11
Counting-out Rhymes   16
- 2.1 IBBLE OBBLE, BLACK BOBBLE   16
- 2.2 ONE, TWO, THREE, FOUR, FIVE, SIX, SEVEN   17
- 2.3 TUPPENCE ON THE WATER   18
- 2.4 RACING CAR NUMBER NINE   19
- 2.5 IPPER DIPPER DATION   20
- 2.6 EGGS, BUTTER, SUGAR, TEA   21
- 2.7 ROUND AND ROUND THE BUTTER DISH   22
- 2.8 ROUND AND ROUND THE APPLE PIE   23
- 2.9 TARZAN IN THE JUNGLE   24
- 2.10 BIG BEN STRIKES TEN   24
- 2.11 MY MUM AND YOUR MUM   25
- 2.12 ONE POTATO, TWO POTATO   26
- 2.13 EENY MEENY MACKER ACKER   27
- 2.14 EENY MEENY MINY MO   29
- 2.15 EASIE PEASIE   31
- 2.16 EENY DEENY DIP   31
- 2.17 ALA ALA MING MONG   32
- 2.18 JINK, JINK, POM, PINK   33
- 2.19 INKY, PINKY, PERKY, PLUM   33
- 2.20 INKY, PINKY, PONKY   33
- 2.21 IM STIM, STAMMER BOMMER   34
- 2.22 IM PIM, SEPTIPIM   34
- 2.23 ICKLETY, PICKLETY, MY BLACK HEN   34
- 2.24 THERE'S A PARTY ON THE HILL   35
- 2.25 MRS. MOP OWNED A SHOP   36
- 2.26 AS I WAS WALKING DOWN INKY-PINKY LANE   37
- 2.27 THERE'S A SOLDIER ON THE GRASS   38
- 2.28 THE GRASS IS GREEN   38
- 2.29 ALL THE MONKEYS   38
- 2.30 IP, DIP, THREEPENNY BIT   39
- 2.31 IP, DIP, SKY BLUE, WHO'S IT? NOT YOU   39

2.32	IP, DIP, SKY BLUE, TOM AND JERRY DOWN THE LOO	40
2.33	IP, DIP, DOGS' SHIT	40
2.34	IP DIP DOO, THE CAT'S GOT THE FLU	41
2.35	IP DIP DOO, THE BOYS LOVE YOU	42
2.36	IP, DIP, ANA MA DA	42
2.37	WHOSE SHOES ARE THE CLEANEST?	43
2.38	DID YOU CLEAN YOUR SHOES LAST NIGHT?	43
2.39	YOUR SHOES NEED CLEANING	44
2.40	DIRTY SHOES, DIRTY SOCKS	45
2.41	TURN THE DIRTY DISH CLOTH	45
2.42	WASH THE DISHES	45
2.43	BOY SCOUT	46
2.44	EACH, PEACH, PEAR, PLUM	46
2.45	MICKEY MOUSE IN HIS HOUSE	47
2.46	HORSY, HORSY IN THE STABLE	48
2.47	NODDY HAS A LITTLE CAR	48
2.48	COWBOY JOE FROM MEXICO	48
2.49	ROSY, ROSY, HOW DO YOU DO?	49
2.50	CHOCOLATE BISCUIT IN THE TIN	49
2.51	LONDON COUNTY COUNCIL	49
2.52	I SAW A FLY	50
2.53	JENNY GOT THE MEASLES	50
2.54	HAM, BACON, PORK CHOP	50
2.55	YOU CAN'T PUT YOUR MUCK IN MY DUSTBIN	51
2.56	CHING CHONG, CHINAMAN	51
2.57	DOCTOR FOSTER WENT TO GLOUCESTER	52
2.58	YUM, YUM, BUBBLEGUM	52
2.59	CINDERELLA, DRESSED IN YELLA	53
Settling a Dispute		53
2.60	RED, GOLD AND GREEN	53

| Contents

SECTION 3   GAMES (WITHOUT SONGS)   55
Introduction   55
3.A   CHASING GAMES   62
3.B   RACING AND SIMILAR GAMES   82
3.C   JUMPING, LEAPING AND HANDSTANDING   92
3.D   SEEKING GAMES   95
3.E   MUDDLES   101
3.F   CONTESTS AND TUSSLES   102
3.G   "ROUGH" OR BULLYING GAMES   108
3.H   BALL GAMES: KICKING   109
3.I   BALL GAMES: HANDLING   115
3.J   BALL GAMES: HITTING BALL WITH BAT OR STICK   119
3.K   GAMES PLAYED WITH OTHER OBJECTS   121
3.L   MISCELLANEOUS OUTDOOR GAMES   128
3.M   PRANKS   130
3.N   MAINLY INDOOR GAMES   131
3.O   PENCIL AND PAPER GAMES   137
3.P   VARIOUS GAMES REPORTED WITH NO DETAILS 1982–84   138

SECTION 4   SINGING AND CHANTING GAMES   139
Introduction   139
4.1   A GIPSY CAME A-RIDING   148
4.2   WHEN SUSIE WAS A BABY   152
4.3   HERE WE GO LOOBEE-LOO   155
4.4   THE HOKEY POKEY   157
4.5   BINGO   158
4.6   WHO HAS STOLE MY WATCH AND CHAIN?   159
4.7   LONDON BRIDGE IS FALLING DOWN   161
4.8   ROW, ROW, ROW YOUR BOAT   163
4.9   QUEENIE, QUEENIE or QUEENIE-I   164
4.10   THE FARMER'S IN HIS DEN   167
4.11   THE GRAND OLD DUKE OF YORK   169
4.12   A-HUNTING WE SHALL GO   170

4.13	RING A RING A ROSES	171
4.14	DOWN IN THE VALLEY	173
4.15	I SENT A LETTER TO MY LOVE	176
4.16	POOR JENNY IS A-WEEPING	178
4.17	FAIR ROSIE WAS A SWEET PRINCESS	179
4.18	IN AND OUT THE DUSTY BLUEBELLS	180
4.19	THE GOOD SHIP SAILS ON THE ALLEE-ALLEE-O	182
4.20	ORANGES AND LEMONS	185
4.21	ARE YOU READY FOR A FIGHT?	187
4.22	PLEASE MOTHER, MAY I GO OUT TO PLAY? (GRANDMOTHER GRAY)	190
4.23	SKIP TO MY LOU	193
4.24	BROWN GIRL IN THE RING	193
4.25	I WENT TO CALIFORNIA	195
4.26	HERE COMES MRS. MACARONI	197
4.27	THERE WERE TEN IN A BED	198
4.28	INTO THE CENTRE AND NOD YOUR HEAD	199
4.29	WHAT CAN YOU DO, PUNCHINELLO?	200
4.30	I'M A LITTLE DUTCH GIRL	200
4.31	HEEL AND TOE	203
4.32	I'M A LOCKED-UP CHICKEN	203
4.33	ORANGE BALLS	206
4.34	SHE WEARS RED FEATHERS	208
4.35	WE ARE THE DEPTFORD GIRLS	208
4.36	WHEN GRANDMAMA MET GRANDPAPA	209
4.37	IN A COTTAGE IN A WOOD	210
4.38	HERE COMES MRS. MOLLY	210
4.39	I'VE GOT A DAUGHTER	211
4.40	I'M A LONDON GIRL (I'M A TEXAS GIRL)	212
4.41	EVERYBODY GATHER ROUND	213
4.42	HEAD, SHOULDERS, KNEES AND TOES	214
4.43	THERE'S A TINY HOUSE	214
4.44	A SHIP SAILS FROM CHINA	215
4.45	THERE WAS A GIRL FROM ITALY	216
4.46	I CAN DO THE CAN-CAN	217

4.47	FAME	218
4.48	MATILDA	218
4.49	KEEP YOUR SUNNY SIDE UP	219
4.50	I'M THE KING OF THE SWINGERS	220
4.51	UNDERNEATH THE SPREADING CHESTNUT TREE	220
4.52	CAT'S GOT THE MEASLES	221
4.53	THIS WAY VALERIE	222
4.54	MY NAME IS SEXY SUE	223
4.55	CRACKERJACK/FIRECRACKER	224
4.56	I'M SHIRLEY TEMPLE	224
4.57	SABRINA, SABRINA	226
4.58	OUT IN ARIZONA	228
4.59	SEVEN LITTLE GIRLS	228
4.60	JIMMY GOT DRUNK	229
4.61	BISCUIT	230
4.62	I'M A SAILOR YOUNG AND GAY	231
4.63	CINDERELLA	233
4.64	AUNT MILDRED	234
4.65	POP GOES THE WEASEL	235
4.66	MILK, MILK, LEMONADE	235
4.67	BOOBY ONE, BOOBY TWO	236
4.68	COCONUT, CARAMEL	236
4.69	CHINESE, JAPANESE	237

SECTION 5   CLAPPING GAMES — 239

Introduction — 239

5.1	A SAILOR WENT TO SEA	242
5.2	HAVE YOU EVER, EVER, EVER	244
5.3	MARIO SE FERA	245
5.4	I AM A PRETTY LITTLE DUTCH GIRL	246
5.5	MY BOYFRIEND GAVE ME AN APPLE	247
5.6	IM POM PAY (OM POM VEE)	250
5.7	I HAD THE GERMAN MEASLES	250
5.8	ONE, TWO, THREE TOGETHER	252

5.9	I HAD A LITTLE BROTHER	252
5.10	I WENT TO A CHINESE RESTAURANT	254
5.11	JOHNNY BROKE A BOTTLE	256
5.12	UNDER THE BROWN BUSH	257
5.13	THREE, SIX, NINE	258
5.14	MY MAMA TOLD ME	259
5.15	MACK, MACK, MACK	260
5.16	MY MOTHER IS A BAKER	262
5.17	SEE, SEE, MY PLAYMATE	263
5.18	WHO STOLE THE COOKIES?	265
5.19	MILLY MOLLY MANDY	266
5.20	I'VE BEEN TO HARLEM	267
5.21	ROSES ARE RED	268
5.22	I SAW MY BOYFRIEND	269

SECTION 6	**SKIPPING GAMES**	271
Introduction		271
6.A	ROPE SKIPPING	278
6.B	ELASTIC SKIPPING	338

SECTION 7	**BALL BOUNCING GAMES**	343
Introduction		343
7.1	BLACK CAT	351
7.2	ALICE IN WONDERLAND	352
7.3	DADDY, MUMMY, UNCLE DICK	352
7.4	DON'T GO TO GRANNY'S ANY MORE	353
7.5	DASHA MARMALADE	353
7.6	UP IN ABERDEEN	354
7.7	D'YOU WANT A CIGARETTE, SIR?	354
7.8	DONALD DUCK WASHING UP	355
7.9	EACH, PEACH, PEAR, PLUM	356
7.10	GIPSY, GIPSY LIVED IN A TENT	357
7.11	FUDGE, FUDGE, CALL THE JUDGE	357
7.12	ORANGES, LEMONS, TWO FOR A PENNY	358
7.13	I'M POPEYE THE SAILOR MAN	359

7.14	MATTHEW, MARK, LUKE AND JOHN	362
7.15	MRS. MINNY WORE HER PINNY	363
7.16	MRS. POLLY HAD A DOLLY	363
7.17	MRS. RUMBLE	364
7.18	DASH, DASH, DASH	364
7.19	I LOST MY ARM IN THE ARMY	365
7.20	IN PRISON YOU GET COFFEE	365
7.21	P.K. PENNY A PACKET	366
7.22	MRS. WHITE HAD A FRIGHT	366
7.23	MY MUM'S A SECRETARY	367
7.24	NIGGER, NIGGER	368
7.25	OLIVER TWIST	368
7.26	ONE, TWO, THREE A-LAIRY	369
7.27	OVER THE GARDEN WALL	370
7.28	WHEN I WENT UP IN A YELLOW BALLOON	371
7.29	ONE, TWO, BUCKLE MY SHOE	372
7.30	RIN-TIN-TIN SWALLOWED A PIN	373
7.31	PLAINSIE JIM SWALLOWED A PIN	374
7.32	PLAINSIE TO AMERICA	374
7.33	PLAINSIE, CLAPSIE	375
7.34	PLAINSIE, UPSIE, DOWNSIE, OVER etc.	375
7.35	ONE, TWO, THREE AND UPSIE/PLAINSIE etc.	377
7.36	SEVENSIES/TENSIES/ALPHABET	378
7.37	PLEASE MISS	379
7.38	QUEENIE, QUEENIE CAROLINE	380
7.39	MRS. MOP OWNED A SHOP	381
7.40	UNDER THE APPLE TREE	381
7.41	MARY MORGAN PLAYED THE ORGAN	382
7.42	SHIRLEY TEMPLE IS A STAR	382
7.43	WINNIE THE WITCH	383
7.44	WHEN THE WAR WAS OVER	383
7.45	WHEN I WAS ONE	384
7.46	ARCHIBALD, BALD, BALD	387
7.47	JOHNNY WENT RIDING	389
7.48	RULE BRITANNIA	389

PART II RHYMES, SONGS, BELIEFS, AND WORDPLAY 391

SECTION 8 SCHOOL RHYMES AND PARODIES 393
Introduction 393
- 8.A SCHOOL AND TEACHERS 394
- 8.B SCHOOL MEALS 409
- 8.C SCHOOL BOASTS, YELLS, AND CHANTS 414
- 8.D PARODIES OF HYMNS, SONGS, AND RHYMES 417

SECTION 9 TEASING AND TAUNTING 455
Introduction 455
- 9.A VERBAL TRICKS AND CATCHING OUT 456
- 9.B TEASES, THREATS, RUSES, AND BOASTS 468
- 9.C TAUNTS AND EPITHETS 477
- 9.D RESPONSES, RETORTS, AND REPARTEE 507
- 9.E PLAY ON (OTHER) CHILDREN'S NAMES 522

SECTION 10 TRADITIONAL BELIEF AND PRACTICE 527
Introduction 527
- 10.A DIVINATIONS 528
- 10.B INCANTATIONS AND RITUALS 537
- 10.C OTHER SUPERSTITIONS (LUCK etc.) 548
- 10.D SAYINGS AND RHYMES 570
- 10.E SEASONAL LORE 574

SECTION 11 JUST FOR FUN 581
Introduction 581
- 11.A NONSENSE RHYMES AND WORDPLAY 582
- 11.B TONGUE TWISTERS etc. 589
- 11.C RIDDLES 598
- 11.D KNOCK-KNOCK RIDDLES 625
- 11.E VERBAL EXCHANGE JOKES 641
- 11.F FUNNY BOOK TITLES AND EPITAPHS 655
- 11.G PUZZLES 659

11.H	LIMERICKS	661
11.I	RHYMES FOR FUN	671
11.J	SONGS	706
11.K	JOKES	731

SECTION 12 MISCELLANY 743
Introduction 743

12.A	FOOTBALL RHYMES AND CHANTS	743
12.B	RHYMES AND SONGS FOR BABIES AND TODDLERS	751
12.C	WRITINGS FOR ALBUMS, etc.	763
12.D	BEING FIRST IN LINE, etc.	769
12.E	FOR MARCHING	771
12.F	STARTING STORIES	771
12.G	EVERLASTING STORIES	773
12.H	SO-CALLED "BACKSLANG"	773
12.I	RHYMING SLANG	777

BIBLIOGRAPHY 779

KEY TO ACRONYMS AND ABBREVIATIONS DESIGNATING PUBLICATIONS CITED 795

DISCOGRAPHY 801

SELECTED FURTHER READING 803

INDEX 811

PART I

GAMES AND GAME RHYMES, CHANTS, AND SONGS

Introduction

Of all children's lore, games have the longest tradition. Archaeology has revealed that a game similar to "Jacks" was played by children in the cities of the ancient civilisations of the Middle East. The Ancient Greeks and Romans are known to have played versions of "Hide and Seek", "Blind Man's Buff", and "Tug of War". Pieter Bruegel the Elder's famous painting, "Children's Games", dating from 1560, illustrates among the numerous activities of children a number of games still played today. Among those in the picture which can be found in the playgrounds of Inner London schools are **3.A.1** to **3.A.17** TAG and variants, **3.A.8.i** THE TUNNEL OF DEATH, **3.A.27** BLIND MAN'S BUFF, **3.C.5** LEAP FROGS, **3.C.6** HANDSTANDS, **3.F.1** PIGGY-BACK FIGHTS, **3.F.6** KING OF THE CASTLE, **3.F.11** PRETEND FIGHTING, **3.K.1** JACKS, **3.K.3** MARBLES, **3.K.4** HOPSCOTCH, and what looks like the verse game **4.22** PLEASE MOTHER, MAY I GO OUT TO PLAY?. Tug of war, also depicted in the painting, is of course a part of games like **4.20** ORANGES AND LEMONS and **4.21** ARE YOU READY FOR A FIGHT?.

Though counting-out rhymes have no recorded history before the nineteenth century, some derive from rustic forms of counting which are very much older. The age of traditional singing games is unknown, though contemporary scholars are not as sure that they perpetuate very ancient folk rituals of courtship, marriage and death, as some folklorists were a century ago. Skipping games probably do not predate the nineteenth century, while hand clapping routines apparently belong to the twentieth. Ball bouncing routines belong primarily to the twentieth century, except for evidence in Gomme regarding the game of "Pots" (1898, pp. 64–65). The oral side of children's games is the virtual monopoly of the girls. The great extent and variety of singing games, skipping, ball bouncing and hand clapping routines and chants deserve separate treatment, and this I have given them.

SECTION 1

STARTING A GAME

As many others have pointed out, the procedure that takes place before a game is of great importance for children. Sometimes it seems to take up more time and arouse more excitement than the actual playing of the game itself. Even before the playground is reached there may already have been arguments and decisions made as to the games to be played and those who are to take part:

> "When we play with the boys we always decide up in the classroom. We go out in the playground and get all the boys together and then we ask them. If they don't want to play (with us) we find something else to play." girl, 10, Dalston 1983.

> "When we play games we all suggest what to play. Sometimes one of the girls suggests what to play, and if we like it we'll play it but if we don't then we play what we like." boy, same class.

In Inner London the integration of boys' and girls' playgrounds did not take place until the 1970s. Separate playgrounds for boys and girls may still have existed when I was collecting children's lore, but I did not come across any in my visits. As already noted, Fr. Damian Webb, in his introduction to the one volume collection of Alice Gomme's *Traditional Games* (1984, p. 15) regrets the passing of the single sex playground, but although there have been some losses as regards the repertoire of girls' singing games and the like, I believe the gains socially outweigh any losses.

The problems of integrated games exist much more in some schools than in others, as does the balance between games played separately by boys and girls and those played together. The urge to "put down" the girls is expressed in some schools:

> "Sometimes when we ask the boys to play in the class they get a bit moany. They're always shouting if they don't want to play a game (if) they think it's a bit of a girls' game. Sometimes when we're in the classroom and we want to play a game with the boys, and the boys want to play a little game with us we surround (sic) all together and make up a game between us so we all like the game." girl, 11, Dalston 1983.

> "Sometimes when we play the games we don't want the rough boys to play because they start trouble and some of us get hurt." girl, same class.

Decisions can be taken by the acknowledged leader or boss:

> "(_____) always organises our games. He bosses us about and he's always in charge." boy, 10, Dalston 1983.

> "(_____) sometimes organises the games and sometimes (_____). She tells us what to do. … and if there's any new ones." girl, same class.

Another boy modified what the first one had said about the absolute power of the leader:

> "When we play a game (_____) decides the game and if we like it we'll play it, but if we don't like it he decides another one." boy, same class.

In some schools there is a completely different approach, and a more democratic spirit prevails:

"Say people want to play 'Family he' and other people want 'Stuck in the mud', somebody will say, 'Well, let's have a vote.' You say, 'People who want to play *Family he*, put your hands up.' They count how many there are. Then the people who want to play 'Stuck in the mud' would put up their hands. The one that had the most hands would win." girl, 11, Finsbury 1983.

"We vote and sometimes it goes wrong so we change the game. Sometimes we each have an idea and then we pick which is the best. Sometimes we have a vote on which games and the most people that think the games are right, play." girl, 10, Kentish Town 1983.

It is not always decided by either the autocratic or the democratic method:

"If there's two games (suggested) we just row about it until we've decided the game. Otherwise we go round shouting, 'Who's going to play … ?' whatever game we're going to play." boy, 11, Kensington 1984.

"We argue a lot about who's going to play. If somebody comes along and says, 'Can I play?' others may say, 'No' or 'It's not my game.' " girl, same class.

When it is finally settled, by whatever method, what the game is that is going to be played, and who is to take part, it is probably a game where somebody has a particular role to play as seeker or catcher. This person has to be selected and the role is usually one to be avoided, though occasionally it is one to be sought. Some method therefore has to be used to decide who is to be "on it", "on", "it" or "he". All four of these terms are used in Inner London. Sometimes two, or rarely three, different terms can be found in the same school, or were when I made my visits to twenty-one schools between 1982 and 1984. To all intents and purposes "on" is not significant. It seems to be a shortened form of "on it".

on it   I found this term used in fourteen out of twenty-one schools in which:
   five used it solely
   three used it as well as "he"
   five used it as well as "it"
   one used it as well as "he" and "it"

he   I found this term used in nine out of twenty-one schools, in which:
   one used it solely
   three used it as well as "on it"
   four used it as well as "it"
   one used it as well as "on it" and "it"

it   I found this term used in eleven out of twenty-one schools, in which:
   one used it solely
   five used it as well as "on it"
   four used it as well as "he"
   one used it as well as "he" and "on it"

Sometimes different terms would be used by different age groups, but more rarely the same class might include children using different terms. The Opies (*CGSP*, 1969, p. 21) show by means of maps that in the London area "he" and "it" predominated, but this information was based on reports before the publication of the book in 1969. My findings would seem to indicate that "on it" had begun to replace the others. The Opies' maps showed that "on it" predominated in the west of Britain only.

Although counting out or "dipping" is overwhelmingly the most often used procedure for deciding who is to be "on it", there are a number of other ways.

"Sometimes people just decide to be 'on it'." boy, 11, Kensington 1984.

"If we can't decide who's going to be 'on' in a game of 'Had', or 'Bulldog' or something, we usually have a race and the last one who finishes is 'on'. We just run to the fence." boy, 10, Stoke Newington 1984.

"Sometimes we pick a person. They close their eyes and the children are round in a circle. The person in the middle sticks their arm out and points to someone." girl, 10, Shepherds Bush 1983.

"We have a race and the last one is 'on it' or the last one to put up their hand or something." girl, 11, Hampstead 1984.

"We say, 'Last one on the bench is on it'." boy, 11, Kentish Town 1983.

There is a much more complicated procedure sometimes called "Chinning Up", which is very popular. I came across versions in thirteen schools out of twenty-one visited. It depends on a routine with the hands and the recital of words: "Ching chang wallah" (Barnsbury, Cubitt Town, Dalston, Finsbury, Mile End 1983/85), "Chin chan channah" (Dalston), "Chin chan cholla" (Stoke Newington 1983), "Spud burst" (Kentish Town and Shepherds Bush 1983). Most versions agree that three children go through the procedure and one is eliminated until one is left who will be "on it". One hand is put forward to hold the others and the hands are vigorously moved up and down while the words are recited. The hands are then made into a shape to represent variously scissors, stone (rock), paper, hammer, cup and saucer, black magic. If two out of the three are the same, the odd one is eliminated.

"You all put your hands together and you go, 'Ching Chang wallah'. Then you make it [hand] into a shape: either a pair of scissors, a piece of paper or a rock. If there's two people who are the same and one person's different, the person who's different is out and not 'on it'." boy, Finsbury 1983.

"When it finally comes to two people, the shape decides. Say you get scissors and you get paper, the scissors can cut paper. If you get stone and paper, the paper wins because paper can wrap the stone up. The stone can blunt the scissors." girl, same class.

"For the scissors you put your fingers sideways. For the paper you put your hand flat. For the cup and saucer you make a fist and put your fist on your [other] hand. For a rock you just clench your fist.

For hammer you clench your fist and put your [other] hand at the end of your fist. For black magic you cross your two [?hands] on your shoulders." girl, Dalston 1983.

"You can either do scissors, bomb, stone, paper or crayon. Scissors can be blown up by a bomb. Scissors can cut paper and stone can blunt scissors. Paper can wrap bombs." boy, Barnsbury 1983.

This is strange logic indeed, but it was not questioned by any of the other children in this particular group.

If there are two left at the end of the elimination a "dummy" is chosen from those eliminated.

"At the end there's usually a dummy. [We say] 'Same as dummy has a choice.' We just pick someone, anyone that's out. If you get the same as the dummy then that's it. If you don't, the other person chooses whether they're 'on it' or not." boy, Barnsbury 1983.

In Mile End the dummy was called "holy" so the chant was, "Same as holy gets the choice." (1983).

"Chinning Up" is not just used for elimination. It can be used to decide an issue between just two players:

"We use it when there's two people, in a car perhaps, (or) when the others are playing something." girl, Kensington 1984.

The Opies (*CGSP*, 1969, pp. 25–28) give several chants under the section entitled "Odd Man Out" or "Chinging Up". They include a number from Inner London: "Ching Chang, Cholly"; "Dib, Dob, Dab"; "Ding, Dang, Dong"; "Dish, Dash, Dosh"; "Zig, Zag, Zog"; "Eee, Pas, Vous"; "Stink, Stank, Stoller". Only the first one was among those I collected. The procedure is presumably not old enough yet to have established a tradition.

As well as "Chinning Up" there are a number of other procedures to decide between two players. The spinning of a coin is probably the most hallowed by tradition. Gomme (1894, p. 200) includes it in her *Traditional Games* under the heading "Heads and Tails".

> "If you're playing a game and someone thinks it not fair, you have to toss a coin. Someone chooses heads and the other person, tails. If the person who chooses heads gets it right, they're not 'on it', the other person is. You can do it another way. You have to do it out of three choices. If you get it heads and then heads again that means you've won and the other person has to be 'on it'." girl, Shepherds Bush 1983.

Another old method is choosing a hand that holds something:

> "When you start a game sometimes, people think it isn't fair to be 'on it' so somebody gets a coin or pebble or anything and then hide it at the back of them. Then you try to guess which hand the pebble or coin is in. When you get it right you're not 'on it'. The one that doesn't get it right is 'on it' and that's fair." girl, same class.

Other methods of deciding include the following:

> "Sometimes when we want to start a game like shooting [for netball] we get a ball and two people stand opposite each other. Someone bounces a ball and the person who catches it is first." girl, Shepherds Bush 1983.

> "'Jumps' is where a person stands opposite another, three metres away and they have to jump at each other. One person has to jump on the other person's toes and then he's won." boy, Stoke Newington 1983.

> "'Bum rab' is where you stand opposite another person three metres away. You've got to put your foot down [heel to toe] until you get near the person. You've got to end up stepping on a person's foot and then you've got first choice." same boy.

There is also sometimes a procedure for opting out of the decision as to who is to be "on it". I do not know the finer points of this:

> "You say, 'Turn around, touch the ground, bagsie not on it'." girl, Barnsbury 1983; also Finsbury, Kentish Town 1983; Hampstead 1984.

"You say, 'Touch black and white, I'm not included'." boy, Cubitt Town 1983; also Kentish Town.

Sluckin (1981, p. 33) lists other uses of "bagsie": to claim precedence; to gain possession of an object; to avoid or obtain a role; to state extra rules in a game. Though I did not come across these uses from the children who were my informants, I was told about the claiming of a respite during the playing of a game by using the word "thanies" or "vanies", usually accompanied by crossing fingers:

"Someone's 'on it' and you want to go to the toilet. You've got to cross your fingers so the person doesn't 'had' you." girl, Shepherds Bush 1983.

"When you're playing catch games and you have to do up your shoelace or something, you cross your fingers over and go 'thanies' so you can't get 'had'." boy, Finsbury 1983; and similar Stoke Newington 1983 and Hampstead 1984 ("vanies").

"Say like someone picked their nose and 'had' someone else, all the other people would say 'thanies'. The person who had just been 'had' can't have anyone, but if they haven't got their fingers crossed they *can* be 'had'." girl, Shepherds Bush 1983.

The procedure is dealt with at length by the Opies. They report the use of *fains* or *fainites*, along with a number of other items.[1] R. D. Jameson (in Leach and Fried, 1949–1950, p. 379) mentions that "Holding up the hand with fingers spread, and crying 'Fingers,' or 'Fins,' is a call for temporary truce or surrender by a player in children's games".

NOTES

1. Opies (*LL*, 1959): *fains*, etc., pp. 140, 151; "Avoiding", pp. 139–140; "Obtaining Respite", pp. 141–153. Whelan (1982, 111) reports using the word *fainites* "if you wanted to stop a game for some reason" in Poplar in the 1920s.

SECTION 2

COUNTING-OUT RHYMES

Introduction

Counting out as a method of deciding who is to be "on it" is probably almost universal. It is certainly to be found among all English-speaking children and by those using the main European languages. As noted in the Introduction, one of the first books to be devoted entirely to children's lore was Henry Bolton's *The Counting-out Rhymes of Children* (1888). He gave the words of 877 rhymes and variants, of which 468 were in the English language (mainly collected in the USA). Another early collection was that of Walter Gregor (*Counting-out Rhymes of Children*, 1891). Many of the examples he gave are still in use, either in exactly the same form as he noted them, slightly modified or radically different. In most schools in Inner London counting-out rhymes are known as "dips" and the process of finding out who is to be chosen for a particular role, usually being "on it" (or "he" or "it"), is known as "dipping". The use of the word "dipping" for counting out does not appear to be a very old one. There are no references to it in Bolton's book and his collection does not include any rhymes beginning "Ip, dip" or "Ipper, dipper". However, he includes rhymes beginning "Eenie, meenie, tipsy/

tippety/tipte-tee/tip de-dee", "Ana, mana, dippery Dick", and "Henry, menry, deeper, dee" (pp. 107 and 108). According to the Opies (*CGSP*, 1969, pp. 28ff), the term was apparently not in general use before the 1940s and is not generally used in Scotland, the USA, or Canada. They state that it began to be used in the 1930s. Some children would "dip" by touching or pointing to the ground before they began to count out (Opies, *CGSP*, 1969, p. 29).

I came across **2.30** IP, DIP, THREEPENNY BIT,/You are not it in 1968 (Mile End). Many counting-out rhymes begin with the words "Ip, dip", including Nos. **2.30–2.36** in this collection. One of these rhymes is almost certain to be in use in Inner London wherever counting out takes place. Despite this, I found some schools where my young informants were not in the habit of using the term "dips" for counting-out rhymes, nor for "dipping" applied to the process of selecting who is to be "on it", even though they may have been using "Ip dip" rhymes.

Counting-out rhymes either let the last syllable of the rhyme decide who is to be "on it" or they eliminate the members of the group, one by one, until the last person left becomes the one who is "on it". The latter procedure appears to be much more common. Many rhymes actually specify this procedure by their endings: "You are not 'he'"; "Out goes you"; "It may not be you"; "O-U-T spells out". An example of the former is to be found in rhyme **2.28** (not a common one): THE GRASS IS GREEN,/The sky is blue,/Everyone's out,/Except for you. Many all-purpose rhymes, of course, can be used for either procedure.

The elimination can be a quick process, even where there are a number of children, by using a very short rhyme like **2.43** BOY SCOUT, Walk out. There are many ways in which the "chance" factor can be reduced by deciding where in the circle the counting is to start, by selecting a particular rhyme with the right number of counts, by extending a particular rhyme, or by deciding whoever is to be the last person pointed to in the rhyme, or by elimination. Sluckin (1981, pp. 16–17) deals with the element of manipulation in detail.

To get round this difficulty there are a number of rhymes where, at a particular point, the child is asked for a number, for the choice of a colour, for a child's name or for a "yes/no" response. Examples include: **2.4** RACING CAR NUMBER NINE and **2.5** IPPER DIPPER

DATION. A colour choice is requested in **2.11** MY MUM AND YOUR MUM, **2.25** MRS. MOP OWNED A SHOP, and **2.26** AS I WAS WALKING DOWN INKY-PINKY LANE.

In **2.8** ROUND AND ROUND THE APPLE PIE a "yes/no" answer can be given as well as a choice of colour. In **2.24** THERE'S A PARTY ON THE HILL there is a "yes/no" choice and the name of a chosen "loved one". The number of syllables in the chosen colour or name will of course dictate the length of the counting-out process. In my experience it is unlikely that reluctance or eagerness to be "on it" would be such as to get round the procedure by "setting up" the count and choice of child with appropriate answers. A "yes/no" answer is asked for in **2.38** DID YOU CLEAN YOUR SHOES LAST NIGHT?. The answer will alter the choice by one count, but as this rhyme as well as **2.39** YOUR SHOES NEED CLEANING and **2.40** DIRTY SHOES, DIRTY SOCKS depend on counting feet rather than people, it might signify no change. Rhyme **2.37** WHOSE SHOES ARE THE CLEANEST? can select the child who has the brightest polish on his/her shoes.

The almost universal rhyme **2.12** ONE POTATO, TWO POTATO, in use in the same form for most of the twentieth century, depends on two fists being extended, and for a player to be eliminated both fists have to be counted out. The result will be different if the ending is "One bad spud" or "One bad spud and out you must go" or "One bad spud and out you go". Ordinary counting takes place in **2.10** BIG BEN STRIKES TEN. The once ubiquitous rhyme, **2.2** ONE, TWO, THREE, FOUR, FIVE, SIX, SEVEN,/All good children go to heaven, seems to have almost disappeared. I found it in only one school out of twenty-one visited.

Equally widespread as the "Ipper dipper" and "Ip dip" rhymes already referred to are the "Eeny meeny" ones, particularly **2.13** EENY MEENY MACKER ACKER. This has many similarities with counting-out rhymes in various European countries, and there is much evidence which links this type of rhyme with sheep counting sequences in Cumberland at the beginning of the nineteenth century, which in turn are thought by some to be derived from numerals in the various Celtic languages of the British Isles, though this is a matter of debate. A later form of counting among children which has clear links with these sequences was called Chinese counting, and in this form, or in rhymes derived from it which were used for counting out, it apparently spread throughout the English-speaking countries in the nineteenth and twentieth centuries.

The "Eeny meeny" rhymes form part of a larger grouping which appeals to children through sounds, rhymes, rhythms, and alliteration, plus a hint of a secret language exclusive to their subculture. So we have the rhymes: **2.1**c ICKY OCKY, HORSE'S COCKY, **2.15** EASIE PEASIE, **2.17** ALA ALA MING MONG, **2.18** JINK, JINK, POM, PINK, **2.20** INKY, PINKY, PONKY, **2.21** IM STIM, STAMMER BOMMER, **2.22** IM PIM, SEPTIPIM, and many others. **2.16** EENY DEENY DIP combines the "Eeny meeny" and the "dip" traditions.

The rhyme EENY MEENY MINY MO,/Catch a nigger by his toe, probably derives from slave bounty laws of the 1850s in pre-emancipation America. (See notes to **2.14**). Although this rhyme was pretty general in the first half of the twentieth century in London, our multiracial school communities and general abhorrence of racism have presented children with problems. These of course arise from the word *nigger* which children realise is an unacceptable term and is offensive to Black people, including children. The problem is avoided either by leaving the first line and changing the rest of the rhyme, or changing the word variously to *piggy*, *pee-pee*, *tigger*, *finger*, *figure*, *fishy* etc. Canadian alternatives include *monkey* and *beatnik* (Fowke, 1969, p. 111) and American ones include *boy*, *tiger* and *rooster*.[1] An example of changing the rhyme drastically is **2.14**c EENY MEENY, MINY, MO,/Sit the baby on the po. Only two schools gave me the traditional version, accompanied by much embarrassed giggling and glances at any Black members of the group to see how they would take it. They would, with obvious selfconsciousness, explain that although they knew the rhyme, they never used it themselves.

Of the fifty-nine counting-out rhymes I collected, at least sixteen are found in broadly similar versions in Bolton's volume of 1888,[2] and four have versions in the nursery rhyme collections of Halliwell.[3] Although twelve were found in only one school each and had no printed versions to compare with, others have printed versions as skipping rhymes, so it would appear that both tradition and innovation are well represented in this genre. The five counting-out rhymes most commonly encountered were **2.1** IBBLE OBBLE, BLACK BOBBLE; **2.12** ONE POTATO,

TWO POTATO; **2.33** IP, DIP, DOGS' SHIT; **2.31** IP, DIP, SKY BLUE, WHO'S IT? NOT YOU, and **2.5** IPPER DIPPER DATION. Their incidence varied from eighteen out of twenty-one schools to thirteen out of twenty-one schools. There are very few really indecent counting-out rhymes. The IP, DIP, DOGS' SHIT rhyme is popular, probably because it provides an excuse to use as many "unacceptable" words as possible.

NOTES

1. "Boy" appears in Hughes and Bontemps (1958, p. 422); "rooster" in Withers, (*CO*, 1970, [p. 1]), and "tiger" in Withers *(RIMP*, 1948, p. 83), and Evans, (*WI*, 1956, p. 8). Leach and Fried (1949, p. 339), state that "when the war (WWII) ended ... they ... continued the trend away from 'nigger' to such variants as 'baby,' 'rooster,' 'black cat,' and 'rabbit.'" "Rabbit" is given by the Solomons (1980, pp. 65, 71) and Abrahams and Rankin (1980, p. 58), who also give "baby". "Robber" appears in Abrahams (1969, p. 47). The Knapps give "tiger", "baby", "lion", "monkey", "dummy", and "rabbit" as alternatives (1976, pp. 5, 197), and Ritchie cites an Australian version, "wombat" (*GC*, 1965, p. 49).
2. Bolton (1888): **2.31** IP, DIP, SKY BLUE, WHO'S IT? NOT YOU (p. 92); **2.2** ONE, TWO, THREE, FOUR, FIVE, SIX, SEVEN and **2.3** TUPPENCE ON THE WATER (pp. 94, 123); **2.14** EENY MEENY MINY MO (pp. 103–106); **2.6** EGGS, BUTTER, SUGAR, TEA (pp. 104, 105); **2.13** EENY MEENY MACKER ACKER (p. 109); **2.4** RACING CAR NUMBER NINE, **2.12** ONE POTATO, TWO POTATO, **2.18** JINK, JINK, POM, PINK, and **2.41** TURN THE DIRTY DISH CLOTH (p. 111); **2.8** ROUND AND ROUND THE APPLE PIE, **2.26** AS I WAS WALKING DOWN INKY-PINKY LANE, and **2.42** WASH THE DISHES (p. 113); **2.56** CHING CHONG, CHINAMAN (p. 116); **2.23** ICKLETY, PICKLETY, MY BLACK HEN (p. 117); **2.57** DOCTOR FOSTER WENT TO GLOUCESTER (p. 119).
3. Halliwell (*NRE*, 1842, p. 116): **2.6** EGGS, BUTTER, SUGAR, TEA; (*NRE*, 1844, p. 166): **2.23** ICKLETY, PICKLETY, MY BLACK HEN; (*NRE*, 1846, p. 31): **2.57** DOCTOR FOSTER WENT TO

GLOUCESTER; (*NRNTE*, c1870, p. 107): **2.23** ICKLETY, PICKLETY, MY BLACK HEN; (*PRNT*, 1849, p. 107): **2.11** MY MUM AND YOUR MUM.

Counting-out Rhymes

2.1   IBBLE OBBLE, BLACK BOBBLE

> A.   Ibble obble, black bobble,
>   Ibble obble out,
>   Turn the dirty dish cloth
>   Inside out.
>   First turn it in,
>   Then turn it out,
>   Ibble obble, black bobble,
>   Ibble obble out.

Sometimes followed by **2.7** ROUND AND ROUND THE BUTTER DISH/bushes or "It's not because you're dirty …" (lines from **2.5B** and **2.31**). See also **2.41**.

> Mile End 1983. Versions of at least the first part of this rhyme are universal in Inner London.

Printed versions Bolton (see below); Daiken, *TTP*, Ittle-attle,/Black bottle, p. 93; Ford (see below); Fowke, Ittle ottle blue bottle, p. 109; Gregor (see below); Gullen, Eetle ottle, Black bottle, … p. 15; Kings (see below); Nicholson (see below); Opies, *CGSP*, pp. 33–34, 196; Parry-Jones, Ickle, ockle, black cockle, p. 139; Ritchie, *GC*, several versions, pp. 46–47; Rodger, Eettle, ottle, black bottle …, p. 20; Rosen and Steele, Ittle, ottle, black bottle, [pp. 1–2]; Ibble [obble], black bobble, [p. 10]; Sutton-Smith, Ickle, ockle, pp. 63, 71; Todd, Ickle ockle chocolate bottle, 3; Turner, both Eetle ottle and Ibble abble, p. 12.

Early notings Wring the dish cloth;/Out, spot, out! Bolton, 1888, p. 111. Eetle, otle,/Black bottle,/ You're out. (Edinburgh), and four further versions, Gregor, 1891, p. 27. Eetly, otly,/Black botlie:/ Out goes she (or he), Nicholson, 1897, p. 307. Ford, 1904, p. 54. Ickle ockle, black bottle, Kings 2, 1930, p. 31.

Recordings MacColl and Seeger, *The Elliotts of Birtley*; BBC 13869 (78) (1949, Edinburgh).

> B. Ibble obble, black bobble,
> My mother's tits wobble.

Dulwich 1983.

Printed versions cf. Hubbard, Ickle ockle, choc'late bockle, mentioned, 263; Opies, *CGSP*, p. 196: Ickle ockle, chocolate bottle, ickle ockle out; if you want a titty bottle please shout out.

> C. Icky ocky, horse's cocky,
> Horse's cocky, out.

Brixton 1982; Brockley 1983.

Printed versions Lowenstein, p. 26; Rosen and Steele, Icky acky/Horses cacky, [p. 20]; Rutherford, Icks, ocks, donkey's cocks, p. 51.

Early noting Iddy oddy cock's body/Inside out, c1890, Northumberland, Opies, *CGSP*, p. 32.

2.2 ONE, TWO, THREE, FOUR, FIVE, SIX, SEVEN

> One, two, three, four, five, six, seven,
> All good children went to heaven.

Brockley 1983.

Printed versions Abrahams, "related to a common counting-out rhyme", pp. 151–152; Bolton (see below); Botkin (see below); Boyce and Bartlett (see below); Brady, rhyme for a ball game, p. 54; Coffin and Cohen, p. 190; Cumnock Academy, p. 29; Daiken, *OGS*, p. 15; Evans, *WI*, p. 15; Ford (see below); Kellett, p. 102 (and see below); Fowke, p. 109; Gadsby and Harrop, No. 38; Gaskell (see below); Gregor (see below); Gullen, p. 35; Hughes and Bontemps, p. 422; Kenney, p. 50; Newell (see below); Opies, *ISE*, p. 56, *CGSP*, p. 37; Petershams, skipping game, p. 46; Ritchie, *GC*, p. 136; Rodger, p. 20; Shaw (1970), p. 73; Solomons, taunt, p. 77; Sutton-Smith, p. 64; Talley (see below); Turner, p. 15; Withers, *CO*, [p. 6].

Early notings 1, 2, 3, 4, 5, 6, 7,/All good children go to heaven, Bolton, 1888, p. 94. Cf. One, two, three, four, five, six, seven,/A' that fisher dodds widna win t'haven. (Fraserburgh), Gregor, 1891, p. 30. One, two, three, four, five, six, seven/All good children go to Heaven, Newell, 1903, p. 202. Ford, 1904, p. 51; Gaskell, 1913, p. 4; Kellett, 1920s, p. 102; Talley, 1922, p. 200; Boyce and Bartlett, 1941, p. 29; Botkin, *TAF*, 1944, p. 773.

2.3   TUPPENCE ON THE WATER

Tuppence on the water,
A penny on the sea,
Penny on the roundabout
And round goes me.

Cubitt Town 1983.

Printed versions Abrahams, "Usually a counting-out or race-starting rhyme", p. 159; Coffin and Cohen, as Bolton, below, p. 190; Daiken, *TTP*, as Douglas, below, p. 95; Douglas (see below); Ford (see below); Gaskell (see below); Gullen, following 1, 2, 3, 4, 5, 6, 7, p. 35; Kellett, following 1, 2, 3, 4, 5, 6, 7, (?early noting), p. 102; Opies, *ISE*, following 1, 2, 3, 4, 5, 6, 7, p. 56; Ritchie, *GC*, following 1, 2, 3, 4, 5, 6, 7, p. 136; Rodger, p. 21; Shaw, 1970, p. 76; Solomons, p. 77; Sutton-Smith (see below).

Early notings One, two, three, 4, 5, 6, 7,/ All good children go to heaven;/A penny by the water,/ Tuppence by the sea,/ Threepence by the railway,/ Out goes she! Bolton, 1888, p. 94; also quoted thus by Sutton-Smith, p. 64 (Nelson, New Zealand, 1890). Ford, 1904, as Bolton, p. 51; Gaskell, c1913, as Bolton, p. 4. Penny on the water, tuppence on the sea,/Threepence on the railway—out goes she—Douglas, 1916, p. 93, 1931, p. 53.

2.4 RACING CAR NUMBER NINE

A.   Racing car number nine
      Losing petrol all the time
      How many gallons did it lose? (e.g.) Five
      The one that comes to number five
      Will surely not be it.
      l, 2, 3, 4, 5.

<u>Battersea</u>, Brixton, Greenwich <u>1982</u>; Borough, Brockley, Cubitt Town 1983.

B.   Engine, engine, number nine
      Running down Kalaga line,
      If the train fell off the track
      Would you want your money back?
      Yes. Y-E-S spells yes
(or)   No. N-O spells no.
      So out you must go
      With a jolly good slap round the jaw.

Clapham 1974.

See also **6.A.33**.

Printed versions Abrahams, p. 48; Bolton (see below); Botkin (see below); Cosbey, p. 72; Evans, *WI,* pp. 18–19; Fowke, p. 110; Knapps, p. 26; Newell (see below); Opies, *CGSP,* pp. 38, 58, 59; Petershams, p. 5; Ritchie, *GC,* p. 47; Solomons, pp. 49, 68; Sutton-Smith, p. 69; Turner, p. 13; Withers, *CO* [pp. 24, 25]; Wood, *FAFR,* p. 53; Worstell, skipping rhyme, p. 36.

Early notings Engine number nine;/Ring the bell when it's time./O-U-T spells out goes he,/Into the middle of the dark blue sea, Bolton, 1888, p. 111. Engine No. 9,/Out goes she, Newell, 1903, p. 203. Botkin, *TAF*, 1944, p. 768.

2.5 IPPER DIPPER DATION

A. Ipper dipper dation (Ibble dibble dation)
My operation,
How many people at the station?
Close your eyes and think, please.
"Four"
The one that comes to number four
Will surely not be He.
One, two, three, four.

(Eliminated one by one; last left is "he".)

<u>Walworth 1974, 1979, 1981</u>; Versions: S. E. London 1967, 1983; E. London 1968, 1983. Current in all parts of Inner London 1982–84.

B. Ipper dipper dation,
My operation,
How many people at the station?
Not because you're dirty,
Not because you're clean,
My mum says you're the fairest queen (fairy queen)
So out you must go with a jolly good smack,
Right round your face,
Like this.

Dalston 1983.

See also **2.31**.

Printed versions Fowke, pp. 77, 116; cf. Kellett, Dic dic dation corporation, (?early noting), p. 47; Opies, *CGSP*, p. 58; Rosen and Steele, [p. 20]; Sluckin, p. 14; Smith, *BBHG*, Dib, dib, dation, p. 64; Turner, Dictation ..., p. 88.

Early noting Dippy dippy dation/My operation/How many people at the station? Tooting, c1930 (correspondent 1980, from memory).

2.6 EGGS, BUTTER, SUGAR, TEA

A. Eggs, butter, sugar, tea,
Fairy on the Christmas tree,
Naughty boy, naughty girl,
Ice cream.

West Norwood 1973.

B. Eggs, butter, sugar, tea,
You are not he.

Mile End 1968.

C. Fairy cake and bumble bee,
What would you like to be?

Mile End 1968.

Printed versions Bolton (see below); Halliwell (see below); Holbrook, p. 122; Lang (see below); Leach and Fried, ll. 4–5 of a rhyme beginning "Eena, meena ...": Eggs, butter, cheese, bread,/Stick, stock, stone dead – O-U-T!, p. 340; Northall (see below); Opies, *ISE*, as Bolton, p. 56, *CGSP*, Eena, meena, mona, my, last two lines like Bolton, p. 43; Withers, *CO*, .../Ease, cheese, butter, bread,/Out goes you!, [p. 13].

Early notings cf. Eggs, butter, cheese, bread,/Stick, stock, stone, dead,/Stick him up, stick him down,/ Stick him in the old man's crown, Halliwell, *NRE*, 1842, p. 116. Bolton, 1888, pp. 104, 110, 111; Northall, 1892, p. 344; Lang, 1897, "A game on the slate", p. 186.

2.7 ROUND AND ROUND THE BUTTER DISH

   A. Round and round the butter dish
      One, two, three,
      You are not he.

Walworth 1974.

   B. Round and round the bushes,
      Is one, two, three,
      Do you want to be he?

   No.

   Then we shall see
   Eggs, butter, sugar, tea
   You are not he.

Marylebone 1967.

Printed versions Abrahams and Rankin, p. 11; Gomme (see below); Holbrook, p. 123; Kellett, pp. 114–115; Opies (see below); Withers, *CO*, …/Ease, cheese, butter, bread [p. 13], All around the butter dish [p. 28], *RIMP*, p. 84.

Early notings Round about the punch bowl,--/One, two, three;/If anybody wants a bonnie lassie,/Just take me, singing game, Gomme, 1898, pp. 84–85. Round and round the butter dish,/One, two, three;/If you want a pretty girl/Just pick me, dipping rhyme "current in both Britain and America since the 1930s", Opies, *SG*, p. 230.

For other early rhymes including "Eggs, butter, sugar, tea", see for example Bolton, 1888, pp. 104, 105, 110, 111, etc., and Chambers, Halliwell, Northall, and Douglas, especially following rhymes beginning "1 2 3 4 5 6 7, All good children …" and "Twopence on the railway".

2.8 ROUND AND ROUND THE APPLE PIE

Round and round the apple pie,
Have you ever told a lie?

No.

Yes you did, you know you did,
You stole your mother's teapot lid.

What colour was it?

Pink.

No, it wasn't it was gold,
That's another lie you told,

(So out you go).

Clapham 1984.

Printed versions Abrahams, Bake a pudding,/Bake a pie, p. 15; Abrahams and Rankin, pp. 20–21, Bolton (see below); Botkin (see below); Briggs, like Bolton, below, p. 91; Ford (see below); Fowke, p. 112; Gregor (see below); Gullen, p. 13; Newell (see below); Opies, *CGSP*, p. 61; Petershams, p. 33; Sutton-Smith, skipping rhyme, p. 76; Withers, *CO*, like Bolton, below [pp. 19, 29].

Early notings As I went up the apple tree,/All the apples fell on me./Bake a puddin', bake a pie,/Did you ever tell a lie?/Yes, I did, and many times./O-U-T spells out goes she,/Right in the centre of the dark deep blue sea. *Variation lines 5 and 6*:-- Yes, you did, you know you did,/You broke your mother's teapot lid, Bolton, 1888, p. 113. As I geed up the aipple tree, (five variants), Gregor, 1891, p. 28; also cf. a rhyme containing the lines As I went by yon pear tree,/All the pears stood by me, Gregor, 1891, p. 16, and another beginning Bake a pudding, bake a pie, Gregor, 1891, p. 24. As I went up the apple-tree/All the apples fell on me;/Bake a pudding, bake a pie,/Did you ever tell a lie?/Yes, you did, you know you did,/You broke your mother's teapot-lid-/L-I-D, that spells lid, Newell, 1903, p. 203. Ford, 1904, p. 49; Botkin, *TAF*, 1944, p. 777.

2.9 TARZAN IN THE JUNGLE

    A. Tarzan in the jungle
         Eating fish and chips,
         Along came a lady
         Scratching her tits.

Borough 1983.

    B. Walking through the jungle,
         Got a bellyache,
         Wanna go toilet,
         Too late!

Brockley 1967.

These are probably based on a series of rhymes popularised in the Charlie Chester radio programmes in the 1940s and 1950s.

Printed versions cf. Lowenstein (version B), pp. 20, 38; cf. Opies, *LLS*, Down in the jungle/Living in a tent,/Better than a pre-fab –/No rent! p. 105; Ritchie, *SS*, football rhyme, p. 129; Rutherford, an amalgamation of the two rhymes given above, p. 124; Turner, similar to B, p. 107.

2.10 BIG BEN STRIKES TEN

    Big Ben strikes ten.
    1, 2, 3, 4, 5, 6, 7, 8, 9, 10.

Brixton 1982; Barnsbury, Kentish Town 1983.

See also **6.A.16** and **6.B.1**.

Printed versions Douglas (see below); Opies, *LLS*, skipping rhyme, p. 4; Ritchie, *SS*, chant, p. 39.

Early noting Douglas, mentioned, 1916, p. 49, 1931, p. 26.

2.11 MY MUM AND YOUR MUM

My mum and your mum
Were drying out the clothes.
My mum gave your mum
A punch on the nose.
What colour was the blood?
Yellow.
Y-E-L-L-O-W.

Shepherds Bush 1983.

Printed versions Abrahams, "Usually a counting-out rhyme", p. 133; Botkin (see below); Boyce and Bartlett (see below); Brady, p. 48; Cosbey, p. 82; Daiken, *OGS*, p. 31, *TTP*, p. 94; Evans, *JRR*, p. 7, *WI*, p. 11; Fowke, skipping rhyme, p. 57; Halliwell (see below); Kenney, p. 50; Knapps, p. 26; Mills and Bishop (see below); Montgomerie, as Halliwell and Northall, p. 48; Northall (see below); Opies, *CGSP*, p. 59; Ritchie, *GC*, p. 39; Rosen and Steele, back cover; Solomons, p. 73; Sutton-Smith, p. 70; Turner, skipping, p. 33; Withers, *CO* [pp. 22, 30]; Worstell, p. 22.

Early notings My mother and your mother/Went over the way;/Said my mother to your mother,/It's chop-a-nose day! Halliwell, *PRNT*, 1849, p. 107, and Northall, 1892, p. 413. My mother, your mother, hanging out the clothes;/My mother gave your mother a punch in the nose./What color did it turn?/Red, yellow, blue, green, violet, orange etc., Mills and Bishop, 1937, 32. Boyce and Bartlett, 1941, as Halliwell and Northall, p. 54. Botkin, *TAF*, 1944, p. 797.

Recording Webb, *Children's Singing Games*.

2.12 ONE POTATO, TWO POTATO

> A. One potato, two potato,
> Three potato, four,
> Five potato, six potato,
> Seven potato, more.
> One bad spud (Bad spud out)
> (And out you must go).

Universal in Inner London.

Printed versions Abrahams, "Usually a counting-out rhyme", p. 149; Boyce and Bartlett (see below); Brady, p. 5; Coffin and Cohen, p. 190; Cumnock Academy, p. 29; Evans, *WI*, p. 30; Fowke, p. 109; Gullen, p. 32; Holbrook, p. 123; Hubbard, mentioned, 263; Kellett, p. 19 (?and early noting); Knapps, p. 25; Opies, *CGSP*, p. 54; Petershams, p. 49; Ritchie, *GC*, p. 41; Rodger, p. 19; Rosen and Steele [p. 2]; Smith, *TGH*, p. 11; Smith, *BBHG*, p. 60; Solomons, p. 70; Sutton-Smith, p. 68; Turner, p. 15; Withers, *CO* [p. 8].

Early noting Boyce and Bartlett, 1941, p. 29.

> B. One potato, two potato, three potato, four,
> Sixteen skinheads knocking at the door,
> One with a hammer, one with a pick,
> One with a water pistol hanging from his prick.

Brockley 1983.

> C. One banana, two banana, three banana, four,
> All went off to the third world war,
> One with a tommy gun, one with a pick,
> One with a hand grenade hanging from his prick.

Hampstead 1984.

B. and C. are reminiscent of version E. and possibly F. of **6.A.36**.

Printed version cf. Shaw, 1970, p. 110.

Early notings This dip has certainly been current since the 1920s and may perhaps be derived from the rhyme noted by Bolton (1888, p. 111): Three potatoes in a pot/Take one out and leave it hot. See also Turner, p. 15. It may also have connections with the many verses playing on the words "One, two, three", e.g. One-ery, two-ery, etc. as in Bolton (1888, pp. 94–101), and Lang (1897, p. 17). Cf. also: One a bin, two a bin, three a bin, four,/Five a bin, six a bin, seven, gie o'er; etc., used to start a hide and seek game, Gomme, 1894, p. 211.

Recording Webb, *Children's Singing Games*.

2.13 EENY MEENY MACKER ACKER

    A.   Eeny meeny macker acker,
          Air eye donnalacker
          Chicker locker, olly popper,
          Om pom push bag.

Deptford 1983.

    B.   Eeny meeny macker acker,
          Dair die dominacker,
          Chicker opper, lolly popper,
          Om pear push.

Brixton 1982.

    C.   Eeny meeny many acker,
          Dair eye dominacker,
          Icker bocker, lolly popper,
          Om pom push.

Battersea 1982.

D. Eeny meeny macker acker,
   Air eye dominacker,
   Chicker ricker, room, boom,
   Chinese bush.

Cubitt Town 1983.

E. Eeny meeny macker acker,
   Air eye dominacker,
   Sugar pooker, lolly popper,
   Om pom poo.

Hampstead 1984.

This rhyme is universal in one of innumerable permutations of the above.

Printed versions Abrahams, Acca, bacca,/Boom a cracka, counting-out rhyme, p. 5; Bolton (see below); Cosbey, Acka backa, soda cracker, p. 62; Daiken, *CGTY*, p. 2, *TTP*, Eena, meener, ricker, racker, p. 93; Evans, *JRR*, p. 7; Fowke, p. 111; Hubbard, mentioned, 263; Kellett, Eeny meeny macker racker, pp. 18–19 (?and early noting); Kelsey, *K1*, 42; Knapps, like Bolton's: Aka, baka, … p. 26; McMorland, part of a song, pp. 88–89; Nelson, Icka backa, icka backa, p. 61; Opies, *CGSP*, pp. 40–41; Petershams, Hacker, packer, soda cracker, p. 48; Ritchie, *GC*, p. 45; Rosen and Steele, back cover; Sluckin, pp. 13, 15; Smith, *BBHG*, p. 58; Sutton-Smith, Icky acky chew the baccy, p. 69; Turner, p. 11; Withers, *CO* [pp. 10–11, 13, 22]; Wood, *FAFR*, Icky-bicky-soda cracker, p. 88.

Early notings Hackabacker, chew tobacco,/Hackabacker chew;/ Hackabacker eat a cracker,/ Out goes you! Bolton, 1888, p. 109. Also cf. many other rhymes in Bolton, e.g. p. 103 rhyme 569; p. 104 rhymes 575, 578, 587; p. 109 rhymes 664, 667, 669, 670.

Recording Webb, *Children's Singing Games.*

2.14 EENY MEENY MINY MO

   A. Eeny meeny miny mo,
       Catch a nigger by his toe.
       If he hollers let him go,
       Eeny meeny miny mo.

Brockley 1967; Mile End 1968; Borough, Cubitt Town 1983.

   B. Eeny meeny miny mo,
       Catch a tigger by the toe.
       If it screams let it go,
       Eeny meeny miny mo.

Blackheath, Kentish Town 1983.

Other replacements for *nigger* were *finger*, Stoke Newington 1983 and Kensington 1984; *fishy*, Dalston 1983; *piggy*, Walworth 1979; *pee pee*, Hampstead 1984; and *fire*, Shepherds Bush 1983.

Printed versions Abrahams, p. 47; Botkin (see below); Cumnock Academy, p. 29; Daiken, *CGTY*, p. 10; Douglas (see below); Evans, *WI*, p. 8; Ford (see below); Fowke, p. 111; Gregor (see below); Gullen, p. 14; Harrowven, pp. 33, 326; Holbrook, p. 121; Hughes and Bontemps, .../ Catch a boy by his toe, p. 422; Knapps, p. 197; Leach and Fried, pp. 339–340; Mills and Bishop (see below); Nicholson (see below); Opies, *ODNR*, pp. 156–157, *CGSP*, p. 36; Parry-Jones, p. 138; Ritchie, *GC*, pp. 45, 49; Rodger, p. 19; cf. Shaw, 1970, p. 84; Sluckin, p. 14; Smith, *BBHG*, p. 59; Sutton-Smith, pp. 62, 63, 70; Turner, p. 11; Withers, *CO* [p. 1]; *RIMP*, p. 83.

Early notings There are counting-out rhymes beginning "Hana, mana, mona mike" and similar noted as early as 1815 (New York, *Notes and Queries*, 1st series, Vol. 11). They were like the "Eeny meeny macker acker" rhymes without any current meaning. See also Bolton, 1888, pp. 103–106; Gregor, 1891, pp. 11ff., and specifically pp. 19, 20;

Nicholson, 1897, p. 308; Ford, 1904, p. 39; Douglas, 1916, p. 78, 1931, p. 44; Mills and Bishop, 1937, 34; Botkin, *TAF*, 1944, pp. 768, 800.

The "Catch a nigger by his toe" versions apparently date from the middle of the nineteenth century. Leach and Fried (p. 339) inform us that at this time, slaves in America were escaping by railway from the Southern states to the north. To deal with this situation, the Fugitive Slave Law was being debated in 1850; in New England some people advocated sending escaped slaves back to the Southern state which they came from, while others were for letting them go free.

> Eeny, meeny, miny, mum,/Catch a nigger by the thumb;/If he hollers send him hum [home]/Eeny, meeny, miny, mum. (Connecticut, 1880s). Also Bolton, 1888, p. 106, rhyme 607, and Knapps, p. 197.

In the Midwest and South it was suggested that escaped slaves should pay a fine.

> Eeny, meeny, miny, mo,/Catch a nigger by the toe;/Ev'ry time the nigger hollers,/Make him pay you fifty dollars. (Nebraska, nineteenth century). Also Bolton, 1888, p. 106, rhyme 604, Cosbey, p. 72, and Knapps, p. 197.

From about the early 1960s the racist versions became more and more unacceptable in most parts of London. *Nigger* had been replaced by such alternatives as *piggy* and *tigger*. Versions of B. were more widespread outside London.

> C. Eeny meeny, miny mo,
>   Sit the baby on the po.
>   When it's done,
>   Wipe its bum,
>   With a piece of chewing gum.
>
> Borough 1983.

Printed versions Gaskell (see below); Kellett, p. 18 (?and early noting); Opies, *LLS,* p. 96, *CGSP,* p. 36; Ritchie, *GC,* p. 45; Turner, p. 12.

Early noting Eenie meenie minie mo,/Put the baby on the poe./When it's done, wipe its bum,/Eenie, meenie, minie mo, Gaskell, c1913, p. 8.

Recording Webb, *Children's Singing Games*.

2.15 EASIE PEASIE

> Easie peasie,
> Japanesee,
> Wash your face
> With lemon squeezie.
>
> Putney 1979; Shepherds Bush 1983.

Cf. the advertising catchphrase "Easy Peasy … Lemon Sqezy". Sqezy, which first came on the market in 1956, was the first washing-up liquid in a squeezy bottle. The catchphrase itself dates from about 1964.

Printed versions Bolton (see below); Gregor (see below); Ritchie, *GC*, Easie, osie, p. 39; Rodger, Eezie, ozie, p. 19.

Early notings cf. Ease, ose,/Man's nose;/Caul parritch,/pease brose, Bolton, 1888, p. 110. Eesy, osy,/ Man's brose,/Eesy, osy,/Out. (Nairn), and fourteen further versions, Gregor, 1891, p. 21.

2.16 EENY DEENY DIP

> Eeny deeny dip,
> My little ship,
> Sails in the water,
> Like a cup and saucer,
> Ip, dip, dip.
>
> Walworth 1981; Stoke Newington 1983.

See also **7.18**.

Printed versions Kellett, Dip dip dip my blue [little] ship, p. 48; Opies, *LLS,* p. 378, *CGSP* (see below); Rosen and Steele, first line, [p. 10]; Smith, *BBHG*, counting-out rhyme beginning "Sailing on the water like a cup and saucer", p. 62; Todd, p. 3.

Early noting the Opies (*CGSP*, Dip, dip, dip,/My blue ship …, p. 36) state that the rhyme had been current for fifty years.

2.17 ALA ALA MING MONG

> Ala ala ming mong,
> Ming mong musy,
> Missy, Missy Aboo,
> Chickaby, chickaboo,
> Chinese donkey.
>
> Brixton 1982.

Printed versions Gregor (see below); Opies, *CGSP*, p. 45 (Enfield) and see below; Ritchie, *GC*, p. 48; cf. Rosen and Steele, Ah rah, chickerah, back cover; cf. Roud, *DM1*, Erli erli/Chickali, Chickali, 25; cf. Shaw, 1970, "Chinese Alphabet", p. 51.

The Brixton version seems to combine the first three lines of the Enfield rhyme in *CGSP*, "Ala mala ming mong,/Ming mong mosey,/Oosey, oosey, ackedy,/I, vi, vack", with two from a much older rhyme in *CGSP* (see below).

Early notings cf. Ra, ra,/Chuckeree, chuckeree,/Ony, pony,/Ningy, ningy, na,/Addy, caddy, westoe,/ Anty, poo,/Chutipan, chutipan,/China, chu. (Fraserburgh), Gregor, 1891, p. 30. The Opies (*CGSP*, 1969, p. 39) quote the *Journal of American Folklore* 10, 1897, 321, referring to the rhyme as an example of "Chinese counting": Rye, chy, chookereye, chookereye,/Choo, choo, ronee, ponee,/Icky, picky, nigh,/ Caddy, paddy, vester,/Canlee, poo./Itty pau, jutty pau,/Chinee Jew.

2.18 JINK, JINK, POM, PINK

Jink, jink, pom, pink,
Inky, pinky, perky, pun.

Barnsbury 1983.

Printed versions Bolton (see below); Gregor (see below); cf. Kellett, Ink pink pen and ink, p. 114 (and see below); cf. Withers, *CO*, Ink, a-bink, a bottle of ink./The cork fell out and-you're It! [p. 30].

Early notings cf. Ink, pink, papers, ink,/Am, pam, push, Bolton, 1888, p. 111, No. 699. Ink, pink, penny, stink. (Fraserburgh), Gregor, 1891, p. 29. Ink pink pen and ink,/Who made that awful stink,/The dog said it was you, Kellett, 1920s, p. 58.

2.19 INKY, PINKY, PERKY, PLUM

Inky, pinky, perky (pear), plum,
Stick a banana (feather) up your bum,
When it's brown, pull it down,
Inky, pinky, perky, plum.

Barnsbury 1983.

Beginning and end similar to **2.44** EACH, PEACH, PEAR, PLUM.

2.20 INKY, PINKY, PONKY

Inky, pinky, ponky,
My daddy bought a donkey,
Donkey died, Daddy cried,
Inky, pinky, ponky.

Dulwich 1983; Kensington 1984.

Printed versions Fowke, p. 109; Opies, *CGSP*, p. 36; Rosen and Steele, front cover; Smith, *BBHG*, p. 61; Sutton-Smith, teasing, p. 97; Turner, p. 14.

2.21 IM STIM, STAMMER BOMMER

Im stim, stammer bommer,
Rommer, borer, rim tim,
Rim tim, bolly rat,
The core me.

Hampstead 1984.

2.22 IM PIM, SEPTIPIM

Im pim, septipim (In pin, septipin),
Im pim, out.

Shepherds Bush 1983.

Printed version Opies, *CGSP*, In pin, safety pin, in pin out, p. 31.

2.23 ICKLETY, PICKLETY, MY BLACK HEN

Icklety, picklety, my black hen,
She lays eggs for gentlemen,
Sometimes nine and sometimes ten,
Icklety, picklety, my black hen.

Brockley 1967.

Printed versions Bolton (see below); Boyce and Bartlett (see below); Briggs, p. 120; Daiken, *CGTY*, Mitty Matty had a hen, p. 10; Ford (see below); Gomme (see below); Gregor (see below); Gullen, two versions, p. 104; Halliwell (see below); Kings (see below); Lang (see below); Newell (see below); Nicholson (see below); Northall (see below); Opies, *ODNR*, pp. 201–202; Sutton-Smith, Games of chance, p. 90; Wood, *FAFR*, p. 84.

Early notings Hickety, pickety, my black hen,/She lays eggs for gentlemen;/Gentlemen come every day/To see what my black hen doth lay, Halliwell, *NRE*, 1844, p. 166, 1870, p. 102; there is another version beginning "Higglepy Piggleby" on p. 107 (5th edn). Hickety, pickety, my black hen,/She lays eggs for gentlemen;/Gentlemen come every day,/To see what my black hen doth lay./Some days five and some days ten,/She lays eggs for gentlemen. (Connecticut), Bolton, 1888, p. 117. For similar verses, see Bolton, pp. 114, 118. Eenity, feenity, my black hen, and five further versions, Gregor, 1891, pp. 18–19. Enniki, benniki, and Hickety, pickety, Northall, 1892, p. 345. Ticky Touchwood, Gomme, 1894, p. 292. Lang, 1897, as Halliwell, p. 222, and a fuller version, Higgley Piggley, p. 238. Nicholson, 1897, several versions, pp. 216–217. Mittie Mattie had a hen, Newell, 1903, p. 202. Ford, 1904: Hickety, pickety, my black hen, p. 27, and Inky, pinky, my black hen, p. 52. Iggledy-piggledy, my black hen, counting-out rhyme, Kings 2, 1930, p. 32. Tiggy, Tiggy Touchwood, my black hen, Boyce and Bartlett, 1941, p. 19.

2.24 THERE'S A PARTY ON THE HILL

There's a party on the hill
Would you like to come?

Yes.

Bring your own cup and saucer
And your own cream bun.

Can't afford it.

Go choose your true loved one.

(boy's name)

(boy's name) will be there
With a ribbon in his hair.
O U T spells out.

Mile End 1967; Walworth 1979; Brixton 1982; Barnsbury, Cubitt Town, Dalston, Deptford, Finsbury, Shepherds Bush 1983.

Tune "Roll Along Covered Wagon", written by Jimmy Kennedy in 1934.

The Opies (*CGSP*, 1969, p. 60) suggest that this rhyme originates from a nineteenth century song: Will you come to my wedding, will you come?"

Printed versions Daiken, *TTP*, Will you come to my wedding,/Will you come?, p. 94; Kellett, p. 21, and see below; Northall (see below); Opies, *CGSP*, p. 60; Ritchie, *GC*, p. 40; Shaw (see below); Smith, *BBHG*, There's a fight on the hill, p. 63, There's a party on the hill, p. 65; Todd, 6.

Early notings Will you come to the wedding, Will you come, Will you come?/Will you come, etc./Bring your own tea and sugar, And your own bread and butter,/And we'll all go a penny to the rum, Northall, 1892, p. 292. Will you come to Abyssinia/Will you come?/Bring your own ammunition and a gun./Mussolini will be there/Shooting peanuts in the air,/Will you come to Abyssinia/Will you come? Kellett, a parody from the 1930s, p. 21. Another version from the 1930s, similar to Kellett's, Shaw, 1970, p. 48.

2.25 MRS. MOP OWNED A SHOP

Mrs. Mop owned (has) a shop,
All she sold (sells) are lollipops,
Red, white or blue,
Which colour suits you?

Mile End 1983.

See also **7.39**.

Early noting Red, white and blue,/All out but you! Bolton, 1888, p. 111.

Recording Webb, *Children's Singing Games*.

2.26 AS I WAS WALKING DOWN INKY-PINKY LANE

As I was walking down Inky-pinky Lane
I met some inky-pinky children.
They asked me this, they asked me that,
They asked me the colour of the Union Jack:

Red, white or blue?
Which colour's for you?

Red.

Red is for danger, so out goes you.

White.

White is for wedding, so out goes you.

Blue.

Blue is for beauty, so out goes you.

Marylebone, Mile End 1967; Brockley 1967, 1983; Walworth 1979, 1982; Battersea, Greenwich 1982; Shepherds Bush 1983.

Red can also be for blood; blue for sky or sea; white for snow.

Printed versions Abrahams and Rankin, As I went down the Icky Picky lane, pp. 17–18; Bolton (see below); Boyce and Bartlett (see below); Brady, As I went up some Chinese steps, p. 50; Daiken, *TTP*, As I went up some Chinese steps, p. 93; Gullen, p. 13; McMorland, p. 29; Opies, *CGSP*, p. 58; Ritchie, *GC*, p. 44; Rutherford, Icky Picky Lane, p. 50; Shaw, 1970, p. 74; Sluckin, p. 16; cf. Solomons, As I went across a steeple, p. 30; Sutton-Smith, As I was going down piggy wiggy track, p. 70, Turner, p. 10.

Early notings As I went up a steeple,/I met a lot of people./Some were white and some were black,/And some the color of a ginger-snap./One, two, three, out goes she! Bolton, 1888, p. 113. A rhyme identical to Bolton's is found in Boyce and Bartlett, 1941, p. 30.

2.27 THERE'S A SOLDIER ON THE GRASS

A. There's a soldier on the grass,
   With a bullet up his arse,
   Pull it out, pull it out, pull it out.
   (You are out).

Battersea, Brixton, 1982; Dulwich, Shepherds Bush 1983.

B. There's a monkey in the grass,
   With a bullet up his arse,
   Stick it out, stick it out,
   If you want to be a scout.
   Red, white or blue,
   What suits you?

<u>Brockley</u>, Deptford, Kentish Town <u>1983</u>.

2.28 THE GRASS IS GREEN

The grass is green,
The sky is blue,
Everyone's out, (We're all right)
Except for you.

Greenwich 1982; Deptford 1983.

2.29 ALL THE MONKEYS

All the monkeys in the zoo,
Have their bollocks painted blue.
l, 2, 3, Out goes *you*.

Mile End 1983.

Printed versions Evans, *WI*, tails painted blue, p. 21; Withers, *CO*, tails painted blue [p. 20].

2.30 IP, DIP, THREEPENNY BIT

A. Ip, dip, threepenny bit,
You are not it.
God's words are true
It may not be you.

Mile End 1968; Dulwich 1983.

B. Ip, dip, sky blue,
Who's it? Not you,
Because the black man says so.
God's words are true,
So it must not be you.

Marylebone 1967.

Printed versions Bolton (see below); Gregor (see below); Newell (see below); Opies, *CGSP*, Ip, dip, sky blue,/Who's it? Not you./God's words are true,/It must not be *you*, p. 31.

Early notings One, two, sky blue,/All out but you! Bolton, 1888, p. 92. The same rhyme, from Cullen, Gregor, 1891, p. 30. Red, white, and blue,/All out but you. (Philadelphia), Newell, 1903, p. 203.

2.31 IP, DIP, SKY BLUE, WHO'S IT? NOT YOU

Ip, dip, sky blue,
Who's it? Not you.
It's not because you're dirty,
It's not because you're clean.
My mum says you're the fairy queen.
O-U-T spells out,
Out you must go.

Putney 1969; Walworth 1974, 1981; Earlsfield, Streatham 1982; Barnsbury, Brockley, Cubitt Town, Dalston, Dulwich, Finsbury, Shepherds Bush 1983.

See also **2.5B**.

Printed versions Bolton (see below); Boyce and Bartlett (see below); Fowke, p. 109; Fulton and Smith, ll. 3–4, p. 55; Gregor (see below); Gullen, pp. 17, 32; Kellett, as Newell, p. 115; Nelson, as Newell and Bolton, p. 61; Newell (see below), Ritchie, *GC*, p. 39; Rodger, p. 20; Sluckin, p. 14; Solomons, p. 72; Sutton-Smith, p. 69; Turner, Dip, red, white, blue,/Who's he? Not you, p. 11; Withers, *CO* [pp. 2, 30].

Early notings One, two, sky blue,/All out but you! Bolton, 1888, p. 92; The same rhyme, from Cullen, Gregor, 1891, p. 30. Red, white, and blue,/All out but you. (Philadelphia), Newell, 1903, p. 203. Boyce and Bartlett, 1941, as Bolton, p. 33.

2.32 IP, DIP, SKY BLUE, TOM AND JERRY DOWN THE LOO

Ip, dip, sky blue,
Tom and Jerry down the loo,
Quick mum, smack his bum,
Before he gets the chewing gum.

Mile End 1983.

See also **2.45**.

2.33 IP, DIP, DOGS' SHIT

A. Ip, dip, dogs' shit,
Boop!
You are not it.

Brixton, <u>Greenwich</u>, Streatham <u>1982</u>; Dalston 1983.

Printed versions Hubbard, a dip using feet, mentioned, 263; cf. Kellett, birds, p. 48; Knapps, dog, p. 26; cf. Lowenstein, p. 26; Opies, *CGSP*, bull's, p. 36; Rutherford, Ip, dip, tom-tit, who shall be it?/ ..., p. 52.

    B.   Ip, dip, dogs' shit,
           Fucking bastard,
           Silly git.

Barnsbury, <u>Blackheath</u>, Borough, Brockley, Cubitt Town, Deptford, Dulwich, Finsbury, Kentish Town <u>1983</u>.

    C.   Ip, dip, dogs' shit,
           Who stepped in it?

Hampstead 1984.

Printed version Sluckin, p. 14.

2.34 IP DIP DOO, THE CAT'S GOT THE FLU

    A.   Ip, dip, doo
           The cat's got the flu,
           The dog's got the measles,
           So out goes you.

Cubitt Town, Mile End 1983.

    B.   Dubba, dubba, doo,
           The cat's got the flu,
           The dog's got the chicken pox,
           And out goes you.

Mile End 1968.

See also **2.53** and **4.52**.

Printed versions Douglas (see below); Nelson, commencing "Red, white and blue", like Douglas, p. 71; Opies, *LLS*, p. 106, *CGSP*, p. 36; Ritchie, *SS*, p. 30, *GC*, p. 136; cf. Rosen and Steele, The cat's got the measles, front cover.

Early noting cf. Mother got the Hooping cough/Father got the gout--/Please (Rosie Milton)/Will you walk out? Douglas, 1916, p. 80, 1931, p. 45.

2.35 IP DIP DOO, THE BOYS LOVE YOU

> Ip, dip, doo,
> The boys love you.
> They took you to the pictures,
> And undressed *you*.
>
> Greenwich 1982; Barnsbury, Dalston, Dulwich, Kentish Town, Shepherds Bush 1983.

Printed versions Lowenstein, Red, white and blue, p. 38; Turner, Red, white and blue, Taunts and insults, p. 74.

2.36 IP, DIP, ANA MA DA

> Ip, dip (Dip, dip), ana ma da
> Dutch cheese centimar,
> Centimar, ana ma da
> Shan (shap).
>
> Clapham 1974/5; Brixton 1982.

Printed version Opies, *CGSP*: "particularly popular around London", pp. 51–52.

2.37 WHOSE SHOES ARE THE CLEANEST?

Whose shoes are the cleanest?
Your shoes are the cleanest.

Marylebone 1967.

Printed version cf. Kellett, p. 48.

2.38 DID YOU CLEAN YOUR SHOES LAST NIGHT?

    A.   Did you clean your shoes last night?
          Yes   (or: No)
          Y-E-S spells yes.   (N-O spells no.)

Streatham 1982; Brockley, Dalston, Finsbury, Shepherds Bush, Stoke Newington 1983; <u>Kensington 1984.</u>

"We all have our feet on the floor. If they say 'No,' you spell NO on the feet. You've got to have two shoes to be taken out and not be it." girl, Kensington 1984.

    B.   Did you clean your shoes last night
          With yellow polish shoe shine?

          Yes/No

          Why I told you so
          So out you must go.

Cubitt Town, <u>Deptford</u>, Mile End <u>1983</u>.

    C.   Did you clean your shoes last night?
          What polish did you clean them with?
          Black, red, blue, pink, yellow?

Black

B-L-A-C-K
You are out.

Barnsbury 1983.

D. Did you wash your shoes this morning
    With cherry, apple, plum?

No I did not.

So out you must go.
O-U-T spells out.

Dalston 1983.

Printed versions cf. Brady, My shoe is black,/Please change your other foot, p. 148; Smith, *BBHG*, When did you last clean your Sunday Best Shoes? p. 66.

2.39 YOUR SHOES NEED CLEANING

Your shoes need cleaning
With Cherry Blossom shoe polish.

West Norwood 1970; Mile End 1983.

Printed versions Hubbard, Your shoe is dirty, mentioned, 263; Opies, *CGSP*, p. 55; Ritchie, *GC*, Your shoe is dirty/;Your shoe is dirty/So please take it out!, p. 49; cf. Turner, Your shoe is dirty,/Please change it, p. 17.

2.40 DIRTY SHOES, DIRTY SOCKS

Dirty shoes, dirty socks,
Out goes Mr. Fox.

Mile End 1968.

Early noting cf. Dirty shoe, dirty shoe,/What will your mother and father do? Northall, 1892, p. 302.

2.41 TURN THE DIRTY DISH CLOTH

Turn the dirty dish cloth,
Inside *out*.

Brixton 1982.

See also **2.1**.

Printed versions cf. Abrahams, O-U-T spells out goes you./You old dirty dishrag you., p. 156, said to be "Usually an ending for a counting-out rhyme."; Bolton (see below); Evans, p. 25; Gaskell (see below); Opies, *CGSP*, p. 35.

Early notings Wring the dish cloth out;/Out, spot, out! Bolton, 1888, p. 111. Cf. Hickassy pickassy pice a pickassy/Pompalora jig./Every man that has no hair/Generally wears a wig./For a rotten cotton dish clout/Boys and girls are often turned out, Gaskell, c1913, p. 4.

Recording MacColl and Seeger, *The Elliotts of Birtley.*

2.42 WASH THE DISHES

Wash the dishes, dry the dishes,
Turn the dishes inside out.

Cubitt Town 1983.

Printed versions ("Turn the dishes over"): Abrahams, p. 202; Bolton (see below); Ritchie, *GC,* p. 11; Sutton-Smith, game, p. 84; Turner, p. 62; Withers, *CO,* similar to Bolton, below [p. 32].

Early noting Wash the ladies' dishes/Hang them on the bushes./… Bolton, 1888, p. 113, Massachusetts. Even at that date, the dishes/dish cloths motifs were becoming interchangeable and, ultimately, mixed up. Bolton adds a Southern US variation on line 1 of the above rhyme: "Ring [sic] the ladies' dish-cloth."

2.43 BOY SCOUT

> Boy Scout, walk out.
>
> Brixton, Greenwich, Walworth 1982; Borough, Cubitt Town, Shepherds Bush 1983.

Printed versions Fowke, p. 109; Opies, *CGSP,* p. 31; Ritchie, *GC,* p. 45; Sutton Smith, Pig snout,/ Walk out, p. 69; Turner, p. 10; Withers, *CO,* Pig's snout,/Walk out [p. 17].

2.44 EACH, PEACH, PEAR, PLUM

> A.   Each, peach, pear, plum,
>   Orange juice and bubble gum.
>
> Mile End 1968; Walworth 1979; Brixton 1982.

Printed versions Opies, *LLS,* pp. 115, 386, *CGSP,* pp. 36, 38, 60; Ritchie, *GC,* p. 91, Rosen and Steele, [p. 2]; Sutton-Smith, p. 69; Turner, p. 11.

> B.   Each, peach, pear, plum,
>   Choose your best chum.

Clapham 1974; Battersea, Brixton, <u>Greenwich</u>, Streatham <u>1982</u>; <u>Borough</u>, Brockley, Cubitt Town, Deptford, Dulwich, Shepherds Bush <u>1983</u>.

See also **2.19** and **7.9**.

Printed versions Abrahams, p. 46; Brady, p. 49; Kelsey, *K1*, 42; Knapps, p. 33; Withers, *CO*, Apple, peach, pear, plum,/When does your birthday come? [p. 28].

2.45 MICKEY MOUSE IN HIS HOUSE

Mickey Mouse in his house,
Pulling down his trousers,
"Quick Mum, smack his bum,"
That's the end of part one. (or: Before he eats his bubble gum.)

Marylebone, Mile End 1967; Walworth 1974, 1979; Brixton 1982; Barnsbury, Borough, Brockley, Cubitt Town, Deptford, Kentish Town, Shepherds Bush 1983; Kensington 1984.

See also **2.32**.

Printed version Opies, *LLS*, p. 111.

Other Mickey Mouse rhymes: Evans, *WI*, p. 24; Fowke, skipping rhyme, p. 54; Opies, *LLS*, several versions, p. 111, *CGSP*, Mickey Mouse bought a house, p. 59; Ritchie, *SS*, Minnie the Mouse came into the house, p. 36, *GC*, Mickey Mouse/He bought a house, p. 47; Smith, *BBHG*, Mickey Mouse built a house, p. 65; Turner, Mickey Mouse,/Haunted house, skipping, p. 32.

Recording Webb, *Children's Singing Games*.

2.46 HORSY, HORSY IN THE STABLE

Horsy, horsy in the stable,
Horsy, Horsy, out,
Horsy, Horsy, done a fart,
And blew the candle out.

Barnsbury 1983.

2.47 NODDY HAS A LITTLE CAR

Noddy* has a little car,
C-A-R.

Stoke Newington 1983.

* Noddy is the central character in a series of stories by Enid Blyton, 1942–63.

2.48 COWBOY JOE FROM MEXICO

Cowboy Joe from Mexico,
Tie up his bum with a little bow,
Out you must go.

Barnsbury 1983.

See also **6.A.29**.

From the popular song, "Ragtime Cowboy Joe", music by Lewis F. Muir and Maurice Abrahams, lyrics by Grant Clarke, published in the USA by F. A. Mills in 1912.

Printed versions Abrahams, skipping, p. 33; Cumnock Academy, skipping, p. 11; Fowke, skipping, p. 59; Smith, *BBHG*, skipping, p. 12;

Turner, skipping, p. 23; Withers, *RIMP*, Joe, Joe, stumped his toe/On the way to Mexico./ …. Rhymes for Fun, p. 28.

2.49 ROSY, ROSY, HOW DO YOU DO?

Rosy, Rosy, how do you do?
Very well thank you,
How about you?
O-U-T spells out.

Barnsbury 1983.

2.50 CHOCOLATE BISCUIT IN THE TIN

Chocolate biscuit in the tin,
Chocolate biscuit out.

Cubitt Town 1983.

See also **6.A.28**.

2.51 LONDON COUNTY COUNCIL

London County Council, L.C.C.
Wrote on the blackboard, A.B.C.
A, B, C, D, E, ……… Z.

Marylebone 1967.

Printed versions Opies, *CGSP*, p. 32; Sutton-Smith, two versions: Wellington (or Auckland) City Council, and Christchurch City Council, p. 69; Turner, Melbourne City Council, p. 14.

Early noting London County Council, L.C.C.,/London County Council,/You're not he. Correspondent (Epping) from memories in London, 1920s.

2.52 I SAW A FLY

    A.   I saw a fly passing by.

Greenwich 1982.

    B.   I saw a bee upon the wall,
         It gave a buzz and that was all.

Earlsfield 1982.

2.53 JENNY GOT THE MEASLES

Jenny got the measles, the measles, the measles,
Jenny got the measles, so out goes you.

Cubitt Town 1983.

See also **2.34** and **4.52**.

Printed versions cf. Rosen and Steele, The cat's got the measles, front cover; Smith, *BBHG*, Cat's got the measles, the measles, the measles …, jumping game, p. 68; Wade 1, 14, Wade 2, 32–33, both as Smith, *BBHG*.

2.54 HAM, BACON, PORK CHOP

Ham, bacon, pork chop,
Out you must hop.

Borough 1983.

2.55 YOU CAN'T PUT YOUR MUCK IN MY DUSTBIN

You can't put your muck in my dustbin,
My dustbin, my dustbin,
You can't put your muck in my dustbin,
My dustbin's full.

Blackheath 1983.

Recording MacColl and Behan, *Streets of Song.*

2.56 CHING CHONG, CHINAMAN

Ching Chong, Chinaman, tried to milk a cow,
Ching Chong, Chinaman, didn't know how,
Ching Chong, Chinaman, pulled the wrong tit,
Ching Chong, Chinaman, got covered in shit.

Barnsbury, Blackheath, Dulwich, Kentish Town, Stoke Newington 1983.

See also **4.1A**.

Printed versions Abrahams, pp. 29–30; Bolton (see below); Daiken, *TTP*, Chin Chin Chinaman/How much are your geese? p. 95; Douglas (see below); Ford (see below); Kellett, similar rhyme to Douglas, below, used for skipping, p. 9 (and see below); Knapps, p. 198; Lowenstein, p. 15; Shaw, 1970, p. 75; Sutton-Smith, pp. 94–95; Turner, p. 88; Withers, *CO*, John says to John, "How much are your geese?", similar to Bolton [p. 26].

Early notings Ching, Chong, Chineeman,/How do you sell your fish?/Ching, Chong, Chineeman,/ Six bits a dish./Ching, Chong, Chineeman,/Oh! That is too dear./Ching, Chong, Chineeman,/Clear right out of here! Bolton, 1888, p. 116. Ford, 1904, similar to Bolton, pp. 52–53. Cf.

Ching Chang Chinaman had a penny doll -/Washed it, scrubbed it, called it pretty poll, Douglas, 1916, p. 95, 1931, p. 54. Kellett (1966, p. 9) suggests that the original inspiration for rhymes beginning with "Ching Chong, Chinaman" and similar was a number called "Chin Chin Chinaman" from the musical comedy "The Geisha", first performed in 1896.

2.57 DOCTOR FOSTER WENT TO GLOUCESTER

> Doctor Foster went to Gloucester,
> In a shower of rain.
> He stepped in a puddle,
> Right up to his middle,
> And never went there again.
>
> Brockley 1967; Brixton 1982.

Printed versions Bolton (see below); Briggs, pp. 36, 43; Cole, p. 42; Ford (see below); Halliwell (see below); MacBain (see below); Opies, *ODNR*, p. 173; Sutton-Smith, skipping, p. 83; Turner, p. 88.

Early notings Doctor Foster went to Glo'ster,/In a shower of rain;/He stepp'd in a puddle up to his middle,/And wouldn't go there again, Halliwell, *NRE*, 1844, two versions, p. 31. Dr. Foster went to Glo'ster/In a shower of rain;/Stepped in a puddle, up to his middle,/Never went there again, Bolton, 1888, p. 119. Ford, 1904, p. 27; MacBain, 1933, p. 194.

2.58 YUM, YUM, BUBBLEGUM

> Yum, yum, bubblegum,
> Stick it up your mum's bum,
> If it sticks, pull her tits,
> And use the milk for Weetabix.
>
> Greenwich 1982; <u>Barnsbury</u>, Kentish Town <u>1983</u>.

Printed version cf. Lowenstein, p. 47.

2.59 CINDERELLA, DRESSED IN YELLA

> Cinderella, dressed in yella
> Turn around,
> Touch the ground.

Blackheath, Borough <u>1983</u>; Kensington 1984.

"You can do it on a step but you don't have to. You do the rhyme to decide who's 'it'. They jump over somebody and go 'Cinderella'. They do the actions and somebody else jumps over, and so on." girl, Blackheath 1983.

See also **4.63** and **6.A.27**.

Settling a Dispute

2.60 RED, GOLD AND GREEN

> "If you say you're not out and the one who's 'on it' says you're out, you all stand in a circle. You choose a colour. If 'red' you have to spell R-E-D and the one it stops on is the one that's wrong." girl, Shepherds Bush 1983.

Although no rhyme is involved, this is a method of settling a dispute about whether a player is "out" or "not out" in a game.

SECTION 3

GAMES (WITHOUT SONGS)

Introduction

In his *London Street Games*, Norman Douglas writes (1916, pp. 156, 157, 1931, pp. 85, 86):

> … if you want to see what children can do, you must stop giving them things. Because of course they only invent games when they have none ready-made for them, like richer folks have—when, in other words, they've nothing in their hands.

> … that's how they come to play any number of games and to discover new ones every day, while better-class lads get into grooves and go on with their frowsy old cricket and one or two more all the time, always the same, year after year.

There was probably much truth in that statement in 1916 or even 1931 when he listed the names of over 600 boys' games, 149 girls' games and twenty-nine played by both sexes, as well as a number of games played by very young children. I think, even so, he overstated his case. Very many of the games he listed, as he himself notes, were duplications of games played in the same way, but with different names. Others would probably have been ephemeral, with very short lives or restricted to small groups of children. He rarely went into detail as to how the games were played. By contrast, the Opies in *Children's Games in Street and Playground* (*CGSP*, 1969) actually catalogue the names of hundreds of games and variants, giving play details for most of them. They exclude ball games, except where a ball is incidental to the game, or games needing other apparatus. At the end of the last century, Gomme (1894, 1898) listed and often explained well over 800 games and singing games. Many of these are duplications of games with different names. She also included a number of indoor games which may have been organised by adults.

In my two-year study I collected around 160 games, not including ball games, indoor games or singing games which I deal with separately. I collected more than thirty ball games plus playground versions of twelve established adult games (American football, basketball, cricket, football, hockey, netball, rounders, rugby, squash, stoolball, tennis, volleyball). Considering that I was noting games from a restricted age group (nine to eleven) from twenty-one different schools, but based on relatively small groups visited only four times or less, I was surprised to find so many. Although I had been interested in children's rhymes and singing games for a number of years before undertaking this study, I had not hitherto noted ordinary games.

In the three schools in which I taught for a number of years, a large number of boys played football, or a variation of it, on almost a daily basis throughout the year, except when the weather or temporary school bans made it impossible. When they were prevented from playing the game, many boys would be at a loss for a time and indulged in various charging or "pretend fighting" activities. Some would interfere in the games of girls or younger children. Few other games seemed to have long-term popularity in the playground, apart from versions of **3.A.4** HE BALL or **3.A.6** STING BALL. Girls' activities mainly consisted of singing games, skipping, ball bouncing, hand clapping, and **3.K.4** HOPSCOTCH.

Seasonally I noticed a few children involved in games of **3.F.5** CONKERS, **3.K.1** JACKS, and **3.K.2** CAT'S CRADLE. More would be involved in playing **3.K.3** MARBLES in the gratings of the drains. A few girls played **3.C.4** BALL IN THE STOCKING. Much of the teasing and chasing between boys and girls appeared to be of an unorganised character, though sometimes it was more formalised, as in **3.D.7** KISS CHASE.

During the course of the study (1982–84) I came to the conclusion that there must have been many more games played than I had noticed and that I must have overlooked the peripheral activities of minority groups in the playground. From the collected data, it seems that the proportion of traditionally received material, as compared with creative variation and newly created items, is far higher in the case of games than in that of rhymes and songs. Obviously, larger social groups are involved in the playing of a game than in routines of skipping or ball bouncing. Too much change would soon lead to argument and wasted time in the case of games.

Apart from standard adult games, the seventeen games most reported (by seven or more schools out of twenty-one) were, in order of frequency: **3.A.28** BULLDOG, **3.B.1** MOTHER, MAY I?, **3.B.6** PEEP BEHIND THE CURTAIN, **3.D.i** I DRAW A SNAKE, **3.B.12** POLO, **3.A.14** ONE HE ALL HE, **3.A.33** PLEASE MR. CROCODILE, **3.A.1** TAG, **3.D.7** KISS CHASE, **3.A.19** STUCK IN THE MUD, **3.D.8** RUN OUTS, **3.A.15** CHAIN HE, **3.A.17** POISON, **3.K.4** HOPSCOTCH, **3.D.2** FORTY FORTY, **3.A.18** WHAT'S THE TIME, MR. WOLF?, and **4.9** QUEENIE, QUEENIE. All of these are mentioned by name by the Opies in *CGSP* (1969), although POLO is described under "Cigarettes", and "Forty-forty" is one of the cries used by the runner reaching home in the game of "Block".[1] These two games are also mentioned in more recent publications such as that of Sluckin.[2] Versions of BULLDOG, MOTHER, MAY I?, TAG, CHAIN HE, HOPSCOTCH, and QUEENIE, QUEENIE are found in the Gomme collection as well as a possible ancestor of I DRAW A SNAKE.[3]

Of the next twenty-three most reported games (from between three and seven schools out of twenty-one), nine are listed by Gomme[4] and thirteen by the Opies.[5] Of the others, four are noted by R. A. Smith,[6] leaving three I have been unable to trace in any printed collection.[7] Sixteen games were reported by only two schools in the sample. Of these, six are noted by the Opies[8] and two by Gomme.[9] Of the games collected from just a single school, nine are reported by Gomme,[10] ten by the Opies,[11] and thirteen appear in other collections both old and new.[12] This leaves fifty playground games which were not reinforced by any other school in the sample nor apparently to be found in printed collections that I am aware of. Of these, in the case of around twenty-five games I have only a name to go on, without any details of how they are played. Summing up, I found twenty-seven playground games and procedures contained in one form or another in the Gomme collection still being played in Inner London a century after her books were published.

It would seem that Douglas was not right in believing that the supply of ready-made games and apparatus would prevent the creation of new games. He was correct, however, in realising that the playing of adult games would absorb the energies of many boys – cricket has been largely replaced by football, even in the summer months. This sentiment is closely echoed by Parry-Jones (1964, p. 238). Possibly without the widespread influence of the national game, a list of contemporary boys' games would rival that of Douglas some seventy years before my survey was undertaken.

The integration of boys' and girls' playing spaces has made a difference in the patterns of games related to gender. Apart from singing games, which remain overwhelmingly the property of the girls, there was only a slight lead for games played mainly by girls (seventy-six), over games played mainly by boys (sixty-eight). There was a bigger lead in games played only by girls (fifty-six) over games played only by boys (forty-three). There were eighty-seven games in at least one school in the sample which were sometimes played by boys and girls together.

The games played only by boys tended to be of the physical tussle type, as one would expect. The games played only by girls included a number relying on individual skills, but several were of a quite energetic type. There were noticeable differences between those schools where few games were played by boys and girls together and those where a number of games were shared. Although there was not an exact correlation between schools and their environment, those in more residential areas with more children from professional and "white collar" families tended to have fewer games played on a separate gender basis. Those from more restricted environments, with more children from semi-skilled, unskilled and unwaged families, were more likely to have games played on a single gender basis. This does not necessarily mean that a particular game was restricted to the boys or the girls in those schools. The general tendency was for more traditional boys' games to be played by girls as well. There was a much smaller contrary process taking place, but even here there was a gradual breaking down of the barriers. Boys may take part in a limited number of singing games and, more rarely, even some skipping games. I have not come across any boys playing any ball bouncing or hand clapping games, though they may watch the routines and be fascinated by them, and learn the words of the accompanying rhymes. There will probably be very interesting developments in the future for observers to note.

I very much regret that the limited time I spent in the schools in the sample did not allow me to observe more than a small number of the games I noted. Taking into consideration the conditions, the size and composition of the groups of children I worked with, and the inconvenience for the school, such observation would have required many more visits, lasting for longer periods. Consequently I had to forgo the advantages of being able to watch many of the games being played.

The descriptions of the games that were popular were numerous and I had to be selective. I also had to edit the children's accounts in some cases to make them intelligible, and sometimes they left out important parts of the games. Nevertheless, I have kept to the children's accounts essentially, though I have not attempted to reproduce the Cockney pronunciations and accents. Pronouns have been altered in many cases to make the accounts understandable; *he/she, they, you* are often used indiscriminately. It is frequently difficult to follow the rhymes in print, though the children have no difficulty in following what is said. *They* or *you* may have to be used instead of *he* or *she* because so many games are no longer gender based. The impersonal *one*, of course, is never used. Children of the age group I studied refer to *boys and girls* sometimes, but hardly ever to *children*. *Person* or *people* were usually preferred.

In the following section I have included all the games that were reported to me as being played in the schools in the study. In the main, the system of classification used by the Opies for the games included in their collection *Children's Games in Street and Playground* (*CGSP*, 1969) is also employed here. For other kinds of games I have had to devise my own. In the case of some games where the singing element has virtually vanished, or at least been reduced to a chant, but which are obviously descended from traditional singing games, I have described them in full in the section on such games, e.g. **4.9** QUEENIE, QUEENIE and **4.21** ARE YOU READY FOR A FIGHT?.

NOTES

1. Opies (*CGSP*, 1969). See **3.A.1** TAG; **3.A.14** ONE HE ALL HE; **3.A.15** CHAIN HE; **3.A.17** POISON; **3.A.18** WHAT'S THE TIME, MR. WOLF?; **3.A.19** STUCK IN THE MUD; **3.A.28** BULLDOG; **3.A.33** PLEASE, MR. CROCODILE; **3.B.1** MOTHER, MAY I?; **3.B.6** PEEP BEHIND THE CURTAIN; **3.B.12** POLO; **3.D.i** I DRAW A SNAKE; **3.D.2** FORTY-FORTY; **3.D.7** KISS CHASE; **3.D.8** RUN OUTS; **3.K.4** HOPSCOTCH; and **4.9** QUEENIE, QUEENIE.
2. Sluckin (1981, p. 21) (Ay-ickie): **3.D.2** FORTY-FORTY; (1981, p. 23) (Polo): **3.B.12** POLO.
3. Gomme (1894, pp. 69–70) (Click), (1894, pp. 72–73) (Cock), (1894, p. 299) (King Caesar): **3.A.28** BULLDOG; (1894, pp. 390–396) (Mother, may I go out to Play?): **3.B.1** MOTHER, MAY I?; (1898, pp. 293) (Tig): **3.A.1** TAG; (1898, p. 107) (Relievo), (1898, p. 216) (Sticky Toffey): **3.A.15** CHAIN HE; (1894, pp. 223–227) (Hopscotch): **3.K.4** HOPSCOTCH; (1898, pp. 90–102) (Queen Anne): **4.9** QUEENIE, QUEENIE; (1894, p. 37) (Blind Man's Buff, II): this may perhaps be the ancestor of **3.D.i** I DRAW A SNAKE.
4. The nine games found in Gomme (1894, 1898) are: **3.A.1** TAG; **3.A.23** FOX AND HOUNDS; **3.A.27** BLIND MAN'S BUFF; **3.D.1** HIDE AND SEEK; **3.F.5** CONKERS; **3.J.1** ROUNDERS; **3.J.5** CRICKET; **3.K.1** JACKS; **3.K.3** MARBLES.
5. The thirteen games found in Opies (*CGSP*, 1969) are: **3.A.1** TAG; **3.A.2** HE ON LINES; **3.A.4** HE BALL; **3.A.6** STING BALL; **3.A.13** OFF GROUND TOUCH; **3.A.21** BUZZ; **3.A.23** FOX

AND HOUNDS; **3.D.1** HIDE AND SEEK; **3.E.2** CHINESE MUDDLE; **3.F.1** PIGGY-BACK FIGHTS; **3.F.5** CONKERS; **3.F.7** KNUCKLES; **3.L.6** TRUE DARE.

6. The four games found in Smith (*BBHG*, 1982, 1983), are: **3.A.4** HE BALL; **3.A.13** OFF GROUND TOUCH; **3.H.1** KNOCKOUT; **3.H.2** SQUASH.
7. The three games not found in any other collection were: **3.H.11** CHINESE FOOTBALL, **3.I.11** FOUR SQUARE, and **3.N.12** WINKING MURDER.
8. The six games found in Opies (*CGSP*, 1969) are: **3.A.26** CAT AND MOUSE; **3.A.32** COLOURS; **3.C.5** LEAP FROGS; **3.D.5** TIN CAN TOLLY; **3.F.6** KING OF THE CASTLE; and **3.F.10** SLAPSIES.
9. The two games in Gomme (1894) are: **3.C.5** LEAP FROGS; and **3.F.6** KING OF THE CASTLE.
10. The nine games in Gomme (1894, 1898) are: **3.A.9** ONE, TWO, THREE, FOUR, FIVE; **3.A.31** SHEEP AND WOLVES; **3.E.1** ROLLER COASTER; **3.F.4** RED ROVER; **3.J.3** STOOLBALL; **3.K.2** CAT'S CRADLE; **3.L.4** TREASURE HUNT; **3.N.1** CHINESE WHISPERS; and **3.O.1** NOUGHTS AND CROSSES.
11. The ten games in Opies (*CGSP*, 1969), are: **3.A.9** ONE, TWO, THREE, FOUR, FIVE; **3.A.11** SMACK RACE; **3.A.30** BLUE PETER; **3.A.31** SHEEP AND WOLVES; **3.B.2** LETTERS; **3.B.4** COLOURS (RACING) (1); **3.B.11** MEGGY PEGGY; **3.C.3** SEVENSIES; **3.D.9** SARDINES; and **3.L.3** BUCKAMAROO.
12. The thirteen games collected from a single school, found in collections other than Gomme and the Opies, are: **3.A.7** ROTTEN EGG; **3.A.10** FRENCH AND ENGLISH; **3.A.34** MONDAY, TUESDAY; **3.C.2** JUMPING A SWINGING ROPE; **3.C.6** HANDSTANDS; **3.F.3** HEAVERS; **3.H.5** THREE AND IN; **3.I.6** PIGGY IN THE MIDDLE; **3.I.10** PAT BALL; **3.N.3** BABY IF YOU LOVE ME, SMILE; **3.N.4** SAUSAGES; **3.N.5** POOR PUSSY; **3.N.6** ON MY HOLIDAY.

3.A CHASING GAMES

3.A.1 TAG, HAD, HE, IT

> "Someone's 'it' and they have to 'had' them and once they've had them, the other person's 'it'." girl, Kensington 1984 (It).

Universal game of chasing, though with varying names.

Printed versions Bett (see below); Brady, Tip and tig, p. 144; Chambers (see below); Gaskell (see below); Gomme (see below); Gregor (see below); Newell (see below); Opies, *CGSP*, Touch, etc., pp. 62–68; Parry-Jones, Tig, Tag and Touch, p. 87; Ritchie, *GC*, Plain Tig, p. 52; Sluckin, Tig, p. 18; Solomons, Tag, p. 26; Sutton-Smith, Tag/Tig, p. 55.

Early notings "it", in Tig, Chambers, 1842, p. 62; … "it", e.g., in the game of "Tackie," or "Tackie among the Rucks", Gregor, 1891, p. 5; Tig, Gomme, 1898, p. 293; "it" in Tag, Newell, 1903, pp. 158–159; "he" in Tig, Gaskell, c1913, p. 3; Tig, Tag, Tiggy, Bett, *TGC*, 1929, pp. 78–79, 87.

3.A.2 HE ON LINES; HE ON THE LINE; ON IT ON THE LINE; LINE HAD; HAD ON THE LINE

> "It's just the famous normal 'He' except it's on lines and you can choose some circle or box as 'home'. If you get off the lines then you're 'he'." boy, Dulwich 1983 (He on lines).

Brixton, Cubitt Town, Dalston, Deptford, <u>Dulwich</u>, Shepherds Bush <u>1982–83</u>.

The game seems to be more popular with boys but is also played by girls on their own or by both sexes together.

Printed versions Opies, *CGSP*, Line touch, p. 70; Ritchie, *GC*, Linie tig, p. 52; Sluckin, Line tig, p. 19.

3.A.3 ON IT ON THE LINE (WITH BALL)

"You can play it two ways. You can just stand along the wall. ('On it') throws the ball and tries to hit someone. If it hits someone, that person's 'on it'. Or you get in a line. A person runs along the wall. ('On it') has got to try and hit them as they run along." girl, Mile End 1983.

3.A.4 HE BALL

"Somebody has the ball and instead of touching them they have to get them with the ball. It's exactly the same as 'Tag' but with a ball." girl, Mile End 1983.

Brockley, Dalston, Deptford, Finsbury, Hampstead, Mile End 1983–84.

Equally popular with boys and girls; rarely played together.

Printed versions Opies, *CGSP*, Ball he, pp. 73–74; Sluckin, Ball tig, p. 19; Smith, *BBHG*, Dobbie ball, p. 89.

3.A.5 HIT AND RUN

"Somebody's 'on it'. People have to stand along the wall. ('On it') has to throw the ball and when they're throwing the ball you have to run up to the other wall and back again and they try and hit you while you're running. If they hit them then they have to sit down." girl, Mile End 1983.

3.A.6 STING BALL; STING UPS; STINGIE; BALLIE; CHINESE STINGER

"The difference between 'Sting Ball' and 'He Ball' is, when you play 'He Ball' you're not allowed to throw it hard. 'Sting Ball' is when you have to throw it fairly hard so that it can hurt them and below the knee." boy, Borough 1983 (Sting Ball).

"My version of 'Sting Up' is to pick someone to throw the ball. The people stand on the bench and they're not allowed to move. The person throws a ball and they just get stinged up. When they get stinged up they have to throw the ball at the other people." boy, Borough 1983 (Sting Ball).

"People line up against the wall and they just have to move back to avoid the ball. The boys boot the ball at you and they've got to try and get you. If they get you then you're 'on it'. It really hurts when the boys do it." girl, Barnsbury 1983 (Sting Ups).

Barnsbury, Battersea, Borough, Brixton, Streatham, Walworth 1982–83.

In some schools this game is banned.

Printed versions Opies, *CGSP*, Stingy, etc., p. 74.

3.A.7 ROTTEN EGG

"You run and the person who's 'he' counts to ten. You stop at ten. ('He') throws the ball and it has to go between your legs. If it goes between your legs, you're 'he'." boy, Borough 1983.

Printed versions Douglas (see below); Sutton-Smith, p. 150.

Early noting A girls' game with this name is mentioned in Douglas, 1916, p. 39, 1931, p. 21.

3.A.8 THREE BAD EGGS; BAD EGGS; SUBJECTS

This game is presumably a development of **3.A.7** ROTTEN EGG. It is usually followed by the "punishment" procedure of "Tunnel of Death" (see **3.A.8.i** below), strangely and ironically termed at one school "Tunnel of Love".

"You pick someone to be 'it'. They go down the other end of the pitch. They say something like 'dogs'. The others would all pick a breed of dogs: alsatian, collie, etc. The person who is 'it' says (say) 'collie'. The person who's 'collie' has to run, get the ball from the person who's 'it', and throw it. The person who's 'it' runs to get the ball and everyone else has to stop running (when he's got it). He can take twenty big steps and nine small steps and after that he can throw the ball at someone. If someone has been caught three times they get the 'tunnel of death'." boy, Finsbury 1983.

"In Bad Eggs there's one ball and one person's 'it'. Everyone crowds around and the person who's 'it' chooses the subject, say it was flowers. Everyone has to name a flower but they don't say who's named that flower. The person with the ball in front or behind her shouts a flower. The person who chose that flower has to run after the ball (get it) and say 'Bad Egg, stop!' When she says that, everyone has to stop running. She throws the ball so it bats them." girl, Blackheath 1983.

"The person that's 'on it' goes in the corner with the ball and the others choose a subject. If they have cars then they all pick a car like Rolls Royce, Jag etc. They call out the names but you've got to guess what names they are. If he says, 'Jag', the one who's 'Jag' goes and gets the ball and he's 'on it'." boy, Mile End 1983 (here called "Subjects").

"The person who's 'on it' thinks of a subject like 'cars' or something like that. Everyone else goes away and they choose one (car name) each and choose one for the person who's 'on it'. One person shouts them all out. The person who's 'on it' has to throw the ball up in the air and say one of the names. Whoever is called out has to get the ball. When they pick up the ball they have to say, 'Stop'. They take three giant steps and five pigeon steps towards the nearest person and throw the ball under their knees. If they hit them they've got one 'bad egg'. If you get three 'bad eggs' you're given a 'dare' by the person who's 'on it'." girl, Hampstead 1984.

Barnsbury, Blackheath, Dulwich, Earlsfield, Finsbury, Hampstead, Mile End, Streatham 1982–84.

This game appears to be played equally by boys and girls.

Early noting Nicholson, Stand but(t), pp. 122–123: a child's name is called to determine who will catch the ball. This child throws the ball at other players. If a player is hit three times, he/she incurs a punishment called "paps" where the child has to hold his/her hand against a wall and other children hit it or throw the ball at it.

3.A.8.i The Tunnel of Death; The Tunnel of Love

This procedure is usually carried out on the loser of the game of THREE BAD EGGS.

> "Everyone leans on a wall or something and they pick say, pinching, kicking or punching. They have to run through the tunnel of death, the tunnel of people. They kick them or punch them." boy, Finsbury 1983.

> "Everyone puts their hands on the wall and bends over. The person has to walk through the middle. They decide on three subjects: kicking, digs or something. If they choose one then they have to go through while everyone digs or whatever. You go through the tunnel and there's kicks and punches, spitting, pinching and tickling. You choose a finger. If it's a certain finger like the index finger. Say it was kicking, you go through the tunnel and they kick you but if you touch it you get let off." boy, Hampstead 1984.

> " 'Tunnel of love' is like 'tunnel of death'. You have to open your legs. As the person comes in you've got to kiss him on the head and that's only if you want to." boy, Stoke Newington 1983.

Barnsbury, Blackheath, Dulwich, Finsbury, Hampstead, Stoke Newington 1983–84.

This procedure was carried out by both boys and girls.

Early noting Newell describes "the punishment of being 'paddled', passing under the legs of the row of players for that purpose." Newell, 1903, p. 183.

3.A.9 ONE, TWO, THREE, FOUR, FIVE

"You give people a number. (You run in turn. 'He' has to) throw the ball and it's got to hit you below the knees. If you get caught you've got to get a ball and help the other person throw the ball until the last person." boy, Stoke Newington 1983.

Printed versions Gomme (see below); Opies, *CGSP*, Kingy, pp. 95–99.

Early noting cf. Gomme, 1894, Monday, Tuesday, pp. 389–390.

3.A.10 FRENCH AND ENGLISH

This game I came across in Dalston has little to do with the game of this name in Opies (*CGSP*, 1969, pp. 9, 146–148, 236, 338). A ball is thrown up and whoever catches it has to throw it and hit someone else in the opposing team. Whoever is hit goes into "jail" and there is a system of scoring points.

Printed version Brewster (*ANG*, p. 85) describes an Armenian game where "players are divided into two groups ... A player of one of the groups throws a ball at the opposite group and runs towards the latter. The player who catches the ball tries to hit the player who threw it. If he succeeds in doing so, the latter becomes a prisoner of the thrower's group." He adds that a Czech variant is called "Nations".

3.A.11 SMACK RACE

"The girls have to chase the boys and when they catch them they have to give them a whack. Then they decide to change and the boys have to go and chase the girls and give them a whack. Most of the time it's the girls chasing the boys." girl, Stoke Newington 1983.

Printed version the Opies (*CGSP*, pp. 72–73), give "Whacko" and "Daddy Whacker", though here a twisted-up scarf and a stick, rather than the hand, are respectively used to convey the "tig".

3.A.12 AGROE

"They all line up and go round the playground shouting, 'Agroe' or they spell it out, 'A-G-R-O-E'. Then they all (go) round the playground chasing the girls, or the girls will chase the boys." girl, Cubitt Town 1983.

Printed versions Sluckin, pp. 56, 109, both used in the context of boys fighting rather than chasing, "aggro" being the then current catchword for aggressive behaviour.

3.A.13 OFF GROUND TOUCH; FEET OFF LONDON

"There's a person who's 'on it' and all the rest have to get off (the) ground. If they're not off the ground the person who's 'on it' can 'had' them. You can't stay on a bench." girl, Borough 1983 (Feet off London).

Battersea, Borough, Dalston, Kentish Town, Mile End 1982–83.

This game appeared to be played by girls or by boys and girls together.

Printed versions Douglas (see below); Holbrook, p. 110; Opies, *CGSP*, Off ground he, p. 81, Budge he, p. 82; Sluckin, Off-ground tig, p. 18; Smith, *BBHG*, Dobbie off-ground, p. 92.

Early noting Off-ground Touch, Douglas, 1916, p. 140, 1931, p. 77.

3.A.14 ONE HE ALL HE; FAMILY HAD; FAMILY HE

"First you have to dip. Then the person who's 'he' has to count to twenty and you all run. If he catches you you're 'he' with him until everyone else gets 'he'. The first one (who was caught) becomes 'he' the next game." boy, Brixton 1982 (One He All He).

"… there's a whole load of people chasing. They don't have to hold hands, as it gets confusing when someone's not 'on it' and they see someone else they like. They put their hands up to show they're not 'on it' (or) cross their arms across their chest, that means they're 'on it'." boy, Finsbury 1983 (Family He).

Barnsbury, Borough, Brixton, Brockley, Cubitt Town, Dalston, Deptford, Finsbury, Hampstead, Kensington, Mile End, Shepherds Bush 1982–84.

This seemed to be mainly a boys' game but was played by boys and girls together in some schools.

Printed version Opies, *CGSP*, Help Chase, p. 89.

3.A.15 CHAIN HE; LONG SAUSAGE; FISH IN THE NET; FRENCH HAD; STICKY TOFFEE

"One person is chosen as 'he' (or 'dipped'). They have to chase after all the other people. Sometimes there's a 'home'. If they get one person he's 'he' with them so they join hands till everybody's joined hands. Sometimes you break if [the chain is] too long." boy, Dulwich 1983.

Borough, Brixton, Deptford, Dulwich, Earlsfield, Finsbury, Hampstead, Mile End, Shepherds Bush, Stoke Newington, Streatham, Walworth 1982–84.

Continuation: in some versions another dip took place; sometimes the first one caught became 'he', sometimes the last one left did.

This game was played by boys, by girls, and by boys and girls together, and it was almost universal. Note that "Sticky Toffee" was also used as a name for other games.

Printed versions Brewster, *ANG*, Link Tag, pp. 67–69; Douglas (see below); Gomme (see below); Opies, *CGSP*, Chain he, pp. 89–91; Ritchie, *GC*, Chainie Tig, p. 51; Sluckin, Chain-he, p. 19; Sutton-Smith, *The Bellahonie*, p. 58, and Chain Tag, p. 60.

Early notings Gomme, 1898, Relievo, p. 107; Sticky Toffey named without details, p. 216. Douglas, Widdy, 1916, pp. 20–21, 1931, pp. 10–11, String-he, 1916, p. 139, 1931, p. 76.

3.A.16 GHOSTS

"You have five people and many people to run away from them. They've got to catch you. (If you're caught) you all line up and you hold hands. The other people who haven't been caught can touch them and they'll be free. There's a home. You can get killed again." boy, Hampstead 1984.

3.A.17 POISON; POISON FINGER; BLACK POISON; BLACK MAGIC

"Someone's 'on it'. First of all you have to put out all ten of your fingers and you have to tell them which one's your poisoned finger. Then you say, 'I went to a shop and I bought (an apple) and in that apple I stuck my poisoned finger.' They all start running away. When you 'had' them they have to go against the wall and put their arms up so the free person can run through them (and free them). If one of them has been caught three times they have to go through the death tunnel." boy, Dalston 1983 (Poison).

For "death tunnel" see **3.A.8.i** The Tunnel of Death.

"Someone's 'it' and they hold out their hands. Each person takes a finger (and holds it). The person whose fingers are being pulled has to make up a story. When they've said 'poison' three times they all have to run. The person who's 'it' has to chase after them. Once they've caught (one) the other person is 'it'." girl, Kensington 1984 (Poison).

Barnsbury, Borough, Brixton, Cubitt Town, Dalston, Dulwich, Kentish Town, Stoke Newington, Walworth 1982–84.

This game was played separately by boys or by girls.

Printed versions Opies, *CGSP*, Poison, pp. 99–100; cf. Smith, *BBHG*, Black Cat, p. 83; Wade 1, Poison, 14.

3.A.18 WHAT'S THE TIME, MR. WOLF?/ MR. CROCODILE?/MR. CLOCK?

"There's a person who can be Mr. Wolf and there's lots of people playing. They have to run after the person who's 'on it' and they keep on saying, 'Mr. Wolf, what's the time?' and he goes up to twelve o'clock. When it's twelve o'clock the wolf has to run to the others and when he gets one, they're 'on it'." girl, Shepherds Bush 1983.

"The children say, 'What's the time, Mr. Wolf?' (and he says) 'Six o'clock.' All the others have to take six steps. They ask again, 'What's the time, Mr. Wolf?' and he says, 'Two o'clock.' They take two steps. When they get quite near him they say, 'What's the time Mr. Wolf?' He goes 'Dinner time!' and they all run away." girl, EC1 1983.

All parts of Inner London.

In some versions the children are in a circle marked like a clock and Mr. Wolf/Clock is in the middle. They ask in sequence "One o'clock, two o'clock", etc. and may move round each time. The game is mainly played by younger children, or by older children playing with younger ones. It is played by boys and girls together or girls on their own.

Printed versions Brady, Mr. Fox, p. 149; Gaskell (see below); Gillington (see below); Opies, *CGSP*, pp. 102–103; Ritchie, *SS*, p. 92; Robertson, p. 35.

Early notings cf. Chicken my wicken, Gaskell, c1913, p. 8. Cf. The Wolf, Gillington, *ODSG*, 1913, p. 15.

3.A.19 STUCK IN THE MUD; RELEASE; FAMILY TREE; ARM RELIEF

"The person who's 'it', when he 'has' somebody they have to stand still with their legs open. Other people have to go underneath them to release them." (boy). "Girls never play it, it's only the boys that play it." (girl). Kensington 1984 (Family Tree).

"First of all it's just like 'He', then when someone gets 'had' the first time they put their hands up against the wall and someone has to run under them. After they've been 'had' three times they're 'on it'." boy, Barnsbury 1983 (Release).

"Somebody is 'it' and they chase after everyone. When they're 'had' they've got to have their legs open and their arms out wide. A friend can release them by going through their legs or under their arm and they're free again. If you're 'had' three times it's the tunnel of terror or death tunnel." boy, Blackheath 1983 (Release).

Barnsbury, Blackheath, Brockley, Dalston, Deptford, Dulwich, Earlsfield, Finsbury, Kensington, Shepherds Bush, Streatham 1982–84.

For "tunnel of terror" and "death tunnel" see **3.A.8.i** The Tunnel of Death.

This game is mainly played by boys, but also by boys and girls together.

Printed versions Opies, *CGSP*, Stuck in the Mud/Underground Tig/Tunnel Touch, pp. 110–112; Sluckin, Scarecrow tig and Stick-in-the-mud, p. 19; Smith, *BBHG*, Dobbie Mud, p. 91, Dobbie Scarecrow, p. 92.

3.A.20 JOEY BEACON

This appeared to be a crude form of STUCK IN THE MUD played by boys who, instead of touching, "They've got to kick you up the bum," I was told. Hampstead 1984.

3.A.21 BUZZ

"Someone's 'it'. You have to go on to the drain. All the people go on to the drain. You have to keep running round. If a person 'has' you before you get to another drain, you're 'it'. You keep running to different drains without the person catching you. When you go on to another drain you say, 'Buzz' before, and push the other person off who has to find another drain to go to." boy, Streatham 1982.

Borough, Shepherds Bush, Streatham, Walworth 1982–83.

The name "Buzz" seems to be a corruption of "Budge". It is mainly a boys' game.

Printed versions Opies, *CGSP*, Budge He, p. 82; children in Fulham also say 'Buzz' and play the game above drains; Ritchie, *GC*, Siver Tig, p. 53; Sluckin, Budge, p. 18.

3.A.22 BOXES; BOX HAD

"Somebody's 'he'. There are two 'boxes' or circles. The people in the boxes have got to try to get from one box to another without being 'had' by the person who's 'he'." girl, Dulwich 1983 (Boxes).

"There's a big 'box' and you run round it and whoever gets caught is 'on it' with the (other) person too." boy, Dalston 1983 (Box Had).

3.A.23 FOX AND HOUNDS

"Say there's five players. You have a dip and one of them's the fox. The other four players have to chase after him. The first one who catches him is the fox." boy, Brockley 1983.

Brockley, Earlsfield, Kensington 1982–84.

This is a boys' game.

Printed versions Brewster, *ANG*, Fox, p. 77; Gomme (see below); Halliwell (see below); Northall (see below); Opies, *CGSP*, p. 178; Solomons, Fox and Hound, p. 29; Strutt (see below).

Early notings Strutt quotes from "an old comedy": "*The longer thou livest the more foole thou art*", written by William Wager in about 1568, spoken by "an idle boy": And also when we play and hunt the fox,/I outrun all the boys in the schoole. Strutt, 1801, Hunt the Fox/Hunt the Hare, p. 284. Whoop, whoop and hollow, Halliwell, 1844, p. 104. Hare and Hounds/ Fox and Hounds, Northall, 1892, p. 357. Hare and Hounds, Gomme, 1894, p. 191.

3.A.24 CHARLIE

"There's about five people standing on a bench and there's someone called 'Charlie'. The people on the bench shout, 'What's your name?' and he says, 'Charlie.' They go 'Charlie who?' and he says 'Chase me'… and they chase him." girl, Shepherds Bush 1983.

3.A.25 ICE AND WATER

"Someone's 'on it' and they have to run around and touch someone and say, 'One, two, three.' If (the person touched) doesn't want to be 'it' they have to stop, put both hands up and say, 'Ice.' They have to wait until someone who's not 'ice' comes along and says, 'Water'." girl, Kensington 1984.

Played by boys and girls.

3.A.26 CAT AND MOUSE

"You all pair up (in a circle). One person's in front, the other behind. You have a pair who are 'on it'. One is the cat and one is the mouse. The cat starts chasing the mouse. If the cat catches the mouse then they swap around. If the mouse becomes tired he can stop behind a pair and the person in front (becomes a mouse). Somebody might say, 'Change' and then they change around." girl, EC1 1983.

Printed versions Opies, *CGSP*, Twos and threes: "the orderly adult-approved form of 'Budge He'.", pp. 82–84; Parry-Jones, Twos and Threes, mentioned, p. 90; Sutton-Smith, Twos and threes, p. 58.

"There are people in a circle and there's a cat and a mouse. The cat goes inside and the mouse goes outside. He has to run round. The people have to close the gap up so that the cat doesn't catch the mouse. When the cat catches the mouse you have to pick somebody else." boy, Streatham 1982.

Finsbury, Streatham 1982–83.

Both games played by boys and girls.

See also **4.15**.

Printed versions Brady, Cat and Mouse, p. 161; Brewster, *ANG*, pp. 61–63; Opies, *CGSP*, pp. 114–115.

3.A.27 BLIND MAN'S BUFF

"There's a person who's 'on it'. You put a scarf round their head so they can't see. Then you've all got to try and keep away from him so he doesn't 'had' you." boy, Mile End 1983.

This is probably universal as a party game. Only in a school in Mile End (1983) was I given it as a playground game.

Printed versions Bett (see below); Ford (see below); Gomme (see below); Holbrook, pp. 106–107; Opies, *CGSP*, pp. 117–120; Solomons, p. 22; Sutton-Smith, p. 57.

Early notings Bett (*TGC*, 1929, p. 4) states that the game is mentioned by Rabelais (*Gargantua*) and Shakespeare (*Hamlet*). Gomme, 1894, pp. 37–40; Ford, 1904, p. 74.

3.A.28 BULLDOG; BRITISH BULLDOG; FAMILY BULLDOG; MAD BULLDOG; SCATTIE

"There's one person 'on it' and the people have to run round. They have to choose a person (who) has to come and the person (who's) 'on it' has to get him, lift him up and count to five. That means he's 'on it'." boy, Barnsbury 1983 (British Bulldog).

"There's a bunch of boys or girls and a person who chases them. They have to run to another side of the wall. They all run and he (the one who's chasing) has to try and catch them. When they all run he has to try and catch them. When he catches them they become 'he' with him. Then afterwards they call a name, any name they like. When that boy runs he shouts out, 'Bulldog'." boy, Kentish Town 1983 (Bulldog).

"I play Bulldog different. There's somebody 'on it' and that person says, 'I bulldog (_____),' or something. If (_____) doesn't want to run on her own she has to say, 'Bulldog all,' and you all run. 'He' has to try and catch them." girl, Kentish Town 1983 (Bulldog).

"They pick someone to be 'on it'. (They pick another) and that person has to run across and try to get to the other side. They can say 'Bulldog' from any time. When they say 'Bulldog' all the others have to run to the other side. People 'had' then join to be 'on it'. The last person 'had' is 'on it' for the new game." Boys, Finsbury 1983 (Bulldog).

"The only difference is in 'Mad Bulldog'. Instead of touching you have to grab them, put them on the floor and hold them down for three seconds." boys, Finsbury 1983 (Bulldog).

"If you get them on the floor they're 'on it'. When you catch them you've got to say, 'Bulldog.' You get them on the floor and say, 'One, two, three, bulldog,' and the whole lot come … The people 'on it' have to get the other people down, and they're 'on it' if they get caught." boy, Dalston 1983 (Bulldog).

"If we play Family Bulldog, if someone 'has' someone they stay 'on' till everyone's 'on'. If someone stays next to the wall for a really long time then all the people … count up to ten and he hasn't run by 'ten' we go and 'had' him and he's 'on'." boy, Stoke Newington 1983.

"When you get them on the floor sometimes you have to turn them on their back. If their legs aren't on the floor or their arms or head are up, you can't say, 'British Bulldog, one, two, three.' " boy, Shepherds Bush 1983 (British Bulldog).

"There's one person who's 'he' and all the rest are lining up against the wall. They call someone's name and the person they call has to say, 'Scattie' and they have to run. All the people who're lining up against the wall have to run over to the other wall and try not to let the person who's 'he' get them." girl, Dulwich 1983 (Scattie).

This is a universal game but seems to have slight differences in almost all schools and some major differences in a few. Versions were collected in almost every school visited. This is mainly a boys' game but it is sometimes played by girls on their own and more rarely by boys and girls together, but not in the "rough" versions, which are probably more traditional, however. See also **3.F.4**.

Printed versions Douglas (see below); Gomme (see below); Kings (see below); Opies, *CGSP*, British Bulldog, pp. 138–142; Parry-Jones, Catcher, p. 67; Ritchie, *SS*, British Bulldog/ Bulldozer, p. 81; Sluckin, British Bulldog, p. 20; Smith, *BBHG*, British Bulldog, p. 93; Sutton-Smith, Bar the door, and many other names, pp. 58–60.

Early notings Gomme, 1894, Click, pp. 69–70, Cock, pp. 72–73, King Caesar, p. 299. Pig in the pot, Douglas, 1916, pp. 147–148, 1931, pp. 80–81. Kings 2, 1930, I spy! p. 9, and note on p. 42.

3.A.29 BULLDOG (SUBJECTS)

"There's one person who catches. We all stand together. He says, like, makes of cars. We pick Escort, Cortina etc. We tell him all of them. He calls one, say, 'Rolls Royce'. The one who's Rolls Royce he has to run. (If he's caught) then both of them are 'on'." boy, Stoke Newington, 1983 (Bulldog).

Cubitt Town, Stoke Newington 1983.

This game has affinities with **3.B.12** POLO.

3.A.30 BLUE PETER

"There's someone 'on it' in the middle of a square. The person in the middle of the square says, 'Who's afraid of Blue Peter?' You can say, 'Not I' and you've got to try and run over to get to the other side. If you're 'had' you're out." girl, Shepherds Bush 1983.

Printed version Opies, *CGSP*, Black Peter, pp. 130–131.

3.A.31 SHEEP AND WOLVES

"There are two walls. There are two wolves and (the others are) sheep. If you get caught you sit … All the rest have got to try and get home. If you get home you're not 'he' and then you run round again." boy, Brockley 1983.

Printed versions This is a much simpler version of the following: Fowke, Old Daddy Tom, p. 46; Gomme (see below); Halliwell (see below); Kidson (see below); Opies, *CGSP*, cf. Wall to wall, pp. 126–128, Johnny Lingo, pp. 314–317; Parry-Jones, Jerry Lango, p. 112; Shaw, 1970, Daddy Bunchy, pp. 31–32; Sutton-Smith (see below).

Early notings Jacky Lingo, Halliwell, *NRE*, 1842, pp. 122–123. Jack a Lingo, Sutton-Smith, p. 36 (Otago, 1890). Who goes round my Stone

Wall, Gomme, 1898, pp. 375–381; Gomme also cites many Jacky Lingo/ Johnny Lingo rhymes. Jackey Ringold (sung version, with the words: "Who goes round my stony wall?"), Kidson, 1916, p. 89.

3.A.32 COLOURS

> "Someone has to be 'he'. (She says) 'You can only cross my bridge if you've got (say she says) blue on.' If you've got blue you can cross without her 'having' you. But if you haven't got that colour on you've got to try and run away. If she 'has' you you're 'in' ('he'). It carries on." girl, Borough 1983.

Borough, Kentish Town 1983.

Printed versions cf. Opies, *CGSP*, Colours, p. 80 (immunity conveyed not only by wearing the colour but by touching it), Farmer, Farmer, May We Cross Your Golden River, pp. 133–135; Ritchie, *SS*, You can't Cross the River, p. 93; Rutherford, Charlie, Charlie, may I cross the coloured water, please?/Not unless you've got *blue* on, p. 47; Sluckin, Jack, Jack, may we cross the water? ... only if you're wearing blue, p. 20; Smith, *BBHG*, Catch, p. 76, with accompanying chant: Please Mr Fisherman,/ May I cross the Chinese water,/On the way to Chinese school,/Eating Fish and Chips one day. The person who is 'on' shouts a colour, and people wearing that colour can cross without getting caught.

3.A.33 PLEASE MR. CROCODILE/MR. BUMBLEBEE; CROCODILE, CROCODILE; ALLIGATOR, ALLIGATOR

This game, preceded by a chant, is to be found in most Inner London schools.

Chants:

A. Please Mr. Crocodile,
   May we cross the water,
   To see your ugly daughter,

>   Sliding on the water,
>   Like a cup of water?

Mile End 1983.

Variants: In a cup and saucer/Inside out, Brockley 1983; Who lives in a cup and saucer, Barnsbury 1983; In a cup and saucer, Kensington 1984.

>   B. Please Mr. Crocodile,
>   May we cross the water,
>   To see the fairies' (pretty) daughter,
>   Before she goes to school?

Battersea, Streatham 1982; Deptford, <u>Dulwich</u>, Finsbury <u>1983</u>.

>   C. Please Mr. Crocodile,
>   May we cross the water,
>   To see the fairy daughter,
>   To have a drop of water,
>   And a slice of bread, please?

Mile End 1967.

>   D. Please Mr. Bumblebee,
>   May we cross the water,
>   In a cup and saucer,
>   Dressed in (blue)?

<u>Greenwich 1982</u>; Dalston 1983.

>   E. Alligator, Alligator,
>   Can we cross the water,
>   To see your lovely daughter,
>   Who'll give us a cup of water?

Brockley 1983.

F. Crocodile, Crocodile,
May we cross the golden river …?

Blackheath 1983.

"One person's the crocodile. (The others) stand on one side touching the wall or something. They say, 'Please Mr. Crocodile etc.' Crocodile says, 'Only if you're wearing (blue).' Anyone who's wearing (blue) can go straight across. Anyone not wearing (blue) has to try and run across without being 'had'. If they're 'had' they're 'it'. It's a bit like British Bulldog." girl, Blackheath 1982.

Printed versions Bett (see below); cf. Brady, Johnny May I Go Across the Water? p. 132; Opies, *CGSP*, Farmer, Farmer, May We Cross Your Golden River?, pp. 133–135; Sutton-Smith, Please, Jack, May We Cross Your Golden River?, p. 66; Turner, Crocodile, Crocodile, p. 54.

Early noting Bett, *TGC*, 1929, a German version, p. 103.

Recording Webb, *Children's Singing Games* (Jack, Jack).

3.A.34 MONDAY, TUESDAY

"We've got some stairs and the stairs go down: Monday, Tuesday, Wednesday, Thursday, Friday, Saturday and Sunday, then North Pole and Dog Kennel Hill. One person's 'he' and they say, 'Monday' and all have to jump on the step: Monday. Then he says 'North Pole' and they have to run up, touch the post and come back. The person who's standing there has got to get them and not let them get up the stairs. They do it until one person's left. The person who is left (or sometimes the first person [who] is caught) is then 'he'." girl, Dulwich 1983.

See also **3.B.1B** and **3.B.3**.

Printed version cf. Ritchie, *GC*, Steps, p. 34.

3.B RACING AND SIMILAR GAMES

STARTING A RACE

The procedure for starting a race takes a number of forms, of which the following are examples.

> 3.B.i One to get ready,
> Two for the show,
> Three to get steady,
> And four to go.

Kensington 1984.

Printed versions Bolton (see below); Briggs, One for money,/Two for show,/Three to make ready,/And four to go, p. 173; Leach and Fried, One to make ready;/Two to show;/Three to start,/And four to go, p. 1017; Wood (see below).

Early notings One for the money, two for the show;/Three to make ready, four for the go! New York and West Tennessee, used to start a race, Bolton, 1888, p. 119. Wood, *AMG*, 1940, like Briggs, p. 96.

Carl Perkins used the first three lines of this version in 1956 to start the song "Blue Suede Shoes", later famously sung by Elvis Presley. The fourth line in that song ("And go, cat, go") is echoed in **3.B.iv**.

> 3.B.ii One to get ready,
> Two to get steady,
> Three to go.

Kensington 1984.

> 3.B.iii Ready,
> Steady,
> Toddy.

Kensington 1984.

3.B.iv   Ready,
         Steady,
         Go, cat.

Kensington 1984.

Printed versions   Abrahams, "Usually used to start a race", p. 147; Botkin (see below); Boyce and Bartlett (see below); Briggs, p. 173, as Halliwell, *NRNTE* (see below); Cansler, 11; Fowke, p. 114; Graves (see below); Gullen, p. 31; Halliwell (see below); Lang (see below); MacBain (see below); Newell (see below); Northall (see below); Opies, *ODNR*, as Halliwell's version, pp. 332–333; Ritchie, *GC*, like version **3.B.ii**, p. 31; Rodger, similar to version **3.B.ii**, p. 35; Solomons, p. 59; Sutton-Smith, skipping game, p. 75; Talley (see below); Withers, *RIMP*, like version **3.B.i**, p. 42.

Early notings   ONE to make ready,/And two to prepare;/God bless the rider,/And away goes the mare. Halliwell, 1846, p. 124. One to make ready,/And two to prepare;/Good luck to the rider,/And away goes the mare. Halliwell, *NRNTE*, c1870, p. 61. Northall, 1892, as Halliwell, c1870, p. 358; Lang, 1897, as Halliwell, c1870, p. 186. One to make ready,/Two to prepare,/Three to *go slambang*,/Right—down—there. Said to be a parody of Halliwell's c1870 rhyme, Newell, 1903, p. 133. Talley, 1922, p. 180; Graves, 1927, as Halliwell, c1870, p. 30. MacBain, 1933, "Learning to Walk", as Halliwell, c1870, p. 281. Boyce and Bartlett, 1941, p. 28; Botkin, *TAF*, 1944, p. 778.

3.B.v.   Bell horses, bell horses,
         What time of day?
         Three o'clock, away.

Brixton 1982.

3.B.vi. Bell horses, bell horses,
         What time of day?
         One o'clock, two o'clock,
         Three o'clock, four o'clock,
         And now it's time to stay.

Brixton 1982.

The girl, aged ten, who gave me the above rhymes, was not sure where she learned them and did not associate them with any particular game. However, a number of collectors record similar versions (see below) and say they were used to start races, so I include them here.

Printed versions Boyce and Bartlett (see below); Briggs, p. 173; Chambers (see below); Daiken, *CGTY*, p. 20; Gomme (see below); Gullen, "a running game", p. 55; Halliwell (see below); Kellett, pp. 113–114 (and early noting); MacBain (see below); Northall (see below); Opies, *ODNR*, pp. 69–70, *CGSP*, p. 184; Rodger, Belluses, Belluses, p. 35; Smith, *TGH*, p. 73; Sutton-Smith, running game, p. 12.

Early notings Bell horses, bell horses, what time o' day,/One a clock, two o'clock, three starts away, Northall, 1892, p. 358, where he states that this rhyme appears in *Gammer Gurton's Garland*, 1783, reprint 1866, p. 42, with the variation "time to away" at the end. Good horses, bad horses,/What is the time of day?/Three o'clock, four o'clock,/Now fare you away, sung by children before starting a race, Halliwell, *NRE*, 1842, p. 147. Bell horses, bell horses,/What time o'day?/One o'clock, two o'clock,/Time to away. Halliwell, *NRE*, 1843, p. 147. Bellasay, Bellasay, what time of day?/One o'clock, two o'clock, three and away! In this case used when children "leap off anything", Halliwell, *PRNT*, 1849, p. 201. Race-horses, race-horses,/What time of day?/One o'clock, two o'clock,/Three—and away! Chambers, 1870, p. 148. Bell-horses, bell-horses, what time of day?/One o'clock, two o'clock, three, and away!/Bell-horses, bell-horses, what time of day?/Two o'clock, three o'clock, four, and away!/Five o'clock, six o'clock, now time to stay!, Gomme, 1894, pp. 26–27. MacBain, 1933, p. 121; Boyce and Bartlett, 1941, p. 28.

The Opies (*ODNR*, pp. 69–70) treat this rhyme as if it referred literally to "bell horses", as may well be the case. On the other hand, Halliwell (*PRNT*, p. 201) compares it with an ancient proverb-rhyme referring to John de Belasye in the fourteenth century, who fought in the Holy Land and who, curiously, was supposed to have been "passionately addicted to 'race horses!'."

Racing as a Game
Racing as a games activity was only reported to me by children in two of the twenty-one schools: Dalston and Shepherds Bush 1983. It is probably more popular than this, but seasonal.

Relay Racing
One school, Deptford, reported relay racing as a playtime activity.

3.B.1 MOTHER, MAY I?/DAYS OF THE WEEK

A. MOTHER, MAY I?

"One person's 'it' and the other people stand against the wall. They have a number. The person who's 'it' calls out the first person, say Number One. He gives them something to do like, 'Take two giant steps', and they go two giant steps. (Before doing so) the person who's against the wall has to say, 'Mother, may I?' 'Mother' says, 'Yes you may!' and the person has to do the action. They do all kinds of actions." girl, Streatham 1982.

"The person says, 'You can take five pigeon steps.' If you just take five pigeon steps then you're out. You've got to start again. You have to say, 'Mother, may I?' and the person who's 'he' can say, 'Yes you may,' or 'No you may not.' You go on until you get home and then you've won." girl, Borough 1983.

Throughout Inner London 1982–84. This appeared to be the second most popular game (after **3.A.28** BULLDOG).

These are some of the possible movements (from various schools): take a pigeon step (a step heel to toe); take giant steps (number specified; long strides); take a trip round the world (round "Mother" and back to place, stop when "Mother" says so); take a trip to London (similar); take an umbrella (turn round and go forward); take water bucket (spit on floor and jump on spit); take a ladder (lie down extended and get up to stand on furthest spot reached); lamp post (similar); watering can (similar to water bucket); toilet (squat, stand up and pull imaginary chain); cartwheel (do or attempt a cartwheel); squashed tomatoes, scissors, spitfire (details unknown).

B. DAYS OF THE WEEK

"You get five people and yourself. You have to be 'mother' and the others are named Monday, Tuesday, etc. You say, 'Monday, take two giant steps.' They say, 'Mother may I?' and if I say they may not they stand still." girl, Shepherds Bush 1983.

Dalston, Kensington, Shepherds Bush 1983–84.

This is mainly a girls' game, but in several schools is played by boys and girls together.

See also **3.A.34**.

Printed versions: Brady, Giant Steps, pp. 132–133; Knapps, Mother, May I, pp. 52–53; Opies, *CGSP*, May I?, pp. 187–190; Ritchie, *SS*, Giant Steps and Baby Steps, pp. 85–86; Sluckin, Mother may I?, p. 22; Smith, *BBHG*, May I?, p. 77; Solomons, Mother, May I?, p. 31, Red Light, p. 38; Sutton-Smith, May I?, pp. 49–50; Steps and Strides, p. 49.

3.B.2 LETTERS

"You have one person who's 'it' and you have to choose a name you want to be. (The person who's 'it') says a letter. If you have two of that letter in your 'name' you take two steps, and so on, until you touch (the person who's 'it')." girl, Streatham 1982.

Printed versions Opies, *CGSP*, p. 191; Sluckin, Red Letter, p. 22; Smith, *BBHG*, Letters in a Name, p. 69; Sutton-Smith, Letters, pp. 48–49.

3.B.3 VINEGAR, MUSTARD, PEPPER

(No connection with the skipping game of that name).

"There's a stair game: Vinegar, Mustard, Pepper. There are three or four steps. If the person says, 'Salt', you have to jump on the step, salt. If they say, 'Tomato sauce', you have to run to the first line, touch it and run back and the last one back is 'he'." girl, Dulwich 1983.

See also **3.A.34**.

3.B.4 COLOURS (RACING) (1)

"Three or any amount of people line up by the wall and a person stands at the other end. This person says a colour like orange and anyone who's wearing it runs to them. The first one to touch the other person (wins)." boy, Streatham 1982.

Printed version Opies, *CGSP*, pp. 191–192.

3.B.5 COLOURS (RACING) (2)

"First you dip and the last one out is 'it'. You go on benches against the wall. There's three posts. You have to run from number one to number two, then to three and then run back to the bench. Everyone has a colour and to run when their colour is called (red, white or blue)." boy and girl, Brixton 1982–84.

Presumably a number of those with, say, colour red, run, and one is the winner.

3.B.6 PEEP BEHIND THE CURTAIN; GRANDMOTHER; PIGGY BEHIND THE CURTAIN

"There's somebody 'on it'. There's a lot of people lined up. The person that's 'on it' has to turn around. When she turns around the people who are lined up have to run as far as they can. When she turns back round again they have to be still. If she sees you, you've got to go right back to the beginning. If somebody runs up and touches her back she's 'on it'." girl, Hampstead 1984.

"They run and when they say, 'Piggy Behind the Curtain 1, 2, 3,' they catch you if you're moving. Then you have to go back to the wall and start all over again." boy, Shepherds Bush 1983.

"One person's 'on it'. They've got to be the 'piggy', the others they're the people. Piggy, the person who's 'on it' behind the curtain, when they say, 'Peep behind the curtain' and turn round, if they see anyone move, that one has to go to the beginning again." girl, Cubitt Town 1983.

"There's one person facing the wall and then there are other people who are trying to creep up behind that person. The person against the wall, who's the grandmother, turns around every so often. If she sees somebody move behind her, that person has to go back to the beginning. It's the first one to touch the grandmother." Inner London 1982–84.

This game appears to be almost ubiquitous in Inner London. Versions were collected in all areas. It was the third most played game (not counting football); sixteen versions collected 1983–84.

See also **3.B.7** and **3.B.8**.

Printed versions Brewster, *ANG*, Red Light, p. 35; Douglas (see below), Opies, *CGSP*, pp. 192–195; Ritchie, *SS*, Red Lights, p. 90; Sluckin, Grandmother's Footsteps, p. 22; Smith, *BBHG*, Sly Fox/Peep Behind the Curtain, p. 75; Sutton-Smith, Creeping Up/Peep Behind the Curtain/Grandmother's Footsteps, plus other names, p. 50.

Early noting Douglas, Peeping Behind the Curtain mentioned as "a hiding game for girls", 1916, p. 48, 1931, p. 26.

3.B.7 STATUES

"There's one person on one side of a wall and a few people on the other side. People walk up to the first person but if he turns around and sees them moving they're out. They've got to stand still when he turns around." boy, Streatham 1982.

See also **3.B.6** and **3.B.8**.

The Opies (*CGSP*, pp. 194–195) note that "Statues" is a name used in Scotland and the Midlands as an alternative to "Peep Behind the Curtain".

Printed versions Ellis (see below); Opies, *CGSP*, p. 195; cf. Ritchie, *GC*, Stookies (also called Dotto, Ditto, and Statues), p. 34; the Streatham game is a much simpler version of games described by Sutton-Smith under "Statues" (p. 50) and "Musical Statues" (pp. 50, 109).

Early noting " 'Statues'. One player stood on the opposite pavement with her back to the rest of the players. The others tried to cross over the road and touch the garden fence without her spotting any movement when she turned around periodically throughout the game." Ellis, 1910s, 39.

3.B.8 FOOTSIE

"If I'm 'on it' you have to go to the other side of the wall. You have to say, 'Footsie, 1, 2, 3.' If I turn around and see someone moving, that means they have to touch the wall. If I see another one moving they have to join hands. If the last one is 'had' they have to go back to the other wall. If I catch one they're 'on it'." girl, Shepherds Bush 1983.

See also **3.B.6** and **3.B.7**.

Footsie, *forty forty* (**3.D.2**) and *foxie* (**3.D.4**), appear to be variants of the same term, which signifies that the chaser is setting off. The Opies (*CGSP*, 1969, p. 195) give "Foxy" as one Midlands name for "Peep Behind the Curtain", see **3.B.6**.

3.B.9 HOT CHOCOLATE

"When the last person links they say, 'Hot chocolate.' They've all got to run back and the person who's 'on it' has to go and chase after them and try and 'had' them. If they catch one they're 'on it'." boy, Blackheath 1983.

Similar to **3.B.8**.

3.B.10 RED, GOLD AND GREEN

"The person who is 'on it' stands one side of the wall. About ten people stand on the other side. When one says, 'Red', (and you are red) you have to run. If you run when (the one who is 'on it') turns round, you have to go back and start again." Inner London 1982–84.

The ending is not clear.

3.B.11 MEGGY PEGGY

"There's many people lined up and there's one person who's 'on it'. The people sing the song:

'Meggy Peggy lost her leggy
On the way to school.'

The person who's 'on it' shouts out a subject like 'shoes'. The people on the line choose different shoes like plimsolls, college shoes, etc. One of them tells the one that's 'on it' all the kinds they've said but doesn't tell them who said each one. The person that's 'on it' might shout, 'college', and the person who chose 'college' and the one who's 'on it' runs. If the one who's 'on it' wins the other is 'on it'." girl, Dalston, 1983.

Printed version cf. Opies, *CGSP*, Eggy Peggy, p. 215.

3.B.12 POLO; COCOA

"In Polo we play with two sides of the playground. The person (who's 'it') shouts (the name of a flower) and the person whose flower it was and the person who's 'it' run say, back and forward. The last one to say 'Polo' is 'it'." girl, Blackheath 1983.

"Someone's 'it' and they say a subject like cars. The other people across the other side have to say the name of a car but they mustn't say (who has chosen different cars). The person who's 'it' has to say someone's (car name) like 'Ford'. Whoever is 'Ford' has to run across to the other side. Whoever is back first to their starting place has to yell, 'Cocoa.' Whoever is back first wins and they call out the subject." girl, Kensington 1984.

Blackheath, Brockley, Cubitt Town, Dalston, Dulwich, Greenwich, Hampstead, Kensington, Kentish Town, Mile End, Shepherds Bush, Stoke Newington, Streatham 1982–84.

This is one of the half dozen most popular games and is played by both boys and girls, but is much more popular with girls. The game has affinities with **3.A.29** BULLDOG (SUBJECTS).

Printed versions Brewster (*ANG*, p. 58) discusses a version of "Prison Base" which has affinities with POLO and is played in the Dominican Republic, where a player reaching the opposite side without being caught is called a "Pololo". Opies, *CGSP*, Cigarettes, p. 138; Sluckin, White horses/ Polo, pp. 22–23; Smith, *BBHG*, Polo, p. 85.

3.B.13 BOMBS

"In our playground there are lots of stones. One person picks on three stones. You've got to try to get to 'home' before you get blown up if you tread on (one of these stones)." girl, Cubitt Town 1983.

Presumably there is a competitive element as well.

3.B.14 SHIPS, SHARKS AND TORPEDOES

"Sometimes we play this game when somebody says, 'Ships!' they have to run to one end of the playground. When they say, 'Torpedoes,' they've got to run to another end. If they say, 'Sharks are coming!' they have to jump on a bench in the playground. The last one to do so is out." girl, Kentish Town 1983.

3.B.15 SHIP, SHORE, DECK

"There's a person who's captain. He stands on the bench. This is the deck. There is a light which is a lighthouse, netball posts are Poland. The dustbin's America. One side is ship and one side is shore. Then the captain says, 'Ship, shore, deck, five times last man,' you have to run from one side to the other and so on. The last person is out. Then he goes, 'Ship, shore, deck, lighthouse, Poland, America, last man.' They go to all these places again and the last man's out." boy, Streatham 1982.

3.B.16 SEA, SKY, EARTH

"There are three circles: sea, sky and earth. One is shouted and children have to run to the particular circle. The last child is out." boy, Battersea 1982.

3.B.17 BOOTS AND SHOES

This appears to be similar to the last three games but directions were unclear. girls, Barnsbury 1983.

3.C JUMPING, LEAPING AND HANDSTANDING

3.C.1 COLOURS (JUMPING ROPE)

"Two hold the rope and they have got a colour. They're so many people over one side and they've got to jump over and say the right colour. Then you become the first on the skipping rope. You have to move it higher and higher and they've got to jump over and say a colour." boy, Streatham 1982.

"You wiggle the skipping rope about and the people who are holding the skipping rope at each end whisper a colour to each other and the people who jump over have to guess what colour it is." girl, Dalston 1982.

Printed version Smith, *BBHG*, Snakes, p. 84.

3.C.2 JUMPING A SWINGING ROPE

"We haven't got a name for this game but there's one person in the middle. They've got some rope with something heavy on the end and they swing it along the ground. People have to jump up, sort of skipping. There's lots of people in it. If you get caught with it round your ankles you have the 'Tunnel of Death'." boy, Hampstead 1984.

For Tunnel of Death, see **3.A.8.i**.

Printed version Ritchie, *GC*, Round Rope Heights, p. 121.

3.C.3 SEVENSIES

"You get seven rulers and you lay them out. The first person has to go over (them). They have to move one further up and they have to jump over that. They can move another one as many times as they like. The person who can't jump over it is out. The next person may not be able to jump over either and they'll be out as well." girl, Borough 1983.

Printed versions cf. the competitive jumping games outlined in Opies, *CGSP*, pp. 253–254.

3.C.4 BALL IN THE STOCKING

"A tennis ball is put in a nylon stocking and tied to one ankle. It is swung from side to side and the child has to jump over it. It is an individual game." girl, Deptford 1983.

3.C.5 LEAP FROGS

Given to me in two schools, with no details (Borough, Kentish Town 1983).

Versions of the usual form of "Leapfrog" where one child bends over and another runs up and vaults over the child's back, are reported as follows:

Printed versions Brewster, *ANG*, pp. 103–106; Douglas (see below); Gaskell (see below); Gomme (see below); Opies, *CGSP*, pp. 247–249, 250–262 passim; Parry-Jones, pp. 70–71; Ritchie, *GC*, Tipenny-Nipenny, p. 36; Sluckin, p. 24; Solomons, p. 21; Strutt (see below); Sutton-Smith, p. 138.

Early notings Strutt (1801, p. 285) says that the game is mentioned in Shakespeare's *Henry V* and in Ben Jonson's *Bartholomew Fair*. Gomme, 1894, pp. 327–328; Gaskell, c1913, Cap-on-back, p. 4; Douglas, 1916, pp. 24–28; 1931, pp. 13–15.

3.C.6 HANDSTANDS

"The girls play this on the grass. You have a person who's 'it'. They say what you have to do and ask you your favourite television programme. You have to do a handstand and say your favourite television programme. If they like that programme and you've done your handstand nicely they say it's your turn. You have to say something they have to do." girl, Streatham 1982.

Printed version cf. Sutton-Smith, p. 53.

3.D SEEKING GAMES

STARTING A SEEKING GAME

3.D.i I Draw a Snake

"You draw a snake behind (somebody's) back and then you put your hands out. They've got to choose (which) finger. You go, 'One hundred,' then if it's the wrong finger, 'Two hundred, three hundred, four hundred. . . .' until it's the right finger. If they get five hundred they've got to put their face behind the post and count to five hundred." girl, Stoke Newington 1983.

"You just draw a snake upon the person's back, an S, and then you sort of hit their back with a finger and say, 'Which finger did that?' and they've got to guess." girl, Kensington 1984.

"You say, 'I draw a snake upon your back, which finger did that?' First you say, 'Which hand was it?' If they choose the wrong hand it's slow. If they choose the right hand it's fast. Each finger represents ten so if they said, 'Second finger' and the finger that poked the back was the fifth one, that would be wrong. If they got it on the third go they'd have to count to thirty (slowly or fast). You do it for 'Stuck in the mud'." girls, Finsbury 1983.

"In my last school the snake upon your back started off a chase game where you run round in a sort of circle (and) catch the person." girl, Kensington 1984.

"Before you play 'Forty forty' one of the hiders goes up to the person who's 'it' and they do this thing, 'Snake, snake on your back, which finger did that?' and they prod the back with one of their fingers." girl, Blackheath 1982.

This game procedure was almost ubiquitous in Inner London schools during the collecting period 1982–84. It usually prefaces a hiding game such as **3.D.1** HIDE AND SEEK or **3.D.2** FORTY FORTY. It is carried out by girls and boys separately, or more usually by boys and girls together.

Printed versions cf. Brewster, *ANG*, Tap-on-the-Back, pp. 48–50; Gomme (see below); Opies, *CGSP*, pp. 157–160; Ritchie, *GC*, pp. 55–56; Sluckin, p. 21: as part of Ay-Ickie "the other children all joined hands and together made as if to touch the back of the seeker, but in reality only one of these many fingers had made contact. They now asked in unison, 'Who did the dot?'." Sutton-Smith, Tip the finger/Draw the snake, and many other names, pp. 67–68.

Early noting cf. How many fingers do I hold up? /Four, three, &c. [at random in reply]./How many horses has your father?/Three [fixed reply]. /What colour?/White, red, and grey./Turn you about three times;/Catch whom you may! Gomme, 1894, under "Blind Man's Buff", pp. 37–38.

3.D.1 HIDE AND SEEK

> "You dip and the last one who's out is left on their own. They close their eyes and count to about a hundred. The others go and hide. When they're all 'had' the first one 'had' is 'he' next time." girl, Borough 1983.

> Borough, Brockley, Cubitt Town, Dalston, Deptford, Shepherds Bush 1983.

Usually played by boys and girls together or girls on their own. The versions known as FORTY FORTY (**3.D.2**) are much more popular.

Printed versions Brady, Hide and Go Seek, p. 147; Chambers (see below); Daiken, *CGTY*, Hide and Spy, p. 4; Gaskell (see below); Gomme (see below); Knapps, Hide and Seek, pp. 6, 7, 21, 34, 36, 49, 50, 51, 261; Parry-Jones, p. 112; Opies, *CGSP*, Hide-and-Seek, pp. 151–155; Strutt (see below); Sutton-Smith, Hide and Seek/Hideygo, p. 56.

Early notings Harry-racket/Hide and Seek/Hoop and Hide, Strutt, 1801, p. 284; Hide-and-Seek, Chambers, 1842, p. 62; Gomme, 1894: All-hid, p. 1, Hide and Seek, pp. 211–213. Cf. "Whip", Gaskell, c1913, p. 3.

3.D.2 FORTY FORTY

"One person's 'he' and everybody runs away and hides. The person has to count up to forty-four, then he opens his eyes. He looks around to see if he can see somebody. If he (thinks he) sees somebody he says, 'Forty forty, I can see (_____) behind the wall, one, two, three.' If he's right the person comes out and she's 'he'." girl, Dulwich 1983.

"When you're counting to forty everyone runs away. (You go) looking for them. The people have to get 'home'. When they get 'home', if they're not the last one they say, 'Forty forty, home' or 'Forty forty, save myself.' If they're the last one home they say, 'Forty forty, save all.' If everybody gets home or if the last person saves all, you're 'it' again. Otherwise the first person seen is 'it'." girl, Blackheath 1983.

Versions collected in all parts of Inner London, 1982–84.

This game is usually prefaced by the "I Draw a Snake" procedures outlined in **3.D.i**. It is equally popular as a girls' game or as a game for boys and girls together. More rarely it is played by boys on their own.

Printed versions Brewster (*ANG*, p. 43) describes a Greek version of Hide and Seek where players count to forty and shout "forty and I'm coming!"; Douglas (see below); Opies, *CGSP*, Block/Forty-Forty/I-acky etc. The Opies add that "custom dictates" that children count to forty "when playing this game in south-east London"; pp. 160–162; Ritchie, *GC*, Forty Buzz Off, p. 59; Sluckin, Ay-ickie, p. 21; Solomons, Hide-and-Go-Seek, pp. 15–16.

Early noting Forty, Douglas, 1916, p. 20, 1931, p. 10.

3.D.3 KARIMPA

"It's a bit like 'Forty forty' except you go, 'One Karimpa, two Karimpa, three Karimpa,' up to ten …" girl, Blackheath 1983.

3.D.4 FOXIE, FOXIE, 1, 2, 3

"You choose one person to go on the wall and count up to fourteen. The rest of you hide. When you hide they have to try to look for you. If a person gets (to home) before you and says, 'Foxie, Foxie, one, two, three,' they're saved." girl, Streatham 1982.

Shepherds Bush, Streatham 1982–83.

A girls' game.

Printed versions Brewster, *ANG*, pp. 42–46; Chambers (see below).

Early notings Chambers, 1842, p. 62. The latter versions of Hide-and-Seek include exemption from being "it" if you reach "the den" before "the tig" catches you.

3.D.5 TIN CAN TOLLY

"We get a tin and we put it on the stone in the patch of green. The person who's 'on it' has to turn round and count to whatever the number is and then the (others) all run and hide. The person (who's 'on it') has to start looking round. He has to go away from the can once in a while and when he sees someone he has to run to the can and say, 'Tin can Tolly, I see (_____) behind (_____)'. Then they come (out) and they're trapped. The other people who're still hiding have to (try to) save the person who got caught, by running up to the can when the person (who's 'on it') isn't looking (and saying), 'Tin can Tolly, I save all.' Then they run off again." boy, Hampstead 1984.

Barnsbury, Hampstead 1983–84.

Played by boys and girls.

Printed versions Brady, Kick the Can, p. 146; Brewster, *ANG*, Kick the Can, pp. 47–48; Douglas (see below), Ellis (see below); Gaskell (see below);

Opies, *CGSP*, Tin Can Tommy, etc., pp. 164–168; Ritchie, *GC*, Kick the Can/Tin-Can Tommy, pp. 57–58, Sutton-Smith, Kick the Tin, p. 58.

Early notings " 'Tin Can Copper'. The one who was 'He' had a tin can (usually a cocoa tin) in which were placed several stones. Everyone else hid, mostly in front gardens. Then 'He' would bang the tin on the ground several times, shout out 'Tin Can Copper', and start searching out the hiding places. The idea was to get back to home without being caught by the 'Copper'." Ellis, 1910s, 39. Kick-can, a game played before World War I, Gaskell, c1913, p. 3. Tin Can Copper, Douglas, 1916, p. 16, 1931, p. 8.

Recording Kicking a tin can down the street, mentioned on MacColl and Behan, *Streets of Song*.

3.D.6 BOO

"You have to sort of hide and this other girl has to sneak up to you very silently and go, 'Boo' right in your ear." girl, Blackheath 1983.

3.D.7 KISS CHASE

"The girls give you ten seconds to hide somewhere or run somewhere. The girls go out looking for you and if they see you they chase after you. The boys try to run away from them. If the girls catch (the boys) they kiss them on the lips. The boys never chase the girls in our school; the boys don't kiss the girls. The boys don't kiss the girls in our school because the girls are so slow they'd be kissing them all day." boy, Stoke Newington 1983.

"Maybe the (boys) are 'it' or maybe it's the girls but it doesn't really matter. You've got to chase the other people and when you catch them you have to kiss them anywhere on the face. When there aren't any boys around the girls play. The girls split up. When they catch each other they have to kiss." girl, Hampstead 1984.

> "When the person's 'it', if it's a girl they have to kiss a boy, and if a boy, they have to kiss a girl. When they're kissed they have to kiss someone else. When they're all kissed another person's 'it'." girl, Blackheath 1983.

This game was almost ubiquitous in Inner London, though disapproved of in some schools by authority. In one or two schools I was told by eleven-year-olds that they played it when they were younger, but that is not the general experience.

Printed versions Opies, *CGSP*, Kiss Chase/Kiss Catch, pp. 169–170; Ritchie, *SS*, Catch-a Kiss, p. 82; Sluckin, Kiss Chase, pp. 20, 70, 102.

3.D.8 RUN OUTS

> "The game is the same as 'Had' but instead of playing in one place, you can go everywhere, anywhere you want, like the flats. You can go in the sheds. When they 'had' you you have to go with them and 'had' (others). (You will be) 'on it' with them." boy, Dalston 1983.

> "There are two teams. You decide which team is 'it'. The other team has to scatter and try to hide somewhere. When the whole team's been 'had' the teams swap over and the other team's 'it'." boy, Blackheath 1983.

> "You dip and the person who's 'he' has to hide. Say you're in one lot of buildings, that person has to stay in them. The others have to run out and hide and the person has to go and find them." girl, Borough 1983.

> Barnsbury, Blackheath, Borough, Brixton, Brockley, Dalston, Dulwich, Earlsfield, Hampstead, Kentish Town 1982–84.

This game is played by boys, or by boys and girls together.

Printed versions Douglas (see below); Opies, *CGSP*, Outs/Outings/Runouts, pp. 168–169.

Early noting Inner and Outer, Douglas, 1916, p. 20, 1931, p. 10.

3.D.9 SARDINES

"One person goes off and hides. Everybody's got to count to a hundred. Then you go off and when you find him you've got to sit next to him, wherever he is. The last one to do it has to go and hide (next time)." boy, Streatham 1982.

Printed versions Knapps, p. 52; Opies, *CGSP*, pp. 156–157.

3.E MUDDLES

3.E.1 ROLLER COASTER

"You've got a long line of people and you all hold hands. Then the front person pulls you around in rings and you go under people's arms and get twisted up. There's two lines and when you break up the other line has to join in." girl, Shepherds Bush 1983.

Printed versions Chase, *SGPPG*, Wind up the Apple Tree, singing game, pp. 30–31; Gomme (see below).

Early notings cf. Gomme, 1894, Bulliheisle, p. 51; Eller Tree, pp. 119–120; 1898, Wind up the Bush Faggot, pp. 384–387.

3.E.2 CHINESE MUDDLE; DOCTOR, DOCTOR; MR. TANGLE

"In 'Chinese Muddle' you dip as usual and the person who's last has to turn round and hide their eyes while the others all stand in a circle. They have to climb over their arms and make themselves all funny.

They say, 'Chinese muddle, we're in a bit of trouble.' The person who's 'he' has to get them out of the muddle. When they've got out of the muddle they dip again till everyone's had a go." girl, Borough 1983.

"You all stand in a circle and hold hands. You could be facing inwards or outwards. The doctor goes away and hides his eyes. Then you all get into a muddle but you have to keep on holding hands. The doctor comes to untangle you. He's not allowed to break hands." girl, Kensington 1984.

Borough, Kensington, Shepherds Bush, Walworth 1982–84.

The game is played by boys and girls together, or girls on their own.

Printed versions Knapps, Doctor (sometimes called Rattlesnake), p. 52; Opies, *CGSP*, Chinese Puzzle, p. 3; also called Chinese Muddle, Chinese Puddle, Jigsaw Puzzle, Chinese Knots, French Knots, Chain Man, Tangle Man, Policeman, Cups and Saucers, p. 8.

3.F CONTESTS AND TUSSLES

3.F.1 PIGGY-BACK FIGHTS

"You have a person on each other's back. Everyone comes in on each other's back. The people on the backs kick and punch each other. The last to fall off is the winner." boy, Stoke Newington 1983.

Finsbury, Shepherds Bush, Stoke Newington 1983.

This game is considered dangerous in schools with hard playgrounds and is consequently banned.

Printed versions Douglas (see below), Opies, *CGSP*, pp. 217–219; Ritchie, *GC*, Collie Backie Fights, p. 24; Sluckin, piggyback fights, p. 23; Strutt (see below); Sutton-Smith, Cockfighting/Piggy back Contest, p. 146.

Early notings cf. Strutt, 1801, under the section "Horses", p. 283. Horse-Soldiers/Flying Angels, Douglas, 1916, p. 19, 1931, p. 10.

3.F.2 PUSHING OFF THE BENCHES

"We all stand up (on the bench). We've got to push each other off the bench. If you want to stay on you hold on to something so they can't push you off. If you stay in the middle and there's two people on (each) side of you, they usually go behind you and push you off, then you can't push them off." boy, Shepherds Bush 1983.

3.F.3 HEAVERS

"Everybody sits on the bench. One side pushes and the other side stops them from pushing. If you push the person off, the next person stays on till you push him off and so it goes on. Sometimes when you squash very hard the other person has to come off because it's too tight." boy, Shepherds Bush 1983.

Printed version cf. Sutton-Smith, Heave Ho, p. 147.

3.F.4 RED ROVER

"We all chain-up in one line, holding hands together. There's two teams, one at each end. When somebody says the rhyme:

'Red rover, red rover
Let (_____) come over.'

they have to run over and try to break through the chain where they're holding hands. They only run if their names are called. If they don't break the chain they go on to the other team's side. If they do break it they go back to their own team. Then the other team says the Red Rover rhyme." girl, Mile End 1983.

This game has affinities with **3.A.28** BULLDOG.

Printed versions Brady, p. 139; Brewster, *ANG*, pp. 170–171; Douglas (see below), Gomme (see below), Newell (see below) Opies, *CGSP*, pp. 239–241; Sluckin, Roll over, roll over, pp. 23–24; Solomons, Red Rover, Red Rover, p. 28; Strutt (see below); Sutton-Smith (see below); Turner, p. 60.

Early notings The game appears to derive from the ancient game of "Prisoner's Base", mentioned twice by Shakespeare: "Indeed, I bid the base for Proteus." *Two Gentlemen of Verona* (1589–92), Act I, Scene II; "He, with two striplings – lads more like to run/The country base than to commit such slaughter …", *Cymbeline* (1623), Act V, Scene III. Base, or Prisoners' Bars, Strutt, 1801, said to date from the time of Edward III, pp. 61–63. Bar the Door, Red Rover, and many other names for similar games, recorded c1870–c1900, Sutton-Smith, pp. 57–62. Prisoner's Base or Bars, Gomme, 1898, pp. 79–83, cf. Jockie Rover, Gomme, 1898, pp. 435–443. Prisoner's Base, or Prisoner's Bars, Newell, 1903, p. 164. Red Rover ("Three steps and I'll be over"), Douglas, 1916, p. 141, 1931, p. 77.

3.F.5   CONKERS

"You both get conkers (horse chestnuts) and tie them on a string. You have to try and break the other one's conker by (them) holding it and you flicking at it (with yours). If it drops out of their hand you know you can stamp on it. At the beginning of the game you can go 'No stampsies' and they can't stamp on it and you have to wait till one conker smashes up. If your conker wins one game you call it a 'oner'. If it wins two games you call it a 'twoer' and however many games it wins without smashing up or breaking into pieces you can call it by however many games it's won." boy, Dulwich 1983.

"If he knocks the conker and makes it go round like a windmill he gets another turn. If your conker is a hundred up and another's is thirteen up, yours becomes (?a hundred and thirteen up)." boy, Stoke Newington 1983.

"Suppose you don't want your conkers any more you can say, 'Scrambles' and throw them up in the air. People who want them can try and get them. First to get them has them." boy, Dulwich 1983.

Barnsbury, Cubitt Town, Deptford, Dulwich, Earlsfield, Finsbury, Stoke Newington 1983.

Printed versions Brady, Chestnuts, p. 38; Daiken, *CGTY*, pp. 161–162; Gomme (see below); Northall (see below), Parry-Jones, p. 108; Opies, *CGSP*, pp. 227–232; Ritchie, *GC*, pp. 24–25.

Early notings Conquerors or Conkers, Gomme, 1894, pp. 77–79; Cobblers or Conkers, Northall, 1892, pp. 354–355.

3.F.6 KING OF THE CASTLE

I'm the king of the castle,
You're the dirty rascal.

Walworth 1979, Greenwich 1982.

No descriptions of how the game was played, but presumably it was a contest to defend a height.

Printed versions Brady, p. 35; Cansler, 12; Chambers (see below); Daiken, *CGTY*, I'm the King of the Castle/Willie Willie Wastell, p. 12; Ford (see below); Fowke, I'm the king of the castle, p. 116; Gomme (see below); Gullen, Willie, Willie Wastell, p. 117; Knapps, King of the Hill, pp. 51–52; Montgomeries, *SC*, I, Willie Wastle, p. 119; Newell (see below); Opies, *ODNR*, pp. 254–255, *CGSP*, p. 234; Parry-Jones, Willie Wastle, p. 122; Ritchie, *GC*, p. 28; Sutton-Smith, p. 147; Turner, p. 73.

Early notings I, Willie Wastle,/Stand on my castle;/And a' the dogs o' your toon/Will no drive Willie Wastle doun. Chambers, 1842, p. 61. Gomme: King o' the Castle, 1894, pp. 300–301; see also Willie, Willie

Wastell, 1898, p. 384. I, William of the Wastle,/Am now in my castle,/ And a' the dogs in the town/Winna gae me gang down. (Dunbar); Hally, hally, hastle,/Come into my new castle! (Pennsylvania); Hally, hally hastle,/Get off of my new castle! (Pennsylvania). Newell, 1903, pp. 164–165. Willie Wastle, Ford, 1904, pp. 70–71.

3.F.7 KNUCKLES

"You put your two fists together (with fingers interlocked). One of your fists has got to try and hit the other person's knuckles. The other person's got to try and move (theirs). If you hit them on the knuckles then you have another go. If they move they've lost a life." boy, Kensington 1984.

"You tell a story and introduce the word 'knuckles'. You hit the person when that word is mentioned, they try to avoid." boy, Streatham 1982.

"Six or seven people play. Each picks a playing card. One is the lowest. The one that gets nearest to one gets hit on the knuckles by everybody that's playing." boy, Barnsbury 1983.

Barnsbury, Deptford, Kensington, Streatham 1982–84.

Printed version Opies, *CGSP*, p. 223.

3.F.8 MERCY/MERCY MERCY

"Two people link hands and then have to bend their (opponent's) hands right over. That person has to say, 'Mercy,' before the other person lets go." girl, Blackheath 1983.

"There are two ways of playing. (In) 'One-hand Mercy' you use only one hand. (In) 'Two hands Mercy, Mercy', you use two hands. The idea is to make your opponent say, 'Mercy, Mercy,' when you twist their hands because it hurts so much." girl, Kensington 1984.

Printed version Sluckin (pp. 24, 39) reports a game called "Mercy" in which "girls ... interlock fingers, squeeze hard until one cries 'mercy', whereupon the other immediately releases her grip."

3.F.9 ONE, TWO, THREE (THUMB WRESTLING)

"You hold your friend's hand (with fingers locked together) and you put your thumbs on either side (of each other). You say, 'One, two, three,' while your thumbs are going to either side. When you've finished saying it your friend has to (try to) hold your thumb down while you try to get him out as well." boy, Stoke Newington 1983.

3.F.10 SLAPSIES/KILLER SLAPSIES

"You have your hands together like you're praying or (palms) outwards. When you say, 'Slapsies, one, two, three,' you've got to slap them on the top of their hands. You've got to try and catch them before they move them away. They can move their hands up or down when they think you're going to slap them. It really hurts." boy, Streatham 1982.

"You put your hands together. You slap them (the other person's hands). If they move them away before you slap them then you get a free slap. If you miss them too many times then it's their turn to slap you." boy, Stoke Newington 1983.

"We play a game of 'Slapsies' called 'Killer Slapsies', which you usually use to settle an argument. You can only resign when it's your turn and your hands are bleeding." boy, Blackheath 1983.

Blackheath, Brockley, Kensington, Stoke Newington, Streatham 1982–84. Reports also from a girl, Brockley, 1983.

Printed version Opies, *CGSP*, Slappies, pp. 224–225.

3.F.11 PRETEND FIGHTING/WARS/FIGHTS

Although I was only given this "game" by children in four schools, it is almost universal and is played by boys, and by boys and girls together. Sometimes it develops into really "rough" play. See **3.G.1–3.G.5**.

Printed versions See Opies, *CGSP*, "War Games", pp. 338–340.

3.F.12 WATER FIGHTING

This game was given to me in three schools but is obviously dependent on accessibility of water, and discipline in school.

3.F.13 KARATE

Children in one school reported playing something based on this martial art but gave no details.

For a contest resembling Tug of War, see **4.21** ARE YOU READY FOR A FIGHT?.

3.G "ROUGH" OR BULLYING GAMES

3.G.1 ZOMBIE

> "There are as many as you like and there's somebody who acts like a zombie. He runs round after us and every time he catches us. He holds his arms out straight and chases us. We stop sometimes to have a rest and when we look he creeps up behind us and when we go past the corner, he's there … When he catches us he punches and kicks you." boy, Kentish Town 1983.

3.G.2 BUNDLE

"If there's somebody we don't like, we all run up to them and 'bundle' them and get them on the floor. We don't play that unless we don't like someone." boy, Stoke Newington 1983.

3.G.3 SPAM

"Spam is where you go round hitting people on the forehead and shouting, 'Spam'." girl, Kensington 1984.

3.G.4 DIGS

"Well first of all we dip and a person is 'on it'. We give them [count to] about twenty two. When we catch them we've got to give them digs, hit them and kick them." boy, Deptford 1983.

3.G.5 BOOTS

"You have to pick somebody and you have to count up to twenty. You say, 'I'm going after you.' (When you've counted) you run and when you catch somebody you boot them." boy, Deptford 1983.

3.H BALL GAMES: KICKING

3.H.1 KNOCKOUT; FINALS

"There's about five players and they've all got to try and score goals. The last one to score a goal is out and then they go into the next round till there's two people left. The one who scored the first goal is the winner." boy, Brockley 1983.

"You've only got one goal. You're against all if it's singles knockout. (You can have doubles and triples.) You all try and score and you're through to the next round if you score. If you're the last person who hasn't scored you're out. It carries on like that till there's only two people left, 'the finals'. The person who's left at the end of the first and second games, they're out. The winner of the knockout can either choose to be on the pitch or in goal." boy, Blackheath 1983.

"You have a certain amount of players. One player kicks the ball (against the wall) then the next person has to kick it but you're only allowed to kick it once. If it rebounds off the wall you're out. The basic idea is to kick the football against the wall and rebound it in such a way that the person after you can't get it." boys, Kensington 1984.

Blackheath, Brockley, Deptford, Kensington, Shepherds Bush, Streatham 1982–84.

This is a boys' game but one girl reported playing it.

Printed versions cf. Smith, *BBHG*, Knockout, p. 80; Ritchie, *GC*, Shapes, similar to the third version above, p. 21.

3.H.2 SQUASH; SMASH

" 'Squash' is a game you play with two or more. You kick the ball against anything that's flat and you have to keep it in a certain area. Only one kick is allowed. If you miss you're out. If you touch it twice you're out." boy, Borough 1983.

"You've got three to five lives. You've got to kick the ball between two posts. If you don't kick it between two posts you've lost a life and it carries on till you've got no lives and then you've lost. The person who's got the most lives at the end, wins. If you get someone out by kicking and it rebounds and hits them and it's not their go you get an extra life." boy, Dulwich 1983.

" 'Smash' is where you use a football and you can have any number of people over two. You have an order: Peter, Fred, Jack etc. Peter starts off by kicking the ball against the wall. Then the next person kicks the ball and so on till somebody misses the wall, then they're out. It goes on until there's a final (between) two people. You can play really difficult shots like making the ball just narrowly hit the wall and go off at a funny angle so the other person can't touch it." boy, Blackheath 1983.

Blackheath, Borough, Brockley, Deptford, Dulwich, Streatham 1982–83.

See also **3.I.2**.

Printed versions cf. Smith, *BBHG*, Knockout, p. 80, Squash, p. 81.

3.H.3 THREE, TWO, ONE

"It's like 'Squash'. First you kick the ball against the wall. You're given three chances. If you miss it in those three chances you're given two. If you miss it in those, you're given one. It's the one who survives longest (who wins)." boy, Streatham.

3.H.4 WEMBLEY

"You have one goal and a field of players, say ten. You say, 'the last three' or whatever number. You've got to score and when you've scored you sit on the wall. When you come to the last three if they haven't scored they're out of the game. Then you go on with the players who scored till the last two, and finally to the winner. Some play that the winner is goalie."

Kensington, Stoke Newington 1983–84.

Printed versions Ritchie, *GC*, pp. 21–22, gives a football game under this name but it consists of heading the ball into goal; cf. Smith, *BBHG*, Knockout, p. 80.

3.H.5 THREE AND IN

"You have to score three goals and then you go in goal." Battersea 1982.

Printed versions Ritchie, *GC*, Three and You're in, p. 21; cf. Smith, *BBHG*, Knockout, p. 80.

3.H.6 CUPPIE

"If you score you go in the goal." boy, Dulwich 1983.

Other versions similar to **3.H.4** WEMBLEY.

3.H.7 TWO TOUCH FOOTBALL

"You have one or two people on each side of the pitch and you get two touch for each side [i.e. the ball can touch the ground twice? Cf. **3.H.8** below]. You've got to score as many goals as possible. You're not allowed to go past the centre line. If the ball rebounds off the wall and goes back into your half of the line you have another go." boy, Hampstead 1984.

3.H.8 THUMB BALL; HEADS AND VOLLEYS

"You have one goalie and a field of players. The idea is to try to score goals with a head or a volley. The ball's not allowed to touch the ground when you kick it in. If the ball touches the ground when you kick it in, the goalie gets a point and if it goes wider than the goal he also gets a point. If you shoot and the goalie parries it, it becomes a thumb ball and you don't need to kick up for a volley." boy, Stoke Newington 1983.

Earlsfield, Hampstead, Stoke Newington 1982–84.

3.H.9 MAD FOOTBALL

Greenwich 1982.

I have no clear description of this game.

3.H.10 BARLEY

"We've got goalposts far away from the wall in this special pitch. When you kick the football you've got to hit the top of the goalpost, that's worth two. If you get it past a certain line on the pitch it's worth ten. If it hits the bar and bounces back on the wall it counts thirty. It's the first with fifty (to win)." boy, Finsbury 1983.

3.H.11 CHINESE FOOTBALL

"You get a ball, any size ball, and you kick it hard and aim for a person. As soon as you've kicked the ball at a person and it hits them they have to sit down somewhere till the rest are out. The first one out is 'he' again and the last one is the winner." boy, Borough 1983.

"Somebody kicks the ball right up in the air and you have to wait till it bounces three times. Then you have to try and kick the ball to touch somebody over the knees. If you kick the ball and nobody else has touched it you can't kick it again. You get one life, or three, four or five lives. If somebody kicks the ball into the air and you catch it they'll lose a life. Sometimes you can gain a life by doing it. If you try to catch it and you don't succeed you lose a life." boy, Dulwich 1983.

Barnsbury, Battersea, Borough, Dulwich 1982–83.

3.H.12 SPACE INVADERS

"There's about ten people (against) this wall and you have to try and get them by kicking the ball and hitting them. If it hits them, then they're out." boy, Shepherds Bush 1983.

The name presumably comes from the popular arcade video shooting game which came out in 1978.

3.H.13 FOOTBALL ROUNDERS

> "You have as many people as you want. You have two captains and they pick boy, girl, boy, girl. They have a choice of fielding or kicking. Sometimes you toss. They have to spread out (in) the field. (The fielders kick the ball.) The way you get a rounder is to pass these four posts. If somebody stumps the post they're running to, they're out." girl, Brockley 1983.

3.H.14 AMERICAN FOOTBALL

> "There's about twelve people in a team and the ref. throws it [the ball] in the middle and one of the team has to get it and the other team has to charge at them." boy, Barnsbury 1983.

Barnsbury, Deptford 1983.

No other details.

3.H.15 RUGBY

Only two schools gave this as one of their games but provided me with no details of how they had adapted it to playground conditions.

3.H.16 FOOTBALL

This game is ubiquitous where conditions allow it to be played, but it varies in frequency of playing. There are schools where it is played every day unless extreme weather conditions or disciplinary action prevent it. In such schools it tends to be a rather "macho" game and it is not played much with the girls. Occasionally a girl who has "proved" herself may be allowed to play football with the boys but this is not common. Where football does not have such "macho" status there will sometimes be mixed teams.

All kinds of difficulties of space, and shape of playground, can be surmounted where there is segregation of the boys in their own space, but there is sometimes a problem when boys of various ages want to play in the same restricted space. I taught in a school where two games of football were played at the same time on the same pitch with two goalies at each end and four teams. Because there was good playground supervision it actually worked.

Printed versions Foakes, game played with a pig's bladder, pp. 24–25; Gomme (see below).

Early noting Football, Gomme, 1894, pp. 134–137.

3.1 BALL GAMES: HANDLING

3.1.1 CHINESE HANDBALL

"You're only allowed to hit the ball once with your hand. It's got to hit the other person from the ankle to the shoulder. If it hits them they're out and you just keep playing it like that." boy, Barnsbury 1983.

3.1.2 TENNIS SQUASH

Played the same as **3.H.2** SQUASH, but the ball is thrown or punched instead of being kicked. Dulwich 1983.

3.1.3 WALL/ SQUARE/ BASE

"There are as many people as you want. One person's got to throw the ball against the wall and leave the ball to bounce. The rest of the children have to try and get it to a base man before the person does. (If he bounces the ball on a square you're out)." boy, Dulwich 1983.

Details not clear.

3.1.4 DONKEY

"You throw the ball against the wall and then it has to go through your legs. If you miss and it doesn't go through your legs you're 'D'. If you do it again and it doesn't go through you're 'O'. This goes on till one is DONKEY." girl, Streatham 1982.

"First you throw the ball and then it goes under your legs and you have to catch it. You give it to the next person. The person who misses the ball gets 'D' and the one who gets DONKEY you ask what they want: tickle or 'Tunnel of Death'." girl, Deptford 1983.

For Tunnel of Death, see **3.A.8.i**.

"Most of the time it's played with a football on the wall and then somebody has to stand there and wait till the ball bounces once and jump over the ball. The one behind who has to jump over the ball has to catch it." boy, Barnsbury 1983.

Barnsbury, Brixton, Dalston, Deptford, Streatham 1982–83.

The last example is the only one I have come across where the game is played by boys.

Printed versions Brady, p. 68; Ritchie, *GC*, p. 25; Sutton-Smith, pp. 150–151.

3.1.5 SARDINES

"It's a ball-throwing game. You have so many on each side. You throw the ball and if you get it in the goal you get two points and if you hit the fence you get one point. Or you can play (so that) if you throw it in the goal you get one point and if you hit the fence you don't get any. At the end of the playtime, whoever's got the most points wins." boy, Streatham 1982.

I did not understand the significance of this name for the game.

3.1.6   PIGGY IN THE MIDDLE

"There's two people and one person in the middle. (The two) throw the ball to each other and the person in the middle has to try and get it. If he gets it the person who threw the ball is 'on'. He has to be in the middle and try to get the ball." boy, Stoke Newington 1983.

Printed version Sutton-Smith, p. 151.

3.1.7   HANDBALL

"You have four sections in a pitch. You have two wide ones and two (narrow) ones at each end. Each team has five in each section. One team has the ball. That team has to throw the ball to a person at the very end, not the team next to them but the one at the very end which is one away. If the person in that part catches the ball you get one point for that. (If somebody from the other team gets the ball they throw.) If somebody goes over the line it's a penalty and the other team gets the ball." girl, Finsbury 1983.

This is obviously not the usual game known by this name.

3.1.8   VOLLEYBALL

Reported as being played in three schools, but with no details.

3.1.9   BASKETBALL OR NETBALL

Reported as a playtime game in three and five schools respectively, but no details.

3.1.10 PAT BALL

A ball patted to the floor and then to a wall, and then another does so until someone is out. girl, Borough 1983 (details not clear).

Early noting Newell, under Hand-ball, refers to girls who "strike … balls with the palm of the hand to keep up their bouncing, or fling them against the wall", 1903, p. 178.

3.1.11 FOUR SQUARE; KING'S SQUARE; KING BALL; CHAMP

"There's one big square with four little squares in it, marked 1, 2, 3, and King. The King throws the ball to 3 or 2 or 1 and they have to throw it back. It has to bounce and if they drop it they're out. If they drop out, a 'spare' goes in and everyone moves up; 'spare' goes to 1, 1 goes to 2, 2 goes to 3 and 3 goes to King. If King drops it the 'spare' goes straight to King." girl, Finsbury 1983.

"There's this box and you have numbers 1, 2, 3, 4. There's a special person on number 4. There is a big ball or a little ball, it doesn't matter which. (Number 4) has to bounce it once then bounce it to another person. You're not allowed to slam it, on the first round. When it's on the second round you can slam it, chuck the ball, twirl the ball, but it has to bounce on the floor before they can catch it. If it bounces more than once they're out. Then the person on the third square moves to the fourth one. The person on the fourth square comes off and another person goes on when they've all moved on. They move around till the end of the game." girl, Brockley 1983.

"We get some chalk and draw four big squares. On the fourth square you have to write CHAMP. You write 1, 2, 3. Number 4 is Champ. There's four people playing, one person on each square. Champ has the ball. Champ has to put his feet on the word CHAMP and has to bat it [i.e. hit it with the hand] to the person he wants to, then Champ can take his feet off. There's a little circle in the middle called DANGER. If not sure if the person was out, all four people have to crowd around. Champ has to bat it to a person. If the ball bounces twice in the square then the person's out or if it goes out of the square." girl, Shepherds Bush 1983.

Barnsbury, Borough, Brockley, Earlsfield, Finsbury, Shepherds Bush, Stoke Newington 1982–83.

The game seems to be played by boys and girls together, or by girls on their own.

For other games involving handling a ball see, for example: **3.A.3** ON IT ON THE LINE (WITH BALL), **3.A.4** HE BALL, **3.A.5** HIT AND RUN, **3.A.6** STING BALL, **3.A.7** ROTTEN EGG, **3.A.8** THREE BAD EGGS, **3.A.9** ONE, TWO, THREE, FOUR, FIVE, **3.A.10** FRENCH AND ENGLISH, **3.C.4** BALL IN THE STOCKING, **4.9** QUEENIE, QUEENIE.

3.J BALL GAMES: HITTING BALL WITH BAT OR STICK

3.J.1 ROUNDERS

Versions are very similar to the official game, though there are modifications such as a catch with one hand means all out, and a catch with both hands means only one out. Sometimes some latitude is given such as "best of three" before having to run, instead of running at the first throw. It is a game for boys and girls, and because it is also a popular teacher-led game it does not lend itself to many deviations.

Dalston, Kentish Town, Walworth 1982–83.

Printed versions Daiken, *CGTY*, mentioned, p. 24; Gomme (see below); Parry-Jones, p. 70.

Early noting Rounders, Gomme, 1898, pp. 145–146.

3.J.2 SKITTLEBALL

Given to me in one school, with no details.

3.J.3 STOOLBALL

Given to me in one school, with no details.

Early notings there are games of this name in Gomme, 1898, pp. 217–220, and Newell, 1903, pp. 179–181.

3.J.4 HOCKEY

Given to me in two schools, without details; boys and girls.

Printed versions Gomme (see below); Parry-Jones, pp. 85–86.

Early noting Gomme, 1894, pp. 216–218.

3.J.5 CRICKET

Given to me in six schools without details; virtually boys only.

Early noting Gomme, 1894, p. 82.

3.J.6 TENNIS

Given to me in three schools, with no details; girls only.

GAMES (WITHOUT SONGS)

3.K GAMES PLAYED WITH OTHER OBJECTS

3.K.1 JACKS; GOBS

"You have six jacks and a bouncy ball. You have to throw the bouncy ball in the air and you have to pick up a jack. After you've picked up all the jacks you throw the jacks in the air and try and put them on the back of your hand. Then you throw them up again and catch them. You put them back on the floor. You have to throw the ball up and pick up two jacks. Then it goes three, four, five.

There's another way. You put six jacks in your hand and throw them up in the air and try and get them on the back of your hand. Say you've got five on the back of your hand (one fell on the floor, so you start with five). You have to pick up one of the jacks when you have thrown the bouncy ball up, and catch it in your hand and so on.

You can also play it with stones without a ball. You get seven little stones. You throw one up and try to get it on the back of your hand, then you throw up two, then three, then four etc." boy, Stoke Newington.

Barnsbury, Cubitt Town, Mile End, Stoke Newington 1983.

Printed versions Brady, Jackstones, pp. 39–44; Daiken, *CGTY*, Fivestones, Jackstones, pp. 37–40; Douglas (see below); Ellis (see below); Gomme (see below); Holbrook, Fivestones, pp. 75–78; Knapps, Jacks, p. 137; Newell (see below); Parry-Jones, Chechstones (sic), Dandies, pp. 99–100; Ritchie, *GC*, Chuckies, pp. 70–73; Shaw, 1970, Jacks, p. 76; Solomons, Jackstones, p. 20; Sutton-Smith, Knucklebones, etc., p. 129 ff; Whelan (see below).

Early notings Checkstone, p. 66, Chucks, p. 69, Dalies, p. 95, Dibbs, pp. 96–97, Fivestones, pp. 122–129, Huckle-bones, pp. 239–240, Gomme, 1894. Five-stones, Jack-stones, Chuck-stones, Newell, 1903, pp. 190–193. Fivestones, Ellis, 1910s, 40. Five-Stones, Douglas, 1916, p. 130, 1931, p. 71; Douglas also describes several games played by boys with five stones, or by girls, either with "gobs" (or "cobs") shaped like dice, or with large marbles called "bonsers" (also called "bonks", "bucks", and "bonsters"), 1916, pp. 126–130, 1931, pp. 69–71. Five stones (gobs), Whelan, 1920s, 111.

3.K.2 CAT'S CRADLE

Kensington 1984.

No details given.

The usual form of this game, using a loop of string on the hands to make different shapes, is described, for example, in:

Printed versions Daiken, *CGTY*, p. 142; Gomme (see below); Holbrook, pp. 46–53; Ritchie, *GC*, p. 70.

Early noting Gomme, 1894, pp. 61–63.

3.K.3 MARBLES

> "We play marbles (on a drain cover). We've got a drain with about ten or fifteen lines on it. We put the marbles on each end. One person flicks (his marble) and it goes on to, say, the second (section of the) drain. The idea is to flick your marble onto your opponent's line on the drain, or turn it off." boy, Kensington 1984.

> "If you're doing it on a big square drain you have to hit the other person's (marble) but if it's a grating you have to get it on the same line as your opponent." girl, Kensington 1984.

> "One person has one marble (on the drain). The other person has the other. You move it with your finger (alternately). The person that gets both marbles on the same line wins both the marbles and keeps them. If you're playing for 'Fundies' you give them the marble back. You can play it with twos but you can

only shoot one marble at a time and all the marbles have to be on the same square." girl, Stoke Newington 1983.

"If you don't have a drain you throw (the marble). Each one has a turn. You put the big marble, the bonker, on a place on the floor. You stand four feet back or more and you have to try and throw the marble to hit the bonker. Whoever hits the bonker, wins." girl, Stoke Newington 1983.

Early noting cf. Douglas's "bonsers" (also called "bonks", "bucks", and "bonsters"), 1916, pp. 126–130; 1931, pp. 69–71.

"You drop two marbles on the floor, one for you and one for the other person. The first one (aims for) the marble and then the second one does. Whoever hits it first wins the game." girl, Stoke Newington 1983.

Barnsbury, Kensington, Stoke Newington, Walworth 1982–84.

Printed versions Brady, Marbles, pp. 151–152; Daiken, *CGTY*, pp. 165–173; Douglas (see below); Gaskell (see below); Gomme (see below); Holbrook, pp. 27–31; Knapps, pp. 37–42; Newell (see below); Parry-Jones, pp. 78–84; Ritchie, *GC*, Bools, pp. 61–67 (several variant games); Sluckin, p. 26; Smith, *BBHG*, p. 88; Solomons, p. 40; Sutton-Smith, pp. 127–129.

Early notings Gomme, 1894, p. 364; Newell, 1903, pp. 185–186; Gaskell, c1913, p. 4; Douglas, 1916, pp. 110–118, 1931, pp. 62–65.

3.K.4 HOPSCOTCH, OXO

"When we play 'Hopscotch' it's the first one to find a stone has to be first." girl, Shepherds Bush 1983.

> Marking A "You throw a stone and then you miss out the one the stone landed on. You start off on 1. You've got to throw the stone on 1. You skip out 1 and on the way back you skip it out again. You collect the stone. You have to throw the stone on 2, then 3, then 4 and so on until you get to OXO. Then you start again." girl, Kensington 1984.

> "This (game) is called 'OXO'. It's quite similar to 'Hopscotch'. You have to hop. When you get all the way round you have to pick a number. You can put both feet on the number you pick, whoever's playing with you." girl, Cubitt Town 1983.

A version also collected from Brixton 1982.

> Marking B "You've got to throw (a stone) on number 1. You've got to hop on the other squares till you get to number 8 and pick up the stone. Then you throw a stone on number 2, on number 3 and number 4 and so on till when you've got it on OXO you can have a lucky number. If anybody jumps on your lucky number they're out. But with your lucky number when you get to it you can stand on it (with two feet) 'cause it's your lucky number." girl, Dalston 1983.

> Marking C "First you throw the stone on number 1 and you hop on number 2 and number 3 and number 4. When you get on to OXO you jump, turn around and your feet have to go in these two rounds. Then you have to go to numbers 5, 6, 7 and 8. You pick your stone up at number 8. You have to throw it to number 2 and you have to jump over 1 and 2 on to number 3. You go up again and you land on OXO. You do the same as before, come down to 7, pick up the stone, and it goes on and on." boy, Shepherds Bush 1983.

A version also collected from Dalston 1983.

> Marking D "You have to throw your stone on number 1, jump on numbers 2 and 3 and go up to 10. You go up to OXO, turn around and come back. You hop on number 2 and pick the stone up from 1. You throw your stone on number 2, you pick your stone up from number 3. (And so on.)" boy, Shepherds Bush 1983.

GAMES (WITHOUT SONGS) 125

HOPSCOTCH MARKINGS

Marking A: Brixton, Cubitt Town, Kensington 1982/4

Marking B: Dalston 1983

Marking C: Dalston, Shepherds Bush 1983

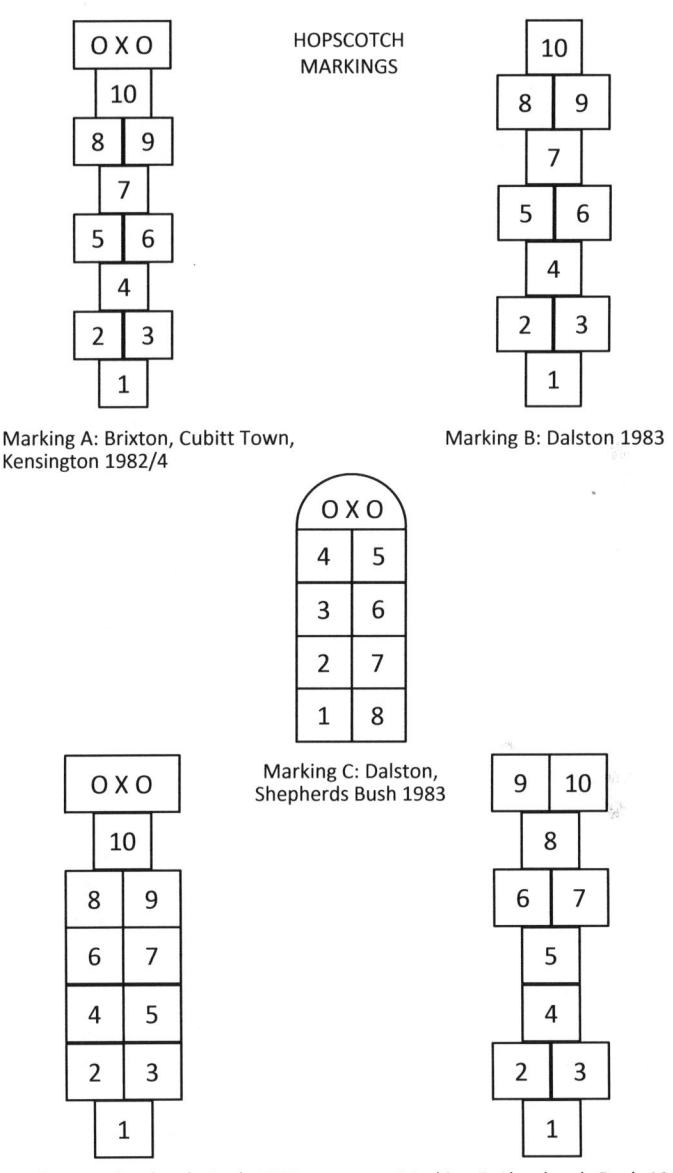

Marking D: Shepherds Bush 1983

Marking E: Shepherds Bush 1983

Marking F: Deptford and Stoke Newington 1983

Marking G: Kensington 1984

Marking H: Shepherds Bush 1983

Marking I: Kensington 1984

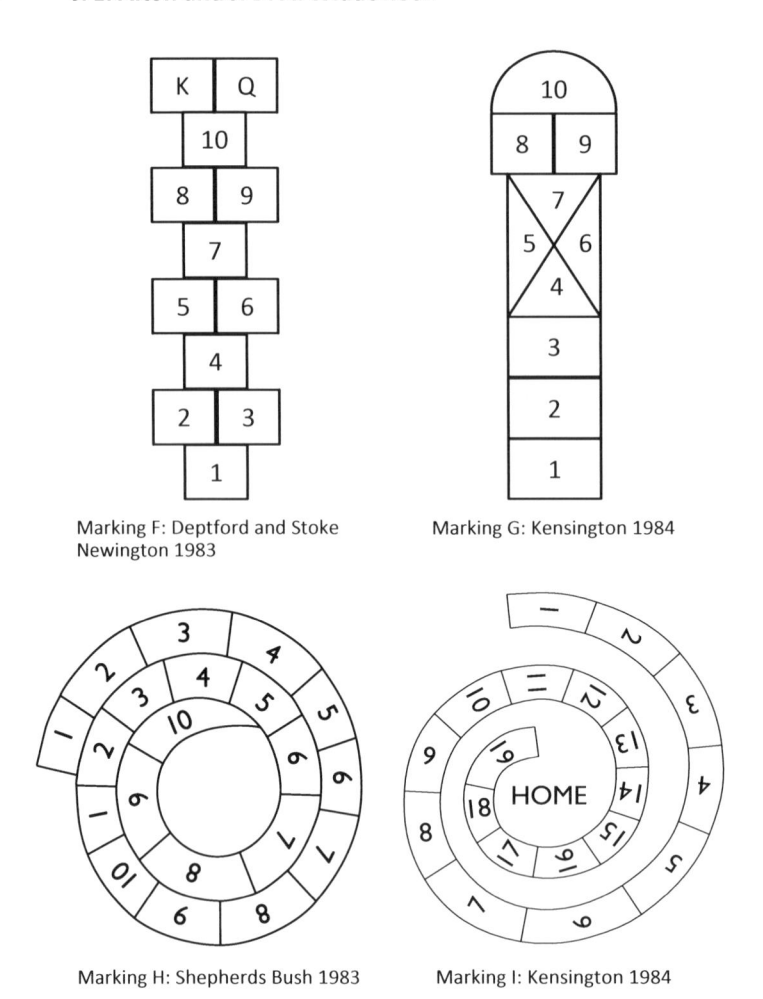

Marking E "First you throw your stone on to number 1 and you jump on 2, 3, 4, 5, 6, 7, 8. When you get to 9 and 10 you jump up in the air, turn round and go back. When you get to 2 and 3 you pick up your stone from number 1 and you jump off. You go on until you get to number 10 then. Then you throw your stone, and whatever number it lands on, that's your lucky number. You can put two feet down on that number." girl, Shepherds Bush 1983.

Marking F "You have about five people. The first one puts the stone on number 1 and jumps on 2 and 3, then 4, then 5, then 7 and 8, then 9 and 10. At the top there's K and Q. You go back on to 2 and 3 and you pick your stone up. Then it's the other person's turn. If the stone gets on the line you say, 'Linesies.' If it goes out of the hopscotch patch you're out and the next person has to go on it." girl, Deptford 1983.

Version from Stoke Newington 1983, exactly the same.

Marking G "You throw your stone and you go up to it. After 3 it has this criss-cross thing and you have to go from 4 to 5, to 6, to 7, in that order. You can't go from 4 to 7." girl, Kensington 1984.

Marking H "You throw your stone on to number 1 and you go on to number 2 and you keep on hopping till you get to number 10. Then you throw your stone on number 2 and keep hopping till you come to number 10. Then you go 9, 8, 7, 6, 5 etc. When you're up to number 5 you have to jump right up to number 6 and so on. It gets harder and harder because you have to jump further and further." girl, Shepherds Bush 1983.

Marking I "One person stands in the middle. You have to jump from one number to another without the person (in the middle) touching you. They have to say, 'Odd' or 'Even.' You jump on an odd one or an even one." girl, Hampstead 1984.

Barnsbury, Brixton, Brockley, Cubitt Town, Dalston, Deptford, Hampstead, Kensington, Kentish Town, Shepherds Bush, Stoke Newington; probably universal.

Printed versions Brady, Beds, pp. 153–159; Daiken, *CGTY*, pp. 41–43; Douglas (see below); Ellis (see below); Foakes, p. 24; Gomme (see below); Holbrook, pp. 71–75; Knapps, pp. 138–140; Lang (see below); Newell, (see below); Parry-Jones, Scotch, Bottle, pp. 96–99; Ritchie, *GC*, Peevers, Beds, pp. 96–110; Sluckin, p. 26; Smith, *BBHG*, p. 87, Solomons, pp. 31–34; Strutt (see below); Sutton-Smith, pp. 136–138, 152–153.

Early notings Strutt, 1801, p. 286, describes a parallelogram "divided laterally into eighteen or twenty different compartments, which were called beds". Hop-Scotch, Gomme, 1894, pp. 223–227. "Hop-scotch is … exceedingly ancient", Lang, 1897, p. 275. Hop-Scotch, Newell, 1903, p. 188; Hopscotch, Ellis, 1910s, 40; Hop-Scotch, several versions mentioned, Douglas, 1916, p. 134, 1931, p. 74.

3.L MISCELLANEOUS OUTDOOR GAMES

3.L.1 ARMIES

"This is a game for young children. If they get 'shot' they lie on the ground and a person who hasn't got shot could touch them and they'd be alive again to shoot the other side." boy, Mile End 1983.

3.L.2 TALLEST BUILDING

"We go on the grass and try to keep still and let the little ones try and get us down on the floor. If they get us down they're the tallest building themselves." boy, Dalston 1983.

3.L.3 BUCKAMAROO

"You give the little children a pigaback and you've got to try and throw them off. You've got to hold on with one hand. You get tired. If you get them off you've won and you get on their backs but it's easy." boy, Hampstead 1984.

Printed version Opies, *CGSP*, Bucking Bronco, p. 216.

3.L.4 TREASURE HUNT

"Somebody collects some sticks or something else, for as many people as there are. They hide the sticks (in various places) and tell the people who have been hiding to look for the sticks. The first person to find a stick gets ten points, the second one gets five points, the last one gets nothing." girl, Shepherds Bush 1983.

Printed versions cf., for example, Gomme (see below), Sutton-Smith, pp. 105–106.

Early notings Hide and Seek (2), Gomme, 1894, pp. 213–214.

3.L.5 NORTH, EAST, SOUTH, WEST

"(There are areas: north, east, south and west.) A person's 'it' and the rest run round. When the person who's 'it' says, 'Stop' you have to stop. They have to guess which areas you're in and then turn around and point at you. If they point at you, then you're 'it' and you have to do it over again." girl, Brockley 1983.

Presumably the person who is 'it' is blindfolded, but this was not mentioned.

3.L.6 TRUE DARE, DOUBLE DARE, LOVE, KISS OR PROMISE

"It goes, 'True Dare, Double Dare, Love, Kiss or Promise.' If you get 'dare' the other people playing have to think of a dare. If it's 'double dare', it has to be an extra, a bad dare. If it's 'love' the person has to go up to someone, say they love them or something, and 'kiss' they have to go and kiss someone. For promise they have to promise to do anything at all. To say who's actually to do it, the person who ends with 'promise' when you've said the rhyme, has to do it." girl, Hampstead 1984.

Borough, Dulwich, Hampstead 1983–84.

Printed versions Knapps, Truth or Dare, pp. 54, 217; Opies, *CGSP*, Truth, Dare, Promise or Opinion etc., pp. 263–267; Ritchie, *GC*, Truth, Dare, Double Dare, Promise, or Repeat, p. 37.

3.M PRANKS

3.M.1 KNOCK DOWN GINGER

"You go into a porch. You tie a bit of string to the letter box and then you pull the string. It knocks the letter box. You run and the people come out to chase you and you hide. When they go back in you do somebody else's and so it goes on till the porter comes." girl, Dalston 1983.

"You knock on a door and you look through the letter box and say, 'Boo!' and run away." boy, Barnsbury 1983.

Barnsbury, Brockley, Dalston, Dulwich 1983.

Printed versions Brady, A Run-away Knock, p. 24; Browne, Knock-and-run, 19; Douglas (see below); Nicholson (see below); Ritchie, *GC*, Tap-a-Door-Run-Fast, p. 35.

Early notings cf. Window-tapping, Nicholson, 1897, p. 93. Knocking Down Ginger, Douglas, 1916, p. 143, 1931, p. 78.

3.M.2 DING DONG THE BELLS

"You jump on all of the cars that have got an alarm. When the owners come running down they all come down at the same time. You hide and say to somebody, 'Will you stay here a minute and watch this thing' when they come down and they get the blame for it." girl, Dalston 1983.

3.M.3 ODD PRANKS

"We go and get bricks and then stick them in front of the door so people can't get in." girl, Brockley 1983.

"We let people's tyres down." boy, Brockley 1983.

"When it's snowing me and my mates throw snowballs at the car windows as they go past." girl, Brockley 1983.

Printed versions of pranks Brady, pp. 24–26; Kellett (see below); Nicholson (see below); Opies, *LLS*, a chapter devoted to pranks, pp. 377–392; Sutton-Smith, pp. 92–93.

Early notings Halloween pranks, Nicholson, 1897, pp. 91–94. Mischievous Night (4th November) pranks, Kellett, 1920s, pp. 88–89.

Recording Knocking on doors and running away, tying doorknockers together, and other street pranks, mentioned on MacColl and Behan, *Streets of Song*.

See also **10.E.5** "Trick or treat".

3.N MAINLY INDOOR GAMES

3.N.1 CHINESE WHISPERS

"Somebody thinks of a sentence. He passes whatever he says on to someone else. That person says what he heard to someone else and so on and so on until it goes to the last person. Before the person who said the sentence (at first), the last person says what he heard. It has often completely changed." girl, Finsbury 1983.

Printed versions Newell (see below); Gomme (see below); Sutton-Smith, Whispers, p. 106.

Early notings Cross-questions, Gomme, 1894, pp. 82–83. Cf. the two whispering games under the heading Present and Advise, Newell, 1903, p. 139.

3.N.2 BUBBLE AND SQUEAK

"People are sitting in a circle. You count, the first person says, 'One', then 'two', then 'three' and 'four.' The next person says, 'Squeak' or 'bubble.' You continue, 'six', 'seven', 'eight', 'nine.' Then it goes, 'squeak,' then count down to five, 'squeak', and so on." girl, Finsbury 1983.

3.N.3 BABY IF YOU LOVE ME, SMILE

"A person is in the middle of a ring. You go up to a boy (if you're a girl) and say, 'Baby, if you love me, smile' and you can do some acting. The boy must answer, 'Baby, I love you, but I just can't smile.' If you smile you have to be the person in the middle. You mustn't smile or laugh. If he doesn't smile he just carries on as normal and the person in the middle does it again (with someone else)." girl, Finsbury 1983.

Early noting [One child holds a wand to the face of another, repeating these lines, and making grimaces, to cause the latter to laugh, and so to the others; those who laugh paying a forfeit.] Buff says Buff to all his men,/And I say Buff to you again;/Buff neither laughs nor smiles,/But carries his face/With a very good grace,/And passes the stick to the very next place! Halliwell, *NRE*, 1842, p. 112.

3.N.4 SAUSAGES

"You all line up and someone says, 'What do you do when you go to school?' You've got to try and say, 'Sausages' without laughing. They all try to say ridiculous things like, 'What's your telly made of?', 'What's your favourite programme?', 'What's your brain made of?' (The answer always has to be 'Sausages'.)" boy, Finsbury 1983.

Printed version Sutton-Smith, Pork and Beans, p. 108.

3.N.5 POOR PUSSY

"They all sit in a line. Somebody's 'Pussy'. 'Pussy' has to come up to one of the people and try and make him laugh by miaowing and looking very sad. The person has to say, 'Poor Pussy,' without smiling. If he smiles he's 'Pussy'. If he doesn't smile the one who is 'Pussy' just carries on." girl, Finsbury 1983.

Printed versions Solomons, Kitty-Wants-a-Corner, p. 43; Sutton-Smith, Poor Pussy, p. 108.

3.N.6 ON MY HOLIDAY

"You stand in a circle. One starts off, 'On my holiday I took my fluffy pillow.' The next one says, 'On my holiday I took my fluffy pillow and my ball.' (Each person adds something. If they forget an item they're out.)" boy, Finsbury 1983.

Printed version Ritchie, *GC*, I Want, p. 28.

3.N.7 PASS THE LEMON; HOT POTATO

"There's an object, say a lemon. Somebody passes it to the next one in the circle and says, 'Pass the lemon.' The person who is given the lemon says, 'Pass the what?' and the first one says, 'Pass the lemon.' (It continues round the circle and if someone makes a mistake they're out.)" girl, Finsbury 1983.

3.N.8 YES HARRY

Similar to above but the procedure is:

> "Harry"
> "Yes Harry"
> "Tell Harry"

"Harry?"
"Yes Harry"

If a mistake is made, for that person it goes:

"One spot"
"Yes Harry"
"Tell Harry"
"Yes, one spot."

Further mistakes become: two spot, wart, verruca, gangrene, pussy scab with a rusty nail. girl, Finsbury 1983.

3.N.9 QUESTIONS

"One person decides on somebody in his class or school. When questioned he has to say, 'Yes' or 'No.' They can only answer, 'Yes' or 'No.' The person who guesses correctly is 'it'." girl, Cubitt Town 1983.

3.N.10 CONCENTRATION

"Children taking part have numbers. They chant in rhythm, 'Concentration now begins, Keep in rhythm all the time.' In turn a child shouts out two numbers, his own and one belonging to a child still in the game, but (they) have to keep up the rhythm. If they fail to do this they're out and others have to remember the numbers of those left." boy, Blackheath 1983.

3.N.11 WINK

"There are five people, one in the middle and one in each corner. One person has to wink at another to change corners. If when they change corners the one in the middle gets to a corner before either, the one without a chair goes in the middle." girl, Finsbury 1983.

Printed version Opies, *CGSP*, Puss in the Corner, pp. 207–209; Strutt (see below).

Early noting Puss in the Corner, Strutt, 1801, p. 285.

"You all sit in a circle with a partner behind you (the ones in front sit on chairs.) Somebody who's 'on' doesn't have a person sitting on their chair. They have to wink at one of the people sitting on a chair and that person has to try to get to the chair. The person behind has to try to stop them by grabbing their shoulders. (If they don't get to the chair the person has to wink at someone else. If they do reach the chair the one behind the empty chair is 'on'.)" girl, Finsbury 1983.

3.N.12 WINKING MURDER; WINK MURDER

"You stand in a circle with your eyes closed. Somebody walks round the circle and picks a murderer. Then you open your eyes and some person picks a detective. The detective has to find the murderer. When the detective is looking for the murderer, the murderer winks at someone. When the person (winked at) sees the murderer wink, they die. The murderer carries on like this until the detective finds the murderer." girl, Battersea 1982.

"Wink murder is a game where you sit in a circle. There's one person who's 'tapper'. There are two taps for murder and one tap for detective. The detective has to find who the murderer is. If the murderer winks at the detective and he's dead, that means the game is over. If the detective finds out, the game's over too." girl, Finsbury 1983.

Battersea, Finsbury, Shepherds Bush 1982–83.

3.N.13 STALKY; KING'S KEYS

"Lots of people sit in a ring. There are some keys in the middle and one person sits in the middle with his eyes blindfolded. One person goes around (the ring) and the person has to try and point where the person is by sound before they get to the keys. If they get the keys they're in the middle." girl, Finsbury 1983.

3.N.14 SIMPLE SIMON SAYS

"You've got to do whatever Simple Simon says if she says, 'Simple Simon says.' If she says, 'Simple Simon says, put your hands on your head,' you do it. If she says, 'Put your hands on your knees,' you don't do it. If you do you're out." girl, Barnsbury 1983.

Barnsbury, Borough 1983.

Printed versions Brady, O'Grady Says, p. 160; Ritchie, *GC*, Do This, Do That, p. 25; Robertson, Mr. O'Grady, p. 31; Solomons, Simon Says, p. 31.

3.N.15 SEA AND FISHES

"You all sit down (on chairs in a circle) and have the name of a fish and they're all different, say I was pike and someone else was salmon. There's a person in the middle. He'll try and remember as many names as he can. He'll go around in the middle and try to say all the names he can remember. Once he's said your name you stand behind him and then you've got a line of people. Then he'll say, 'The king is coming, the king is coming,' and you all have to sit down but there's one chair short and the person who doesn't get a chair is 'it'." girl, Finsbury 1983.

3.N.16 LADDERS

"You need about sixteen people playing (in pairs). Each pair sit with their legs out in front of them, touching feet. Pairs are numbered one to eight. Someone who is out says a number and those people (with that number) have to jump over people's legs and run between them. The first person to get back wins a point (for their team)." girl, Blackheath 1983.

Blackheath, Shepherds Bush 1983.

3.0 PENCIL AND PAPER GAMES

3.0.1 NOUGHTS AND CROSSES

Cubitt Town 1983.

Printed versions Brewster, *ANG*, pp. 128–129; Douglas (see below); Gomme (see below); Sutton- Smith, pp. 110–111.

Early notings Noughts and Crosses, Gomme, 1894, pp. 420–421. A chalk-game also known as Oxen-Crosses, played out of doors, mentioned in Douglas, 1916, p. 134, 1931, p. 74.

3.0.2 HANGMAN

Cubitt Town 1983.

Early noting A possible forerunner of games like HANGMAN is reported in Douglas under the section on "chalk-games". Among a number of "Body-Building" games is "Germans-English" where two players aim a stone into a chalked target, and if they succeed are allowed to draw, successively, the head, body, limbs and rifle of a "soldier". Once one player has completed the drawing of the soldier, on the next successful throw of the stone he can draw a "bullet" and "shoot" and destroy the other player's (uncompleted) soldier with it. Douglas, 1916, pp. 135–136, 1931, pp. 74–75.

3.0.3 SPACE INVADERS

Shepherds Bush 1983.

The name presumably comes from the popular arcade video shooting game which came out in 1978.

These three games, although only reported from one school apiece, are representative of games played between two children with pencil and paper, and in one form or another are pretty universal. A more complicated game, "Battleships", was not reported though I know it is played in schools.

3.P VARIOUS GAMES REPORTED WITH NO DETAILS 1982–84

GARDEN GATE, HIDE THE SILVER PLATE, ON THE RED, WEREWOLF (Battersea); HORSES, OBSTACLES, ROUND THE CLOCK, STRONGEST MAN (Dalston); LOLLYSTICKS, MURDERATION, PARTNERS, RING ARROW (Deptford); THREE UGLY MONSTERS (Greenwich); GRANDMOTHER'S FOOTSTEPS (Hampstead); GAME WATCH, JINGLE JANGLE, SUICIDE (Kensington); CHANCE, GIVE US A CLUE, QUEEZIES (Mile End); PENNIES, WAR CHAMP (Shepherds Bush); BLACK JACK, BUTTERFLY HE, GHOST TRAIN (Walworth).

Not included are the following games which were teacher-led or teacher-organised:

SEVEN UP/THUMBS UP (Cubitt Town, Dulwich, Earlsfield); BASHBALL (Dalston); COLOURED BAND TAG; also, in swimming pool: SUBMARINES AND TORPEDOES (Kensington); FIFTY PENNY PIECE (Stoke Newington).

SECTION 4

SINGING AND CHANTING GAMES

Introduction

Children enjoy ritual; they enjoy dramatisation and mime; they enjoy the ingredients of popular verse: rhythm, metre, rhyme, alliteration, imagery, and humour. They enjoy singing. At least girls enjoy all these, but boys consider them, when they are all found together in singing games, as "cissy", especially if they are linked with elements of courtship etc. Changes over the years have led to a decline in the ritual side as well as in the dramatic aspects and the imagery. However, there has been a certain compensation in the growth of improvised mime and humour. Singing games seem to divide themselves into two groups. There are those which have a long tradition and have either continued to exist using similar words, melodies, and movements, or have been subject to more radical change over the generations. The other group consists of those adapted by the children from popular song or other sources, or which appear to be completely improvised by them. In their turn some may enter the tradition and others will have a brief ephemeral life.

The old traditional singing games were fixed in versions developed by the end of the nineteenth century by finding their way into printed collections, sometimes with musical accompaniments. Many of them have been used over the years by teachers as part of educational activities, mainly with younger children. Some of these versions appear in the playground as part of the repertoire of older children in the final years of the junior stage. Singing games like **4.12** A-HUNTING WE SHALL GO or **4.18** IN AND OUT THE DUSTY BLUEBELLS may differ very little from the received patterns. Occasionally a song taught in the classroom is adapted for playground use, even if only for a brief period. In one school in which I was head teacher, a song learned in music lessons appeared in the playground. It was **4.62** I'M A SAILOR YOUNG AND GAY, which is related to "Paper of Pins" and "Keys of Canterbury" that have been in the tradition in the past or are in use in some other English-speaking countries. Another song taught in the classroom, **5.20** I'VE BEEN TO HARLEM, was adapted for a clapping routine by a group of girls in another school.

Many of the old nineteenth century singing games might have completely disappeared if it had not been for the work of teachers. There was a regular Singing Games Festival held in South London for a number of years, based on Redriff Primary School, Bermondsey. A group of teachers from that school produced a record and accompanying booklet, *The Festival Book of Singing Games* (Wilson and Gallagher, 1969). Boys and girls took part in the festival on equal terms as they do in folk dancing in many junior schools. Girls can be seen taking part in singing games in every primary school playground. In the upper part of the junior school, however, boys sometimes look on, rather shamefacedly. They often learn the words of the rhymes, and will giggle at those which are obviously directed to them or which refer to boys generally. Occasionally they join in, but in my experience their selfconsciousness is liable to lead to showing off, or even disruption. I believe these barriers may well be broken down in the future. The developments in the integration of boys' and girls' play had not reached finality at the time I was collecting information. I tend to believe that the behaviour expected in the so-called "latency period" is more likely to have resulted from social and cultural influences than to have arisen from natural stages in physical development.

The sustaining of the male image, which many boys think is expected from them, works against their participation in singing games. It seems quite likely that boys originally played the male role in courtship rhymes, and the rituals were certainly participated in by a wider age group. However, by the latter half of the nineteenth century such games had become overwhelmingly a girls' activity, apart from the early years of childhood. Where school education was extended to adolescence, the games were played by girls throughout their school years. The reorganisation of elementary schools into junior and senior in the 1930s, and completed in the postwar years into primary and secondary, usually meant, in Inner London at any rate, that the tradition was left to the younger girls to maintain.

Separate playground versions of singing games rarely coexist with the use of received versions in the classroom. Perhaps because **4.20** ORANGES AND LEMONS is not used so much nowadays, it is one of the few singing games in which boys participate. Performed versions often vary greatly from those in the handed down printed texts. Two other singing games whose contemporary versions are very different from the nineteenth century's are **4.21** ARE YOU READY FOR A FIGHT? and **4.4** THE HOKEY POKEY. The latter is a modernised composition based on **4.3** HERE WE GO LOOBEE-LOO, which usually follows the traditional form when it is occasionally played in the playground. ARE YOU READY FOR A FIGHT? is a very truncated contemporary version of "Have you any bread and wine?" which appears in Gomme.[1] In the earlier form it would not be played by older boys, but the newer version gives plenty of scope for very vigorous movement. ARE YOU READY FOR A FIGHT? can get quite rough. Old versions usually featured English versus French, or English versus Romans. Two world wars changed it to English versus Germans, but I have noted English versus Americans (1982), and English versus Spanish (1983). In 1984 I also came across a revival of the traditional enemies: English versus French.

4.24 BROWN GIRL IN THE RING was played in many schools by both boys and girls when it had become familiar through a version in the pop charts.[2] A correspondent[3] sent me an interesting form of this song which was apparently played and sung in North West London before 1922. The first verse has the lines, "There's a black boy in the ring/.../He likes sugar and I like jam". The game had been taken up by several Inner London schools, before it had become a pop song, through the efforts of Caribbean cultural representatives who visited a number of schools on behalf of the Commonwealth Institute, or perhaps by children brought up in the Caribbean, although I have no evidence of this. **4.33** ORANGE BALLS is the only contemporary singing game that I have come across in which boys will participate without any selfconsciousness, but there are probably others in some schools.

Newell in the USA (1883) and Gomme in the British Isles (1894, 1898) were the first compilers of extensive collections of singing games, along with other games. Gomme's collection was much fuller, and she included many alternative versions from various regions, and accompanied them with anthropological explanations. In the old singing games she saw survivals of old rituals connected with courtship, marriage, and death. Alice Gillington published four shorter collections of singing games from Southern England, with musical accompaniments, in the early years of the twentieth century (*OHSG, OIWSG, OSSG*, 1909; *ODSG*, 1913). Since then, many books of singing games have been printed and reprinted. Out of the many local variants a kind of standard form was arrived at, as happened in an earlier century with the nursery rhymes, which has been used mainly by teachers of young children. Sometimes a few of these games are played in this form by children without adult organisation, but by the age of nine or ten they will be relegated to occasional party use, though girls may continue to play them with younger children. Of these I have come across a few during the present study (1982–84): **4.3** HERE WE GO LOOBEE-LOO; **4.10** THE FARMER'S IN HIS DEN; **4.13** RING A RING A ROSES; **4.16** POOR JENNY IS A-WEEPING, and **4.18** IN AND OUT THE DUSTY BLUEBELLS. My informants told me they had stopped playing them when they were six or seven, but their memories may not have been accurate.

There are others which older girls play occasionally but which seemed to be fading out in Inner London. They were still subject to change and variation, and sometimes only survived in decadent forms. Most of my notings of these, however, come from the late 1960s and the 1970s, and only one or two turned up in the later survey. **4.12** A-HUNTING WE SHALL GO was noted in 1983 but I was not sure if it was still played by my informants. **4.11** THE GRAND OLD DUKE OF YORK I last noted in 1974; **4.7** LONDON BRIDGE IS FALLING DOWN I noted in 1974 in its old form; **4.17** FAIR ROSIE WAS A SWEET PRINCESS I noted in 1970 and **4.6** WHO HAS STOLE MY WATCH AND CHAIN? in 1967. They may now be out of the living tradition in Inner London.

I found versions of **4.19** THE GOOD SHIP SAILS ON THE ALLEE-ALLEE-O in only six of the twenty-one schools in the survey. This singing game, which was ubiquitous in the 1950s, is apparently now less popular. Some claim that it was derived from "Round and round went the gallant ship" (Kidson 1916, p. 91; Montgomerie, 1966, p. 99) which in its turn came from an old ballad, "The Golden Vanity". There does not appear to be any direct link between the two in any printed collection. I thought that **4.22** PLEASE MOTHER, MAY I GO OUT TO PLAY?, which consists of spoken dialogue instead of singing, had disappeared from the living tradition. Then I came across versions in Mile End (1967), Deptford (1983), and Brockley (1983).

There are a few singing games which appear to have been in a thriving oral and performing tradition since they were first noted. They have undergone continual change, reflecting new social conditions and resulting changes in the children's subculture. In this respect they are very different from the games kept alive by teachers and other adults. **4.2** WHEN SUSIE WAS A BABY obviously derives from "When I was a Young Girl", noted in Gomme (1898, pp. 362–374). It is now used for clapping and mimed actions, and its contemporary form reflects changes in home, school, and attitudes to sex. **4.14** DOWN IN THE VALLEY has changed from a marriage game in the 1890s to an action rhyme usually incorporating the actions of washing, scrubbing etc. It is not easy to explain the popularity of this action song while the universality of launderettes and washing machines is taken for granted. No doubt it will change or eventually die out.

No. **4.9** QUEENIE, QUEENIE, a universal ball game, has been reduced in the wording of the chant to the bare essential, a far cry from the lovely verses of "Lady Queen Anne" of ancient times. No. **4.1** A GIPSY CAME A-RIDING was still popular, but not so universal as it was a few years before the survey was undertaken. Sometimes it is a duke, reduced from the old versions of three dukes riding. Even Gomme's collection contains a version: "One duck comes a-ridin'", however (1898,

p. 247). In Douglas's version the word is spelt "duk" (1916, pp. 75–76, 1931, p. 42).

Rutherford (1971, pp. 31–32) gives a list of twenty-three traditional singing games from Gomme which he says had "lately been found" in the North East. These include eight which I cannot trace being played in Inner London, that is outside the classroom or school assembly hall. These are: "Oats and beans and barley", "Sally Water", "Sunday night", "Wallflowers", "The wind", "Mulberry bush", "Hop, hop, hop", and a version of **4.5** BINGO which was given to me by a boy who played it at his Cub Scouts. A number of Gomme singing game variants were given a new very active lease of life as hand clapping or skipping rhymes when the singing game with which they were associated died out.

Apart from **4.2** WHEN SUSIE WAS A BABY, referred to above, there are several less obvious transformations to the requirements of clapping routines. The game "Priest of the Parish", noted by Gomme (1898, p. 79), includes the exchange: "'Is it me, sir?'/'Yes you, sir.'/'You lie, sir.'/'Who then, sir?'" The clapping rhyme **5.18** WHO STOLE THE COOKIES? has: "Who me?/Yes, you./ Couldn't have been./Then who?" A version of "Salmon Fishers", also noted by Gomme (1898, pp. 179–181), is ubiquitous in Inner London as **5.5** MY BOYFRIEND GAVE ME AN APPLE. Similarly "Alligoshee", with the lines: "Betsy Blue came all in black,/Silver buttons down her back." (Gomme 1894, pp. 7–8), has become **5.15** MACK, MACK, MACK,/ All dressed in black, black, black,/With silver buttons, buttons, buttons,/All down her back, back, back. Divinatory skipping rhymes adapted from nineteenth century singing games include: **6.A.54** ALL THE GIRLS IN OUR TOWN, **6.A.58** ROSY APPLE, LEMON TART and **6.A.59** ON A MOUNTAIN STANDS A LADY.

The publication of the Opies' book *The Singing Game* (*SG*, 1985) provided us with a worthy companion to their works on children's lore and children's games. It is the first major collection of singing games which covers both the old traditional singing games that belong to the nineteenth century and probably, in many cases, earlier centuries, as well as the contemporary action games, often inspired by popular songs. The Opies' classification has some similarities to that used by Gomme, but in many aspects is very different. I have not attempted to follow either system of classification. Where I was able to obtain a description of the movements and actions used in a particular singing game I have included it, but I was not able to do so in all cases.

Nearly half of the singing games of today which are derived from nineteenth century ones are based on a circle formation. Many of the contemporary singing games and action rhymes are similarly based. Some examples are: **4.25** I WENT TO CALIFORNIA, **4.26** HERE COMES MRS. MACARONI, **4.29** WHAT CAN YOU DO, PUNCHINELLO?, **4.33** ORANGE BALLS, **4.39** I'VE GOT A DAUGHTER, and of course **4.4** THE HOKEY POKEY. Most other action rhymes are performed, either in a single line like a stage chorus line, or by couples facing each other. Examples of the former are: **4.42** HEAD, SHOULDERS, KNEES AND TOES, **4.46** I CAN DO THE CAN-CAN, **4.54** MY NAME IS SEXY SUE, and **4.61** BISCUIT. Typical of the action rhymes where participants go through their routines facing a partner are: **4.32** I'M A LOCKED-UP CHICKEN, **4.43** THERE'S A TINY HOUSE, **4.49** KEEP YOUR SUNNY SIDE UP, and **4.53** THIS WAY VALERIE. In some games played this way, partners represent a boy and girl, as in **4.30** I'M A LITTLE DUTCH GIRL, or a man and woman: **4.36** WHEN GRANDMAMA MET GRANDPAPA.

Sometimes contemporary singing games and action rhymes are based on variations of popular song hits, though there may be a long time gap between the initial popularity of the song and the playing of the singing game. This time gap invites conjecture as to whether the song was rediscovered by a group of children or whether it went through a long period of gestation, perhaps confined to a particular school or area. **4.39** I'VE GOT A DAUGHTER, popular in the 1960s and 1970s, derives from a song of 1895. **4.58** OUT IN ARIZONA, possibly an ephemeral song confined to one school, parodies one from the ragtime era at the beginning of the twentieth century. I encountered this version in 1983. **4.49** KEEP YOUR SUNNY SIDE UP is based on a song from a 1929 film, but it has only been around as a singing game since the 1960s. More than a decade separates the popularity of song **4.34** SHE WEARS RED FEATHERS from the singing game based upon it. **4.4** THE HOKEY POKEY is of course from the "Hokey Cokey", which could be termed an adult singing game, and which became very popular at dances during the

Second World War (Opies, *SG*, 1985, p. 392). It did not reach the playgrounds till the late 1950s. The popularity of American folk music in the 1960s was probably responsible for the introduction of **4.23** SKIP TO MY LOU to the playground repertoire.

Another source for playground singing games is the routines and games played in children's organisations: Brownies, Cubs etc. These include **4.5** BINGO, **4.51** UNDERNEATH THE SPREADING CHESTNUT TREE, an adult popular action song of the 1930s which was taken up by Scouts and other groups, and **4.27** THERE WERE TEN IN A BED, which I was only aware of as a community song until I came across an adaptation with actions in 1983. Brownies and Cubs do not usually originate these songs but they help to perpetuate them.

In the course of the survey I came across a number of action rhymes which appeared to be limited to one school. Some of them had unknown origins and had not been rounded into a form which was likely to be widely disseminated. Two of these came from the same school (**4.31** HEEL AND TOE and **4.59** SEVEN LITTLE GIRLS). The latter comes from a song which was a big hit in the pop charts.[4] Three came from other schools. The first of these, **4.37** IN A COTTAGE IN A WOOD, appears in *Okki-tokki-unga* (Harrop, Friend, and Gadsby, 1976, p. 24), so perhaps it might have been learned in the classroom originally, as it was evidently taught in some infants' schools. The other two were **4.41** EVERYBODY GATHER ROUND and **4.48** MATILDA. I expect examples of the same kind of possible ephemera could be found in many schools. If this is the case, there must be hundreds of rhymes which are potential playground standards if they changed in the direction of widening their appeal. Nearly all, however, will have a brief existence, confined to a single school or neighbourhood. No doubt some of the unique examples in a few printed collections come into this category.

Although I have included details given to me by the players as to the actions and routines accompanying some of the rhymes, these movements are subject to much greater variation than the words, and there is a lot of improvisation. Within groups there are often leading children, usually girls, who introduce changes in the actions and add new ones. Sometimes they are very creative, and the others are often keen to follow such leads. From area to area, from school to school, these games may show wide variations, and there may even be differences between classes and groups within a single school. The accompanying actions to **4.32** I'M A LOCKED-UP CHICKEN, **4.53** THIS WAY VALERIE, **4.54** MY NAME IS SEXY SUE, **4.55** CRACKERJACK (FIRECRACKER), and **4.61** BISCUIT, all action songs which were very popular in Inner London at the time of the survey, lent themselves to a very great variety. Indeed I do not think I ever saw two performances which were absolutely the same.

A number of action rhymes are accompanied by exaggerated hip movements, the raising of skirts etc., which the girls call "sexy". Showing off, an element of "daring" and teasing the boys, are no doubt all involved. **4.55** CRACKERJACK (FIRECRACKER) includes the line: "The girls have got the sexy legs". **4.61** BISCUIT has "Take a sexy leg". In **4.46** I CAN DO THE CAN-CAN the girls lift up their skirts. **4.54** MY NAME IS SEXY SUE has "I've got a cute, cute figure/And a busty bra". **4.56** I'M SHIRLEY TEMPLE includes "And I wear my skirts up there,/I'm not able to do the sexy cable", and **4.57c** SABRINA, SABRINA contains "Hands up there, skirts up there". These are typical; similar examples can be found among the clapping routines. Perhaps having little claim to be included in the section dealing with singing games are the mildly or grossly indecent little rhymes consisting of pointing to parts of the (usually female) anatomy, indicating their functions in crudely symbolic references (**4.66** to **4.68**). **4.69** CHINESE JAPANESE is perhaps less offensive and involves some actions as well as merely pointing.

Finally, I do not share the belief of some observers of children's lore that the singing game is on its way to extinction, but I do believe that the old traditional singing games are probably doomed to disappear, at least in their traditional forms. There will always be dedicated adults who value the old rituals and they will sustain them, as the old nursery rhymes are sustained, but they will cease to have any part in living folklore. On the other hand, the creative and adaptive skills of children will continue, perhaps in new forms and perhaps in unisex ones. As long as enjoyment in movement, song, and wordplay, whether separately or in combinations, continues, the singing game will continue. I see no signs of this enjoyment diminishing among children.

NOTES

1. See Gomme (1898). "We are the Rovers", pp. 343–360.
2. Boney M (1978). "Brown Girl in the Ring", *Nightflight to Venus*, MCI.
3. Mrs. Gerrard of Cheshunt remembering a singing game from North West London, in circulation before 1922.
4. Evans, P. (1959). "Seven Little Girls". Guaranteed Records (subsidiary of Carlton Records).

4.1 A GIPSY CAME A-RIDING

TRADITIONAL SINGING GAME:

A. A gipsy came a-riding, a-riding,
A gipsy came a-riding,
Ching Chong Chinaman.

What you riding here for? Here for? Here for?
What you riding here for?
Ching Chong Chinaman.

I'm riding here for marriage, marriage, marriage.
I'm riding here for marriage,
Ching Chong Chinaman.

Who are you going to marry? Marry? Marry?
Who are you going to marry?
Ching Chong Chinaman.

I'm going to marry (nickname of girl) (nickname, nickname),
I'm going to marry (nickname),
Ching Chong Chinaman.

Her real name is (____, ____, ____), (You can't have (____)),
Her real name is (____),
Ching Chong Chinaman.

Well I want (____, ____, ____),
I want (____),
Ching Chong Chinaman.

Here's your smelly (____, ____, ____),
Here's your smelly (____),
Ching Chong Chinaman.

Walworth 1974; <u>Greenwich 1982</u>; Deptford 1983.

See also **2.56**.

Nicknames might be: "white socks", "fairy", "hairy monster", "ginger nob", etc.

B. A duke came a-riding, a-riding, a-riding,
    A duke he came a-riding,
    On a summer's day.

   What you riding here for? etc.

   I'm riding here to marry, etc.

   What you going to marry? etc.

   I'm going to marry a dustbin (skeleton) etc.

   Who is the dustbin? etc.

   (Girl's name) is the dustbin, etc.

West Norwood 1970, 1972.

C. There came three dukes a-riding,
    A-riding, a-riding,
    There came three dukes a-riding,
    One, two, three.

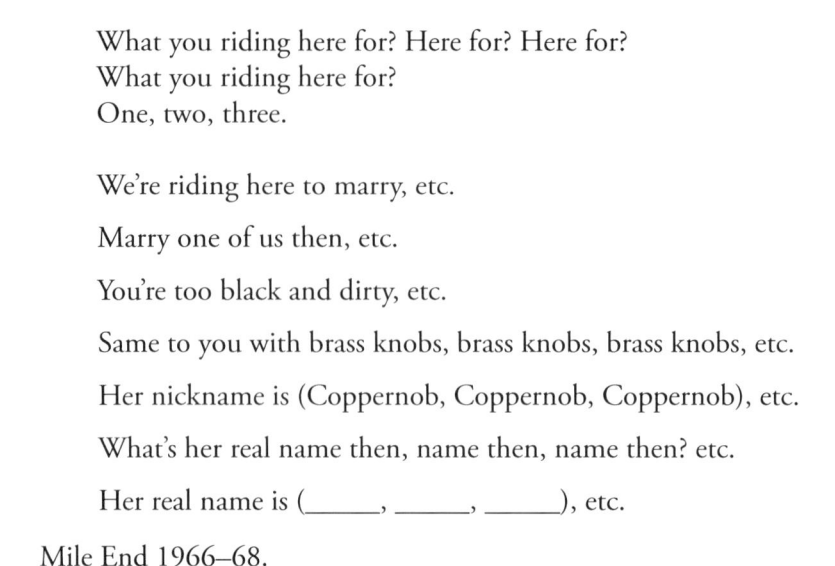

What you riding here for? Here for? Here for?
What you riding here for?
One, two, three.

We're riding here to marry, etc.

Marry one of us then, etc.

You're too black and dirty, etc.

Same to you with brass knobs, brass knobs, brass knobs, etc.

Her nickname is (Coppernob, Coppernob, Coppernob), etc.

What's her real name then, name then, name then? etc.

Her real name is (_____, _____, _____), etc.

Mile End 1966–68.

"There's a person singing, 'A gipsy came a-riding' and they have to go forwards and backwards. They have to choose a funny name for a person who's in front of them. Say it was (_____) and she was called 'Blondie', they would say, 'I want Blondie.' The others would say, 'You can't have (_____),' twice. Then they would say, 'Here's your stinky (_____).' " girl, 10, Deptford 1983.

Printed versions Beckwith (see below); Bolton (see below); Botkin (see below); Brady, pp. 106–110; Chase, *SGPPG,* pp. 16–19; Daiken, *CGTY,* p. 76; Douglas (see below); Fowke, p. 36; Gaskell (see below); Gillington (see below); Gomme (see below); Gullen, p. 95; Hopkin, p. 20; Kellett, p. 63; Kelsey, *K1,* 43; Kidson (see below); Knapps (see below); MacBain (see below); Newell (see below); Nicholson (see below); Opies, *SG,* pp. 76–92; Plunket (see below); Rodger, 2 versions, pp. 31, 32; Rohrbough (see below); Rutherford, pp. 33–34; Sutton-Smith, p. 25; Swift, 149; Talley (see below); Thornhill (see below); Turner, pp. 55–56: begins "Here come two Dukes", but the main part of the rhyme is like "Three Jews from Spain"; Webb, There came a gypsy riding, 639.

Early notings Here come three tinkers, Plunket, 1886, pp. 28–29; Here come three Dukes a-riding, Plunket, 1886, pp. 38–39. Here comes a dude a-riding by,/So ransom, tansom, titty bo tee./And what are you riding here for?/So ransom, …/I'm riding here to be married! Bolton, 1888, p. 118 (Virginia). Here come three dukes a-riding,/A-riding, a-riding;/Here come three dukes a-riding,/With a rancy, tancy, tay!//What is your good will, sirs? etc.//Our good will is to marry, etc.//Marry one of us, sirs, etc.//You're all too black and greasy [or dirty], etc.//We're good enough for you, sirs, etc.//You're all as stiff as pokers, etc.//We can bend as much as you, sirs, etc. //Through the kitchen and down the hall,/I choose the fairest of you all;/The fairest one that I can see/Is pretty Miss ___, walk with me. One of thirty versions in Gomme, 1898, pp. 234–235, collected in Shropshire 1891; other versions in Gomme: 1894, p. 206, 1898, pp. 233–255. Nicholson, 1897, pp. 150, 151, 155. Here come three soldiers three by three, and Here comes a duke a-roving, Newell, 1903, pp. 46–49. Gillington, *OSSG,* 1909, p. 4; Thornhill, 1911, p. 14; Gaskell, c1913, p. 5; Douglas, 1916, pp. 75–76, 1931, p. 42; Kidson, 1916, 2 versions: pp. 25, 92; Talley, 1922, pp. 85–86. "In Cincinnati in 1927, children played a variant of the popular singing game … Three Dukes … in which they substituted Jews for the nobility", Knapps, p. 200. Beckwith, *JFL,* 1928, pp. 48–49. Cf. "A Game Rhyme", MacBain, 1933, pp. 226–227. Botkin, *APPS,* 1937, p. 329. A version like Three Jews from Spain (see note on Halliwell below), Rohrbough, *SSG,* 1938, p. 8, also Two Dukes A-Roving, Rohrbough, *HPPB,* 1940, p. 134.

There is a version in Halliwell (*PRNT,* 1849, pp. 123–124) which is nearer to the singing game "Three Jews from Spain", which has links with "Three Dukes" but is a different game (Lang has a similar version, 1897, p. 181). The Opies discuss the differences, which lie chiefly in verse pattern, in *SG* (1985, pp. 93–94).

Recordings BBC 16075 (78) (1951, Sidbury, Devon); MacColl and Behan, *Streets of Song*; MacColl and Seeger, *The Elliotts of Birtley*; Ritchie, *Children's Songs and Games from the Southern Mountains*; Webb, *Children's Singing Games.*

4.2 WHEN SUSIE WAS A BABY

ACTION or CLAPPING SONG, descended from traditional singing game:

A. When Susie was a baby,
    A baby Susie was,
    She went, "A-ga-ga, ga-ga-ga,
    Ga-ga-ga-ga-ga-ga-ga."

    When Susie was a toddler,
    A toddler Susie was,
    She went waddle, waddle, waddle, waddle, waddle, waddle,
    Waddle, waddle, waddle, waddle, waddle, waddle, waddle.

    When Susie was a schoolgirl,
    A schoolgirl Susie was,
    She went, "Miss, Miss, I can't do this,
    I think I've got my knickers in a twist."

    When Susie was a teenager,
    A teenager Susie was,
    She went, "Oo-ah, I lost my bra,
    I think I left it in my boyfriend's car."   (See also **5.11**)

    When Susie was a mother,
    A mother Susie was,
    She went a-rock, rock, rock, rock, rock,
    Rock, rock, rock, rock, rock, rock, rock.

    When Susie was a granny,
    A granny Susie was,
    She went knit, knit ("I lost my zip"), knit, knit, knit,
    "I think I lost my little stitch."

    When Susie was a skeleton,
    A skeleton Susie was,
    She went click-clack, click-clack, clack,
    Click-clack, click-clack, click-clack-click.

When Susie was a ghost,
A ghost Susie was,
She went, "Ooooooooooooooooooooo."

Mile End 1967; West Norwood 1970, 1972; Clapham 1974; Walworth 1974, 1979; Brixton, Earlsfield, Greenwich, Streatham 1982; Blackheath, Cubitt Town, Dalston, Shepherds Bush 1983.

Variations include:

Baby: "er, er, er," Mile End 1967; "yum, yum, yum," Walworth 1974; "ga, ga, ga," Brixton, Greenwich 1982.
Toddler: "oink, oink, oink," West Norwood 1972.
Schoolgirl: "yes, no, yes, no," West Norwood 1970; "l, 2, 3, 4, 5," West Norwood 1972, Walworth 1979; "Miss, Miss, I wanna go a piss. I don't know where the toilet is.", Brixton, Greenwich 1982.
Teenager: "Ts, ts, ts" (kissing sound), West Norwood 1970; "I don't know where my knickers are, I left them in my boyfriend's car," Walworth 1979, Streatham 1982, Blackheath 1983.
Mother: "sh, sh, sh," West Norwood 1972; spank, spank, spank, Blackheath 1983; "bake, bake, bake," Streatham 1982.
Skeleton: rattle, rattle, rattle, Greenwich 1982.

Additional "stages" include:

Stripper: "Oo-ah, off with your bra, /Down with your knickers, / Oo-ah."
A-dying: "ooooo, ooooo, ooooo," West Norwood 1972.
Goner: Mile End 1967.
Dead: Streatham 1982.
Nothing: Mile End 1967, Greenwich 1982, Cubitt Town 1983.

The last three are accompanied by a brief "freeze". All versions are accompanied by appropriate actions.

B. When Mary was a baby, a baby, a baby,
When Mary was a baby, a baby was she.
She went this way and that way
And this way and that way.
When Mary was a baby, a baby was she.

When Mary was a child, a child, a child,
When Mary was a child, a child was she.
She went this way and that way
And this way and that way
When Mary was a child, a child was she.

When Mary was a teenager, a teenager, a teenager,
When Mary was a teenager, a teenager was she.
She went (long scream)
And (long scream)
When Mary was a teenager, a teenager was she.

When Mary was a wife, a wife, a wife,
When Mary was a wife, a wife was she.
She washed pots and pans,
And cups and plates,
When Mary was a wife, a wife was she.

When Mary was a grandma, a grandma, a grandma,
When Mary was a grandma, a grandma was she.
She went, "Oh dear! Oh dear!"
"Oh my poor back, oh my poor back."
When Mary was a grandma, a grandma was she.

When Mary was a ghost, a ghost, a ghost,
When Mary was a ghost, a ghost was she.
She went, "Ooooooooooooooo."

Mile End 1964; Putney 1966.

Putney's version includes schoolgirl, sweetheart and angel. This version seems to be a transitional one between the traditional singing game where the "stages" are accompanied by actions but the actions are not described, and the contemporary action song where the actions are described, or a suitable sound is made.

Printed versions Brady, two versions, pp. 124–127; Daiken, *CGTY,* There was a girl in our school, pp. 47–48; Ford (see below); Fowke, p. 22; Gillington (see below); Gomme (see below); Hubbard, 253–254; Jorgensen, *SWF,* 63–64, *LL,* 114; Kelsey, *K2,* 104–109; Kenney, p. 35; Kidson (see below); Montgomerie, When I was a baby, p. 98; Newell (see below); Nicholson (see below); Opies, *SG,* pp. 458–461; Plunket (see below); Roud, *DM1,* 28–29; Shaw, 1970, pp. 84–85; Sims, p. 33; Sluckin, a clapping game, pp. 28–29; Sutton-Smith, p. 19; Swift, 150; Wade (1), 14, (2), 35–36; Wilson, 980, 981.

Early notings When I was a young girl, a young girl, a young girl,/When I was I (sic) young girl, how happy was I./And this way and that way, and this way and that way, and this way and that way, and this way went I; continues: When I was a school-girl, etc.//When I was a teacher, etc.// When I had a sweetheart, etc.//When I had a husband, etc.//When I had a baby, etc.//When my baby died, etc.//When I took in washing, etc.// When I went out scrubbing, etc.//When my husband did beat me, etc.// When my husband died, etc. … (Hurrah!), Gomme, 1898, pp. 364–365, from Barnes, Surrey. When I was a lady, Plunket, 1886, p. 47. When I was a lady, and When I was a maiden, Nicholson, 1897, pp. 164–169. When I was a shoemaker, Newell, 1903, p. 88. When I was a young thing, Ford, 1904, pp. 78–79. When I was a school girl, Gillington, *OHSG,* 1909, pp. 20–21. When I was a young girl, Kidson, 1916, p. 5.

Recording Webb, *Children's Singing Games.*

4.3   HERE WE GO LOOBEE-LOO

TRADITIONAL SINGING GAME:

Here we go loobee-loo,
Here we go loobee-li,
Here we go loobee-loo,
All on a Saturday night.

You put your right arm in,
You put your right arm out,
You shake it a little, a little,
And turn yourself about.
  Here we go loobee-loo, etc.

Successively: left arm, right leg, left leg.

You put your whole self in,
You put your whole self out,
You shake it a little, a little,
And turn yourself about.
  Here we go loobee-loo etc.

Mile End 1967.

See also **4.4**.

Printed versions Chase, *SGPPG,* Hullabaloo, pp. 6–9; Daiken, *CGTY*, p. 156; Dennison, 293–294; Douglas (see below); Ford (see below); Fowke, pp. 18–19; Gillington (see below), Gomme (see below); Graves (see below); Halliwell (see below); Harrop, Friend, and Gadsby, p. 4; cf. Kenney, Willowbee, p. 66; Kidson (see below); Kings (see below); MacBain (see below); Montgomerie, pp. 102–103; Newell (see below); Nicholson (see below); Northall (see below); Plunket (see below); Ritchie, *GC*, Halliballoo Ball-aye, pp. 160–161; cf. Robertson, Sally go round the moon, pp. 8–9; Rodger, Hallabuloobaloo, p. 5; Rohrbough (see below); Sutton-Smith, Baloo Baloo Balight, p. 13; Thornhill (see below); Uttley, p. 68; cf. Wilson and Gallagher, Sally go Round the Moon, No. 13, Lubin Loo, No. 29.

Early notings Now we dance looby, looby, looby,/Now we dance looby, looby, light./Shake your right hand a little/And turn you round about. etc., Halliwell, *PRNT*, 1849, p. 129. Here we dance Lubin, Lubin, Plunket,

1886, pp. 16–17. Northall, 1892, p. 361; Gomme, 1894, pp. 352–361. Hilli ballu ballai, Nicholson, 1897, pp. 176–184. Put your right elbow in,/ Put your right elbow out,/Shake yourselves a little,/And turn yourselves about. "The words we give were in use some sixty years since ... The English name is 'Hinkumbooby'", Newell, 1903, p. 131. Ford, 1904, pp. 59–60; Gillington, *OSSG*, 1909, pp. 22–23. Looby Loo, Thornhill, 1911, p. 18. Douglas, 1916, pp. 74–75, 1931, pp. 41–42; Kidson, 1916, p. 56; Graves, 1927, p. 26. Ha-la-ga-loo-ga-loo, Kings 2, 1930, pp. 33–34. MacBain, 1933, pp. 159–161; Rohrbough, *HPPB*, 1940, p. 135.

Recording Wilson and Gallagher, *Children's Singing Games*.

4.4 THE HOKEY POKEY

You put your right arm in,
You put your right arm out,
 In out, in out, shake it all about.
You do the Hokey Pokey,
Turn around
That's what it's all about.

Oh the Hokey Hokey Pokey!
Oh the Hokey Pokey Pokey!
Oh the Hokey Pokey Pokey!
Knees bend, arms stretch,
Ra, ra, ra.

Then left arm, right leg, left leg, whole self in turn.

Mile End 1967; <u>Streatham 1982</u>; Cubitt Town, Shepherds Bush 1983.

Mainly played by younger children. It is of course similar to the old singing game "Loobee-Loo" (see **4.3**). It has not changed much from the song by Jimmy Kennedy (1941).

Printed versions Chambers (see below); Dennison, Hokey Cokey, mentioned, 293; Hubbard, Okey Cokey, mentioned, 263; Opies, *SG*, Okey Kokey, pp. 391–392; Ritchie, *GC*, The Hokey Pokey, p. 168.

Early noting "to the tune of Lullibullero": Fal de ral la, fal de ral la;/ Hinkumbooby, round about,/Right hands in, and left hands out,/…/ Right foot in, and left foot out/ etc., Chambers, 1842, p. 65.

4.5 BINGO

TRADITIONAL SINGING GAME:

There was a man who had a dog,
And Bingo was his name,
B-I-N-G-O, B-I-N-G-O, B-I-N-G-O,
And Bingo was his name.

There was a man who had a dog,
And Bingo was his name,
*-I-N-G-O, *-I-N-G-O, *-I-N-G-O,
And Bingo was his name.

* Further verses reduce one letter each time until:

There was a man who had a dog,
And Bingo was his name,
--*-*-*, *-*-*-*-*, *-*-*-*-*,
And Bingo was his name.

Streatham 1982.

A slight movement may be made to indicate missing letters.

Ultimately derived from a comic song "Little Bingo" sung at the Theatre Royal, Haymarket c1780, see Opies (*SG*, 1985, p. 410).

See also **6.A.46**.

Printed versions Abrahams, p. 191; Beckwith (see below); Chase, *SGPPG*, pp. 52–53; Cumnock Academy, p. 17; Fowke, p. 91; Gaskell (see below); Gillington (see below); Gomme (see below); Kidson (see below); MacBain (see below); Montgomerie, p. 102; Opies (see below); Parry-Jones, p. 89; Plunket (see below); Rohrbough (see below); Sims, pp. 40–41; Sutton-Smith, pp. 20–21; Uttley, p. 69; Webb, mentioned, 639; Wilson and Gallagher, No. 28; Withers, *CO* [p. 33].

Early notings "One child holds a stick; the others dance round [that child] & sing—B-I-N-G-O, B-I-N-G-O, B-I-N-G-O,/Bingo was his name/Oh! Bingo was his name. Then the child with the stick touches, first one, then another; the 1st touched says 'B,', the 2nd 'I,', the 3rd 'N,', the 4th 'G,', the 5th 'Oh! Bingo was his name.' Whoever fails to do so must take the place in the middle", Plunket, 1886, p. 8. "There was a farmer had a boy, And his name was Bobby Bingo": this song, according to the Opies, *SG*, p. 411, as reported in *Strand Magazine*, ii, 517, was sung by London street children in 1891. There *was* a farmer *had* a dog,/ His name was Bobby Bingo./B-i-n-g-o, B-i-n-g-o, B-i-n-g-o/His name was Bobby Bingo, Gomme, 1894, p. 30, one of eight versions, pp. 29–33. Gillington, 1909, *OHSG*, p. 22, *OIWSG*, p. 6; Gaskell, c1913, p. 7; Kidson, 1916, p. 111; Beckwith, *JFL*, 1928, p. 60; MacBain, 1933, p. 36; Rohrbough, *SSG*, 1938, pp. 3–4, *HPPB*, 1940, pp. 15, 35.

Recordings BBC 16075 (78) (1951, Sidbury, Devon); Webb, *Children's Singing Games*; Wilson and Gallagher, *Children's Singing Games*.

4.6 WHO HAS STOLE MY WATCH AND CHAIN?

TRADITIONAL SINGING GAME:

Who has stole my watch and chain?
Watch and chain, watch and chain,
Who has stole my watch and chain?
My fair lady.

Off to prison you must go,
You must go, you must go,
Off to prison you must go,
My fair lady.

Mile End 1967.

Printed versions Brady, pp. 140–141; Daiken, *CGTY*, p. 99; Douglas (see below); Elder, See da robbers passin' by, p. 103 – tune of "London Bridge"; Fowke, "Tune: London Bridge", p. 31; Gillington (see below); Gomme (see below); Kidson (see below); Kings (see below); Newell (see below); Nicholson (see below); Opies, *SG*, pp. 68–72; Plunket (see below); Ritchie, *GC*, See the robbers passing by, pp. 152–153; Sutton-Smith, p. 22; Turner, p. 61.

Early notings A version of "London Bridge" which includes the line ".. stole my watch and broke my chain" ("New version"), Plunket, 1886, pp. 22–23. Hark the robbers/Coming through, coming through,/My fair lady.//They have stolen my watch and chain,/Watch and chain, watch and chain.//Off to prison they shall go,/They shall go, they shall go,/My fair lady, Gomme, 1894, p. 193, Wolstanton, Stoke-on Trent; one of seven versions (similar tune to "London Bridge"), pp. 192–199. Similar tune to "London Bridge", referred to as "Sheriffmuir", Nicholson, 1897, pp. 340–342. What did the robber do to you?/My fair lady!/He broke my watch and stole my keys,/My fair lady! Newell, 1903, verses to "London Bridge", pp. 208–210. Here come three robbers just from town (tune similar to Nicholson), Gillington, 1909, *OHSG*, p. 18; Hark the robbers coming through, Gillington, *OIWSG*, 1909, p. 18. Douglas names "an old catch game", "Hark the Robbers Coming Through", 1916, p. 39, 1931, p. 21. See the robbers passing through (tune as Nicholson), Kidson, 1916, p. 58. See the robbers passing by, tune similar to London Bridge, Kings 2, 1930, p. 19.

Recording MacColl and Behan, *Streets of Song*.

4.7 LONDON BRIDGE IS FALLING DOWN

TRADITIONAL SINGING GAME:

A. London Bridge is falling down,
   Falling down, falling down,
   London Bridge is falling down,
   Roll, roll the …
   Gently down the street,
   Merrily, merrily, merrily, merrily,
   Life is but a dream.

Brixton 1982; Mile End, Shepherds Bush 1983 (first part).

B. London Bridge is falling down,
   Falling down, falling down,
   Roll, roll, roll the boat,
   Gently down the stream,
   Merrily, merrily, merrily, merrily,
   Life is but a dream.

Brixton 1982.

Here, the first three lines of the traditional singing game have been combined with what the Opies term a "minstrel song" copyrighted in 1852 (*SG*, 1985, p. 454): "Row, row, row your boat,/Gently down the stream;/Merrily, merrily, merrily, merrily,/Life is but a dream.". See **4.8** and **8.A.14**.

C. Get the keys and lock her up,
   Lock her up, lock her up,
   Get the keys and lock her up,
   My fair lady.

   London Bridge is falling down,
   Falling down, falling down,
   London Bridge is falling down,
   My fair lady.

> Build it up with sticks (bricks) and stones, etc.
>
> Sticks (bricks) and stones will break and fall, etc.
>
> Build it up with silver and gold, etc.
>
> Silver and gold will wash away, etc.
>
> Build it up with clay and straw, etc.
>
> Clay and straw will burn away, etc.
>
> Build it up with bricks and cement, etc.
>
> Bricks and cement will just do,
> Just do, just do,
> Bricks and cement will just do,
> My fair lady.
>
> Walworth 1974.

It is interesting that Gomme (1894, p. 198), comments that verses from "Hark the Robbers" (**4.6 WHO HAS STOLE MY WATCH AND CHAIN**) came into "London Bridge" in her day. The first verse of variant C. shows that the tradition remains.

Printed versions Bett (see below); Briggs, p. 126; Chase, *AFTS*, p. 189: the tune given is similar to the third version cited by Gomme (1894, p. 333); Daiken, *CGTY*, pp. 95, 96; Douglas (see below); Ford (see below); Fowke, p. 30, followed by "Here are the robbers"; Gillington (see below); Gomme (see below); Halliwell (see below); Kidson (see below); Lang (see below); MacBain (see below); McMorland, p. 83; Mills and Bishop (see below); Newell (see below); Northall (see below); Opies, *ODNR*, p. 76, *SG*, pp. 61–67; Plunket (see below); Sutton-Smith, p. 22; Thornhill (see below); Wilson and Gallagher, No. 16.

Early notings According to the Opies (*SG*, 1985, pp. 63–64), this song first appeared in print in *Tommy Thumb's Pretty Song Book,* c1744.

London bridge is broken down,/Dance o'er my lady lee;/London bridge is broken down,/With a gay lady. (seven more verses), Halliwell, *NRE*, 1843, p. 194. London bridge is broken down ("Old version"), Plunket, 1886, pp. 20–21. Northall, 1892, pp. 365–366; Gomme, 1894, pp. 333–350; Lang, 1897, like Halliwell, p. 98; Newell, 1903, pp. 204–211; Ford, 1904, pp. 69–70. London Bridge is broken down, broken down, broken down/London Bridge is broken down,/Heigh ho! Merry O!//Build it up with pins and needles etc.// third and following verses of a song entitled "London Bridge" beginning "Where are you three foxes going", sung to a different tune and played like "Oranges and Lemons", said to be a similar game to "Hark the Robbers", Gillington, *OHSG*, 1909, p. 17. Thornhill, 1911, pp. 1, 2; Douglas, mentioned, 1916, p. 96, 1931, p. 55; Kidson, 1916, p. 6; Bett, *TGC*, 1929, pp. 99–100; MacBain, 1933, like Halliwell, pp. 155–157. Discussed in Mills and Bishop, 1937, 34.

Recording Wilson and Gallagher, *Children's Singing Games*.

4.8 ROW, ROW, ROW YOUR BOAT

Row, row, row your boat,
Merrily down the stream,
Smoke your pipe and ride your bike,
Life is just a dream.

Shepherds Bush 1983.

"We pretend to be rowing a boat and we sing it with actions." girl, Shepherds Bush 1983.

See also **4.7B** and **8.A.14**.

Printed versions Gadsby and Harrop, No. 27; Opies, *SG*, p. 454.

4.9 QUEENIE, QUEENIE or QUEENIE-I

TRADITIONAL GAME with chant or singing:

A.   Queenie, Queenie, who's got the ball?
           Is she fat, or is she tall?
           Or is she hanging on the garden wall,
(chanted)   You see I haven't got it!
           You see I haven't got it! (in my pocket)
           Twist right round and still hasn't got it.
           I am Queen and I know who's got the ball
           (_____'s) got it.

West Norwood 1972; <u>Walworth 1974</u>; Brixton 1982; Brockley, Deptford, Dulwich 1983.

Variations:

        Is she fat, or is she thin?
        Or is she like a rolling pin?

Mile End 1964.

        Is she fat or is she small?
        Or is she like a tennis ball?

Finsbury 1963.

B.   (sung)
        Quee-ee-nie, Quee-ee-nie, Quee-ee-nie-I,
        Who's go-ot the ball?
        I-is she bi-ig, or i-is she small?
        See I haven't got it!
        See I haven't got it!
        Who's got the ball?

Marylebone 1967; <u>Barnsbury 1983</u>.

"You get about six people and an extra person who's going to be the Queen. She gets the ball and she turns around so she's not facing the other people. She throws the ball over her head and whoever gets it puts it behind their back. The Queen turns round and the other people say, 'Queenie, Queenie, who's got the ball? ... See I haven't got it.' Then the person who's the Queen says, '(_____'s) got it.' If they haven't got it she's got to keep on trying. If she gets it right then she's Queen again." girl, 11, Deptford 1983.

This game was usually played by girls, but in two places boys told me how they played it:

"Somebody's 'on it' and there's three people standing behind him. The person in front turns his back to the three people, then he throws the ball over his head and one of the three people behind picks it up and hides it behind his back. Then the person turns around and says, 'Queenie, Queenie, who's got the ball?' and the three people are spaced out. 'Queenie' can run through but the person with the ball has to try and turn round so he don't see the ball. After so many goes, running through them, he's got to try and guess who's got the ball." boy, 11, Finsbury 1983.

"There's this person called Queenie-I and he throws the ball over his shoulder. One person gets it and hides it behind his back. He has to say all sorts of things to try to see who's the person who's got the ball. If he gets it right he's 'he' again and if he gets it wrong the person who's got the ball has got to be the man." boy, 10, Cubitt Town 1983.

Printed versions Brady, Queenie eye o, p. 67; Daiken, *CGTY*, Alla-balla, alla-balla, p. 32; Ellis (see below); Fowke, p. 77; Opies, *CGSP*, pp. 5, 290–292; Shaw, 1969, p. 17, 1970, p. 25; Sluckin, pp. 25–26; Sutton-Smith, Queenie, Alla Balla, p. 51; Todd, Birella, Queeneeo, 8; Turner, Ali Baba, p. 53.

Early noting … "Queenie" where the one who throws the ball over her shoulder has to guess who picked it up. If the ball was caught the thrower is out, Ellis, 1910s, 39.

Recording Webb, *Children's Singing Games.*

This game appears to be derived from "Queen Anne", an old singing game. The versions of Kidson and Searle form a link between "Queen Anne" and the contemporary "Queenie, Queenie".

Printed versions of "Queen Anne": Chambers (see below); Daiken, *CGTY*, p. 79; Douglas (see below); Gomme (see below); Gillington (see below); Graves (see below); Gullen, p. 86; Halliwell (see below); Holbrook, pp. 68–69; Lang (see below); MacBain (see below), Newell (see below); Northall (see below); Opies, *ONRB*, p. 132; Plunket (see below); Uttley, p. 72.

My Lady, My Lady and similar versions: Kidson (see below); Searle, 133.

Early notings Here we come a piping,/First in spring and then in May,/The queen she sits upon the sand,/Fair as a lilly (sic), white as a wand;/King John has sent you letters three,/And begs you'll read them unto me;/We can't read one, without them all,/So pray Miss Bridget deliver the ball! Halliwell, *NRE*, 1842, p. 108. Queen Anne, queen Anne, you sit in the sun,/As fair as a lily, as white as a wand./I send you three letters, and pray read one,/You must read one, if you can't read all,/So pray, Miss or Master, throw up the ball, Halliwell, *NRE*, 1842, p. 113*,* 1843, p. 137. Queen Anne, Queen Anne, who sits on her throne,/As fair as a lily, as white as a swan;/The king sends you three letters,/And begs you'll read one.//I cannot read one unless I read all,/So pray, --------, deliver the ball.//The ball is mine, and none of thine,/So you, proud Queen, may sit on your throne,/While we, your messengers, go and come. Or, sometimes: The ball is mine, and none of thine,/You are the fair lady to sit on: (sic)/And we're the black gipsies to go and come, Halliwell, *PRNT*, 1849, pp. 133–134. Lady Queen Ann she sits in her stand,/And a pair of green gloves upon her hand, Chambers, 1870, p. 136. Lady Queen Anne she sits in the sun/As fair as a lily, as white as a swan/ King John has sent you three letters to read/And begs you'll read one. I cannot read one unless I read all/So pray Miss … deliver up the ball. The ball is mine it is not thine (twice)/ So you proud Queen sit on your throne/While we poor gipsies come and go, Plunket, 1886, pp. 14–15. Northall, 1892, pp. 409–411. Queen Anne, as Halliwell, Lang, 1897, p. 172. Gomme, 1898, pp. 90–102; Newell, 1903, p. 151; Gillington, *ODSG*, 1913, p. 3; Douglas, 1916, p. 65, 1931, p. 35. My Lady, My lady, she's sent me to town,/For something she lost, when she was last down,/It's something that's round and something that's small,/I intend to ask *you* to give me the ball, Kidson, 1916, p. 39. Graves, 1927, p. 9; MacBain, 1933, p. 93.

4.10 THE FARMER'S IN HIS DEN

TRADITIONAL SINGING GAME:

A. The farmer's in his den,
   The farmer's in his den,
   Ee-o, ee-o,
   The farmer's in his den.

   The farmer wants a wife, etc.

   The wife wants a child, etc.

   The child wants a nurse (nanny), etc.

   The nurse wants a dog, etc.

   The dog wants a cat (bone), etc.

   The cat wants a mouse, etc.

   The mouse wants some cheese, etc.

   We all want some cheese, etc.

Walworth 1974, 1979; Finsbury 1983 (The cat wants a mouse/He chased the mouse through the hole.)

B. The farmer's in his den,
    The farmer's in his den,
    Ee-i, atty-o,
    The farmer's in his den.

    The farmer wants a wife, etc.

    The wife wants a child, etc.

    The child wants a nurse, etc.

    The nurse wants a dog, etc.

    The dog wants a bone, etc.

    We all pat the bone, etc.

Mile End 1967, Dalston 1983.

Printed versions Bolton (see below); Botkin (see below); Brady, pp. 101–102; Chase (see below); Douglas (see below); Fowke, p. 13; Gillington (see below), Gomme (see below); Hubbard, mentioned, 263; McMorland, p. 67; Montgomeries, *HBSNR*, pp. 69–70; Newell (see below); Opies, *SG*, pp. 183–189; Parry-Jones, p. 124; Rodger, p. 5; Todd, 10; Uttley, pp. 65–66; Webb, mentioned, 639; Wilson and Gallagher, No. 10.

Early notings The farmer in the den,/Hi-oh, my cherry, ho!/The farmer takes a wife, Hi-oh, my, cherry, oh!/The wife takes a child, etc. (Virginia), Bolton, 1888, p. 119. Gomme, 1898, p. 420. The farmer in the dell,/.../Heigh ho! for Rowley O!, Newell, 1903, pp. 129–130. Gillington, 1909, *OHSG*, p. 19, *OIWSG*, pp, 4–5; Douglas, 1916, p. 68, 1931, p. 37; Botkin, *APPS*, 1937, pp. 29 (mentioned), 97; Chase, *OSASG*, 1938, pp. 35–36.

Recordings MacColl and Behan, *Streets of Song*; Wilson and Gallagher, *Children's Singing Games*; Wales, *Folk Songs and Ballads of Sussex*.

4.11 THE GRAND OLD DUKE OF YORK

TRADITIONAL SINGING GAME, longways:

The grand old Duke of York,
He had ten thousand men,
He marched them up to the top of the hill,
And he marched them down again,
And when they were up, they were up,
And when they were down, they were down,
And when they were only half way up,
They were neither up nor down.

Rule Britannia, Britannia rules the waves,
Britain never, never, never, shall be slaves.

Mile End 1967; Walworth 1974.

Printed versions Briggs, p. 25; Chase, *SGPPG*, pp. 10–13 (and see below); Douglas (see below); Fowke, p. 37; Gillington (see below); Gomme (see below); Graves (see below); Halliwell (see below); Harrop, Friend, and Gadsby, p. 53; Kidson (see below); Lang (see below); MacBain (see below); Nicholson (see below); Northall (see below); Opies, *ODNR*, p. 176, *LLS* (see below), *SG*, pp. 214–215 (and see below); Rohrbough (see below); Smith, *TGH*, pp. 64–66; Sutton-Smith, p. 29; Thornhill (see below); Wilson and Gallagher, No. 32.

Early notings The king of France, and four thousand men,/They drew their swords, and put them up again, Halliwell, *PRNT*, 1849, p. 10: "an early variation ... in MS. Sloane 1489". The King of France went up the hill/With forty thousand men;/The King of France came down the hill,/And ne'er went up again, Opies, *LLS*, p. 99, "noted three times in Charles I's reign". The king of France went up the hill, Halliwell, *NRE*, 1842, p. 12, 1843, p. 20. Oh the mighty Duke of York, Northall, 1892, p. 99. Gomme, 1894, p. 121; Lang, 1897, p. 35. Napoleon was a general, Nicholson, 1897, pp. 232–233. Gillington, *OIWSG*, 1909, p. 13;

Thornhill, 1911, p. 19; Douglas, 1916, pp. 66–67, 1931, p. 36; Kidson, 1916, pp. 14, 15. The Opies (*SG*, p. 215) state that "in some places they add 'Rule Britannia'", quoting the "Macmillan Collection", 1922. The Duke of Cumberland, Graves, 1927, p. 12. MacBain, 1933, pp. 164–165, 303; Chase, *OSASG*, 1938, pp. 41–42; Rohrbough, *HPPB*, 1940, p. 132.

Recording Wilson and Gallagher, *Children's Singing Games*.

4.12 A-HUNTING WE SHALL GO

TRADITIONAL SINGING GAME:

A-hunting we shall go,
A-hunting we shall go,
To catch a fox,
And put him in a box,
And never let him go.

A-hunting we shall go,
A-hunting we shall go,
To catch a frog,
And put him in a bog,
And then we start again.

Shepherds Bush 1983.

"We get partners. There's a great big row with everybody joining in, even the boys. The first partners go right through the middle and come back again. Then they split up and go each side. Then they make an arch and everyone goes through." girl, Shepherds Bush 1983.

Printed versions Abrahams, p. 5; *Ballads and Songs* [9], Chase, *SGPPG*, p. 10, records verse 1 of the Shepherds Bush version as verse 3 to "The

Noble Duke of York" (and see below); Fowke, p. 36; Gillington (see below); Gomme (see below); Northall (see below); Opies, *SG*, pp. 212–213 (and see below); Sutton-Smith, p. 28; Thornhill (see below); Uttley, p. 69; Wilson and Gallagher, No. 31.

Early notings A hunting we will go (*repeat*),/We'll catch a little fish,/And put him in a dish,/And never let him go. *Ellesmere, Shropshire*. ... In Derbyshire they say—We'll catch a fox, and put him in a box,/And a-hunting, etc., Northall, 1892, pp. 386–387. Oh, a-hunting we will go, a-hunting we will go;/We'll catch a little fox and put him in a box,/And never let him go, Gomme, 1894, p. 243, one of three versions (Bath), pp. 243–245. Gillington, *OIWSG*, 1909, p. 14. According to the Opies (*SG*, 1985, p. 215), Cecil Sharp in 1909 had suggested that the two rhymes "The Noble Duke of York" and "A-Hunting We Shall Go" could be combined (cf. Chase, above). Thornhill, 1911, p. 6. Chase, *OSASG*, 1938, p. 41, records verse 1 of the Shepherds Bush version as verse 3 to "The Noble Duke of York".

Recording Wilson and Gallagher, *Children's Singing Games*.

4.13 RING A RING A ROSES

TRADITIONAL SINGING GAME:

A. Ring a ring a roses,
    A pocket full of posies,
    A-tishoo, a-tishoo,
    We all fall down.

    Picking up the daisies,
    Picking up the daisies,
    A-tishoo, a-tishoo,
    We all stand up.

<u>Walworth 1979</u>; Brixton 1982; Barnsbury, Cubitt Town, Dalston (one verse), Deptford, Shepherds Bush 1983 (one verse).

B. Ring a ring a roses,
    A pocket full of posies,
    A-tishoo, a-tishoo,
    We all fall down.

   Ashes in the water,
   Ashes in the sea,
   They all jump out,
   With a one, two, three.

Greenwich 1982; Finsbury 1983.

"You have a circle of people. They link hands and gallop around. They all fall down. You have to smell the 'pocketful of posies'." Finsbury 1983.

Printed versions Bett (see below); Brady, p. 12; Dennison, mentioned, 293; Fowke, p. 11; Gaskell (see below); Gomme (see below); Gullen, p. 126; Hubbard, mentioned, 263; Kellett, counting-out rhyme, p. 102 (and see below); Kidson (see below); Kings (see below); MacBain (see below); Newell (see below); Northall (see below); Opies, *ODNR*, pp. 364–365, *SG*, pp. 220–227; Parry-Jones, p. 92; Petershams, p. 52; Ritchie, *GC*, p. 166; Rodger, p. 4; Sutton-Smith, p. 12; Uttley, p. 66; cf. Wilson and Gallagher, No. 26; Wood (see below).

Early notings Ring a ring a rosie,/A bottle full of posie,/All the girls in our town,/Ring for little Josie, Newell, 1903 (rhyme said to be from c1790), with three further versions, pp. 127–128. A ring, a ring o' roses,/A pocket full of posies,/One for Jack, and one for Jim, and one for little Moses./Atisha! atisha! atisha! Northall, 1892, p. 360. Ring, a ring a roses,/A pocketful of posies;/ Hush, oh! hush, oh!/All fall down! Gomme, 1898, p. 109, Colchester, Essex; one of eleven versions, pp. 108–111. Gaskell, c1913, p. 5; Kidson, 1916, p. 68; Kellett, 1920s, p. 92; Bett, *TGC*, 1929, p. 89; Kings 2, 1930, p. 11; MacBain, 1933, p. 38; Wood, *AMG*, 1940, p. 102.

Recording Wilson and Gallagher, *Children's Singing Games*.

4.14 DOWN IN THE VALLEY

A. Down in the valley where the green grass grows,
Dear old (_____) she grows like a rose.

She grows, she grows, she grows so sweet,
And she calls for her lover down the street.

Down in the dark valley where nobody goes
I saw a young lady picking her nose.

Greenwich 1982.

Printed versions cf. Fulton and Smith, skipping, p. 31; Gillington (see below); Kellett, p. 16, (another version, ?early noting, similar to Northall and Gomme, below), p. 129.

Early noting Down in the meadow where the high grass grows/See *Grace Kellaway* (*Girl's name*), she grows like a rose!/She grows and she grows, and she grows so sweet!/Will you come and tell your thoughts to me? Gillington, *OIWSG*, 1909, pp. 28–29.

B. Down in the jungle where nobody knows,
There's a big fat woman, washing her clothes,
With a rub-a-dub here, and a rub-a-dub there,
That's the way she washes her clothes.

> Tiddle-i-i, cootchy-cootchy woman,
> Tiddle-i-i, hootchy-cootchy woman,
> Tiddle-i-i, cootchy-cootchy woman,
> That's the way she washes her clothes.

Down in the jungle where nobody knows,
There's a big fat woman picking her nose,
With a pick-pick here and a pick-pick there,
That's the way she washes her clothes.
> Tiddle-i-i, cootchy-cootchy woman, etc.

Down in the jungle where nobody knows,
There's a big fat woman scrubbing her toes,
With a scrub-scrub here, and a scrub-scrub there,
That's the way she scrubs her toes.
  Tiddle-i-i, cootchy-cootchy woman, etc.

<u>Mile End 1983</u>; Dalston 1985.

C. Down in the valley where nobody knows,
There was an old woman washing her clothes,
With a scrub-scrub here and a scrub-scrub there,
That's how the old woman washes her clothes.

  Diddly-um-dum, a scoobeedoo bedoobe
  Diddly-um-dum, a-scoobeedoo bedoobe
  Diddly-um-dum, a scoobeedoo bedoobe dum
  That's how the old woman washes her clothes.

Mile End 1967 (Inky-pinky woman); <u>Walworth 1974, 1979</u>.

D. Down by the crossings of the Green Cross Code*,
There sat someone undressing their clothes.

Walworth 1982.

* The Green Cross Code was a guide introduced by the National Road Safety Committee in 1970 to teach children how to cross the road safely.

E. Down by the river where nobody knows,
There's a little old woman who washes her clothes,
With a wish-wash here and a wish-wash there (cha-cha here and a cha-cha there)
That's how the old lady washes her clothes.

  Tiddly-ump-hump, boogie-woogie,
  Tiddly-ump-hump, boogie-woogie,
  Tiddly-ump-hump, boogie-woogie,
  That's how the little lady washes her clothes.

Down by the river where nobody knows,
There's a little dog, washing his clothes,
With a woof-woof here and a woof-woof there,
That's how the little dog washes his clothes.
    Tiddly-ump-hump etc.

Down by the river where nobody knows,
There's a little cat washing his clothes,
With a miaow here and a miaow there,
That's how the little cat washes his clothes.
    Tiddly-ump-hump etc.

Down by the river where nobody knows,
There's a little chicken washing her clothes,
With a peck-peck here and a peck-peck there,
That's how the little chicken washes her clothes.
    Tiddle-ump-hump etc.

Barnsbury 1983.

Girls kneel facing each other and do appropriate actions. They waggle hips, etc., for the chorus.

The Opies (*SG*, 1985, pp. 127–130) imply a connection between the traditional singing game where the girl "blows like a rose" and the lady "who washes her clothes", and there are many variants which connect the two. Furthermore, in *LLS* (1959, p. 364), they state a connection explicitly.

Printed versions Abrahams, skipping rhymes, pp. 40, 43; Bett (see below); Botkin (see below); Brady, p. 92; Briggs, p. 170; Coffin and Cohen, skipping rhyme, p. 189; Cosbey, p. 71; Daiken, *CGTY*, p. 81; Douglas (see below); Evans, *JRR*, a skipping rhyme, p. 11; Fowke, p. 68; Gillington (see below); Gomme (see below); Kellett (see below); Kenney, skipping game, p. 6; Kings (see below); Knapps, skipping games, pp. 116, 186, 209; Lowenstein, p. 18; McMorland, p. 45; Montgomeries, *HBSNR*, p. 51; Northall, (see below); Opies, *ONRB*, p. 122, *LLS*, p. 364, *SG*, pp. 127–130,

426–428; Ritchie, *SS*, p. 31, also a football rhyme, p. 129, *GC*, p. 122; Shaw, 1969, pp. 45, 58, 1970, pp. 82, 99; Smith, *BBHG*, p. 45, clapping game, p. 49; Solomons, p. 55; Worstell, skipping rhyme, p. 1.

Early notings (a courtship game, probably still played, though not in Inner London playgrounds): Down in the meadows where the green grass grows,/ To see (*girl's name*) blow like a rose,/She blows, she blows, she blows so sweet,/Go out (*girl's name*) who shall be he? (*Here a partner is chosen.*)/(*Girl's name*) made a pudding,/She made it so sweet,/And never stuck a knife in/ Till (*partner's name*) came to eat. … Northall, 1892, p. 368. Down in the valley where the green grass grows/Stands E___ H___, she blows like a rose./She blows, she blows, she blows so sweet./In came F___ S___ and gave her a kiss./E___ made a pudding, she made it nice and sweet,/F___ took a knife and fork and cut a little piece./Taste of it, taste of it, don't say nay,/For next Sunday morning is our wedding day.* Gomme, 1894, p. 99, Cowes, Isle of Wight, one of three versions, pp. 99–100. Douglas, 1916, pp. 61, 93, 1931, pp. 32, 53. Down by the waterside the green grass grows, Kellett, 1920s, ring game, p. 15. Botkin, *TAF*, 1944, skipping rhyme, p. 792.

* For later versions of the second half of this verse, see Gomme, 1898, pp. 416–418; Gillington, 1909, *OHSG*, p. 23, *OSSG*, p. iv; Bett, *TGC*, 1929, pp. 15–16; Kings 2, 1930, p. 6; Shaw, 1970, p. 35.

Recordings BBC 13869 (78) (1949, Edinburgh); MacColl and Behan, *Streets of Song*; Webb, *Children's Singing Games*.

4.15 I SENT A LETTER TO MY LOVE

TRADITIONAL SINGING GAME:

I sent a letter to my love,
And on the way I dropped it,
One of you has picked it up,
And put it in your pocket.

It wasn't you, it wasn't you,
   But it's you.

Mile End 1967; <u>Walworth 1974</u>; Brixton, Greenwich 1982; Dalston, Finsbury 1983.

"There's a circle and someone has a piece of paper in their hand. The person goes around the outside and picks someone. They drop the letter in their lap and then they go around as many times as they want, saying, 'Was it you?'. When they say, 'It was you,' it means you've got to race them around the outside, back to their seat and the last one there is 'on it'." girl, 11, EC1 1983.

See also **3.A.26**.

Printed versions Abrahams, p. 90; Beckwith (see below); Bett (see below); Botkin (see below); Brady, pp. 116–117; Douglas (see below); Elder, "I los' my glove on a Satu'day night" p. 75; Ford (see below); Fowke, p. 11; Gomme (see below); Halliwell (see below); Harrop, Friend, and Gadsby, A-tisket, a-tasket, p. 49; Hopkin, p. 28; Hubbard, Lucy Locket "(played with a glove)", mentioned, 263; Kenney, p. 60; Kidson (see below); Kings (see below); Knapps, p. 81; McMorland, Lucy Locket, p. 61; Newell (see below); Northall (see below); Opies, *CGSP*, pp. 185, 198–202, 203–206 passim; Parry-Jones, described, pp. 89–90 (played without a rhyme but otherwise the same); Petershams, p. 56; Ritchie, *GC*, p. 163; Sutton-Smith, pp. 20, 58; Turner, p. 58; Uttley, p. 57; Wilson and Gallagher, No. 7.

Early notings ... I sent a letter to my love,/I lost it, I lost it!/I found it, I found it!/It burns, it scalds! Halliwell, *PRNT*, 1849, p. 130 (Drop-glove; cf. also game of Drop-Cap, p. 113). Northall, 1892, p. 364. Drop Handkerchief, Gomme, 1894, pp. 109–112; Kiss in the Ring, Gomme, 1894, pp. 305–310; Newell, 1903, pp. 168–169; Ford, 1904, pp. 60–61; Douglas, 1916, p. 42, 1931, p. 22; Kidson, 1916, pp. 22, 23; Beckwith, *JFL*, 1928, pp. 29–30. "Drop Handkerchief", mentioned, p. 16, but partly written out on p. 29, Bett, *TGC*, 1929. Kings 2, 1930, p. 16; Botkin, *TAF*, 1944, p. 806.

Recordings BBC 16074 (78) (1951, Sidbury, Devon); Wilson and Gallagher, *Children's Singing Games;* MacColl and Behan, *Streets of Song.*

4.16 POOR JENNY IS A-WEEPING

TRADITIONAL SINGING GAME:

Poor Jenny is a-weeping,
A-weeping, a-weeping,
Poor Jenny is a-weeping,
On a bright summer's day.

Stand up and choose a partner, (lost one), etc.

Shake hands before you leave her, etc.

Mile End 1967; Cubitt Town, EC1 1983.

"You have a ring. The person in the middle pretends to be crying and does the actions to the song. Everyone goes around her singing. She stands up and chooses a person and then they shake hands. The person she shakes hands with is then the person in the middle. Jenny joins the people around her." girl, 11, EC1 1983.

Printed versions Daiken, *CGTY*, Mary, p. 75, Jennie, p. 138; Dennison, mentioned, 293; Douglas (see below); Gillington (see below); Gomme (see below); Hubbard, mentioned, 263; Kings (see below); McMorland, p. 66; Montgomeries, *SC*, p. 82, *HBSNR*, p. 70; Opies, *SG*, p. 325; Rutherford, p. 25; Starn, Jennie, p. 99; Sutton-Smith, pp. 14–15; Uttley, pp. 61–62; Wilson and Gallagher, No. 1.

Early notings Oh, what is Jennie weeping for,/A-weeping for, a-weeping for?/ Oh, what is Jennie weeping for,/All on this summer's day?//I'm weeping for my own true love, etc., Gomme, 1898, p. 55, one of nineteen versions. Gillington, *OSSG*, 1909, p. 7; Douglas, mentioned, 1916, p. 96, 1931, p. 55. Jinny, Kings 1, 1926, p. 13.

Recordings BBC 16074 (78) (1951, Sidbury, Devon); MacColl and Behan, *Streets of Song*; Wilson and Gallagher, *Children's Singing Games*; Webb, *Children's Singing Games*; Wales, *Folk Songs and Ballads of Sussex*.

4.17 FAIR ROSIE WAS A SWEET PRINCESS

DRAMATIC GAME based on Grimms' "Brier Rose":

Fair Rosie was a sweet princess,
A sweet princess, a sweet princess,
Fair Rosie was a sweet princess,
Long, long ago.

A wicked fairy cast a spell, etc.

Fair Rosie slept for a hundred years, etc.

A great big forest grew around, etc.

A handsome prince came riding by, etc.

He chopped the trees down one by one, etc.

He kissed Fair Rosie on the cheek, etc.

The wedding bells went ding, dang, dong, etc.

West Norwood 1970.

Children make an enclosed circle while the wicked fairy, the handsome prince and Fair Rosie do their individual mimes.

Printed versions Daiken, *CGTY*, Briar Rosebud was a pretty child, p. 89; Harrop, Friend, and Gadsby, p. 20; Kellett (see below); McMorland, p. 81; Newell (see below); Opies (see below); Robertson, The princess was a charming child, pp. 18–19; cf. Rutherford, There once lived a princess, p. 79; Wilson and Gallagher, Briar Rosebud was a pretty child, No. 24.

Early notings cf. Newell, 1903, The Enchanted Princess, pp. 223–224. According to the Opies (*SG*, 1985, pp. 266–269), this song comes from an American translation from German, c1908: "The game, which tells the story of the Sleeping Beauty, is a direct translation of the German 'Dornröschen war ein schönes Kind'. It was imported during the years leading up to the First World War …" (p. 267). Fair Rosebud was a lovely child …, Kellett, 1920s, pp. 64–65.

Recordings BBC 19003 (78) (1953, Kentish Town); Wilson and Gallagher, *Children's Singing Games.*

4.18 IN AND OUT THE DUSTY BLUEBELLS

TRADITIONAL SINGING GAME:

A. In and out the dusty bluebells,
    In and out the dusty bluebells,
    In and out the dusty bluebells,
    Who shall be your master?

    Pitter-patter, pitter patter, on my shoulder (pitty pitty, pat pat),
    Pitter-patter, pitter-patter, on my shoulder,
    Pitter-patter, pitter-patter, on my shoulder,
    You shall be my master.

Mile End 1967, 1982–84; West Norwood 1970, 1972; Walworth 1981; Brixton 1982; Dalston, Shepherds Bush 1982–84 (dancing bluebells); <u>Inner London 1983</u>.

B. In and out the dusting bluebells,
    In and out the dusting bluebells,
    In and out the dusting bluebells,
    I am your master.

    Jimmy-jammy, Jimmy-jammy, on your shoulder,
    Jimmy-jammy, Jimmy-jammy, on your shoulder,
    Jimmy-jammy, Jimmy-jammy, on your shoulder,
    I am your master.

Barnsbury, Cubitt Town 1983.

"You're all in a circle, linking hands up high. The person goes around underneath the arches. When we go, 'pitter-patter, pitter-patter' they go and stand behind someone and pat on their shoulders. When we've finished 'master' they join the end of the line. It goes on till only two or three people are left." girl, 11, Finsbury 1983.

Printed versions Beckwith (see below); Brady, pp. 120–121; Daiken, *CGTY*, p. 154; Douglas (see below); Gomme (see below); Hubbard, mentioned, 263; Kellett, In and out those shaking bluebells, pp. 62–63 (and see below); McMorland, p. 82; Montgomeries, *HBSNR*, p. 67; Opies, *SG*, p. 366; Ritchie, *GC*, p. 164; Rutherford, p. 33; Todd, 10; Wilson and Gallagher, No. 14.

Early notings Round and Round the Village, Gomme, 1898, pp. 122–143. Cf. Outside Bluebell, thro' de window,/Outside Bluebell, thro' de window,/Outside, Bluebell, thro' de window,/tra la la la la.//Den you take a little girl an' pat her on de shoulder … Beckwith, *JFL*, 1928, pp. 69–70. Running in and out the Bluebells, ring game, mentioned, Douglas, 1916, p. 43, 1931, p. 23. In and out those shaking bluebells, Kellett, 1920s, pp. 62–63.

Recordings BBC 13869 (78) (1949, Edinburgh); BBC 16074 (78) (1951, Sidbury, Devon); BBC 19926 (78) (1953, Edinburgh); BBC 19003 (78) (1953, Kentish Town); Wilson and Gallagher, *Children's Singing Games*; Webb, *Children's Singing Games*.

This singing game is probably related to "In and out the windows" and similar songs:

Printed versions Beckwith (see below); Bett (see below); Brady, p. 115; Chase, *AFTS*, We're marchin' 'round the levee, pp. 191–193; Dennison, mentioned, 293; Douglas (see below); Fowke, p. 22; Gaskell (see below); Gomme (see below); Kings (see below); Newell (see below); Parry-Jones, pp. 123–124; Rohrbough (see below); Sutton-Smith, p. 23; Swift, mentioned, 146; Thornhill (see below); Uttley, Round and Round the Village, p. 58; Wilson and Gallagher, No. 11; Wood (see below).

Early notings Round and Round the Village, Gomme, 1898, pp. 122–143. Go Round and Round the Valley, Newell, 1903, pp. 128–129. Thornhill, 1911, p. 3. In and out the windows (repeat twice)/As you have done before./Stand and face your lover (repeat twice)/As you have done before. (etc.), Douglas, 1916, p. 74, 1931, p. 41. Gaskell, similar to Thornhill, c1913, p. 7. Kings 1, 1926, p. 33. Cf. Walking Round the Valley, Beckwith, *JFL*, 1928, pp. 67–68. Round and round the village, Bett, *TGC*, 1929, p. 7. Go in and out the window, Rohrbough, *HPPB*, 1940, p. 131. We're marching round the levee, Wood, *AMG*, 1940, pp. 98–100.

4.19 THE GOOD SHIP SAILS ON THE ALLEE-ALLEE-O

TRADITIONAL SINGING GAME:

A. The good ship sails on the Allee-allee-o,
The Allee-allee-o, the Allee-allee-o,
The good ship sails on the Allee-allee-o,
On the first day of September.

We all dip our heads in the deep blue sea,
The deep blue sea, the deep blue sea,
We all dip our heads in the deep blue sea,
On the last day of September.

> The captain said he would never, never leave,
> Never, never leave, never, never leave,
> The captain said he would never, never leave,
> On the last day of September.

West Norwood 1972; Walworth 1974.

B.
> The big ship sails on the Allee-allee-o,
> The Allee-allee-o, the Allee-allee-o
> The big ship sails on the Allee-allee-o,
> On the last day of September.
>
> The captain says it will never, never do,
> Never, never do, never, never do,
> The captain says it will never, never do,
> On the last day of September.
>
> The big ship sank in the Allee-allee-o,
> The Allee-allee-o, the Allee-allee-o,
> The big ship sank in the Allee-allee-o,
> On the last day of September.
> Shoot! Bang! Fire! (Crash! Bang! Woosh!)

Mile End 1964; Putney 1966; Borough 1983 (one verse only).

C. Additional verse:

> The big ship sails too slow, too slow,
> Too slow, too slow, too slow, too slow,
> The big ship sails too slow, too slow,
> On the last day of September.

Shepherds Bush 1983.

Printed versions Brady, p. 162; Chase, *SGPPG*, pp. 46–47; Daiken, *CGTY*, p. 153; Dennison, 293; Douglas (see below); Fowke, p. 37; Gaskell (see below); Gillington (see below); Gomme (see below); Hubbard, mentioned, 263; Kellett (see below); McMorland, pp. 70–71; Opies, *SG*, pp. 50–54; Ritchie, *SS*, pp. 27–28, *GC*, pp. 153–154; Rodger, ball game, p. 24; Rutherford, mentioned as an alternative name to "Round and round went the gallant ship", cf. Gomme, below, p. 32; Searle, 133; Shaw, 1969, p. 44; 1970, pp. 79–80; Sims, pp. 24–25; Sutton-Smith (see below); Swift, *The Illy Ally O*, 148; Wilson and Gallagher, Ily Aly O (or Ali Ali O), No. 19.

Early notings The big ship sails/Through the Eely Ily Oh,/On the nineteenth of December, Nelson, New Zealand, 1870. "In this game, one player placed a hand against a wall and all the other players joined hands in a line with him or her. While singing the rhyme, all the players passed through the arch until head and tail joined and then separated again", Sutton-Smith, p. 24. Sutton-Smith suggests a comparison with a winding game, Eller Tree (Gomme, 1894, p. 119). Cf. Round and round went the gallant, gallant ship,/And round and round went she;/Round and round went the gallant, gallant ship,/Till she sank to the bottom of the sea, the sea, the sea,/Till she sank to the bottom of the sea, Gomme, 1898, p. 143. Three times round goes the galley, galley ship,/And three times round goes she;/Three times round goes the galley, galley ship,/And she sank to the bottom of the sea, Gomme, 1898, pp. 422–424. The big ship sails thro' the Holly, Holly, O! Holly, Holly, O! Holly, Holly, O! /The big ship sails thro' the Holly, Holly, O!/On the last day of December! Gillington, *OHSG*, 1909, p. 24. The big ship sailed through the alley alley alley oh, Gaskell, c1913, p. 8. The big ship sails on the holly holly ho …, Douglas, 1916, p. 66, 1931, p. 36. The big ship sails through/The Illi alli O, Kellett, 1920s, pp. 2–3.

The Opies suggest connections with the game "Barley Bridge" as recorded by Halliwell in 1849 (*PRNT*, p. 118), and to a number of games in Gomme (1894, pp. 231–238, 1898, p. 230). These appear to be either winding games or games played more like "Oranges and Lemons". For a discussion of possible origins of the game, see Opies (*SG*, 1985, pp. 51–54).

Recordings BBC 16075 (78) (1951, Sidbury, Devon); Webb, *Children's Singing Games*; Wilson and Gallagher, *Children's Singing Games*.

4.20 ORANGES AND LEMONS

TRADITIONAL SINGING GAME:

Oranges and lemons,
Said the bells of St. Clements.

I owe you five thousand,
Said the bells of St. Martins.

When will you pay me?
Said the bells of Old Bailey.

When I am rich,
Said the bells of Shoreditch.

I do not know,
Said the bells of Big Bow.

Here comes a chopper to chop off your head,
Here's a candle to light you to bed.
Chip, chop, the last man's head.

Mile End 1966; Brixton 1982; Blackheath, Cubitt Town, Dalston, Finsbury, <u>Mile End 1983</u>.

"What we do is, two people hold their hands and make an arch. They run underneath our hands and when they say, 'Here comes a chopper to chop off your head,' they bring their arms down. Whoever's in between their arms gets rocked, fast or slow. There's two people on the arch, one's orange and one's lemon. The people going under the arch don't know that. After they've done fast or slow, the two persons say, 'Oranges or lemons?' The person that has had his head chopped off says, 'orange' or 'lemon'. At the end when we've got a few people on oranges or lemons, they have a tug of war." boy, 10, Mile End 1983.

Variations:

Chip-chop, chip-chop
The last one in.

Brixton 1982.

(at end)
Off to prison you must go,
You must go, you must go,
Off to prison you must go,
My fair lady.

Brixton 1983.

Children of ten and eleven may have forgotten a singing game they played when they were younger, or perhaps it is not played so much by younger schoolchildren. Certainly the words change and some verses are forgotten. Almost everywhere I noticed that "five farthings" (coins that of course are not known to today's children), had become "five thousand". The bells of Shoreditch and Bow may disappear. Old Bailey may become Shorebailey or Old Lady; the bell of Bow may be St. Bow or Big Bow as in the example above; St. Martin may be St. Marvin, Shoreditch may become St. Ditch. Older versions include extra verses referring to a number of additional churches (cf. Halliwell, see below) but these disappeared from playgrounds generations ago.

Printed versions Briggs, pp. 138–139; Daiken, *CGTY*, p. 93; Dennison, mentioned, 295; Douglas (see below); Fowke, p. 31; Gillington (see below); Gomme (see below); Gullen, begins "Gay go up and gay go down," p. 47; Halliwell (see below); Hubbard, mentioned, 263; Lang (see below); MacBain (see below); Northall (see below); Opies, *ODNR*, pp. 337–339; *SG*, pp. 54–60; Parry-Jones, p. 90; Plunket (see below); Sutton-Smith, p. 21; Uttley, mentioned, p. 68; Webb, 639; Wilson and Gallagher, No. 12.

Early notings *Tommy Thumb's Pretty Song Book*, II, 1744, Two Sticks and Apple, Ring ye Bells at Whitechapple, pp. 50–51 (cited by the Opies, *SG*, 1985, p. 55). Halliwell, *NRE*, 1842, pp. 111–112 (13 verses), 1843, pp. 135–136 (15 verses), c1870, pp. 61–62 (16 verses). The third edition in 1844 was the first version to contain the "head-chopping" final verse, and it was not until 1853 that Halliwell included a description of the game. The versions in Halliwell reveal that "Oranges and lemons" was not originally the first verse, but was preceded by four others, beginning "Gay go up, and gay go down,/To ring the bells of London town." Plunket, 1886, pp. 44–45; Northall, 1892, p. 399; Lang, 1897, pp. 172–174; Gomme, 1898, pp. 25–35; Gillington, *ODSG*, 1913, pp. 12–13; Douglas, 1916, p. 99, 1931, p. 56; MacBain, 1933, p. 107.

Recordings Wales, *Folk Songs and Ballads of Sussex*; Wilson and Gallagher, *Children's Singing Games*.

4.21 ARE YOU READY FOR A FIGHT?

TRADITIONAL GAME with chant:

Alternately chanted by two sides:

Are you ready for a fight?
We are the English.

> Yes, we're ready for a fight.
> We are the Germans.

We want (_____) on our side,
We are the English.

> You can have him if you try,
> We are the Germans.

<u>West Norwood 1970</u>; Walworth 1974; Brixton, Streatham 1982; Borough, Brockley, Cubitt Town, Finsbury, Shepherds Bush, Stoke Newington 1983.

Variations:

> Who d'you want upon your side?
> We are the English.
>> We want (_____) on our side.
>> We are Americans.

Brixton.

We'll have (_____) for a fight,
We are the English.
> We'll have (_____) for a fight,
> We are the Germans.

Come on (_____).
> Come on (_____).

Walworth.

We are getting stronger.
We are ready for a fight.
> We are getting weaker,
> We are ready for a fight.

We'll have (_____) for a fight.
> We'll have (_____) for a fight.

Then a tug of war between the two sides.

Cubitt Town.

After tug of war between the two sides:

> They've not got him for a fight.

Borough.

English and Spanish

Shepherds Bush.

English and French

Stoke Newington.

"There's supposed to be six girls on each side and each girl is from each country (English or French). They say, 'Are you ready for a fight?' They choose each other and they have to pull each other to their side." girl, Stoke Newington 1983.

"There's two teams. One of the teams pick a country like Spain, and the other side pick a country like England. The first team goes up to the English and says, 'Are you ready for a fight?' Then the English go to the Spanish people and say, 'Yes, we're ready for a fight.' The Spanish say, 'We take (_____) for a fight.' The English go up to the Spanish and say, 'We take (_____).' The Spanish take hands with the English and try to pull them over a line, like tug of war. Whoever wins the most people wins." boy, Shepherds Bush 1983.

Printed versions Brady, pp. 112–115; Chase, *SGPPG*, pp. 26–29; Daiken, *CGTY*, pp. 17, 19; Dennison, 294; Douglas (see below); Elder, "We are the Romans", p. 111; Fowke, p. 34; Gaskell (see below); Gillington (see below); Gomme (see below); Gullen, pp. 26–28; Harrop, Friend, and Gadsby, Have you any bread and wine, p. 50; Kellett (see below); Kidson (see below); Kings (see below); Newell (see below); Opies, *SG*, pp. 280–285 (and see below); Ritchie, *GC*, pp. 148–150; Shaw, 1970, p. 79; cf. Sutton-Smith, French and English, p. 144, "a capturing game" (no rhyme mentioned); Swift, mentioned, 149.

Early notings The Opies (*SG*, 1985, pp. 283–284) refer to possibilities that the words may have religious significance: Romans and English referring to Roman Catholics and Protestants, and the bread and wine referring to the Eucharist. They add that the game is very old, and that it might refer to many different battles, perhaps dating back at least to the time when William III and James II were fighting each other in Ireland in 1690. Have you any bread and wine?/We are the English!/Have you any bread and wine?/We are the English soldiers!//No, we have no bread and wine,/We are the Romans!/No, we have no bread and wine,/We are the Roman soldiers! After another seven verses it finishes: Are you ready for a fight? &c.//Yes, we're ready for a fight, &c. "We are the Rovers"; one of eighteen variants, Gomme, 1898, pp. 348–349. Have you any bread and wine,/*My fairy and my fory?*/Have you any bread and wine,/*Within the golden story?* …, first of several versions, Newell, 1903, p. 248. English soldiers (Boers and English), Gillington, *OIWSG*, 1909, p. 19; Roman Soldiers, Gillington, *OSSG*, p. 15. Gaskell, c1913, p. 5. The Gallant Sailors, in which the contest is between teams of "sailors" and "soldiers", Gillington, *ODSG*, 1913, p. 6. Douglas names several possibly similar games: "We are Romans", two parties of girls, 1916, p. 44, 1931, p. 23; "We are British Soldiers", 1916, p. 45, 1931, p. 24, and "Will You Give Us Bread and Wine", 1916, p. 101, 1931, p. 57. Kidson, 1916, p. 13. Here we're on the battle field/…/We are the English soldiers, Kellett, 1920s, pp. 10–11. Kings 1, 1926, similar to Gomme, pp. 18–19.

Recordings BBC 16075 (78) (1951, Sidbury, Devon); Webb, *Children's Singing Games*, MacColl and Seeger, *The Elliotts of Birtley*.

4.22 PLEASE MOTHER, MAY I GO OUT TO PLAY? (GRANDMOTHER GRAY)

TRADITIONAL GAME with chanting:

A. One child (Mother) and three others as children.
Ch. Please Mother, may I go out to play?
M. No.
Ch. Please Mother, may I go out to play?
M. No.
Ch. Please Mother, may I go out to play?
M. Yes, shoo all the ducks away.

(Children go and return.)

	M.	Children, where have you been?
	Ch.	To see the queen.
	M.	What did she give you?
	Ch.	A loaf of bread as big as my head,
		A lump of cheese as big as my knees,
		A lump of jelly as big as my belly,
		And a Chinese sixpence.
	M.	Where's mine?
	Ch.	Up in the sky.
	M.	So how do I get there?
	Ch.	A broken chair.
	M.	In case I fall.
	Ch.	I don't care.

(Mother chases children to other wall.)

Brockley 1983.

B.	Ch.	Please Nanny Granny may we go out to play?
		We won't go near the duckpond to frighten the ducks away.
	NG.	No.

Children ask and are refused again.

The third time they beg on their knees and Nanny Granny agrees.

Then basically as above.

Deptford 1983.

C.	(fragment)	
	Ch.	Grandmother Gray, may I go out to play?
	GG.	Yes.
		Come in.
	Ch.	We can't, the geese are in the way.

Mile End 1967.

Printed versions Beckwith (see below); Brady, p. 149; Daiken, *OGS*, p. 28; Douglas (see below); Gaskell (see below); Gillington (see below); Gomme (see below); Holbrook, p. 111; Kellett (?early noting), p. 130; Kings (see below); Newell (see below); Opies, *CGSP*, pp. 307–310; cf. Robertson, Children, Children, p. 28; Rosen and Steele, [pp. 13–14]; Shaw, 1970, p. 72; Sutton-Smith, Old Mother Gray, p. 37; cf. Turner, "Mother, may I go in for a swim?", p. 58; Wood (see below).

Early notings Mother, may I go out to play?/No, my child, it's such a wet day./Look how the sun shines, mother./Well, make three round curtseys and be off away.//[Child goes, returns, knocks at door. Mother says, "Come in."] What have you been doing all this time? /Brushing Jenny's hair and combing Jenny's hair./What did her mother give you for your trouble?/A silver penny./Where's my share of it?/Cat ran away with it. … (London), Gomme, 1894, pp. 390–391. "Oh, mother, mother, may I go out to play?"/"No, no, no, it's a very cold day."/"Yes, yes, yes, it's a very warm day,/So take three steps, and away, away, away."/"Where's your manners?"/"I haven't any". The indignant mother now pursues the disobedient children. A game of "little girls in Philadelphia", Newell, 1903, p. 172. Gaskell, c1913 p. 3; Gillington, *ODSG*, 1913, pp. 10–11; Douglas, 1916, pp. 101–102, 1931, p. 58. Grandmother Gray, Kings 1, 1926, p. 31. Cf. Children, children, Beckwith, *JFL*, 1928, p. 19. Grandmother, grandmother grey, Kings 2, 1930, p. 17. Cf. Mother may I go out to swim? Wood, *AMG*, 1940, p. 7.

This game can be found intertwined with the games of "Hewley Puley" (Halliwell, *NRNTE*, c1870, p. 223; Gomme, 1894, p. 207); with "Dump" (Halliwell, *PRNT*, 1849, pp. 128–129; Gomme, 1894, pp. 117–119); with "Old Witch" (Gomme, 1898, pp. 391–396; Newell, 1903, pp. 259–263); with "Hawk and Chickens" (Newell, 1903, pp. 155–158); and with "Old Dame" (Holbrook, p. 112).

4.23 SKIP TO MY LOU

SINGING GAME:

Lou, Lou, skip to my Lou,
Lou, Lou, skip to my Lou,
Lou, Lou, skip to my Lou,
Skip to my Lou, my darling.

I've lost a partner, what shall I do? etc.

Lou, Lou, skip to my Lou, etc.

I'll get another one prettier (better) than you, etc.

Lou, Lou, skip to my Lou, etc.

West Norwood 1972; <u>Walworth 1979</u>; Borough, Mile End 1983.

This is an American play party singing game imported into the London playgrounds in the 1960s and 1970s.

Printed versions Abrahams, p. 179: "Usually collected as a singing or play-party game"; Botkin (see below); Chase, *AFTS*, pp. 193–199; Opies, *SG*, pp. 319–320; Rohrbough (see below); Sims (with many more verses), pp. 44–45.

Early notings Botkin, *APPS*, 1937, pp. 75–80; Rohrbough, *HPPB*, 1940, p. 16.

4.24 BROWN GIRL IN THE RING

Brown girl in the ring,
    Tralalalala
There's a brown girl in the ring,
    Tralalalala

Brown girl in the ring,
 Tralalalala
She looks like a sugar in a plum.

Show us your motion,
 Tralalalala
Show us your motion,
 Tralalalala
Show us your motion,
 Tralalalala
She looks like a sugar in a plum.

Dance and get your partner,
 Tralalalala, etc.

Hug and kiss your partner,
 Tralalalala, etc.

<u>Earlsfield 1982</u>; Brixton, Greenwich, Streatham <u>1982</u> (only one or two verses); Cubitt Town, Dalston, Mile End, Shepherds Bush 1983 (only one or two verses).

This is a singing game from Jamaica. Given that a version of this rhyme was in use in London in the 1920s, it may have persisted since that time, or it may have been introduced into schools more recently by Caribbean cultural representatives and/or children of Jamaican origin. However, its popularity at the time of the survey may have been enhanced by the popular song "Brown Girl in the Ring" performed by Boney M on the LP *Nightflight to Venus* (1978).

Printed versions Beckwith (see below); Elder, p. 59; Fowke (echoes in both "Round the mountain", p. 17, and "Here stands a red bird", p. 20, especially the tune, here); Robertson, pp. 6–7.

Early notings There's a black boy in the ring/Tra-a-la-a-la/There's a black boy in the ring/Tra-a-la-a-la/He likes sugar and I like jam.//There's a black boy in the ring/Tra-a-la-a-la /There's a black boy in the ring,/Tra-a-la-a-la/Wheel and take you[r] partner (Grabs a partner (girl) from circle)/

Jump Shenadoah./Wheel and take your partner/Jump Shenadoah. (Jumps over chalk line), London, circulating before 1922, from memory, Mrs Gerrard (correspondent, Cheshunt). Dere's a brown gal in de ring, tra la la la la/…/Fo' she like sugar an' I like plum.//Den you wheel an' take yo' pardner/ … Beckwith, *JFL*, 1928, p. 74; the tune given here is similar to that performed by Boney M. A second version also contains a verse beginning: Then show you me your motion ("a kind of cake-walk"), Beckwith, *JFL*, 1928, pp. 74–75.

4.25 I WENT TO CALIFORNIA

SINGING GAME (also skipping):

A. I went to California, far, far away,
I met a senorita with flowers in her hair.
O shake it, shake it, shake it,
Shake it if you can,
And if you cannot shake it,
Do the best you can,
Turn around, round, round,
Stop.

West Norwood 1970, 1972.

B. I saw a signorina going to the fair,
I saw a signorina with flowers in her hair.
Hey shake it, shake it, shake it,
Shake it, turn around,
Shake it, shake it, shake it,
Turn around and turn around.

Finsbury 1983.

C. I was going through the traffic lights,
Going to the fair,
When I met a Cinderella,

> With a flower in her hair.
> O twist it, twist it, twist it,
> Twist it all you can,
> Twist it like a milk shake,
> Shaking in the can.
> O rumble to the bottom,
> Rumble to the top,
> Turn around, and turn around,
> Until it's time to stop.

Dalston, Shepherds Bush 1983.

"Everyone has to go round holding hands. Someone is in the middle. They have to skip round and sing, and then they have to stop. The person in the middle has to wiggle her thighs up and down. When they say, 'Turn around' they turn around 'until it's time to stop'. They (the one in middle) close their eyes, they turn around and land on someone. It's their turn." girl, 10, Dalston 1983.

"There's someone in the middle of the ring. When you sing, 'We're going to the fair,' then everyone goes around her. Then she shakes her hips again, and then she rumbles (twist and go up and down). When it comes to 'turn around' she turns round with her hand out pointing. When she stops, the person she's pointing to is 'senorita'." girl, 10, Shepherds Bush 1983.

Printed versions Boyes, 38; Fowke, We're going to Chicago, p. 26; Kellett, As I was going to Honkey Tonkey,/The Honkey Tonkey Fair (?early noting), p. 55; Knapps, I went to old Kentucky, p. 149; Nelson, Oh, we're going to the circus, an "inner city game" from Puerto Rico, p. 34; Opies (see below); Rutherford, I went to Kentucky, singing game, p. 39, I'm going to Kentucky, skipping rhyme, p. 57; Wilson, 981, and letter in reply to this article from Anna Levison, aged 12, *New Statesman*, 4.1.1980, giving her version from Harrow: I went to see Kentucky,/To see a summer fair,/I saw a senorita,/With flowers in her hair. My own response to the Wilson article, dated 22.12.1979, was evidently not published.

Early notings The Opies (*SG*, 1985, p. 423) report that they were unable to trace the source of this rhyme but mention that the use of the word "shimmy" in some versions may place it in the 1920s.

Recording Webb, *Children's Singing Games*.

4.26 HERE COMES MRS. MACARONI

CIRCULAR SINGING GAME:

Here comes Mrs. Macaroni,
Riding on a big fat pony,
Here she comes in all her glory, (sometimes "with all her money",)
Mrs. Macaroni.

Om, pom, Susianna,
Om, pom, Susianna,
Om, pom, Susianna,
Mrs. Macaroni.

West Norwood 1973; Clapham 1974; Walworth 1979; Brixton 1982; Borough, Deptford, Dulwich 1983.

Tune "Dusty bluebells".

"Someone rides around in the circle. She's Mrs. Macaroni. They pick somebody else and dance around with them. That's when they sing, 'Om pom Susianna'. The person who was picked is now Mrs. Macaroni." Cubitt Town 1983.

Printed versions Abrahams, p. 61; Briggs, p. 162; Fowke, ball bouncing rhyme, p. 76; cf. Kellett, Old King Solomon and his glory/Riding on his lily white pony, skipping game (?early noting), p. 39; McMorland, p. 68; Nicholson (see below); Opies (see below); Ritchie, *SS*, p. 37, *GC*, pp. 123–124; Rutherford, Old King Solomon, p. 68.

Early notings The Opies (*SG*, 1985, p. 338) suggest that perhaps "the game-song evolved from 'Come, my Lads'," collected by Baring-Gould "probably in 1889": Solomon in all his glory,/Told us quite another story,/In our cups to sing and glory./When we're met together (cf. Kellett, above). Mrs Brown, clapping rhyme, Nicholson, 1897, p. 188.

Recordings BBC 19926 (78) (1953, Edinburgh); Webb, *Children's Singing Games.*

4.27 THERE WERE TEN IN A BED

> There were ten in a bed,
> And the little one said,
> "Roll over, roll over."
> So they all rolled over,
> And one fell out,
> And gave a shout.
>
>> "Please remember to tie a knot in your pyjamas,
>> Single beds are only made for one, two, three, four,"
>
> There were nine in a bed,
> And the little one said,

and so on until there are "none in the bed".

Dalston, Kentish Town, Shepherds Bush 1983.

The rhyme and tune are commonly found in children's songbooks. The reference to pyjamas was a recent addition at the time the survey was undertaken.

> "The children sit on each others' laps in one line. Five is a more convenient number to start with. We're sitting on each other and the one underneath gets all squashed. The first person to roll over sits on the other end (of the bench) and that person becomes the last person when it starts all over again." girl, 10, Shepherds Bush 1983.

Printed versions Fowke, p. 132; Harrop, Blakeley, and Gadsby, p. 18; Opies, *LLS*, mentioned, p. 31; Ritchie, *SS*, p. 109; Roud, *DM1*, 31; Sims, pp. 46–47; Whyton, p. 48.

4.28 INTO THE CENTRE AND NOD YOUR HEAD

A. Into the centre and nod your head,
   Parlee voo,
Into the centre and nod your head,
   Parlee voo.
Into the centre and round you go,
Round and round and round you go,
   Inky pinky parlee voo-oo-oo.

Into the centre and shake your hands,
   Parlee voo, etc.
Into the centre and shake your hands,
Shake your hands, shake your hands
   Inky pinky parlee voo-oo-oo.

Into the centre and round again,
   Parlee voo, etc.
Into the centre and round again,
Round and round and round again,
   Inky pinky parlee voo-oo-oo.

Mile End 1967.

B. Mademosel from Armenteers,
   Parlee voo,
Hasn't been kissed for forty years,
   Parlee voo.
The King of Wales was put in jail
For riding a horse without any tail,
   Inky pinky parlee voo.

Marylebone 1967.

See also **8.D.18**.

Many versions of this song were sung by troops in both World Wars and after. The original, "Mademoiselle from Armentières", is attributed variously to Edward Rowland and Glitz Rice, Harry Carlton and Joe Tunbridge, Harry Wincott, and Alfred Charles Montin.

Printed versions Opies, *LLS*, p. 92; Ritchie, *SS*, p. 26; Shaw, 1970, p. 60.

4.29 WHAT CAN YOU DO, PUNCHINELLO?

> What can you do, Punchinello, little fellow?
> What can you do, Punchinello, little man?
> I can do this, Punchinello, little fellow,
> I can do this, Punchinello, little man.
> We can do it too, Punchinello, little fellow,
> We can do it too, Punchinello, little man.

Borough 1983.

Printed versions Fowke, p. 14; Fulton and Smith, Look who's here, Punchinella, p. 26; Hopkin, p. 26; Kenney, p. 62; McMorland, p. 52; the Opies (*SG*, pp. 412–413) believe the rhyme was purpose-written and is not part of oral tradition; Ritchie, *GC*, p. 167; Sutton-Smith (see below).

Early noting Sutton-Smith (p. 30) says the rhyme was introduced into New Zealand schools in the 1940s by "physical education specialists".

Recordings BBC 19003 (78) (1953, Kentish Town); BBC 19926 (78) (1953, Edinburgh).

4.30 I'M A LITTLE DUTCH GIRL

> A. I'm a little Dutch girl, Dutch girl, Dutch girl,
>   I'm a little Dutch girl, two, four, six.

I'm a little Dutch boy, Dutch boy, Dutch boy,
I'm a little Dutch boy, two, four, six.

Will you marry me? etc.

I cannot marry you, etc.

Why can't you marry me? etc.

'Cos you stole my silver shoes, etc.

Here are your silver shoes, etc.

Now will you marry me? etc.

I cannot marry you, etc.

Why can't you marry me? etc.

'Cos you stole my silver cloak, etc.

Here is your silver cloak, etc.

Now will you marry me? etc.

I cannot marry you, etc.

Why can't you marry me? etc.

'Cos you stole my wedding ring, etc.

Here is your wedding ring, etc.

Now will you marry me? etc.

Now we're getting married, etc.

Now we're getting old, etc.

Mile End 1968, 1983.

B. I'm a little Dutch girl, Dutch girl, Dutch girl,
I'm a little Dutch girl, far across the sea.

I'm a little Dutch boy, Dutch boy, Dutch boy,
I'm a little Dutch boy, far across the sea.

I've a frilly apron, etc.

I've got baggy trousers, etc.

Go away I hate you, etc.

Why do you hate me? etc.

'Cos you stole my ring, etc.

Here is back your ring, etc.

Go away I hate you, etc.

Why do you hate me? etc.

'Cos you stole my bracelet, etc.

Here's back your bracelet, etc.

Now we're getting older, etc.

Now we are dying, etc.

Now we are dead, etc.

Now we are angels, etc.

Walworth 1979, 1981; Brockley, Dalston 1983; <u>Barnsbury 1982–84.</u>

Other verses may include ones for "wedding ring", "silver shoes", "silver cloak", "necklace", "teddy bear", "pearls", etc.

This singing game for partners seems to have affinities with the traditional courtship games of the last century but I have been unable to trace an early version so far. Two girls usually face each other, advancing and retreating. In the Mile End version the girl and "boy" alternately skipped or did a dance step around the partner while doing the particular mimes. Mimes of "showing off", pushing away, pointing to fingers etc. are pretty simple and obvious ones.

See also **5.4**.

Printed versions Fowke, pp. 40–41; Opies, *SG*, pp. 307–308; Rutherford, p. 35; Sluckin, p. 29; Smith, *BBHG*, pp. 43–44; Turner, p. 59; Wade 2, 35.

Recording Webb, *Children's Singing Games.*

4.31 HEEL AND TOE

> Heel and toe,
> Heel and toe,
> Gallop to the side you go.

Shepherds Bush 1983.

"You get partners and you make a line (about ten of you). You sing the rhyme and you gallop to the side. You say the rhyme and you go: Clap! Clap! Clap! and Smack! Smack! Smack! on your knees, on your thighs, and then on your partner's hands. Then you go 'Heel and toe' and gallop to the side again, and keep going." girl, Shepherds Bush 1983.

4.32 I'M A LOCKED-UP CHICKEN

> A. I'm a locked-up chicken, I'm a locked-up hen
> I've been locked up since I don't know when.
> So she walks with a wiggle and a wriggle and a waddle,
> Doing the Tennessee (telephone) ping pang pong.
>
> The cowboys come from the U.S.A.
> The Indians go from the other way
> So she walks, etc.
>
> The girls are watching B.B.C.
> The boys are watching I.T.V.
> So she walks, etc.

> The girls are wearing red, white and blue,
> The boys are saying, "I love you"
> > So she walks, etc.

Borough 1983.

B. There's a knock-kneed (bow-legged) chicken and a back-boned hen,
> Never been so happy as I don't know when,
> > When she walks with a wiggle and a wiggle and a woggle,
> > Doing the Tennessee bing-bang-bong.
>
> Put your knees together and your toes apart,
> Bend your elbows and get ready to start,
> > When she walks, etc.
>
> Won't you be my honey, won't you be my bride,
> Walk together side by side,
> > When she walks with a wiggle and a wiggle and a woggle,
> > Doing the Tennessee bing – bang – bong – King Kong.

Stepney 1967.

C. I'm a bald-headed chicken with a feather in my hair,
> I don't know this and I don't much care,
> > I'm going to walk with a wiggle and a wriggle and a waddle,
> > Doing the taxi ping, pang, pong.
>
> You're the Queen and I'm the King,
> You're the one who stole my ring,
> > I'm going to walk, etc.
>
> The grass is green and the sky is blue,
> The sun is yellow and so are you,
> > I'm going to walk, etc.
>
> The Indians come from far away,
> The cowboys come from the U.S.A.,
> > I'm going to walk, etc.

Dalston 1983.

Other beginnings:

> D. I'm a stuffed-up chicken and a knock-kneed hen,
> My mother goes to heaven and I don't know when …

Walworth 1980.

> E. I'm a one-legged chicken and I got no sense,
> I haven't been in heaven since I dunno when …

Greenwich 1982.

> F. I'm a ballet chicken and I got no sense,
> I wanna get married but I don't know when …

Brixton 1982.

> G. I'm a bald-headed chicken with a feather in my head,
> I don't know where to go to bed …

Barnsbury 1983.

The movements are different in each school and vary between class groups in the same school, even when the words are the same. Bird movements are usual. "Knock-kneed", "bow-legged", "ballet", "stuffed-up", all suggest the kind of actions, but sometimes the actions are copied from another version, though the words have changed, probably through mishearing, and there is not always a match between words and movement. Creative girls alter the words sometimes to match their particular movements.

> "You stand up and you bounce down and hold your hands as if you're praying. When it comes to 'The cowboys come from the U.S.A.' you get three fingers (saluting). When it comes to 'The Indians' you go far away and swing your arms round. On 'B.B.C.'

you push the switches down and for 'I.T.V.' turn a knob or something. When it goes, 'Wiggle, woggle' you walk, wiggling your bum." Borough 1983.

Derived from an action dance song, "The Tennessee Wig-Walk" (1953), words by Norman Gimpel and music by Larry Coleman.

Printed versions Abrahams, p. 68; Kellett, p. 127; Kelsey, *K1*, 44; Opies, *LLS*, p. 18, *SG*, p. 433; Webb, 638.

Recording Webb: *Children's Singing Games.*

4.33 ORANGE BALLS

CIRCULAR GAME (The children all chant while going round in a circle):

Orange balls, orange balls,
Here we go again,
Orange balls, orange balls,
Here we go again,
Orange balls, orange balls,
Here we go again.
The last one to sit down (hit the floor).

Children sit down in a hurry and the last one to sit down goes into the circle. Then they chant to the child in the circle:

(Boy's or girl's name) says he/she loves you, loves you, loves you,
(Boy's or girl's name) says he loves you,
And we shall say no more.

Children then tease the child in the middle who has to do the actions demanded (usually one or two actions) such as the following:

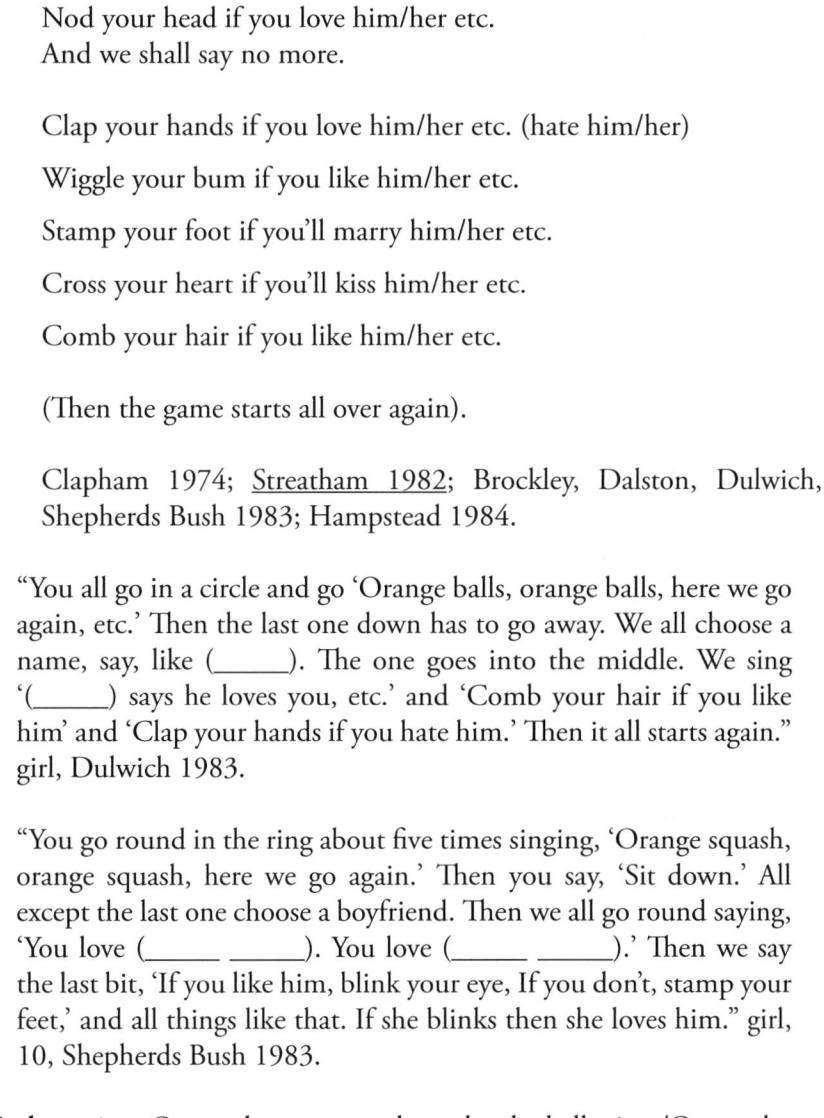

Nod your head if you love him/her etc.
And we shall say no more.

Clap your hands if you love him/her etc. (hate him/her)

Wiggle your bum if you like him/her etc.

Stamp your foot if you'll marry him/her etc.

Cross your heart if you'll kiss him/her etc.

Comb your hair if you like him/her etc.

(Then the game starts all over again).

Clapham 1974; <u>Streatham 1982</u>; Brockley, Dalston, Dulwich, Shepherds Bush 1983; Hampstead 1984.

"You all go in a circle and go 'Orange balls, orange balls, here we go again, etc.' Then the last one down has to go away. We all choose a name, say, like (____). The one goes into the middle. We sing '(____) says he loves you, etc.' and 'Comb your hair if you like him' and 'Clap your hands if you hate him.' Then it all starts again." girl, Dulwich 1983.

"You go round in the ring about five times singing, 'Orange squash, orange squash, here we go again.' Then you say, 'Sit down.' All except the last one choose a boyfriend. Then we all go round saying, 'You love (____ ____). You love (____ ____).' Then we say the last bit, 'If you like him, blink your eye, If you don't, stamp your feet,' and all things like that. If she blinks then she loves him." girl, 10, Shepherds Bush 1983.

Early noting Orange boys, orange boys, let the bells ring,/Orange boys, orange boys, God save the King./*Teddy Jones* says he loves her,/All the boys are fighting for her,/Let the boys say what they will/But *Teddy Jones* loves her still … Gilchrist MSS, c1920, quoted by the Opies (*SG*, 1985, p. 235). The Opies say this game should be compared with "All the boys in our town", see **6.A.54**.

4.34 SHE WEARS RED FEATHERS

> She wears red feathers and a hula-hula skirt,
> She wears red feathers and a hula-hula skirt,
> She lives on fresh coconuts and fish from the sea,
> With a rose in her hair,
> And a gleam in her eye,
> And a heart set free for me,
> Hollay!
>
> Mile End 1968.

From a popular song, words and music by Bob Merrill, recorded by Guy Mitchell, which reached No. 19 in the pop charts in 1953. The chorus went: "She wears red feathers and a huly-huly skirt./She wears red feathers and a huly-huly skirt./She lives on just cokey-nuts and fish from the sea,/A rose in her hair, a gleam in her eyes,/And love in her heart for me."

Printed version Opies, *SG*, pp. 425–426.

4.35 WE ARE THE DEPTFORD GIRLS

> ACTION AND CLAPPING RHYME:
>
> We are the Deptford girls;
> We wear our hair in curls;
> We wear our fathers' shirts
> As mini skirts;
> We have a smoke or drink,
> That's what the teachers think.
> And when we come to boys,
> We treat them just like toys,
> La la la la la la
> La la la la la la.
>
> Palmers Green 1967; Brockley, Dalston, <u>Deptford 1983</u>.

This is part of a long tradition of school or neighbourhood boasting rhymes going back at least to the start of the twentieth century.

Tune The Knapps report that sixth grade girls sang a similar rhyme to the tune of "Ta-Ra-Ra-Boom-De-Re" (p. 180).

Printed versions Knapps, We are the tomboy girls, p. 180; Opies, *LLS*, p. 355, *SG*, p. 478; Ritchie, *SS*, We are the Leith Walk Boys, p. 109; Shaw, 1969, We are the Huyton lads, p. 10.

Recording Webb, *Children's Singing Games.*

4.36 WHEN GRANDMAMA MET GRANDPAPA

SINGING GAME, with dancing:

When grandmama met grandpapa
They danced the milulet [sic].
The milulet was far too slow,
So they danced to rock and roll.
Heel, toe, heel, toe, kick that leg,
Heel, toe, heel, toe, kick that leg,
Heel, toe, heel, toe, kick that leg.
That's the way to do it.
Sit down, turn around, drop down dead,
Sit down, turn around, drop down dead,
Sit down, turn around, drop down dead.
That's the way you do it.
Dededededededede,
Dededededededede,
Dededededededede,
Olé.

Walworth 1974; Walworth 1980.

Tune The first three lines are danced in slow and stately style to the tune of the traditional German folksong "O Tannenbaum". Then it speeds up, actions suiting the words.

Printed version Opies, *SG*, pp. 436–437.

4.37 IN A COTTAGE IN A WOOD

ACTION GAME:

In a cottage in a wood
A little old man at the window stood.
Saw a rabbit running by,
Knocking at the door.
"Help me, help me, help me," he said
"Before the hunters shoot me dead."
Come little rabbit, come with me,
Happy we shall be.

Dalston 1983.

"We get our hands and make the shape of a house. We all put our two fingers up on our heads and we're the rabbits. For the hunters and their guns we get our fingers and shoot round as if we're shooting the rabbits. With our hand we stroke our other hand 'cause the old man is stroking the rabbit." girl, 10, Dalston 1983.

Printed version Harrop, Friend, and Gadsby, p. 24.

4.38 HERE COMES MRS. MOLLY

RING GAME, with actions and dancing:

Here comes Mrs. Molly around the ring,
Here comes Mrs. Molly around the ring,

Here comes Mrs. Molly around the ring,
She opens the door and she lets herself in.

She does a boom cha-cha, boom cha-cha round the ring,
She does a boom cha-cha, boom cha-cha round the ring,
She does a boom cha-cha, boom cha-cha round the ring,
She opens the door and she lets herself in.

To dance with her she choose her best friend,
To dance with her she choose her best friend,
To dance with her she choose her best friend,
She opens the door and she lets herself out.

Shepherds Bush 1983.

"Someone acts as Mrs. Molly. Children form a ring and Mrs. Molly goes around and lets herself into the ring. She starts wiggling her hips around and then she chooses her best friend and dances with her. Then they both go out. Her friend then acts as Mrs. Molly and it starts all over again." girl, Shepherds Bush 1983.

Early noting This game may perhaps be linked to "Knocked at the rapper": Here comes ,/He knocked at the rapper, and he pulled at the string,/ Pray, Mrs. _____, is _____ _____ within?/O no, she has gone into the town:/Pray take the arm-chair and sit yourself down. ... Gomme, 1894, pp. 312–313.

4.39 I'VE GOT A DAUGHTER

I've got a daughter,
Lives in Gibraltar,
I'd give her anything,
To keep her alive.
She's got a wooden leg,
Just like a wooden peg,
That's how the story go-o-oes.

>Oompah, oompah, stick it up your jumper,
>Ah, ah, ah, ah, ah.

>West Norwood 1970, 1972; Walworth 1979; <u>Borough</u>, Dulwich <u>1983</u>.

"You're in a circle with lots of children. A girl goes around the outside. You're all singing this song and when you go 'Ahahahah' she touches you on the back and then you're the girl from Gibraltar." girl, Dulwich 1983.

"When it goes 'Keep her alive', they clap their hands under their knees." girl, Borough 1983.

The Opies (*SG*, 1985, p. 424) suggest the song is derived from "My Girl's a 'Corker' or The Race Track Girl", 1895, words by William Jerome, music by John Queen. Cf. also "My Best Girl's a New Yorker", written by John "Honey" Stromberg in 1895. Parodies of the latter appear in Cray, 1970, pp. 126–127.

Printed versions Opies, *SG*, pp. 423–425; Ritchie, *GC*, p. 126; Rutherford, pp. 37–38; Smith, *BBHG*, p. 38.

Recording Webb, *Children's Singing Games.*

4.40 I'M A LONDON GIRL (I'M A TEXAS GIRL)

>A. I'm a London girl,
>I'm a London girl,
>I'm a London girl,
>'Cause I live in the land of London.
>
>>I can ride my bike, I can show my tattoo,
>>I can ride my bike, I can show my tattoo,
>>I can ride my bike, I can show my tattoo,
>>And I live in the land of London.

I can touch the boys, I can kick 'em in the shins,
  I can touch the boys, I can kick 'em in the shins,
  I can touch the boys, I can kick 'em in the shins,
  And I live in the land of London.

Walworth 1980.

B. I'm a Texas girl,
    I'm a Texas girl,
    I'm a Texas girl,
    And I come from the land of Texas.

   I can ride, I can shoot, I can swing a lassoo (do the hula hoop),
   I can ride, I can shoot, I can swing a lassoo,
   I can ride, I can shoot, I can swing a lassoo,
   And I come from the land of Texas.

   Stick your hands up and shoot, drop down dead,
   Stick your hands up and shoot, drop down dead,
   Stick your hands up and shoot, drop down dead,
   You come from the land of Texas.

Walworth 1980; <u>Deptford</u>, Dulwich, Mile End <u>1983</u>.

4.41 EVERYBODY GATHER ROUND

ACTION GAME:

Everybody gather round,
Everybody gather round,
Listen to the bumble sound,
Listen to the bumble sound,
Grab the first one in your reach,
Grab the first one in your reach,
Now we're going to shake the beat,
Yeah, Yeah, Yeah, do the clown,
Do the clown.

Take your baby by the hand,
Dig right in and do it.

Walworth 1974.

4.42 HEAD, SHOULDERS, KNEES AND TOES

Head, shoulders, knees and toes, knees and toes,
Head, shoulders, knees and toes, knees and toes,
Eyes and mouth and ears and nose,
Head, shoulders, knees and toes, knees and toes.

Brixton, Streatham 1982; Dalston, Deptford, Mile End, Shepherds Bush 1983.

Tune "There is a tavern in the town" (traditional).

The actions include touching the various features mentioned. In a version collected in 1967 in Palmers Green, the song is sung over and over again, but humming replaces the first mention of head, then of head and shoulders and so on, until it is all hummed. Then it is sung as at the beginning.

Printed versions Fowke, p. 46; Harrop, Friend, and Gadsby, p. 1.

4.43 THERE'S A TINY HOUSE

There's a tiny house (repeat)
By a tiny stream, (repeat)
There's a lovely lad (repeat)
Had a lovely dream, (repeat)
And the dream came true (repeat)
Quite unexpectedly

> In a gilly gilly ossan pepper casanella bogun
> By the sea ea ea ea ea.

She was out one day (repeat)
Where the tulips grow, (repeat)
Where a lovely lad (repeat)
Stopped to say hallo, (repeat)
And before she knew, (repeat)
He kissed her tenderly
    In a gilly gilly etc.

The happy pair were married
One Sunday afternoon,
They left the church and ran away
To spend their honeymoon.
    In a gilly gilly etc.

In a long summer night (repeat)
By the Mexico, (repeat)
Where a little bird (repeat)
Stopped to say hallo, (repeat)
(unfinished)

Mile End 1967; Walworth 1974.

Two lines, facing partners, mimed actions. With the nonsense chorus, cross over with partners, and skip back to place.

From the popular song "Gilly Gilly Ossenfeffer Katzenellen Bogen by the Sea", written by Al Hoffman and Dick Manning, with which Max Bygraves reached No. 7 in the pop charts in 1954 (HMV Records, B10734).

4.44 A SHIP SAILS FROM CHINA

ACTION GAME:

A.   A ship sails from China with a cargo of tea,
      All laden with flowers for you and for me,

> They gave me a fan, just imagine my bliss,
> When I found myself going like this, like this, like this.

Dalston 1983.

B. My ship sailed to China with a cargo of tea,
    All laden with presents for you and for me,
    They gave me a flag to wave like this,
    And I found myself going like this, like this, like this.

Mile End 1968.

"You sit on the floor and sway. When you sing about tea you pretend to drink tea and when you sing about a fan, you pretend to wave one." girl, Dalston 1983.

Printed version Harrop, Blakeley, and Gadsby, p. 7. From *An Australian Campfire Book*, published by the Girl Guides Association of Victoria, which suggests that children may have learned it at Guides meetings.

4.45 THERE WAS A GIRL FROM ITALY

ACTION RHYME:

There was a girl from Italy,
There was a girl from Spain,
There was a girl from over the seas,
And this is how she came:

>   Woosh-a-la-la
>   Woosh-a-la-la
>   Woosh-a-la-la
>   Woosh-a-la, Woosh-a-la
>   Woosh-a-la-la-la.

Marylebone 1967.

Printed version Abrahams, There came a girl from France, p. 190.

Recording BBC 19003 (78) (1953, Kentish Town).

4.46 I CAN DO THE CAN-CAN

ACTION RHYME:

I can do the can-can,
I can do the splits,
I can do the turn around
I can do the kicks (show my knicks).
The Queen does a curtsey,
The King does a bow,
The boys go Ts! Ts! (kissing sound with lips, or a whistle)
The girls go, "Wow!"

Mile End 1968; Hampstead 1971; Borough 1983.

"For, 'I can do the can-can', you just turn around and try to do the splits. For 'I can do the kicks', you kick your legs up high. You do the curtsey and the bow. You put your hands to your lips and blow a kiss. When the girls go 'Wow!' they jump up on the benches, lifting their skirts up." girl, 11, Borough 1983.

See also **6.A.52**, and some parts of **6.A.26**.

Printed versions Cumnock Academy, p. 14; Douglas (see below).

Early noting Douglas mentions a girls' rhyme, "I Can Do the Tango", 1916, p. 95, 1931, p. 54.

4.47 FAME

SINGING GAME, with dancing:

"You dance and when you sing, 'Fame' you jump up in the air; you turn around; do head over heels; walk on your hands; do the splits, and all that kind of thing." girl, 11, Borough 1983.

Popular in 1983, probably because of the television programme of the same name, imported from America, about a school where singing and dancing were learned. The opening credits had teenagers jumping and shouting "Fame!" as the first word of a song.

4.48 MATILDA

CIRCLE GAME:

Wash those dirty faces,
Matilda, Matilda,
Wash those dirty faces,
With (_____ _____).

Stoke Newington 1983.

"There's a whole circle. They all put their arms up and you sing the song. Then you choose yourself a partner, (a girl is in the middle):

Choose yourself a partner,
Matilda, Matilda,
Choose yourself a partner
For (_____ _____).

Then you jump. She goes in and joins in and starts singing. The person who started goes in and out the hands." girl, 11, Stoke Newington 1983.

4.49 KEEP YOUR SUNNY SIDE UP

A. Keep your sunny side up, up,
   And the other side too, too,
   See the boys saying, "We love you,"
   And see those girls saying, "How do you do?"
   So keep your sunny side up, up,
   And the other side too, too.
   See those soldiers marching along,
   See Cliff Richards singing a song,
   So keep your sunny side up, up,
   And the other side too, too,
   Don't be nannygoats,
   Show your petticoats,
   Keep your sunny side upside down,
   Boom! Boom!

Walworth 1979; Greenwich 1982; <u>Brockley</u>, Dalston <u>1983</u>.

B. Keep your sunny side up, up,
   And the other side blue, blue,
   All those soldiers marching along,
   All those angels singing a song,
   Get down upon your knees,
   Look like a Japanese,
   All those fellows in red, white and blue,
   All those girls say, "How do you do?"
   Come on bandy legs,
   Show those pretty legs,
   Keep your sunny side, keep your sunny side,
   Keep your sunny side up, and down.

Mile End 1967.

From the song "Keep your sunny side up" written for the film *Sunny side up* by Ray Henderson in 1929.

Printed versions Boyes, 36; Kellett, pp. 53–54; Kelsey, *K1*, 43; Opies, *SG*, pp. 429–430; Ritchie, *GC*, p. 8; Rutherford, p. 58; Webb, 640.

Recording Webb, *Children's Singing Games.*

4.50 I'M THE KING OF THE SWINGERS

> I'm the king of the swingers too,
> A jungle V.I.P.
> When I reach the top,
> Well I have to stop,
> And that's what's bothering me.
>
>> Oh scoobeedoo, scoobeedoo, scoobeedoo,
>> I want to be like you, scoobeedoo, scoobeedoo,
>> I want to walk like you,
>> Talk like you,
>> Oh scoobeedoo.

Walworth 1974.

From a song in the Walt Disney film *Jungle Book*, released in 1967. Although the words "scooby dooby doo" appear occasionally in the jazz-style original, the playground version of the chorus may also have been associated with the popular American cartoon character Scooby-Doo, created for Hanna-Barbera Productions by writers Joe Ruby and Ken Spears in 1969.

4.51 UNDERNEATH THE SPREADING CHESTNUT TREE

ACTION SONG:

> Underneath the spreading chestnut tree,
> Where I sat her on my knee,

All the little birds went Tweet! Tweet! Tweet!
Underneath the spreading chestnut tree.

Earlsfield 1982.

Cf. "The Chestnut Tree" written by Jimmy Kennedy, Tommie Connor and Hamilton Kennedy in 1938. Children's versions and other parodies of this action song echo the opening line of Longfellow's poem, "The Village Blacksmith" (1842).

Printed versions Harrop, Friend, and Gadsby, p. 23; Opies, *LLS*, mentioned, p. 37, a parody, p. 101.

4.52 CAT'S GOT THE MEASLES

ACTION RHYME:

A. Cat's got the measles,
   Dog's got the 'flu,
   Chicken's got the chicken pox
   And so have you.

Greenwich 1982.

B. Cat's got the measles, the measles, the measles
   Cat's got the measles,
   The measles got the cat.

Brixton 1982; Blackheath 1983.

See also **2.34** and **2.53**. Also used for skipping, and as a taunt.

Printed versions Douglas (see below); cf. Fulton and Smith, pp. 16–17, 27; Nelson, like Douglas, skipping game, p. 71; Rodger, p. 18; Rohrbough (see below); Rosen and Steele, [p. 25]; Smith, *BBHG*, p. 68; Wade (1), 14, (2), 32–33.

Early notings cf. Mother got the Hooping cough/Father got the gout--/ Please (Rosie Milton)/Will you walk out? Douglas, 1916, p. 80, 1931, p. 45. Mary's got the whooping cough,/Johnnie's got the measles,/That's the way the money goes,/Pop goes the weasel, second verse of a play party game from Iowa, recorded in 1929, Rohrbough, *HPPB*, 1940, p. 95.

4.53 THIS WAY VALERIE

ACTION SONG:

A. This way Valerie, that way Valerie,
This way Valerie, all day long,
Scatter Mr. (_____), scatter Mr. (_____),
Scatter Mr. (_____), all day long.

Here comes the other one, just like the other one,
Here comes the other one, all day long,
Here comes the other one, just like the other one,
Here comes the other one, all day long.

<u>Brixton</u>, Streatham <u>1982.</u>

B. Step back Charlie, Charlie, Charlie,
Step back Charlie, all night long,
Walking down the alley, alley, alley,
Walking down the alley, all night long.

Here comes the other one, other one, other one,
Here comes the other one, all night long,
Step back Charlie, Charlie, Charlie,
Step back Charlie, all night long.

Walworth 1974.

Printed versions Fulton and Smith, pp. 21–24; Kenney, p. 69; Opies, *SG*, This Way Hen-er-y, pp. 402–404.

4.54 MY NAME IS SEXY SUE

ACTION RHYME:

A. My name is Sexy Sue,
    And I'm a superstar,
    I've got the hips, the lips,
    The legs for a star,
    So if you want to come and see me,
    If you want to come and see me,
    If you want to come and see me,
    I'm eight, seven, four.

Earlsfield 1982.

B. My name is Dinah Dors*
    And I'm a movie star,
    I've got a cute, cute figure
    And a busty bra.
    I've got the hips, the lips,
    The legs of the star.
    And if you want to see me
    Just jump in the car.

Barnsbury, Borough, Dalston, <u>Dulwich</u>, Mile End <u>1983.</u>

* Diana Dors was a glamorous English actress and cabaret artist who made many film and television appearances from the 1950s to the 1980s. See also **11.I.20**.

Sometimes **4.55** CRACKERJACK (FIRECRACKER) was included in the routine where the girls featured exaggerated movements with hips, hands and legs, in what they considered to be a "sexy" way.

Printed versions Opies, *SG*, like B, pp. 415–417; Rutherford, I'm Matt Munro, I'm a famous star, p. 36; Smith, *L&L*, My name is dinosaur, 29.

Recording Hammond, *Green Peas and Barley*, O.

4.55 CRACKERJACK/FIRECRACKER

ACTION GAME:

Crackerjack, crackerjack, Boompity boom,
Crackerjack, crackerjack, Boompity boom,
The boys have got the muscles,
The teacher's got the brains,
The girls have got the sexy legs,
And that's our game. (So here we are again.)

One, two, three, four,
D'you want to see some more? (Come on boys if you want to see more.)
   (turn up skirts)
Five, six, seven, eight,
Sorry boys, you're far too late.

Walworth 1980 (first part only); Battersea, Blackheath 1982 (second part only); Brockley, Dalston, <u>Deptford</u>, Shepherds Bush, Stoke Newington <u>1983</u>.

Sometimes the first part of this routine was included in **4.54** MY NAME IS SEXY SUE.

Printed versions Opies, *SG*, parts of song "Diana Dors", p. 416; Wilson, 980.

4.56 I'M SHIRLEY TEMPLE

ACTION RHYME:

A. I'm Shirley Temple,
    The one with curly hair,
    I've got two baby dimples,
    And I wear my skirts up there,
    I'm not able to do the sexy cable,

>   I'm Shirley Temple,
>   The girl with curly hair.

<u>Walworth 1979</u> (followed by **4.57c** SABRINA, SABRINA; Greenwich 1982 (part); Dalston 1983 (followed by **4.57d** SEMINA, SEMINA).

"When you go 'I've got curly hair', you twiddle your hair and pretend you've got curly hair. For 'got two dimples', you press your cheeks. You flash your skirt up for 'Wear my skirts up here'. Then you do the 'sexy cable' with your hand on your hip and you shake your bum." girl, 10, Dalston 1983.

> B. I'm Shirley Temple,
>   With curly, curly hair;
>   I've got two pimples,
>   I wear my skirts up there.
>   I won't be able
>   To do the Betsy Gable,
>   But I'm Shirley Temple,
>   With curly, curly hair.

West Norwood 1973.

> C. My name is Shirley Temple,
>   And I've got curly hair.
>   I've got two dimples (pimples)
>   And I wear my skirts up there.
>   I've got hair like Ginger Rogers,
>   And a figure like Marimin Rowe,
>   I've got legs like Shirley Bassey,
>   And a face like ….

Walworth 1974.

> D. I'm Shirley Temple,
>   The one with curly hair,
>   I've got two dimples,

> Lift my skirts up there.
> I'm not able to do the six times table,
> I'm not able to do the turn around.
> Shirley, Shirley,
> I am Shirley, (I love Shirley)
> Shirley, Shirley,
> I am Shirley. (I love Shirley)
>
> Hampstead 1984.

This singing game was most popular with girls from seven to nine. It was one of several teasing games where little girls pulled up their skirts and did a "sexy" routine.

Shirley Temple, with her curly hair and dimpled cheeks, was most famous as a child film star in the 1930s – see also **7.42**. "Betsy Gable" is evidently a reference to Betty Grable, the 1940s–1950s film actress, modified in two versions to "sexy cable" and "six times table" (see also **7.9B**). Ginger Rogers is best known for appearing in films as a dancer alongside Fred Astaire in the 1930s. "Marimin Rowe" is what the children had made of Marilyn Monroe, the iconic 1950s screen actress. Dame Shirley Bassey, the Welsh singer, was well-known through television at the time of my survey.

Printed versions Lyons (followed by Shirlomy, Shirlami), 50; McMorland (followed by Salome, Salome), p. 78; Opies, *SG* (followed by Salome), pp. 417–419; Ritchie, *SS* (followed by Salome, Salome), p. 46, *GC* (followed by Salome, Salome), p. 163; Rutherford, p. 36; Turner, p. 57; Wilson (followed by Salami, salami), 980, 981.

Recording Webb, *Children's Singing Games.*

4.57 SABRINA, SABRINA

ACTION RHYME (Usually follows **4.56** in one version or other, but sometimes it is on its own, as A. or B):

A. Sabrina, Sabrina,
   You ought to see Sabrina,
   Standing there with her legs all bare,
   She does a wiggle-woggle and the boys all stare,
   She swings it, she flings it,
   She turns around and swings it,
   There's a boy over there and he winks his eye,
   He says, "Will you be mine?"
   But his shoes aren't clean,
   And his hair isn't combed,
   So he won't be mine.

Marylebone 1967.

Sabrina was a film star and singer of the 1950s and 1960s.

B. Sal-o-me, Sal-o-me,
   You ought to see Salome,
   Standing there with her legs all bare,
   Every little wiggle makes the boys all stare,
   She swings it, she sings it,
   She turns around and swings it,
   Swings it, swings it, swings it …

West Norwood 1970 (also used for skipping).

Early noting The Opies state (*SG*, 1985, p. 419) that "The Salome verse (which is also used for skipping) came into being when Maud Allen … was scandalizing London with her dance 'The Vision of Salome' first performed … on 17 March 1908."

C. Sabrina, Sabrina,
   We're off to see Sabrina,
   Hands up there, skirts up there,
   We're off to see Sabrina.

Walworth 1979.

D. Oh Semina, Semina,
    We're off to see Semina,
    I'm not there, skirts up there,
    We're off to see Semina.

Dalston 1983.

Printed versions (on its own): Abrahams, pp. 174–175; Evans, Salome was a dancer, p. 30; Fowke, Salami was a dancer, p. 62; Rutherford, Sarina, Sarina, p. 36.

4.58 OUT IN ARIZONA

Out in Arizona where the cowboys are,
The only thing to guide 'em is the shooting star,
The roughest, toughest man on earth
Is Blackboy, Cowboy Joe, O.K.

Barnsbury 1983.

From the popular song, "Ragtime Cowboy Joe", music by Lewis F. Muir and Maurice Abrahams, lyrics by Grant Clarke, published in the USA by F. A. Mills in 1912.

4.59 SEVEN LITTLE GIRLS

ACTION SONG:

Seven little girls, sitting in the back row,
Kissing and hugging with Fred,
Then they say, "Hey Fred,
Go back to the driving seat,
And keep your eyes on the road,
Not on us."

Shepherds Bush 1983.

"There's seven girls and a boy's been chosen to be Fred. He's driving. Then he stops the bus and goes to the back seat. Well they don't really kiss, they just pretend. Then he has to go back to the driving seat." girl, 10, Shepherds Bush 1983.

From a popular song, chorus: "Seven little girls,/Sitting in the back seat,/Kissin' and a-huggin' with Fred,/We're having fun,/Sitting in the back seat,/Kissin' and a-huggin' with Fred." Song composed and performed by Paul Evans and released by Guaranteed Records, subsidiary of Carlton Records (1959).

4.60 JIMMY GOT DRUNK

ACTION RHYME or SINGING GAME, also a CLAPPING GAME:

A. Jimmy (Charlie) got drunk on a bottle of gin,
Called for the doctor and the doctor came in.
Have you got the rhythm to your head? Ding dong!
Have you got the rhythm to your head? Ding dong!
Have you got the rhythm to your hands? (clap, clap)
Have you got the rhythm to your hands? (clap, clap)
Have you got the rhythm to your feet? (stamp, stamp)
Have you got the rhythm to your feet? (stamp, stamp)
Have you got the rhythm to the (move hips) hot dog?
Have you got the rhythm to the (move hips) hot dog?
Put them all together and what do you get?
Ding dong! (clap, clap, stamp, stamp)—hot dog.

Walworth 1980.

B. Doctor Knickerbocker, Knickerbocker number nine,
You sure got stuck on the bumpety line.
Now let's get the rhythm of the hands (clap, clap)
Now let's get the rhythm of the hands (clap, clap)
Now let's get the rhythm of the feet (tap, tap)
Now let's get the rhythm of the feet (tap, tap)
Now let's get the rhythm of the aaaaaa (stretch up)

> Now let's get the rhythm of the hips whoo-oooo
> Now let's get the rhythm of the number nine. (bend down).

Stoke Newington 1983.

"When we say 'number nine' then somebody goes into the middle (of a ring). They close their eyes and they turn around. When they finish turning round they point to somebody. The person counts to a hundred (ten, twenty, thirty, etc.). Whatever one they land on they pick to go into the middle of the circle. Then they do it by themselves. It goes on and on until it comes to another girl in the middle." girl, 11, Stoke Newington 1983.

Printed versions Cosbey, p. 69; Kenney, p. 64; Knapps, Mr. Knick Knack, pp. 133–34; Opies, *SG*, p. 479. A clapping/singing game, said by the Opies to originate in America.

4.61 BISCUIT

ACTION AND CLAPPING GAME:

A. Shamerla, my darling (clap, clap)
Biscuit,
Shamerla, my darling (clap, clap)
Biscuit,
My sister, an actress,
Biscuit,
My brother, a doctor,
Biscuit.
Down by the alley,
Down by the alley,
Love me,
Love me,
Take a sexy leg,
Take a statue.

Walworth 1980.

B.   O cha cha wa wa – a biscuit,
       I've got a sister – a biscuit,
       She plays the guitar – a biscuit,
       Ice cream, chuckaberry,
       Cherry on the top.

Actions and movement, facing a partner.

Brixton 1982.

C.   Donna, donna, donna – biscuit,
       Oo chick a wah wah – a biscuit,
       How do you know-ow
       Oo I love you – biscuit,
       Just like a cherry,
       Wah what a biscuit
       After me ice cream – ice cream
       Lolly pop.

       Now you know your ABC,
       Join in, after me,
       ABCD etc.
       Cool it, cool it,
       Here's the fun.

Dalston 1983.

Printed version   Hopkin, 11, 34.

4.62 I'M A SAILOR YOUNG AND GAY

I'm a sailor young and gay,
Just come back from sea today,
Will you marry, marry-marry-marry,
Will you marry me?

Though you're a sailor, young and gay,
Just come back from sea today,
I won't marry, marry-marry-marry,
I won't marry you.

If I give you a golden ball,
To bounce from the kitchen right through the hall,
Will you marry, marry-marry-marry,
Will you marry me?

If you give me a golden ball,
To bounce from the kitchen right through the hall,
I won't marry, marry-marry-marry,
I won't marry you.

If I give you the key to my chest,
And all the money that I possess,
Will you marry, marry-marry-marry,
Will you marry me?

If you give me the keys to your chest,
And all the money that you possess,
I will marry, marry-marry-marry,
I will marry you.

Ha ha ha, now isn't that funny,
You don't want me but you want my money,
I won't marry, marry-marry-marry,
I won't marry you.

Ha ha ha, that's funnier still,
I've got a husband whose name is Bill,
I won't marry, marry-marry-marry,
I won't marry you.

Walworth 1974.

This song was learned by the children in the classroom but it was re-adopted as a singing game in the playground.

Printed versions cf. Brady, I'm a Soldier Brave and Strong, pp. 110–111; Halliwell (see below); Lang (see below); Newell (see below); cf. Opies, I'll Give to You a Paper of Pins, *SG*, pp. 140–143.

Early notings The earliest forms of this song are usually versions of "The Keys of Canterbury" with examples in Halliwell, *NRNTE*, c1870, pp. 92–93, and Lang, 1897, pp. 204–205. See also I'll Give To You a Paper of Pins, Newell, 1903, pp. 51–55.

4.63 CINDERELLA

ACTION RHYME or BALL BOUNCING RHYME:

A. Cinderella, dressed in yella,
   Twist right round.
   "More's the pity," father said,
   Twist right round.
   Cinderella at the ball,
   Twist right round,
   Drop down.

West Norwood 1970, 1972.

B. Cinderella, dressed in yella,
   Please turn round.
   Cinderella, dressed in yella,
   Please turn round.
   Cinderella, dressed in yella,
   Please stand up.
   Cinderella, dressed in yella,
   Please stand up.
   Cinderella, dressed in yella,
   Clap your hands.
   Cinderella, dressed in yella,

Clap your hands.
Cinderella dressed in yella,
Jump down.

Walworth 1979.

See also **2.59** and **6.A.27**.

Printed versions Botkin (see below); Brewster (see below); Evans, *JRR*, p. 13; Jorgensen, *SWF*, 67–68, *LL*, action rhyme, 113; Lyons, 51; Mills and Bishop (see below); Ritchie, *GC*, ball-bouncing rhyme, p. 82; Rutherford, ball-bouncing rhyme, p. 84; Turner, skipping rhyme, p. 22.

Early notings Cinderella, dressed in yellow,/Gone downtown to buy an umbrella;/On the way she met her fellow./How many kisses did she receive?/Five, ten, fifteen, twenty, etc., Mills and Bishop, 1937, this and a version beginning Cinderella, dressed in red, 34. Cinderella dressed in yellow/Went uptown to meet her fellow./How many kisses did he give her? (*Count until there is a miss.*), skipping rhyme, Brewster, *RCORC*, 1939, 173–178. Botkin, *TAF*, 1944, p. 791, as Brewster, and two further versions, as Mills and Bishop, pp. 800–801.

4.64 AUNT MILDRED

ACTION RHYME:

Aunt Mildred's crooked,   (You all go crooked)
Aunt Jenny is bent,   (You all go bent)
Aunt Jenny farted,
And Aunt Mildred went.   (And then you got to go away.)

girl, Hampstead 1984.

4.65 POP GOES THE WEASEL

Half a pound of tuppenny rice,
Half a pound of treacle,
That's the way the money goes,
Pop goes the weasel.

West Norwood 1972.

See also **8.D.38**.

Printed versions Abrahams, pp. 58–59, 199; Briggs, p. 100; Daiken, *TTP*, several versions, p. 11; Fowke, Johnny's got the whooping cough, p. 51; Gomme (see below); Gullen, p. 41; Harrowven, pp. 272–273; Holbrook, p. 55; MacBain (see below); McMorland, p. 12; Montgomeries, *SNR*, Roon aboot the parritch pat, pp. 94–95; Opies, *ONRB*, p. 71, *SG*, pp. 216–218; Ritchie, *SS*, parody, p. 97, *GC*, p. 19; Rodger, p. 6; Rohrbough (see below); Turner, parody, p. 91; Withers, *RIMP*, "I went down to JOHNNY'S house", parody, p. 197.

Early notings Gomme, 1898, a game, pp. 63–64; skipping rhymes, pp. 202, 203. MacBain, 1933, p. 195; Rohrbough, *HPPB*, 1940, p. 95.

Recording MacColl and Behan, *Streets of Song*.

4.66 MILK, MILK, LEMONADE

ACTION RHYME:

A. Milk, milk, lemonade,
Round the corner
Chocolate's made.

(Point to nipples, genitals and anus in turn.)

Battersea 1982; Barnsbury 1983.

Printed versions Rutherford, p. 119, Turner, p. 96.

B. Eyes, nose, mouth and chin,
All walk (go) round to Uncle Jim.
Uncle Jim makes (sells) lemonade,
And round the corner
Chocolate's made.

(Point to face as named, and then as above.)

Greenwich 1982.

4.67 BOOBY ONE, BOOBY TWO

ACTION RHYME:

A. Booby one, booby two,
Blackwall tunnel,
Waterloo.

Greenwich 1982.

B. Begin: B.B.C. 1, B.B.C. 2.

(Point to nipples, anus and genitals in turn.)

Brockley 1983.

4.68 COCONUT, CARAMEL

ACTION RHYME:

Coconut, caramel, cherries and chocolate.

(Point to head, mouth, nipples and anus in turn.)

Greenwich 1982.

4.69 CHINESE, JAPANESE

ACTION RHYME:

Chinese, Japanese,   (pull skin near eyes up, then down)
These are knees,   (point)
And what are these?   (point to breasts)

Brockley (dirty knees), <u>Mile End 1983</u>.

Printed versions Kellett, p. 67; Knapps, p. 199; Wilson, 981; Roud, *DM1*, 25; Turner, p. 70.

SECTION 5

CLAPPING GAMES

Introduction

Although the present day clapping games are to be found in almost every school where there are girls of primary school age, they do not appear to be very old and they have received far less attention than skipping or ball bouncing activities. The Opies (*SG*, 1985, pp. 440ff) trace the early history of hand clapping rhymes from "Pat-a-cake, pat-a-cake, baker's man", noted in 1698. They outline the development of this activity and point out that it reached a peak at the end of the nineteenth century and up to the First World War. It apparently declined during the inter-war period but revived after the Second World War, due to the import of American clapping rhymes of an exciting character.

Douglas, whose collection dates from the First World War, mentions the genre under girls' games: "hand-clapping games", and gives three titles (1916, p. 43; 1931, p. 23), one of which, "One-two-three", may be an earlier version of **5.8** ONE, TWO, THREE TOGETHER which was in use in the 1980s. The examples which the Opies give of nineteenth century clapping rhymes (*SG*, 1985, pp. 440ff) do not appear to have survived for contemporary use, though **6.A.37** MY MOTHER SAID, now (rarely in Inner London) used as a skipping rhyme, may be in use as a clapping rhyme, taken at a different tempo.

As already mentioned in the remarks on singing games, the popular clapping rhyme **5.5** MY BOYFRIEND GAVE ME AN APPLE is in part based on words of a singing game in the Gomme collection,[1] likewise **5.18** WHO STOLE THE COOKIES?.[2] **5.15** MACK, MACK, MACK was a part of "the wave of sparkling and spirited chants" which the Opies (*SG*, 1985, p. 443) no doubt included among those which came from the U.S.A. and led to the revival of the popularity of hand clapping at the end of the Second World War. It contains lines which can be found in a counting-out rhyme in Bolton's 1888 collection (No. 795, p. 117).

I included **4.2** WHEN SUSIE WAS A BABY in the section on singing games because I have come across as many examples of this game played with mimed actions without clapping as those based on clapping plus actions. It is also part of a continuous tradition which I have outlined in a brief article elsewhere (*K2*, 1981, 104–109).

Despite these links with the past, most contemporary hand clapping rhymes are much more likely to owe their inspiration to pop songs, re-adapted entertainment rhymes or ball bouncing rhymes, or from songs learned at Brownies or Guides. As hand clapping routines require no apparatus, no walls, balls, ropes etc., but consist of rapid sequences of clapping one's own hand and that of a partner, usually supplemented by other movements and mimes, they can be played anywhere, indoors or outdoors, to warm up, or to while away any odd boring periods. Facility increases with practice, and girls as young as six can be introduced to the activity by older girls. By the time they are ten or eleven they may have a repertoire of quite complicated routines.

More rarely, clapping games are played in a circle (or in a line occasionally). In the circle a player may simultaneously or alternately clap hands with the girl on her right and her left, or the actions may be passed around the circle. **5.18** WHO STOLE THE COOKIES? is an example of the former, and **5.3** MARIO SE FERA of the latter. The actions of clapping palm to opposite palm, crosswise, two hands, right hand, left hand, horizontally or vertically, using backs of hands or clenched fists, clapping knees, thighs etc., lend themselves to many permutations.

Collectors and others interested in children's play have taken the trouble to analyse some of the sequences. Hubbard (1982, 246–264) has done so on the basis of games played in Birdsedge and has devised a system of notation for the various movements. Roud (*DM1*, 1984, 21–32; *DM2*, 1985, 10–15) has analysed some games that his daughter played in Andover, R. A. Smith (*BBHG*, 1982, pp. 48–56) gives some details of a number of clapping rhymes from Nottingham, and Kenney (1975, pp. 20–45) provides information on clapping games not only from the American South but also from Washington, DC, Boston, New York State and Pennsylvania. No doubt many more American schoolteachers and folklorists have made similar studies.

A clapping game may have a number of verses, with different actions for each verse, such as **5.2** HAVE YOU EVER, EVER, EVER. With **5.1** A SAILOR WENT TO SEA and **5.16** MY MOTHER IS A BAKER there is a different mime for each verse, but in the final verse all the actions are incorporated. This adds to the general amusement, particularly if an action is omitted or some other mistake is made. In the commentary on singing games I mentioned that a number of the rhymes include elements of showing off or teasing by emphasising hip movements, pulling up skirts etc. Sometimes this is followed by an emphasised "Sexy!" at the end of the routine. This is a feature of several clapping games such as **5.10** I WENT TO A CHINESE RESTAURANT, **5.12** UNDER THE BROWN BUSH, and **5.17** SEE, SEE, MY PLAYMATE.

The element of words without meaning, which is a feature of many counting-out rhymes, adds a complicating factor to one or two hand clapping rhymes such as **5.3** MARIO SE FERA and **5.6** IM POM PAY. In the case of the former, there is the added complication of a circular clapping routine. This may help to explain why I only encountered this rhyme in one school.

The use of "pop" songs by inventive schoolgirls for various purposes is sometimes reciprocated by pop singers. Just as the popularity of the pop song "Brown Girl in the Ring", recorded by Boney M in 1978, reinforced the playing and singing of this Caribbean singing game in the playground, so did the song by the Black recording artist Shirley Ellis in 1965, which tied together "My Mama told me" and "Three, six, nine", so that the playing of these games separately became rare. Words were usually amended to follow those of the pop version and generally superseded those already in use. Probably now they have been modified and may have gone their separate ways.

NOTES

1. Gomme (1898). "Salmon Fishers", p. 180.
2. Gomme (1898). "Priest of the Parish", p. 79.

5.1 A SAILOR WENT TO SEA

CLAPPING AND ACTIONS:

A. A sailor went to sea, sea, sea,
To see what he could see, see, see,
But all that he could see, see, see,
Was the bottom of the deep blue sea, sea, sea.

A sailor went to chop, chop, chop,
To see what he could chop, chop, chop,
But all that he could chop, chop, chop,
Was the bottom of the deep blue chop, chop, chop.

A sailor went to knee, knee, knee,
   To see etc.

A sailor went to toe, toe, toe,
   To see etc.

A sailor went to sea, chop, knee, toe,
To see what he could see, chop, knee, toe,
But all that he could see, chop, knee, toe,
Was the bottom of the deep blue sea, chop, knee, toe.

Brockley, Mile End 1967; West Norwood 1970; Battersea, Brixton, Earlsfield 1972; Walworth 1974, 1979; <u>Borough</u>, Deptford <u>1983</u>.

B. A sailor went to Hawaii,
To see what he could Hawaii,
But all that he could Hawaii,
Was the bottom of the deep blue Hawaii.

A sailor went to Jamaica,
　　To see etc.

A sailor went to China,
　　To see etc.

A sailor went to Africa,
　　To see etc. etc.

A sailor went to Hawaii, Jamaica, China, Africa,
To see what he could Hawaii, Jamaica, China, Africa
But all that he could Hawaii, Jamaica, China, Africa
Was the bottom of the I love you.

Other actions include: heel, ear, head, eye, horizon.

Walworth 1980.

"They put their hands to their foreheads and go looking round. When it goes 'chop, chop, chop', they put the side of their hand on their elbow, pretending to chop it. When it's 'knee, knee, knee', they get their hands and put them on their knees. When it's 'toe, toe, toe', they put them on their toe. When it's 'sea, chop, knee, toe', they do everything that they've done." girl, 10, Borough 1983.

The Opies say "this joke originated, or was perpetuated, in the Fred Astaire and Ginger Rogers song": "We Joined the Navy" from the film *Follow the Fleet* (1936).

Printed versions Abrahams, "Collected in many functions", p. 173; Boyes, 39; Cosbey, Three sailors went to Disneyland, p. 92; Fowke, p. 79; Hubbard, 255; Kellett, p. 117; Knapps, p. 129; McMorland, p. 33; Nelson, p. 62; Opies, *SG*, pp. 467–468; Roud, *DM1*, 26–27; Rutherford, p. 77; Sluckin, p. 27; Smith, *BBHG*, p. 53; Turner, p. 42; Withers, *RIMP*, p. 52.

Recording Webb, *Children's Singing Games*; Hammond, *Green Peas and Barley, O.*

5.2   HAVE YOU EVER, EVER, EVER

Have you ever, ever, ever,
In your long-legged life
Seen a long-legged chicken
With a long-legged wife?

No, I've never, never, never,
In my long-legged life
Seen a long-legged chicken
With a long-legged wife.

Have you ever, ever, ever,
In your short-legged life
Seen a short-legged chicken
With a short-legged wife?

No, I've never, never, never,
In my short-legged life
Seen a short-legged chicken
With a short-legged wife.

Have you ever, ever, ever,
In your bow-legged life (also bone-legged and back-boned)
Seen a bow-legged chicken
With a bow-legged wife?

No, I've never, never, never,
In my bow-legged life
Seen a bow-legged chicken
With a bow-legged wife.

Have you ever, ever, ever,
In your long-legged life
Seen a short-legged chicken
With a bow-legged wife?

No, I've never, never, never,
In my long-legged life
Seen a short-legged chicken
With a bow-legged wife.

Mile End 1964, 1968; Putney 1966; Walworth 1982; Mile End 1983.

The above is the only full version I have come across.

The Opies (*SG*, 1985, p. 457) state that "the ancestors of the rhyme are American".

Printed versions Abrahams, p. 37; Gardner (see below); Kellett, pp. 117–118; Kirshenblatt-Gimblett, pp. 93–94; Knapps, p. 129; Opies, *SG*, pp. 456–457; Rutherford, skipping game, p. 69; Turner, p. 42; Withers, *RIMP*, Did you ever ever ever/In your life, did you ever/See a whale catch a snail by the tail? p. 8; also p. 183.

Early noting Did you ever, ever, ever,/In your life, life, life,/See a nigger, nigger, nigger,/Kiss his wife, wife, wife? Counting-out rhyme, Gardner, 1918, 531.

Recording Webb, *Children's Singing Games*.

5.3 MARIO SE FERA

Mario se fera,
Mario se fera
Lara, lara, pee, pee, pee
Lera, lera, pee, pee, pee
One, two, three.

Earlsfield 1982.

Girls sit in a ring, they clap neighbours' hands and then turn round one at a time, clapping the hand of the girl on the right. I think the words were made up by the girls who showed it to me.

5.4   I AM A PRETTY LITTLE DUTCH GIRL

   A.   I am a pretty little Dutch girl,
As pretty as can be,
And all the boyfriends around
Go crazy after me.
I have a boyfriend Paddy,
Who comes from Cincinnati,
With forty eight toes and a pickle up his nose,
And this is how the story goes:
One day as I was walking
I heard my boyfriend talking
To a pretty little girl with a strawberry curl,
And this is what he said to her:
I L-O-V-E love you,
I K-I-S-S, kiss you,
I K-I-S-S, kiss you
On the F-A-C-E, face,
Face, face.

Walworth 1982.

   B.   I am a pretty little Dutch girl,
As pretty as can be, be, be,
And all the boys in my home town
Go crazy over me, me, me.
My boyfriend's name is Tony,
He comes from Macaroni,
With ten black toes and a cherry on his nose,
And this is what he said to me:
I'm going to T-A-K-E, take you to the P-A-R-K, park,
I'm going to K-I-S-S, kiss you in the D-A-R-K, dark.
I'm going to L-O-V-E, love you all the T-I-M-E time,
I'm going to H-O-L-D, hold you in my A-R-M-S, arms.

      Birds in the wilderness, birds in the wilderness,
Drop dead!

Other versions: Mile End 1964; West Norwood 1972, 1973; Walworth 1974; EC1 1983. Sometimes the sequence continues with **5.5** MY BOYFRIEND GAVE ME AN APPLE.

See also **4.30**.

Printed versions Abrahams, skipping rhyme but "Usually a handclapping rhyme", p. 69; Cosbey, skipping game with elements of "My boyfriend gave me peaches" p. 77; Fowke, pp. 88 and 89: the version on p. 88 continues as "My boyfriend gave me peaches"; versions of ll. 1–4 and 5–8 appear on p. 89 as separate rhymes, and a version of ll. 9–12 on p. 94; Kellett, a version of ll. 5–8, p. 120; Kenney, a version of ll. 1–4, p. 26; a version of ll. 5–8, p. 27; Knapps, pp. 115 and 123 as skipping games with elements of "My boyfriend gave me apples"; p. 116, ll. 5–8 as a separate skipping rhyme; also ll. 5–8 of version A. appear on p. 129 as a separate clapping game; Lowenstein quotes verses beginning "He offered me some peaches", p. 24; Opies, *SG* (see below); Rutherford, pp. 74–75; Turner, three versions out of five containing "My boyfriend gave me apples", p. 45; cf. Wade 2, 35; Withers, *RIMP*, My boy friend's name is Jello, p. 3.

Early noting the Opies (*SG*, 1985, pp. 451–452) state that the song came to Britain from the USA in the late 1950s, but add that the earliest reference (New York, NY, c1940) was documented by Carl Withers in his collection *Ready or Not, Here I Come* (1947). New York, NY: Grosset and Dunlap (p. 100).

Recording Webb, *Children's Singing Games*.

5.5 MY BOYFRIEND GAVE ME AN APPLE

    A. My boyfriend gave me an apple,
         My boyfriend gave me a pear,
         My boyfriend gave me a kiss on the lips,
         And threw me down the stair.

I gave him back his apple,
I gave him back his pear,
I gave him back his kiss on the lips,
And I threw him down the stair.

One day he took me to the pictures,
To see a sexy film,
And when I wasn't looking
He kissed another girl.
Bloody hell!

<u>Walworth 1981</u>; Greenwich 1982 (two verses); Dalston, Deptford (two verses), Shepherds Bush 1983.

B. My boyfriend gave me apples,
My boyfriend gave me pears,
My boyfriend gave me kiss, kiss, kiss,
And kicked me down the stairs.

I gave him back his apples,
I gave him back his pears,
I gave him back his kiss, kiss, kiss,
And kicked him down the stairs.

I kicked him over London,
I kicked him over France,
I kicked him over the U.S.A.
And he lost his underpants.

<u>Blackheath 1983</u>. Versions without a third verse: Mile End 1967; Walworth 1979; Battersea, Brixton, Streatham 1982; Barnsbury, Borough, Brockley 1983.

C. One day he gave me peaches,
One day he gave me pears,
One day he gave me fifty pence,
And kissed me on the stairs.

I gave him back his peaches,
I gave him back his pears,
I gave him back his fifty pence,
And kicked him down the stairs.

I made him wash the dishes,
I made him scrub the floor,
I made him change the baby,
And a very great deal more.

Finsbury 1983.

Various versions of B. or C. without a third verse: Mile End 1967; Walworth 1979; Battersea, Brixton, Streatham 1982; Barnsbury, Borough, Brockley 1983; Kensington 1984.

Printed versions Abrahams, p. 100; Botkin (see below); Brady, p. 37; Cosbey, I'm a pretty little Dutch girl, p. 77; Daiken, *CGTY*, First he bought me apples, p. 80; Douglas (see below); Evans, *JRR*, skipping rhyme, p. 18; Fowke, like Gomme's version, p. 59; Gainer, 45; Gillington (see below); Gomme (see below); Jorgensen, *SWF*, I wish I had a nickel, 68, *LL*, 113; Kelsey, *K1*, 46; Kenney, p. 28; Knapps, skipping games, as ll. 5–8 of "I'm a pretty little Dutch girl", p. 115, and p. 123; Lowenstein, p. 24; Montgomeries, *SC*, both like Gomme's version, p. 112, *HBSNR*, p. 73; Nicholson (see below); Opies, *SG*, part of "I Am a Pretty Little Dutch Girl" p. 451; Ritchie, *SS*, close to Gomme's version, p. 97; Roud, *DM1*, 28; Wilson, 980.

Early notings 'Mother, the nine o'clock bells are ringing;/Mother, let me out;/For my sweetheart is waiting;/He's going to take me out.//He's going to give me apples,/He's going to give me pears,/He's going to give me a sixpence/To kiss him on the stairs.' (with two further verses), Nicholson, 1897, p. 155; another version from Cheshire, pp. 344–345. Mother, struck eight o'clock,/Mother, may I get out?/For my love is waiting/For to get me out./First he gave me apples,/Then he gave me pears,/Then he gave me a sixpence/To kiss him on the stairs. Part of "Salmon Fishers", Gomme, 1898, p. 180. Many of the older versions begin with "Eight o'clock bells are ringing,/Mother, may I go out" and similar, e.g. Gillington, 1909, *OSSG*, p. 24; Douglas, 1916, pp. 69–70, 1931, p. 38; Botkin, *TAF*, 1944, skipping rhyme, p. 792.

5.6   IM POM PAY (OM POM VEE)

   A.   Im pom pay, polonay, polonesky,
        Im pom pay, polonay,
        Acker dormy, acker dormy,
        So fah me, so fah me,
        Boof, boof.

Brockley 1968 (similar); <u>West Norwood 1970</u>.

   B.   Om pom vee, diddlee, diddle ishu,
        Om pom vee, om pom vee,
        Om pom vee, diddlee, diddle ishu,
        Om pom vee, and om pom,
        Va ra.

Mile End 1967.

Printed versions Opies, *SG*, p. 464; Roud, *DM1*, 29, Smith, *BBHG*, p. 52.

5.7   I HAD THE GERMAN MEASLES

   CLAPPING and BALL BOUNCING RHYME:

   A.   I had the German measles,
        I had them very bad,
        They wrapped me up in tissue paper,
        And threw me in a van.
        The van was very shaky,
        It really shook me up,
        But when I reached the hospital,
        I heard the children shout,
        "Mummy, Daddy, take me home,
        The boys won't leave the girls alone.
        I've been here a year or two,
        Now I want to be with you.
        Here comes Dr. Allister,

Sliding down the banister,
Halfway down he split his pants,
Now he's doing the cha cha dance."

Hampstead 1972, 1984; Walworth 1979; <u>Barnsbury</u>, Blackheath, Dalston, Kentish Town <u>1983</u>.

B. I had the scarlet fever,
   I had it very bad, bad, bad,
   They wrapped me in a blanket,
   And threw me in the van, van, van,
   The van was very loaded,
   I nearly tumbled out, out, out,
   And when I got to hospital,
   I heard the children shout, shout, shout,
   "Mummy, Daddy take me home,
   I've been here a year or so.
   Here comes Dr. Splannister,
   Sliding down the banister,
   Halfway down he split his pants,
   Now he's doing the ballet dance,
   Om diddy om pom, pom pom."

Shepherds Bush 1983.

Printed versions Brady, pp. 94–95; Opies, *SG*, pp. 455–456, and see below; Shaw, 1970, Mother, Mother, take me home, p. 62; I had the scarlet fever, p. 91.

Early notings Mother, Mother, take me home/From this convalescent home,/ I will wait a day or two/If you'll let me come home to you. Correspondent (Welwyn) remembering a song sung in the 1900s in London SE17 by children sent for fortnight holidays by charitable bodies like the Ragged School Union and Country Holiday Homes. The Opies (*SG*, 1985, p. 456) give a similar version, and suggest that "Mother, mother, fetch me home" mentioned in Douglas (1916, p. 95, 1931, p. 54) is likely to be the same song.

Recording Webb, *Children's Singing Games.*

5.8 ONE, TWO, THREE TOGETHER

CLAPPING WITH ACTIONS:

(Continue repeating)
One, two, three together,
Up together, down together,
Back, front, knees together.
Boom!

West Norwood 1972; <u>Walworth 1974</u>.

Printed version Smith, *BBHG*, p. 55.

Early noting Douglas mentions a clapping game called "One-two-three", 1916, p. 43, 1931, p. 23.

5.9 I HAD A LITTLE BROTHER

CLAPPING or ACTION RHYME:

A. I had a little brother,
    His name was Tiny Tim.
    I put him in the bathtub
    To teach him how to swim.
    He drank up all the water,
    He ate up all the soap.
    He died last night
    With a bubble in his throat.
    In came the doctor,
    In came the nurse,
    In came the lady
    With the alligator purse.

"Dead," said the doctor,
"Dead," said the nurse,
"Dead," said the lady
With the alligator purse.
Out went the doctor,
Out went the nurse,
Out went the lady
With the alligator purse.

Barnsbury, <u>Finsbury 1983</u>.

B. Susie had a baby,
Its name was Tiny Tim,
She put it in the bathtub,
And taught it how to swim.
It drank up all the water,
And swallowed all the soap,
It tried to eat the bathtub,
But it wouldn't fit its throat.
Susie called the doctor,
Susie called the nurse,
Susie called the lady
With the alligator purse.
"Measles," said the doctor,
"Mumps," said the nurse,
"Chicken pox," said the lady
With the alligator purse.

Mile End 1966; Hampstead 1972; Streatham 1982; <u>Finsbury 1983</u>.

See also **11.I.24**.

Printed versions Abrahams, skipping rhyme, pp. 79–80, 126; Botkin (see below); Cosbey, p. 75; Douglas (see below); Evans, *JRR*, a version of ll. 9–16 of both A. and B, p. 3; Fowke, p. 50; Gomme (see below);

Jorgensen, I had a little sister, her name was Suzy Q, *LL*, 111–112; Kellett (see below); Kenney, Miss Lucy had a Baby, p. 29; Knapps, p. 113; Mills and Bishop (see below); Nelson, Miss Lucy had a baby, p. 66; Opies, *SG*, The Johnsons had a baby, etc., pp. 472–473, and see below; Rosen and Steele, [p. 25]; Shaw, 1970, pp. 109–110; Smith, *BBHG*, singing game, pp. 41–42; Solomons, pp. 57–58; Withers, *RIMP*, p. 30; Wood, *FAFR*, I had a little dog, his name was Tim, p. 35.

Early notings Up came the doctor, up came the cat,/Up came the devil with a white straw hat./Down went the doctor, down went the cat,/Down went the devil with a white straw hat, Gomme, 1894, p. 4, "All the boys in our town". Douglas has a version of "All the boys in our town" ending "Up goes the doctor, up goes the cat,/Up goes a little boy in a white straw hat", 1916, pp. 59–60, 1931, p. 32. Lulu had a baby, she called it Sunny Jim,/She took it to the bathroom to see if it could swim./It swam to the bottom, it swam to the top,/Lulu got excited and grabbed it by the—/ Cocktails, ginger ale, two and six a glass … Bawdy verse of the 1920s, Opies, *SG*, 1985, p. 473. Kellett, 1920s, similar to the Opies' version, p. 27. Mills and Bishop, 1937, 32. Botkin, *TAF*, 1944: Virginia had a baby, p. 794; I had a little brother, as Mills and Bishop, p. 797.

5.10 I WENT TO A CHINESE RESTAURANT

A. I went to a Chinese restaurant
 To buy a loaf of bread.
 He wrapped it up in a five pound note
 And this is what he said:
  "My name is Ell i chickali,
  Chick ell i,
  Hong Kong hooya,
  Chinese chopsticks,
  Indian bells go woo oo oo oo,
  How!"

Walworth 1979 (similar quoted words); Battersea 1982 (similar quoted words); <u>Blackheath</u>, Dalston <u>1983</u>; Kensington 1984.

Endings:

    B.   Oo ee ah ha ha,
          Walla walla whisky,
          Bang Bang.

West Norwood 1973; Brockley 1983 (mixture of A and B).

    C.   My name is Elvis Presley,
          Girlfriend Lesley,
          Kissing in the garden,
          Kiss, kiss, kiss.

Greenwich 1982; Deptford 1983.

    D.   Haila, chicka lom pom Suzianna,
          You deserve a jolly good kiss.

Brixton 1982.

    E.   My name is Elvis Presley,
          Looks sexy,
          Sitting in the back row,
          Drinking Pepsi,
          Kissing the girls,
          That look sexy,
          Hi chi, bang, bang,
          Pepsi Cola.

Barnsbury, Borough, Dulwich, Hampstead, Mile End, Shepherds Bush 1983.

    F.   Air I chickali, chickali air I,
          Om pom poodle
          Walla walla whispers,

> Chinese whispers.
> Indian chief says "How!"

<u>Barnsbury</u>, Cubitt Town, Dalston, Shepherds Bush <u>1983</u>.

The nonsense endings are very similar to certain dips (see notes to **2.17**). The Opies (*SG*, p. 466) state that the verse beginning "I went to a Chinese laundry" was used as part of a counting-out rhyme before the clapping game craze of the 1960s.

Printed versions Boyes, 33; Hubbard, 256–257; Kings (see below); Lyons, 49; Opies, *CGSP*, p. 41, *SG*, I went to a Chinese laundry, p. 465; Rosen and Steele, front cover; Roud, *DM1*, 24–25; Shaw, 1969, p. 26; 1970, pp. 42–43, p. 51; Smith, *BBHG*, p. 48; Turner, p. 43; Wilson, 981.

Early noting cf. Ari-ari chikari-chari, Kings 2, 1930, p. 21.

5.11 JOHNNY BROKE A BOTTLE

> A. Johnny broke a bottle,
> And blamed it on to me,
> I told Mama, Mama told Papa,
> Johnny got a spanking
> And this is what he said,
> "Oh ah, I lost my bra,
> I left my knickers in my boyfriend's car." (See also **4.2A**)

<u>Walworth 1980, 1981</u>, Finsbury 1983.

> B. Johnny went over the ocean,
> Johnny went over the sea,
> Johnny smashed a window,
> And blamed it on to me.
> I told Ma, Ma told Pa,
> Johnny got a spanking, Ha ha ha!

<u>West Norwood 1970</u>, Borough 1983.

Printed version Fulton and Smith, p. 13.

> C. Under the brown bush,
> Under the sea,
> Johnny broke a window,
> And blamed it on to me.
> I told my mother,
> My mother told my brother,
> Johnny broke another
> And I didn't get my tea.

<u>Battersea</u>, Blackheath <u>1982</u>.

See also **5.12** below.

Printed versions Abrahams, pp. 101–102; Barltrop and Wolveridge (see below); Botkin (see below); Evans, *JRR*, skipping rhyme, p. 25; Fowke, p. 79; Jorgensen, *SWF*, 64; Kellett (see below); Kenney, p. 36; Knapps, p. 113; Northall (see below); Ritchie, *GC*, p. 136; cf. Shaw, 1970, p. 23; Solomons, like A and B, p. 102; Withers, *RIMP*, p. 67; Worstell, p. 39.

Early notings cf. "You'll catch it when you get home!"/"What for?"/"Breaking the bottle, and spilling the rum,/And kissing your sweetheart all the way home", Northall, 1892, p. 318. Cf. When you broke the organ/And you blamed it on to me, Kellett, 1920s, p. 37. Sally broke the jampot, and blamed it onto me, skipping rhyme from the 1920s and 1930s, Barltrop and Wolveridge, p. 64. Botkin, *TAF*, 1944, skipping rhyme, p. 791.

Recording *Ring Games, Line Games and Play Party Songs of Alabama.*

5.12 UNDER THE BROWN BUSH

> Under the brown bush,
> Under the sea,
> Boom, boom, boom.

True love for you, my darling,
True love for me,
And when we're married
We'll raise a fam-il-lee
So, a boy for you,
A girl for me,
How's your father? Sexy.

<u>West Norwood 1972</u>; Walworth 1974, 1979; Brixton 1982; Dalston, Deptford, Mile End 1983; Kensington 1984.

See also **5.11c**.

According to the Opies (*SG*, 1985, p. 453), this is based on the composite "The Cannibal King Medley", a student song made up from "A Cannibal King" (Harry Harndin, 1895) and "Under the Bamboo Tree", written by Bob Cole and John Rosamond Johnson in 1902 and featured in their vaudeville act; the song was included in the Broadway musical *Sally in Our Alley* (1902), and performed as a song and dance duet by Judy Garland and Margaret O'Brien in the film *Meet Me in St. Louis* (1944).

Printed versions Boyes, 41; Hubbard, Under the bramble bushes, 251–252; Knapps, p. 131; Lyons, 50; Opies, *SG*, Under the bram bush, pp. 453–455; Sluckin, p. 27; Smith, *BBHG*, p. 51; Turner, p. 47.

Recording Webb, *Children's Singing Games.*

5.13 THREE, SIX, NINE

CLAPPING SONG:

Three, six, nine, the goose drank wine,
The monkey chewed tobacco on the street car line (Caroline).
The line broke, the monkey got choked,

And they all went to heaven in a little rowing boat.
(Clap, clap, clap), black cat.

Borough, <u>Brockley 1983</u>.

This is usually sung together with **5.14 MY MAMA TOLD ME**, as in "The clapping song" by Lincoln Chase, recorded by Shirley Ellis in 1965 and re-released, among a number of other cover versions, by the Belle Stars in 1982, though I collected it separately in Twickenham in 1967. It very often begins: "Once upon a time", and I remember my father in the 1920s using, "Once upon a time, when pigs drank wine, and monkeys chewed tobacco" to introduce a story. Almost all the printed versions begin, "Once upon a time …"

Printed versions Abrahams, p. 145; Brady, p. 37; Chambers (see below); Gaskell (see below); Hubbard, mentioned, 262; Hughes and Bontemps, p. 435; Kenney, p. 23; Opies, *LLS*, p. 22, *SG*, p. 450; Ritchie, *SS*, p. 97; Rodger, p. 44; Rutherford, p. 123; Shaw, 1970, p. 8; Talley (see below); Turner, p. 99; Withers, *RIMP*, p. 21.

Early notings Lang syne, when geese were swine,/And turkeys chewed tobacco,/And birds biggit their nests in auld men's beards,/And mowdies del't potawtoes– Chambers, 1847, p. 209. That was langsyne, when geese were swine,/And turkeys chewed tobacco,/And sparrows biggit in auld men's beards,/And moudies delv't potatoes! Chambers, 1870, p. 395. Cf. Once upon a time/When there were no lime/An' brickters had no mortar,/There came a little bird/An' dropped a little turd,/An' that was the brickter's mortar, Gaskell, c1913, p. 9. Talley, 1922, p. 99.

5.14 MY MAMA TOLD ME

CLAPPING SONG:

My mama told me, comma, comma, full stop,
If I was a goody, comma, comma, full stop,

That she would buy me, comma, comma, full stop,
A rubber dolly, comma, comma, full stop.
My auntie told her, comma, comma, full stop,
I kissed a soldier, comma, comma, full stop,
Now she won't buy me, comma, comma, full stop,
A rubber dolly, comma, comma, full stop.

<u>West Norwood 1970, 1972</u>, without "comma, comma …";
Walworth 1974; Streatham 1982; Borough, Mile End 1983.

When linked together with **5.13** above, "comma, comma, full stop" is not used, possibly because these words did not occur in the version recorded by Shirley Ellis and the Belle Stars. Lincoln Chase evidently borrowed the lyrics of "The Clapping Song" from the song "Little Rubber Dolly" recorded by the Light Crust Doughboys in the 1930s, which includes instructions for a clapping game.

Printed versions Hopkin, like Roud, 31; Hubbard, mentioned, 263; Knapps, p. 129; Opies, *SG*, pp. 447–449; see also "Popeye the Sailor Man", p. 471 for spoken punctuation at the ends of lines; Roud, *DM1*, Full stop/Comma comma/Dash dash/Turn around/Touch the ground/Om pom push, tagged on to a Popeye rhyme, 30–31; Rutherford, p. 76; Turner, p. 44.

5.15 MACK, MACK, MACK

CLAPPING AND ACTIONS:

Mack, Mack, Mack,
All dressed in black, black, black,
With silver buttons, buttons, buttons,
All down her back, back, back.
She asked her mother, mother, mother,
For fifty cents, cents, cents,
To watch the elephant, elephant, elephant,
Jump over the fence, fence, fence.

They jumped so high, high, high,
That they reached the sky, sky, sky,
They didn't come back, back, back,
Till the end of July, July, July.

Dalston 1983.

The Opies (*SG*, 1985, p. 469), state that "These words ... are a combination of an old English rhyme [from Halliwell, *NRE*, 1844 – roughly ll. 1–4 of the Dalston version] and an oldish American one [a reference from Boston, c1865]." A version from Jamaica almost identical to the Dalston rhyme is given by Hopkin (1979, 28–29). The version I recorded in Dalston was given to me by a girl with Jamaican-born parents.

Printed versions Abrahams, Hi ho! Skippety toe, p. 64; variant of ll. 5–12, p. 72; ll. 1–4, p. 120; Bolton (see below); Botkin (see below); Boyes, 37; Brady, p. 66; Briggs, Darby and Joan were dressed in black, p. 203; Daiken, *CGTY*, p. 65, *TTP*, Judy and Jack dressed in black/Silver buttons way down her back, p. 15, *OGS*, p. 41; Fowke, p. 89; cf. Fulton and Smith, Chitty, chitty bang bang sittin' on a fence/Tryin' to make a dollar out of fifteen cents./He missed, he missed, he missed like this, p. 43; Gaskell (see below); Gomme (see below); Graves (see below); Gullen, Turvey, turvey, clothed in black, p. 92; Halliwell (see below); Harrop, Friend, and Gadsby, p. 12; Hopkin, 28–29; Hughes and Bontemps, pp. 430–431; Kenney, p. 42; Kirshenblatt-Gimblett, a version of ll. 5–12 only, p. 103; Knapps, p. 136; Lang (see below); Leach and Fried, Ask your mother for fifty cents/To see the elephant jump the fence:/He jumped so high he touched the sky/And never came down till Fourth of July, p. 1017; Mills and Bishop (see below); Nelson, p. 64; Northall (see below); Opies, *SG*, Miss Mary Mack, pp. 469–470; Petershams, version of ll. 5–12 only, p. 2; Sluckin, p. 27; Solomons, p. 58; Talley (see below); Turner, p. 44; cf. Withers, *CO*, Monkey, monkey, sitting on a fence,/Trying to make a dollar out of fifteen cents, counting-out rhyme [p. 21]; Wood, *FAFR*, Jaybird settin' on a barbed-wire fence,/Tryin' to make a dollar out of fifteen cents, p. 24 (and see below).

Early notings cf. Darby and Joan were dress'd in black,/Sword and buckle behind their back;/Foot for foot, and knee for knee,/Turn about Darby's company, Halliwell, *NRE*, 1844, p. 194. Miss Mary Mack, dressed in black,/Silver buttons on her back./I love coffee, I love tea,/I love the boys, and the boys love me./I'll tell ma when she comes home,/The boys won't leave the girls alone, Bolton, 1888, p. 117. (For ll. 3–4 of this version, see **6.A.31**). Northall, 1892, pp. 387–388, 395. Betsy Blue came all in black,/Silver buttons down her back. … Gomme, 1894, one of five versions under the head "Alligoshee", pp. 7–8. Lang, as Halliwell, above, 1897, p. 270. Mrs Boardman dressed in black, Gaskell, c1913, p. 7. Talley, 1922, p. 116. Darby, Darby, dressed in black, Graves, 1927, p. 10. A version of ll. 5–12, Mills and Bishop, 1937, 42. I asked my mother for fifteen cents, Wood, *AMG*, 1940, p. 19. Botkin, *TAF*, 1944, as Mills and Bishop, p. 803.

Recording *Ring Games, Line Games and Play Party Songs of Alabama.*

5.16 MY MOTHER IS A BAKER

ACTION and CLAPPING SONG:

A. My mother is a baker, yum yummy, yum yummy!
    My father is a dustman, yum, yummy, yum yummy, pooee!
    My sister is a show-off, yum yummy, yum yummy, pooee, tinker tinker tooee!
    My brother is a cowboy, yum yummy, yum yummy, pooee, tinker tinker tooee, turn around BANG!

<u>Walworth 1980</u>; Battersea, Brixton, Greenwich 1982; Borough, Dalston, Deptford, Mile End 1983.

B. My mother is a baker, yum yum,
    My father is a dustman, yum yum, hoo-oo,
    My sister is a hairdresser, yum yum, hoo-oo, rat-a-tat too-oo,
    My grandmother is a telephone lady, yum yum, hoo-oo, rat-a-tat too-oo, hallo, hallo!

> My grandfather is a train driver, yum yum, hoo-oo, rat-a-tat too-oo, hallo, hallo, choo choo.

Mile End 1967.

"They just sing it. Someone acts the dustman. They stand up and pretend they're taking the lid off, putting the dust in the cart. When it goes 'baker' they pretend they're their mother doing baking. If they just do the 'show off' they put their hands on their head and their hands on their hips and go, 'nyeu, nyeu.' When they go 'My brother is a cowboy,' they turn around, touch the ground, pretend they've got a gun and go 'Bang! Bang! you're dead.'" Borough 1983.

Printed versions Boyes, 38; Fowke, p. 57; Kenney, p. 30; Knapps, pp. 128–129; Opies, *SG*, pp. 476–477.

Recording Webb, *Children's Singing Games.*

5.17 SEE, SEE, MY PLAYMATE

> A. See, see my playmate,
> Come up and play with me. (I cannot play with you.)
> And bring your dollies three. (My dolly got the 'flu.)
> Slide down the rainbow
> Into the cellar door,
> And we'll be jolly friends
> For evermore.

Blackheath 1982.

> B. See, see my baby,
> One, two, three,
> Come out and play with me.
> My sister's got the flea.
> She caught it off of you

>   When you were in the loo.
>   Tra la la la.

Barnsbury 1983.

> C. See, see my mama,
>   Come out and play with me,
>   Under the apple tree,
>   My boyfriend said to me,
>   Kiss me, cuddle me,
>   Tell me that you love me.
>   A boy for you,
>   A girl for me,
>   Um tiddly um tum, sexy.
>   What's for dinner? Turkey.
>   What's for afters? Jelly.
>   What's for drink? Pepsi.
>   What's on telly? Fonzie.*

Dalston 1983.

* The principal character in the American sitcom *Happy Days*, which ran on British television from 1974 to 1984.

> D. See, see my baby,
>   I cannot play with you,
>   My sister's got the 'flu
>   In 1972.
>   Slide down the drainpipe,
>   Slide down the cellar door,
>   Until we meet again,
>   For evermore, more,
>   Shut that door!*

Shepherds Bush 1983.

* A catchphrase used by the television personality Larry Grayson.

Various other versions, sometimes with "See, see my brownie" as first line: West Norwood 1973; Clapham 1973–74; Walworth 1974, 1982–84; Earlsfield, Greenwich 1982; Borough, Brockley, Cubitt Town, Deptford, Mile End 1983; Hampstead, Kensington 1984.

These rhymes are originally based on a popular song of 1894 entitled "I Don't Want to Play in Your Yard" by Philip Wingate, to music by H. W. Petrie. Horace Kirby ("Saxie" Dowell), based a song called "Playmates" on Wingate and Petrie's song in 1940.

Printed versions Boyes, 40; Cosbey, p. 82; Fowke, p. 95; Kelsey, *K1*, 46; Kenney, p. 38; Knapps, p. 131; Opies, *SG*, p. 475; Roud, *DM1*, 27–28, *DM2*, 10; Smith, *BBHG*, p. 54.

5.18 WHO STOLE THE COOKIES?

A. Who stole the cookies from the Kookaburra shop (cookery stall)?
She stole the cookies from the Kookaburra shop.   (pointing)
Who me?
Yes you.
Couldn't have been.
Then who?
(_____) stole the cookies from the Kookaburra shop.
Who me? etc. (all the girls in turn)
We all stole the cookies from the Kookaburra shop
Even me, even me … and even me.

Walworth 1974.

B. Who stole the apples from the greengrocer's shop (bread from the baker's shop)?
Was it number one?
Who me?
Yes you.
Couldn't have been.
Then who?

> Number two stole the apples from the greengrocer's shop.
> Who me? etc.
> (until all numbered).

Stepney 1966; Brockley 1967; West Norwood 1970; <u>Streatham 1982</u>; Earlsfield 1982–84; Shepherds Bush 1983.

> C. Who stole the cookies from the cookie jar?
> (_____) did, (_____) did ra ra ra.
> (Repeat, with different names).

Borough 1983.

Printed versions Fowke, Who stole my chickens and my hens, p. 93; Fulton and Smith, p. 52; Gomme (see below); Hopkin, 8, 24–25; Kenney, p. 56; Knapps, p. 132; Turner, p. 48.

Early noting perhaps derived from a game called "Priest of the Parish" in Gomme, 1898, p. 79, which goes, in part: The priest of the parish has lost his considering-cap …/ 'Is it me, sir?'/'Yes you, sir.'/'You lie, sir.'/'Who then, sir?'/ 'Black Cap.' …

Recording Webb, *Children's Singing Games.*

5.19 MILLY MOLLY MANDY

> Milly Molly Mandy,
> Sweet as sugar candy,
> Pretty little eyes of blue;
> Everybody would be,
> If they only could be,
> Walking out with you.
>
> Wishing on a Monday,
> Then I saw you Sunday,
> Makes my heart feel blue,

Milly Molly Mandy,
Sweet as sugar candy,
I'm in love with you.

Milly Molly Mandy
Is the girl that lives next door,
Milly Molly Mandy
Is the girl that I adore.
She teases me and pleases me,
She knows it's very wrong,
But all I have to do to her
Is sing this little song.

Walworth 1974.

Printed version Opies, *SG*, p. 480.

5.20 I'VE BEEN TO HARLEM

CLAPPING RHYME AND SKIPPING SONG:

I've been to Harlem,
I've been to Dover,
I've travelled this wide world over,
Over, over, three times over.
Drink what you have to drink,
And turn the glasses over.
Sailing east, sailing west,
Sailing over the ocean,
You'd better watch out,
When the boat begins to rock,
Or you'll lose your girl in the ocean.

West Norwood 1972.

See also **6.A. 51**.

Printed versions Chase, *SGPPG*, Oh, I've been to Winchester, I've been to Dover, p. 2; Rohrbough (see below).

Early noting I've been to Harlem I've been to Dover;/I've travelled this wide world all over,/Over, over, three times over;/Drink all the brandy-wine and/Turn the glasses over.//Sailing east sailing west,/Sailing over the ocean,/Better watch out when the boat begins to rock/Or you'll lose your girl in the ocean, Rohrbough, *HPPB*, 1940, p. 14.

5.21 ROSES ARE RED

RING GAME WITH CLAPPING:

Roses are red,
Violets are blue,
When God made brains (looks)
Where were you?
You! You! You!

Earlsfield 1982.

Girls sit in a ring. A girl claps hands with a girl on her left and the clap goes all round the ring. This is followed by three claps on the lap. The head is touched on the word "brains". The clap goes round again and it finishes with every girl pointing to three others.

See also **8.D.44**, **9.C.1c**, **9.C.13**, **9.C.21**, **9.C.31d**, and **12.C.1** ("Roses are red" rhymes).

Printed version cf. Hepburn and Roberts, 303.

5.22 I SAW MY BOYFRIEND

ACTION AND CLAPPING GAME:

I saw my boyfriend walking down the street,
Walking down the street, walking down the street,
I saw my boyfriend walking down the street,
Oh Susiana.

And under his arm he carried a box, etc.

And in that box there was a dress, etc.

And in that dress there was a pocket, etc.

And in that pocket there was a note, etc.

And on that note there was three words, etc.

And those three words were, "I love you," etc.

Walworth 1980.

See also **9.A.1**.

Printed version cf. Opies, This is the key of the kingdom, *ONRB*, p. 125.

SECTION 6

SKIPPING GAMES

Introduction

Although skipping, like many other playground activities, is seasonal, it depends on other factors as well. One day it may be absent from the playground completely, but the next day a few girls will have begged, borrowed or found a long rope and started skipping. Soon many groups may be involved in the activity and other games will be dropped. A few weeks later it may have almost disappeared, apart from the odd group. It is not dependent on warm spring weather. Skipping is almost exclusively a girls' activity, along with ball bouncing routines, hand clapping, and action songs. It was not so always, however. In 1801 Strutt wrote (pp. 286–287):

> Boys often contend for superiority of skill in this game, and he who passes the rope about most times without interruption is the conqueror. In the hop season, a hop-stem stripped of its leaves is used instead of a rope, and in my opinion it is preferable.

Of a dozen skipping rhymes included in the Gomme collection (1898, pp. 202–204), none were sung or chanted in the London area in the same form at the time of my fieldwork, though it is possible to recognise lines or rhythmic patterns that indicate a connection: "Lady, lady, drop your handkerchief,/Lady, lady, pick it up.", seems to relate to: **6.A.40** TEDDY BEAR, Teddy Bear, turn around,/Teddy Bear, Teddy Bear, touch the ground. Douglas (1916, p. 66, 1931, p. 36) provides the link with:

> Lady, lady, drop your purse,
> Lady, lady, pick it up,
> Lady, lady, touch the ground,
> Lady, lady, turn right round,
> Lady, lady, show your foot,
> Lady, lady, sling your hook.

Douglas (1916, pp. 49–50, 1931, p. 26) gives the names of specific games, very few of which are performed today with those names. Of all his rhymes, however, no less than twenty or so were still used for skipping in Inner London playgrounds when I was conducting my survey. According to the Opies (*LLS*, 1959, p. 65), these include what is perhaps an early version of **6.A.31** I LIKE COFFEE, I LIKE TEA which I found in nineteen schools. I also noted **6.A.53** BLUEBELLS, COCKLE SHELLS from thirteen schools, **6.A.43** MOTHER'S IN THE KITCHEN from twelve schools, **6.A.41** VOTE, VOTE, VOTE and **6.A.45** ALL IN TOGETHER from six schools each, and **6.A.55A** I KNOW A BOY from four schools.

There is another skipping rhyme which is widespread and popular: **6.A.26** I'M A GIRL GUIDE, from fourteen schools, is similar to rhymes current at the time of the First World War, and perhaps ultimately derives from the nursery rhyme: "Hector Protector" (Opies, *ODNR*, 1951, p. 200). **6.A.31** I LIKE COFFEE, I LIKE TEA, already referred to, can trace its ancestry back to Halliwell (1842, p. 86, 1843, p. 105). **6.A.3** EEVER, WEEVER, CHIMNEY SWEEPER and **6.A.36** NOT LAST NIGHT BUT THE NIGHT BEFORE both have versions in Bolton's collection of counting-out rhymes.[1] Thus it would appear that, although skipping as a popular children's activity with accompanying chants may not be very old, it demonstrates a continuity and persistence of tradition comparable to that of the singing games. Abrahams (1969, p. xv) quotes from William Hugh Jansen who stated that in at least one region of the USA, boys' skipping still prevailed in the 1920s. However, it is generally accepted that in the British Isles the changeover to skipping as a girls' activity occurred in the last decades of the nineteenth century. The type of clothing then worn by girls prevented the development of complicated skills and variation of movement until the inter-war years of the twentieth century.

Gomme (1898, pp. 200–201) gives examples of a number of skipping games with "more or less complicated movements of the rope and feet", unaccompanied by any singing or chanting. These all seem to have disappeared. One example she cites that has an accompanying chant is "Pepper, salt, mustard, cider, vinegar", where the rope is turned increasingly quickly. This is still played as **6.A.18** SALT, VINEGAR, MUSTARD, PEPPER, though versions with various actions are usually preferred such as "High low dolly pepper". Another category referred to by Gomme (1898, pp. 201–204) is the divinatory one where the skipper's sweetheart is named, and possibly the details of courtship, marriage and children are indicated by the point in the chant where the skipper trips. A number of rhymes are now used for the business of divination (**6.A.53–6.A.61**). Usually they are just looked upon as good fun, but reference to marriage and the actual naming of the sweetheart might be regarded in a kind of semi-serious fashion by the girls taking part. The longstanding tradition of these skipping sequences and their popularity along with a number of other divinatory practices all seem to point in this direction. The boys who happen to be around when these rhymes are chanted go through the expected mocking and the pretended indignation if their names are mentioned.

A number of traditional singing games have been saved from possible extinction by their being adopted for use as skipping rhymes. As Sutton-Smith points out (1959, p. 5, p. 30, passim), not only the greater freedom of girls' clothing but the changing social conditions and way of life allowed more vigorous and lively activity than many of the old singing games provided, and skipping is one of the activities which offers this greater excitement and humour. Such adaptations have been and still are used in a number of Inner London schools, including: **6.A.45** ALL IN TOGETHER, **6.A.46** HERE'S A LITTLE FRENCH GIRL from "Bingo", **6.A.54** ALL THE GIRLS IN OUR TOWN, and **6.A.58** ROSY APPLE, LEMON TART from "Blackcurrant, Redcurrant". **6.A.59** ON A MOUNTAIN STANDS A LADY is probably the most popular of these adaptations.[2]

Rhymes used originally for other purposes also sometimes become adopted as skipping rhymes. The Opies (*LLS*, 1959, p. 23) give an example of a rhyme which was popular for a century and a half before being printed in 1909: "It warn't last night bu' th' night before,/Three big beggars knockt at the door; …". This was taken up for skipping and was still very popular as **6.A.36** NOT LAST NIGHT BUT THE NIGHT BEFORE. **6.A.41** VOTE, VOTE, VOTE, sung to the tune of the chorus in "Tramp! Tramp! Tramp! (The Prisoner's Hope)", was a partisan street song for election times. It told the electorate to vote for the favoured candidate and informed the candidate not so favoured that he might expect a hostile and even violent reception. Later it was adapted for skipping, no doubt because of its strong rhythm and because one could name the girls alternately as they were welcomed and rejected from the turning rope.

Although solo skipping is an activity which can be indulged in when there are no friends around to play with, the skipper tends to get out of breath while turning the rope, jumping, and possibly doing additional movements as well as trying to chant the rhyme. The song may come out between puffs of breath to help the rhythm of the turning rope but the melody will tend to get lost and the volume muted. The skipper is limited in her movements compared with those possible when the actions can be concentrated on while the rope is turned by others. She can change her steps, the direction of the rope and its speed; she can swing the rope to one side etc., but as the point of many games is being "out" or "not out" in competition with others, much of the fun is missing. I once knew a girl who imagined she was different people in turn while she was skipping, but she was an exception. Gomme (1898, p. 200) believed that solo skipping was probably developed later than group activities.

Although the possible permutations of actions in group skipping are extensive, they tend to fall into certain categories. Apart from divinatory skipping or repeated chanting of verses until the skipper trips, certain groupings can be distinguished:

1. The skippers, one at a time, go through a series of movements.
2. The skipper is joined by one or more others. Skippers are called out or pushed out and are replaced by others who are called in or invited in.
3. The skipper goes out and comes in again, sometimes having to perform certain actions.
4. Similarly to the divinatory rhymes, the skipper continues until tripped on a particular line of the rhyme, or on a particular number or letter.
5. The rope changes speed, usually getting faster and faster.

Series of movements by skipper This may take the form of a series of unrelated movements, usually numbered, e.g. skipping with hands up, crouching down with the rope being turned overhead as in **6.A.8** MY AUNT DAISY, or of actions of a miming nature similar to the "One, two, buckle my shoe" kind, as in **6.A.34** NUMBER ONE, SUCK YOUR THUMB. In **6.A.39** JELLY ON THE PLATE the original simple action of wobbling the body to imitate jelly in a rhyme which is almost ubiquitous, has been developed to include many other actions as in the several examples given, usually involving the miming of picking something up or removing it. Actions of a more acrobatic character are called for in **6.A.52** CHARLIE CHAPLIN WENT TO FRANCE. These include turning round, kicking high, doing the splits (by suggestion). This routine has an ingredient of "showing off" already referred to in connection with a number of singing games and action rhymes. Narrative elements are included in **6.A.30** NELSON, NELSON where the hero suffers various physical losses involving increasing difficulty until further skipping is impossible; **6.A.40** TEDDY BEAR has to perform a number of actions before he can "say goodnight" (leave the rope); the Girl Guide in **6.A.26** I'M A GIRL GUIDE also has to perform a series of actions. This rhyme is very popular and has been subject to much variation throughout the English-speaking world. Version **6.A.26A** contains an element of teasing.

Skipper joined by one or more who are invited in They replace the original skipper or are expelled.

This can be a simple replacement at the end of the rhyme, usually indicated. Examples are: **6.A.50** TWO LITTLE MEN IN A FLYING SAUCER and **6.A.25** SKIP A LULU. In **6.A.2** CHANGE KEYS, two girls cross over a turned rope, doing a kind of do-si-do movement. In **6.A.43** MOTHER'S IN THE KITCHEN, a girl is replaced by another (representing a burglar, bogeyman or animal) who pushes her out. In several popular rhymes the skipper invites another girl in to the rope. They skip together for a few turns and then the first one leaves. This is a feature of: **6.A.5** I WISH TONIGHT WAS SATURDAY NIGHT, where the first skipper merely retires. In **6.A.31** I LIKE COFFEE, I LIKE TEA, the chosen one is later rejected. In **6.A.38** THERE'S SOMEONE UNDER THE BED, a "sister" is invited in to help. She is later insulted and told to leave. In **6.A.41** VOTE, VOTE, VOTE, the singers applaud the skipper, then another one is called in and the first one is rudely rejected. Perhaps this type of skipping game persists because it reflects, in an exaggerated form, the often rapid turnover of attraction and repulsion in personal relationships among girls of this age group. Sometimes more than two girls are involved in the changeover. In **6.A.46** HERE'S A LITTLE FRENCH GIRL, three girls come in to the rope when called and leave, one by one. More than two girls skip together in **6.A.44** OLD MOTHER HUBBARD and in some versions of **6.A.45c** ALL IN TOGETHER.

Running in and out of the rope, or running round it In **6.A.10** OVER THE MOON AND UNDER THE STARS, girls run in, one after the other, either dodging under or skipping over a turning rope, while in **6.A.20** UNDER AND OVER, CASANOVA the skipper has to run under or jump over a rocking rope and then skip in and out; similarly for **6.A.21** DIP, DIP, DO A SKIP, except that the rope is turned faster and faster. For **6.A.36** NOT LAST NIGHT BUT THE NIGHT BEFORE the skipper is knocked out by robbers etc., as in **6.A.43** MOTHER'S IN THE KITCHEN, already mentioned. She comes back to do a series of actions, but sometimes has to run right round the rope before returning. In **6.A.32** I'M A LITTLE BUMPER (BUBBLE) CAR, which is very popular, the running round is the important part, representing the little car going round the "coooooooorner", which is chanted by all.

Skipping till tripped, sometimes on a special word, a letter or number This, of course, is the special feature in a divinatory rhyme and is repeated a number of times to ascertain different details. There are several other ways in which this device is used. It might be a simple "Miss a loop you're out" as in **6.A.6** KEEP THE KETTLE BOILING or **6.A.42** DOWN TO MISSISSIPPI. Another very popular rhyme: **6.A.53** BLUEBELLS, COCKLE SHELLS, not only has a divinatory version (**6.A.53F**) but other versions decide on a birthday month (**6.A.53A**), how many boys the skipper kissed the night before (**6.A.53E**), or how many stitches Mother did in the kitchen (**6.A.53B**), by adding on a fragment from **6.A.43** MOTHER'S IN THE KITCHEN. Similarly **6.A.27** CINDERELLA DRESSED IN YELLA may be used to enquire how many doctors were needed to cure a tummy ache (**6.A.27A**), how many kisses were given to her "fella" (**6.A.27B**) or how many people were disgusted when her knickers fell down (**6.A.27C**). How many gallons of petrol used by **6.A.33** RACING CAR NUMBER NINE is another of the same kind of rhyme. Numbers also feature in all versions of **6.A.26B** I'M A GIRL GUIDE which I recorded, while letters of the alphabet are recited in **6.A.1** INGLE, SPINGLE, SPANGLE and **6.A.16** BIG BEN. Various actions have to be performed according to which of four letters the skipper trips on in **6.A.15** H-E-L-P which is repeated continuously until she does trip.

Rope turned with increasing speed This kind of skipping is referred to by Gomme over a century ago (1898, p. 200). Examples usually finish with a recital of various condiments, the last one, "pepper", involving the turning of the rope very fast indeed. **6.A.17** FISH AND CHIPS AND VINEGAR, **6.A.18** SALT, VINEGAR, MUSTARD, PEPPER, and **6.A.24** FAR AWAY IN GERMANY are good examples. Fast and slow speeds are used in a version of **6.A.3A** EEVER, WEEVER, CHIMNEY

SWEEPER. "Bumps", where the rope is turned so fast that it passes twice under the feet for one jump, as dealt with by Ritchie (*GC*, 1965, pp. 118–120), and by Violet Ellis (1979, 38–40), does not appear to be so popular in Inner London as in Edinburgh. Interesting examples of skipping rhymes being adapted from dips are to be seen in **6.A.3B** PETER, PETER, PUMPKIN-EATER, **6.A.16** BIG BEN, **6.A.29** COWBOY JOE FROM MEXICO (which is accompanied by actions and retains the "O-U-T spells out" formulation), **6.A.33** RACING CAR, NUMBER NINE, and **6.A.36** NOT LAST NIGHT BUT THE NIGHT BEFORE.

NOTES

1. Bolton (1888): "Heeper, weeper, chimney-sweeper/Got a wife and couldn't keep her …" p. 116; "All last night, and the night before/Twenty robbers at my door …" p. 117.
2. For a discussion of this rhyme and its analogues, see Kelsey (*K2*, 1985, 78–85).

6.A   ROPE SKIPPING

6.A.1   INGLE, SPINGLE, SPANGLE

> Ingle, spingle, spangle, One, two, three,
> Do you know your ABC?
> ABCDEFG … Z.

> Cubitt Town 1983.

See also **6.B.2**.

Printed version Opies, *CGSP*, dip, pp. 33–34.

6.A.2 CHANGE KEYS

> Change keys with your next door neighbour,
> Change keys with your next door neighbour,
> Change keys with your next door neighbour,
> Early in the morning.

> Walworth 1979.

> Two girls approach the rope from both sides; they skip and go round each other something like a do-si-do in a folk dance.

Printed versions Cosbey draws a parallel between this (English) game as described here, and the Saskatchewan one: Changing bedrooms 1, 2, 3, pp. 7, 66. See also Holbrook's description of a skipping game called "Visiting" (pp. 54–55): "… While … skipping they change places, one saying to the other as they cross, 'Give me some bread and butter', and the other answering, 'Try my next-door neighbour'."

6.A.3 EEVER, WEEVER, CHIMNEY SWEEPER

> A. Eever, weever, chimney sweeper,
>   Had a wife and couldn't keep her,
>   Had another, did not love her,
>   Please turn fast.
>
> Eever, weever, chimney sweeper,
> Had a wife and could not keep her,
> Had another, did not love her,
> Please turn slow.

Mile End 1968.

> Rhymes are recited at contrasting speeds.

> B. Peter, Peter, pumpkin eater,
>   Had a wife and could not keep her.

Deptford 1983.

Printed versions Abrahams, p. 46; Bolton (see below); Brady, p. 89; Daiken, *CGTY*, p. 64; Douglas (see below); Gaskell (see below); Kellett (see below); Nelson, p. 68; Northall (see below); Opies, *ISE*, Eaper Weaper, chimney sweeper, p. 18, *ODNR*, Peter, Peter, pumpkin eater, p. 346, *LLS*, Eaver Weaver, chimney sweeper, pp. 20, 21; Shaw, Eeper, Weeper, chimbley sweeper, 1969, p. 43, 1970, p. 71; Smith, *BBHG*, p. 16; Todd, 6.

Early notings Heeper, weeper, chimney-sweeper,/Got a wife and couldn't keep her;/Got another, couldn't love her,/Heeper, weeper, chimney-sweeper, Bolton, 1888, p. 116, No. 779, Newcastle; Peter, Peter, pumpkin eater,/Had a wife and couldn't keep her;/Put her in a pumpkin-shell,/And then he kept her very well, Bolton, 1888, p. 116, No. 780, New York. Northall, 1892, counting-out rhyme, p. 345. Eever iver, chimney sweeper, Gaskell, c1913, p. 7. Eaper Weaper, chimbley-sweeper, Douglas, 1916, p. 53, 1931, p. 28. Eever Weaver chimney sweeper, Kellett, 1920s, p. 58.

6.A.4   EGGS A PENNY EACH

> Eggs a penny each,
> Eggs a penny each,
> Quick mum, buy some,
> Eggs a penny each.
> Eggs are tuppence each,
> Eggs are tuppence each,
> Quick mum, buy some,
> Eggs are tuppence each.
> Eggs are threepence each (and so on).

> <u>Mile End 1966</u>; Brixton 1982; Borough 1983.

Printed version   Rosen and Steele, [p. 2].

Early noting A correspondent (Romford, 1981) remembers skipping to this rhyme in London c1930.

6.A.5   I WISH TONIGHT WAS SATURDAY NIGHT

> I wish tonight was Saturday night,
> Tomorrow will be Sunday,
> I'll be dressed in all my best,
> To walk along with (_____).   (new girl enters)
> (_____) likes candy,
> I like shandy.
> (_____) likes kissing the boys,
> Whoops a diddle a dandy.   (first girl leaves)
>
> Verse repeated for each girl.
>
> Mile End 1968.

Printed versions Abrahams, p. 97; Douglas (see below); Ritchie, *GC*, p. 113, p. 124.

Early noting (first two lines only) O tonight is Saturday night,/Tomorrow will be Sunday— Douglas, 1916, p. 89, 1931, p. 51.

Recordings BBC 19004 (78) (1953, Kentish Town); BBC 19926 (78) (1953, Edinburgh).

6.A.6   KEEP THE KETTLE BOILING

> Keep the kettle boiling,
> Never miss a loop.   (Boiling, boiling)
>
> Keep the kettle boiling,
> Miss a loop you're out.

Mile End 1968; Borough 1983; Kensington 1984.

"You jump in and you jump out but you've got to keep in time." girl, Kensington 1984.

Printed versions Abrahams, p. 105; Brady, p. 79; Cosbey, p. 79; Evans, *JRR*, p. 6; Kellett, rhyme begins: "Duck, a quack, a chicken and a hen," p. 61; Ritchie, *GC*, p. 114; Turner, p. 31; Worstell, p. 6.

6.A.7   MADEMOISELLE WENT TO THE WELL

SKIPPING or BALL BOUNCING RHYME:

A. Mademoiselle
    Went to the well
    She washed her face,
    And dried it well.

B. Little Nell,
    She didn't feel well,
    She washed her face,
    And dried it well.

Mile End 1966.

Printed versions Abrahams, pp. 116, 117; Brady, p. 78; Daiken, *CGTY*, Parnell/Went to the well, ball bouncing, p. 34, Mademoiselle, skipping, p. 64; Douglas (see below); Opies, *ISE*, p. 57; Rutherford, p. 17; cf. Shaw, Parlee vouze Fransie madam-mer-selle/Went to the lavatory and in she fell—, 1970, p. 11; Sutton-Smith, Madam Morel,/She went to the well, p. 82; Mademoiselle,/She goes to the wall (sic), p. 88; Turner, pp. 50–51.

Early noting "… MADEMOISELLE WENT TO THE WELL (which is interesting because they have forgotten what 'mademoiselle' means and now call it ADAM AND ELL) …", Douglas, 1916, pp. 95–96, 1931, p. 55.

6.A.8 MY AUNT DAISY

A. My Aunt Daisy drives me crazy,
Up the ladder, (skip with hands up)
Down the ladder, (bend down, turn rope above head)
One up to Lulu, two up to Lulu, (two skips then turn rope above head etc.)
Three up to Lulu, etc. (till):
Ten up to Lulu.

Walworth 1974, 1980.

B. One, two, three, Auntie Lulu,
Four, five, six, Auntie Lulu,
Seven, eight, nine, Auntie Lulu,
Ten Auntie Lulu, ten Auntie Lulu, ten Auntie Lulu,
You're out.

West Norwood 1970; Dalston 1983.

Printed versions Botkin (see below); Evans, *JRR*, Old Man Lazy, drives me crazy, p. 15; Fowke, Old Man Daisy, p. 65; Kenney, Old man Daisy,/He's gone crazy, p. 8; Smith, *BBHG*, Up the ladder, down the ladder,/Over the garden wall./1 2 3 4 5, etc., p. 25; also "1, 2, 3, on to Lulu", p. 18; Turner, p. 41; Withers, *RIMP*, Old Man Daisy,/You're driving me crazy, p. 61.

Early noting Old Man Lazy/Drives me crazy;/Up the ladder,/Down the ladder,/H-O-T spells hot! Botkin, *TAF*, 1944, p. 793.

6.A.9 DOCTOR, DOCTOR, HOW DO YOU DO?

Doctor, Doctor, how do you do?
Very well, thank you, How about you?
O-U-T spells out,
U-N-D-E-R spells under,
O-V-E-R spells over,

I-N spells in.
Once you're in you can't get out,
'Less you turn around.
Once you're in you can't get out,
Unless you touch the ground.
Once you're in you can't get out,
Unless you do the kicks,
Once you're in you can't get out,
Unless you do the splits.

Barnsbury 1983.

Actions are obvious from the above. If you do all the actions without missing, you stay till the end of the verse.

Printed versions (last eight lines) cf. Brady, p. 77; Kellett (see below), with a longer version for skipping on p. 87; Opies, *LLS*, p. 3 (and see below); Rutherford, p. 60; cf. Shaw, 1970, Little Black Doctor, how is your wife?/Very well, thank you, she's all right./She won't eat salt-fish,/Or a stick of licquorice (sic)./O-U-T spells out, p. 89.

Early notings The Opies (*LLS*, 1959, p. 3) state that the rhyme was known as early as 1818. Cf. Little fatty doctor, how's your wife,/Very well thank you, that (sic) all right,/Can't eat a bit of fish or a stick of liquorice,/Out spells out, Kellett, 1920s, counting-out rhyme, p. 19.

6.A.10 OVER THE MOON AND UNDER THE STARS

Over the moon and under the moon (stars)

Mile End 1967.

Run in, one after the other, skipping over or dodging under.

Printed versions Brady p. 99; Rutherford, p. 67; Smith, *BBHG*, Over the stars/And under the moon, p. 25; Turner, p. 40.

6.A.11 SMITH'S CRISPS ARE THE BEST

>Smith's Crisps* are the best,
>North and south
>And east and west.
>
>Marylebone 1967.

* A well-known brand of potato crisps.

Printed versions cf. Brady, part of rhyme: Keep it boiling,/On the glimmer,/If you don't/You won't get your dinner./North, South, East and West/Cadbury's chocolates are the best, p. 76; cf. Turner, Baby's biscuits are the best/From north, south, east and west, plus two other versions, p. 20.

6.A.12 SKINAMALINKY LONG LEGS

>Skinamalinky long legs
>Eating banana split.
>If you want a piece of jelly,
>Just jump out.
>
>Marylebone 1967.

Printed versions Abrahams, p. 178; cf. Browne, 18; Opies, *LLS*, p. 168; Ritchie, *SS*, p. 76; Rodger, p. 10; Rosen and Steele, [p. 2]; Smith, *BBHG*, p. 13; Sutton-Smith, teasing rhyme, p. 93.

6.A.13 MRS. SQUIRREL

>Mrs. Squirrel up the tree,
>Came to school at half past three.
>
>Marylebone 1967.

6.A.14 RED ROSE

Red Rose, picked her nose,
Wiped it on her clean clothes.

Walworth 1979.

6.A.15 H-E-L-P

H-E-L-P, H-E-L-P ...

West Norwood 1970; Walworth 1974, 1979; Cubitt Town 1983.

"You skip really fast until you stop. Whatever letter you stop on, you have to do it:

> H is high. You have to jump ten times.
> E is everything, you skip very fast.
> L is low. You have to jump over a low rope ten times.
> P is a pirate, with one eye and one leg."   girl, 11, EC1.

"E stands for ender (take ends)."   Cubitt Town.

Printed versions Cosbey, p. 75; Knapps, p. 120; Turner, p. 26.

6.A.16 BIG BEN

SKIPPING GAME, sometimes used for elastic skipping:

Big Ben strikes one, tick-tock, two tick-tock,
Three, four, five tick-tock, six tick-tock.
ABC, ABC, ABCDE ... Z
You're out.

Mile End 1964.

See also **2.10** and **6.B.1**.

Printed versions Abrahams, pp. 17–18; Douglas (see below); Kellett, p. 125; Opies, *LLS*, p. 4; Ritchie, *GC*, p. 140; Searle, 132; Smith, *BBHG*, p. 24; Turner, ball-bouncing, p. 49.

Early noting Big Ben Strikes One, skipping game, Douglas, 1916, p. 49, 1931, p. 26.

6.A.17 FISH AND CHIPS AND VINEGAR

Fish and chips and vinegar, vinegar, vinegar,
Fish and chips and vinegar, pepper, pepper pot.

Blackheath 1983.

6.A.18 SALT, VINEGAR, MUSTARD, PEPPER

Salt, vinegar, mustard, pepper, salt, vinegar, mustard, pepper …

"Pepper" is very fast skipping.

Walworth 1974.

Printed versions Abrahams, p. 175; Botkin (see below); Brady, p. 78; Daiken, *CGTY*, p. 63; Douglas (see below); Gaskell (see below); Gillington (see below); Holbrook, p. 54; Hubbard, 262; Kellett (see below); Leach and Fried, My mother uses salt,/Ginger, mustard, *pepper*, p. 1016; Ritchie, *GC*, p. 137; Rosen and Steele, [p. 2]; Smith, *BBHG*, p. 26; Starn, p. 97; Todd, 7; Turner, p. 37.

Early notings Lay the cloth,/Knife and fork,/Don't forget the salt;/Mustard—/Vinegar—/Pepper—. At the last word the one in the rope has to skip very quickly till she breaks down, and another takes her place, Gillington, 1909, *OHSG*, Skipping-Rope Rhyme No. II, [p. iii]. "Doing pepper" (turning the rope rapidly), Gaskell, c1913, p. 7. [Some skipping rhymes] end … with the things in the cruet-stand (salt, mustard, vinegar, pepper), Douglas, 1916, p. 52, 1931, p. 27. Kellett, 1920s, p. 59; Botkin, *TAF*, 1944, p. 768.

6.A.19 HIGH, LOW, DOLLY, PEPPER

A. High, low, dolly, pepper,
    High, low, dolly, pepper,
    One, two, three.

Earlsfield 1982; Blackheath 1983.

B. High, low, swinging, dolly,
    High, low, swinging, dolly,
    High, low, swinging, dolly,
    Mrs. Macaroni.

Barnsbury 1983.

C. High, low, slow, dolly, rocker, pepper …

Kensington 1984.

"After saying it twice, the rope is turned very fast. Then if you land on 'high' you have to turn the rope high in the air. For 'low' you have to crouch low and touch the floor. For 'dolly' you're a sort of Russian dancer. For 'rocker' they turn the rope from side to side, not right over. For 'pepper', the rope is turned fast and you have to keep your eyes shut."

girl, 11, Kensington 1984.

Printed versions Abrahams, pp. 35, 63; Cosbey, pp. 75–76; Douglas (see below); Gomme, (see below); Hubbard, 262; Kenney, p. 11; Ritchie, *GC*, pp. 118, 130; Rutherford, p. 55; Shaw, 1970, Pitch, patch, pepper, mentioned, p. 72; Slow down Sally/What do you like the best?/ High-low-dolly-sweeper-/baby-jig, p. 89; Smith, *BBHG*, p. 15; Turner, p. 27.

Early notings Knife and fork,/Lay the cloth,/Dont forget the salt,/ Mustard, vinegar,/Pepper! Gomme, 1898, p. 204, Deptford. Slow skip, what you like,/A dolly or a pepper, Douglas, 1916, p. 91, 1931, p. 52.

Recording MacColl and Seeger, *The Elliotts of Birtley.*

6.A.20 UNDER AND OVER, CASANOVA

> Under and over, Casanova,
> Under and over, Casanova,
> In and out, in out, in out,
> Boom! Boom! Boom!
>
> In and out, Casanova,
> In and out, Casanova,
> In and out, Casanova,
> Boom! Boom! Boom!

Rock the rope, run under, jump over, skip in and out, etc.

> Earlsfield 1982; Barnsbury 1983.

6.A.21 DIP, DIP, DO A SKIP

> Dip, dip, do a skip,
> Dip, dip, do a skip,
> If you skip, do a dip,
> Dip, dip, do a skip.

Rock the rope, jump over, skip etc., getting quicker and quicker.

> Barnsbury 1983.

6.A.22 ALICE IN WONDERLAND

Alice in Wonderland,
Skipping brown mouse,
Stepped in the puddle,
And that was the end
Of her and the mouse.

Kensington 1984.

6.A.23 TWO LITTLE SAUSAGES

Two little sausages, frying in the pan,
One went pop and the other went bang.

Sometimes start with five sausages, then reducing, four, three, two, one.

Brockley 1967; Mile End 1968; West Norwood 1973.

Printed versions Brady, p. 81; Dennison, counting out, 292; Fowke, p. 55; Opies, *CGSP*, p. 237; Rosen and Steele, [p. 19]; Turner, p. 40.

6.A.24 FAR AWAY IN GERMANY (UP IN THE NORTH)

Far away in Germany, a long way off,
Hitler's got the whooping cough,
What shall we give him to make him better?
Salt, vinegar, mustard, pepper.
"Pepper" means turning the rope very quickly.

Hampstead 1984.

Printed versions Abrahams, Down in the meadow not far off, p. 43; Up in a loft/A long way off, p. 200; Botkin (see below); Douglas (see below); Holbrook, as Abrahams, p. 57; McMorland, p. 19; Northall (see below); Ritchie, *GC*, p. 138; cf. Shaw, Up yonder hill a far way off/The wind near blew/My billycock off. …, 1970, p. 76; Withers, *RIMP*, Far over the hills, p. 3.

Early notings there are more of the "Billycock" rhymes in other collections: cf. Northall, 1892, p. 565: Over the hills and a long way off,/And the wind has blown my topknot off. However, these couplets were used as the last lines to the song "Tom, Tom, the Piper's Son". Up in the North, a long way off,/The donkey's got the whooping cough— Douglas, 1916, p. 92, 1931, p. 53. Over the hills and a good way off,/A woodchuck died with the whooping-cough, Botkin, *TAF*, 1944, p. 785.

6.A.25 SKIP A LULU

> Skip a Lulu, skip a Lulu,
> Skip a Lulu, you must do,
> Skip a Lulu, you must do,
> Out you go, in you come.

Barnsbury 1983.

Printed versions Abrahams, Little Lulu/Dressed in bluelu, p. 112; Smith, *BBHG*, 1, 2, 3, on to Lulu, /4, 5. 6, on to Lulu, p. 18.

6.A.26 I'M A GIRL GUIDE

SKIPPING SONG, ACTION SONG:

> A. I'm a Girl Guide, dressed in blue,
>   These are the actions I must do:
>   Salute to the captain,
>   Bow to the Queen,
>   Show your knickers to the football team,
>   The football team, the football team,
>   Close your eyes and count sixteen:
>   1, 2, 3, 4, 5, 6, 7, 8 … 16.

Clapham 1983; <u>Walworth 1979, 1981</u>; Brixton, Greenwich 1982; Dalston, Kentish Town, Shepherds Bush 1983; Hampstead, Kensington 1984.

   B.   I am a Girl Guide, dressed in blue,
         These are the actions I must do:
         Salute to the captain, bow to the Queen,
         Turn right round and count sixteen:
         1, 2, 3, 4, 5, 6, 7, 8 … 16.

         I am a Girl Guide dressed in green,
         Close your eyes and count fifteen:
         1, 2, 3, 4 … 15.

         I am a Girl Guide dressed in yellow,
         These are the times I kiss my fellow:
         1, 2, 3, 4 …

         I am a Girl Guide dressed in red,
         These are the times I go to bed:
         1, 2, 3, 4 …

         I am a Girl Guide dressed in brown,
         These are the times I go to town:
         1, 2, 3, 4 …

         I am a Girl Guide dressed in black,
         These are the times I'll get the sack:
         1, 2, 3, 4 …

<u>Marylebone 1967</u>; <u>Mile End 1968</u> (one verse only); Barnsbury 1983.

This is the only extended version I have come across. Other versions include:

   C.   Twist right round to the fairy queen.

       Walworth 1974; Battersea 1982.

D. Turn my back to the fairy queen.

Borough 1983.

E. Turn right round to the L.C.C.

Mile End 1967.

See also **4.46** and **6.A.52**.

Printed versions Abrahams, p. 70; Botkin (see below); Brady, p. 86; Cosbey, p. 76; Cumnock Academy, p. 26; Daiken, *CGTY*, p. 65, *TTP*, p. 15; Douglas (see below); Fowke, p. 48; Halliwell (see below); Holbrook, p. 56; Kellett, ball bouncing and skipping, pp. 16, 17 (and see below); Kenney, Salad Girl, p. 16; Kings (see below); Lang (see below); Mills and Bishop (see below); Opies (see below); Ritchie, cf. Kings and Queens/And partners two … *SS*, p. 27, *GC*, pp. 114–115; I'm a Girl Guide/Dressed in blue, *GC*, p. 132; Rodger, p. 22; Rutherford, a version of Douglas's rhyme, below, p. 69; Shaw (see below); Sutton-Smith, p. 81; Turner, p. 28; Withers, *CO*, Jean, Jean, Dressed in green, [p. 33]; Worstell, p. 35.

Early notings This rhyme may perhaps ultimately derive from the following: Hector Protector was dressed all in green;/Hector Protector was sent to the Queen./The Queen did not like him,/Nor more did the King:/So Hector Protector was sent back again, Halliwell, *NRNTE*, c1870, p. 5, and Lang, 1897, p. 37. I'm a little Girl Guide dressed in blue,/These are the actions I have to do,/Salute to the king and bow to the Queen,/And turn my back on the Kaiser Bill, Kellett, "from the '14–18 War", p. 16. Salute the King/Salute the Queen,/Salute the German submarine, Opies, *LLS*, 1959, p. 319, "During and after the First World War". I had a dolly dressed in green,/I didn't like her—I gave her to the Queen—/The Queen didn't like her—she gave her to the cat—/The cat didn't like her, because she wasn't fat, Shaw, 1970, said to date from c1915, p. 74. Douglas, 1916, p. 52, 1931, p. 27. I am a Girl Scout, Kings 2, 1930, p. 23. Cf. rhyme beginning "One, two, three, four", Mills and Bishop, 1937, 40. Botkin, *TAF*, 1944, as Mills and Bishop, p. 802.

In some more recent collections, versions appear which may be intermediate between the "Hector Protector" and "Girl Guide" rhymes. Cf. for example, Abrahams, p. 69: I'm a girl dressed in green./ My mother didn't want me/So she sent me to the Queen: …; Kellett, p. 17; and Ritchie, *GC*, pp. 132–133: "I'm a Girl Guide dressed in green" which continues rather like Douglas's and Abrahams's examples.

Recording BBC 3539 (78) (1941, Yorkshire).

6.A.27 CINDERELLA DRESSED IN YELLA

A. Cinderella (Arabella) dressed in yella,
Went upstairs (downstairs) to kiss a fella,
Kissed a snake by mistake,
Then she had a tummy ache,
How many doctors did it take?
1, 2, 3, 4 …

Earlsfield, Greenwich 1982.

B. Cinderella dressed in yella,
Went upstairs to kiss her fella,
How many kisses did she give?
1, 2, 3, 4 …

Finsbury 1983.

C. Cinderella dressed in red,
Went to town to buy some bread.
On the way her knickers busted,
How many people were disgusted?

Dulwich 1983.

See also **2.59** and **4.63**.

Printed versions Abrahams, pp. 30–31; Botkin (see below); Cole, counting-out rhyme, p. 36; Cosbey, p. 67; Cumnock Academy, p. 21;

Evans, *JRR*, p. 13; Fowke, p. 49; Fulton and Smith, p. 39; Hubbard, mentioned, 263; Jorgensen, *SWF*, 67; Kenney, p. 3; Knapps, pp. 125–126; Lowenstein, p. 3; Mills and Bishop (see below); Nelson, p. 71; Smith, *BBHG*, p. 24; cf. Sutton-Smith, Cinderella at a ball,/Cinderella had a fall,/ …, p. 77; My little sister,/Dressed in pink,/ …, p. 79; Todd, 6; Turner, pp. 22–23 (and see below); Withers, *RIMP*, p. 65; Worstell, p. 4.

Early notings Cinderella, dressed in yellow,/Gone downtown to buy an umbrella;/On the way she met her fellow./How many kisses did she receive?/Five, ten, fifteen, twenty, etc., Mills and Bishop, 1937, 34. Cinderella, dressed in red,/Went downtown to buy some thread./Along came a fellow whose name was Red,/And shot her with a bullet that was made of lead, Mills and Bishop, 1937, 34. Botkin, *TAF*, 1944: skipping rhyme, p. 791, "sidewalk rhyme", as Mills and Bishop, pp. 800–801. Turner (1972, p. 23) states that "This rhyme is almost certainly of American origin" and cites Mills and Bishop as the earliest reference.

6.A.28 CHOCOLATE BISCUITS

> Chocolate biscuits down the lane,
> If you want to spell your name,
> (M-A-R-Y   S-M-I-T-H)
> Spells (Mary Smith).
>
> Walworth 1979.

See also **2.50**.

Printed version Kellett, p. 125.

6.A.29 COWBOY JOE FROM MEXICO

> Cowboy Joe from Mexico,
> Hands up, stick 'em up,

Drop your guns, pick 'em up.
O-U-T spells out.

Marylebone 1967, Mile End 1967, 1983; West Norwood 1970; Walworth 1974, 1979; <u>Greenwich 1982</u>.

See also **2.48**.

From the popular song, "Ragtime Cowboy Joe", music by Lewis F. Muir and Maurice Abrahams, lyrics by Grant Clarke, published in the USA by F. A. Mills in 1912.

Printed versions Abrahams, Cowboy Joe, p. 33, Old Black Joe, p. 141; Cosbey, p. 83; Cumnock Academy, p. 11; Fowke, p. 59; Hubbard, mentioned, 263; Kellett, p. 61; Ritchie, *SS*, p. 33; Smith, *BBHG*, p. 12; Turner, p. 23; cf. Wood, *FAFR*, Joe, Joe, broke his toe,/on the way to Mexico, p. 106.

6.A.30 NELSON, NELSON

Nelson, Nelson, lost one eye,
Nelson, Nelson, lost the other eye,
Nelson, Nelson, lost one arm,
Nelson, Nelson, lost the other arm,
Nelson, Nelson, lost one leg,
Nelson, Nelson, drop down dead.

Walworth 1974.

Child skips with one eye closed, then both, then with one arm doubled up, then two arms, then with only one leg, then out.

Printed versions Fowke, p. 63; Turner, p. 32.

6.A.31 I LIKE COFFEE, I LIKE TEA

A. I like coffee,
I like tea,
I like (_____) in with me.

I don't like coffee,
I don't like tea,
I don't like (_____) in with me.

Sometimes "I hate coffee" etc. for second verse.

Child invited joins skipping and then has to leave.

West Norwood 1970; Walworth 1979; Brixton, Greenwich, Streatham 1982; Barnsbury, Blackheath, Borough, Dalston, Deptford, Dulwich, Mile End, Shepherds Bush, Stoke Newington 1983; Hampstead, Kensington 1984.

Printed versions Abrahams, pp. 85, 180; Knapps, p. 121; Opies, *LLS*, p. 117; Ritchie, *GC*, p. 131; Rosen and Steele, [p. 9]; Shaw, 1969, p. 52, 1970, p. 90; Solomons, p. 58.

B. I like coffee,
I like tea,
I like (_____) in with me.

Now she's in she can't get out,
So I'll have to push her out,
How many pushes shall I give her?
1, 2, 3 …
Hard, soft, hard, soft …

Mile End 1967; Barnsbury, <u>Dalston</u>, Finsbury, Kentish Town <u>1983</u>.

"When you say the name she jumps in with you. When you say, 'How many pushes?' you skip until the number it stops at. Then you say, 'Hard, soft …' until it stops. If it stops on 'hard' you have to push her as many times but hard." girl, 11, Dalston 1983.

Some omit the "hard" and "soft" decision.

    C. (_____) likes coffee,
        (_____) likes tea,
        (_____) likes sitting on (_____) knee.

<u>Battersea 1982</u>; Kentish Town

Printed versions Opies, *LLS*, p. 65; Rutherford, p. 72; Sutton-Smith, p. 79.

    D. I like coffee,
        I like tea,
        I'm going to do
        A great big wee.

Streatham 1982.

Other printed versions Abrahams, pp. 84–86; Bolton (see below); Botkin (see below); Boyce and Bartlett (see below); Daiken, *CGTY*, p. 33; Evans, *JRR*, p. 32; Fowke, p. 63; Halliwell (see below); Kellett (see below); Kings (see below); Knapps, p. 116; Mills and Bishop, (see below); Opies, *ODNR*, p. 334; *LLS*, p. 65, *SG*, p. 358; Ritchie, *GC*, pp. 28, 132; Rutherford, p. 70; Shaw, 1969, p. 52; 1970, p. 73; Sutton-Smith, p. 79; Withers, *RIMP*, p. 63; Worstell, p. 4.

Early notings One, two, three,/I love coffee,/And Billy loves tea./How good you be,/One, two, three,/I love coffee,/And Billy loves tea, Halliwell, *NRE*, 1842, p. 86, 1843, p. 105. Miss Mary Mack, dressed in black,/Silver buttons on her back./I love coffee, I love tea,/I love the boys, and the boys love me./ …, Bolton, 1888, p. 117. I like coffee I like tea,/I like sitting on a black man's knee, Kellett, 1920s, p. 58. Kings 2, 1930, p. 29; Mills and Bishop, 1937, 33; Boyce and Bartlett, 1941, as Halliwell, p. 18; Botkin, *TAF*, 1944, pp. 791, 795.

The Opies (*LLS*, 1959, p. 65) compare their rhyme "Do you like coffee?/ Do you like tea?/Do you like sitting on a blackman's knee?" with Douglas, 1916, p. 53: "Do you like silver and gold?/Do you like brass?/Do you like looking through/The looking-glass? …"

6.A.32 I'M A LITTLE BUMPER (BUBBLE) CAR

    A. I'm a little bumper (bubble) car,
         Number forty eight,
         I run round the coooooooorner
         And slam on the brakes.
         Bang—
         On—
         My—
         Brakes, brakes, brakes.

At "corner", the skipper runs round the end rope turner and continues skipping. In this version, there is fast skipping until the end.

<u>Earlsfield 1982</u>; without last part: Marylebone, Mile End 1967; Hampstead, West Norwood 1972; Walworth 1974; Brixton 1982.

Printed versions Abrahams, p. 80; Cosbey, p. 74; Fowke, p. 60; Hubbard, 260; cf. Kellett, I'm a corporation bus,/My number's forty-eight,/I whizzed round a corner,/And bumped into a gate, for skipping and ball bouncing, p. 97; Rutherford, p. 66; Turner, p. 26; Wade (1), 14, (2), 33–34.

    B. I'm a little bubble car,
         Number forty eight,
         I went (live) round the cooooooorner,
         And I pulled down the brakes.
         The brakes didn't work,
         So I tumbled down the hill.
         I had to go (ended up)(in) to hospital,
         I had to take some pills,

How many pills did you take?
1, 2, 3, 4 ...

Walworth 1979; Borough, <u>Dalston 1983</u>.

C.   Bumper car, bumper car,
Number forty eight,
Went round the cooooooorner,
And pulled on the brakes.
The brakes didn't work,
It skidded down the hill,
It landed in the duckpond,
And then stood still,
How many gallons did she lose?
1, 2, 3, 4 ...

Greenwich 1982; <u>Blackheath 1983</u>; Deptford 1983 (How many hours were you there?); Barnsbury 1983 (How many ducks could I count?)

D.   I'm a little bumper car,
Number forty eight,
Had to go to the doctor's
Round the cooooorner
1, 2, 3, 4, 5, 6 ...

"... and then you have to jump. Then you stop and play again." girl, 11, Hampstead 1984.

E.   Bumper car, bumper car,
Number forty eight,
I went round the coooooorner
And pulled up my brakes.
My brakes wouldn't work,
I tumbled down the hill,
I fell into a fish shop eating jellied eels.
How many jellied eels did I eat?
1, 2, 3, 4 ...

Mile End 1983; Finsbury 1983 (I landed in the baker's shop and had to pay the bill, 1, 2, 3, 4 …)

> F. I'm a little bumper car,
> Number forty eight,
> I went round the coooooorner,
> I stopped at the traffic lights,
> And pulled down my brake.
> The policeman caught me,
> And put me in jail,
> And all I had was a ginger ale.
> How many bottles did I drink?
> 5, 10, 15, 20 …

<u>Shepherds Bush</u>, Stoke Newington <u>1983</u>; Kensington 1984.

"And it's up to where you stop. When it comes to 'corner' you run out. You have to try and jump back in. When it comes to 'brakes' you have to make sure that the rope is between your legs." girl, 10, Shepherds Bush 1983.

Printed versions Fowke, p. 60; Rosen and Steele, [p. 16].

6.A.33 RACING CAR NUMBER NINE

> Racing car number nine,
> Using petrol all the time,
> How many gallons did you use?
> 10, 20, 30 … 100

Shepherds Bush 1983.

See also **2.4**.

Printed versions cf. Abrahams, Engine, engine, number nine,/Running on the Chicago (Frisco) line, p. 48; Bolton (see below); Newell (see below); Sluckin, dip, p. 16; Worstell, Engine, engine, p. 36.

Early notings It seems possible that the early versions referring to a (railway) engine developed into versions referring to a racing car. Engine number nine;/Ring the bell when it's time./O-U-T spells out goes he,/Into the middle of the dark blue sea, Bolton, 1888, p. 111. Engine No. 9,/Out goes she, Newell, 1903, p. 203.

Recording MacColl and Seeger, *The Elliotts of Birtley.*

6.A.34 NUMBER ONE, SUCK YOUR THUMB

> Number one, suck your thumb,
> Number two, touch your shoe,
> Number three, touch your knee,
> Number four, touch the floor,
> Number five, take a dive, (jump out, run round and come in again)
> Number six, show your knicks,
> Number seven, close your eyes,
> And count to eleven,
> 1, 2, 3, … 11.

> Finsbury 1983.

"You're skipping all the time and you do all the movements."

See also **7.29** and **7.45**.

Printed versions Fowke, ball bouncing, p. 81; Halliwell (see below); Nelson, ball-bouncing, p. 68; Sutton-Smith, p. 82; Turner, p. 51.

Early noting This rhyme may be a development from "One, two, buckle my shoe", cf. Halliwell, *NRE*, 1842, p. 132 and 1843, p. 161.

6.A.35 PEPSI COLA

> Pepsi Cola, Pepsi Cola, up,
> Pepsi Cola, Pepsi Cola, down.

> Walworth 1979.

6.A.36 NOT LAST NIGHT BUT THE NIGHT BEFORE

SKIPPING RHYME, ENTERTAINMENT RHYME:

A. Not last night but the night before,
Twenty five robbers came knocking at the door,
I opened the door to let them in,
They hit me on the head with a rolling pin.

Mile End 1968; Hampstead 1982; Dulwich 1983.

Addition:
The rolling pin was made of glass,
Do not slide it on my arse.

Deptford 1983.

Printed versions Abrahams, p. 110; Coffin and Cohen, p. 189; Evans, *JRR*, p. 14; Fulton and Smith, for hide and seek, pp. 54–55; cf. Hughes and Bontemps, p. 421; Knapps, pp. 122–123; Solomons, p. 107; Withers, *CO*, [p. 37], *RIMP*, p. 34.

B. Not last night but the night before,
Twenty four robbers came knocking at the door.
As I ran out to let them in,
This is what they said to me:
    Chinese lady*, turn around,   (* most versions have "Spanish lady")
    Chinese lady, touch the ground,
    Chinese lady, do the kicks,
    Chinese lady, do the splits.

West Norwood 1970; Battersea, Brixton, Earlsfield 1982; Cubitt Town, Mile End, Dalston (Mrs. Pill …) 1983.

Printed versions Botkin (see below); Cosbey, Not last night, p. 83, Spanish dancers, p. 89; Fowke, p. 48; Kenney, p. 2; Rutherford, p. 59; Solomons, Spanish dancer, p. 62; see also p. 51; Smith, *BBHG*, p. 20.

Early noting Last night and the night before/Twenty-four robbers came to my door,/And this is what they said:/"Buster, Buster, hands on head;/Buster, Buster, go to bed;/Buster, Buster, if you don't,/I'm afraid they'll find you dead." Botkin, *TAF*, 1944, p. 793.

Recording Webb, *Children's Singing Games.*

> C. Not last night but the night before,
>   Twenty four robbers came knocking at the door,
>   I ran ouuuuuut to let them in, (run round and come in again)
>   This is what they said to me:
>   (_____, _____), do the kicks,
>   (_____, _____), do the splits.

Barnsbury 1983.

> D. Not last night but the night before,
>   Two tom cats came knocking at my door.
>   I went downstairs to let them in,
>   They hit me on the head with a rolling pin,
>   They picked me up and smacked my
>   Ask no questions, tell no lies,
>   I see a little boy doing up his
>
>   Flies are bad but bugs are worse,
>   That's the end of my little verse.

Barnsbury 1983.

Printed versions Opies, *LLS*, tom cats/black cats/A lemon and a pickle, p. 23; Rodger, tom cats, p. 16.

> E. Not last night but the night before,
>   Three little monkeys came knocking at the door,
>   One with a tommy gun, one with a stick,

> One with a hand grenade hanging on his prick,
> One with a stick, one with a drum,
> One with a pancake stuck to his bum.   (See also **11.I.14**)

Hampstead 1984.

Printed versions Fowke, p. 48; Kellett (see below); Lowenstein, three tom cats, p. 33; Shaw, 1970, p. 110; Turner, three tomcats, entertainment rhyme, p. 97.

Early noting You know last night, you know the night before,/Two tom cats came knocking at mi (sic) door,/One had a fiddle, one had a drum,/ And one had a pancake stuck to his bum, Kellett, 1920s, p. 46.

> F.   Father Christmas came last night,
>   Brought two men, dressed in white,
>   One had a pistol, one had a gun,
>   Shoot! Bang! Fire!
>   Off he run.

Mile End 1968.

"When it says 'downstairs' it's made to last so you can jump out, run round and jump in again. When it says, 'turn around, touch the ground', and all that, you have to do what it says. You have to do the kicks and do the splits." girl, 11, Dalston 1983.

Many versions of this rhyme are used just for entertainment and it is difficult to disentangle the two uses. The last three are probably unlikely to be used for skipping.

See also **2.12B** and **2.12C**.

Other printed versions Bolton (see below); Gaskell (see below); Opies, *LLS*, p. 23; Rutherford, p. 59; Turner, p. 97.

Other early notings All last night, and the night before,/Twenty robbers at my door./Wake up, wake up, ginger blue,/And don't be afraid of the bugaboo! Bolton, 1888, for counting out, p. 117. There was a little man,/He had a little gun,/An' o'er yon field he run run run,/He'd a white sthraw hat/A bally full o' fat/An' a pancake stitched to his bum bum bum, Gaskell, c1913, p. 8. You know last night, well the night before/There came three monkeys knocking at my door./I went downstairs to let them in,/They knocked me down with the rolling pin./The rolling pin was made of ash,/They ran away with all my cash./I went upstairs to get in bed,/Fell on the floor and cracked my head./My poor old head gave me no peace,/I rubbed it o'er with candle grease./Candle grease it made it smart,/I wish I'd never let it start, Gaskell, c1913, p. 10.

6.A.37 MY MOTHER SAID

> A. My mother said I never should
> Play with the gipsies in the wood.
> If I did she would say:
> "Naughty girl to disobey,
> Your hair shan't curl,
> Your shoes shan't shine."
> My father said that if I did,
> He'd hit my head with the teapot lid.

Mile End 1967; <u>Shepherds Bush 1983</u>.

> B. My mother said I never should
> Play with the gipsies in the wood.
> January, February, … December.

Mile End 1967.

Printed versions Briggs, p. 159; Browne, 18; Daiken, *CGTY*, p. 158; Douglas (see below); Gillington (see below); Graves (see below); Gullen, clapping game, p. 6; Hubbard, clapping game, mentioned, 263; Kellett, pp. 17–18; Kings (see below); MacBain (see below); McMorland, contains elements of Gullen's rhyme, p. 41; Opies, *ODNR*, p. 315, *ONRB*, p. 127, *PBNR*, pp. 152, 153, *SG*, clapping game, p. 441 (and see below); Parry-Jones, p. 96; Ritchie, *GC*, pp. 127, 142; Shaw, 1969, p. 53; Starn, p. 98; Sutton-Smith, pp. 85–86; Taylors, clapping game, pp. 44–46; Turner, p, 44.

Early notings the Opies quote a version from the Crofton Manuscript (c1875): My mother *said* (clap)/That I never *should* (clap)/Play with the gipsies (clap)/In the wood (clap)/Because she said (clap)/That if I did (clap)/She'd smack my bottom (clap)/With a saucepan lid! (clap), *SG*, 1985, p. 441. Gillington, 1909, *OHSG*, ring game with chasing, p. 20; *OIWSG*, pp. 12–13. Cf. Douglas, Ma she said that this won't do,/To play with the boys at half-past two--, 1916, p. 94, 1931, p. 54; also a rhyme containing the lines If I do, mother will say,/Naughty girl to disobey,/And play with the boys down yonder, 1916, p. 87, 1931, p. 50. According to the Opies (*ODNR*, 1951, pp. 315–316), although this rhyme was known in the early nineteenth century it did not appear in print until the early 1920s in Walter de la Mare, *Come Hither* (London: Constable, 1923; new ed., London: Constable, 1960, p. 535). Kings 1, 1926, p. 29; Graves, 1927, p. 12; MacBain, 1933, pp. 127–128.

Recording MacColl and Seeger, *The Elliotts of Birtley.*

6.A.38 THERE'S SOMEONE UNDER THE BED

> There's someone under the bed,
> I don't know who it is.
> I feel so shocking nervous,
> I call my sister in.
> Once she lit the candle,
> Under the bed she goes.
> Get out you fool,
> Get out you fool,
> Get out from under the be-e-ed.

Mile End 1966; Dalston 1983.

"Someone has to go in. When they skip they bend down as if they're looking under the bed. When their sister comes in, someone else jumps in. Then they pretend they've lit the candle and the person who was in there before has to get out. Then they sing it again."

Printed versions Abrahams, pp. 190–191; Brady, p. 78; Cosbey, p. 88; Daiken, *CGTY*, p. 63, *TTP*, p. 16; Douglas (see below); Fowke, p. 58; Kellett (?early noting), p. 34; Rutherford, p. 60; Shaw, 1969, p. 51; Turner, p. 37.

Early noting Douglas, title of a "song", 1916, p. 95, 1931, p. 55.

Recordings BBC 6669 (78) (1941, Bristol); BBC 19003 (78) (1953, Kentish Town); Webb, *Children's Singing Games*.

6.A.39 JELLY ON THE PLATE

A. Jelly on the plate, jelly on the plate,
Wiggle-woggle, wiggle-woggle,
Jelly on the plate.

Sausage on the floor, sausage on the floor, (Sausage in the pan) (Sizzle, sazzle!)
Pick it up, pick it up,
Sausage on the floor.

Washing on the line, washing on the line,
Take it off, take it off,
Washing on the line.

Apple on the tree, apple on the tree,
Pick it off, pick it off,
Apple on the tree.

Paper on the stairs, paper on the stairs,
Pick it up, pick it up,
Paper on the stairs.

Marylebone 1967.

Additional verses:

B. Custard by the side, custard by the side,
Wibble-wobble, wibble-wobble,
Custard by the side.

Prunes on the top, prunes on the top,
Wibble-wobble, wibble-wobble,
Prunes on the top.

Banana split, banana split,
Banana, banana,
Banana split.

Mile End 1967/68. Various combinations of these verses: Earlsfield 1982; Barnsbury, Borough, Cubitt Town, Dalston, Mile End, Shepherds Bush, 1983.

See also **6.B.1**.

C. Burglar in the house, burglar in the house,
Kick him out, kick him out,
Burglar in the house.

Baby on the floor, baby on the floor,
Pick it up, pick it up,
Baby on the floor.

"When it's 'jelly' we 'wibble-wobble'. When it's 'pick it up' we pretend to pick up something. When it's 'burglar' we pretend we're kicking someone. When it's 'baby', you sort of rock it." girl, 11, Stoke Newington 1983.

Printed versions Abrahams, pp. 15, 99; Brady, p. 86; Cosbey, Banana splits, p. 64, Jelly in the bowl, p. 79; Cumnock Academy, p. 8; Fowke, p. 55; Kellett (?early notings), pp. 25, 126; Kenney, p. 7; Banana splits,

p. 16; Ritchie, *SS*, pp. 55, 58, *GC*, p. 133; Rodger, p. 21; Rosen and Steele, [p. 11]; Rutherford, p. 58; Smith, *BBHG*, p. 13; Turner, p. 31; Withers, *RIMP*, p. 59.

Recordings BBC 3539 (78) (1941, Yorkshire); MacColl and Behan, *Streets of song*; Webb, *Children's Singing Games*.

6.A.40 TEDDY BEAR

Teddy Bear, Teddy Bear, turn around, (turn right round)
Teddy Bear, Teddy Bear, touch the ground,
Teddy Bear, Teddy Bear, run upstairs, (climb, roll, go)
Teddy Bear, Teddy Bear, say your prayers,
Teddy Bear, Teddy Bear, switch off the light, (turn out, blow out)
Teddy Bear, Teddy Bear, spell good night. (say)
G-O-O-D   N-I-G-H-T, good night!

Also: "do the splits/count to six"
"show your shoe/that will do"

Mile End 1966; Marylebone 1967; West Norwood 1970, 1972; Walworth 1974, 1980; Greenwich 1982; Dalston 1983; Hampstead, Kensington 1984.

Printed versions in addition to "Teddy Bear", these include "Spanish Lady", "Spanish Dancer", "Lady", "Lady bird", "Old Lady", "Dolly", "Butterfly", "Aeroplane", "Dilly-dilly", "Buster", and "Teddy Teddy". Abrahams, pp. 180, 186; Botkin (see below); Brady, p. 84; Coffin and Cohen, p. 189; Cosbey, pp. 90–91; Daiken, *CGTY*, p. 64, *TTP*, p. 15; Douglas (see below); Evans, *JRR*, pp. 16, 17; Fowke, p. 54; Fulton and Smith, p. 54; Gomme (see below); Kellett, p. 49 (and see below); Kenney, p. 5; Knapps, p. 117; Leach and Fried, Butterfly, p. 1016; Ritchie, *GC*, pp. 114, 137; Rodger, p. 21; Rutherford, p. 64; Shaw, 1969, p. 51; Smith,

BBHG, p. 22; Solomons, p. 51; Sutton-Smith, p. 81; Todd, 7; Turner, pp. 36, 38; Withers, *RIMP*, p. 69; Worstell, pp. 20, 27.

Early notings Lady, lady, drop your handkerchief,/Lady, lady, pick it up, Gomme, 1898, p. 204, part of a skipping routine. Lady, lady, drop your purse,/Lady, lady, pick it up,/Lady, lady, touch the ground,/Lady, lady, turn right round,/Lady, lady, show your foot,/Lady, lady, sling your hook, Douglas, 1916, p. 66, 1931, p. 36. Ali Bali Buster the king of the Jews/ Bought his wife a pair of shoes,/When the shoes began to wear/Ali Bali Buster began to swear/And this is what he said./"Lady, lady, touch the dirty ground,/Lady, lady, turn yourself around,/Lady, lady read a dirty book,/Lady, lady take your dirty hook", Kellett, 1920s, skipping rhyme, pp. 74–75. Botkin, *TAF*, 1944: Teddy bear, pp. 791, 792, Old lady, p. 793, Teddy, p. 794, Spanish dancer, p. 795.

6.A.41 VOTE, VOTE, VOTE

    A.   Vote, vote, vote, for (_____ _____),
She calls (_____) at the door,
(_____) is the one who likes a bit of fun,
So we don't want (_____) any more,
Shut the door!

<u>Marylebone</u>, Mile End <u>1967</u>.

Tune chorus in the song "Tramp! Tramp! Tramp! (The Prisoner's Hope)", written during the American Civil War and published in 1864 by George F. Root.

    B.   Vote, vote, vote, for little (_____),
Call in (_____) at the door, How d'you do?
(_____) is the one with a pimple on her bum,
So we don't like (_____) any more.

Clapham, <u>Walworth 1974</u>.

C. Vote, vote, vote for little (_____),
    In comes (_____) at the door,
    Because (_____) is the one with the automatic bum,
    And we don't want (_____) any more,
    Shut the door, piss off, goodbye.

Finsbury 1983.

"When they go, 'Vote, vote, vote', they just sing it. When they sing, 'In comes …' they both jump in. When they sing, 'automatic bum', they wiggle their bums. Then one is pushed out and it continues. If you trip you take the rope." girl, 11, EC1 1983.

D. Vote, vote, vote, for little (_____),
    In comes (_____) at the door,
    (_____) is the lady,
    And she's going to have a baby,
    So we don't need (_____) any more.
    Chuck her out.

Stoke Newington 1983.

Printed versions Abrahams, p. 201; Brady, p. 80; Cosbey, pp. 94–95; Daiken, *CGTY*, p. 69, *OGS*, p. 25; Douglas (see below); Evans, *JRR*, For, for, for, for Sherry./In come [sic] Judy at the door, p. 29; Fowke, p. 57; Fulton and Smith, Knock, knock, knocking at the door,/calling Janice at the door, p. 55; Hubbard, mentioned, 263; Kellett (see below); Kenney, p. 18; Knapps, three versions, including Douglas's, with the comment that they have lost their political meaning, pp. 120, 210–211; Opies, *ISE*, p. 59, *LLS*, political rhyme, pp. 348–349; Ritchie, *SS*, not said to be political, p. 109, *GC*, skipping rhyme, p. 128; Rutherford, p. 62; Shaw, election jingle, 1969, p. 61, 1970, p. 105; Turner, p. 41, Wade 2, 34; Whelan (see below).

Early notings Vote, vote, vote for (Billy Martin),/Chuck old (Ernie) at the door—/If it wasn't for the law,/I would punch him on the jaw,/And we won't want (Billy Martin) any more, Douglas, 1916, p. 60,

1931, p. 32. Tramp, tramp, tramp, the boys are marching,/Cheer up the bobbies at the door,/If you do not let us in,/We will kick your winders in/And you won't be a Tory anymore, one of three polling day songs from Leeds in the 1920s, Kellett, pp. 90–91. Whelan, 1920s, 109.

Recording MacColl and Behan, *Streets of Song*.

6.A.42 DOWN TO MISSISSIPPI

   A. Down to Mississippi,
Where the girls are very pretty,
If you miss a loop, you're out.

       Up to Mississippi,
Where the girls are very pretty,
If you miss a loop you're out.

Similarly with
    Stand to Mississippi …
    Swim to Mississippi …
    Hop to Mississippi …
    Skip to Mississippi …

Mile End 1966.

    Get to Mississippi …
    Turn to Mississippi …
    Clap to Mississippi …
    Jump to Mississippi …

at end: Down to Mississippi, where the steamboats push (push the child out).

One or two girls in the middle carry on skipping till out.

Putney 1966.

> Down to Mississippi … (bend and touch ground)
> Back to Mississippi …
> Twist to Mississippi … (turn round)
> One leg to Mississippi … (skipping on one leg)
> Other leg to Mississippi …
> Drop to Mississippi …
> Scissors to Mississippi … (scissor movement with legs)
> Frog to Mississippi … (bend right down)

Walworth 1974, 1979.

Some of the above, plus:

> Read a book to Mississippi …
> Comb your hair to Mississippi …
> Pray to Mississippi …
> Walk to Mississippi …

Brixton 1982.

Selections from the above: Deptford, Dulwich, Shepherds Bush 1983.

B. Up to Mississippi,
    Miss a loop you're out.

> Cut, In, Down, Up-down-turn-around, Read, Pray, Shout hurray.

Finsbury 1983.

Tune "Ten green bottles".

C. Down to Mississippi with the girls in blue,
    Skip to Mississippi with the girls in white,
    Jump to Mississippi with the girls in green.
        ("You stop with the colour the girl's got on.")
    Skip to Mississippi, if you miss a loop you're out.

Barnsbury 1983.

Printed versions Abrahams, p. 44; Cosbey, p. 70; Evans, *JRR*, p. 6; Hubbard, mentioned, 263; Nelson, p. 71; Rosen and Steele, back cover; Rutherford, p. 61; Smith, *BBHG*, p. 17; Turner, p. 25; Withers, *RIMP*, p. 59.

6.A.43 MOTHER'S IN THE KITCHEN

    A. Mother's in the kitchen,
        Doing a bit of knitting,
        In comes a burglar (robber)
        And knocks (pushes) her out.

Brockley 1960s; Mile End 1968; West Norwood 1970s; Walworth 1970s, 1979; Brixton, Streatham 1982; Borough 1983.

    B. Granny in the kitchen,
        Doing a bit of knitting, (stitching)
        In comes a bogeyman,
        And pushes her out.

Battersea, Earlsfield 1982; Deptford 1983 (Nanny in the kitchen); Shepherds Bush 1983; Kensington 1984.

"Someone else comes in as 'burglar' and pushes 'Granny' out. Then you start again. The 'burglar' becomes 'Granny'." girl, 11, Kensington 1984.

    C. Mother's in the kitchen,
        Doin' a bit of stitchin',
        In comes a polar bear,
        And pushes Mother out.

Mile End 1968.

Sometimes the stitching/knitting is mimed.

See also **6.A.53B**.

Printed versions Abrahams, p. 12; Brady, Bluebells, cockle shells, p. 83; Cumnock Academy, p. 12; Daiken, *CGTY*, p. 63, *TTP*, p. 13, *OGS*, p. 33; Douglas (see below); Evans, *JRR*, p. 15; Fowke p. 59; Holbrook, p. 57; Kellett, p. 50 (and see below); Ritchie, *GC*, p. 114; Rosen and Steele, [p. 12]; Shaw, 1969, p. 50; Smith, *BBHG*, p. 21; Turner, p. 32; Wade, Katie in the kitchen, (1), 14, (2), 33.

Early notings I-N spells in—/I was in my kitchen/Doing a bit of stitching,/Old Father Nimble/Came and took my thimble,/I got up a great big stone,/Hit him on the belly bone—/O-U-T spells out, Douglas, 1916, p. 68, 1931, pp. 37–38. When I was in the kitchen/Doing a bit of stitching,/In came a bogey-man/And pushed me out, Kellett, ?1920s, p. 50.

6.A.44 OLD MOTHER HUBBARD

> Old Mother Hubbard,
> Doing a bit of knitting,
> Takes a cup, drinks it up,
> And calls her neighbours in.

Walworth 1982.

6.A.45 ALL IN TOGETHER

> A. All in together,
>   Never mind the weather,
>   If you get to two,
>   Touch your shoe,
>   One, two.

Dalston 1983.

> B. All in together, girls,
>   Never mind the weather, girls,
>   When I call your birthday,
>   Please jump out (in).

January, February, …

All in together, girls,
Never mind the weather, girls,
When I call your birthday,
Please jump out.   (number, i.e. date)

Hampstead 1972, 1984; Greenwich 1982; Shepherds Bush*, Stoke Newington* 1983 (*chanting months only).

C.   Mrs. One goes in, Mrs. Two goes in,
Mrs. Three goes in,
All in together, girls,
Never mind the weather, girls.
When I call your birthday,
Please run out.

Mile End 1966.

Printed versions   Abrahams, p. 6; Brady, pp. 13, 95–96; Coffin and Cohen, p. 189; Cosbey, pp. 62–63; Daiken, *CGTY*, p. 71; Douglas (see below); Ellis (see below); Foakes, p. 28; Fowke, p. 55; Holbrook, p. 56; Hubbard, mentioned, 263; Kellett, pp. 59–60 (and see below); Kenney, p. 13; Kings (see below); Nelson, p. 70; Ritchie, *GC*, pp. 113, 129; Rodger, p. 23; Rutherford, p. 63; Shaw, 1969, p. 51, 1970, pp. 78, 89; Smith, *BBHG*, p. 23; Sutton-Smith, p. 75; Turner, pp. 18–19; Withers, *RIMP*, p. 60; Worstell, p. 38.

Early notings   All in together, all sorts of weather,/When the wind blows we all go together./I spy Nelly hanging out the window,/Tallyho, Tallyho, Shoot, Bang, Fire! Ellis, 1910s, 38. All in together—all sorts of (or *frosty*) weather—/When the wind blows we all go together— Douglas, 1916, p. 88, 1931, p. 50. All in together girls,/Never mind the weather girls,/By I count twenty this rope must be empty,/5 10 15 20, Kellett, 1920s, p. 59. Kings 2, 1930, p. 29.

Recordings   BBC 19005 (78) (1953, Kentish Town); Webb, *Children's Singing Games*.

6.A.46 HERE'S A LITTLE FRENCH GIRL

SKIPPING SONG developed from singing game:

Here's a little French girl, E-I-E-I-O,
Here's a little Spanish girl, E-I-E-I-O,
Here's a little Italian girl, E-I-E-I-O,
And this is how they dance, E-I-E-I-O,
E-I-E-I-O, E-I-E-I-O, E-I-E-I-O, E-I-E-I-O.
Out goes little French girl, E-I-E-I-O,
Out goes little Spanish girl, E-I-E-I-O,
Out goes little Italian girl, E-I-E-I-O,
E-I-E-I-O, E-I-E-I-O, E-I-E-I-O, E-I-E-I-O.

Finsbury 1983.

See also **4.5**.

Tune "Bingo" as in the Scout song (see, for example, Sims, p. 40).

6.A.47 THREE WHITE HORSES

Three white horses in a stable,
Pick one out and call it Mabel.

Walworth 1974.

Printed versions cf. Abrahams, Mabel, Mabel/set the table, p. 115, Mabel, Mabel, strong and able, p. 116; Botkin (see below); Douglas (see below); Evans, *JRR*, p. 21; Fowke, p. 55; Fulton and Smith, Mabel, Mabel set the table don't forget the hot potatoes, p. 55; Kenney, p. 6; Knapps, p. 112; Nelson, Mabel, Mabel, strong and able, p. 70; Ritchie, *GC*, p. 40; Rutherford, counting-out rhyme, p. 52; Smith, *BBHG*, counting-out rhyme, p. 60; Sutton-Smith, p. 76; Turner, p. 32; Withers, *RIMP*, p. 60; cf. Wood, *FAFR*, Joe, Joe, strong and able, p. 78, and Mabel, Mabel, set the table, p. 99; Worstell, p. 23.

Early notings cf. "a very naughty one" Mabel, Mabel,/Lay the table—Douglas, 1916, p. 91, 1931, p. 52. Botkin, *TAF*, 1944, p. 792.

6.A.48 I WENT DOWN THE LANE

> I went down the lane to get a penny whistle,
> A copper came along and stole my penny whistle.
> I asked him for it back, he said he hadn't got it,
> Hi, Hi! Curlywig! You've got it in your pocket.

Mile End 1968.

Printed versions Douglas (see below); Kellett (see below); Opies, *LLS*, p. 370; Shaw 1970, p. 51.

Early notings I went down the lane to buy a penny whistle,/A copper come by and pinch my penny whistle./I ask him for it back, he said he hadn't got it—/Hi, Hi, Curlywig, you've got it in your pocket, Douglas, 1916, p. 55, 1931, p. 29. I went down the lane to buy a penny whistle,/A bobby took it off me, and gave me a lump of gristle,/I asked him for it back, he said he hadn't got it,/You liar te (sic) you liar te (sic) you've got it in your pocket, Kellett, 1920s, p. 96.

6.A.49 MICKEY MOUSE IS DEAD

> Mickey Mouse is dead,
> He died last night in bed,
> He cut his throat with a five pound note,
> And this is what he said,
> "It's not because I'm dirty,
> It's not because I'm clean
> It's all because of whooping cough,
> And measles in between."

Mile End 1966.

Printed versions Brady, last four lines, p. 55, Cosby, last four lines, p. 77; Fowke, last four lines, p. 110, last four lines, in rhyme beginning "My father is a king", p. 116; Fulton and Smith, lines 5–6, p. 55; Kellett, p. 23 (and see below); Northall (see below); Opies, *LLS*, ten Mickey Mouse versions, plus Jack the Ripper and Kruger, first four lines, p. 111, last four lines, p. 175; Ritchie, *SS*, p. 36; Rutherford, last four lines, p. 57, the Kaiser, p. 114; Shaw, My poor donkey's dead, 1969, p. 62, Micky Mouse is dead, 1970, p. 73; Sutton-Smith, Poor old Ernie, p. 99; Turner, Donald Duck, p. 88; Wilson, 981.

Early notings Ned, Ned the donkey's dead,/He died last night with a pain in his head, Northall, 1892, p. 310, Warwickshire. Poor old Kruger's dead,/He died last night in bed,/He cut his throat with a ten bob note,/ Poor old Kruger's dead, one of two versions, Kellett, 1920s, p. 4.

6.A.50 TWO LITTLE MEN IN A FLYING SAUCER

Two little men in a flying saucer,
Went round the world in a minute and a quarter,
One found a skellington,
And put it in his wellington,
So out you go.

Walworth 1982.

Printed version Rutherford, p. 61.

6.A.51 I'VE BEEN TO HARLEM

SKIPPING SONG AND CLAPPING RHYME:

I've been to Harlem,
I've been to Dover,
I've travelled this wide world over,
Over, over, three times over.

> Drink what you have to drink,
> And turn the glasses over.
> Sailing east, sailing west,
> Sailing over the ocean,
> You'd better watch out,
> When the boat begins to rock,
> Or you'll lose your girl in the ocean.

West Norwood 1972.

See also **5.20**.

Printed versions Chase, *SGPPG*, Oh, I've been to Winchester, I've been to Dover, p. 2; Rohrbough (see below).

Early noting I've been to Harlem I've been to Dover;/I've travelled this wide world all over,/Over, over, three times over;/Drink all the brandy-wine and/Turn the glasses over.//Sailing east sailing west,/Sailing over the ocean,/Better watch out when the boat begins to rock/Or you'll lose your girl in the ocean, Rohrbough, *HPPB*, 1940, p. 14.

6.A.52 CHARLIE CHAPLIN WENT TO FRANCE

> Charlie Chaplin went to France,
> To show (teach) the ladies how to dance,
> First you do the can-can,
> Then you do the splits,
> Then you do the turn-around,
> And then you do the kicks.
> The Queen does a curtsey,
> The King does a bow,
> The boys go (whistle),
> The girls go "Wow!"

Mile End 1967/68.

See also **4.46,** and some parts of **6.A.26.**

Printed versions Abrahams, p. 26; Botkin (see below); Brady, p. 85; Cumnock Academy, p. 23; Daiken, *CGTY*, p. 34; Evans, *JRR*, p. 8; Fowke, p. 60; Gillington (see below); Gregor (see below); Harrowven, p. 319; Holbrook, p. 57; Kellett (see below); Kings (see below); Knapps, The Jackson Five went to France, p. 122; Mills and Bishop (see below); Opies, *LLS*, p. 110; Ritchie, first two lines, *SS*, p. 24, *GC*, p. 129; Shaw, 1970, pp. 11, 74; Smith, *BBHG*, p. 14; Solomons, Marco Polo, p. 102; Sutton-Smith, pp. 82, 87; Turner, p. 21; Withers, *RIMP*, p. 65; Worstell, pp. 2, 3.

Early notings cf. three rhymes containing the lines: And when he's done he takes a dance/Up to London, down to France, Gregor, 1891, p. 26. My young man is gone to France,/To learn the ladies how to dance!/ When he comes home he'll marry me,/Cockalorum, Gee, Gee, Gee! Second verse of a ring game song beginning "I have a bonnet trim'd with blue", Gillington, *ODSG*, 1913, p. 11. Charlie Chaplin went to France/ To teach the ladies how to dance,/And this is what he taught them,/Heel, toe, over you go,/Heel, toe, over you go, Kellett, 1920s, ball-bouncing rhyme, p. 10. Kings 1, 1926, ball bouncing rhyme, p. 7; Kings 2, 1930, p. 24. Cf. One, two, three, four,/Charlie Chaplin went to war, Mills and Bishop, 1937, 40. Botkin, *TAF*, 1944, p. 793.

6.A.53 BLUEBELLS, COCKLE SHELLS

A. Bluebells, cockle shells,
Eevy ivy over.
Mother said that I was born in
January, February, March, …

Mile End 1968; Borough 1983.

B. Seashells, cockle shells,
Eevy ivy over. (Lillywhite, lillywhite over)
Mother's in the kitchen

> Doing all the stitching,
> How many stitches can she stitch?

Marylebone 1967; Hampstead 1972; Barnsbury, Cubitt Town, Finsbury, Mile End 1983.

See also **6.A.43, 9.A.9c** and **11.B.3b**.

Printed version Rosen and Steele, [p. 1].

> C. Bluebells, cockle shells,
>   Eevy ivy over.
>   Long John Silver went to sea,
>   With a buckle on his knee.
>
> then as MY AUNT DAISY, **6.A.8**.

Walworth 1974.

> D. Bluebells, cockle shells,
>   Please turn over.
>
> (Squiggle rope and then jump over. Continue skipping.)

Mile End 1968.

> E. Bluebells, cockle shells,
>   Eevy ivy over.
>   How many boys did you kiss last night?
>   5, 10, 15, 20, …

<u>Battersea</u>, Brixton, Earlsfield <u>1982</u>.

> F. Bluebells, cockle shells,
>   Eevy ivy over.
>   I saw you in the cellar,
>   Kissing (_____ _____).
>   How many kisses did he give you?
>   1, 2, 3, …

> How many babies will you have?
> 1, 2, 3, …
> What sort of ring will you get?
> Gold, silver, plastic, bronze. …
> What colour babies will you get?
> Black, white, black, white, …

<u>Streatham 1982</u>; Deptford 1983; Hampstead 1984.

Printed versions Abrahams, pp. 18–20; Brady, p. 83; Cosbey, pp. 64–65; Cumnock Academy, p. 5; Douglas (see below); Evans, *JRR*, p. 19; Fowke, p. 55; Fulton and Smith, p. 37; Kenney, p. 3; Knapps, p. 116; Montgomeries, *HBSNR*, p. 63, *SC*, p. 80 (same version in both; first two lines only are similar to the Streatham version: Evie-Ovie,/Turn the rope over); Parry-Jones, p. 101; Ritchie, *SS*, Bluebells, dummie dummie shells/ Evie ivy o-over!/Charlie Chaplain [sic] went to France/To teach the ladies how to dance, p. 24, *GC*, p. 116; Rodger, one line only: Eevy, ivy, turn the rope over, p. 21; questions only, p. 22; Shaw, 1970, p. 72; Smith, *TGH*, pp. 66–67; Sutton-Smith, p. 76; Todd, one line only: Eevy, ivy, turn the rope over, 6; Turner, p. 20; Worstell, pp. 19, 25.

Early noting Evie, Ivy, over,/The kettle is boiling over— Douglas, 1916, p. 92, 1931, p. 53.

Recordings BBC 19926 (78) (1953, Edinburgh); BBC 3539 (78) (1941, Yorkshire); Webb, *Children's Singing Games*.

6.A.54 ALL THE GIRLS IN OUR TOWN

SKIPPING RHYME with divinatory sequence, developed from traditional singing game.

All the girls in our town lead a happy life,
Except for (_____) she wants to be a wife;
A wife she shall be, according to the lad.

Along comes (____ _____),
He kisses her, he cuddles her,
He sits her on his knee,
He says, "My darling, will you marry me?"
Yes, No, Yes, No, …
How many babies shall she have?
1, 2, 3, … 10

(continues with colour, wedding dress, dwelling place)

Mile End 1964; Marylebone 1967; Hampstead 1972; <u>Shepherds Bush 1983</u>.

See also **4.33**.

Printed versions Abrahams, p. 7; Douglas (see below), Fowke, p. 69; Gomme (see below); Halliwell (see below); Holbrook, pp. 94–95; Kellett (?early noting), p. 76; cf. Montgomeries, *HBSNR*, p. 80; Opies, *ISE*, p. 46, *SG*, pp. 130–133; Ritchie, *GC*, lines 5–7 only, p. 123; Rodger, p. 29; Swift, 148; cf. Wade 2, All the boys in Hollywood, 34.

Early notings cf. There is a girl of our town,/She often wears a flowered gown, ring game, Halliwell, *PRNT*, 1849, p. 119. (Part) All the boys in our town/Shall lead a happy life,/Except 'tis _____ _____, and he wants a wife./A wife he shall have, and a-courting he shall go,/Along with _____, because he loves her so./He huddles her, he cuddles her,/He sits her on his knee;/He says, My dear, do you love me?/I love you, and you love me,/And we shall be as happy/As a bird upon a tree, Gomme, 1894, pp. 2–6, Hampshire; see also additional Scottish versions in Gomme, 1898, p. 403. All the boys in our town, eating apple-pie,/Excepting (Georgie Groves), he wants a wife— Douglas, 1916, p. 59, 1931, p. 32.

Recording BBC 16076 (1951, Sidbury).

6.A.55 I KNOW A BOY

A. DIVINATORY SKIPPING RHYME:

I know a boy who's double jointed,
He kissed (_____) and made her disappointed.
All right (_____), [? I'll] tell your mother,
Kissing (_____) round the corner.
(_____) laid her on the bed,
Said, "My darling do you love me?"
Yes, no, …
    (if on yes:)
How many kisses did you give him?
5, 10, 15, 20, …
Did you get married?
Yes, no, …
    (if on yes:)
What did you wear at the wedding?
Silk, satin, see-through, rags, …

What did you live in?
House, mansion, pigsty, loo, …

How many children did you have?
1, 2, 3, 4, …

What colour were they?
Black, white, pink, yellow, …

Did you get divorced?
Yes, no, …

<u>Blackheath</u>, Cubitt Town, Deptford, Mile End <u>1983</u>.

Printed versions Abrahams, p. 77; Douglas (see below); Gaskell (see below); Kings (see below); Opies, *ISE*, p. 21; Ritchie, *GC*, p. 132; Rodger, question part only, p. 22; Smith, *BBHG*, p. 10; Sutton-Smith, part, p. 80; Turner, p. 29.

Early notings Who will she marry, tinker, soldier, sailor, rich man, poor man, beggar man, thief? What will she be married in, silk, satin, muslin, rags? What will she be carried in, coach, carriage, wheelbarrow, muck-cart? Gaskell, c1913, p. 8. I had a black man, he was double-jointed,/I kissed him, and made him disappointed./ All right, Hilda, I'll tell your mother,/Kissing the black man round the corner./How many kisses did he give you?/One, two, three, etc., Douglas, 1916, pp. 56–57, 1931, p. 30. Silk, satin,/Velvet, cotton,/Rags, Kings 2, 1930, p. 30.

    B.   SKIPPING GAME (part, usually added on to **6.A.59** ON A MOUNTAIN STANDS A LADY, with divination):

> All right (_____) I'll tell your mother,
> Kissing (_____ _____) around the corner.
> How many kisses did you give him?
> Five, ten, fifteen, twenty ...
> Do you love him?
> Yes, no, yes, no ...
> Are you going to marry him?
> Yes, no, yes, no ...
> What are you getting married in?
> Silk, satin, cotton, rags ...
> What are you going to live in?
> House, palace, dustbin, pigsty ...
> How many babies will you have?
> One, two, three, four ...
> What is their colour?
> Black, white, yellow, red ...   (or Black, white, half caste ...)
> (Sometimes): What colour you getting married in?   White, gold, silver ...

Walworth 1974, 1979; Brixton 1982; Borough, Dulwich 1983.

Printed versions Gillington (see below); cf. Gullen, p. 19; Kings (see below); Smith, *BBHG*, I know a little boy, p. 10; Sutton-Smith, part, p. 80; Turner, p. 29.

Early notings David Bailey (Boy's name), Do you love me? Yes, No, etc. … Silk, satin, cotton, or rags; … Little house, big house, pigstye, barn, etc., Gillington, 1909, divination sequence, Skipping-rope rhyme No. IV, *OHSG*, p. iii. Kings 2, 1930, p. 30.

Recordings BBC 19004 (78) (1953, Kentish Town); MacColl and Seeger, *The Elliotts of Birtley*; Webb, *Children's Singing Games*.

6.A.56 GREEN GRAVEL

SKIPPING RHYME with divinatory sequence, developed from traditional singing game:

Green gravel, green gravel,
Your age is sixteen.
I sent you a letter
Complaining the weather.
Turn your back you saucy cat,
I saw you kissing (_____)
In the parlour.
How many kisses did you give him?
5, 10, 15, 20, …
Do you love him?
Yes, no, yes, no, …
Will you marry him?
Yes, no, yes, no, …
Will you have children?
Yes, no, yes, no, …
How many children are you going to have?
1, 2, 3, 4, …
What will you get married in?
Silk, cotton thread, silk, …
Are you going to live happy?
Yes, no, Yes, no, …
What are you going to live in?

> Toilet, bungalow, house, …
> Where you going to get married?
> Church, house, flat, …
> What colour babies?
> Black, white, black, …

West Norwood 1970.

The first four lines of this rhyme are reminiscent not only of the singing game "Green Gravel", but also of similar games beginning "Queen Mary" or "Queen Anne", all of which are found in many of the older collections. Early printed versions, in addition to the reference to "Green Gravel", also allude to a letter, and the weather, e.g. Douglas (see below). Line 5 occurs in a number of rhymes of the Green Gravel type, including the Keeping example (see below) and another fragment in Douglas, both from London.

Other printed versions include phrases and fragments indicating a line of descent from the original singing game. The fragments in Douglas, for example, point to an intermediate stage in the development of the rhyme from the earlier purely singing game rhymes to more recent versions. The divinatory sequence is apparently not part of older versions of this rhyme.

Printed versions (singing games without divinatory sequence) Abrahams, p. 56; cf. Boyes, 39 (rhyme 11); Brady, Wallflowers, pp. 117–118 and cf. Apple Jelly, pp. 90–91 and Dear Anne, p. 123; Daiken, *CGTY*, p. 139, *TTP*, p. 10; Douglas (see below); Fowke, p. 25; Gaskell (see below); Gillington (see below); Gomme (see below); Gullen, "Queen Mary", p. 105; Halliwell (see below); Holbrook, p. 64; Keeping, p. 161; Kidson (see below); Lang (see below); MacBain (see below); Montgomeries, *SNR*, "Queen Mary", p. 123, *HBSNR*, "Queen Mary", p. 84; Newell (see below); Nicholson (see below); Northall (see below); Opies, *SG*, pp. 239–242; Plunket (see below); Ritchie, *GC*, "Queen Mary", p. 152; Rohrbough (see below); Sutton-Smith, p. 17; Swift, 149; Turner, p. 55; Uttley, "Green Gravel", p. 63; Wilson and Gallagher, No. 21.

Early notings Around the green gravel the grass grows green,/And all the pretty maids are plain to be seen;/Wash them with milk, and clothe them with silk,/And write their names with a pen and ink, Halliwell, 1842, p. 148, 1843, p. 186. Green gravel, green gravel, the grass is so green/The prettiest fair maid that ever was seen/We'll wash her with new milk and clothe her in silk/And write down her name with a brass pen and ink/Dear Mary, Dear Mary, your true love is dead/He sends you this letter, so turn round your head, Plunket, 1886, p 13. Green gravel, green gravel, your grass is so green,/The fairest young damsel that ever was seen;/We washed her, we dried her, we rolled her in silk,/And we wrote down her name with a glass pen and ink./Dear Annie, dear Annie, your true love is dead,/And we send you a letter to turn round your head, Gomme, 1894, p. 171, Belfast, one of seventeen versions; see also Gomme, 1898, p. 426. Lang, as Halliwell, 1897, p. 268. My name is Sweet William,/My age is sixteen,/My father's a farmer behind the tree,/With plenty of money/To dress me in silk/But nobody loves me but you, Gillington, 1909, *OSSG*, p. 5. Greengravel, Greengravel, the grass is so green/And all your pretty fairies are fit to be seen./Greengravel, Greengravel, your sweetheart is dead,/I wrote you this letter so turn back your head, Gaskell, c1913, clapping game, p. 7. Green gravel, green gravel,/Your grass is so green, (or: Your voice is not heard)/I'll send you a letter/To call (Florrie) in./I'll wash you in milk, and dress you in silk,/And write down your name with a gold pen and ink, Douglas, 1916, p. 58, 1931, p. 31. My name is sweet (Jennie), my age is sixteen,/My father's a father [farmer] and I am a Queen./Got plenty of money to dress me in silk,/But nobody loves me but (Gladys dear), Douglas, 1916, p. 72, 1931, p. 40. (Two fragments): Turn your back, you saucy cat,/And say no more to me— and immediately following: Send a letter, send a letter,/Be content in the weather, Douglas, 1916, p. 92, 1931, p. 53.

Other early notings Northall, 1892, p. 362; Nicholson, 1897, "Queen Mary" and "Green Gravel", pp. 132–147; Newell, 1903, p. 71; Gillington, 1909, *OHSG*, "Green Gravel", two versions, pp. 10, 11, *OIWSG*, Yellow gravel, pp. 20–21; Kidson, 1916, "Queen Mary" p. 4, "Green Gravel" p. 7; MacBain, 1933, "A Game Rhyme", p. 272; Rohrbough, *HPPB*, 1940, p. 130.

Recordings BBC 16076 (78) (1951, Sidbury, Devon); BBC 19004 (78) (1953, Kentish Town); Ritchie, *Children's Songs and Games from the Southern Mountains*; Wilson and Gallagher, *Children's Singing Games*.

6.A.57 LOOK WHO'S COMING DOWN THE STREET

DIVINATORY SKIPPING SONG:

Look who's coming down the street,
(_____ _____), ain't she sweet?
She's been married twice before,
And now she's knocking on (_____'s) door.
She kisses him, she cuddles him,
She sits upon his knee,
She says, "Oh darling, won't you marry me?"
Yes, no, yes, no, …
Where did they get married?
Church, toilet, dustbin, …
How many children did they have?
1, 2, 3, …
What colour were they?
Red, yellow, black, white, …
What did they marry in?
Silk, satin, cotton, rags, …

Battersea*, Brixton, <u>Earlsfield 1982</u>.

*In the Battersea version, the genders are reversed: "Why it's (_____) isn't he sweet?" etc.

Tune "Organ Grinder's Swing", by Irving Mills and Will Hudson, 1936.

Printed versions Brady, p. 80: said to be "only known for the past six or seven years" (book published 1975); Fowke, p. 72; Kellett (see below); Kings (see below); Opies, *LLS*, Who's that coming down the street?/ Shirley Temple, ain't she sweet? p. 113; Rutherford, p. 127.

Early notings Silk, satin,/Velvet, cotton,/Rags, Kings 2, 1930, p. 30. "The reference to being married twice before, which would be otherwise inexplicable, occurs because the rhyme has developed from one current in the late 1930s and for some time afterwards, which referred to Mrs. Simpson and King Edward VIII, later Duke of Windsor. This is a typical version: 'Who's that coming down the street,/ Mrs. Simpson, ain't she sweet,/She's been married twice before/Now she's knocking at Edwards (sic) door.'" Kellett, p. 40.

6.A.58 ROSY APPLE, LEMON TART

DIVINATORY SKIPPING RHYME from an old singing game still played (see Opies, *SG*, 1985, pp. 164–166).

A. Rosy apple, lemon tart,
   Tell me the name of your sweetheart
   A, B, C, D, …

   "If she trips on 'P' perhaps:"

   Peter, Peter, will you marry me?
   Yes, no, yes, no, … ("getting faster")

   "If it lands on 'yes' you carry on:"

   What sort of wedding shall we have?
   Red, black, blue, white, …

   "If it lands on 'white', you say:"

   That shall be the colour of the wedding dress.

   What sort of house shall we live in?
   Dustbin, toilet, bungalow, house, flat, …

"If you land on, say, 'house' or 'flat', you say:"

That's what you should live in.

How many babies shall we have?
1, 2, 3, 4, 5, 6, 7, 8, 9, 10.

How many kisses shall we have?
1, 2, 3, 4, … ("till you trip")

Mile End 1968; <u>Barnsbury</u> (girl, 10), Dalston, Finsbury, Kentish Town <u>1983</u>; Hampstead 1984.

B. Apple crumble, apple tart,
Tell me the name of your sweetheart.
A, B, C, D, …

(Then follows a sequence on boy's name, marriage, place of marriage, colour of wedding dress, number of babies, their colour, whether the girl loves the boy or not.)

Earlsfield 1982; <u>Shepherds Bush 1982–84</u>; Kensington 1984.

"Some people like it, when they get a 'yes' (for marriage) 'cause they want to skip. They don't want anyone else to have a go, no matter which boy, even if they don't like him because they want a long skip. Some trip on 'yes' on purpose." girl, 10, Shepherds Bush 1983.

C. Jam tart, marmalade tart,
Tell me the name of your sweetheart,
A, B, C, D, …

Greenwich 1982.

Printed versions Abrahams, Ice cream soda, Delaware Punch, p. 73; also Douglas's rhyme, quoted, p. 171; Botkin (see below); Brady, p. 90; Cosbey, Icecream soda, lemonade tart, p. 76; Daiken, *CGTY*, p. 82; Dennison, Raspberry, strawberry, gooseberry jam, 294; Douglas (see below); Ellis (see below); Evans, *JRR*, as Abrahams, p. 8; Fowke, p. 68; Fulton and Smith, Ice cream soda with the cherry on top, p. 29; Gaskell (see below); Gillington (see below); Gomme (see below); Holbrook, p. 20; Hubbard, Raspberry, strawberry, gooseberry jam, 261; Jorgensen, *SWF*, Ice cream soda with a cherry on top, 64; Kellett, Rosy apple, lemons and pear, p. 76; Kenney, p. 8; Kings (see below); Knapps, pp. 115, 254; Nicholson (see below); Northall (see below); Opies, *ISE*, p. 22, *LLS*, p. 339, *SG*, pp. 164–166; Ritchie, *GC*, version like Gomme below, p. 144; Rodger, Black sugar, white sugar, p. 22; Shaw, 1969, pp. 49, 52, 1970, pp. 86, 90; Smith, *BBHG*, p. 8; Solomons, three versions, all starting Ice cream soda, pp. 52, 53; Starn, Blackcurrent, redcurrent (sic), raspberry tart, p. 98; Sutton-Smith, p. 78; Turner, p. 20; Wilson and Gallagher, No. 5; Withers, *RIMP*, p. 61; Worstell, p. 17.

Early notings Rosy apple, lemon, or pear,/Bunch of roses she shall wear;/Gold and silver by his side,/I know who will be the bride./Take her by the lilywhite hand,/Lead her to the altar,/Give her kisses, one, two, three,/Mrs. —'s daughter, Northall, 1892, p. 380. First line only: Rosy apple, lemon or pear, associated with "Queen Mary" rhymes, Nicholson, 1897, pp. 139, 140. Black currant,/Red currant,/Raspberry tart,/Tell me the name/Of my sweetheart./A, B, C, D, &c., Gomme, 1898, p. 195. Rosy apple, lemon or pear, Gillington, 1909, *OIWSG*, pp. 8–9. Blackcurrant, redcurrant, raspberry tart, tell me the name of your sweetheart, followed by "the gamut of names, where we would live, what we would use to drive to the church, material and colour of our wedding dress, number of children, etc." Ellis, 1910s, 38. Orange and a lemon, apple and a pear, similar to Northall, Gaskell, c1913, p. 6. Black-currant—red-currant—raspberry tart:/Tell me the name of your sweet-heart,/ and then they begin with A. B. C, and all through the alphabet … Douglas, 1916, p. 51, 1931, p. 27. Kings 2, 1930: Rosy apple, a-la-ba-la pear, p. 8, Raspberry, strawberry, marmalade jam, p. 30. Botkin, *TAF*, 1944, p. 792.

Recordings BBC 6669 (78) (1941, Bristol); Webb, *Children's Singing Games*; Wilson and Gallagher, *Children's Singing Games*.

6.A.59 ON A MOUNTAIN STANDS A LADY

>SKIPPING SONG descended from courtship singing game, descended from folksong.

>On a mountain stands a lady,
>Who she is I do not know.
>All she wants is gold and silver;
>All she wants is a nice young man.

>Mile End 1964, 1966; Marylebone 1967; Walworth 1974, 1979; Barnsbury, Borough, <u>Dulwich</u>, Finsbury <u>1983</u>.

At the time the fieldwork was undertaken, one of three further rhymes (**6.A.55B**, **6.A.60**, and **6.A.61**) could be added to ON A MOUNTAIN STANDS A LADY to make a complete skipping game.

According to the Opies (*SG*, 1985, p. 176), the original singing game underwent a revival in 1975–76 after it was performed on schools television.

Printed versions this rhyme hardly ever stands on its own. As a singing game it was followed by verses common to other singing games such as: "Rosy Apple and Pear"; "Pretty Little Girl of Mine"; "Oats and Beans"; "Sally Water"; "Isabella", or verses from "The Keys of Canterbury". Such versions are contained in: Brady, pp. 103–105; Chase, *SGPPG*, pp. 20–23; Daiken, *CGTY*, p. 75; Douglas (see below); Gillington (see below); Gomme (see below); Kelsey, *K1*, 44, *K3*, 78–85; Kings (see below); Kirshenblatt-Gimblett, p. 90; Mills and Bishop (see below); Northall (see below); Opies, *SG*, pp. 174–178; Shaw, 1969, pp. 50–51, followed by "So call in my very best friend …"; Smith, *BBHG*, p. 9.

Other printed versions of the song standing alone, appear in Abrahams, p. 155; Botkin (see below); Cosbey, p. 85; Cumnock Academy, p. 16; Evans, *JRR*, p. 11; Fowke, p. 66; Halliwell (see below); Kellett, p. 13 (and see below); Nicholson (see below); Swift, mentioned, 146; Turner, pp. 36, 56, and 122 (the latter quoting *The Bulletin*, Sydney, 26.2.1898).

Some versions, particularly the older ones, are closer to the folksong "On Yonder Hill there Stands a Creature" and its relative "Yonder Sits a Spanish Lady". Typical is Newell's version (see below).

Early notings cf. a similar rhyme beginning: Madam, I am come to court you,/If your favour I can gain, Halliwell, *NRNTE*, c1870, p. 96. Northall, 1892, p. 376; Gomme, 1894, pp. 320–324; Nicholson, 1897, p. 149. There she stands, a lovely creature,/Who she is, I do not know;/I have caught her for her beauty,—/Let her answer, yes or no.//Madam, I have gold and silver,/Lady, I have houses and lands,/Lady, I have ships on the ocean,/All I have is at thy command.//What care I for your gold and silver,/What care I for your houses and lands,/What care I for your ships on the ocean—/*All I want is a nice young man*. (New York), Newell, 1903, pp. 55–56. Gillington, 1909, *OHSG*, p. 8, *OIWSG*, pp. 23–25, *OSSG*, p. 16; Douglas, 1916, p. 85, 1931, p. 49; Kellett, 1920s, p. 13; Kings 1, 1926, p. 20. Part of a rhyme beginning Happy Hooligan, number nine, Mills and Bishop, 1937, 39. Yonder comes a heavenly creature, Botkin, *APPS*, 1937, p. 61n. Botkin, *TAF*, 1944: as Mills and Bishop, p. 801, and There she stands, a lovely creature, pp. 804–805.

Recording Webb, *Children's Singing Games*.

6.A.60 DRIP, DROP, DROPPING IN THE SEA

SKIPPING SONG (part, usually added to **6.A.59** ON A MOUNTAIN STANDS A LADY):

A. Drip, drop, dropping in the sea,
Please turn the rope for me.
Come, come, come to the fair,
No, no, the fair's not there.
Along came a Chinaman and said to me,
Do you know your ABC?
A, B, C, D, E, F, G, H, … till "You're out".

Mile End 1968.

B. Drip, drop, drops in the sea,
    Up came a mermaid and said to me,
    Do you know your ABC?
    'Cause I do.
    Then speak to me
    A, B, C, D, E, F, G, H, ...

Walworth 1979.

Children do two skips each in turn, then they alternate from each end, one at a time.

Printed versions Brady, pp. 72, 77.

6.A.61 SO CALL IN ...

SKIPPING SONG, (part, usually added to **6.A.59** ON A MOUNTAIN STANDS A LADY):

A. So call in my (_____ _____)
    And I'll be married to him straight away.

Marylebone 1967; <u>Barnsbury 1983</u>.

B. So come in (_____ _____, _____ _____, _____ _____),
    So come in (_____ _____),
    (_____) loves you.

Finsbury 1983.

Printed versions Abrahams, p. 73, quoting Ritchie; cf. Evans, *JRR*, Everybody, everybody,/ Come on in./The first one misses/Gonna take my end, p. 5; Ritchie, *GC*, p. 112; Shaw, 1969, p. 51.

6.B ELASTIC SKIPPING

The development of a kind of skipping with elastic bands was a relatively minor spin-off from rope skipping in the two or three decades prior to my collecting project. It requires more skill than ordinary skipping and some girls achieve a high degree of virtuosity. A number of elastic bands are knotted together to produce a large circle which is stretched between the ankles of two girls. In the middle, the skipper has to perform a series of movements with her feet and legs, creating various patterns and shapes with the bands. When she has gone through the progression at ankle level the bands are raised to calf, knee level, and so on, according to the skill of the performer. It becomes increasingly difficult (see notes to **6.B.3**). Most of the rhymes used are adapted from other skipping rhymes. Some are exclusively used for this activity, while a few still do service for more traditional kinds of skipping. Ritchie (*GC*, 1965, p. 121) gives details of how this activity, known variously as Chinese ropes, American ropes, and Elastications, was performed in Edinburgh in 1965.

6.B.1 ENGLAND, IRELAND, SCOTLAND, WALES

> England, Ireland, Scotland, Wales,
> Inside, outside, monkeys' (donkeys') tails,
> Catapult! catapult! please jump in,
> Catapult! catapult! please jump out,
> Double Diamond* insies,
> Double Diamond outsies,
> Lady in the tight skirt, please jump out,
> Lady in the tight skirt, please jump on,
> Big Ben strikes one,   (See also **2.10** and **6.A.16**)
> Over the bridge, in the bridge, and on the bridge,
> Lemonade in, cherryade out,
> In, out, in, out, shake it all about.
> Banana, banana, banana, split,   (See also **6.A.39B**)
> Fanny (Granny) put her knickers on, inside out,   (See also **6.B.3**)
> One scoobeedoo,

Two scoobeedoo,
Four scoobeedoo.

Dalston 1983.

* Double Diamond is an English pale ale, first brewed in 1876 by Samuel Allsopp and Sons and very popular during the 1960s and 70s.

Many elastic bands are joined together to make a large circle. A girl puts her legs inside the stretched circle at each end. A third girl in the middle goes through a sequence of movements, sometimes of a very complicated nature. The skill of the participants determines the routine. In some versions the bands are raised from ankle, to knee, to thigh and even to hip level. The game seems to be international. I have seen a girl from Vietnam go through a long sequence of movements requiring great skill which none of the other girls of her age in the school were able to achieve, at ankle, calf, hip, waist and chest levels.

Here are a few of the possibilities:

> "We make two lines out of the elastics and we jump over them. We put one leg in and one leg out until we finish, then another person does the same thing." girl, 11, Stoke Newington 1983.

> "You have elastic bands. You jump on it, then in, then out. You do all the different actions. When it says, 'catapult' you step on it and jump out, then jump in and jump out again. When it says, 'Big Ben strikes ten,' you do all different actions. When it says, 'split,' you do the splits." girl, 11, Dalston 1983.

> "In, on, in out"—step on elastic, others stretch elastic.
> "Twist, twist, jump"—twist elastic.
> "Envelope"—bring one side over.
> "Carrotsie"—make a long kite shape.
> "Diamond"—make diamond shape, similar to "Envelope".

Hampstead 1984.

Printed versions Roud, *DM2*, 11–13; Rutherford, p. 64; Shaw, 1969, p. 11, Wade 2, 33.

6.B.2   JINGLE JANGLE

> Jingle, jangle, centre spangle.
> Jingle, jangle out.
>
> Hampstead 1984.

See also **6.A.1**.

Printed version Roud, *DM2*, 11.

6.B.3   GRANNY PUT HER KNICKERS ASIDE

> Granny put her knickers aside (three times)
> Inside out.
>
> Granny put her knickers on (three times)
> Inside out.
>
> Kentish Town 1983.

See also **6.B.1**.

This is the longest sequence of movements explained to me:

> "You keep jumping in and out of the two elastics very fast.
>
> (Jingle, jangle)   You go from one side to the other, then to the middle, then, very slow, out.
>
> Then it's from one side to the other. Then you jump out, then in, out, etc.

You jump in, then you jump on the two elastics, then you jump out, then in and out.

You take a big jump and you put your two feet on the elastics, and then you jump off again.

Also we do envelopes. You bring the back one under the first one.

You've got to jump on the first one and then from the first one to the second one."

Hampstead 1984.

SECTION 7

BALL BOUNCING GAMES

Introduction

Although rubber balls evidently existed as long ago as the Olmec civilisation, children's ball bouncing games gained in popularity following the availability of cheap indiarubber balls following the inventions of vulcanisation by such manufacturers as Goodyear in 1839 and Parkes in 1846. Also in 1846, Macintosh and Company listed rubber balls among their manufactures and they were apparently displayed at the Great Exhibition of 1851. It seems likely that two-ball bouncing became more popular after the invention of the sponge rubber ball in the 1920s. Nowadays ball bouncing consists of bouncing one or two balls on the ground and of bouncing one, two (and rarely, three) balls against a wall, occasionally deliberately letting a ball bounce on the ground. It would not hold the interest of a player for very long if it were not for the innumerable variations of throwing, bouncing, dropping and catching, interspersed with various movements, that have been invented by generations of schoolgirls. These activities are accompanied by some of the most ingenious, humorous and intriguing songs and rhymes to be found among contemporary children's traditional verse.

In his study of the games of New Zealand children, Sutton-Smith (1959, p. 86) says that there are no records of ball bouncing before 1900. However, in Gomme's collection (1898, pp. 64–65) there are two examples of the game of "Pots". The first consists of a series of bounces against a wall, first in ordinary fashion, then with twisting of hands, clapping hands behind and before, turning round, bouncing the ball on the ground etc. The version printed was reported from Hexham. The second example, from Scotland, is in the addenda to the collection (Gomme, 1898, pp. 405–406) under the heading of "Ball". This latter version had thirteen variations in all, which also include touching both shoulders in turn, touching alternate knees, catching the ball on the back of the hand, etc. No rhymes or songs to accompany these actions are given by Gomme. However, under the same heading, rhymes are given to accompany the activity of patting the ball against the ground for as long as possible.

Newell (1883, 1903), in his study of American children's games, does not include ball bouncing. It is very likely, however, that some time around the beginning of the twentieth century, words and actions came together and ball bouncing as a major activity for girls at play began, instead of just being one game among many others, occasionally played. Presumably, bouncing and catching, and pat bouncing preceded bouncing against a wall, and certainly came before the greater skill required for two-ball bouncing. The "alairy" rhymes which accompanied the raising of a leg over the ball while bouncing it appear to be the oldest specifically ball bouncing rhymes noted. I doubt if they were the oldest used, because the type of clothing that girls still wore at the beginning of the twentieth century would have made this activity difficult unless they tucked their skirts up. A correspondent from Hamdon, Somerset, whose memory went back to 1908, told me that she used to sing a rhyme: "One, two, three o'lairy,/I spy sister Mary/Outside the Maypole dairy/Kissing (Billy Tomkins)." The Maypole company ran a chain of provision shops for many years.[1] In London, and presumably other cities, the rhyme usually went: "One, two, three alairy, /My ball's down the airy …" and then something like "Don't forget to give it to Mary,/Not to Charlie Chaplin." *Airy* was dialect or slang for "area", the space in front of the basement floor in buildings of the eighteenth and early nineteenth centuries. It usually had access to street level by a steep metal staircase, while railings stopped people from falling into it. Despite these, and a gate at the top of the stairs, if balls were played with in the vicinity, inevitably, sooner or later, they went "down the airy". In country districts such buildings were rare, so *dairy* replaced *airy*. Versions of the "alairy/airy" rhyme were still going strong in the early 1960s, even though most of the buildings with basement areas had been replaced by council housing. Many of the dark basements had been bricked in, and many of the railings removed during the Second World War, ostensibly for use as scrap metal for munitions. I was therefore very surprised to collect two versions of the "down the airy" rhyme in schools in 1983, so strong is the folk tradition.

In his chapter on ball bouncing, Rutherford (1971, p. 80) refers to an Anglo-Saxon scholar, Bertram Colgrave, who suggested that the word *alairy* might have connections with the Middle English word *alery*, which meant folding the leg under, like a beggar pretending to have lost a leg. *Collins English Dictionary* (1979) has an entry for the word *alary*, meaning referring to, or like, wings; this dates from the seventeenth century. Whatever the derivation of the word, or whether children somewhere made it up, variations of it have become ubiquitous throughout the English-speaking world: England, Scotland, Ireland, Wales, New Zealand, Canada, and the U.S.A. have a form of the word, e.g. *cockalairy, a-leary, o'lary, o'leary, alairer, o'laier, a-larry, alara*.

Ball bouncing requires a different rhythm from that of a turning rope. Some skipping rhymes have been adapted for ball bouncing but changes usually take place. The skipping rhyme: "Nebuchadnezzar, King of the Jews,/Sold his wife for a pair of shoes," underwent a change and became the ball bouncing rhyme: **7.46** ARCHIBALD, BALD, BALD,/King of the Jews, Jews, Jews,/Bought his wife, wife, wife,/A pair of shoes, shoes, shoes ... .

Sometimes the change is very slight. A skipping version went: "Rin-Tin-Tin swallowed a pin,/He went to the doctor's and the doctor wasn't in,/He went to the nurse and she said a curse,/And that was the end of Rin-Tin-Tin." The ball bouncing version is sharper: **7.30** RIN-TIN-TIN SWALLOWED A PIN,/Went to the doctors', doctors weren't in,/Opened the door, fell through the floor,/That's the end of Rin-Tin-Tin.

While ball bouncing is not an activity with a very long history, traditional rhymes are incorporated into the repertoire, though they do not play a large part. **7.24** NIGGER, NIGGER and **7.38** QUEENIE, QUEENIE CAROLINE, to be found in Bolton's 1888 collection of counting-out rhymes (pp. 115, 116) are examples of old traditional rhymes being brought into use. **7.14** MATTHEW, MARK, LUKE AND JOHN has retained the first line and rhythmic pattern of the old rhymes, and **7.29** ONE, TWO, BUCKLE MY SHOE is, of course, an old standard counting rhyme which has filled several roles in its long history. However, even if not of longstanding tradition, most of the rhymes existed before my survey was undertaken.

An interesting illustration of how a rhyme can be adapted for a particular use and then amended and added to, came my way when I was a class teacher in East London in 1968. A drama production was being worked on by my class, involving a number of traditional rhymes connected with London. One of these was the nursery rhyme in the Opies' paperback collection (*PBNR*, 1963, p. 54): "Mother and Father and Uncle Dick/Went to London on a stick;/The stick broke and made a smoke,/And stifled all the London folk." A few months later I noticed a number of girls playing two-balls, accompanied by a slightly amended version of what they had used in the classroom: "DADDY, MUMMY, UNCLE DICK/Went to London on a stick;/The stick broke,/What a joke,/Daddy, Mummy, Uncle Dick." (**7.3**). They had, however, added another verse: "Daddy, Mummy, Uncle Tom/Went to London on a bomb;/The bomb broke,/What a smoke,/Daddy, Mummy, Uncle Tom."

Any sequence of ball bouncing would include a number of variations from an innumerable store: *Alairsie, Archie, Backsie, Bendsie, Blinksie, Bowsie, Bumsie, Clapsie, Curtsey, Dancie, Digsie, Downsie, Dropsie, Dumb Hipsie, Dumbsie, Farsie, Floorsie, Footsie, Gatesie, Highsie, Hopsie, Kneesie, Legsie, Loopsie, Lowsie, Nearsie, One handsie, One legsie, Other handsie, Other legsie, Overs, Plainsie, Roundsie, Round the Worldsie, Shoesie, Slipsie, Smallsie, Stillsie, Tallsie, Thumpsie, Twistsie, Unders, Upsie, Winksie.* These are a selection from those I have come across in Inner London. Many of the actions are self-evident. Here are a few which may not be so straightforward:

Digsie: "You throw it at the corner of the wall and the ground."
Downsie: "You bounce it on the ground and let it drop on the ground before you catch it."
Dumbsie: "You don't say anything."
Farsie: "You jump away."
Loopsie: "You throw it over your shoulder."
Nearsie: "You jump towards the wall."
Stillsie: "You mustn't move."

Archie is more complicated. Two legs make an arch. The ball is bounced from behind, to bounce on the floor and off the wall, before it is caught. Some actions are imitative mimes, such as *Birdsie*, *Policeman*, and *Milkman*, though this is not always clear to the uninitiated.

"For 'policeman' you just bow like a policeman does."

"For 'milkman' you got to go down and touch the floor." (Presumably imitating a milkman putting down a bottle of milk).

Most school groups had a particular sequence of movements usually known as *tensies* or *sevensies*. This is an example of *sevensies* from Kensington (1984):

Sevensie: Let the ball bounce on the ground seven times.
Sixie: Bounce and catch the ball without it touching the ground six times.
Fivesie: Throw the ball up and catch it five times.
Foursie: Bounce the ball under the leg four times.
Threesie: Throw the ball against the wall and touch the floor three times.
Twosie: Hit the ball, using the hand as a bat, twice.
Onesie: Throw the ball against the wall, let it bounce and catch it.

Then the sequence was done in reverse, so the last action was done seven times and then each activity reduced until the original first one was done first again.

It is interesting to note that almost all the movements contained in the sequence under the name "Pots" in Gomme (1898, pp. 405–406) were still in use at the time of my survey, though not necessarily linked in the same way. Another kind of sequence was to repeat a particular movement throughout a verse of a song and then have a different movement for the second verse, and so on. The first verse might be ordinary throwing against the wall and catching it (*plainsie*):

> **7.34B**   Plainsie Mrs. Brown, plainsie Mrs. Brown
> Plainsie, plainsie, plainsie, plainsie,
> Plainsie Mrs. Brown.
> > then
>
> Upsie Mrs. Brown, upsie Mrs. Brown etc.
> > then
>
> Clapsie Mrs. Brown, clapsie Mrs. Brown etc.

and so on until the continuity has been broken or the bouncer gets tired of the game. A similar procedure was gone through in **7.32** PLAINSIE TO AMERICA. Another variation is *Dasha*, as in **7.5** DASHA MARMALADE. The ball was thrown on the ground to bounce on the wall and then caught. In some schools, however, the action consisted of the ball being thrown and allowed to bounce on the ground to go between the legs before being caught.

Sometimes the rhyme describes the movement which accompanies it, as in **7.33** PLAINSIE, CLAPSIE: Plainsie, clapsie,/Round the wall and backsie,/First your knee,/Then your toe,/Give it a bounce,/And let it go. The OLIVER TWIST rhymes, **7.25A** and **7.25B**, have a boasting element, e.g. **7.25B** Oliver Twist, Oliver Twist,/Bet you five thousand you can't do this./Stand at ease,/Stamp your knees,/Quick march!/Over the arch. **7.29** ONE, TWO, BUCKLE MY SHOE has already been referred to above, but **7.45** WHEN I WAS ONE was much more popular. This also had a series of mimes, the actions representing various ages instead of just numbers. It was found in almost every Inner London school but the mimes would vary from school to school, from group to group, and often between individual bouncers.

A dramatic element can be found in several ball bouncing rhymes. **7.27** OVER THE GARDEN WALL deals with a domestic crisis, the critical dropping of the baby represented by the dropping of the ball. **7.44** WHEN THE WAR WAS OVER, which has a refusal of admission to heaven by the Lord, is a very interesting rhyme and deserves its recognition by the *Encyclopaedia Britannica* in an article on children's games and sports (1973, p. 518). I doubt if Josephine was the first subject for the rhyme, but none of the girls who gave me a version with Josephine had ever heard of Napoleon's wife. Of eight notings I only came across one alternative applicant for celestial bliss, namely Queen Victoria. Other collectors, however, have noted the Kaiser, Mussolini, Hitler (in the *Encyclopaedia Britannica* article), and Tommy Steele. I have given a version where the Lord relents in a second verse, but this is not the usual ending.

I think that the most dramatically fascinating of all play rhymes is probably the ball bouncing rhyme: **7.11** FUDGE, FUDGE, CALL THE JUDGE. This rhyme is almost certainly an import from the United States and two versions were printed in an American collection as long ago as 1944 (Botkin, pp. 794, 801). The version I selected for the present collection was recorded in 1983:

> **7.11** Fudge, fudge, call the judge,
> Me mother's having a baby.
> Is it a boy? Is it a girl?
> Or is it a human baby?
> Wrap it up in tissue paper,
> Throw it down the escalator,
> First floor, drop,
> Second floor, drop,
> Third floor, shut (kick) the door,
> Me mother's not having a baby no more.

Obviously *escalator* is an attempt to Anglicise *elevator* contained in the American versions. An elevator is of course a lift, not a moving staircase, but the words are similar and the word *lift* would not fit the rhythm. There is a contradiction contained in most English versions: the lift goes up, but the baby is thrown down. In American versions they both ascend, or both descend. Some English and American variants deny that the baby is a boy or girl, but say: "It's just an ordinary baby". In some American versions it is a "fair young lady", "a new-born baby", or a "plain old baby". Another series of versions, as is the case with one from Edinburgh (Ritchie, *GC*, 1965, pp. 83–84) and one from the USA (Botkin, 1944, p. 801), welcome the baby: "Joy, joy/It's a boy", and "It's a boy, full of joy". However, in most versions from either side of the Atlantic, the baby is wrapped in tissue paper and disposed of by sending it up (or throwing it down) the escalator/elevator and Mother is not going to have another baby.

Despite the nonsensical elements in some versions, I do not think this is a nonsense rhyme. It belongs to environments where there are medium- or high-rise dwellings. I did not come across any versions in suburbs consisting of detached or semi-detached houses. The basic core of the rhyme in most versions seems to suggest the disposal of a baby (stillborn or alive) which is unwanted and whose birth may have been concealed. In one version, however (Fulton and Smith, 1978, p. 48), a diaper is disposed of instead of a baby. The fact that a judge is called for in almost all versions tends to indicate that some breach of law has been committed. Of course the girls do not think about what the words may mean when the balls are being bounced, but I am sure that the imagery contained in many rhymes influences their popularity, their survival and their spread. In this case, for example, it might be argued that the rhyme reflects a degree of sibling rivalry. Cosbey (1980, pp. 50–51) analyses the Canadian version in terms of teenage pregnancy, its attendant anxieties, and society's disapproval of it. Actions to accompany this rhyme varied, but the ball was usually dropped on the ground for the lines which indicate the arrival of the lift on the first and second floors, and a kick accompanied its final destination when the door is shut or kicked. I have given this particular attention here because I think it is an example of the interesting character of a number of ball bouncing rhymes.

Wordplay features in several ball bouncing rhymes such as **7.7** D'YOU WANT A CIGARETTE, SIR?, **7.23** MY MUM'S A SECRETARY, and

7.37 PLEASE MISS. The insertion of *Sir* or *Miss* at every possible point is of course a feature of the language of schoolchildren when talking to their teachers.

NOTES

1. This is remarkably similar to one of Brady's rhymes (1975, p. 57): "1, 2, 3, O'Leary,/I spy my Auntie Mary/Coming out of Merville Dairy,/Eating chocolate ice-cream.". Brady explains that many tenants on the Finglas Corporation housing estate (Dublin) worked in the local "Merville Dairies".

7.1 BLACK CAT

TWO-BALLS RHYME:

A. Black cat sat on the mat,
    Eating a tin of Kit-e-Kat,
    Swallowed a bone,
    Started to moan,
    That's the end of black cat.

Mile End 1968; West Norwood 1973; Walworth 1982; <u>Dulwich 1983</u>.

Printed version Rosen and Steele, front cover.

B. Black cat sat on the mat,
    Fell through,
    One, two.

West Norwood 1970.

7.2 ALICE IN WONDERLAND

TWO-BALLS RHYME:

Alice in Wonderland,
Alice in Wonderland
Alice oh Alice,
Alice oh Alice,
Alice in Wonder-la-a-and.

Mile End 1968; Walworth 1979; <u>Dalston 1983</u>.

7.3 DADDY, MUMMY, UNCLE DICK

TWO-BALLS RHYME:

Daddy, Mummy, Uncle Dick,
Went to London on a stick,
The stick broke,
What a joke,
Daddy, Mummy, Uncle Dick.
Daddy, Mummy, Uncle Tom,
Went to London on a bomb,
The bomb broke,
What a smoke,
Daddy, Mummy, Uncle Tom.

Mile End 1969.

Printed versions Briggs, p. 87; Daiken, *TTP*, Mother, Father, Uncle Dick, p. 94; cf. Montgomerie, Father and Mother and Uncle John, p. 83; Opies, *PBNR*, Mother and Father and Uncle Dick, p. 54.

7.4 DON'T GO TO GRANNY'S ANY MORE

TWO-BALLS RHYME, CLAPPING:

Don't go to Granny's any more, more, more,
There's a great big copper at the door, door, door,
He'll grab you by the collar,
And charge you half a dollar,
Don't go to Granny's any more, more, more.

<u>Mile End</u> 1968, <u>1983</u>; West Norwood 1973; Walworth 1981; Brixton, Greenwich 1982; Cubitt Town 1983.

Printed versions Botkin (see below); Evans, *JRR*, to Macy's, p. 5; Kellett, p. 127; Mills and Bishop (see below); Opies, *SG*, to school, p. 478; Rosen and Steele, [p. 15]; Turner, to the pictures, p. 43; Withers, *RIMP*, to Macy's, p. 68.

Early notings I won't go to Macy's any more, more, more,/There's a big fat policeman at the door, door, door,/He grab me by the collar and he make me pay a dollar,/So I won't go to Macy's any more, more, more, Mills and Bishop, 1937, 36. Botkin, *TAF*, 1944, as Mills and Bishop, p. 801.

7.5 DASHA MARMALADE

SINGLE-BALL RHYME:

Dasha marmalade,
Dasha marmalade,
All the nurses, lost their purses,
Dasha marmalade.

"You throw the ball against the wall, over your head and through your legs." girl, Cubitt Town 1983.

Walworth 1974, 1979; <u>Borough</u>, Cubitt Town <u>1983</u>.

Printed version Brady, Plainy marmalade, p. 64.

7.6   UP IN ABERDEEN

Up in Aberdeen,
I met the fairy queen,
Her name is Alice,
She lives in a palace,
Up in Aberdeen.

West Norwood 1973; Walworth 1979; <u>Battersea 1982</u>; Borough 1983.

7.7   D'YOU WANT A CIGARETTE, SIR?

BALL BOUNCING RHYME:

D'you want a cigarette, sir?
No sir. Why sir?
'Cause I got a cold, sir.
Where d'you get the cold, sir?
Up the North Pole, sir.
What you doing there, sir?
Catching polar bears, sir.
How many did you catch, sir?
One, sir, two, sir.
The rest caught me, sir.
Climbing up the tree, sir.
That's the end of me, sir.

Mile End 1966; Putney 1967; Walworth 1979; Battersea, Brixton 1982; Barnsbury 1983.

See also **8.A.4**, **11.I.6** and **11.I.7**.

Printed versions (also used for "dipping" and skipping): Abrahams, "Generally used as a ball-bouncing rhyme", p. 60; Brady, Where are you going Bob,/Down the lane Bob, p. 52; Please get off the grass, Sir, p. 64; Coffin and Cohen, p. 188; Daiken, *CGTY*, p. 33; Evans, *JRR*, skipping rhyme, p. 17; Fowke, Are you coming out, sir? p. 77; Graves (see below); Kelsey, *K1*, 45; Kenney, p. 48; Kings (see below); Opies, *CGSP*, dip, p. 37; Ritchie, *GC*, Are you going to golf, sir? p. 85; cf. Rosen and Steele, Please keep off the grass, sir, [p. 5]; Rutherford, pp. 82–83; cf. Shaw, Where you goin', Joe? Down the lane, Joe. ... 1969, p. 34, 1970, p. 59; Turner, pp. 49–50; Withers, *RIMP*, p. 62.

Early notings I have a little cough, sir, Graves, 1927, p. 22. Are you going to golf, sir? Kings 2, 1930, p. 22.

Recordings MacColl and Seeger, *The Elliotts of Birtley*; Behan and McColl, *Streets of Song*.

7.8 DONALD DUCK WASHING UP

TWO-BALLS RHYME:

Donald Duck washing up,
Broke a saucer and a cup.

Marylebone 1967; Mile End 1968; West Norwood 1970; Walworth 1982; Borough 1983.

Printed versions Abrahams, Charlie Chaplin, p. 26; Opies, *LLS*, Charlie Chaplin, p. 108; Ritchie, *GC*, Charlie Chaplin, p. 87; Rosen and Steele, back cover; Rutherford, Cinderella, p. 84.

7.9 EACH, PEACH, PEAR, PLUM

TWO-BALLS RHYME:

A. Each, peach, pear, plum,
I spy Tom Thumb,
Tom Thumb in the cellar,
Making love to Cinderella,
Cinderella at the ball,
Making love to Henry Hall,
Henry Hall at the pictures,
Making love to Cliff Richards,
Cliff Richards is a star,
S-T-A-R.

<u>West Norwood 1973</u>; Walworth 1979 (shorter); Barnsbury 1983 (fragment).

At Walworth, the rhyme, which is used for "two balls" against the wall, stopped at Frankie Hall (replacing Henry Hall).

B. First six lines as above, then:

Henry Hall at the stable,
Making love to Betty Grable,
Betty Grable in the wood,
Making love to Robin Hood,
Robin Hood up a tree,
Making love to a bumble bee,
L-O-V-E spells love.

<u>Mile End 1968</u>; West Norwood 1970 (shorter); Battersea 1982 (shorter); Brockley 1983 (fragment).

Henry Hall was an English dance band leader, well-known from BBC Radio from the 1920s to the 1960s. Cliff Richard is the British pop singer who would have been familiar to the children in my survey from television, and his stage name is often misquoted as "Richards" as here. Betty Grable was an American film star in the 1940s and 1950s – see also **4.56B**.

See also **2.19** and **2.44**.

Printed versions Kelsey, *K1*, 42; Opies, *LLS*, p. 115; Ritchie, *SS*, p. 45; Rutherford, p. 61; Turner, p. 49.

Recording Webb, *Children's Singing Games*.

7.10 GIPSY, GIPSY LIVED IN A TENT

BALL BOUNCING RHYME:

Gipsy, gipsy lived in a tent,
Gipsy, gipsy wouldn't pay the rent,
The rent man came around one day,
And gipsy, gipsy ran away,
Over the fields and far away.

Brockley, Marylebone 1967; Mile End 1968; <u>Dulwich 1983</u>.

Printed versions Abrahams, Gypsy, p. 57; Indian, p. 86; Brady, Little Nellie, p. 55; Fowke, p. 74; Kellett, p. 60; Nelson, counting-out rhyme, p. 61; Opies, *CGSP*, counting-out rhyme, p. 29; Ritchie, *SS*, pp. 33–34, *GC*, p. 93; Rutherford, counting-out rhyme, p. 53, ball bouncing, pp. 78, 85; Smith, *BBHG*, p. 28; Turner, p. 31.

Recording Webb, *Children's Singing Games*.

7.11 FUDGE, FUDGE, CALL THE JUDGE

BALL BOUNCING AND SKIPPING RHYME:

Fudge, fudge, call the judge,
Me mother's having a baby,
Is it a boy? Is it a girl?
Or is it a human baby?
Wrap it up in tissue paper,

Throw it down the escalator,
First floor, drop,
Second floor, drop,
Third floor, shut (kick) the door,
Me mother's not having a baby no more.

Marylebone 1967; Hampstead 1972; Walworth 1974, 1979, 1982; <u>Barnsbury</u>, Borough <u>1983</u>.

From the variety of printed sources, and the use of the word *escalator* – obviously substituted for *elevator* – this is almost certainly an American rhyme. I have only collected it in Inner London in areas with fairly high-rise blocks of flats.

Printed versions Abrahams, pp. 51–52; Botkin (see below); Cosbey, pp. 51, 73; Cumnock Academy, p. 19; Evans, *JRR*, p. 24; Fowke, p. 60; Fulton and Smith, clapping, p. 48; Kelsey, *K1*, 45; Kenney, p. 2; Knapps, p. 113; Mills and Bishop (see below); Ritchie, *GC*, pp. 83–84; Rutherford, p. 85; Solomons, pp. 58, 83; Withers, *RIMP*, p. 64; Worstell, p. 14.

Early notings Judge, judge, tell the judge/Mamma has a baby./It's a boy, full of joy,/Papa's going crazy./Wrap it up in tissue paper,/Send it down the elevator./How many pounds did it weigh?/One, two, three, etc., Mills and Bishop, 1937, ball bouncing, 36. Fudge, fudge, tell the judge/Mother has a newborn baby;/It isn't a girl and it isn't a boy;/It's just a fair young lady./Wrap it up in tissue paper/And send it up the elevator:/First floor, miss;/Second floor, miss;/Third floor, miss;/Fourth floor,/Kick it out the elevator door, Botkin, *TAF*, 1944, p. 794; as Mills and Bishop, p. 801.

7.12 ORANGES, LEMONS, TWO FOR A PENNY

TWO-BALLS RHYME:

Oranges, lemons, two for a penny,
Mother got rich she bought so many.

Father died, he ate so many.
Oranges, lemons, two for a penny.

Barnsbury 1983.

Printed versions Bolton (see below); Chambers (see below); Douglas (see below); Ford (see below); Gregor (see below); Gullen, Lemons and oranges, p. 16; Montgomeries, *SC*, Apples and oranges,/ Four a penny, p. 149; Newell (see below); Opies (see below).

Early notings Oranges, Oranges, four a penny,/All went down the donkey's belly;/The donkey's belly was full of jelly,/Out goes you, Opies, *CGSP*, counting-out rhyme, p. 38. The Opies comment: "The first line introduced several other puerile rhymes in the nineteenth century." cf. Lemons and oranges, two for a penny, "chappin out" (counting-out) rhyme, Chambers, 1842, p. 62, 1870, p. 121. Bolton (1888) notes several versions on p. 112, including one very similar to the Barnsbury example. Eringes, oranjies,/Two for a penny, Gregor, 1891, two variants, pp. 26, 30. Apples and oranges, two for a penny,/Takes a good scholar to count as many; O-u-t, out goes she, counting-out rhyme, Newell, 1903, p. 201. Ford, 1904, p. 53. Douglas mentions a "hand-clapping game" played by girls (title only): "Oranges, oranges, four a penny", 1916, p. 43, 1931, p. 23.

7.13 I'M POPEYE THE SAILOR MAN

BALL BOUNCING, DIPPING AND ENTERTAINMENT RHYME:

Popeye appeared in many cartoon films in the 1930s. The song "I Yam Popeye the Sailor Man" was featured in the film *Popeye Starring in Choose your Weppins* (1935–36, Paramount): I yam Popeye,/The Sailor Man./I yam what I yam/'Cause tha's what I yam./I yam Popeye,/The Sailor Man.

A.   I'm Popeye the sailor man,
       I live in a caravan,

When I go swimming,
I kiss all the women,
I'm Popeye the sailor man.

Mile End 1968, 1983; Walworth 1974; Greenwich, Streatham 1982; Borough, Brockley, Cubitt Town, Dalston, Dulwich, Finsbury, Kentish Town, Shepherds Bush 1983; Hampstead 1984.

Printed versions Fowke, p. 62; Kellett (see below); Knapps, p. 188; Opies, *LLS*, p. 112, *SG*, p. 471; Roud, *DM1*, 30; Ritchie, *GC*, p. 90; Smith, *BBHG*, p. 50.

Early noting I'M Popeye the sailor man,/I live in a caravan;/Before I go swimming/I kiss all the women,/I'M Popeye the sailor man. Kellett, 1930s, p. 24.

B. I'm Popeye the sailor man, Whoo ooh!
    I live in a caravan, Whoo ooh!
    There's a hole in the middle,
    Where I do my piddle,
    I'm Popeye the sailor man, Whoo ooh!

Walworth 1974; Streatham 1982; Dalston, Dulwich, Finsbury, Mile End 1983; Hampstead 1984.

Printed versions Lowenstein, p. 25; cf. Shaw, Our Sally's new drawers,/ Our Sally's new drawers,/ There's a hole in the middle/For Sally to piddle/ In our Sally's new drawers, 1970, p. 17.

C. I'm Popeye the sailor man,
    I live in the caravan,
    I open the door
    And fall flat on the floor,
    I'm Popeye the sailor man, Tooh! Tooh!

Greenwich 1982; Dalston, Deptford 1983.

Printed versions Kellett (see below); Opies, *LLS*, p. 112, *SG*, p. 471; Turner, p. 93.

Early noting Popeye the sailor man/He lived in a caravan;/He opened the door/And he fell through the floor,/Popeye the sailor man. Kellett, 1930s, p. 24.

> D.   Popeye the sailor man,
>   Lives in a pot of jam,
>   The jam is so sticky,
>   It sticks to his dicky,
>   Popeye the sailor man.

Dulwich, Kentish Town 1983.

Printed versions Richards and Stubbs, p. 153; Turner, p. 93.

> E.   Popeye the sailor man,
>   He lived in a caravan,
>   He said to his granny,
>   "Can I see your fanny?
>   I'm Popeye the sailor man."

Battersea 1982.

Printed version Opies, *SG*, p. 472.

> F.   I'm Popeye the sailor man,
>   I live in a caravan,
>   I bought a pianner,
>   For two and a tanner
>   And sold it for half-a-crown.

Mile End 1968.

Printed versions Browne, 18; Kellett (see below); Opies, *LLS*, p. 112; Ritchie, *SS*, p. 35.

Early noting Popeye the sailor man/He lived in a caravan,/I bought a piana/For one and a tanner,/ Popeye the sailor man, Kellett, 1930s, p. 24.

Printed versions of other "Popeye" rhymes Botkin (see below); Hopkin, 31; Kellett (see below); Knapps, pp. 164, 184; Opies, *LLS*, p. 112, *SG*, pp. 471–472; Richards and Stubbs, p. 153; Rutherford, p. 123, Solomons, pp. 116, 117; Turner, p. 93.

Early notings of other "Popeye" rhymes Kellett, 1930s, pp. 24, 98. Eight versions, Botkin, *TAF*, 1944, pp. 254–255.

7.14 MATTHEW, MARK, LUKE AND JOHN

TWO-BALLS AND BOUNCING RHYME:

A. Matthew, Mark, Luke and John,
    Next door neighbour carry on,
    Next door neighbour's got the 'flu,
    So I pass the balls to you.

Mile End 1968; West Norwood 1973; Walworth 1974, 1979; Battersea 1982; Barnsbury, Borough, Cubitt Town, Dalston, Deptford, Dulwich, Mile End 1983.

B. With addition:
    If not now, then later on,
    Now it's time to pass them on.

Brockley 1983.

A girl has to take over from another the two balls in motion against the wall without holding them or dropping them. Some skill is called for.

There are very many printed versions of other "Matthew, Mark" rhymes, mainly of the traditional "Bless the bed that I lie on", or "Hold the horse that I leap on", some even going back to the seventeenth century (Opies, *LLS*, 1959, pp. 21–22). Several correspondents sent me the alternative version "Went to bed with their trousers on". A correspondent from Reading provided me with a link between the traditional rhyme and the current ball bouncing one: "Next apostle follow on."

Printed versions Kellett (see below); Opies, *LLS*, pp. 21–22; Ritchie, *SS*, skipping, p. 57, *GC*, ball-bouncing, p. 86, skipping, p. 135; Rodger, p. 11.

Early noting The traditional version, plus: Matthew, Mark, Luke and John/Hold me hoss while I get on, Kellett, ?1920s, p. 38.

Recording MacColl and Seeger, *The Elliotts of Birtley*.

7.15 MRS. MINNY WORE HER PINNY

BALL BOUNCING RHYME:

Mrs. Minny wore her pinny,
Upside down,
First she wore it, then she tore it,
Upside down.

West Norwood 1970; Battersea 1982.

Printed versions cf. Daiken, *TTP*, Little Minnie wore her pinnie/Inside out, counting-out rhyme, p. 94; cf. Sutton-Smith, Mrs. B. went to town,/ With her britches upside down, p. 98.

7.16 MRS. POLLY HAD A DOLLY

TWO-BALLS RHYME:

Mrs. Polly had a dolly,
Who was sick, sick, sick,
And she called for the doctor,
Very quick, quick, quick,
And the doctor came

With his bag and hat,
And he knocked at the door
With a rat-tat-tat.

Walworth 1979.

Printed versions Fowke, p. 40; cf. Leach and Fried, as Mills and Bishop, and Botkin (see below), skipping, p. 1016.

Early notings cf. Mother, Mother, I am sick;/Send for the doctor, quick, quick, quick. Doctor, Doctor, shall I die? Yes, my darling, do not cry./How many coaches shall I have?/Ten, twenty, thirty, etc. [till the skipper misses], Mills and Bishop, 1937, 32. Botkin, *TAF*, 1944, as Mills and Bishop, p. 798.

7.17 MRS. RUMBLE

BALL BOUNCING RHYME:

Mrs. Rumble, apple crumble,
Mrs. Rumble, in the jungle.

Dalston 1983.

7.18 DASH, DASH, DASH

BALL BOUNCING RHYME:

Dash, dash, dash,
My blue sash,
Floating on the water,
Like a cup and saucer,
Dash, ash, dash.

Marylebone 1967.

See also **2.16**.

7.19 I LOST MY ARM IN THE ARMY

BALL BOUNCING RHYME

I lost my arm in the army,
I lost my leg in the navy,
I lost me balls in the butcher's shop,
And found them in my gravy.

Dulwich, Mile End 1983.

Printed versions Opies (see below); cf. Webb, I lost my love in the Kerney, 640.

Early noting cf. O, I've lost my lad an' I care-nae,/I've lost my lad an' I care-nae,/I've lost my lad an' I ca-are-nae,/A ramshy-damshy-doo! Willa Muir in *Living with Ballads,* 1965 (quoted in Opies, *SG,* 1985, p. 376) dates the rhyme back to c1902.

Recording Webb, *Children's Singing Games* ("Lost my Love in the Kerney").

7.20 IN PRISON YOU GET COFFEE

BALL BOUNCING RHYME:

In prison you get coffee,
In prison you get tea,
In prison you get everything,
Except the prison key.

Mile End 1983.

7.21 P.K. PENNY A PACKET

TWO-BALLS RHYME:

P.K.* penny a packet,
First you lick it then you crack it,
Then you stick it in your jacket.
P.K. penny a packet.

Mile End 1966; West Norwood 1970; Dulwich, Mile End 1983.

* P.K. is a brand of chewing gum made by Wrigley's. K.P., a brand of salted peanuts, was more likely to be used at the time of the survey.

Printed versions Abrahams, p. 160; Kellett, pp. 19–20 (also known "pre-war"); cf. Lowenstein, P.K. chewing gum, p. 37, Yum, yum, bubble gum, p. 47; Ritchie, *SS*, "double ballie", p. 34, *GC*, skipping, p. 143; Rosen and Steele, [p. 1]; Rutherford, Cream crackers, penny a packet, p. 55; Sutton-Smith, Crackers, crackers, p. 77; Turner, p. 52.

Recording Webb, *Children's Singing Games.*

7.22 MRS. WHITE HAD A FRIGHT

BALL BOUNCING RHYME:

A. Mrs. White had a fright,
 In the middle of the night,
 Saw a ghost eating toast,
 Halfway up the lamp-post.

Brockley, Marylebone 1967; Mile End 1968; Battersea, Streatham 1982; Borough, Dalston, Dulwich 1983; Kensington 1984.

B. (____ _____)* had a fright,
   In the middle of the night,
   Saw a ghost eating toast
   Halfway up a lamp-post.
   The ghost was (_____)*
   Eating (yogurt)*

* Names etc. substituted as required.

Greenwich 1982.

Printed versions Brady, Mrs Dunne made her bun, p. 64; Briggs, Three little ghostesses,/Sitting on postesses, p. 209; Cole, There were three ghostesses …, p. 32; MacBain (see below); McMorland, p. 29; Northall (see below); Opies, *ISE*, like Northall's version, below, p. 57; *LLS*, p. 37; Ritchie, *GC*, p. 89; cf. Smith, *BBHG*, John Wayne, went to Spain, counting-out rhyme, p. 61.

Early noting I saw the ghostesses,/Sitting on the postesses,/Eating of their toastesses,/And fighting with their fistesses, Northall, 1892, p. 294; this version from Sussex, another from Northamptonshire. There were three ghosties-es …, MacBain, 1933, p. 66.

7.23 MY MUM'S A SECRETARY

BALL BOUNCING RHYME:

My mum's a secretary,
Born to be a secretary,
If you find it necessary,
Look it up in the dictionary.

Walworth 1979; Battersea, Greenwich 1982; Borough 1983.

Printed versions cf. Kenney, p. 46; cf. Ritchie, *GC*, p. 90; cf. Withers, *RIMP*, p. 51. All these examples begin with a formula like "One, two, three o'lary".

7.24 NIGGER, NIGGER

BALL BOUNCING RHYME:

A. Nigger, nigger, pull the trigger,
   Bang! Bang! Bang!

   (a drop on the floor for each "Bang!")

Walworth 1979.

B. Little nigger pulled a trigger,
   Bang! Bang! Bang!
   If this ball should touch the wall,
   I've surely won one game.

Mile End 1966.

For obvious reasons this rhyme, like some versions of the counting-out rhyme EENY MEENY MINY MO (**2.14A** and **2.14B**), was disappearing from Inner London schools by the 1980s.

Printed versions Bolton (see below); Knapps (see below); Ritchie, *GC*, p. 91.

Early noting Nigger, Nigger,/Pull a trigger/Up and down the Ohio river;/Rigger, jigger, /Nary snigger,/In a row we stand and shiver, Bolton, 1888, p. 115. Knapps, a version from the 1920s, p. 193.

7.25 OLIVER TWIST

TWO-BALLS RHYME AND SKIPPING RHYME:

A. Oliver, Oliver, Oliver Twist,
   I bet you three farthings you can't do this:
   One, touch your tongue, (suck your thumb)
   Two, touch your shoe, (buckle your shoe)

Three, touch your knee, (climb a tree)
Four, touch the floor,
Five, touch your thigh, (kick a hive)
Six, touch your knicks, (pick up sticks/do the splits)
Seven, jump to heaven (close your eyes and count to eleven)
Eight, pinch your mate,
Nine, touch your spine,
Ten, start again.

Deptford, Dulwich, Finsbury 1983; <u>Kensington 1984</u>.

B. Oliver Twist, Oliver Twist, (twist twice)
    Bet you five thousand you can't do this. (stand straight)
    Stand at ease,
    Stamp your knees, (stamp feet)
    Quick march! (march movement)
    Over the arch. (over-arm bounce)

Mile End 1968; <u>Walworth 1979</u>.

Printed versions Abrahams, p. 145; Cumnock Academy, p. 8; cf. Fulton and Smith, Come on girls let's do our thing, p. 55; Ritchie, *GC*, pp. 92, 142; Robertson, p. 22; Rosen and Steele, [p. 4]; Rutherford, p. 23; Smith, *BBHG*, p. 33; Turner, pp. 51–52.

7.26 ONE, TWO, THREE A-LAIRY

BALL BOUNCING RHYME:

A. One, two, three a-lairy,
    My balls went down the airy.
    Don't forget to give them to Mary,
    Not to Charlie Chaplin.

Mile End 1964, 1968; <u>Barnsbury</u>, Dalston <u>1983</u>.

Printed versions Fowke, p. 74; Kelsey, *K1*, 44; Opies, *LLS*, p. 108.

Recording BBC 19005 (78) (1953, Kentish Town).

> B. One, two, three, a-lairy,
> Four, five, six, a-lairy,
> Seven, eight, nine, a-lairy,
> Ten, a-lairy, drop the ball.

Mile End 1964.

See introduction to this section for early "a-lairy" references.

Printed versions Brady, p. 57; Cumnock Academy, p. 24; Fowke, p. 74; Gullen, p. 33; Kenney, pp. 46, 47; Ritchie, *GC*, p. 90; Rodger, p. 25; Rutherford, p. 81; Worstell, skipping, p. 32.

Recordings MacColl and Behan, *Streets of Song*; MacColl and Seeger, *The Elliotts of Birtley.*

Printed versions of other "a-lairy" rhymes Abrahams, p. 154; Botkin (see below); Brady, p. 57; Cumnock Academy, p. 25; Daiken, *CGTY*, p. 33; Evans, *JRR*, skipping, p. 22; Fowke, p. 74; Kellett, pp. 127–128 (and see below); Kenney, p. 46; Nelson, p. 67; Opies, *LLS*, p. 115; Ritchie, *SS*, p. 37, *GC*, p. 90; Rodger, p. 24; Rutherford, p. 80; Shaw, 1969, p. 43, 1970, p. 71; Smith, *BBHG*, p. 33; Sutton-Smith, p. 87; Withers, *RIMP*, pp. 51, 52.

Early notings One two three alairy,/Four five six a bear,/Seven eight nine a beauty,/What a lovely teddy bear, with three further versions, similar to Botkin, below, Kellett, 1920s, pp. 55–56. One, two, three a-lairy,/I spied Missus Sary,/Sitting on a bumble-airy,/Just like a choc'late fairy, Botkin, *TAF*, 1944, p. 796.

7.27 OVER THE GARDEN WALL

SINGLE OR TWO-BALLS RHYME:

> Over the garden wall,
> I let the baby fall.

My mama came out,
She gave me a clout,
I asked her who she was bossing about.
She gave me another,
To match the other,
Over the garden wall.

Mile End 1966; Marylebone 1967; West Norwood 1970; Walworth 1974, 1979; Battersea, Greenwich 1982; Barnsbury, Borough, Dalston 1983.

On the line: "I let the baby fall", a ball is dropped.

Printed versions Abrahams, p. 156; Botkin (see below); Cumnock Academy, p. 26; Daiken, *OGS*, part of "Auld Granny Gray", p. 28; Kellett (see below); Kelsey, *K1*, 45; Mills and Bishop (see below); Ritchie, *GC*, p. 90; Rosen and Steele, back cover; Smith, *BBHG*, p. 34; Sutton-Smith, p. 78; Turner (see below).

Early notings Over the garden wall/I let the baby fall,/Me mother came out/She gave me a clout/Over the garden wall, Kellett, ?1920s, skipping, p. 74. Cf. Bouncy, Bouncy ballie,/I lost the leg of my dollie;/My mother came out/And gave me a clout/That turned my petticoat/Inside out, Mills and Bishop, 1937, 32. Over the garden wall,/I let the baby fall;/My mother came out/She gave me a clout/And sent me over the wall, Turner, Melbourne, c1937, p. 36. Botkin, *TAF*, 1944, p. 797.

Recordings BBC 19005 (78) (1953, Kentish Town); Webb, *Children's Singing Games*.

7.28 WHEN I WENT UP IN A YELLOW BALLOON

TWO-BALLS RHYME:

When I went up in a yellow balloon,
The yellow balloon went pop,

I fell down in the deep blue sea
And caught a fish in me frock.

<u>Greenwich 1982</u>. "Penny balloon": Marylebone, Mile End 1966; West Norwood 1970, 1973; Walworth 1979, 1982; Borough, Dulwich 1983.

Printed version Rosen and Steele, [p. 21].

7.29 ONE, TWO, BUCKLE MY SHOE

BALL BOUNCING RHYME:

One, two, buckle my shoe,
Three, four, knock at the door,
Five, six, pick up sticks,
Seven, eight, lay them straight,
Nine, ten, a big fat hen,
Eleven, twelve, dig up and drown (sic).

Brixton 1982.

See also **6.A.34** and **7.45**.

Printed versions Abrahams, p. 149; Botkin (see below); Boyce and Bartlett (see below); Coffin and Cohen, p. 187; Douglas (see below); Ford (see below); Gomme (see below); Graves (see below); Halliwell (see below); Kidson (see below); Lang (see below); Opies, *ODNR*, pp. 333–334; Smith, *BBHG*, inside cover and p. 32; Sutton-Smith, p. 82; Turner, p. 52; Withers, *RIMP*, p. 59; Wood (see below).

Early notings Halliwell, *NRE*, 1842, p. 132, 1843, p. 161, similar to above but counting up to twenty. Lang, 1897, p. 52; Gomme, 1898, under "Shuttlefeather" p. 195; Ford, counting-out, pp. 41–42; Douglas, skipping, 1916, p. 63, 1931, p. 34; Kidson, 1916, p. 41; Graves, 1927, p. 23; Wood, *AMG*, 1940, pp. 47–51; Boyce and Bartlett, 1941, p. 20; Botkin, *TAF*, 1944, p. 795.

7.30 RIN-TIN-TIN SWALLOWED A PIN

BALL BOUNCING RHYME:

Rin-Tin-Tin swallowed a pin,
Went to the doctors', doctors weren't in,
Opened the door, fell through the floor,
That's the end of Rin-Tin-Tin.

Mile End 1968.

Rin-Tin-Tin was a remarkably well-trained dog who appeared in many silent films. Successor dogs of the same name appeared in films, radio, and television series thereafter.

Printed versions Abrahams, pp. 169–170; Botkin (see below); Kellett (see below); Mills and Bishop (see below); Opies, *LLS*, p. 113 (and see below); Turner, skipping, p. 37; Withers, *RIMP*, p. 32.

Early notings Rin Tin Tin swallowed a pin,/He went to the doctor's,/The doctor wasn't in./He opened the door,/And fell through the floor,/And that was the end of Rin Tin Tin, Kellett, 1920s, p. 44. Kellett notes that "Nos 4 + 5 lines also appear in Popeye the Sailor man jingles" (see **7.13** above). The Opies (*LLS*, 1959, p. 114) mention a version collected by Dr. Howard in the US in 1936. Two versions, Mills and Bishop, 1937, 39. Botkin, *TAF*, 1944, as Mills and Bishop, p. 802.

7.31 PLAINSIE JIM SWALLOWED A PIN

SINGLE BALL BOUNCING RHYME:

Plainsie Jim, swallowed a pin,
And that's the end of plainsie Jim.

Upsie Jim, swallowed a pin,
And that's the end of upsie Jim.

Likewise with "One-handsie Jim", "Turnsie Jim", "Lazy Jim", "Basket Jim", etc.

Brockley, Cubitt Town, <u>Dalston</u>, Mile End <u>1983</u>.

Printed versions Brady, Tiger Tim, p. 65; Smith, *BBHG*, Plainy Tim, p. 35.

7.32 PLAINSIE TO AMERICA

SINGLE BALL BOUNCING RHYME:

Plainsie to America,
Plainsie to Japan,
Plainsie to the Isle of Wight,
And plainsie back again.

Upsie to America etc.
Downsie to America etc.
Oversie to America etc.
    and so on.

Walworth 1979; Greenwich 1982; <u>Barnsbury</u>, Borough, Dulwich <u>1983</u>.

7.33 PLAINSIE, CLAPSIE

SINGLE BALL BOUNCING RHYME:

Plainsie, clapsie,
Round the wall and backsie,
First your knee,
Then your toe,
Give it a bounce,
And let it go.

Walworth 1979.

The routine was: bounce the ball against wall, bounce and clap, turn around, step backwards, touch your knee, touch your toe, bounce the ball under your leg etc.

Printed versions Brady, Plainy, clappy, rolley, to-backy, p. 62; Cumnock Academy, Plainey, clappy,/Wee burley backy, p. 28; Ritchie, *GC*, Plainie, Clappie, Rollie-pin, To backie, p. 81; Turner, ... Round the world to Baxies, p. 52.

Recording BBC 20536 (78) (1952, Northamptonshire).

7.34 PLAINSIE, UPSIE, DOWNSIE, OVER etc.

SINGLE BALL ROUTINES:

A. Upsie Mrs. Dee,
    Upsie Mrs. Dee,
    Upsie, Upsie, Upsie, Upsie, Upsie,
    Upsie Mrs. Dee.
    Downsie Mrs. Dee etc.

Marylebone 1967.

B. Plainsie Mrs. Brown, etc.

Mile End 1968, 1983; West Norwood 1970; Brockley, Cubitt Town, Dalston, Deptford 1983.

C. Over Scotland Yard, etc.

Walworth 1974; Borough 1983.

D. Plainsie, Billy Balloo,
Plainsie, Billy Balloo,
Plainsie, plainsie, plainsie, plainsie
Plainsie Billy Baloo-oo-oo.

Dalston 1983.

"After 'plainsie' you go overs, then upsies, downsies, dancies, clapsies, digsies, twisties, blinksies, other blinksie, winksie, other winksie, legsie, other legsie, hopsie, other hopsie, jumpsie, alairsie, one handsie, curtsey, bowsie, dropsie, floorsie, bendsie, shoesie, thumbsie, gatesie, farsie, nearsie, smallsie, tallsie, milkman, policeman. When it goes 'farsie' you jump away, for 'nearsie', you jump towards the wall, for 'smallsie' you go down when it says so, for 'tallsie' you got to get up a little bit more, for 'milkman' you got to quickly go down and touch the floor, for 'policeman' you just bow like a policeman does." girl, Dalston 1983.

This was the longest routine I was given from any one school. Other movements I have come across are: "turn aroundsie, bumsie, stillsie" (Dulwich 1983); "unders, kneesies, kingsies, footsies, dumb hipsies" (Mile End 1983); "archie, dumbsies, slipsies, loopsie, batsie, loopsie, round the world" (Cubitt Town 1983).

Downsie: bounce on the ground; upsie: throw up in the air; overs: throw overhand, higher up the wall; dumbsie: must not talk; stillsie: must not move; loopsie: over the shoulder; digsie: throw at corner between ground and wall.

Permutations of the above from Mile End 1967; Walworth 1979; Battersea, Earlsfield 1982; Barnsbury, Borough, Deptford, Stoke Newington, 1983; Kensington 1984.

Printed versions Brady, p. 62 ff.; Fowke, p. 76; Gomme (see below); Ritchie, *SS*, passim, *GC*, pp. 80 ff.; Rodger, p. 24; cf. Rosen and Steele, [p. 1], Plainsy went to work, Plainsy bought a shirt/ Plainsy wore it, Plainsy tore it, Plainsy what a twerp.

Early notings cf. Gomme, 1898, Pots, or Potts, pp. 64–65, Ball, pp. 405–406.

Recordings BBC 20536 (78) (1952, Northamptonshire); BBC 19926 (78) (1953, Edinburgh).

7.35 ONE, TWO, THREE AND UPSIE/PLAINSIE etc.

SINGLE BALL BOUNCING:

One, two, three and upsie,
Four, five, six and upsie,
Seven, eight, nine and upsie,
Turn (ten) and upsie, drop the ball.

One, two, three a-plainsie,
Four, five, six a-plainsie,
Seven, eight, nine a-plainsie,
Turn and upsie, drop the ball.

Then in sequence it might be: "one hand", "same hand", "one leg", "other leg", "over", "dropsie", "under leg", "farsie", "nearsie", etc.

First game over,
Second game coming up,
What shall it be?

It's up to me,
Comma, comma, full stop.

Then the whole sequence could be gone through again, but this time including "dumbsie" (saying nothing).

Second game over,
Third game coming up,
What shall it be?
It's up to me,
Comma, comma, full stop.

Marylebone 1967; Mile End 1968, 1983; <u>West Norwood</u> 1970, <u>1973</u>; Cubitt Town 1983.

As the song says: "It's up to me." The ball bouncer might decide to do the whole sequence with one hand, or with the other hand. The permutations are inexhaustible.

Printed versions Fowke, *One, two, three, a-twirlsy*, p. 76; Ritchie, *GC*, One two three a-wallie, p. 90; Roud, *DM1*, Full stop/Comma comma/ … ending to a clapping game, 31.

Recordings BBC 16076 (78) (1951, Sidbury, Devon); Webb, *Children's Singing Games*.

7.36 SEVENSIES/TENSIES/ALPHABET

A. *Sevensies*: "You've got a tennis ball and you throw it at the wall seven times. You throw it at the wall and turn round six times, and then throw it under your legs five times. You do clapsies four times, crossies three times, one legsies two times twice and clapsies one time."   girl, 10, Barnsbury 1983.

With different routines: Battersea 1982; Cubitt Town, Stoke Newington 1983; Kensington 1984.

B. *Tensies*: (starting with ten times and reducing to once).

Mile End 1966, 1967; Earlsfield 1982; Deptford 1983.

C. *Alphabet*: "You bounce the ball once, going through the first letter of the alphabet. My name is Anthea, I come from America, I eat apples …" (similarly for other letters). girl, Kensington 1984.

Other similar games: Battersea 1982; Mile End 1983.

Printed versions Brady, pp. 53–68; Fowke, pp. 74–86, Alphabet, p. 86; Gomme (see below); Holbrook, Pots, pp. 78–79; Ritchie, *SS*, passim, *GC*, pp. 80–95; Rodger, pp. 25–26; Sutton-Smith, pp. 86–88, including "Tens" and "Sevens"; Todd, Kaifie, 8; Turner, pp. 49–52; Withers, Alphabet Ball, *RIMP*, p. 54.

Early notings cf. Gomme, 1898, Pots, or Potts, pp. 64–65, Ball, pp. 405–406.

7.37 PLEASE MISS

SINGLE OR TWO-BALLS RHYME:

A. Please Miss,
   Me mother, Miss,
   She forgot to tell you this, Miss,
   I, Miss, won't, Miss,
   Be at school tomorrow, Miss.

<u>Walworth 1979, 1982</u>; Battersea, Brixton 1982; Barnsbury, Borough, Cubitt Town, Dalston, Deptford, Dulwich 1983.

B. Please Miss,
   Mother, Miss,
   I'm coming to tell you this, Miss,
   Ey Miss,

> Thank you, Miss,
> I'm coming to school tomorrow, Miss.

Mile End 1968.

Printed version Rosen and Steele, [p. 28].

7.38 QUEENIE, QUEENIE CAROLINE

TWO-BALLS RHYME:

> Queenie, Queenie Caroline,
> Washes her hair in turpentine,
> Turpentine makes it shine,
> Queenie, Queenie Caroline.

Mile End 1968, 1983; Walworth 1979; <u>Dalston</u>, Dulwich <u>1983</u>.

Printed versions Bolton (see below); Brady, p. 57; Briggs, p. 196; Cumnock Academy, p. 25; Douglas (see below); Ford (see below); Fowke, p. 79; Gregor (see below); Kellett, pp. 56–57 (and see below); Opies, *ISE*, p. 48, *LLS*, pp. 20, 21; Ritchie, *GC*, counting-out, pp. 40, 47; Rosen and Steele, [p. 17]; Rutherford, Good Queen Arabella, p. 85; Turner, skipping, p. 37.

Early notings Queen, queen, Caroline,/Dipped her hair in turpentine,/Turpentine made it shine./ Queen, queen Caroline, Bolton, 1888, p. 116. Queen, queen Caroline/Dipped her face in turpentine;/ Turpentine made it shine,/Queen, queen Caroline,—"direct reference is made to Queen Caroline of Brunswick, consort of George IV", Gregor, 1891, p. 11, and several further versions on p. 24. Queen, Queen Caroline, Ford, 1904, counting-out, p. 50. Sweete, sweet Carroline, Douglas, 1916, p. 61, 1931, p. 33. Queen Queen Caroline, Kellett, 1920s, pp. 56–57.

Recording Webb, *Children's Singing Games*.

7.39 MRS. MOP OWNED A SHOP

BALL BOUNCING RHYME:

Mrs. Mop owned a shop,
All she sold was lollipops,
Red, white and blue.

Dalston 1983.

"First of all you just do 'plainsies' and when it comes to 'red, white and blue', you throw it over. Then it carries on till 'upsies' and 'downsies'. Then you go on to another song. When you've finished one song, you say, 'I've finished the first song, now I'm on the second,' and you spell your name." girl, 10, Dalston 1983.

See also **2.25**.

Printed version Cumnock Academy, Mrs Dunlop had a wee shop, p. 27; Rosen and Steele, [p. 1]; Turner, p. 51.

Recording Webb, *Children's Singing Games*.

7.40 UNDER THE APPLE TREE

BALL BOUNCING RHYME:

Under the apple tree,
My true love said to me:
"Kiss me darling,
Kiss me darling,"
Under the apple tree.

Brockley 1967.

7.41 MARY MORGAN PLAYED THE ORGAN

TWO-BALLS RHYME:

Mary Morgan played the organ,
And her father played the drum, bompety bom!
And her sister, she's a twister,
And her mother's deaf and dumb.

Battersea 1982; <u>Borough</u>, Deptford <u>1983</u>.

Tune The song is normally sung to the tune of "Clementine".

Printed versions Opies, Johnny Morgan played the organ, *LLS*, p. 13 (and see below); Ritchie, *SS*, p. 116.

Early noting According to the Opies (*LLS*, 1959, p. 13) the song is "a … recollection of the chorus of John Read's music-hall song 'Johnny Morgan' published in 1877".

7.42 SHIRLEY TEMPLE IS A STAR

TWO-BALLS RHYME:

Shirley Temple is a star.
S-T-A-R.

Mile End 1966; <u>Cubitt Town 1983</u>.

This short rhyme can form part of longer sequences.

See also **4.56**.

Printed versions For this and other Shirley Temple rhymes, see Abrahams, pp. 177–178; Opies, *LLS*, p. 113; Ritchie, *SS*, p. 35; Turner, p. 37.

7.43 WINNIE THE WITCH

BALL BOUNCING RHYME:

Winnie the witch fell down the ditch,
Ha! Ha! Ha!
Found a penny and thought she was rich,
Ha! Ha! Ha!

Walworth 1979; Battersea, <u>Greenwich 1982</u>; Borough 1983.

Kellett, writing in 1966, states (p. 19): "The modern trend of counting-out formulas is influenced by the T.V. commercials and … the reading of comics. I wondered where Winnie the Witch came from until I saw a Reveille and there she was." *Reveille* was a tabloid newspaper, later a magazine, published between 1940 and 1979, in which Winnie the Witch featured as a glamorous character in a strip cartoon. The author Valerie Thomas later used the name Winnie the Witch for the main character in her popular children's book series beginning in 1989.

Printed versions Abrahams, Old Mother Rich, p. 143; Brady, Minnie the witch, p. 65; Evans, *JRR*, Old Mother Rich, p. 23; Fowke, Old Mother Witch, p. 59; Kellett, p. 19; Rutherford, Winnie the witch, p. 81; Smith, *BBHG*, Willy the witch, p. 29; Withers, *CO*, Rich, Rich, fell in the ditch [p. 31]; *RIMP*, Rich, Rich,/Fell in the ditch, p. 118.

7.44 WHEN THE WAR WAS OVER

TWO-BALLS RHYME:

When the war was over,
And Josephine was dead,
She wanted to go to heaven,
With a crown upon her head,
But the Lord said, "No,

You've been a naughty girl,
You can't go up to heaven,
But you can go down to hell."

So she prayed all night,
And she prayed all day,
She prayed to go to heaven,
With a crown on her head,
But you shan't (can't) go down to hell,
But you can go up to heaven.

Mile End 1966; Marylebone 1967; <u>West Norwood 1970, 1972</u>; Walworth 1974, 1979; Battersea 1982; Borough 1983.

Printed versions *Encyclopaedia Britannica*, article on children's games and sports, Vol. 5, p. 518; Opies, *LLS*, "Hitler", and "Mussolini", p. 104; Rosen and Steele, back cover.

7.45 WHEN I WAS ONE

BALL BOUNCING OR ACTION RHYME:

A. When I was one I sucked my thumb
Going out to sea,
I jumped aboard a pirate ship.
And the pirate said to me:
"We're going this way, that way,
Forward and backward,
Over the Irish Sea,
With a bottle of rum,
To fill my tum,
And that's the life for me."

When I was two I buckled my shoe,
    Going out to sea,   etc.

When I was three I grazed my knee,
    Going out to sea,   etc.

When I was four I kicked the door,
    Going out to sea,   etc.

When I was five I sat on a hive,
    Going out to sea,   etc.

When I was six I laid down sticks,
    Going out to sea,   etc.

When I was seven I went to heaven,
    Going out to sea,   etc.

When I was eight I sat on the gate,
    Going out to sea,   etc.

When I was nine I drank some wine,
    Going out to sea,   etc.

Mile End 1966, 1983; Marylebone 1967; <u>West Norwood 1970</u>; Walworth 1974, 1979; Greenwich, Streatham 1982; Borough, Brockley, Cubitt Town, Dalston, Shepherds Bush 1983; Hampstead 1984.

B.   When I was one I'd just begun,
    Going over to sea,
    I jumped aboard a ferryman's boat,
    And the ferryman said to me:
    "Going this way, that way,
    Backwards and forwards,
    Over the Irish Sea
    A bottle of rum to fill me tum,
    And that's the life for me."

        (Then two, three etc.)

Dulwich 1983.

C. When I was one I sucked my thumb,
My mother said to me:
"Can you do unders and overs,
Pepsi Colas,
One, two, three?"

(Then two, three etc.)

Walworth 1980; Mile End 1983.

D. When I was one I sucked my thumb,
The day I went to sea,
I jumped upon a pirate ship,
And the pirate said to me:
"We're going north, east, south, west,
Over the Irish Sea,
A bottle of rum to fill me tum,
A bottle of gin to fill me chin,
And that's the life for me,
Whoopee!"

When I was two, I touched my shoe, (done a poo) etc.

When I was three I touched my knee, (done a wee) etc.

When I was four I touched the floor, etc.

When I was five I touched a hive (me side) etc.

When I was six I touched me knicks (done the splits) etc.

When I was seven I went up to heaven, etc.

When I was eight I touched me mate (had a mate) etc.

When I was nine I touched me spine (stood on a line) etc.

When I was ten I done it again (Dad bought me a hen) etc.

Greenwich 1982.

See also **6.A.34** and **7.29**.

Printed versions Abrahams, p. 206; Botkin (see below); Chambers (see below); Cumnock Academy, p. 27; Daiken, *CGTY*, p. 155, *OGS*, p. 14; Fowke, p. 84; Fulton and Smith, Cross town when Billy was one/he learned to suck his thumb, clapping, pp. 38–39; Gullen, as Chambers, below, p. 40; Kellett (see below); Kenney, p. 32; Kings (see below); McMorland, p. 43; Mills and Bishop (see below); Montgomeries, *SNR*, p. 63, *HBSNR*, p. 108 (both very like Chambers, below); Nelson, p. 68; Ritchie, *GC*, pp. 94–95; Rutherford, p. 80; Sluckin, p. 28; Smith, *BBHG*, p. 30; Turner, p. 51; Withers, *RIMP*, pp. 70–73.

Early notings When I was ane, I was in my skin;/When I was twa, I ran awa';/When I was three, I could climb a tree;/When I was four, they dang me o'er;/When I was five, I didna thrive;/When I was sax, I got my cracks;/When I was seven, I could count eleven;/When I was aught, I was laid straught;/ When I was nine, I could write a line;/When I was ten, I could mend a pen;/When I was eleven, I gaed to the weaving;/When I was twall, I was brosy Wull, Chambers, 1870, p. 159. When I was one I ate a bun,/Going out to sea, Kellett, 1920s, pp. 57–58. Kings 2, 1930, p. 21. When Buster Brown was one, Mills and Bishop, 1937, 39. Botkin, *TAF*, 1944, as Mills and Bishop, p. 801.

Recordings BBC 19005 (78) (1953, Kentish Town); BBC 19926 (78) (1953, Edinburgh).

7.46 ARCHIBALD, BALD, BALD

BALL BOUNCING RHYME:

Mother calls me Archie,
Me father calls me Bald,
They didn't know what to call me,
So they called me Archibald.

Marylebone 1967.

and then:

Archibald, bald, bald,
King of the Jews, Jews, Jews,
Bought his wife, wife, wife,
A pair of shoes, shoes, shoes,
When the shoes, shoes, shoes,
Began to wear, wear, wear,
Archibald, bald, bald,
Began to swear, swear, swear,
When the swear, swear, swear,
Began to stop, stop, stop,
Archibald, bald, bald,
Bought a shop, shop, shop.
When the shop, shop, shop,
Began to sell, sell, sell,
Archibald, bald, bald,
Bought a bell, bell, bell,
When the bell, bell, bell,
Began to ring, ring, ring,
Archibald, bald, bald,
Began to sing, sing, sing,
(Doh, ray, me, fah, soh, la, te, doh)

Mile End 1966, 1968, 1983; Putney 1966; Walworth 1974, 1979; Borough, Dalston 1983.

Printed versions Abrahams, Nebuchadnezzar, p. 138; Bolton (see below); Brady, Johnston Mooney and O'Brien, echoes ll. 8–14 of second part above, p. 67; Cumnock Academy, Archie-bald, -bald, -bald, p. 24; Daiken, *OGS*, Holy Moses, King of the Jews, p. 17; Fowke, Nebuchadnezzar, p. 126; Halliwell (see below); Kellett, Nebuchadnezzar, counting out, p. 101 (and see below); Kelsey, *K1*, 45; Knapps, Holy Moses, p. 202; Northall (see below); Ritchie, *GC*, Archie-*ball-ball-ball*, pp. 135, 139; Rodger, Scottie MaLottie, the King o' the Jews, p. 10; Rutherford, Allebeloosha, King of the Jews, p. 83; Shaw, oly Moses, 1970, p. 94; Starn, Nebuchadnezzah [sic], skipping, p. 98; Sutton-Smith,

Ikey Moses, skipping, p. 95: could also begin "Nebuchadnezzar" or "Pontius Pilate"; Turner, Nebuchadnezzar, Ikey Moses, I King Mo, hand clapping, p. 45; Wood (see below).

Early notings Thomas a Didymus, king of the Jews,/Jumped into the fire and burned both his shoes, Halliwell, *NRE*, 1842, p. 149. Nebuchadnezzar, king of the Jews,/Slipped off his slippers and slipped on his shoes, Bolton, 1888, p. 116; see also p. 114: "A knife and a razor,/ Spells Nebuchadnezzar;/ .../Spells Nebuchadnezzar,/The king of the Jews". Rhymes beginning "Thomas-a-Didymus" and "Nebuchadnezzar", Northall, 1892, p. 293. Skipping rhymes: Nebuchadnezzar King of the Jews, Kellett, early 1900s, pp. 75–76, and Ali Bali Buster the king of the Jews, Kellett, 1920s, pp. 74–75. Cf. Wood, *AMG*, 1940, like Bolton (p. 114), p. 53.

Recordings BBC 19927 (78) (1953, Edinburgh); Webb, *Children's Singing Games.*

7.47 JOHNNY WENT RIDING

> Johnny went riding,
> Riding in the park,
> He even went to Waterloo,
> And then to Noah's ark.

> Walworth 1979.

7.48 RULE BRITANNIA

> Rule Britannia,
> And marmalade for tea ...

> Borough 1983.

Printed versions Kellett (see below); Rosen and Steele, part of a football rhyme, [p. 10]; Rutherford, "Entertainment rhymes", pp. 102, 124; Shaw, 1969, p. 4, 1970, p. 2; Turner, "For amusement only", pp. 102, 103.

Early noting cf. Rule Brittania [sic] two monkies [sic] up a stick,/One fell down and broke his/ Prickles grow on bushes prickles grow on trees … Kellett, 1920s, p. 37.

PART II

RHYMES, SONGS, BELIEFS, AND WORDPLAY

SECTION 8

SCHOOL RHYMES AND PARODIES

Introduction

The place where most of the circulation of children's lore takes place is the school playground, but it also occurs in the street or the playing areas near housing estates, usually before or after school, at playtime or dinnertime. However, as a theme of children's lore, school does not play an unduly prominent part compared with the whole repertoire. Nevertheless, rhymes and songs about school, teachers and school meals are so universal that it is worthwhile devoting a separate section to them, though some also serve other purposes besides commenting on aspects of school. Parodies can be linked with school because they are often inspired by school assemblies, or by music or poetry lessons. Parodies of nursery rhymes or of popular songs, television commercials and the like may have no direct links with school, apart from being passed around there. I have put them together here for convenience.

8.A SCHOOL AND TEACHERS

Scurrilous rhymes about school and teachers are probably as old as formal education itself, though few have been noted. Some early collectors perhaps did not want to recognise the existence of disaffection among schoolchildren. Writers of autobiographies, who often recount some of their traumatic experiences, particularly in boarding schools, do not usually consider such ephemera worth mentioning. The Opies (*LLS*, 1959, p. 298, n. 1) quote a Robert Graves version of a breaking-up day song at his prep school in 1908. Usually writers did not consider such rhymes would be of interest to their readers, or perhaps they took for granted that their readers would be familiar with them. Perhaps, like me, they forgot them, but why?

School was not much beloved by my fellow schoolboys and girls at the mixed elementary school (seven to fourteen) in South London that I attended in the late 1920s and early 1930s. I remember many rhymes from those days, but cannot recall the rhymes we chanted at the end of term about school and our teachers. I know we had them; we had rhymes for all possible occasions and situations, and many parodies. I can remember an oblique reference to school in a parody of the hymn: **8.D.7** FIGHT THE GOOD FIGHT which went: "Fight the good fight with all your might,/Sit on a box of dynamite,/Set it alight and you will be/Far away from the L.C.C." The L.C.C. (London County Council) was of course the forerunner of the Inner London Education Authority, and of the Greater London Council (G.L.C.). A version of the parody was collected in 1967 but without the reference to the L.C.C.

We probably made up ephemeral rhymes to suit our particular need at the time and that might be why they are forgotten. My particular circle of friends delighted in reading comics and magazines about the exploits of fifteen-year-old boys in four imaginary public schools: Greyfriars (*The Magnet*), St. Jim's (*The Gem*), Rookwood (*The Boys' Friend*), and St. Frank's (The Nelson Lee Library). Very much later I learned that all these stories were written by the same author, Frank Richards. Particularly unpopular masters and the infliction of corporal punishment played an important part in many of the weekly episodes during term time in these stories. The episodes usually featured "pranks", "japes", "practical jokes", and other breaches of school discipline. They were usually dealt with by the command to "bend over" and the infliction by cane or birch of "six of the best".

Most of my other classmates (the boys that is – the girls had separate playgrounds and sat on the other side of the classroom and the other side of the hall during assembly) read penny comics like *Funny Wonder*, *Comic Cuts*, or *Merry and Bright*. These featured four large pages of comic strips. There would be at least one strip where a class of little "toughies" was in continual warfare with a teacher wearing a gown and mortarboard (which none of us had ever seen in real life). The teacher was usually thin and very sharp nosed and he was equipped with a cane or a weapon of birch twigs. Later these comics were supplanted by others such as *Dandy* and *Beano* which continued this tradition. The magazines, with their long weekly accounts of the doings of young teenage boys in boarding schools, disappeared. The legendary cane-wielding teacher continued to fascinate children and held a place in their folklore. This stereotype can still be featured in the dramatic games of young children, even though the actual teachers, in the primary stage at any rate, are liked, and in many cases loved, by them.

The legend is still perpetuated in the end-of-term rhymes, though in more than thirty years of teaching in typical inner city type schools I can only recall two or three occasions when **8.A.2** ONE MORE DAY AT SCHOOL or **8.A.1** WE BREAK UP, WE BREAK DOWN which was supplanting it, were chanted. Yet they are universally known both in primary and secondary schools. They perpetuate, however, more the traditions of secondary schools. Very few junior schools teach French, though many did so when resources were more generously provided. Nearly all versions of **8.A.1** WE BREAK UP, WE BREAK DOWN include the lines: "No more English, no more French,/No more sitting on the old school bench." The rebellion aspect which most children go through during adolescence when they leave the stage of complete dependence on the adult plays a part, but these rhymes are recited by children in the years before puberty as well.

The fantasies of putting teachers on bonfires or blowing them up, to be found in rhymes like **8.A.3** COME TO OUR SCHOOL or **8.A.1B** WE BREAK UP, WE BREAK DOWN, are not to be taken too seriously, though the revenge taken against a teacher in **8.A.7** ON TOP OF A SANDPIT seems to reveal a degree of real cruelty among the fantasy. It was by no means a very common rhyme in primary schools. Most of my examples were collected in schools in more affluent areas which seem to reflect an attitude of less high regard and less affection for teachers than in the schools with a spread of lower social categories, where I did most of my teaching.

A fellow researcher in the USA collected a number of parodies of "On Top of Old Smoky", including the following from Southern California, c1965: "On top of Old Smoky, all covered with blood/I saw my old teacher, her face in the mud/An axe through her belly, a knife through her head/I think my old teacher is certainly dead./I plucked out her eyeballs, I cut off her toes/I took Daddy's hammer and bashed in her nose."[1] The London version referred to above (**8.A.7**) tells of shooting "my poor teacher,/With a green rubber band." and "I couldn't have missed her,/She was forty feet wide." In the London version we can see some traces of humour. In the American version above there is only sick violence. I never came across anything approaching this level of violence in any rhyme dealing with school or teachers. Most of them are light and good humoured.

8.A.9 GLORY, GLORY, HALLELUIA is very widespread. The event in the rhyme is not very far from possibility. One can imagine a teacher who lost his/her temper and hit a child with a ruler. Humiliated when the ruler breaks and the children all laugh, the teacher has temporarily lost control of discipline. This rhyme was current before corporal punishment was abolished in primary schools. I would be interested to see whether it becomes less prevalent.

8.A.13 TEACHER, TEACHER, DON'T BE DUMB is an import from the USA, but version D came from a recent immigrant from Jamaica. It had not changed its dialect form at all when I recorded it.

NOTES

1. Jorgensen, M. G. (1981). *Anti-school parodies of 'The Battle Hymn of the Republic' and 'On Top of Old Smoky' as speech play and social protest* (Unpublished dissertation). Austin, TX, University of Texas at Austin.

8.A.1 WE BREAK UP, WE BREAK DOWN

A. We break up, we break down,
We don't care if the school falls down,
There'll be no more English, no more French,
No more sitting on the old school bench.
If the teachers interfere,
Blow them up and box their ears.
There'll be no more pencils, no more books,
No more teachers' grumpy old looks,
No more sorrow, shout away,
Because today's a holiday.

Brixton, Earlsfield 1982; Barnsbury, Borough, Brockley, Cubitt Town, Dalston, Deptford, Dulwich, Kentish Town, Shepherds Bush 1983; Hampstead, Kensington 1984.

Tune "This old man" (traditional).

B. We break up, we break down,
We don't care if the school falls down,
No more Latin, no more French,
No more sitting on the old hard bench.
In my cabbages no more slugs,
No more drink out of dirty mugs.
This time next week, where shall we be?
Out of the gates of misery.
Kick up tables, kick up chairs,
Kick the teachers down the stairs.
If that doesn't serve them right,
Blow them up with dynamite.
No more spiders in my tea
Making googly eyes at me.

Stoke Newington 1983.

Although I collected this in an authority aided junior school, the rhyme would appear to be more usually associated with the private sector tradition.

Printed versions (rhymes with similar themes) Botkin (see below); Brady, p. 98; Cansler, 15; Cosbey, No more pencils, no more books, p. 82; Daiken, *OGS*, p. 35; Gainer, fragment, 45; Kellett, p. 30; Knapps, p. 224; Opies, *ISE*, pp. 74–75, *LLS*, pp. 298, 299 (and see below); Leach and Fried, No more pencils, no more books, and three other versions, p. 1017; Mills and Bishop (see below); Rosen and Steele, [pp. 27, 28]; Rutherford, p. 42; Sutton-Smith, p. 45; Turner, p. 67; Withers, *RIMP*, fragment, p. 191; Wood (see below).

Early notings An early reference to this theme is quoted by the Opies (*LLS*, 1959, p. 298) from Robert Graves who apparently sang the following at his prep school (Rugby, c1908): "No more mucky potted meat/ Scraped from dirty Tommy's feet." (The headmaster was Thomas Eden, M.A.). Tonight, tonight,/The pillow fight,/ Tomorrow's the end of school;/ Break the dishes, break the chairs,/Trip the teachers on the stairs, Mills and Bishop, 1937, 32, and two further rhymes, 33. Jay bird, Jay bird, settin' on a rail,/Pickin' his teeth with the end of his tail,/Mulberry leaves and calico sleeves/All school teachers are hard to please, Wood, *AMG*, 1940, p. 67. Botkin, *TAF*, 1944, as Mills and Bishop, pp. 797, 798.

8.A.2 ONE MORE DAY AT SCHOOL

> A. One more day at school,
> One more day of sorrow,
> One more day at this old dump,
> I'll be home tomorrow.

Mile End 1966, 1968; Brockley 1967; Walworth 1974; Streatham 1982; <u>Blackheath</u>, Dalston <u>1983</u>.

Tune "One Man Went to Mow" (traditional).

Printed version Opies, *LLS*, p. 299.

> B. One more day at school,
> One more day of sorrow

One more day of this old dump,
And we'll be going tomorrow.
No more teachers, no more books,
No more teachers' dirty looks.
When Mr. (_____) rings the bell,
Grab your things and run like hell.

Walworth 1980.

C. No more school tomorrow, no more school today,
Kick the teachers up the bum and let's be on our way.

Deptford 1983.

Early noting (theme of breaking up from school): O! for August and September,/De'il tak' October and November, Chambers, 1826, pp. 296–297.

8.A.3 COME TO OUR SCHOOL

Come to our school, come to our school
It's a place of misery.
Round the corner there's a signpost
Saying, "Welcome unto thee."
Don't believe it, don't believe it,
It is just a pack of lies.
If it wasn't for the teachers
We'd be home in paradise.
Build a bonfire, build a bonfire,
Put (name of school) on the top,
Put the teachers in the middle
And burn all the lot.

Brockley, Marylebone 1967; Mile End 1968; Earlsfield 1982 (last part).

See also **11.I.58** and **12.A.12**.

Tune "Oh My Darling, Clementine", an American folk ballad, usually credited to Percy Montrose (1884).

The rhyme in this form seems to have disappeared in London. Two later notings deal with Argentinians (**11.I.58,** Blackheath 1983) and football teams (**12.A.12,** Battersea 1982). Both start with "Build a bonfire". In Earlsfield (1982) it was used for skipping.

Printed versions *Ballads and Songs*, No. 4 [9]; Hubbard, mentioned, 263; Kellett, p. 29; Kelsey, *K1*, 47; Rutherford, p. 42; *Spin*, 5; Stork, 4; Turner, p. 65.

8.A.4 PLEASE KEEP OFF THE GRASS, SIR

> Please keep off the grass, sir,
> To let the lady pass, sir.
> You know the rules of all the schools,
> Please keep off the grass, sir.

> Brockley 1967; <u>Walworth</u> 1979, <u>1982</u>; Battersea, Brixton 1982; Borough, Dulwich 1983.

See also **7.7** and **11.I.7** (repetition of "sir").

Printed versions Brady, ball bouncing, p. 64; Kellett, p. 55 (and see below); Rosen and Steele, [p. 5]; Rutherford, skipping, p. 60.

Early noting Please keep off the grass/To let the ladies pass,/A copper came by and spit in me eye,/So please keep off the grass, Kellett, 1920s, p. 29.

8.A.5 HI HO! HI HO!

> PARODY of a song from the Walt Disney film "Snow White and the Seven Dwarfs", 1937.

A. Hi ho! Hi ho!
Off to school we go
With singing songs and dropping bombs
Hi ho! Hi ho!

Mile End 1968.

A version from Palmers Green, 1967, was more explicit:

B. Hi ho! Hi ho!
It's off to school we go
With a bucket and spade and a hand grenade,
Hi ho! Hi ho!

Hi ho! Hi ho!
It's home from school we go,
With a bucket and spade and no hand grenade,
Hi ho! Hi ho!

Printed versions Knapps, pp. 176, 201; Rutherford, p. 115; Turner, amusement rhyme, p. 91.

8.A.6 ONE, TWO, THREE, FOUR

One, two, three, four,
Teachers are a great big bore.

Stoke Newington 1983.

Printed version Turner, pp. 66–67.

8.A.7 ON TOP OF A SANDPIT

PARODY of American folksong "On Top of Old Smoky".

On top of a sandpit,
All covered with sand,
I shot my poor teacher,
With a green rubber band.
I shot her with pleasure,
I shot her with pride,
I couldn't have missed her,
She was forty feet wide.
I went to her funeral,
I went to her grave,
Some people threw flowers,
I chucked a grenade.
I came to the conclusion,
She wasn't quite dead,
So I brought my bazooka,
And blew off her head.

Earlsfield, Walworth 1982; Blackheath, Finsbury 1983; <u>Kensington 1984</u>.

Of five schools (see above), only examples from Kensington and Blackheath mentioned a teacher in the rhyme. I believe this kind of rhyme is widespread in the USA. It is certainly the most extreme of all the anti-school or anti-teacher rhymes I have encountered. The other examples mentioned unpopular or personally disliked children, instead of teachers.

See also **8.D.14**.

Printed versions Cansler, 8; Jorgensen, *LL*, p. 113; Knapps, pp. 174–175; cf. Lowenstein, p. 35; Rosen and Steele, [p. 28]; Solomons, p. 117; Wilson, 980.

8.A.8 POUNDS, SHILLINGS AND PENCE

Pounds, shillings and pence,
Teachers have no sense.

They go to school,
To act the fool,
Pounds, shillings and pence.

Stoke Newington 1983.

This was an interesting survival from pre-decimalisation days.

Printed versions Brady, p. 56; Opies, *LLS*, p. 363; Rutherford, p. 23.

8.A.9 GLORY, GLORY, HALLELUIA

A. Glory, glory, halleluia,
Teacher hit me with a ruler.
The ruler broke in half,
So she hit me with a staff,
And we all began to sing.

Brixton 1982.

B. Glory, glory, halleluia,
Teacher hit me with a ruler.
The teacher done a fart,
And we all began to laugh,
On the last day of September.

Borough 1983.

C. Glory, glory, halleluia,
Teacher hit me with a ruler.
The ruler snapped,
And the whole class clapped,
Glory, glory, halleluia.

Kentish Town 1983.

D. Glory, glory, halleluia,
Teacher hit me with a ruler.
Mother hit me with a rolling pin,
And the saints go marching in.

Dalston 1983.

E. Glory, glory, halleluia,
Teacher hit me with a ruler.
I got her in the eye,
With a steak and kidney pie,
And that was the end of school.

Battersea 1982; Barnsbury, Cubitt Town, EC1, Mile End 1983, Kensington 1984.

Tune "Glory, glory, halleluia", the chorus to "Battle Hymn of the Republic" written by Julia Ward Howe in 1861.

See also **12.A.3**, which is sung to the same tune.

Printed versions Abrahams, p. 54; Cansler, 9; Fowke, p. 146; Jorgensen, *LL*, 113; Kellett, p. 31 (and see below); Knapps, p. 173; Rosen and Steele, [p. 27]; Rutherford, p. 112; Solomons, p. 100; cf. *Spin*, 22; Turner, p. 65.

Early noting Glory glory halleluiah,/Teacher hit me with the ruler,/The ruler broke in two,/So she hit me with her shoe,/And we all went marching on, Kellett, 1920s, p. 31.

Recording Webb, *Children's Singing Games*.

8.A.10 TING-LING-LING

Ting-ling-ling,
School bell rings,
Teacher's batty,

Full of strings,
Strings pop,
Knickers drop,
That's what you call
A lollipop.

Dulwich 1983.

This bit of doggerel may perhaps have been influenced by the poem of W. H. Davies, "School's out": Girls scream, / Boys shout; / Dogs bark, / School's out.

8.A.11 READING, WRITING, ARITHMETIC

Reading, Writing, Arithmetic,
Teacher comes with a great big stick.
What did I tell you a minute ago?
Get on with your work and don't be slow.

Mile End 1966.

8.A.12 MY TEACHER'S GOT A BUNION

My teacher's got a bunion,
A face like a pickled onion,
Nose like a squashed tomato,
And eyes like green peas.

Mile End 1968; Blackheath, Dalston 1983.

Tune "The Ash Grove" (traditional, Welsh).

Printed versions Kellett, O Johnny is a funny 'un, and Oh corns warts and bunions (tune as above), p. 77; Opies, *LLS*, pp. 171, 364; Ritchie, *GC*, p. 18; Rosen and Steele, [p. 28]; Shaw, skipping, 1970, pp. 72–73.

Early noting A correspondent from Croydon in 1980 recalled the following version from Walworth (c1930): My teacher's got a bunion,/Her face is a pickled onion,/Her nose is a squashed tomato,/Her legs are two pins.

8.A.13 TEACHER, TEACHER, DON'T BE DUMB

    A.   Teacher, teacher, don't be dumb,
          Give me back my bubble gum.
          If you don't I'll tell my mum,
          Teacher, teacher, don't be dumb.

Walworth 1982.

    B.   Teacher, teacher, don't be dumb,
          (You) Take away my bubble gum.
          If she hits (beats) me I don't care,
          Just pack my books and go away.

Battersea 1982.

    C.   Teacher, teacher, don't be dumb,
          Give me back my bubble gum.
          Teacher, teacher, I declare,
          Tarzan lost his underwear.
          Teacher, teacher, don't be mean,
          Give me a go with the Coke machine.

Shepherds Bush 1983.

    D.   Teacher, teacher, Humpty Dumpty,
          Take away my bubble gum.
          If she beat me I don't care,
          I'm gonna pack my bags and go away.
          Hey you boy!
          You looking at me,
          You think you can buy my belly skin,
          No ping, no pang, no chang chang,

> Me gotta penny in my belly,
> Going umpah, umpah!

Battersea 1982.

Printed versions for several rhymes beginning "Teacher, teacher", cf. Cansler, 14–15, and Hopkin, p. 20. The version given by Hopkin, recorded in Kingston, Jamaica in 1979, is very similar to D above. Version D was recorded from an eleven-year-old girl whose parents were born in Jamaica. It was used in Jamaica as a clapping rhyme, but although it was known to all the girls in the group I was not clear whether it was so used in London.

> E. Policeman, policeman, Hullo! Hullo!
>   Give me back my Polo*.

Walworth 1980.

* Polo is the name of a popular mint sweet.

8.A.14 ROW, ROW GENTLY DOWN THE STREAM

> Row, row gently down the stream,
> Throw the teacher overboard,
> And listen to her scream.

Finsbury 1983.

See also **4.7B** and **4.8**.

Printed versions Cosbey, p. 87, Kenney, p. 3.

8.A.15 TEACHER'S KIND

> Teacher's kind, teacher's gentle,
> Teacher's strong, teacher's mental.

Streatham 1982; <u>Dulwich 1983</u>.

Printed version Opies, *LLS*, p. 365.

8.A.16 HO! HO! HO!

> Ho! Ho! Ho! He! He! He!
> What! Nobody here to welcome me?
> There sit some children quiet and good,
> I'll soon make them noisy and rude.

> Dalston 1983.

Early noting cf. Ha ha ha he he he/I put a tanner on a gee gee gee/The gee gee fell and broke its back/ But I didn't get my tanner back, Kellett, parody set to the tune of "Little brown jug" (traditional), sung during the 1920s, p. 129.

8.A.17 PRINCE CHARMING

> Prince Charming, Prince Charming,
> Don't you ever, don't you ever,
> Pick your nose and flick it at the teacher,
> Pick your nose and flick it at the teacher.

> Dalston 1983.

This was possibly influenced by the popular song, "Prince Charming" released by the New Romantic band Adam and the Ants in 1981, which has a chorus beginning "Don't you ever, don't you ever".

8.A.18 TEACHER, TEACHER, IT'S NOT FAIR

> Teacher, teacher, it's not fair,
> We can't see your underwear.
> Is it black, or is it white?

Oh my God, it's dynamite!

Stoke Newington 1983; Shepherds Bush

Printed versions Abrahams, p. 186; Cansler, 4; Kirshenblatt-Gimblett, p. 103; Knapps, pp. 89, 90.

8.A.19 COME ALL YE FAITHFUL

CAROL PARODY:

Come all ye faithful,
Teachers are disgraceful.

Brockley 1983.

Printed version cf. Opies, *LLS*, p. 88.

8.A.20 SCHOOL HUMOUR

A. In case of fire, grab as many school books as you can and run towards the fire.

Blackheath 1983.

B. My teacher loves me because she puts crosses at the ends of my sums.

Greenwich 1982.

8.B SCHOOL MEALS

School meals have no long tradition. They were first introduced generally during the Second World War. When I began collecting children's lore in the 1960s from the children in a school in East London in which I was teaching, the now ubiquitous rhyme **8.B.2** OUR SCHOOL DINNERS was not current. I first came across it in an Outer London school in 1967, though it was obviously much older than this. For many children in more deprived areas, the midday cooked meal at school is the most important meal of the day, and the number of children who will ask for seconds when (rarely) available indicates their popularity with many children. Just as in the case of "breaking up" rhymes referred to in the preceding section, this rhyme has been recited by many children without much enthusiasm. On the other hand, a number of children dislike school meals and will prefer to bring a packed lunch or to spend their dinner money on "junk" food.

At the time this material was collected, Inner London had retained the daily hot meals service in primary schools. The references to being sick on the plate were in universal usage in Inner London at this period. A similar kind of rhyme, though not so widespread, is **8.B.1** IF YOU STAY TO SCHOOL DINNERS. The revolting **8.B.3** SNOT AND BOGEY CUSTARD PIE has a limited circulation, mainly in areas where school dinners play a less important role. An even more unpleasant version of this rhyme, if that is possible, was given to me by a most charming, polite and well spoken little girl. School meals give a chance to the school wit, and **8.B.5** and **8.B.6** are typical of such humour.

8.B.1 IF YOU STAY TO SCHOOL DINNERS

A. If you stay to school dinners,
You better chuck it aside.
A lot of kids didn't,
A lot of kids died.
The meat and veg. are iron,
The spuds are made of steel.
If the spuds don't get you
The afters will.

Mile End 1968; Earlsfield 1982; <u>Borough</u>, Dulwich <u>1983</u>.

Printed versions Hubbard, mentioned, 262; cf. Kellett, Say what you will/ School dinners make you ill, p. 101; Kelsey, *K1*, 46–47; Opies, *LLS*, p. 162.

B. If you go to school dinners
    You sit side by side.
    You cannot escape,
    Many have tried.
    You look at the gravy,
    All lumpy and still,
    If that doesn't get you,
    The afters will.

Stoke Newington.

8.B.2 OUR SCHOOL DINNERS

A. Our school dinners, our school dinners,
    Mushy little peas, mushy little peas,
    Soggy semolina, soggy semolina,
    I feel sick, toilet quick.
    It's too late,
    I've done it on the plate.

Streatham 1982.

Tune "Frère Jacques", the traditional French nursery song.

Printed versions Kelsey, *K1*, 46; Opies, *LLS*, p. 162; Rosen and Steele, [p. 28].

B. Concrete chips, concrete chips,
    Bad baked beans, bad baked beans,
    Soggy semolina, soggy semolina,
    Doctor quick, I feel sick,
    You're too late,
    I've done it on my plate.

Blackheath 1983.

Versions of this rhyme were current in Outer London in the 1960s; I collected versions in Twickenham, Croydon and Palmers Green, 1967–68.

It first appeared to be widely current in Inner London in the early 1960s and was later to be found in every part of Inner London. I collected versions from eighteen schools.

8.B.3 SNOT AND BOGEY CUSTARD PIE

    A.   Snot and bogey custard pie,
           Dead bird, dog giblets, (Mix it up with a)
           Green cat's eye.
           Spread it on butter,
           Spread it on thick,
           Wash it down
           With a cup of cold sick.

<u>Barnsbury 1983</u>; Hampstead 1984.

    B.   Red and yellow custard,
           Snot and bogey pie
           All mixed up
           With a dead dog's eye.

           Stir it, stir it,
           Till it's thick
           Then drink it down
           With a cup of cold sick.

Marylebone 1967; <u>Mile End 1968</u>; Stoke Newington 1983.

Printed versions Gainer, 44; Kellett, pp. 129, 132 (and see below); Lowenstein, pp. 22, 36; Opies, *LLS*, p. 162; Turner, Ooey gooey custard, p. 101.

Early noting Caterpillar sandwich spread on thick/Then washed down [or: Then drink it down] with a cup of cold sick, Kellett, ?1920s, pp. 129, 132.

8.B.4 APPLE TART MAKES YOU FART

Apple tart makes you fart,
Apple crumble makes you rumble,
Apple snow makes you go.

Stoke Newington 1983.

8.B.5 SCHOOL MEALS HUMOUR

A. We've got hot sick today. That's a change, we usually have shit.

Barnsbury 1983.

B. Our school cook's been cooking for six years. She ought to be done by now.

Blackheath 1983.

C. Did you know that pygmies come from Africa to our school just to dip their spears in our cook's gravy?

Blackheath 1983.

D. What is worse, a spider or half a spider in your soup?

Blackheath 1983.

E. Greens put colour in your cheeks. Who wants green cheeks?

Blackheath 1983.

8.B.6 NICKNAMES FOR SCHOOL FOOD

A. Ravioli: dead tea bags.
B. Boiled cabbage: gangrene.
C. Boiled potatoes: ping pong balls.
D. Beans on toast: skinheads on a raft.

8.C SCHOOL BOASTS, YELLS, AND CHANTS

School boasts appear to be made up separately in different schools, apart from ones like **8.C.1** WE WON THE WAR which has been in universal use for many years. They are usually chanted on special combat occasions on a coach or in the playground after a game or competition with another school. The singing game: **4.35** WE ARE THE DEPTFORD GIRLS can be regarded as a local boast and is in the tradition that was going strong in the early years of the twentieth century. The boast usually began: "We are the (*neighbourhood or school*) boys,/We know our manners,/We spend our tanners,/We are respected wherever we go." The Opies (*LLS*, 1959, p. 355) give an example from 1952, from a junior secondary school in Scotland.

Most yells and chants represent the less pleasant side of competitive team games. Either they are dying out or children were unwilling to report them because they were ashamed of them. A number of the football rhymes and chants contained in the last section of this collection are of course adapted for school use.

Boasts

8.C.1 We won the war in 1984 (or 1944, 1964, etc.)
Guess what we done:
We kicked 'em up the bum.

Mile End 1956, 1983; Battersea, Brixton, Greenwich, Streatham 1982; Blackheath, Dalston, Dulwich 1983.

See also **11.I.21**.

Printed versions Rutherford, p. 125; Turner, p. 108.

8.C.2 We are the boys in red and white
Come on boys (girls) do you want a fight?

Borough 1983.

8.C.3 We're all marching for the army
We're all off to Blackheath
And we'll really shake it up,
When we win the Blackheath cup,
'Cause (_____) are the greatest football team.

Deptford 1983.

Tune chorus of the song "Tramp! Tramp! Tramp! (The Prisoner's Hope)" written by George F. Root in 1864.

8.C.4 A. We are the (nickname for school)
Jolly, jolly (_____)
Everywhere we go-o
(another school) wants to know-o
So we'll tell 'em so-o.

Kentish Town 1983.

Every line is repeated either in unison or solo and chorus response. The whole is then repeated with the name of another rival school, and so on.

B. Everywhere we go   (x 2)
People always ask us   (x 2)
Where we come from   (x 2)
So we tell them   (x 2)
We're from (name of school)   (x 2)
The mighty, mighty (_____)   (x 2)
And if you can't hear us,   (x 2)
You must be DEAF   (x 2)

        (much louder the second time)

    Shepherds Bush 1983.

This is repeated at least once more.

See also **4.35**.

Early noting cf. Who are, who are we,/We are the boys of the L.P.C./First in love, first in war,/And first in the hands of the Leeds Police, Kellett, from World War I, pp. 73–74.

Yells and Chants

8.C.5   Give (us) me an S   S
            Give me a T   T
            Give me an L   L
            Give me a U   U
            Give me a K   K
            Give me an E   E
            Give me an S   S
            Give me an S   S
            Give me a C   C
            Give me an H   H
            Give me an O   O
            Give me an O   O
            Give me an L   L

        What have you got?   (What does it spell?)

        <u>Cubitt Town 1983</u>; similar Shepherds Bush 1983.

Solo and response in chorus, shouted at the end.

8.C.6   A.   Two, four, six, eight,
                  Who do we appreciate?

The name of the school is then spelled out and shouted. Sometimes the rival school is shouted out after:

> B. Two, four, six, eight,
> Who do we really hate?

> Almost universal.

Printed versions Kellett, football rhyme, p. 80; Knapps, p. 209; Opies, *LLS*, pp. 350, 351; Rutherford, p. 99; Turner, p. 68.

8.C.7 Two, four, six and a quarter
Who are we going to slaughter? (do we intend to slaughter?)

> The name of the rival team is shouted out.

> Earlsfield 1982; Blackheath 1983; Hampstead 1984.

Printed version Rutherford, p. 98.

8.C.8 We hate (name of another school) and we hate (_____) (repeated twice more)
We are (_____) haters.

> Stoke Newington 1983.

See also Section **12.A**, Football Rhymes and Chants.

8.D PARODIES OF HYMNS, SONGS, AND RHYMES

The most popular and widespread parodies to be found in Inner London schools, as elsewhere I should imagine, were of well established carols and songs which the children repeatedly sang in school assemblies or in singing lessons. There are a few parodies of so-called "community songs" or long established music hall ditties. Very little contemporary material was parodied, apparently, apart from the odd commercial television jingle.

Nursery rhymes inspire the largest body of parodies, a number of which are of an "indecent" character. Although I only came across parodies of five carols, four of these are quoted by the Opies (*LLS*, 1959, pp. 88, 89). Two of them are almost universally known: "We three kings" (**8.D.4**) and "While shepherds watched" (**8.D.5**). No. **8.D.3** SLAP, SLAP, HEAVILY ON THIGH, a parody of "Ding dong merrily on high", may have started a tradition and be more well-known than my single noting would suggest. It is wittier than many other parodies.

The temptation to parody something that is repeated many times in school to the point of boredom is very great, even if the resulting parody is nonsense, but only a few items lend themselves to this kind of obvious treatment. It is easy to replace "kumbaya" by "cucumber", as in **8.D.24** CUCUMBER, MY LORD. The parody of **8.D.7** FIGHT THE GOOD FIGHT was probably made up because this particular hymn was over-used.

Many of the parodies have lasted through several generations and are part of the general pool of children's entertainment material. They could just as logically have been included in the section "Just for Fun". Examples of these are: **8.D.8** HERE COMES THE BRIDE, **8.D.9** OH DEAR WHAT CAN THE MATTER BE?, **8.D.18** PARLEE VOO, and **8.D.31** THE BOY STOOD ON THE BURNING DECK. Versions of these were giggled at by children in the 1920s and probably before.

"Mrs. Brown went to town" (**8.D.27D**), a parody of "Yankee Doodle", has been extensively collected and is in the Douglas book (in a respectable version) which dates it before the First World War (1916, p. 62, 1931, p. 33). The joke about a powerful fart is also to be found in versions of **8.D.18B** PARLEE VOO and is widespread. The rhyme about a "Batmobile", **11.I.3** RUNNING DOWN THE HIGHWAY, is equally popular. Incidentally the "Batmobile" also appears in a parody of JINGLE BELLS (**8.D.30A**). Hitler and the Second World War inspired several parodies which have been handed down to later generations of schoolchildren: **8.D.12** LAND OF SOAP AND BUBBLES, **8.D.13** WHISTLE WHILE YOU WORK, and a version of PARLEE VOO (**8.D.18A**) are examples.

Parodies which have become popular in the last few years all seem to come into the risqué category, ranging from the mild references to knickers in **8.D.19A** TA RA RA BOOM DE AY, and references to "bum" and "balls" in **8.D.20** JESUS CHRIST, SUPERSTAR, to the indecent, represented by **8.D.21B** IF YOU GO DOWN IN THE WOODS TODAY and **8.D.22** DAISY, DAISY, and the explicit sex of "Tra la la boom de ay" (**8.D.19B**). It is interesting to note that in 1983, during a series of visits, I collected both a decent and an indecent parody of this latter song from the same school. There was apparently no connection between the versions except the title line. "On top of Old Smoky" became popular in Britain with the awakened interest in American folksongs in the late 1950s and although it is not so familiar now to adults, parodies of it abound. In addition to the anti-teacher version referred to above (**8.A.7**), I found three completely different parodies. **8.D.14A** is an innocuous rhyme about a meatball, **8.D.14B** is an example of constructing a rhyme so that a particular "rude" word appears to be inevitable and then changing it into something else, and **8.D.14C** is an unpleasant violent rhyme.

Nursery rhymes, because of children's familiarity with them, are favourites for parodying. Of fourteen examples, **8.D.36** MARY HAD A LITTLE LAMB is the most parodied. The Opies (*LLS*, 1959, p. 90) give eleven different ones. I have collected eight from Inner London, some consisting of more than one verse. The form most encountered uses the trick of turning an expected rhyming word into something else, as noted above. A similar verbal trick can be found in a version of I HAD A LITTLE BROTHER (**11.I.24C**).

8.D.39 HUMPTY DUMPTY is another nursery rhyme which has inspired several different parodies with no particular relationship with each other apart from their original base. The version in **8.D.39A**, referring to eating bananas, is the one most frequently encountered. **8.D.44** ROSES ARE RED and **8.D.10** HAPPY BIRTHDAY TO YOU are a little rhyme and a little song which have produced dozens of parodies. Examples are also included in the sections on Clapping Games (**5.21**), Taunts and Epithets (**9.C.1C**, **9.C.13**, **9.C.21**, **9.C.31D**, and **9.C.49**), and Writings for Albums (**12.C.1**).

Parodies of Carols and Hymns

8.D.1 GOOD KING WENCESLAS

    A. Good King Wenceslas looked out,
         On the eve of Stephen,

           Someone donked him on the snout,
           And made it look uneven.

Dulwich 1983.

Printed versions Opies, *LLS*, p. 89; Rutherford, p. 113.

   B.   Good King Wenceslas looked out,
        In his mother's garden,
        He walked into a Brussels sprout
        And said, "I beg your pardon."

<u>Borough</u>, Dulwich 1983.

Printed versions Cole, p, 75; Opies, *LLS*, p. 89; Ritchie, *SS*, p. 115; *Spin*, 4; Turner, p. 91.

Other parodies of Good King Wenceslas Hubbard, mentioned, 263; Kellett, p. 40; Opies, *LLS*, pp. 21, 89; cf. Rosen and Steele, Adam and Eve/In the Garden of Eden, [p. 23]; Rutherford, pp. 113–114; *Spin*, as B. above, and five further versions, 4; Turner, p. 91.

Some printed versions are similar to the HUMPTY DUMPTY versions below (**8.D.39**) and, like **8.D.39A**, include references to bananas (Opies, *LLS*, 1959, p. 89; *Spin*, 4; Turner, p. 91).

8.D.2 HARK THE HAIRY ANGELS SING

   A.   Hark the hairy angels sing,
        Beecham's pills are just the thing.

Hampstead 1984.

   B.   Hark the jelly babies sing,
        Beecham's pills are just the thing.
        They are meek and they are mild,
        Two for an adult and one for a child.
        If you want to go to heaven

Then the dose is exactly seven.
If you want to go to hell
Try swallowing the box as well.

Finsbury 1983.

Printed versions Kellett (see below); Opies, *LLS*, p. 89; *Spin*, 4; Turner, p. 91.

Early noting Hark the herald angels sing/Beechams Pills are just the thing,/They're so gentle, they're so mild/Two for adults and one for a child,/If you want to go to heaven/Then you have to swallow seven./If you want to go to hell/You must swallow the box as well/Hark the herald angels sing/Beechams Pills are just the thing. Kellett, ?1920s, p. 72.

8.D.3 SLAP, SLAP, HEAVILY ON THIGH

PARODY OF CAROL "Ding dong merrily on high".

Slap, slap, heavily on thigh,
In heaven the thighs are stinging,
Slap, slap, heavily on thigh,
Is written with angels singing.
Ah Ah Ah Ah Ah Ah Ah
Hosanna's thigh is stinging.

Kensington 1984.

8.D.4 WE THREE KINGS OF LEICESTER SQUARE

A. We three kings of Leicester Square,
Selling ladies' underwear,
How fantastic, no elastic,
Not very safe to wear.

Brockley, Mile End 1967; Streatham 1982; <u>Finsbury 1983</u>.

Printed versions Abrahams (quoting Opies, *LLS*), p. 204; Kellett, pp. 39, 40, 100 (and see below); Opies, *LLS*, We are three spivs of Trafalgar Square, p. 105; Ritchie, *SS*, as Opies, p. 109; *Spin*, 5; Stork, 4.

Early notings We three Kings of Leicester Square/Selling corsets three pence a pair,/They're fantastic, no elastic,/Buy your mother a pair. Kellett, one of three versions, 1920s, p. 39.

    B. We three kings of Orient are,
         One in a taxi, one in a car,
         One in a scooter beeping his hooter,
         And following yonder star.

         O star of wonder, star of light,
         Charlie caught his pants alight,
         So fantastic, broke his elastic
         Shooting round the world.

Earlsfield 1982; Brockley, <u>Cubitt Town</u>, Dalston, Dulwich <u>1983</u>.

Printed versions Cansler, 9; Kellett, handwritten insertion between pp. 40–41; Opies, *LLS*, p. 88; Ritchie, *SS*, We four lads from Liverpool are, following lines like first verse of B., p. 52; Wilson, 980.

    C. We three kings of Orient are,
         Tried to light a rubber cigar.
         It was loaded and it exploded,
         BANG!
         Silent night! Holy night!

Finsbury 1983.

Printed versions Cansler, 9; Fowke, p. 145; Knapps, p. 167; *Spin*, 5; Turner, p. 107.

    D. We three kings of Orient are,
         George in a scooter, John in a car,*

One drove a go-cart to see the star.

Greenwich 1982.

* "George" is George Harrison, and "John", John Lennon, of the Beatles pop group (cf. the Ritchie reference under B. above).

Printed versions Ritchie, *SS*, p. 52; *Spin*, 5; Stork, 4; Turner, p. 107.

Other parodies of We Three Kings Turner, p. 107.

8.D.5 WHILE SHEPHERDS WASHED THEIR SOCKS BY NIGHT

A. While shepherds washed their socks by night
All seated round the tub,
A bar of Sunlight soap came down,
And they began to scrub.

Borough, Mile End 1983; Hampstead 1984.

Printed versions Fowke, p. 146; Kellett (see below); Opies, *LLS*, p. 88; *Spin*, 5.

Early noting While shepherds washed their sweaty socks/All seated round the tub,/A bar of Watsons soap came down/And they began to scrub. Kellett, ?1920s, p. 39.

B. While shepherds watched their flocks by night,
While watching ITV,
The angel of the Lord came down,
And switched to BBC.

Streatham 1982; Kensington 1982–84; Blackheath, Brockley, Dulwich, Kentish Town, Shepherds Bush 1983; Hampstead 1984.

Printed version *Spin*, 5.

> C. While shepherds cooked their supper by night,
> All seated round the pot,
> The angel of the Lord came down,
> And scoffed the blinking lot.

Mile End 1968.

Printed versions Kellett (see below); cf. Opies, *LLS*, p. 88; cf. *Spin*, 5.

Early noting cf. While shepherds watch their turnip tops/All boiling in a pot,/A great big lump of soot came down/And spoiled the bloody lot. Kellett, ?1920s, p. 39.

Other printed versions Hubbard, mentioned, 263; Rutherford, p. 127; *Spin*, three further versions, 5.

8.D.6 ONWARD CHRISTIAN SOLDIERS

> A. Onward Christian soldiers,
> Marching as to school,
> With the cross of teachers
> Scribbled on the wall.

Blackheath 1983.

Printed version cf. Turner, p. 90.

> B. Onward Christian soldiers,
> Marching up the stairs
> In their pink pyjamas
> With their teddy bears.

Blackheath 1983.

8.D.7 FIGHT THE GOOD FIGHT

> Fight the good fight with all thy might,
> Sit on a box of dynamite.
> Set it alight and you shall see
> The quickest way to the cemetery.

Brockley 1967.

Early noting I remember an earlier version from the 1930s: Fight the good fight with all your might, /Sit on a box of dynamite,/Set it alight and you will be/Far away from the L.C.C.

Parodies of Songs and Poems

8.D.8 HERE COMES THE BRIDE

> PARODY of "Bridal Chorus" from Wagner's 1848 opera *Lohengrin*.

> A. Here comes the bride,
>   All dressed in pink,
>   She's been eating onions,
>   Don't she stink.

Mile End 1968.

> B. Here comes the bride,
>   Forty inches wide,
>   Here comes the groom,
>   With a face like a moon.

Greenwich 1982; Finsbury 1983.

> C. Here comes the bride,
>   All fat and wide,
>   Jumped in a taxi,

And fell out the other side.

Mile End 1968; <u>Dulwich 1983</u>.

D.   Here comes the bride,
     All dressed in white.
     Pull down her knickers,
     Oh what a sight!

Mile End 1968; West Norwood 1983; <u>Stoke Newington 1983</u>.

E.   Here comes the bride,
     Ninety foot wide.
     They had to break the door down,
     To get her inside.

Finsbury 1983.

Printed versions Knapps, p. 212; Opies, *LLS*, p. 303; Ritchie, *SS*, p. 73; Rutherford, p. 44.

Other printed versions Abrahams, quoting Withers, p. 62; Brady, p. 16; Morrison, p. 41; Rutherford, p. 44; Solomons, p. 113; Turner, p. 72; Withers, *RIMP*, p. 63.

8.D.9 OH DEAR WHAT CAN THE MATTER BE?

PARODY of the traditional nursery rhyme.

A.   Oh dear what can the matter be?
     Three old ladies locked in the lavatory.
     They were there from Monday to Saturday,
     Nobody knew they were there.

<u>Greenwich 1982</u>; Cubitt Town, Dulwich, Finsbury 1983; Hampstead 1984.

B.   Oh dear what can the matter be?
     Margaret Thatcher got stuck in the lavatory.

She was there from Monday till Saturday
Nobody knew she was there, so there!

<u>Brixton 1982</u>. Children's names used (one or two): Mile End 1967; Blackheath, Dulwich, Finsbury, Kentish Town 1983.

Printed versions Bolton (see below); Boyce and Bartlett (see below); Gullen, p. 128; Halliwell (see below); Kellett, p. 103 (?early noting); MacBain (see below); Opies, *LLS*, p. 364; Stork, 5; Turner, p. 97.

Early notings The Opies (*ODNR*, 1951, pp. 248–250) give the texts of original eighteenth century songs from which these parodies were made. OH, dear, what can the matter be?/Two old women got up in an apple tree;/One came down,/And the other staid till Saturday, Halliwell, *NRE*, 1844, p. 98. One, two, three,/What can the matter be? Bolton, 1888, p. 93. MacBain, 1933, as Halliwell, p. 275. One, two, three,/What can the matter be?/Three old maids/Tied up to an apple tree, Boyce and Bartlett, 1941, p. 18.

8.D.10 HAPPY BIRTHDAY TO YOU

Happy birthday to you,
Squashed tomatoes and stew,
If you want it, come get it,
Squashed tomatoes and stew.

See also **9.C.49**.

Printed versions Kellett, one of three versions, p. 43; Turner, p. 72.

8.D.11 TEN STICKS OF DYNAMITE

PARODY of "Ten Green Bottles".

A. Ten sticks of dynamite hanging on the wall,
    Ten sticks of dynamite hanging on the wall,

And if one stick of dynamite should accidentally fall,
There'd be no more dynamite and no more wall.

<u>Streatham 1982</u>; Cubitt Town 1983.

B. A version from Palmers Green (1967) ended "and no flipping school".

See also **11.J.6**.

Printed versions Hubbard, mentioned, 263; cf. Sims, Ten bluebottles sitting on the meat, p. 46.

8.D.12 LAND OF SOAP AND BUBBLES

PARODY of "Land of Hope and Glory" (the trio theme from Elgar's *Pomp and Circumstance March No. 1*).

Land of soap and bubbles,
Hitler's having a bath,
Churchill's looking through the keyhole,
Having a jolly good laugh.

Kensington 1984.

Printed version (different theme): Barltrop and Wolveridge, p. 64.

8.D.13 WHISTLE WHILE YOU WORK

PARODY of a song from the Disney film *Snow White and the Seven Dwarfs*, 1937.

A. Whistle while you work,
Hitler is a twerp,
He is barmy,

So's his army,
Whistle while you work.

Finsbury 1983; Kensington 1984.

B. Whistle while we work,
Hitler is a berk,
Someone silly,
Pulled his willy,
Now it doesn't work.

Kensington 1984.

Printed versions Abrahams, quoting Ritchie, p. 207; Harrowven, p. 325; cf. Opies, *ISE*, p. 93, *LLS*, pp. 101, 102; Ritchie, *GC*, p. 112; Turner, p. 67.

8.D.14 ON TOP OF SPAGHETTI

PARODY of the American folksong "On Top of Old Smoky".

A. On top of spaghetti,
All covered in cheese,
I lost my poor meatball,
When somebody sneezed.

It rolled off the table,
And on to the floor,
And then my poor meatball,
Rolled out of the door.

It rolled round the garden
And into a bush,
And then my poor meatball,
Was nothing but mush.

Two years later
It grew to a tree,
It grew lovely meatballs
For you and for me.

So if you eat spaghetti
All covered in cheese,
Hang on to your meatball,
In case somebody should sneeze.

Mile End 1966; <u>Earlsfield 1982</u>; Hampstead, Kensington 1984.

Printed versions Knapps, pp. 175–176; Turner, p. 100.

B. On top [of] Old Smoky,
All covered in grass,
There sat a bald eagle,
Scratching his _____.

Don't get excited,
Don't be misled,
'Cause that bald eagle,
Was scratching his head.

Blackheath, Borough, <u>Shepherds Bush 1983</u>.

See also **8.A.7**; and **9.A.3, 11.I.24c** and **12.C.2** for similar wordplay.

C. I had an old stocking,
I filled it with lead,
I knocked an old lady,
Right over the head.

A policeman came up to me,
And asked me my name,
I gave him the answer,
With a bicycle chain.

The judge said to me,
"Boy, wipe up those tears,"
....
....

My mother fainted,
My daddy dropped dead,
My little brother,
Shot the judge in the head.

Blood on the ceiling,
Blood on the floor,
Blood on the window,
And blood on the door.

Hampstead 1984.

Printed versions cf. Ritchie, *SS*, p. 47; cf. Shaw, 1970, p. 53.

Other printed versions Turner, pp. 100–101.

8.D.15 IF I HAD THE WINGS OF A SPARROW

PARODY of a verse from "Botany Bay", a song from the musical burlesque, "Little Jack Sheppard", 1885.

If I had the wings of a sparrow,
The dirty black arse of a crow,
I'd fly over (_____)* tomorrow,
And crap on the buggers below.

* Name of a rival school.

Hampstead 1984.

Printed version Rosen and Steele, football rhyme, first line, [p. 9].

8.D.16 ROBIN HOOD AND ALL HIS MEN

PARODY of "The King's Horses, the King's Men", a "fox-trot song", written by Noel Gay and Harry Graham in 1930.

Robin Hood and all his men
Went to school at half past ten.
Teacher said, "You're late again"
Robin Hood and his men.

Walworth 1982.

Printed versions Abrahams, quoting Ritchie, p. 170; Ritchie, *GC*, Ali Baba, p. 139; Robin Hood, p. 144.

8.D.17 ROBIN HOOD, ROBIN HOOD

PARODY of theme song from the television series *Robin Hood*, originally shown on ITV from 1955 to 1960.

Robin Hood, Robin Hood, riding through the trees,
Robin Hood, Robin Hood, with his band of fleas,
Loved by the bad, hated by the good,
Robin Hood, Robin Hood, Robin Hood.

Mile End 1968.

Other printed versions Kellett, p. 104; Rutherford, p. 124; Turner, p. 102.

8.D.18 PARLEE VOO

PARODY of "Mademoiselle from Armentières", First World War song.

A. Hitler in his submarine,
    Parlee voo,

>   Hitler in his submarine,
>   Parlee voo,
>   Hitler in his submarine,
>   Pissed all over the window screen,
>   Inky, pinky parlee voo.
>
>   Churchill in a rowing boat, etc.
>   Pissed all over his overcoat, etc.

Hampstead 1984.

> B. There was an old lady of ninety two,
>   Parlee voo,
>   There was an old lady of ninety two,
>   Parlee voo,
>   There was an old lady of ninety two,
>   Did a fart and missed the loo,
>   Inky pinky parlee voo.
>
>   The fart went rolling down the street, etc.
>   Knocked a copper off his feet, etc.
>
>   The copper got out his rusty pistol, etc.
>   Knocked the fart from here to Bristol, etc.
>
>   Bristol City (Rovers) were playing at home, etc.
>   Kicked the fart from here to Rome, etc.
>
>   Julius Caesar was drinking gin, etc.
>   Opened his mouth and the fart rolled in, etc.
>
>   The fart went rolling down his spine, etc.
>   Knocked his bollocks out of line, etc.

Walworth 1981; Greenwich 1982; Cubitt Town, Finsbury, Kentish Town, Mile End, Stoke Newington 1983; Hampstead 1984.

See also **4.28**.

Other printed versions Kellett, a version from the early 1930s, p. 69; Opies, *LLS*, ball-bouncing game, p. 104; Shaw, 1970, p. 60.

8.D.19 TA RA RA BOOM DE AY

PARODY of song copyrighted by Henry J. Sayers in 1891, apparently derived from an old American traditional song, introduced by Mamie Gilroy in the variety show *Tuxedo* and later popularised by Lottie Collins in London music halls from 1892.

A. Ta ra ra boom de ay,
    My knickers flew away.
    I went on holiday,
    They came back yesterday.

West Norwood 1973; <u>Battersea 1982</u>; Dulwich, Shepherds Bush 1983.

B. Tra la la boom de ay,
    I met a boy today.
    He gave me fifty pence,
    To go behind the fence.
    He stuffed it up my shirt,
    He said it wouldn't hurt.
    My mummy was surprised
    To see my tummy rise,
    My father jumped for joy
    To see a baby boy.

Shepherds Bush 1983.

Printed versions Turner, p. 104.

Other printed versions Barltrop and Wolveridge, p. 64; Knapps, pp. 176, 188; Lowenstein, p. 40; Opies, *LLS*, pp. 107–108; Turner, p. 104.

8.D.20 JESUS CHRIST, SUPERSTAR

PARODY of a song from the rock opera of the same title written by Tim Rice and Andrew Lloyd Webber in 1970.

A. Jesus Christ, superstar,
    Came down from heaven in a peanut jar,
    Did a skid, killed a kid,
      Scraped his bum on a dustbin lid.

Hampstead 1984.

B. Jesus Christ, superstar,
    Riding around on a Yamaha,
    Did a skid, killed a kid,
    Scraped his balls on a dustbin lid.

Brixton, Earlsfield, Streatham 1982; Blackheath, Borough, Cubitt Town, Dulwich, Finsbury, Mile End 1983.

Printed version Opies, *SG*, Georgie Best, Superstar, p. 479.

8.D.21 IF YOU GO DOWN IN THE WOODS TODAY

PARODY of "Teddy Bears' Picnic", written in 1907 by John Walter Bratton.

A. If you go down in the woods today,
    Don't let the bear see you.
    She'll take your jelly and cake away,
    Your crisps and chocolate too.
    She'll climb a tree and gobble the lot,
    And then she'll see what else you've got,
    So please take care,
    Don't let that bear surprise you.

Dulwich 1983.

B. If you go down to the woods today,
    You're sure to have a surprise,
    If you go down to the woods today,
    You'd better do up your flies,
    'Cause Mum and Dad are having a shag,
    And Uncle Frank is having a wank,
    And Auntie Floss is having a toss,
    With Grandad.

Mile End, Dulwich 1983.

8.D.22 DAISY, DAISY

PARODY of music hall song "Daisy Bell", composed by Harry Dacre in 1892.

A. Daisy, Daisy,
    Give me your tits to chew,
    I cannot
    Because I haven't got
    Any to expose to you.

Kentish Town 1983.

B. Daisy, Daisy, give me your answer, do,
    Daisy, Daisy, my balls are turning blue,
    I can't afford a Durex,
    But plastic bags will do.
    You'll look sweet,
    Upon a seat,
    With me on top of you.

Barnsbury, Brockley, Kentish Town 1983.

Other printed versions Kellett (see below); Opies, *LLS*, pp. 100, 371; Rutherford, p. 110; Turner, p. 88.

Early notings Daisy, Daisy the coppers are after you,/If they catch you they'll give you a month or two,/They'll tie you on with wire/Behind the Black Maria,/So tinkle your bell/And peddle like hell/On a bicycle built for two, Kellett, a version from the late Edwardian period, p. 31; two further versions referring to Amy Johnson, from the 1930s, pp. 50–51.

8.D.23 OLD MACDONALD HAD A FARM

PARODY of traditional song.

Old Macdonald had a farm,
Ee-i-ee-i-o,
And on that farm he had some police,
Ee-i-ee-i-o,
With a nick-nick here and a nick-nick there,
Here a nick, there a nick
Everywhere a nick-nick,
Old Macdonald had a farm,
Ee-i-ee-i-o.

Stoke Newington 1983.

8.D.24 CUCUMBER, MY LORD

PARODY of "Kumbaya", a spiritual song originating in South Carolina in the 1930s.

Cucumber, my Lord, cucumber,
Cucumber, my Lord, cucumber,
Cucumber, my Lord, cucumber,
Oh Lord, cucumber.

Walworth 1981; Cubitt Town, Dalston, <u>Deptford 1983</u>.

8.D.25 GUANTANABEERA

PARODY of popular song, "Guantanamera", attributed to José Fernàndez Diaz (Cuba, 1929).

Too much Guantanabeera,
Makes you do Guantadiarrhoea.

Dulwich 1983.

8.D.26 THE YELLOW ROSE OF TEXAS

PARODY of a traditional song, an early manuscript version of which possibly dates from 1836.

The yellow rose of Texas
And the man from Laramie
Invited Davy Crockett,
To have a cup of tea.
The tea was so delicious,
They had another cup,
But poor old Davy Crockett,
Had to do the washing up.

Mile End 1967/68.

Printed version Opies, *LLS*, p. 120.

8.D.27 YANKEE DOODLE WENT TO TOWN

PARODY of a song dating back to the Seven Years War (1754–1763).

A. Yankee Doodle went to town,
    Riding on a pony,
    Stuck a feather up his nose,

And called it bogey roney.

Walworth 1982.

Early noting Botkin, *TAF*, 1944, p. 780.

> B. Yankee Doodle rode to town,
>   Riding on a pony,
>   Done a fart behind the cart,
>   And paralysed the pony.

Dulwich 1983; Kensington 1984.

Printed versions Lowenstein, p. 47; Turner, p. 108.

> C. Yankee Doodle stayed at home,
>   Cooking for a pony,
>   Put a muffler in its mouth
>   And called it macaroni.

Kensington 1984.

> D. Mrs. Brown went to town,
>   Riding on a pony,
>   Done a fart behind the cart,
>   And paralysed the pony.
>
>   The fart went rolling down the street,
>   Knocked a copper off his feet.
>   A man came up, drinking gin,
>   Opened his mouth and the fart rolled in.

Brockley 1967.

Printed version Kelsey, *K1*, 48.

Other printed versions Barltrop and Wolveridge, p. 66; Brady, p. 65; Daiken, *CGTY*, Rosie Apple went to Chapel, p. 81, *OGS*, Rosie Apple went to Chapel, p. 19; cf. Hughes and Bontemps, pp. 433–434; Kings (see below); Knapps, Yankee Doodle, pp. 170, 202; Lowenstein, (Mrs. A) went to town, p. 31; MacBain (see below); Montgomerie, p. 85; Sutton-Smith, p. 98; Turner, Yankee Doodle, p. 108.

Early noting cf. Missis Brown/Went to town,/Riding on a pony:/When she came back/She took off her hat/And gave it to Miss Maloney, Kings 1, 1926, p. 28, said in the notes (p. 40) to be a clapping game; a variant of the third line was "With her breeches hanging down". MacBain, 1933, pp. 89–90.

8.D.28 FATHER CHRISTMAS, FATHER CHRISTMAS

PARODY sung to the tune of the French nursery song "Frère Jacques".

Father Christmas, Father Christmas
What bad luck! What bad luck!
Coming down the chimney, coming down the chimney,
He got stuck, he got stuck.

Mile End 1983.

8.D.29 CHRISTMAS IS COMING

PARODY of folk rhyme.

Christmas is coming,
The goose is getting fat,
Please put a penny in the old man's hat,
If you haven't got a penny,
A phone call will do,
If you haven't got the number,
It's 852 [local exchange].

Blackheath 1983.

See also **10.E.7**.

8.D.30 JINGLE BELLS

PARODY of song written by James Pierpont of Massachusetts in 1850.

A. Jingle bells, jingle bells,
    Robin ran away,
    The Batmobile has lost its wheels
    And won't be here today.

Brockley 1967; Finsbury 1983.

This refers to a series of films and television programmes about Batman, his assistant, Robin, and his vehicle the Batmobile, first shown in the 1960s and repeated and remade periodically ever since.

Printed versions Knapps, p. 168; Rutherford, p. 116; *Spin*, 4; Turner, p. 95.

B. Jingle bells, jingle bells,
    Robin flew away,
    Kojak* lost his lollipop
    And didn't know what to say.

Brockley, Finsbury, Stoke Newington 1983.

* This refers to an American television series about a detective called Kojak, screened in England in the 1980s.

Printed version Richards and Stubbs, p. 154.

C. Jingle bells, jingle bells,
    Jingle all the way,
    Father Christmas lost his knickers,
    On the motorway.

Finsbury 1983.

Other printed versions Knapps, p. 168; Rosen and Steele, football rhyme, [p. 10].

8.D.31 THE BOY STOOD ON THE BURNING DECK

PARODY of poem by Felicia Dorothea Hemans (1793–1835): "Casabianca" appeared in: R. S. Holland. (Ed.). 1912. *Historic poems and ballads*. Philadelphia, PA: George W. Jacobs.

   A. The boy stood on the burning deck,
       Picking his nose like mad,
       He rolled it up in little balls,
       And threw it at his dad.

Mile End 1969; <u>West Norwood 1973</u>.

Printed versions Barltrop and Wolveridge, p. 66; Opies, *LLS*, p. 93; Turner, p. 104.

   B. A boy stood on a burning deck,
       His legs were all a-quiver,
       He gave a cough, his head fell off,
       And floated down the river.

<u>Walworth 1982</u>; Mile End 1969, 1983.

Printed version Kellett, p. 73.

   C. A boy stood on the burning deck,
       Having a game of cricket,
       The ball ran up his trouser leg,
       And hit the middle wicket.

Mile End 1969.

Printed version Opies, *LLS*, p. 93.

Other printed versions Barltrop and Wolveridge, p. 66; Botkin (see below); Brady, 3 versions, one like the 1928 West Norwood version below, p. 79; Lowenstein, p. 13; Opies, *LLS*, pp. 93, 365; Shaw, 1970, pp. 38, 54, 100–101; Withers, *RIMP*, p. 40; Wood, *FAFR*, p. 76 (and see below).

Early notings I remember a version from the late 1920s: The boy stood on the burning deck,/His feet were covered in blisters,/He had no trousers to his arse/So he had to wear his sister's. West Norwood, c1928. See also one of the versions in Opies, *LLS*, p. 93. Wood, *AMG*, 1940, p. 66. Three versions, Botkin, *TAF*, 1944, p. 784.

Recording   MacColl and Behan, *Streets of Song*.

Nursery Rhyme Parodies

8.D.32   TWINKLE, TWINKLE, LITTLE STAR

> Twinkle, twinkle, little star,
> What you say is what you are,
> Twelve and twelve is twenty four,
> So shut your gob and say no more.

> Dulwich 1983.

Printed versions Knapps, pp. 68–69; Opies, *LLS*, lines 3–4, p. 43.

8.D.33   THERE WAS AN OLD WOMAN WHO LIVED IN A SHOE

> There was an old woman who lived in a shoe,
> She done a poo and off she blew.

> Greenwich 1982.

8.D.34 LITTLE MISS MUFFET

    A.   Little Miss Muffet sat on a tuffet,
           Eating her Christmas pie,
           There came a big spider
           That sat down beside her
           And little Miss Muffet squashed it.

Streatham 1982.

    B.   Little Miss Muffet sat on a tuffet,
           Eating her Irish stew,
           When down came a spider
           And sat down beside her
           So she ate him up too.

Streatham 1982.

Printed version cf. Shaw, 1970, p. 108.

8.D.35 MARY, MARY, QUITE CONTRARY

    Mary, Mary, quite contrary,
    How does your garden grow?
    With mush and muck,
    And feathers from a duck
    All in a little row.

Streatham 1982.

Printed version cf. Knapps, p. 166.

8.D.36 MARY HAD A LITTLE LAMB

    A.   Mary had a little lamb,
           She thought it fun and frolic,

She threw it up into the air,
And caught it by its tail.

Mary had a little lamb,
She thought it very silly,
She threw it up into the air,
And caught it by its hair.

Finsbury 1983.

B. Mary had a little lamb,
Its feet were made of lard.
And every time it took a step,
It fell back half a yard.

Earlsfield 1982.

C. Mary had a little lamb,
You've heard this tale before,
And did you know she passed her plate
And had a little more.

Blackheath 1983.

Printed version Opies, *LLS*, p. 90.

D. Mary had a little lamb,
Its feet were black as soot
And into Mary's dinner
He put his sooty foot.

<u>Borough</u>, Finsbury <u>1983</u>.

Printed versions Opies, *LLS*, p. 90.

E. Mary had a little lamb,
She also had a bear.

> I've seen Mary's little lamb,
> But I've never seen her bear.

Streatham 1982.

Printed versions Kellett (see below); Lowenstein, p. 30; Opies, *LLS*, p. 90; Turner, for albums, p. 116.

Early noting Mary had a little lamb,/She also had a bear,/I've often seen poor Mary's lamb,/But I've never seen her bear, Kellett, one of three versions, 1920s, p. 54.

> F. Mary had a little lamb,
>   She also had a cat.
>   She called it Tommy Cooper
>   And it died, "just like that."*

Streatham 1982.

* A catch phrase popularised by the English comedian Tommy Cooper (1921–1984).

> G. Mary had a little lamb,
>   She thought it rather silly.
>   She threw it up into the air
>   And caught it by its
>   Willy was a sheepdog
>   Sitting on the grass
>   Along came a bumble bee
>   And stung it up its
>   Ask no questions, tell no lies
>   Have you ever seen a copper
>   Doing up his
>   Flies are a nuisance, bugs are worse
>   And that's the end
>   Of my silly little verse.

Earlsfield 1982; Barnsbury, Blackheath, Finsbury, Kentish Town 1983; Hampstead, Kensington 1984.

See also **11.I.24c** for a similar ending, and **8.D.14b**, **9.A.3** and **12.C.2** for similar wordplay.

Printed versions (like lines 9–12 in Version G): Barltrop and Wolveridge, p. 66; Boyes, Helen had a steamboat, 34; Cosbey, Mary had a steamboat, p. 80; Fowke, Helen had a steamboat, p. 146; Kellett, The higher up the mountain …, p. 94 (and see below); Knapps, p. 183; cf. Lowenstein, pp. 31, 40; Opies, *LLS*, lines 9–12, p. 94; Shaw, fragment, 1970, p. 46.

Early notings (like lines 9–12 in Version G): Lulu had a baby, Kellett, 1920s, p. 27, and Rule Brittania [sic] two monkies [sic] up a stick, Kellett, 1920s, p. 37.

    H. Mary had a little dog,
         Little dog, little dog,
         Mary had a little dog,
         All covered in _____ (shit)

         And everywhere that Mary went,
         Mary went, Mary went,
         And everywhere that Mary went
         The dog was covered in _____

         It made the teacher cry one day,
         Cry one day, cry one day,
         It made the teacher cry one day,
         'Cause teacher's hand was covered in _____

         Mary had a little dog,
         Little dog, little dog,
         Mary had a little dog,
         And now it's covered in _____

Borough 1983.

Tune This was sung to the same tune as **4.17** FAIR ROSIE WAS A SWEET PRINCESS, a traditional singing game.

Other printed versions Hughes and Bontemps, p. 515; Kellett, 1920s, p. 54; Knapps, p. 167; Opies, *LLS*, p. 90; Petershams, p. 4; Ritchie, *SS*, p. 39, *GC*, pp. 164, 165; Rutherford, p. 119; Solomons, p. 101; Turner, p. 96; Withers, *RIMP*, p. 189.

Recording Webb, *Children's Singing Games*.

8.D.37 BAA BAA WHITE SHEEP

>Baa baa, white sheep,
>Have you any wool?
>No sir, no sir,
>Not even three bags full.
>None for the master,
>And none for the dame,
>And none for the little boy
>Who lives down the lane.

>Shepherds Bush 1983.

8.D.38 HALF A POUND OF NUTS AND BOLTS

>Half a pound of nuts and bolts,
>Half a pound of elastic,
>Put them together and what do you have?
>One known as a spastic.

>Mile End 1968.

I collected this unpleasant rhyme in 1966 and hoped it was a "one off" effort. However, I collected it again two years later. Happily I have not come across it since.

See also **4.65**.

Other printed versions Fowke, p. 51; Lowenstein, p. 21; McMorland, p. 12; Ritchie, *SS*, Don't go out with Jane any more, p. 97, *GC*, p. 19; Turner, p. 91; Withers, *RIMP*, I went down to JOHNNY'S house, p. 197.

8.D.39 HUMPTY DUMPTY

A. Humpty Dumpty sat on a wall,
   Eating green bananas,
   Where d'you think he put the skins?
   Down the king's pyjamas.

Mile End 1968; Brixton, Streatham 1982; Cubitt Town, Finsbury, Shepherds Bush 1983.

Printed versions Rosen and Steele, front cover; Shaw, 1970, p. 73; Sluckin, p. 30.

B. Humpty Dumpty sat on a wall,
   Humpty Dumpty had a great fall,
   All the king's horses and all the king's men
   Trod on him!

Brixton, Earlsfield, Streatham 1982.

Printed version Rosen and Steele, [p. 6].

C. Humpty Dumpty sat on a wall,
   Humpty Dumpty had a great fall,
   All the king's horses and all the king's men
   Had scrambled eggs for tea again.

Brixton, Streatham 1982; Finsbury 1983.

Printed version Withers, *RIMP*, p. 190.

D. Humpty Dumpty fell on the grass,
   Humpty Dumpty hurt his arse.

Walworth 1982.

Other printed versions Rosen and Steele, [p. 7]; Rutherford, football rhyme, p. 95.

8.D.40 HEY DIDDLE DIDDLE

Hey diddle diddle
The cat done a piddle
All over the bathroom mat.
The little dog laughed
To see such fun,
It piddled all over the cat.

Marylebone 1967; <u>Battersea</u>, Streatham <u>1982</u>; Shepherds Bush 1983.

Another printed version Turner, for an album, p. 114.

8.D.41 I HAVE A BLACK CAT

PARODY of the nursery rhyme "There was a little girl".

I have a black cat and I gave him a pat,
Right in the middle of his forehead.
When he's good, he's ever so good,
But when he's bad he's horrid.

Borough 1983.

8.D.42 JACK AND JILL WENT UP THE HILL

Jack and Jill went up the hill,
To fetch a pail of water.

I don't know what they did up there,
But now they've got a daughter.

<u>Earlsfield 1982</u>; Kentish Town 1983.

Printed versions Lowenstein, p. 27; Turner, p. 95.

8.D.43 OLD KING COLE

Old King Cole was a merry old soul,
And a merry old soul was he,
He woke up one night with a terrible fright,
And phoned for the w.c.
It had to be done, it had to be done,
So out of the window he popped his bum.
Queen Victoria walking by,
Heard a rumbling in the sky.
Up she looked and down it came,
And she was never seen again.

Streatham 1982.

Printed versions Abrahams, p. 144; cf. Lowenstein, p. 35; Shaw, 1970, pp. 16–17; Turner, p. 98.

8.D.44 ROSES ARE RED

A. Roses are red,
    Violets are blue,
    The shorter the skirt,
    The better the view.

Dulwich 1983; Kensington 1984.

B. Roses are red,
    Violets are bluish, (blue)
    If it wasn't for Jesus,

> We'd all be Jewish. (a Jew)

Hampstead 1984.

Printed version Knapps, autograph rhyme, p. 203.

> C. Roses are red,
> Violets are blue,
> Most poems rhyme
> But this one doesn't.

Blackheath 1983.

Printed version Hepburn and Roberts, 303.

See also **5.21**, **9.C.1c**, **9.C.13**, **9.C.21**, **9.C.31d**, and **12.C.1** ("Roses are red" rhymes).

Other printed versions Botkin (see below); Hepburn and Roberts, 302–304; Kirshenblatt-Gimblett, p. 104; Kellett, pp. 110–111; Knapps, pp. 73–74, 180, 216; Mills and Bishop (see below); Opies, *LLS*, pp. 48, 171, 177; Shaw, 1970, p. 109.

Early notings Roses are red,/Violets are blue,/I like pecans,/Nuts to you, and four further versions, Mills and Bishop, 1937, 32. This and four further versions, Botkin, *TAF*, 1944, p. 796.

Parodies of Themes from Television Advertisements

8.D.45

> PARODY of Cadbury's "Flake" chocolate advertisement:
>
> Only the crumbliest flakiest chocolate,
> Misses the mouth and makes a mess on the floor.

Stoke Newington 1983.

8.D.46

PARODY of Wall's "Cornetto" ice cream advertisement:

Just one Cornetto,
Take it from me,
Disgusting ice cream,
From Hack-e-ney,

La la, the worst ice cream,
Take from me Cornetto
The worst ice cream.

Stoke Newington 1983.

Tune "O Sole Mio", Neapolitan song, lyrics by Giovanni Capurro, melody by Eduardo di Capua, 1898.

8.D.47

PARODY of Clinic "All Clear" anti-dandruff shampoo advertisement:

All Clear is a shampoo
That takes care of your hair,
It's kind to your dandruff,
And it kills all your hair.

Dulwich 1983.

SECTION 9

TEASING AND TAUNTING

Introduction

Exchanging the apt insult or taunt; making the witty rejoinder; playing with words to trick another child; making fun of another child to be "one-up" on him/her; showing the unpopular child why he/she is disliked (particularly if the offence is a social one, like tale-bearing, trying to get round the teacher, telling lies or breaking promises) – these may be improvised for the occasion by the child who has a facility with language. Most children, however, have to rely on a repertoire of words, phrases, and routines which have been used by many others before. They may have been used by many generations of children; or they may be a repetition of remarks that have been heard somewhere and have been remembered, and so a new tradition may be helped on its way. This kind of lore is used by both boys and girls, but physical threats and the like are obviously more the province of the boys, though by no means exclusive to them. Wordplay as a whole appears to be used more by boys, but most of the ruses with a practical element were given to me by girls.

9.A VERBAL TRICKS AND CATCHING OUT

The essence of these verbal tricks is that the child on whom the trick is played is a willing participant, even if at the end he/she may have to put up with a minor embarrassment or self-accusation. Teases and ruses, on the other hand, usually involve a practical element and can be uncomfortable or even painful. A child who goes through the ritual of repeating something like "just like me", a number of times, expects some trick, but is prepared to put up with a joke at his/her expense because of curiosity, or because the child thinks he/she will be able to play the trick on somebody else. There are rhymes which rely on the element of surprise for those who have not heard them before. Versions of **9.A.1** IN A DARK, DARK STREET have two alternative kinds of surprise. In version **9.A.1a**, the listener is led to expect something strange or eerie, if the telling of the story is done with the necessary skill, but he/she gets an anticlimax instead. In version **9.A.1b** the climax, though half expected, can still contain an element of surprise through the noises or actions accompanying the revelation of the "ghost". In **9.A.2** HIS HAND WAS ROUND HER SHOULDER the listener is led to expect a different kind of ending by the way the rhyme begins. In **9.A.3** MARY ATE JAM, MARY ATE JELLY the listener may be encouraged to supply a rhyming word in the second line, but is put right by the reciter of the rhyme. Examples of a similar kind can be found in the sections dealing with parodies and with album rhymes.

Sometimes the trick consists of telling the "victim" that he will say a particular word, e.g. "black", as in **9.A.4** below, and then putting him in a situation where he will almost certainly say the word. He may be tricked into giving a particular answer which will put the initiator in a "one up" situation (e.g. **9.A.5–9.A.12**). Another kind of trick is to get the other child to say something which will be self-incriminating, such as admitting that he stinks (**9.A.13**), uses secondhand toilet paper (**9.A.14**), or uses his hand instead of toilet paper (**9.A.15**). A long-established piece of verbal catching out is to ask how many s's in "that" (**9.A.9**) or how to spell "it" (**9.A.10**). Another traditional trick, continually being adapted to new situations, consists of getting somebody to repeat the same phrase after every line supplied by the initiator, such as: **9.A.20** BEHIND THE BUSH, **9.A.21** SO DID THE FAT LADY, **9.A.22** SO DO I, **9.A.23** I

DO, or **9.A.24** JUST LIKE ME. Getting somebody to say, "I one it,/I two it,/I three it," etc. until the child says "I eight (ate) it", thus admitting he ate something very unpleasant, has tricked children for more than a century (**9.A.25** I ATE IT).

9.A.1 IN A DARK, DARK STREET

    A.   In a dark, dark street,
There was a dark, dark house,
In the dark, dark house,
There was a dark, dark room,
In the dark, dark room,
There was a dark, dark corner,
In the dark, dark corner,
There was an electrician
Fixing the lights.

Dulwich 1983.

    B.   In the dark, dark world,
There was a dark, dark space,
In the dark, dark space,
There was a dark, dark forest,
In the dark, dark forest,
There was a dark, dark house,
In the dark, dark house,
There was a dark, dark room,
In the dark, dark room,
There was a dark, dark cupboard,
In this dark, dark cupboard,
There was a dark, dark shelf,
On this dark, dark shelf,
There was a GHOST!

Finsbury, Shepherds Bush 1983.

See also **5.22**.

Printed versions Abrahams, like A, p. 88; like B, p. 87, both quoting Ritchie; cf. Kellett, Down on the beach there's a cave, p. 126; Opies, *LLS*, like B, p. 36; Ritchie, *SS*, like A, p. 51; like B, p. 30; Rutherford, introductory lines to "Allebeloosha, King of the Jews", p. 83 (see **7.46**).

Recording of similar sequence (skipping): BBC 20536 (78) (1952, Northamptonshire).

9.A.2 HIS HAND WAS ROUND HER SHOULDER

> His hand was round her shoulder,
> His hand was on her cheek,
> He pulled her gently closer,
> Soothing words to speak.
> This may sound romantic,
> Though she wished she wasn't there,
> Though you may not think it,
> She was in the dentist's chair.

Finsbury 1983.

9.A.3 MARY ATE JAM, MARY ATE JELLY

> Mary ate jam, Mary ate jelly,
> Mary went to bed with a pain in her …
> Now don't be mistaken,
> Now don't be misled,
> Mary went to bed with a pain in her head.

Borough 1983.

See also **8.D.14B**, **8.D.36G**, **11.I.24C** and **12.C.2** for similar wordplay.

Printed versions Fowke, John had some cake, p. 126; Kellett, pp. 49–50 (and see below); Leach and Fried, p. 1018; Opies, *ISE*, Annie ate jam,/ Annie ate jelly, p. 30 (not a catch), *LLS*, p. 97; Shaw, 1970, p. 38; Turner, p. 112.

Early noting Mary ate jam, Mary ate jelly, Kellett, ?1920s, pp. 49–50.

9.A.4   A.   I bet I can make you say "black".
              I bet you can't.
              O.K. Say something after me:
              Yellow and blue equals green.
              Yellow and blue equals green.
              I told you I could make you say "blue".
              You said "black"!
              You see, you said, "black".

   Kensington 1984.

         B.   I bet I can make you say "black".
              I bet you can't.
              What are the colours of the Union Jack?
              Red, white and blue.
              I told you I could make you say "blue".
              You said "black"!
              You see, you said "black".

   Kensington 1984.

Printed version Opies, *LLS*, p. 58.

9.A.5   What's your name?
            (_____)
            What's this? (pointing to nose)
            What's in my hand? (holding out empty hand)
            Nothing.
            (_____)—knows (nose)—nothing.

   Finsbury 1983.

9.A.6   What's your favourite animal?
            A dog.

What's your favourite colour?
Blue.
What's your lucky number?
Eight.
I've never seen a blue dog with eight legs.

Cubitt Town 1983.

This bit of nonsense has been around for quite some time and was used mainly by little children.

9.A.7 Where's the chocolate?
In the fridge.
Where's the fridge?
In the kitchen.
Where's the kitchen?
In the house.
Where's the house?
In London.
Where's London?
In England.
Where's England?
In the world.
Where's the world?
In the solar system.
Where's the solar system?
In the galaxy.
Where's the Galaxy*?
In the fridge.

Barnsbury, Kentish Town 1983.

* "Galaxy" is the name of a popular chocolate bar made by Mars.

See also **9.D.32**.

9.A.8 What is the difference between a weasel, a stoat and a monkey?
A weasel is weasily disguised; a stoat is stoatally different.

Where does the monkey come in?
It doesn't, you've been here already.

Mile End 1968.

9.A.9   A.   I saw Esau sitting on a seesaw,
How many S's in that?
Answer: None.

Deptford 1983.

See also **11.B.23**.

Printed version Opies, *LLS*, p. 68.

B.   See-saw, see-saw, sitting on a see-saw,
See-saw, see-saw, sitting on a see-saw,
How many S's in that?

Brockley 1983.

C.   Seashells, cockle shells,
How many S's in that?

Borough 1983.

See also **6.A.53B** and **11.B.3B**.

9.A.10   Constantinople is a very long word Now spell it.
C-O-N-S ...
No. I-T.

Greenwich 1982; Deptford 1983.

Similar printed versions Knapps, "Are you smart? Okay, what's your name? Okay, spell it. Dummy, that's not how you spell 'it.' ", p. 98; Opies, *LLS*, p. 69; Shaw, 1969, p. 11, 1970, p. 12.

9.A.11 I know what you're going to say.
What?
You just said it.

Greenwich 1982.

Printed version Opies, *LLS*, p. 58.

9.A.12 Do you know about the man going round saying, "No."?
No.
You're it.

Shepherds Bush 1983.

9.A.13 What's frozen water?
Ice.
What's frozen cream?
Ice cream.
What's frozen ink?
Iced ink.
I know you do.

Hampstead 1984.

Printed version Opies, *LLS*, p. 58.

9.A.14 What's the worst thing you can get in a second-hand shop?
I don't know.
Second-hand toilet paper. Do you get it?
Yes.
You get second-hand toilet paper.

Streatham 1982; Brockley, Cubitt Town 1983.

9.A.15 What hand do you use to wipe your bum with?
The right hand.
I don't, I use toilet paper.

Similar printed versions Knapps, Which hand do you eat with? My right. You dirty kid. Why don't you use a spoon?, p. 99; Opies, *LLS*, similar to Knapps, p. 67.

9.A.16   I can prove you're a Red Indian.
             How?
             Just proved it.

Printed versions cf. Knapps, Bet I can make you say an Indian word. How?, p. 92; cf. Opies, *LLS*, p. 58.

9.A.17   There were two horses in a field, one called "Shut up" and one called "Because". Because ran away, which one was left? "Shut up".
             I'm not telling you because you said, "Shut up".

9.A.18   Are you scared of squirrels?
             No.
             Why do you keep your nuts in a bag then?

   Brockley 1983 (boys).

9.A.19   "At dinner time if you're the only boy on a table with five girls, someone on another table might say, 'Is that the first time you've been on an all-girls' table?' If you say, 'Yes,' they might say, 'That means you're a girl 'cause it's an all-girls' table." boy, 11, Blackheath 1983.

9.A.20 BEHIND THE BUSH

A child is told to say "Behind the bush" after each statement:

> I went to the park.
> Behind the bush.
> There was an old woman.

Behind the bush.
She took off her clothes.
Behind the bush.
Where were you?
Behind the bush.

Mile End 1983.

9.A.21 SO DID THE FAT LADY

A child is told to say "So did the fat lady" after each statement:

I went up one stair.
So did the fat lady.
I opened the door.
So did the fat lady.
I walked round the shop.
So did the fat lady.
I bought some sweets.
So did the fat lady.
I bought a balloon.
So did the fat lady.
The balloon popped.
So did the fat lady.

Borough 1983.

9.A.22 SO DO I

A child is told to say "So do I" after each statement:

I get up.
So do I.
I go to the shops.
So do I.

I buy some nappies.
So do I.
I put them on the baby.
So do I.
The baby wears them.
So do I.

Streatham 1982.

9.A.23 I DO

A child is told to say "I do" after each statement:

I went to the shop.
I do.
I bought some dog food.
I do.
I gave it to my dog.
I do.
The dog didn't like it.
I do.

Stoke Newington 1983.

9.A.24 JUST LIKE ME

A child is told to say "Just like me" after each statement:

A. Go up the first flight of stairs.
    Just like me.
    Go up the second flight of stairs.
    Just like me.
    Go into the bedroom.
    Just like me.
    Look in the mirror.
    Just like me.

See a fat monkey.
Just like me.

Barnsbury, <u>Dulwich</u>, Stoke Newington <u>1983</u>.

B. I went to the library.
Just like me.
I got out a book.
Just like me.
I opened a page.
Just like me.
I looked at a picture.
Just like me.
It was a big fat gorilla.
Just like me.

Dalston 1983.

C. I went down the road.
Just like me.
I got on a bus.
Just like me.
I went to the zoo.
Just like me.
I saw a monkey.
Just like me.

Mile End 1983.

Printed versions Botkin (see below); Halliwell (see below); Lang (see below); cf. Leach and Fried, pp. 196, 1017; MacBain (see below); Newell (see below); Opies, *ISE*, p. 24, *LLS*, p. 66; Shaw, 1969, p. 43, 1970, p. 72; cf. Turner, similar to MacBain, p. 80.

Early notings I went up one pair of stairs,/Just like me./I went up two pair of stairs./Just like me./I went into a room;/Just like me./I looked out of a window;/Just like me./And there I saw a monkey;/Just like me, Halliwell, *NRE* [1870], p. 66. Lang, 1897, one version as Halliwell, p. 180. "I went up one pair of stairs."/"Just like me."/"There was a monkey."/"Just like me."/"I one'd it."/"I two'd it,"etc./"I ate [eight] it." Newell, 1903, p. 141; this version encompasses both the catch at **9.A.24** and the one at **9.A.25**. MacBain, 1933, p. 122, and cf. I am a gold lock./ I am a gold key/.../ I am a monk lock./I am a mon(k) key, as Lang's second version, p. 237. Botkin, *TAF*, 1944, p. 774.

9.A.25 I ATE IT

The catcher-out and his "victim" alternate: "I one it", "I two it" and so on till "I eight (ate) it."

> A. There was a dead frog in the road,
> I one it,
> I two it,
> I three it,
> I four it,
> I five it,
> I six it,
> I seven it,
> I eight (ate) it.

Blackheath (boot, monster); Brockley; Dalston (a lump of dog muck); Dulwich; Kentish Town (a lump of poo); Stoke Newington (a spider) 1983.

> B. I went to the funfair,
> I saw a smelly sock.
> I won (one) it,
> You two it ... etc.

Printed versions Botkin (see below); Cansler, 6; Newell (see below); Opies, *ISE*, p. 25, *LLS*, pp. 57, 65n, 66; Shaw, I 'ate the Pope, 1969,

p. 44, 1970, p. 81; Sutton-Smith, As I was going over London bridge, counting out, p. 71; Todd, counting out, 5; Turner, p. 80.

Early notings Newell, 1903, see Early notings to **9.A.24** above. Botkin, *TAF*, 1944, p. 775.

9.B TEASES, THREATS, RUSES, AND BOASTS

The examples in this section are more unpleasant than the verbal tricks in the previous one, and all either have some element of pain (usually mild), embarrassment, or making the other child feel "put down". The long-established ADAM AND EVE AND PINCH-ME trick (**9.B.12A**), leading to a mere token pinch, has become firmly established in nursery lore, as the Opies suggest (*LLS*, 1959, p. 59). A contemporary version (**9.B.12B**) gives the recipient a choice of being kicked, punched or slapped, and is less acceptable. No. **9.B.3** is a typical bully's excuse for hitting someone. No. **9.B.11** has an element of trickery, but the only connection of "a punch in the belly" with "you get lots of jelly" is simply the rhyme. However, it has been hallowed with a tradition going back at least to the 1920s. Other longstanding traditions are maintained in the versions of **9.B.7** A PINCH AND A PUNCH and **9.B.5** SEE MY FINGER. No. **9.B.7** does not involve any trickery but a particular occasion. Nos. **9.B.1** and **9.B.8**–**9.B.10** use the flimsiest of pretexts for hitting another child. More complicated ways of seeming to get the victim's acceptance of a situation leading to an unpleasant ending are also found. It might be a punch (**9.B.18**); some kind of scratch (**9.B.21**); spitting (**9.B.22**) or just "putting down" (**9.B.17**, **9.B.19**). A child may be tricked into saying a "rude" word and then made fun of for doing so (**9.B.23**, **9.B.24**), or tricked into saying something embarrassing (**9.B.27**). Sometimes the objective is to put the other child in an inferior or degrading position (**9.B.16**). I include a couple of boasts (**9.B.28**, **9.B.29**) which adopt the same arrogant tone.

9.B.1   Talking to me or chewing a brick,
      Both ways you lose your teeth.

   Walworth 1982; Dulwich 1983.

9.B.2 FROM HERE TO THERE IS AN INCH

   From here to there is an inch,
   From there to there is a pinch,
   From there to there is pull your hair.

   Mile End 1983.

9.B.3   Hit me. What did I say?
      "Hit me."
      All right I will.

   Deptford, Kentish Town 1983.

Printed version Opies, *LLS*, p. 60.

9.B.4 YOUR MONEY OR YOUR LIFE

   Your money or your life,
   Or your bald-headed wife.

   Dalston 1983.

9.B.5 SEE MY FINGER

   See my finger, see my thumb,
   See my fist and here it comes.

   Mile End 1968; Greenwich, Walworth 1982; Borough, Brockley, Cubitt Town, Deptford, EC1 1983.

Printed versions Knapps, p. 99; MacBain (see below); Northall (see below); Opies, *LLS*, pp. 61, 196; Sutton-Smith, p. 100; Turner, p. 76; Withers, *RIMP*, p. 124.

Early notings cf. "In Gloucestershire they say, showing first one fist and then the other- 'Here's your bread, and here's your cheese,/And here's your master when you please.'" Northall, 1892, p. 305. Cf. Here stands a fist, MacBain, 1933, p. 310.

9.B.6 HERE'S A TREE, HERE'S A BUSH

Here's a tree, here's a bush, (making shapes with fingers)
Here it comes right in your mush.

Dalston 1983.

9.B.7 A PINCH AND A PUNCH

A. A pinch and a punch,
    (On the) first day of the month.

Universal.

Printed versions Sutton-Smith, *end* of the month, p. 99; Turner, p. 79.

Replies:

B. A pinch and a kick for being so quick.

C. A slap and a kick for being so quick (slick).

Universal.

Printed version (like B.) Turner, p. 79.

D. A punch (poke) in the eye for being so sly.

Walworth 1982; Blackheath, Brockley, Dulwich 1983.

E. Pinch, punch, first day of the month,
    And no returns (of anything).

Earlsfield, Greenwich, Walworth; Brockley 1983.

F. Pinch and a punch, join in the ring,
    Or tell me your boyfriend's name.

Greenwich 1982.

Printed versions Opies, *LLS*, p. 300, *CGSP*, to start a game, p. 18.

G. A kick up the bum,
    For not being my chum.

Walworth 1982.

9.B.8 STICKS AND STONES

Sticks and stones can't break my bones.
But my fist will.

Borough 1983.

See also **9.D.33**.

9.B.9 Royal Mail, one, two, three, (knocking with knuckles)
And no returns.

Earlsfield 1982.

9.B.10 You'd better not or I'll give you a knuckle sandwich.

Hampstead 1984.

9.B.11 Do you want to come to my party?
Yes.
You get lots of jelly (You get ice cream and jelly)
With a punch in the belly.

Barnsbury 1983.

Printed versions Botkin (see below); Fowke, p. 122; Sutton-Smith, p. 101; Turner, p. 71; Wilson, 981.

Early noting Do you like jelly?/Punch in the belly! Botkin, *TAF*, 1944, p. 769.

9.B.12 ADAM AND EVE AND PINCH-ME

A. Adam and Eve and Pinch-me,
Went down to the river to bathe,
Adam and Eve got drowned,
Who d'you think was saved?

Deptford, Kentish Town, Shepherds Bush 1983.

B. Kick-me, Punch-me and Slap-me,
Went down to the sea to bathe,
Two of them got drowned,
Who do you think was saved?

Kentish Town 1983.

Printed versions Botkin (see below); Cansler, 6; Fowke, Peter and Paul and Pinch Me, p. 122; Leach and Fried, p. 9; Northall (see below); Opies, *ISE*, p. 25, *LLS*, pp. 59, 60 (and see below); Petershams, p. 35; Turner, p. 79; Withers, *RIMP*, p. 11; Wolfenstein, p. 115; Wood (see below).

Early notings According to the Opies (*LLS*, 1959, p. 59, n. 1), quoting *Notes and Queries*, 10th series, Vol. IV, 1905, the lines were well known in 1855. Adam and Eve, and Pinch-me,/Went over the water to bathe;/ Adam and Eve were drownded,/And who do you think was saved? Northall, 1892, p. 298. Wood, *AMG*, 1940, p. 92; Botkin, *TAF*, 1944, p. 782.

9.B.13 DO ME A FAVOUR

Do me a favour,
Lick my bum,
And tell me the flavour.

Dalston 1983.

9.B.14 I'M TELLING ON YOU

I'm telling on you,
You flushed me down the loo.

Kensington 1984.

Printed versions cf. Lowenstein, p. 25; cf. Opies, *LLS*, p. 49; cf. Turner, p. 73.

9.B.15 "The person holds out their hand. You say, 'Dogs go Woof! Woof! (and move to their fingers) Cats go Mee.' You pull back, or pinch, their finger and they go, 'Ouw.'" boy, 11, Hampstead 1984.

Hampstead, Kensington 1984.

Printed version Opies, *LLS*, p. 59.

9.B.16 "Your shoelace is undone."
(The child bends down).
"Don't bow, I'm only your master."

Kensington 1984.

9.B.17 "The second sign of madness is hairs on the palm of your hand." (The child probably looks at his hand).
"The first sign is looking for them."

Shepherds Bush 1983.

9.B.18 "You put your fist on the palm of your hand and you ask someone to smell your hand. You say, 'Smell cheese.' When they smell it you punch them on the nose." boy, 11, Blackheath 1983.

Blackheath, Finsbury 1983.

9.B.19 "You have your hand in a sort of tube shape. You ask someone to put their finger inside and turn it round. Then you say, 'Thank you for cleaning my toilet.' " boy, 11, Blackheath 1983.

Blackheath, Finsbury 1983.

Printed version Knapps, p. 96.

9.B.20 "You put the hand of a person, palm upwards, on a piece of paper. You say, 'Johnny starts off walking to school.' You start drawing from one side of the hand, round to the thumb. You say, 'When he gets to school, he suddenly remembers, "Oh no! I've forgotten my Maths book and I've got to go all the way back again." He goes all the way back again. He goes on and he says, "I've forgotten my dinner money." This time he says, "I'll take a short cut." ' With the pen you draw a line across the palm from thumb to little finger. It tickles." girl, 11, Finsbury 1983.

Printed version cf. Knapps, p. 95.

9.B.21 THE RED BRIDGE/RED RIVER

"This is called 'The red bridge'. You go up to someone and say, 'Hold out your arm.' You give them a scratch. A sparrow would be very light. You might say, 'Here's an animal with a claw,' and you work it up their arm. Then you say, 'Here the elephant comes along,' and you punch their arm very hard. Because of the scratch it makes a red mark. That's why it's called the red bridge. Or it could be a kangaroo, then you punch them." girl, 11, Finsbury 1983.

I heard a very involved version called "Red River" on similar lines in Kensington (1984).

9.B.22 HOLD OUT YOUR HAND

"You say, 'Hold out your hand, I'm going to read your palm; I can see a big house with a wood and in the middle of that wood I can see a lake,' and you spit on her hand." girl, 11, Finsbury 1983.

"You say, 'You're going to have a big house and lots of children. You're going to have a garden with a swimming pool.' Then you spit on their hand. This is when you're pretending to tell their fortune." girl, 11, Kensington 1984.

Printed versions cf. Knapps, p. 93; cf. Opies, *LLS*, p. 63.

"You say, 'You've just met a person. You'll fall madly in love with them. You ask them to marry you. They say, 'Yes,' so you go off together straight away and get married. At the wedding you have wine. Can you see the wine?' Then you spit on their hand." girl, 11, Kensington 1984.

"When you're on your honeymoon you're having a bath. Can you see yourself in the bath?" (Then you spit on their hand). girl, 11, Kensington 1984.

9.B.23   IF YOU EVER SEE A BUNNY

A child is told to say quickly:

A. If you ever see a bunny,
    With its nose very runny,
    Don't think it funny,
    'Cause it's not.

Mile End 1983.

B. Similarly: "Polish it."

Printed versions cf. Opies, *ISE*, p. 68; *LLS*, p. 67; cf. Turner, tongue twister, p. 80.

9.B.24   A child is told to stretch his/her mouth with fingers and then to try to say, "My dad's a banker," or "bucket".

Kentish Town 1983.

9.B.25   "When I was little they used to say, 'Don't walk on the cracks or we'll kick you. The first one to walk on the line gets a kick up the bum.'"

Barnsbury 1983.

See also **10.C.17** and **10.C.18**.

9.B.26   "You stand up and another person says, 'There's a hole in your back; it's getting bigger and bigger. You must close your eyes and really concentrate.' The person says, 'I'm going to thread a piece of string through the hole and bring it through a hole in your tummy.' They pretend to bring it through and then say, 'I'm pulling, I'm pulling.' They go away from you and automatically you go towards them because of their voice. You follow them." girl, 11, Finsbury 1983.

9.B.27   "A person takes a hair out of her head, one single hair. She holds it up. They say, 'Tap out a boy's name, any boy you love.' (If it's a boy he says, 'Tap out a girl's name'). Then they say, 'Tap out the colour of his/her eyes, the number of letters, that is.' She has to close her eyes and the person who is holding the hair takes it away. They say, 'In a dark alleyway you're with a boy you love and he pulls down his pants, tap out what you would say.' They can't find the hair because (the other person) has taken it away so they say, 'Where is it?' It always works."

girl, 11, Finsbury 1983.

9.B.28   DON'T MESS WITH THE BEST

Don't mess with the best
Till you've passed the test.
When you've passed the test
You can mess with the best.

boy, Dalston 1983.

9.B.29   MY NAME IS (____)

My name is (____) and I've got freckles on my face.
I found a barrel and I beat (____) in a race.
Everybody knows that I can sing,
I fought in a boxing ring.
My name is (____) and I've got freckles on my face.

Dulwich 1983.

9.C   TAUNTS AND EPITHETS

I have a strong belief that at the time of the survey there was much less taunting of other children because of their physical shape or appearance than there was fifty or sixty years earlier when I was a schoolboy. Boys then were continually reminded of the fact that they were tall or short, overweight or thin, had rare hair coloration, wore glasses or had any unusual features of limbs. Much of this was no doubt fairly good-natured, but if there was a quarrel, or if the child concerned was unpopular, then the physical peculiarities were very likely to play a part in the exchange of verbal attack. If a child was ragged or dirty, or had a poor complexion, this might be used against him/her. Children who were prone to crying, were nervous, had learning difficulties, and boys who were considered to be effeminate, would receive the epithets of "cry baby", "cowardy custard", "dunce", "cissy", "pansy" etc. Most cruel of all were the insults directed at a child's parents or other relations.

In the course of my researches it was difficult to find epithets for physical differences. Those I did collect were mainly good-natured nicknames or "one-off" insults. One exception was the common use of "four eyes" or "goggle eyes" (**9.C.5**) for children who wore spectacles. A doggerel rhyme sung to the conga tune (**9.C.27**) was quite common, suggesting the cheapness, poor quality, or dowdiness of another child's clothing. Though these suggestions were not necessarily meant to be taken seriously, they would make sensitive children very unhappy, particularly because of an implied criticism of their parents. The old "dunce" (**9.C.32**) and "cowardy custard" happily seemed to be almost extinct, though the latter had been replaced by "scaredy cat" (**9.C.36**). "Cry baby" rhymes (**9.C.37**) were uncommon; tears from boys are more acceptable than they used to be. "Tale tellers" (**9.C.33**), "copy cats" (**9.C.35**), and "showoffs" (**9.C.44, 9.C.45**) would still be at the receiving end of insults or rhymes, pointing out that their weaknesses are not socially acceptable. General insults, suggesting that a child is not very good looking, is like a monkey etc. were quite common, but were usually expressed jokingly in variations of the ROSES ARE RED rhyme (**9.C.1c, 9.C.13, 9.C.21,** and **9.C.31d**) or, on a child's birthday, a parody of HAPPY BIRTHDAY TO YOU (**9.C.49**). Taunts suggesting that a child smells were widespread, and often expressed in the "Roses are red" formula.

The multi-ethnic character of many Inner London schools and the varying attitudes which children acquire from their neighbours and family meant that racial and national-chauvinist taunts were used in many parts of the city. My experience as a class and head teacher in several multi-ethnic areas, however, indicated that most children of junior school age (apart from a small number heavily indoctrinated from home) only used overt racial taunts when they were involved in a serious quarrel. Children would go out of their way not to use the word "nigger" in traditional rhymes and would usually change the word to a more innocuous one. They were not so sensitive in the use of the obnoxious word "Paki", often applied indiscriminately to children of a southern Asian appearance, nor were they so sensitive when it came to retelling jokes with racial, anti-Semitic or anti-Irish implications. In this they reflected the adult world around them.

Unpleasant or critical remarks about other children, rather than those addressed to them, may suggest that the child mentioned is rather unpopular. Sometimes an unpopular girl might be referred to in a rhyme used for skipping or ball bouncing, as in the long established **9.C.23** I KNOW A GIRL. Similarly, girls' names were used in a few rhymes where the effect was just to embarrass, as in the ball bouncing rhymes **9.C.54** K-I-S-S-I-N-G and **9.C.55** MY NAME IS CHINKY CHINA. I have included a few such rhymes which suggest that girls have boyfriends and which sometimes include the boy's name as well.

Features

9.C.1 *Nose*

    A.   Pinocchio.*

* Carlo Collodi's book and Disney cartoon character whose nose grew longer when he told lies.

    B.   Your nose is so long it knocks me over when you turn round.

Finsbury 1983.

C. Roses are red, violets are blue,
You have a nose like a B52.

Hampstead 1984.

See also **5.21**, **8.D.44**, **9.C.13**, **9.C.21**, **9.C.31D**, and **12.C.1** ("Roses are red" rhymes).

9.C.2 *Teeth*

A. Goofy.

Disney cartoon character with prominent teeth.

B. Your teeth are like stars, come out at night.

Finsbury 1983.

C. (_____, _____), got false teeth.

Mile End 1983.

Printed version Knapps, cf. version C, p. 63.

9.C.3 *Ears*

A. F.A. Cup handles.
B. Elephant ears.

9.C.4 *Hair*

A. Carrot top.
B. Ginger.
C. Ginger nut.

See also **9.E.2G**, **9.E.5B**.

D. There's a jungle in his hair,
    With a monkey swinging there.
    Just like him, just like him.

    (to a boy with frizzy hair).

Shepherds Bush 1983.

E. Baldy (skinhead).
F. Hey! you up there,
    What's it like to have no hair?
    Skinhead!

Walworth 1982.

Printed version Knapps, as A, p. 67.

9.C.5 *Spectacles*

A. Goggles for girls,
    Goggles for guys.
    (_____ _____'s) got shit in his eyes.

Mile End 1983.

B. Four eyes, goggle eyes,
    Don't forget to wash your eyes.

Mile End 1983.

C. "Four eyes" and "Goggle eyes" are used extensively.

See also **9.D.7**.

Printed versions Barltrop and Wolveridge, as A, line 3, p. 44; Daiken, *OGS*, p. 37; Knapps, p. 66; Opies, *LLS*, p. 172; Sluckin, p. 67.

Height

9.C.6 *Tall*

    A. Lanky.
    B. Lofty.

9.C.7 *Short*

    A. Hobbit.
    B. Titch.

Legs

9.C.8

    A. Knobbly knees.
    B. Lanky legs.

Weight

9.C.9 *Thin*

Thin as a lamp-post.

9.C.10 *Overweight*

    A. Beefy.
    B. Fatso.
    C. Fatty.
    D. Georgie Porgie, pudding and pie …

Printed version Knapps, as B, p. 66.

    E. You can't stand it with (_____),
        He'll break the bridge down.
        You can't stand it with (_____),
        He'll make us all drown.

You can't stand it with (____),
He'll float on the top,
You can't stand it with (____)
We'll all be popped. (sic)

Shepherds Bush 1983.

See also **9.C.48**.

Appearance

9.C.11 GOD MADE THE SEA

God made the sea,
God made the lakes,
God made you (____ ____)
But we all make mistakes.

Earlsfield 1982; Blackheath 1983.

Printed version Knapps, pp. 72–73.

9.C.12 THE RAIN MAKES ALL THINGS BEAUTIFUL

The rain makes all things beautiful,
Flowers and grasses too,
The rain makes all things beautiful,
So why doesn't it rain on you?

Earlsfield 1982; Finsbury 1983.

See also **9.C.13A** below.

9.C.13 ROSES ARE RED

A. Roses are red, violets are blue,
    God made things beautiful (When God made the world)

What happened to you?

Earlsfield 1982; Kensington 1984.

B. Roses are red, violets are blue,
    I'm so handsome, what happened to you?

West Norwood 1973; Kensington 1984.

C. Roses are red, violets are blue,
    But no-one can be as ugly as you.

Battersea 1982.

See also **5.21**, **8.D.44**, **9.C.1c**, **9.C.21**, **9.C.31d**, and **12.C.1** ("Roses are red" rhymes).

Other printed versions (appearance) Botkin (see below); cf. Fowke, p. 120; cf. Hepburn and Roberts, 302–303; cf. Knapps, pp. 73–74; cf. Mills and Bishop (see below); Opies, *LLS*, p. 171.

Early noting Roses are red,/Violets are blue,/If I had your mug,/I'd join the zoo, Mills and Bishop, 1937, 32, also quoted in Botkin, *TAF*, 1944, p. 796.

9.C.14 A. You look like a pig's backside.
            B. You look like a pig's rear end.

Walworth 1982.

Attributes

9.C.15 (_____, _____), covered in snot.

Mile End 1983.

Printed version cf. Knapps, p. 63.

9.C.16 (____ THE ____) (Child's name, and a rhyme of the name)

(____ the ____)
He had a rubber bum,
He rubbed it and scrubbed it,
He couldn't get it done.
So he called for the doctor,
The doctor couldn't come,
Poor little (____)
He had a rubber bum.

Shepherds Bush 1983.

9.C.17 PRATTIE ANNIE

Pratty Annie, Pratty Annie,
Where are you, where are you,
You are sitting, you are sitting,
On the loo, on the loo.

9.C.18 BUM, TIT, BUM, TIT

Bum, tit, bum, tit,
Willy Willy Wanker,
Bum, tit, bum, tit,
Willy Willy Wanker.

9.C.19 SAM, SAM, DIRTY OLD MAN

A. Sam, Sam, dirty old man,
    Washed his hair in a frying pan,
    Combed his hair with the leg of a chair,
    Sam, Sam, dirty old man.

Brockley 1967; West Norwood 1979; Greenwich, Streatham 1982; Finsbury 1982–84; Kentish Town 1983; Hampstead 1984.

B. Sam, Sam, the dirty man,
    Washed his face in a frying pan,
    Combed his hair with a donkey's tail,
    And picked his nose with a big toe nail.

Kensington 1982–84; Dalston 1983.

C. Dan, Dan, the lavatory man,
    Cleans the loo with his frying pan.

EC1 1983.

The Opies say this is "a relic of a once famous song 'Old Dan Tucker' composed by the black-faced minstrel Daniel Decatur Emmett, of 'Dixie' fame, and printed in 1843." (*LLS*, 1959, p. 13).

Printed versions Abrahams, title "Old Dan Tucker", only, mentioned, p. 142; Barltrop and Wolveridge, p. 67; Botkin (see below); Daiken, *OGS*, p. 32; Douglas (see below); Hewins, p. 19; cf. Hughes and Bontemps, The Waffle Man, pp. 416–417; Kings (see below); McMorland, p. 30; Mills and Bishop (see below); Montgomeries, *SC*, Slap, bang,/The dirty man, p. 170; Nelson, ball-bouncing, p. 67; Opies, *ISE*, p. 50, *LLS*, pp. 13 (Sam), 159 (Dan); Ritchie, *SS*, Tam, Tam, p. 107; Rodger, p. 12; Rohrbough (see below); Shaw, Daddy Bunchy (i), 1969, p. 17, Dan (or Sam), 1970, pp. 25–26, 32; Sutton-Smith, Dan, p. 99; Talley (see below); Turner, both Dan and Sam, pp. 70–71; Withers, *CO*, Sam, [p. 35], *RIMP*, p. 32.

Early notings Sam, Sam, dirty old man,/Washed his face in a frying pan,/Combed his hair with the leg of a chair—/Sam, Sam, dirty old man. "For a shuttlecock game", Douglas, 1916, p. 55, 1931, p. 29. Cappun Dime, Talley, 1922, p. 5; Kings 2, 1930, p. 35; cf. Mills and Bishop, 1937, 32. Old Dan Tucker, Rohrbough, *HPPB*, 1940, p. 82. Botkin, *TAF*, 1944, pp. 783, 797.

Recording MacColl and Behan, *Streets of Song*.

9.C.20 HEY, YOU'RE A DIRTY KANGAROO

> Hey, you're a dirty kangaroo,
> I put you up a chimney pot
> And made you black and blue.

Walworth 1982.

9.C.21 ROSES ARE RED

> A. Roses are red, violets are blue,
>   Onions stink and so do you (just like you).

Walworth 1982.

Printed version Opies, *LLS*, a version from London, p. 48.

> B. Roses are red, violets are blue,
>   You stink like a lump of poo.

Cubitt Town 1983.

> C. Roses are red, violets are blue,
>   You are smelly, and I hate you.

Barnsbury 1983.

> D. Roses are red, violets are blue,
>   Your knickers stink like the back of the zoo.

Dalston 1983.

> E. Roses are red, violets are blue,
>   Dustbins smell and so do you.

Battersea 1982.

> F. Roses are red, violets are blue,
> No-one farts as good as you.

Brockley 1983.

Other printed versions (attributes) Botkin (see below); cf. Knapps, p. 216; Mills and Bishop (see below); cf. Opies, *ISE*, p. 68.

Early notings Roses are red,/Violets are blue,/Everybody stinks/And so do you; Roses are red,/ Violets are blue,/I use Lifebuoy,/Why don't you? Mills and Bishop, 1937, 32, also quoted in Botkin, *TAF*, 1944, p. 796.

Personality, Behaviour, etc.

> G. Roses are red, violets are blue,
> They are sweet, so why aren't you?

Walworth 1982.

> H. Roses are red, violets are blue,
> Sugar makes me sick, and so do you.

Greenwich 1982; Hampstead 1984.

> I. Roses are red, violets are blue,
> Sugar is sweet, but what happened to you?

Borough 1983.

Other printed versions (personality) Opies, *LLS*, p. 177.

See also **5.21**, **8.D.44**, **9.C.1c**, **9.C.13**, **9.C.31d**, and **12.C.1** ("Roses are red" rhymes).

9.C.22 (____ ____) AIN'T NO GOOD

(____ ____) ain't no good,
Chop up the head in the firewood,
When them dead, burn them head,
Make it into bulla bread.

Battersea 1982.

This is a Jamaican dialect version.

Printed versions a typical English version might be: Micky Roche is no good,/Chop him up for fi-erwood,/When he's dead/Bile his head,/Then we'll all have gingerbread. Shaw, 1969, p. 31, 1970, p. 55, Liverpool. See also Brady, p. 98; Fowke, p. 119; Gaskell (see below); Opies, *LLS*, p. 176; Sutton-Smith, p. 97; Turner, p. 73.

Early noting (Someone named) is no good,/Chop him up for firewood./When he's dead, jump on his head,/Then we'll have some currant bread, Gaskell, c1913, p. 8.

9.C.23 I KNOW A GIRL

SKIPPING RHYME

I know a girl who's sly and deceitful,
Every little tit-tat, she goes and tells the people,
Long nose, ugly face, and fit to put in a glass case.
If you want to know her name,
Her name is (____ ____).
Oh, (____ ____) keep away from me,
Not because you're dirty,
Not because you're clean,
Because you play with other kids
And never play with me.

Dalston 1983.

Printed versions Douglas (see below); Fowke, p. 117; Fulton and Smith, ll. 7–8, p. 55; Opies, *LLS*, p. 175; Turner, p. 73.

Early noting I know a girl, sly and deceitful,/Every little tittle tat she goes and tells her people./Long nose, ugly face, ought to be put under a glass case,/If you want to know her name,/Her name is (Evie Allen)./O (Evie Allen), get away from me,/I don't want to speak to you,/Nor you to speak to me./Once we were playmates,/But now we can't agree—/O (Evie Allen), get away from me, Douglas, 1916, pp. 84–85, 1931, p. 48.

9.C.24 (_____) IS A NUTTER

(_____) is a nutter,
She lives on bread and butter,
La la la la,
La la la la.

Kentish Town 1983.

Tune "I Came I Saw I Conga'd", written by James Cavanaugh, John Redmond, and Frank Weldon in 1940 and performed by Edmundo Ros and His Orchestra.

See also **9.C.27**, **11.I.38** and **12.A.10** for similar uses of the rhythmic formula of "I came I saw I conga'd".

9.C.25 (_____) IS CROOKED, (_____) IS BENT

(_____) is crooked, (_____) is bent,
(_____) farted, and off she went.

Kensington 1984.

9.C.26 THERE WAS (____) STANDING IN THE SNOW

There was (_____) standing in the snow,
Saying, "I'm a prostitute,
Come and have a go."

Kentish Town 1983.

Clothes

9.C.27 YOU GO (____ GOES) TO TESCO'S/MOTHERCARE

A. You go (_____ goes) to Tesco's*
That's where you get (she gets) her best clothes,
Tra la la la,
Tra la la la.

* Tesco: a major supermarket chain selling, among much else, inexpensive children's clothing.

Same or similar: Earlsfield, Greenwich 1982; Borough, Brockley, Kentish Town, Mile End 1983.

B. You go (_____ goes) to Mothercare,*
Where you get (she gets) your (her) underwear,
Tra la la la,
Tra la la la.

* Mothercare: a chain of stores specialising in everything for expectant mothers, mothers, and babies.

See also **9.C.24**, **11.I.38**, and **12.A.10** for similar uses of the rhythmic formula of "I Came I Saw I Conga'd".

9.C.28   A.   Who's a posh boy (girl)? (new clothes).
         B.   Oxfam. (in reference to the chain of shops run by the charity).

Clothes: colours

9.C.29   A.   Oi, you in the red,
              You wet the bed.

   Borough 1983.

         B.   If you wear blue
              Go and do a poo.

   Borough 1983.

Printed versions cf. Knapps, pp. 62–63; a version similar to A but an insult to a redhead, p. 67.

Intelligence

9.C.30   A.   Clever clocks.
         B.   Smarty boots.
         C.   Smart moccasins.

Lack of Intelligence:

9.C.31   A.   I'm sorry you missed (? took) the wrong turning
              When God was giving out the brains.

   Blackheath 1983.

         B.   You were made with two bricks short.
              God must have forgotten your brains.

   Blackheath 1983.

C. No wonder (____)'s that thick;
They forgot to put his brains in.

Blackheath 1983.

D. Roses are red, violets are blue,
When God made brains, where were you?

Earlsfield 1982.

See also **5.21**, **8.D.44**, **9.C.1c**, **9.C.13**, **9.C.21**, and **12.C.1** ("Roses are red" rhymes).

Printed versions Botkin (see below); Hepburn and Roberts, 302–304; Kellett, pp. 110–111; Knapps, pp. 73–74; Mills and Bishop (see below); Opies, *LLS*, Version B, p. 48; other versions pp. 171, 177, 352; Rutherford, p. 71; Turner, p. 74.

Early notings Roses are red,/Violets are blue,/I like pecans,/Nuts to you, and four further versions, Mills and Bishop, 1937, 32. This and four further versions, Botkin, *TAF*, 1944, p. 796.

9.C.32 DUNCE, DUNCE, DOUBLE D

Dunce, dunce, double D,
Cannot learn his A B C.
Put a hat on, then you'll see
What a silly boy is he.

Walworth 1979.

A rhyme which is almost extinct, I am glad to say.

Printed versions Browne, Dunce, dunce stubble-ee, 18; Opies, *LLS*, p. 180 (and see below); Turner, p. 71.

Early noting Dunce, dunce, double D,/Doesn't know his A.B.C. A popular rhyme noted in Joseph Wright's *English Dialect Dictionary* (1898–1905), quoted by the Opies (*LLS*, 1959, p. 180).

Tale tellers

9.C.33 TELL TALE TIT

    A. Tell tale tit,
         Your tongue's all split (shall split),
         And all the doggies in the town
         Shall have a little bit.

Barnsbury, Blackheath, Dulwich, Finsbury, Kentish Town 1983; Kensington 1984.

Printed versions Cansler, 13; Daiken, *OGS*, p. 12; Fowke, pp. 114, 116; Halliwell (see below); Kings (see below); Lang (see below); MacBain (see below); Northall (see below); Opies, *ISE*, p. 58, *LLS*, pp. 189, 190; Rosen and Steele, [p. 18]; Sutton-Smith, p. 93; Turner, p. 77.

Early notings Tell tale, tit!/Your tongue shall be slit,/And all the dogs in the town/Shall have a little bit, Halliwell, *NRE*, 1842, p. 135, 1843, p. 165, *PRNT*, 1849, p. 183. Northall, 1892, p. 314; Lang, 1897, p. 44; Kings 2, 1930, p. 10; MacBain, 1933, p. 309.

    B. Tell tale tit,
         Your mother can't knit.
         Your dad can't walk
         Without a walking stick.

Streatham 1982; Barnsbury 1983.

Printed versions Opies, *LLS*, p. 190; Rutherford, p. 93.

Other "tell-tale" rhymes in print Abrahams, p. 185; Knapps, p. 61; Northall, p. 314; Opies, *LLS*, pp. 189–191; Rodger, pp. 10, 12; Sutton-Smith, p. 97.

Recording MacColl and Behan, *Streets of Song*.

Liars

9.C.34 YOU LIAR, YOU LIAR

A. You liar, you liar,
    Your butty's (bum's) on fire,
    Your nose is as long as a telephone wire.

Battersea, Greenwich, Streatham 1982; Barnsbury, Blackheath, Cubitt Town, Dalston 1983.

B. You liar, you liar,
    Your bum's on fire,
    Your knickers are twisted
    In the telephone wire.

Mile End 1983.

C. Liar, liar, your pants (tongue's) on fire,
    Your ears are stuck up
    With telephone wire.

Kentish Town 1983.

Printed versions Fowke, p. 114; Knapps, p. 60, Opies, *LLS*, p. 48; Solomons, p. 80.

Other "liar" rhymes in print Chambers, 1847, p. 279, 1870, p. 145; Gaskell, c1913, p. 9; Halliwell, *NRE*, 1842, p. 135, 1843, p. 164, *PRNT*, 1849, pp. 13, 182; Montgomeries, *SC*, p. 88; Northall, pp. 337, 549; Opies, *ISE*, p. 59; Solomons, p. 80.

Children who copy

9.C.35 COPY CAT, COPY CAT

    A. Copy cat, copy cat,
          Sitting on a door mat.

Finsbury 1983; Kensington 1984.

    B. Copy cat, copy cat,
          I don't know what you're looking at.

Barnsbury, Cubitt Town, Dalston, <u>Mile End</u>, Shepherds Bush, Stoke Newington, <u>1983</u>.

    C. Copy cat, copy cat,
          Till I kiss your bottom,
          Follow pattern, follow pattern,
          Till I kiss your bottom.

Mile End 1983.

Other copy cat rhymes in print Knapps, p. 60; Opies, *LLS*, p. 182; Sutton-Smith, p. 98; Turner, p. 70.

Cowards (so called)

9.C.36 SCAREDY CAT, SCAREDY CAT

    A. Scaredy cat, scaredy cat,
          Who (What) d'you think you're looking at?

Clapham 1974; Walworth 1979, 1982; Streatham 1982; Barnsbury, Borough, Dalston, Dulwich, Mile End, Stoke Newington 1983.

B. Scaredy cat, scaredy cat,
     What you doing on a door mat?

   Streatham 1982.

The rhyme: "Cowardy, cowardy custard" seems to have become extinct in Inner London. I only came across one recital in twenty years. It is not a loss to be mourned. In my fieldwork I noted only the first line.

Early noting Cowardy, cowardy custard, eat your father's mustard,/ Catch me if you can, Gomme, under "One Catch-all", 1898, p. 25.

Cry babies

9.C.37 CRY, BABY BUNTING

   Cry, Baby Bunting,
   Daddy's gone a-hunting,
   Gone to get a rabbit skin,
   To wrap the Baby Bunting in.

   Streatham 1982; Dulwich 1983.

Cry baby rhymes in print Barltrop and Wolveridge, p. 120; Botkin (see below); Fowke, p. 117; Halliwell (see below); Kellett (see below); Knapps, p. 60; Opies, *ISE*, p. 58, *LLS*, pp. 186–188; Sutton-Smith, p. 93; Withers, *RIMP*, p. 114; Wood (see below).

Early notings Bye, baby bunting,/Daddy's gone a hunting,/To get a little hare's skin,/To wrap a baby bunting in, Halliwell, *NRE*, 1842, p. 102, 1843, pp. 124, 125. Cf. Oh Johnny's a baby/Dipped himself in the gravy/ Combed his hair with the leg of a chair/Oh Johnny's a baby, Kellett, 1920s, p. 123. Cf. Cry-Baby, cry,/Take your little shirt-tail/And wipe your little eye/And go tell your mammy/ To give you a piece of pie, Wood, *AMG*, 1940, p. 28. Botkin, *TAF*, 1944, the ordinary nursery rhyme, p. 786.

Babyishness

9.C.38   Little boys and their silly toys!

   Finsbury 1983.

Said to boys playing with Action Man dolls: figures in the shape and dress of a soldier, popular during the 1980s.

9.C.39 GROW UP, GROW UP

   Grow up, grow up,
   Every time I look at you, I throw up.

   Dulwich 1983.

Printed version   Similar to the Knapps' response to the words "Shut up!": "I don't shut up,/I grow up!/But when I see you,/I throw up!", p. 71.

Weakness

9.C.40   A.   Weakling.
    B.   Cissy.

Teacher's pet

9.C.41 TEACHER'S PET

   A.   Teacher's pet, teacher's pet,
      You're going to get your panties wet.

   Brixton 1982; Kensington 1984.

   B.   You're teacher's pet. She keeps you in a cage at the back of the class.

   Barnsbury 1983.

Bargain breakers

9.C.42 GIVE A THING, TAKE A THING

    A. Give a thing, take a thing,
         Never give it back again.

Mile End 1983.

    B. Give a thing, take a thing,
         Never going to go to God.

Barnsbury 1983.

    C. Swopsie, swopsie,
         Never going to give it you back.

Barnsbury 1983.

    D. Once you give you can't have back,
         Things you give you can't have back.

Kentish Town 1983.

    E. Touch black,
         You can't have it back.

Greenwich 1982.

Printed versions Chambers (see below); Halliwell (see below); Opies, *LLS*, as B, p. 133; Withers, *RIMP*, as E, p. 172.

Early notings Give a thing,/And take a thing,/To weare the divell's gold ring, Cotgrave (1632): *Dictionarie of the French and English Tongues*, quoted in Halliwell, *PRNT*, 1849, pp. 181–182. Gi'e a thing, tak' a thing,/Auld man's deid ring;/Lie butt, lie ben,/Lie amang the deid men, Chambers, 1826, p. 296.

Other bargain breaker rhymes in print Brady, p. 19; Chambers, 1842, p. 59, 1870, pp. 146–147; Halliwell, *PRNT*, pp. 181–182, Montgomeries, *SNR*, p. 60; Northall, pp. 334–335; Opies, *ISE*, pp. 64, 92, *LLS*, pp. 133–134; Turner, p. 72.

9.C.43 You're an Indian giver!

Finsbury 1983; Hampstead 1984.

"If someone gives you something and wants it back, we call them an 'Indian giver'. I don't know why." girl, 11, Finsbury 1983.

Printed versions Knapps, p. 45; Opies, *LLS*, said to be an American custom, p. 134.

Showing off

9.C.44   A.   You think you're fly.

Finsbury 1983.

B.   You think you're cool.

Finsbury 1983.

C.   You're flash.

Universal.

9.C.45 SHOW OFF, SHOW OFF

Show off, show off,
Pick your nose and blow off.

Barnsbury, Kentish Town, Stoke Newington 1983.

Gender

9.C.46 A. Girls are fantastic, boys are elastic.

Dalston 1983.

B. Boys are fantastic, girls are elastic.

Streatham 1982.

C. Eye, eye, ackers,
Boys are crackers.

Mile End 1983.

D. All join in,
The boys are in the dustbin.

Mile End 1983.

Racial epithets

9.C.47 A. "Bubble" (Bubble and squeak): for Greek child.
B. "Turkish delight": for Turkish children and for relevant Cypriots; quite common.
C. "Spanish onion": for Spanish child, Barnsbury 1983, not common.
D. "Black Jack": for a black child, Barnsbury 1983, not common.

Names

9.C.48 GEORGIE PORGIE

A. Georgie Porgie, pudding and pie,
Kissed the girls and made them cry.
When the boys came out to play,
Georgie Porgie ran away.

Mile End 1968; Battersea 1982; Barnsbury, Deptford, Shepherds Bush 1983.

B. Georgie Porgie, pudding and pie,
    Kissed the boys and made them cry.
    When the girls came out to play,
    All the boys ran away.

Dulwich 1983.

C. Georgie Porgie, pudden' and pie,
    Kissed the girls and made them cry.
    When the boys came out to play,
    He kissed them too then ran away.

Finsbury 1983.

D. (_____, _____), custard pie,
    Kissed the girls and made them cry.
    When the boys came out to play
    (_____, _____) ran away.

Stoke Newington 1983.

See also **9.C.10D** above.

This seems to be a multi-purpose rhyming taunt. It is used sometimes for boys called George (Barnsbury 1983). It is used for boys thought to be overweight (Deptford 1983), and also as a universal taunt for any boy who fancies the girls (Stoke Newington 1983). The Finsbury and Dulwich versions suggest a hint of homosexual taunting.

Printed versions cf. Abrahams, Charley, Charley, wheat and rye, p. 24; Briggs, p. 80; Fowke, p. 114; Halliwell (see below); Kings (see below); Knapps, p. 216; Lang (see below); cf. Leach and Fried, Charley, Barley, Pudding and Pie, p. 1017; MacBain (see below); Northall (see below); Opies, *ODNR*, pp. 185–186, *LLS*, pp. 159, 188; Turner, p. 71.

Early notings Rowley Poley, pudding and pie,/Kissed the girls and made them cry;/When the girls begin to cry,/Rowley Poley runs away, Halliwell, *NRE*, 1844, p. 158. Gorgey Porgey, Pudding and Pie,/Kiss'd the girls and made them cry;/When the girls came out to play/Gorgey Porgey ran away, Northall, 1892, p. 303. Lang, 1897, p. 215; Kings 2, 1930, p. 35; MacBain, 1933, p. 16.

Birthdays

9.C.49 HAPPY BIRTHDAY TO YOU

    A. Happy birthday to you,
          Squashed tomatoes and stew,
          You look like a monkey
          And you act like one, too.

Mile End 1968; West Norwood 1973; Battersea, Greenwich 1982; Barnsbury, Blackheath, Borough, Cubitt Town, Dalston, Deptford, Dulwich, Finsbury, Mile End, Shepherds Bush 1983; Kensington 1984.

    B. Happy birthday to you,
          Squashed tomatoes and stew,
          Bread and butter down the gutter,
          Happy birthday to you.

Borough, Kentish Town 1983; Kensington 1984.

    C. Happy birthday to you,
          Squashed tomatoes and stew,
          You look like an elephant
          And you smell like one, too.

West Norwood 1973.

Printed versions Kellett, p. 43; Turner, p. 72.

D. Happy birthday to you,
   Stick your head down the loo,
   If you taste it, don't waste it,
   Happy birthday to you.

Greenwich 1982; Kentish Town 1983.

E. Happy birthday to you,
   The cat done a poo,
   A poo in your shoe,
   Happy birthday to you.

Cubitt Town 1983.

F. Happy birthday to you,
   I went to the zoo,
   I saw a fat monkey,
   And I thought it was you.

Mile End 1968; Brixton 1982; Finsbury, Stoke Newington 1983; Kensington 1984.

See also **8.D.10**.

According to Jean Harrowven (1977, pp. 281–282), the original lyrics of "Happy Birthday to You" were "Good morning to you" and were composed by the Misses Hill in the 1890s as a welcome song for children in their school, later adapted for singing on the children's birthdays. It was first published in 1896 and copyrighted in the form of "Happy Birthday to You" in 1936. It is now one of the songs most frequently sung in the world.

Printed versions of parody Kellett, p. 43; Knapps, p. 223; Rutherford, p. 44; Turner, p. 72.

Boyfriends, girlfriends

9.C.50 WHEN (_____) WAS YOUNGER

> When (girl's name) was younger,
> It was toys, toys, toys,
> Now (_____) is older,
> It's boys, boys, boys.

Blackheath, Finsbury 1983.

Printed versions Kellett, autograph album rhymes, pp. 49, 109; Turner, autograph album rhyme, p. 120.

9.C.51 TULIPS IN THE GARDEN

> Tulips in the garden,
> Tulips in the park,
> All that (_____ _____) wants
> Are two lips in the dark.

Putney 1967.

9.C.52 IF ALL THE BOYS LIVED OVER THE HILLS

> If all the boys lived over the hills (overseas),
> What a good climber (swimmer) (_____) would be.

Earlsfield 1982.

Printed version Turner, autograph album rhyme, p. 114.

9.C.53 THERE'S A BOAT LEAVING FOR CALAIS

There's a boat leaving for Calais today,
Bound from Liverpool bay.
There is (_____) with tears in her eyes,
Out pops (_____) from out of the skies.
"Oh darling, I love you I do,
Darling I'll always be true."
He bent down and kissed her,
And said that he missed her,
"Darling I'll always be true,
To you."

9.C.54 K-I-S-S-I-N-G

BALL BOUNCING RHYME

A. (_____) and (_____) sitting in a tree,
K-I-S-S-I-N-G,
First comes love,
Then comes marriage,
Then comes (_____) with a baby carriage.

Brockley 1967.

B. (_____) and (_____) in a tree,
K-I-S-S-I-N-G,
First comes love,
Then comes marriage,
Now they're snugging in my back garage.

Blackheath, Stoke Newington 1983.

Printed versions Abrahams, p. 99; Botkin (see below); Cosbey, p. 68; Fowke, p. 72; Knapps, p. 217; Mills and Bishop (see below); Ritchie, *GC*, pp. 87–88; Solomons, p. 64; Turner, [John and Mary] up a tree, p. 119.

Early notings First comes love,/Then comes marriage;/Then comes Edith/With a baby carriage, Mills and Bishop, 1937, 33. Botkin, *TAF*, 1944, as Mills and Bishop, p. 800.

9.C.55 MY NAME IS CHINKY CHINA

This rhyme is normally used for ball bouncing.

> My name is Chinky China,
> I live in Chinatown,
> I do my washing every day,
> And it costs me half a crown.
> Ohhh (_____, _____, _____)
> You ought to be ashamed,
> To marry, marry, marry,
> A boy without a name.
>
> Clapham 1984.

Printed versions Abrahams, p. 77; Cumnock Academy, p. 11; Ritchie, *SS*, I live in Chinkie China, skipping, p. 38.

Recording BBC 19926 (78) (1953, Edinburgh).

9.D RESPONSES, RETORTS, AND REPARTEE

The apposite response to a single over-used word, to a breach of good manners, or to a taunt, will probably have the effect of "putting down" the recipient. It often requires quick thinking, but it can become almost an automatic response, in which case it will tend to lose its effect. The irrelevant response has a long history. The Opies (*LLS*, 1959, p. 42) quote Dean Swift giving "Hay is for Horses" in response to "Eh?" (**9.D.3**). Only a few of the responses that I collected were very widespread. Some themes apparently inspire several responses, though no particular one was very widespread. I collected, for example, four different responses to "Shut up!" (**9.D.4**).

A follow-up to a successful attempt to get a child's attention by saying MADE YOU LOOK, MADE YOU STARE (**9.D.23**) in some form is almost universal. The reply to the charge "You're chicken!" in the form of "If I'm a chicken you're a duck,/I lay eggs and you lay muck" (**9.D.6**) was also used in every school I visited. Several schools gave me a version of a response to the query "What's the time?" usually in the form of "Half past nine,/Hang your knickers on the line" (**9.D.29**). Printed versions of this have been collected in New Zealand (Sutton-Smith, 1959, p. 102) and Australia (Turner, 1969, p. 108). The Opies also give examples (*LLS*, 1959, pp. 44–45). At least one of several responses following the breaking of wind by a child is to be found in almost all schools (**9.D.18**). The traditional **9.D.33** STICKS AND STONES WILL BREAK MY BONES, ubiquitous in the English speaking world, perpetuates a lie. Most children experience being at the receiving end of words that give them very much pain and unhappiness and which can lead to disrupted friendships, quarrels and fights.

9.D.1 So?

Sew buttons.

Kentish Town 1983.

9.D.2 What?

Watt died years ago and Pardon took his place.

Cubitt Town 1983.

Printed version Opies, *LLS*, p. 50, other versions pp. 50–51.

9.D.3 Eh?

Horses eat hay.

Cubitt Town 1983.

Printed versions MacBain (see below); Northall (see below); Opies, *LLS*, two examples, one like Northall's below, and "Eh?/B./Cat's in the cupboard/And can't see me", p. 51, and see below; Sutton-Smith, p. 101.

Early notings the Opies quote an example included in a collection by Dean Swift (1738): *Mr. Neverout.* Hey, Madam, did you call me?/*Miss Notable.* Hay; why, Hay is for Horses, *LLS*, 1959, p. 42. "Eh?" "Straw!" "What you can't eat you may gnaw/put in the draw", Northall, 1892, p. 303. Cf. MacBain, 1933, p. 238.

9.D.4 Shut up!

   A. You going to make me?
      I don't make shit (dirt), it comes naturally.

Cubitt Town, Kentish Town, Stoke Newington 1983.

   B. Shut up!
      It's not closing time.

Barnsbury 1983.

   C. Shut up!
      I don't shut up, I grow up.
      That's not the way you're acting.

Kentish Town 1983.

Printed version cf. Knapps, p. 71.

   D. Shut up!
      I won't shut up, I was brought up.

Barnsbury 1983.

Printed version Sutton-Smith, p. 102.

9.D.5 I thought … :

A. You know what thought did?
No.
He fought and lost the battle.

Shepherds Bush 1983.

B. I thought …
You know what thought done?
No.
He thought he farted but he pooped himself.

Cubitt Town 1983.

Printed versions Northall (see below); Shaw, two versions, 1970, p. 120.

Early noting You thought a lig,/Loike Hudson's pig. Northall, 1892, Leicestershire, p. 297.

9.D.6 You're chicken:

If I'm a chicken you're a duck,
I lay eggs and you lay muck.

This was ubiquitous in Inner London (1982–84).

9.D.7 Four eyes:

Four eyes are better than one.
– Not if two of them are glass.

Kensington 1984.

See also **9.C.5**.

9.D.8 ... she did:

Who's she, the cat's mother?

Kentish Town 1983.

Printed versions Barltrop and Wolveridge, p. 123; Brady, p. 22; Daiken, *OGS*, p. 37; Opies, *LLS*, p. 52.

9.D.9 A. **You cow!**
A cow is nature. Nature is beautiful. Thank you for the compliment.

Kentish Town 1983.

Similar printed version Knapps, p. 71.

B. **You pig!**
A pig is an animal. An animal is nature. Nature is wonderful. Thanks for the compliment.

Mile End 1983.

9.D.10 You've got sawdust in your head:

Sawdust makes wood
Wood makes paper
Paper makes books
Books make knowledge
And knowledge makes brains.

Streatham 1982.

9.D.11 (Name is called):

That's my name, don't wear it out.

Blackheath 1983.

Printed version Knapps, p. 69.

9.D.12 (A request is made):

Sorry, it's against my religion.

Blackheath 1983.

9.D.13 Do you want a sweet?

Go upstairs and wash your feet.

Barnsbury 1983.

Printed version cf. Do you like lollies? … Then go upstairs and kiss your dollies, Sutton-Smith, p. 100.

9.D.14 Do you want to photograph me?

No, you might break the camera.

Mile End 1983.

9.D.15 (Someone touches a child's best clothes):

Don't touch the Oxfam.

Barnsbury 1983.

9.D.16 Manners!

Manners, pianners, tables and chairs,
All belong to the woman upstairs.

Mile End 1968; Barnsbury 1983.

To get silence, or following silence:

9.D.17 SILENCE IN THE GALLERY/COURTYARD

    A.   Silence in the gallery,
         Silence in the court,
         The big fat monkey's
         Just about to talk.
         Starting now:

Stoke Newington 1983.

    B.   Silence in the courtyard,
         Silence in the street,
         The world's fattest monkey
         Is just about to speak.
         Talk, monkey, talk.

Cubitt Town, Dulwich 1983; Kensington 1984.

Printed versions cf. Abrahams, skipping, pp. 155–156; Botkin (see below); Cansler, 12; cf. Evans, skipping, p. 16; Fowke, p. 120; MacBain (see below); Mills and Bishop (see below); Northall (see below); Opies, *ISE*, p. 27, *LLS*, pp. 194–195; Ritchie, *GC*, p. 33; Shaw, 1970, p. 104; Solomons, p. 78; Turner, p. 76; Withers, *RIMP*, p. vii.

Early notings Order in the gallery, silence in the pit;/The people in the boxes can't hear a bit, Northall, 1892, p. 312. MacBain, 1933, as Northall, p. 262. Silence in the courtroom!/The judge wants to spit, Mills and Bishop, 1937, 32, and Botkin, *TAF*, 1944, p. 798.

9.D.18 (Following a child breaking wind):

    A.   The one who smelt it, dealt it.

         Streatham 1982; Blackheath, Finsbury 1983.

B. The one who denied it, supplied it.

Streatham 1982; Blackheath 1983.

C. Who let Polly out of prison?

Finsbury 1983.

D. The last one to say "frazzles" did it.

Blackheath 1983.

Printed versions Barltrop and Wolveridge, p. 42; Gregor (see below); Knapps, as A., p. 215; Northall (see below).

Early notings cf. I think, I think,/I fin a stink,/It's comin from y-o-u. On whom "u" fell was beaten with bonnets till he cried "Peas", Gregor, 1891, p. 32. Cf. Hailey bailey, *barley straw*,/Forty pinches in the law,/Pinch me now, pinch me then,/Pinch me when I ___ again. "… an ancient [Warwickshire] nominy … by which the speaker claims partial immunity after the offence of crepitation from the anus", Northall, 1892, p. 338n.

9.D.19 An accusation might be followed by:

You said the rhyme, so you did the crime.

Finsbury 1983.

(A child looks at another one):

9.D.20 A. What are you looking at?
    I don't know, it's not in its cage.

   Kensington 1984.

   B. What are you looking at?
    I don't know, it hasn't got a label.

   Dulwich, Kentish Town, Stoke Newington 1983.

Printed versions Brady, p. 17; Opies, *LLS*, pp. 184–185.

9.D.21 Who do you think you're looking at?

A.B.C.
What's that?
African bum cleaner.

Shepherds Bush.

9.D.22 Response to someone giving a prolonged look:

Stare, stare; over there,
Would you like to have no hair?

Kentish Town 1983.

Early noting cf. Stare stare you big fat bear,/When you grow up you'll have no hair, Kellett, 1920s, p. 49.

Other versions Opies, *LLS*, p. 184; Sutton-Smith, p. 98; Turner, p. 76.

After attracting attention:

9.D.23 MADE YOU LOOK, MADE YOU STARE

   A.   Made you look, made you stare,
        Made you show (lose) your underwear.

   Streatham 1982; Blackheath, Brockley, Dulwich, Finsbury 1983.

   B.   Made you look, made you stare,
        Made your mother (the barber) cut your hair.
        Cut it long, cut it short,
        Cut it with a knife and fork.

   Mile End 1968; Blackheath, Brockley, Cubitt Town, Dalston 1983.

Printed versions Brady, p. 18; Opies, *LLS*, p. 62; Shaw, 1969, p. 67; 1970, p. 115; Turner, pp. 77, 80.

> C. Made you look, made you stare,
> What are you doing up there?

Borough 1983.

Other versions Brady, p. 17; Opies, *LLS*, pp. 62–63; Turner, p. 77; Withers, *RIMP*, p. 168.

9.D.24   Look up, look down,
> Your trousers are falling down.

Blackheath 1983.

Printed version Knapps, p. 98.

9.D.25   Beauty! Beauty!
(child pays attention)
Don't look at me, I said "Beauty" not "Beast".

Borough 1983.

9.D.26   What are you doing?:

I'm feeding the cat, what does it look like?

Kentish Town 1983.

9.D.27   (No reply to a retort):

Sussed out?

Blackheath 1983.

Please, please!

9.D.28 BREAD AND CHEESE

> … Bread and cheese,
> Never remember to wash your knees,
> Goes to bed at half past nine,
> All the nappies on the line.

Mile End 1968.

What time is it?

9.D.29 WHAT'S THE TIME?

> A. What's the time?
>   Half past nine,
>   Hang your knickers on the line.
>   When the copper comes along,
>   Hurry up and put them on.

Mile End 1968; Dulwich, Stoke Newington 1983.

> B. What's the time?
>   Half past nine,
>   Hang your knickers on the line.
>   When it's time to bring them in,
>   Hang them on a safety pin.

Hampstead 1984.

> C. What's the time?
>   Half past nine,
>   Hang your knickers on the line.
>   When the policeman comes along,
>   Take yours off and put his on.

Hampstead 1984.

D. What's the time?
Number nine,
Hang your knickers on the line.
When the teacher rings the bell,
Pull her tits and run like hell.

Shepherds Bush 1983; Kensington 1984.

Printed versions Botkin (see below); Mills and Bishop (see below); Opies, *LLS*, p. 44; Sutton-Smith, p. 102; Turner, p. 108.

Early notings cf. Happy Hooligan, number nine,/Hung his breeches on the line;/When the line began to swing,/Happy Hooligan began to sing, Mills and Bishop, 1937, 39, and Botkin, *TAF*, 1944, p. 801.

9.D.30 A. What's the time?
Time you bought (had) a watch.

Stoke Newington, Shepherds Bush 1983.

Printed version Opies, *LLS*, p. 44.

B. What's the time?
Same as this time yesterday.

Stoke Newington 1983.

The following question and answer routines depend on a shared familiarity with the sequences.

9.D.31 WHAT'S YOUR NAME?

A. What's your name?
Puddeny Tame (Mary Jane)
Where do you live?
Down the lane.
What number?
Cucumber.

What street?
Dogs' meat.

Borough, Shepherds Bush 1983.

Printed versions Abrahams, p. 205; Botkin (see below); Cansler, 12; Fowke, p. 70; Northall (see below); Opies, *ISE*, pp. 28, 50, *LLS*, p. 156; Rosen and Steele, [p. 1]; Shaw, 1969, p. 7, 1970, p. 6; Solomons, p. 82; Turner, p. 78.

Early notings (What's your name?)/Pudding and tame,/If you ask me again,/I'll tell you the same, Northall, 1892, p. 316. What's your name?/Pudden tame;/Ask me again/And I'll tell you the same, Botkin, *TAF*, 1944, p. 778.

Recording Behan and MacColl, *Streets of Song*.

B. What's your name?
    Mary Jane.
    Where d'you live?
    Down the lane.
    What do you keep?
    A little shop.
    What d'you sell?
    Ginger pop.
    How many bottles do you sell a day?
    Twenty four, now go away.

West Norwood 1970, 1973.

Printed version cf. Opies, *LLS*, skipping, p. 157.

Other versions Botkin (see below); Brady, p. 7; Daiken, *OGS*, pp. 10, 37; Northall (see below); Opies, *ISE*, p. 28, *LLS*, pp. 156–158; Rutherford, p. 92.

Early notings "What's your name?" "Mary Jane."/"Where do you live?" "Womber Lane."/"What do you do?" "Keep a school."/"How many scholars?" "Twenty two."/"How many more?" "Twenty four."/"What's your number?" "Cucumber!" Northall, 1892, one of four versions, pp. 316–317. Cf. "Third form" of the rhyme in Botkin, *TAF*, 1944, p. 778.

9.D.32 WHERE DO YOU LIVE?

A. Where do you live?
In a house.
Where's your house?
In a street.
Where's the street?
In a place.
Where's the place?
In London.
Where's London?
In England.
Where's England?
In the world.
Where's the world?
In the solar system.
Where's the solar system?
In the universe.
Where's the universe?
In space.
Where's space?
It's all around.

Dulwich 1983.

See also **9.A.7**.

B. Where do you live?
That's for me to know and you to find out.

Cubitt Town 1983.

A response to a taunt:

9.D.33 STICKS AND STONES WILL BREAK MY BONES

Sticks and stones will break my bones,
But names will never hurt me.
When I'm in my grave and dead,
You'll be sorry.

Dulwich 1983. First half only: Mile End 1968, 1983; West Norwood 1973; Barnsbury, Blackheath, Borough, Deptford, Stoke Newington 1983.

See also **9.B.8**.

Printed versions Brady, p. 17; Cansler, 12; Daiken, *OGS* pp. 11, 13; Fowke, p. 117; Gaskell (see below); Knapps, p. 69; Montgomeries, *SC*, p. 88, *HBSNR*, p. 115; Northall (see below); Opies, *ISE*, p. 19, *LLS*, p. 160; Ritchie, *GC*, p. 20; Rodger, p. 10; Rutherford, p. 27; Sluckin, p. 66; Solomons, p. 75; Sutton-Smith, p. 93; Turner, p. 76; Withers, *RIMP*, p. 128.

Early notings "… the well-known saw, 'Hard words break no bones.'" Northall, 1892, p. 559. Sticks and stones will break my bones/But names won't break my head,/But when I'm dead and in my grave/You'll be sorry for all you've said, Gaskell, c1913, p. 9.

A response to a question:

9.D.34 ASK NO QUESTIONS

Ask no questions, tell no lies,
Shut your mouth, you'll catch no flies.

Mile End 1983.

Printed versions Barltrop and Wolveridge, p. 66; Opies, *LLS* p. 183; Shaw, 1970, p. 46; Withers, *RIMP*, p. 128.

9.E PLAY ON (OTHER) CHILDREN'S NAMES

Play on children's names is universal, though not all schools in this study furnished me with examples. Adults may be traditionally known as "Dusty" Miller or "Nobby" Clark, but these are not usually found among children. Children either choose words that rhyme with a child's first name or maybe something suggested by the surname. The very common "Georgie Porgie", probably inspired by the Prince Regent who became King George IV, can be used as a taunt (**9.C.10E**, 9.C.48), or as a play on a name (**9.C.48D**). The interesting rhymes that the Opies refer to as the "new spelling" (*LLS*, 1959, p. 158), which have a particular rhyming pattern, are only represented by one example which I found in a single school.

9.E.1 New spelling:

> Tracey-bombacey,
> Stick a lacey,
> Fi lacey
> Fi lacey
> Stick a lacey,
> That's how you spell Tracey.
>
> Greenwich 1982.

Printed versions the Opies refer to a particular rhyming pattern for children's names, known as "new spelling" and give a couple of examples (*LLS*, 1959, p. 158). I only came across one example of this: the Greenwich version above. The Opies go on to give the typical "formula" among American children, e.g. "Annie bom bannie, tilly Annie, go sannie, tea legged, tie legged, bow legged Annie", adding that this "follows fairly closely the formulas current in Britain at the end of the nineteenth century." (cf. Mills and Bishop, and Botkin, below). The Knapps give a similar example, saying that children adapt "this long-popular rhyme" according to the name to be inserted, e.g. "Jimmy, bum binny,/Tee aligo, Jimmy,/Tee leg-ged,/Tie leg-ged,/Bow leg-ged, Jimmy!" (p. 64). See also Brady, Doyle, the boil,/The rick stick stoil, etc., p. 17; Fowke, Bill the rill, the rick stick still,/The reebo, the ryebo, the scabby-headed Bill, p. 120.

Early notings George, Porge, the rix-tix Torge,/The rhibo, the rhambo,/The cocktail'd George, Northall, 1892, p. 304. Northall says this rhyme was "at least fifty years old". Annie bolanny,/Tillie annie, go sanny,/Tee-legged, tie-legged,/Bow-legged Annie, Mills and Bishop, 1937, 40. Botkin, *TAF*, 1944, as Mills and Bishop, p. 803.

9.E.2 Rhyming nicknames:

Other schools had rhyming nicknames for individual children:

A. Guesty Besty

Blackheath 1983.

B. Curly Whirly

C. Cooper Whooper

D. Anny Fanny

E. Bobby Snobby

F. Ricky Dicky

G. Gingy Mingy

Borough 1983.

H. Lucy Poocy

Kensington 1984.

Early noting Kings 2, 1930, Charlie-barlie, p. 36.

9.E.3 Other surnames:

A. "Mustard" for Coleman

B. "Black Label" for Carling

C. "Gear stick" for Gear

D. "Picture" for Drew

E. "Long Johns" for Johns

9.E.4 Other first names:

A. "Flash Gordon" for Gordon

B. "Laly Bayleaf" for Leila

C. "Wheezy Lulu" for Louise

D. "Chopsticks" for Charlotte

E. "Noodles" for Naomi

F. "Mental" for Michelle

G. "Nosaj" for Jason (backwards)

Barnsbury, Blackheath, Stoke Newington 1983.

It was not always made clear how the nicknames were arrived at.

9.E.5 Appearance or personality:

A. "Angel" for a girl (She's called Angel because she's always up in the air harping about something.)

B. "Duracell"* for a boy with copper-coloured hair.

* Duracell is the trade name of an electric battery, one end of which is copper-coloured.

For derogatory examples see **9.C** Taunts and Epithets above.

9.E.6 Rhymes:

    A. (_____) did a whiffy
         Trying out the new Jiffy.

Blackheath 1983.

    B. (_____) broke an egg,
         (_____) broke his leg.

Stoke Newington 1983.

    C. There was a girl called (_____),
         She had a fat belly,
         She ate too much jelly
         That was the end of (_____).

Inner London 1982–84.

9.E.7 THERE WAS (_____, _____), PULLING OUT HIS TEETH

There was (_____),(_____), pulling out his teeth,
In the store, in the store,
There was (_____),(_____), pulling out his teeth,
In the quartermaster's stores.

    There was (_____),(_____), playing the piano, etc.

    There was (_____),(_____), doing a wee wee, etc.

    There was (_____),(_____), looking like a bear, etc.

    There was (_____),(_____), singing like a lark, etc.

    There was (_____),(_____), chatting up _____, etc.

Also others.

Borough, Cubitt Town, Kentish Town, Mile End 1983.

Only the Kentish Town version had a refrain:

> My eyes are dim I cannot see,
> I left my specs in the lavatory.

Parody of "The Quartermaster's Store", an army and Scout song originating in the First World War.

Other examples of name play Brady, pp. 16–17; Chambers (see below); Knapps, pp. 66–68; Northall (see below); Opies, *LLS*, pp. 159–160; Sluckin, pp. 65–66, p. 101; Withers, *RIMP*, pp. 114–118.

Early notings "A jocular vituperation of boys named David:" Davie Doytes, the Laird o' Loytes,/ Fell ower the mortar stane;/A' the lave got butter and bread,/But Davie Doytes got nane, Chambers, 1842, p. 59. Mary Pary Pinder/Peeped thro' the winder;/Mother come/And smack'd her bum,/And cut her little finger. (And she jump'd thro' the winder). Warwickshire. Sometimes used as a street shout to any obnoxious Mary, Northall, 1892, p. 310.

SECTION 10

TRADITIONAL BELIEF AND PRACTICE

Introduction

The Opies (*LLS*, 1959, pp. 206–231) describe the superstitions of children as "half-belief". I think this is a very useful term which covers a wide range of practices, rituals, sayings and beliefs. Some of these rightly belong to genuine children's lore which is passed on through the subculture of the playground and the street. Others are taken from the adult world but often become muddled up and changed in the process. Thus the superstition of seven years of bad luck, resulting from the breaking of a mirror, is often applied to other situations where the taboos of received superstition have been breached. The good luck/bad luck represented by a black cat often appears to be an individual matter of "half-belief", complicated no doubt by the different interpretations of encounters with black cats in the folklore of Britain and the USA.

Superstitious rituals and beliefs belonging to the children's own traditions and owing little to adult influence include ritual counting; divining sweethearts, etc.; confirming promises; sealing bargains; protective rituals, including those invoked when children duplicate the same words; making up after quarrels; finding things; various procedures in connection with paving stone cracks and milk teeth; and miscellaneous beliefs associated with the weather, flowers, birds, insects, spiders, vehicles etc.

Adult superstition is not so very different from the half-belief of children. Lucky and unlucky numbers and colours, open umbrellas in the house, four-leaved clovers, broken mirrors, crossed knives and crossed fingers, touching wood, horseshoes, ladders, spilled salt, palm reading, lucky mascots, and astrology – these represent a small part of the folklore of the adult world even in the inner cities. Adult attitudes range from the extreme of intense belief and fear, or the attitude of "there might be something in it", to complete disregard, or the absolute extreme of a kind of recognition of the importance of the superstition by deliberate defiance of it. These attitudes, of course, affect the children's belief and disbelief.

10.A DIVINATIONS

Most of the rhymes or procedures for finding out whether a favoured boy returns one's love, or who one's lover or husband is going to be, are long-established rituals associated with daisy petals (**10.A.3**), cherry or plum stones (**10.A.6**) or skipping routines (**6.A.53–6.A.61**). Procedures involving peeling apples (**10.A.8B**) or putting nuts in the fire (**10.A.10**) are reported by the Opies[1] and the Radfords[2] respectively. Palm reading is of course well established in the adult world, though **10.A.11B**, referring to lines on the palm, seems to be a child's creation, probably limited to one school. Some other procedures I came across do not appear to have been noted by other collectors: for instance twisting off the stalk of an apple and then stabbing the apple with the stalk (**10.A.8A**). I encountered this in two schools. Others involving wood (**10.A.7**), bus tickets (**10.A.9**), fingers, legs and nose (**10.A.12–10.A.14**) I found mainly in one school, which suggests that is where they originated, though it is of course possible they were picked up from friends or relations. The old rhyme usually associated with the counting of magpies (**10.A.4**, here referring to blackbirds) was quite commonly known. The Opies (*LLS*, 1959, pp. 333–334) give examples of how versions of this rhyme are used to tell fortunes from bus tickets, but several versions of the rhyme that I collected mention blackbirds specifically (**10.A.4a**). These birds are more common in Inner London than magpies, but the references may also be to crows (black birds). As might be expected, most of the magpie or blackbird rhymes came from schools in the greener areas where children tended to live in houses with gardens rather than in blocks of council flats.

NOTES

1. Opies (*LLS*, 1959), pp. 274, 338 (apples).
2. Radfords (1961), p. 17 (apples – and cf. apple pips in the fire), p. 252 (nuts).

10.A.1 Buttercups

"If you have a buttercup and you put it under someone's chin, you say, 'Do you like butter?' If the buttercup shines yellow on your chin, which it nearly always does, then you like butter." girl, 11, Finsbury 1983.

Similar: Dalston, Kentish Town, Shepherds Bush 1983; Hampstead 1984.

Printed versions Daiken, *CGTY*, p. 115; Knapps, p. 259; Leach and Fried, p. 176; Ritchie, *GC*, p. 12.

10.A.2 Dandelions

"If you have a dandelion [in seed] you can blow it and count how many are left and that's what the time's meant to be." girl, 10, Hampstead 1984.

Similar: Shepherds Bush 1983.

See also **10.C.48**.

Printed versions Daiken, *CGTY*, p. 115; Leach and Fried, p. 296; cf. Morrison, Dandelion, dandelion, tell me pray,/Must I go home or may I stay? *If all seeds are gone at the third puff, you may stay*, p. 60.

Daisies, etc.

10.A.3 HE/SHE LOVES ME

> A. She loves me,
> She loves me not,
> I love you,
> I love you not.

Borough 1983.

> B. He loves me,
> He loves me not.

Dalston, Finsbury, Kentish Town, Shepherds Bush 1983; Hampstead 1984.

> C. He loves me, yes,
> He loves me, no.

Barnsbury 1983.

> D. Love me, love me not.

> E. "You pick the petals off a daisy. One petal stands for 'loves me' and the next one stands for 'loves me not'. You go on till the last one.
>
> If you pick a rose and love a boy, you can tell if he loves you or not by picking off the rose petals and saying, 'He loves me, he loves me not.' You count the head and stalk as two, and you pull the head away from the stalk and things like that to find the one that it ends up on." girl, 11, EC1 1983.

Blackheath 1983; Kensington 1984.

> F. "If you're walking along the road and you love someone you pick a flower and you go, 'He loves me, yes, he loves me, no.' You might say, 'Shall I go out with him, shall I not?' If you don't really love him you're doing it for a joke. If you land on 'I shall' then you go out with him." girl, 11, Barnsbury 1983.

See also **10.C.49**.

Printed versions Abrahams, skipping, p. 39; Bolton (see below); Daiken, *CGTY*, p. 115; Leach and Fried, p. 275; Morrison, p. 11; Withers, autograph album rhymes, *RIMP*, pp. 158, 159.

Early noting He loves me (or she),/He loves me not./He loves me,/He loves me not./Etc., etc. Used in the US by children counting petals of daisies; to each petal one line is assigned, and the fortune is determined by the last petal, Bolton, 1888, p. 120.

Magpies, blackbirds etc.

10.A.4 ONE FOR SORROW

> A. How many blackbirds in a tree?
> Count them and you will see:
> One for sorrow, two for joy,
> Three for a girl, four for a boy,
> Five for silver, six for gold,
> Seven for a secret that's never been told.

Cubitt Town, <u>Dulwich</u>, Shepherds Bush <u>1983</u>. Brief versions: Earlsfield 1982; Blackheath, Finsbury 1983.

> B. One for the ice cream,
> One for the cat,
> One for the blackbird,
> Sitting on the lap.

Barnsbury, 1983.

See also **10.B.3** (magpies) and **10.C.38** (crows).

Printed versions (similar to A) Boyce and Bartlett (see below); Briggs, p. 121; Chambers (see below); Gullen, p. 22; Halliwell (see below); Leach and Fried, magpies, p. 663; Montgomeries, *SC*, p. 34; Morrison, pp. 52–53; Northall (see below); Opies, *ONRB*, p. 74, *LLS*, magpies, p. 217, bus tickets, pp. 333, 334; Radfords, p. 225, applied to sneezes, p. 314; Shaw, bus tickets, 1970, p. 73; Turner, p. 82; Wood (see below); and many other collections.

Early notings Ane's joy; twa's grief;/Three's a marriage; four's death, Chambers, 1826, p. 285; 1842, p. 35 (magpies). Chambers (1847, p. 122) quotes an interesting rationale for this rhyme, cited in this edition as "One's sorrow—/two's mirth—/Three's a wedding—/four's death;/ Five a blessing—/six hell—//Seven the deil's ain sel'! Sir Humphry Davy, *Salmonia*: 'For anglers in spring it is always unlucky to see single magpies; but two may always be regarded as a favourable omen: and the reason is, that in cold and stormy weather one magpie alone leaves the nest in search of food, the other remaining sitting upon the eggs or the young ones; but when two go out together, it is only when the weather is mild and warm, and favourable for fishing.' " One for anger,/Two for mirth,/ Three for a wedding,/Four for a birth,/Five for rich,/Six for poor,/Seven for a witch,/I can tell you no more, Halliwell, *PRNT*, 1849, p. 168. Northall, 1892, pp. 167–168 (magpies). Wood, *AMG*, 1940, p. 6; Boyce and Bartlett, 1941, as Halliwell, p. 34.

Counting: General use

10.A.5 ONE'S A WISH

    A.   One's a wish,
          Two's a kiss,
          Three's a letter,
          Four's much better.

Putney 1967.

B. First a wish,
Second a kiss,
Third a letter,
Fourth a loving kiss. (Give us a loving kiss)

Printed versions Opies, *LLS*, touching a mail van, p. 218; Turner, magpies, p. 82.

Cherry or plum stones etc.

10.A.6 TINKER, TAILOR, SOLDIER, SAILOR

A. Tinker, tailor, soldier, sailor,
Rich man, poor man, beggar man, thief.
This year, next year, someday, never.

Shepherds Bush 1983, and many others.

B. Tinker, tailor, soldier, sailor,
Doctor, lawyer, Indian chief.
Silk, satin, cotton, rags.
Coach, carriage, wheelbarrow, cart.

Kensington 1984, etc.

See also **6.A.53–6.A.58**.

Printed versions Abrahams, p. 168; Bolton (see below); Brady, skipping rhyme, Apple Jelly, p. 90; Cansler, buttons, fruit stones, 13–14; Cosbey, p. 93; Daiken, *CGTY*, pp. 63, 68, *OGS*, p. 26; Douglas (see below); Fowke, skipping, p. 70; Gomme, (see below); Gullen, A laird, a lord,/A rich man, a thief, button counting, p. 11; Tinker, tailor, part of a fortune-telling fruit stone count, p. 19; Kellett, p. 61 (and see below); Kings (see below); Knapps, pp. 254–255; Montgomeries, *SC*, p. 139; Morrison, buttons, pp. 28–29; Newell (see below); Opies, *ODNR*, pp. 404–405, *LLS*, fruit stones, p. 339; Ritchie, *SS*, p. 96, *GC*, pp. 23, 48, 127, 160; Rutherford, p. 65; Solomons, p. 24; Sutton-Smith, rye grass, or skipping p. 41; Todd, 5; Turner, skipping, p. 34, charm, p. 83; Withers, *RIMP*, p. 177; Worstell, p. 18.

Early notings (While counting waistcoat buttons) My belief,—/A captain, a colonel, a cow-boy, a thief, Halliwell, *PRNT*, 1849, p. 222. Then she shall marry a tinker, tailor … Bolton, 1888, p. 120. "Battledore and Shuttlecock", Gomme, 1898, p. 194. Plucking one by one the petals of the ox-eye daisy (*Leucanthemum vulgare*), children ask: Rich man, poor man, beggar-man, thief,/Doctor, lawyer, Indian chief. … Played also on buttons, Newell, 1903, pp. 105–106. Then she shall marry a tinker, tailor etc., Douglas, 4th line of 1st verse, 1916, p. 67, 1931, p. 37. Whom shall I marry,/Tinker, tailor, soldier, sailor,/Rich man, poor man, beggar man, thief?/When shall I marry/ This year, next year, sometime, never? … Kellett, ?1920s, p. 61. Kings 2, 1930, two skipping rhymes, p. 30.

10.A.7 Wood

A boy or girl says of a member of the opposite sex: "If I break this piece of wood [in one try] I'll go out with her/him."

10.A.8 Apples

A. "If you have an apple you turn the little stalk round on the top and go, 'A, B, C …' When it comes off, that letter will be your boyfriend's first letter. If the stalk comes off at F, his name will be Freddy or something like that.

After you know the first name you find out the surname by stabbing the apple (with the little stalk). When it pierces the skin, the letter you're up to is going to be your boyfriend's surname. If it's B, his name will be Barraclough, or Breen, or Bloggs—Fred Bloggs." girl, 11, Finsbury 1983.

Similar: Kensington, 1984.

Printed version (first part of the above) Knapps, p. 253.

B. "Another way of deciding your boyfriend's name is by peeling an apple continuously, and then throwing the peel over your head. Whatever shape the peel makes is the first letter of your boyfriend's name." girl, 11, Finsbury 1983.

Similar: Shepherds Bush 1983.

Printed versions Knapps, p. 253; Leach and Fried, reference to the apple as a love charm and a means of divination, p. 68; Morrison, p. 24; Northall (see below); Opies, *LLS*, as version B, Halloween practice, pp. 274, 338 (and see below); Radfords, p. 17; Ritchie, *SS*, Halloween practice, p. 118.

Early notings The Opies (*LLS*, 1959, p. 338) trace the first recording of this practice back to Gay, *The Shepherd's Week*, 1714. See also Northall, 1892, p. 114: "St. Simon and Jude (Oct. 28) on you I intrude,/By this paring I hold to discover,/Without any delay to tell me this day,/The first letter of my own true lover."

10.A.9 Bus tickets

"Sometimes when we're on the bus we get numbers on the tickets. If you have a six you say somebody was married six times. Then you say if there's number five, they'll have five children. If there's number three you say three died and there were two left." girl, 11, Kentish Town 1983.

See also **10.C.27D**.

Printed versions Opies, *LLS*, p. 333; other versions pp. 329–334; Shaw, 1970, p. 73.

10.A.10 Nuts

"If you put a nut or pea into the fire and it crackles, it means you're going to have quarrels [when you marry].

If it doesn't crackle it means you're going to have a happy marriage, a good life, and not quarrel a lot." girl, 10, Shepherds Bush 1983.

Printed versions Halliwell (see below); Lang (see below); Morrison, a chestnut, rhyme like Halliwell, below, p. 16; Nicholson (see below); Opies, *LLS*, similar belief, p. 274; Radfords, rhyme as Halliwell, below, and both the Shepherds Bush beliefs, but in respect of apple pips rather than nuts, p. 17; nuts on bars of grate, p. 252.

Early notings If you love me, pop and fly,/If you hate me, lay and die! Halliwell, *PRNT*, 1849, apple pips thrown in the fire, p. 224. Lang, as Halliwell, 1897, p. 145. Similar beliefs, Nicholson, 1897, p. 95.

10.A.11 Palm of the hand

A. "Ask someone if you can look at their hand. The line on the bottom going from the pointing finger down to the wrist is the life line. The line in between both of the deep lines is the love line. If it's short you've only got a little life. If there are two lines there, you get divorced and marry again. The top line is how far you travel, and how long you've travelled." girl, 11, Kensington 1984.

B. "On the bottom of each finger you've got lines. You count the ones going across. If you've got any lines going straight down, in between the two lines there, they'll tell you how many babies you're going to have. If you haven't got any lines you're not going to have any babies." girl, 10, Kensington 1984.

Printed version cf. Opies, *LLS*, p. 340.

10.A.12 Fingers

"You get your hand and you pull one finger and if it goes crack you've got a girlfriend, and so on." boy, 10, Kensington 1984.

Printed versions Leach and Fried, p. 379; Opies, *LLS*, p. 328.

10.A.13 Legs

"When a boy crosses his legs and a girl crosses her legs at the same time it means they are in love." boy, 10, Kensington 1984.

10.A.14 Nose

"You can tell how many people a person loves by putting your hand over their head and holding their nose. Count till they put their hand on their nose." girl, 10, Kensington 1984.

10.B INCANTATIONS AND RITUALS

The oldest incantation in use is probably the one asking the rain to go away (**10.B.1**). The version I learned as a tiny child told the rain to go to Spain, but I did not come across this one in the survey. Most came nearer to the proverb noted by Aubrey in 1686–87: "Raine, raine, goe away,/ Come againe a Saterday (sic)." Saturday was not mentioned by the children I recorded, but in one version it was told not to come back at all, and in another to come back on Mother's washing day. Maybe in these days of tumble-driers the child had misunderstood the version which tells the rain *not* to come back on Mother's washing day. Yet another version tells it not to come on Mother's shopping day (**10.B.1D**).

The ladybird rhyme (**10.B.2**) likewise shows a wide variation from the normal received versions. Only one version I collected came near to the traditional hiding under a stone (**10.B.2A**), but three referred to the later tradition of hiding under a frying pan (**10.B.2B**). The very wide variation of different rhymes showed that this rhyme is not very well known in traditional forms, thus leaving a clear field for improvisation. The versions where "your kids are away" (**10.B.2C**) and where the insect is told: "Your wife's out for the day" (**10.B.2D**) certainly bring the rhyme a little nearer to the children's contemporary experience.

The precaution of touching wood (**10.B.10**), invariably accompanied by the words "touch wood", is general, though the examples (**10.B.10A–F**) show that it has various applications. The incantations accompanying the making of a promise or affirming the truth are rather awesome oaths (**10.B.4**, **10.B.5**). They suggest sticking a needle in the eye or losing an eye, cutting one's throat, or invoking the life or deathbed of mother or grandmother. Such oath swearing is universal among the age group covered by this collection. Of course, with such serious oaths, there has to be a get-out. This usually takes the form of crossing legs or fingers (**10.B.6**). This procedure will nullify the oath, but the child to whom the oath is sworn may be unaware that it has been revoked.

The declaring of "hares" or "white rabbits" (**10.B.7**) at the beginning of the month appears not to have been noticed by collectors until the second half of the twentieth century. The rituals accompanying the sealing of a bargain (**10.B.8**) were certainly not new, though the complicated procedure of **10.B.8**c appears to have been a recent development. The reciting of the word *injection* (**10.B.11**), sometimes followed by a few words and accompanied by a miming of giving an injection, seemed to be fairly new. The circumstances giving rise to it varied among different groups of children. Perhaps a new tradition may emerge eventually. The saying of the word *jinx* (**10.B.12**), as a response by two children who duplicate what is said, was well established. Additional words and the detail of the ritual varied greatly.

10.B.1 RAIN, RAIN, GO AWAY

> A. Rain, rain, go away,
>   Come back (again) another day.

Walworth 1975; Battersea 1982; Brockley, Cubitt Town, Deptford, Kentish Town, Mile End, Shepherds Bush 1983; Kensington 1984.

Printed versions Briggs, p. 10; Chambers (see below): Daiken, *CGTY*, … go to Spain, p. 107; … go away, p. 175; Halliwell (see below); Hubbard, mentioned, p. 262; Kellett (see below); Knapps, like Halliwell's *NRE* version, p. 241; MacBain (see below); cf. Montgomeries, headed "Hailstanes", *SNR*, p. 70, *SC*, p. 101, *HBSNR*, p. 95; Morrison, p. 146; Nicholson (see below); Northall (see below); Opies, *ODNR*, pp. 360–361,

LLS, p. 218 (and see below); Radfords, p. 278; Ritchie, *SS*, p. 62; Rodger, 3 versions, p. 4; Turner, p. 82.

Early notings Halliwell (*PRNT*, 1849, p. 157) quotes James Howell, *Proverbs* (1659), p. 20: Rain, rain, go to Spain;/Fair weather, come again, and Aubrey's MS, *Remaines of Gentilisme and Judaisme*, 1686–87, rpt. Britton, J. (Ed.). (1881). Folklore Society Publications, No. 4. London: Satchell, Peyton, p. 180: Raine, raine, goe away,/Come againe a Saterday (sic). The Opies (*LLS*, 1959, p. 218, fn. 1) quote Howell as follows: "Raine, raine, goe to Spain: faire weather come againe". Rain, rain,/Gang to Spain,/And never come back again, Chambers, 1842, p. 40. Rain, rain, go to Spain;/Come again another day:/When I brew and when I bake,/I'll give you a figgy cake, Halliwell, *PRNT*, 1849, p. 156. Northall, 1892, several versions, one as Aubrey, pp. 331–333. Nicholson, 1897, like Montgomeries, p. 233. Kellett, 1920s, p. 114; MacBain, 1933, p. 13.

> B.   Rain, rain, go away,
>   Little Johnny wants to play.
>   (For the children want to play)

Barnsbury, Borough, Dulwich, Shepherds Bush 1983.

Printed versions Knapps, p. 241; Lang (see below); Halliwell (see below); Withers, *RIMP*, p. 171.

Early notings Rain, rain, go away,/Come again another day;/Little Arthur wants to play, Halliwell, *NRE*, 1843, p. 214. Lang, 1897, as Halliwell, p. 270.

> C.   Rain, rain, go away,
>   Come back on Mother's washing day.

Brixton 1982; Deptford, Dulwich, Shepherds Bush 1983.

> D.   Rain, rain, go away,
>   Don't come back on mum's shopping day.
>   (Don't come back another day)

Barnsbury 1983; Kensington 1984.

10.B.2 LADYBIRD, LADYBIRD

    A.   Ladybird, ladybird, fly away home,
           Your house is on fire and your children alone,
           All except one who lives under a stone,
           Ladybird, ladybird, fly away home.

<u>Walworth 1979</u>; Kensington 1984 (part).

    B.   Fly away ladybird, fly away home,
           Your house is on fire and your children have gone,
           All except for one, her name is Ann,
           She's hiding under a big frying pan.

<u>Battersea</u>, Brixton <u>1982</u>; Kentish Town 1983; Hampstead 1984.
Part: Dulwich, Mile End 1983.

    C.   Ladybird, ladybird, fly away home,
           Your house is on fire and your kids are away,
           So ladybird, ladybird, fly away,
           Come back tomorrow, come back today.

Earlsfield 1982.

    D.   Ladybird, ladybird, fly away,
           Your house is on fire,
           Your wife's out for the day.

Borough 1983.

    E.   Ladybird, ladybird, fly away,
           Your house is on fire and your children gone.
           Ladybird, ladybird, fly away,
           And come back another day.

Brockley 1983.

    F.   Ladybird, ladybird, fly away,
           Your house is on fire and your children crying.

Barnsbury; Shepherds Bush 1983.

G. Ladybird, ladybird, fly away,
    Your house is on fire,
    And your children have run away.

Cubitt Town 1983.

See also **10.C.45**.

Printed versions Abrahams, p. 107; Chambers (see below); Daiken, *CGTY*, pp. 116–119; Eckenstein (see below); Gullen, p. 89; Halliwell (see below); Holbrook, p. 124; Knapps, p. 239; Lang (see below); Leach and Fried, p. 599; MacBain (see below); Mills and Bishop (see below); cf. Montgomeries, *SNR*, p. 30; Morrison, pp. 32, 89; Northall (see below); Opies, *ISE*, p. 52, *ODNR*, pp. 263–264, *LLS*, p. 217; Petershams, p. 10; Radfords, p. 211; Turner, p. 82; Withers, *RIMP*, p. 174; Wood (see below).

Early notings Lady-bird, lady-bird, fly away home;/Your house is afire, your children's at home,/All but one that ligs under a stone;/Ply thee home, lady-bird, ere it be gone, Chambers, 1842, p. 43 (first two lines); 1870, p. 201 (all four lines). Lady-cow, lady-cow, fly thy way home,/Thy house is on fire, thy children all gone,/All but one that ligs under a stone,/Ply thee home, lady-cow, ere it be gone, Halliwell, *NRE*, 1842, p. 158, *PRNT*, 1849, p. 3. Northall, 1892, pp. 119, 326–327. Lang, 1897, similar to B. above, but with "pudding-pan", p. 235. Eckenstein, 1906, pp. 92–100. MacBain, 1933, like B. above, but with "warming pan", p. 207. Ladybug, ladybug, fly away home,/Your house is on fire, your children will burn, Mills and Bishop, 1937, 33. Cf. Doodle-bug, Wood, *AMG*, 1940, p. 80.

10.B.3 MAGPIE, MAGPIE

Magpie, magpie, flutter and flee,
Turn up your tail and show to me.

Dalston 1983.

See also **10.A.4** (blackbirds) and **10.C.38** (crows).

Printed versions Halliwell (see below); Morrison, pp. 32, 94.

Early noting Magpie, magpie, chatter and flee,/Turn up thy tail, and good luck fall me, Halliwell, *PRNT*, 1849, p. 168.

10.B.4 Oaths

    A.   Cross my heart, hope to die,
          Stick a needle in my eye. (your eye)

Battersea, Blackheath, Deptford, Earlsfield, Kentish Town, Mile End, Shepherds Bush 1982; Hampstead, Kensington 1984.

Printed versions Cansler, 10; Knapps, p. 46.

    B.   Cross my heart, hope to die,
          Cut my throat if I tell a lie.

Cubitt Town 1965.

Printed versions Morrison, p. 83; cf. Stork, Cross my heart and hope to die,/If I ever tell a lie, 4; Turner, as Stork, p. 82.

    C.   Cross my heart and hope to die,
          If I don't I'll lose my eye.

Dulwich 1983.

    D.   See this wet, see this dry,
          Stick a needle in my eye.

Dulwich 1983.

    E.   Break my cross and hope to die.

Earlsfield 1982; Borough, Finsbury 1983.

F. If I tell a lie,
    Stick a needle in my eye.

Finsbury 1983.

Other printed versions (oaths) cf. Kellett, See this wet, see this dry,/God cut my throat/If I tell a lie (?early noting), p. 82; Leach and Fried, p. 452; Northall (see below); Opies, *LLS*, pp. 124–127; cf. Radfords, finger wet, finger dry, cut my throat if I tell a lie, p. 319.

Early noting See that wet, see that dry,/ Cross/cut my throat before I die/lie, Northall, 1892, p. 336.

10.B.5 Other solemn "swears"

A. "I swear on my mother's life."

B. "I swear on my mother's deathbed."

C. "I swear on my granny's life."

Almost universal.

D. "I swear on the Holy Bible."

Rare.

Printed versions Cansler, from "a generation ago", 10; Knapps, p. 46.

E. "Cubs'/Brownies' honour."

F. "God's honour."

Printed versions cf. Cansler, 10; Knapps, Scout's honor, p. 46; Opies, *LLS*, God's honour, Scout's honour, p. 122.

G. "Stick a needle in my heart."

H. "Someone puts their fingers in the shape of a cross and says, 'Break my cross' or 'God's honour' or they swear on their mother's life. I think it should be your own life." girl, 11, Finsbury 1983.

Printed version Opies, *LLS*, p. 125.

10.B.6 Nullifying promises

A. "If you lift your feet up or cross your fingers, your promise doesn't count." boy, 10, Dulwich 1983.

B. "If you promise but you're crossing your legs it's not a true promise."

Blackheath 1983.

Printed versions Cansler, 11; Knapps, p. 46; Leach and Fried, crossing fingers while telling a lie, p. 379; Opies, *LLS*, as B., p. 125.

Recording MacColl and Behan, *Streets of Song*.

10.B.7 Hares, rabbits

A. "Before the first day of the month you say, 'Hares' and in the morning you say, 'White rabbits' and that's supposed to give you good luck."

Kensington 1984.

B. "If you say, 'White rabbits' at the beginning of the month you have good luck for the rest of the month."

Hampstead 1984.

Printed versions Opies, *LLS*, pp. 299–300; Radfords, p. 276.

10.B.8 Sealing bargains

A. "Shake hands if you make a bargain or a promise."

Barnsbury, Shepherds Bush 1983.

B. "One person puts out their hand and the other person claps it. Then the other person puts out their hand and you clap it."

Stoke Newington 1983.

C. "Somebody put their two hands in front and the other one smacks them. Then they put their hands on their back and the other smacks them. They turn around and smack the other person's hands. They touch the ground, then they bang each other's heads together and that's it."

Stoke Newington 1983.

Printed versions Opies, *LLS*, pp. 122, 130; Radfords, shaking hands on "a promise or contract", p. 178.

10.B.9 "All the time things go wrong for me, so for good luck I say, 'I hope I get smacked today,' and I don't get smacked."

London, 1980s.

10.B.10 Touching wood

A. "I say, 'I'll go out tomorrow if it doesn't rain—touch wood!' and I touch wood."

Barnsbury 1983.

B. "When you talk about someone who is dead, touch your head and say, 'Touch wood!'"

Mile End 1983.

C. "If you hear of someone's illness you say, 'I hope I don't get it, touch wood!' and you touch wood."

Finsbury 1983.

D. "If you buy a new toy and say it's going to last a long time, you have to touch wood, or knock on wood, to make it come true."

Shepherds Bush 1983.

E. "If you say you want something to happen, you say 'Touch wood!'"

Kensington 1984.

F. "If someone asks you how many fillings you've got (and you haven't got any) you say, 'None, touch wood!' and hope you don't ever get any."

Kensington 1984.

G. "Some say, 'Touch wood!' and they touch their head."

Barnsbury 1983.

Printed versions Leach and Fried, knocking on wood, pp. 585–586; Opies, *LLS*, pp. 9, 212, 218, 227, 230, 310, 311; Radfords, p. 61; *ODEP* (see below).

Early noting Touch wood; it's sure to come good, *ODEP*, 1935, p. 554, earliest citation from 1908.

10.B.11 Injections

A. "If someone touches something horrible, they turn to someone else and say, 'Injection!' and pretend to inject them. They say: 'Eyes, nose, mouth, ears, Injection for a thousand years.'" boy, 10, Mile End 1983.

B. "When someone does something rude (farts) you stab her arm and say, 'Injected.' You can't inject yourself." girl, 11, Finsbury 1983.

C. "If someone touches you and says you'll catch a disease, you say, 'Injection or my life!' so you don't catch it." girl, 11, Finsbury 1983.

10.B.12 Jinx

A. "If two people say the same thing, you say, 'Jinx.' Then the other one can't talk until someone says his name."

Hampstead 1984.

B. "If two people say the same word at the same time they both say, 'Jinx.' The first person to knock on wood, well the other person is not allowed to talk until the person who knocked on wood first, says his name."

Kensington 1984.

C. Jinx, Jinx, Double Jinx,
If you talk you get
Ten pounds of cheese.

"If two people say the same thing at the same time, one of them would say, 'Jinx' etc. If they talk they get ten pound of cheese (two fists) unless the other person says their name."

Kentish Town 1983.

D. "If you say the same word at the same time as another person you get 'Jinx', the first one to say, 'Jinx.' If you break the Jinx without them saying the name three times, you get seven years' bad luck."

Finsbury 1983.

E. "Sometimes me and my brother say the same thing and then we have to say, 'Jinx, touch wood.' If I'm the first one to touch wood, my brother is not allowed to speak until I say he can. If he does I have to hit him. He's not allowed to speak till someone says his name."

Shepherds Bush 1983.

Other notings from Greenwich 1982; Barnsbury, Brockley, Dulwich, Stoke Newington 1983.

Printed versions of various similar rituals Kellett, "When meeting a friend and you both say the same thing together, you must both crook your little fingers together and make a wish. When you have made a wish, you must say – I wish, I wish your wish comes true … the reply will be – I wish, I wish the same to you" (?early noting), p. 84; Opies, *LLS*, pp. 310–312; cf. Radfords, p. 160.

10.C OTHER SUPERSTITIONS (LUCK etc.)

Belief as to what constitutes lucky or unlucky phenomena and how to deal with them is subject to great variation. This sometimes arises from misunderstandings of traditional superstitious beliefs. However, several examples I was given appear to have originated from children's imagination. I found four different beliefs about spiders (**10.C.42**) from the same group of children in a particular school. One of these had absolutely no connection with the other three (**10.C.42D**). I have been unable to trace the connection between spiders and rain in other Inner London schools.

The belief that seven years' bad luck will follow the breaking of a mirror (**10.C.9**) is pretty general, but I was also informed that the same period of misfortune would follow new shoes being put on a table (**10.C.4B**). Other informants said that an umbrella open indoors would have the same dire results (**10.C.14**). One school yielded the belief that catching falling leaves resulted in seven years' good luck (**10.C.47C**) and in another it was said that the number seven was lucky (**10.C.25B**); these reflect the traditional superstitious associations with that number. The wide variety of cat superstitions has already been referred to in the Introduction to Section 10 above, and examples of these are presented below (**10.C.31**).

Turning to superstitions that more specifically belong to the folklore of children, there is the widespread linkage of dandelions with wetting the bed (**10.C.48B**). Many children are not discriminating about the plant world and I have heard the term "wet-the-beds" applied to a number of yellow flowers such as hawkweed, hawksbeard, ragwort and coltsfoot. The longstanding and widespread practice of putting milk teeth (**10.C.1**) under the pillow, or in a specific receptacle, to be changed into money, is of course sustained by many parents. The going rate in the early years of the twentieth century was six (old) pence (a shilling in more affluent circles), but inflation has long since made these amounts out of date. There does not appear to be a consensus as to what little children should expect these days.

The superstition contained in rhyme **10.C.10** SEE A PIN AND PICK IT UP,/And all that day you'll have good luck, is still widespread, but there were more schools where "penny" had superseded "pin" in the rhyme. The very low purchasing value of the penny in the early 1980s led to a general carelessness in retrieving these coins. The decline in hand needlework probably meant that finding a penny was more likely than finding a pin. The widespread avoidance of paving stone lines (**10.C.17, 10.C.18**), which has featured in anthologies of children's poetry,[1] was still flourishing and was not just restricted to very young children. Superstitions attached to ambulances (**10.C.22**), funerals (**10.C.23**), graveyards (**10.C.24**), etc., with the accompanying rituals, seem to have fewer adherents than they did in earlier generations. Children in several schools had no knowledge of these superstitions.

NOTES

1. See, for example, Milne, A. A. (1924). "Lines and Squares". In *When We Were Very Young* (pp. 12–13). London: Methuen.

Human Beings

10.C.1 Teeth

It is a general practice among little children, when their teeth come out, to put them under the pillow for the fairies who will leave money in replacement. Children in six schools told me of the practice.

- A. "When I was little and I pulled my tooth out I said, 'Better go to bed early, wipe my tooth and put it under the pillow and the fairies will come and give me 50p.'"

Barnsbury 1983.

- B. Alternatives were: putting the tooth in an eggshell and the eggshell in a glass (Barnsbury, 1983), and throwing the tooth over the roof of the house (Dulwich, 1983). I was not told what the results of the latter action would be.

Printed versions Opies, *LLS*, sprinkling with salt, burning, throwing, leaving out for fairies, pp. 304–305; cf. Radfords, beliefs in A. and B. above not recorded; milk teeth had to be destroyed by fire or buried in a mousehole, pp. 337–338.

10.C.2 Fingers

- A. "If you're scared, cross your fingers!"
- B. "If you want someone to win you cross your fingers, but if you do so twice they won't win."

Blackheath 1983.

Printed versions Opies, *LLS*, pp. 122–125 passim, 142–153 passim, 206, 208, 211–217 passim, 231; Radfords, p. 160.

10.C.3 Legs

"Some people say if you sit on a chair and you're swinging your legs, it means your mother will die."

Shepherds Bush 1983.

Human Life

10.C.4 Shoes

A. Any shoes on a table mean bad luck.

Barnsbury 1983.

B. New shoes on a table mean bad luck.

Brockley, Dulwich 1983.

According to the Dulwich child, it was followed by seven years' bad luck.

See also **10.C.14** and **10.C.16**.

Printed version Radfords, p. 305.

10.C.5 Food

A. "If you've got seven pieces in your satsuma you can give a wish on each one."

Hampstead 1984.

B. "Don't eat the last slice of cake. Offer it to an unmarried lady with 'another thousand a year.' "

Blackheath 1983.

Printed version Radfords, similar to Version B, associated with bread, p. 67.

10.C.6 Salt

A. "If you spill salt on the table, throw a bit over your shoulder and the bad luck goes away."

Dalston 1983.

B. "If you drop some salt and then pick it up and throw it over your right shoulder, you get good luck."

Shepherds Bush 1983.

C. In Blackheath (1983) I was informed that it had to be your left shoulder.

See also **10.C.9B** and **10.C.29A**.

Printed versions Knapps, p. 239; Radfords, p. 298.

10.C.7 Knives

Crossed knives are unlucky; they used to mean a sword fight.

Dalston 1983; Hampstead 1984.

Printed versions Leach and Fried, p. 584; Opies, *LLS*, p. 329; Radfords, p. 210.

10.C.8 Broken glass and plates

A. Good luck if you find a piece of broken glass.

B. If a plate is broken accidentally it is good luck.

Stoke Newington 1983.

10.C.9 Mirrors

A. Seven years' bad luck follows the breaking of a mirror.

Battersea 1982; Barnsbury, Deptford, Shepherds Bush 1983.

B. Averted by the throwing of salt over the shoulder.

Stoke Newington 1983; Kensington 1984.

See also **10.C.6** and **10.C.29A**.

Printed versions Opies, *LLS*, p. 208; Nicholson (see below); Radfords, p. 232.

Early noting "To break a looking-glass, it is said, means 'Ill-luck.'" Nicholson, 1897, p. 85.

Pins and coins

10.C.10 SEE A PIN AND PICK IT UP

A. See a pin and pick it up,
And all that day you'll have good luck.

Battersea, Streatham 1982; Borough, Mile End 1983.

Printed versions Botkin (see below); Brady, p. 23; Halliwell (see below); Kellett (?early noting), p. 83; Morrison, p. 55; Nicholson (see below); Northall (see below); Opies, *LLS*, p. 224; Radfords, p. 266; Ritchie, *SS*, p. 64; Turner, p. 83; Withers, *RIMP*, p. 168.

Early notings See a pin and pick it up,/All the day you'll have good luck;/See a pin and let it lay,/Bad luck you'll have all the day! Halliwell, *NRE*, 1842, p. 98. See a pin, and let it stay (lie)/You'll want a pin another day (before you die);/See a pin, and pick it up/All the day you'll have good luck, Northall, 1892, p. 174. See a pin and let it stay/lie,/You'll want a pin another day/before you die./See a pin and pick it up,/All the day you'll have gook (sic) luck, Lang, 1897, p. 78. Nicholson, 1897, pp. 86–87; Botkin, *TAF*, 1944, p. 790.

> B. Find a penny, pick it up,
>   Then all day you'll have good luck.
>   (All the week you'll have good luck).

Barnsbury, Blackheath, Borough, Cubitt Town, Dalston, Dulwich, Finsbury, Kentish Town, Stoke Newington 1983; Kensington 1984.

10.C.11   A. For good luck, find a penny, spit on it and throw it away.

Dulwich 1983.

> B. "If you find a penny, and drop it again, you sometimes find a pound note."

Shepherds Bush 1983.

> C. "Good luck to find a 5p. piece."

Hampstead 1984.

Printed versions Kellett, spit on money found before pocketing it (?early noting), p. 83; Knapps, p. 238; Opies, *LLS*, some similar beliefs, pp. 223–224.

10.C.12   Staircases

"Don't walk downstairs if someone else is walking up. Never cross on the stairs, it's unlucky."

Dalston 1983; Hampstead, Kensington 1984.

Printed versions Nicholson (see below); Radfords, p. 321.

Early noting It is not considered lucky to meet and pass anyone on the stairs, Nicholson, 1897, p. 86.

10.C.13 Blinds

Unlucky to have blinds down during the day.

Borough 1983.

10.C.14 Umbrellas

Many children told me it is unlucky to have an umbrella open indoors. Those interviewed in Kentish Town (1983) told me it meant seven years' bad luck, but in Deptford (1983) this spell of misfortune would follow having an umbrella up when it was not raining, I was told.

See also **10.C.4B** and **10.C.16B**.

Printed versions Knapps, p. 239; Radfords, p. 345.

10.C.15 Coal

Lucky to find a piece of coal.

Blackheath 1983.

Printed versions Opies, *LLS*, p. 223; Radfords, pp. 107–108.

10.C.16 Ladders

> A. It seems to be universally believed that walking under ladders is very unlucky. It results in seven years' bad luck according to informants in Cubitt Town (1983) and twelve years'(!) bad luck the other side of the river in Deptford (1983).

Some want to be on the safe side:

> B. "I've put an umbrella up (indoors) and been under a ladder. Although I said I don't believe in the stuff, I still kind of think, 'Oh dear, I've already done it now, what's going to happen to me?'"

Finsbury 1983.

See also **10.C.4B** and **10.C.14**.

Printed versions Kellett, if walking under a ladder, spit three times to avert bad luck (?early noting), p. 84; Leach and Fried, p. 598; Opies, *LLS*, p. 216; Radfords, p. 211.

Paving stones

10.C.17 IF YOU STEP ON A CRACK

> A. If you step on a crack,
> You're going to break your (mother's) back.

Brockley, Finsbury 1983.

> B. If you tread on a nick,
> You'll marry a pick, (sic)
> And a beetle will come to your wedding.

Kentish Town 1983.

Printed version Kellett, If you tread on a nick/You marry a brick, which may be followed by: And a beetle shall come/To your wedding, p. 82.

> C. If you step on a line
> You are a swine.

Dulwich 1983.

Printed versions Knapps, like Version A, p. 237; Morrison, A, p. 61; Opies, *LLS*, one like B, cf. one like C, pp. 221–222; cf. Ritchie, *SS*, p. 70 (C) and one like A; Turner, A, p. 83; Withers, *RIMP*, A, p. 171.

10.C.18 A. "If you walk on a line, some people say your mother's blind."

Shepherds Bush 1983.

> B. "When I was little I would never walk on the lines. I thought a bear would come out and get me from behind the corner."

Cubitt Town 1983.

Similar ideas from: Battersea 1982; Dulwich, Kentish Town, Shepherds Bush 1983; Hampstead 1984.

Crocodile replacing bear: Hampstead 1984.

> C. "If you don't step on the cracks on the pavement all the way home you won't get bad luck, or you're going to meet a boy or girl, or something like that."

Finsbury 1983.

> D. "Pavements ... have a kind of hole. You should only tread on those. If you tread on the whole pavement itself, bears go after you."

Hampstead 1984.

E. Treading on lines unlucky.

Barnsbury 1983; Kensington 1984.

See also the chasing games **3.A.2** HE ON LINES and **3.A.3** ON IT ON THE LINE, and the threatening **9.B.25**, in each of which there is the implication that treading on lines has unfortunate consequences.

Printed versions cf. Opies, *LLS*, pp. 220–222; Ritchie, *SS*, If you stand on a line/You'll break your spine, and two other versions, p. 71.

10.C.19 Taxi

"If you see a taxi, particularly a red taxi, say, 'No returns.' "

Kensington 1984.

10.C.20 Truck

"When three men are in a truck it's unlucky."

Hampstead 1984.

10.C.21 Telecom van

"If you see a British Telecom van, shut your eyes and make a wish."

Kensington 1984.

10.C.22 Ambulance

"If you see an ambulance, cross your heart if it's not for one of your relations."

Borough 1983.

See also **10.C.23** and **10.C.24**.

Printed versions cf. Kellett, on seeing an ambulance, child holds coat lapel, until he or she sees a dog, p. 83; Opies, *LLS*, p. 211; Whelan (see below).

Early noting "If we saw a fever ambulance we used to have to say: Touch your collar/Never catch the fever." Whelan, 1920s, 106.

10.C.23 Funeral

    A. "If you see a funeral hearse, hold your collar till you see a four-legged animal."

Brockley 1983.

See also **10.C.22** and **10.C.24**.

    B. "If you see a funeral, bless yourself or cross your heart."

Borough 1983.

Printed version Opies, *LLS*, p. 215.

10.C.24 Graveyard or cemetery

    A. "Hold on to your collar till you see a four-legged animal or cross your heart."

Borough 1983.

    B. "If you pass a graveyard you have to put your thumb in your mouth till you see a four-legged animal."

Brockley 1983.

See also **10.C.22** and **10.C.23**.

10.C.25   Football

A.   "If you're a footballer always go fifth in the line."

Barnsbury 1983.

B.   "Neil Brady used to play for Arsenal, the best team. He wore number seven. Now whenever I play football I wear number seven on my shirt and I feel lucky."

Barnsbury 1983.

C.   "If you want good luck at football, kiss the ball."

Stoke Newington 1983.

10.C.26   Friday the 13th

A.   "Friday the 13th is a scary night."
B.   "You're unlucky if your birthday is on Friday the 13th."

Kentish Town 1983.

Printed version   Radfords, p. 250.

10.C.27   Numbers

A.   Thirteen is an unlucky number.

Barnsbury, Dalston, Deptford, Kentish Town, Shepherds Bush 1983.

B.   Seven is a lucky number.

Dalston, Kentish Town 1983.

C.   "Your birthday date is your lucky number."

D. "On tube tickets if you get two numbers and they add up to twenty-one it means you'll have good luck."

Finsbury 1984.

See also **10.A.9**.

E. "When I do something on the first or second time it doesn't work out but on the third time it always does, third time lucky."

Stoke Newington 1983.

Printed versions Leach and Fried, A and B, p. 651; Opies, *LLS*, A, p. 226, B, p. 330; D, p. 330; Radfords, pp. 249–250.

10.C.28   Colour

"My best colour's green, 'cause I love the Queen."

Barnsbury 1983.

10.C.29   Fear

A. "If you're frightened of Dracula, sprinkle yourself with salt or put garlic near you."

Kensington 1984.

See also **10.C.6** and **10.C.9B**.

B. "My mum used to say, 'Don't chalk outside the front door or this big creature will come down from a helicopter and take you away.'"

Barnsbury 1983.

C. "I'm scared when I go to bed because I think there's a dead man rotting away under my bed and he's reaching up for me. When I go to bed I jump right up to the top of my bunk bed from the floor."

Hampstead 1984.

D. "My mum used to say, 'If you don't go to bed the bogeyman's going to come and get you.'"

Barnsbury 1983.

E. "Seven-year-olds say, 'Don't go in the toilets, there's a bogeyman there. He might get you.'"

Barnsbury 1983.

Printed versions Knapps, pp. 249–250; Leach and Fried, p. 153.

10.C.30 Wishes

A. "You have to close your eyes and put your hands together as if you're praying. Someone asks you to fold two fingers down and they say, 'Wish.' Then they say, 'To make that one come true you put your next two fingers down.' Then you make another wish and then, to make that one come true you fold the next two fingers down and make a wish. To make that wish come true you fold the other two fingers down and make a wish.

To make all these wishes come true you pick a number from one to twenty, say four. If somebody swears, you've got to lick your finger and put it in the palm of your hand and then toss it over your shoulder. If you do that for four days you'll get all those wishes." girl, 11, Finsbury 1983.

B. "I do it the same way, but you lick two fingers and you stamp your hand, you just hit it. The number you choose between one and twenty you do it that number of days." girl, 11, Finsbury 1983.

The Natural World and the Cosmos

Animals

10.C.31   Cats

Beliefs were very divided on the question of black cats. While children of Cubitt Town, EC1 and Kensington told me that just to see a black cat was lucky, in Barnsbury I was told the opposite. In Blackheath I had both opinions expressed at the same time, though the consensus was that it was lucky, and was especially lucky if one owned a black cat. In Stoke Newington I was told that it was lucky to trip over a black cat and in Shepherd's Bush it was lucky to see one cross the pavement. In Blackheath I was informed that if a black cat went past, you would have seven years' good luck. In Hampstead I was told it was good luck for a black cat to cross your path. On the other hand I learned in Dalston that on no account should a black cat be allowed in your garden. Children of Barnsbury, Dalston, Battersea, Kensington, Blackheath and EC1 adhered to the popularly-held view that it is unlucky to have a black cat cross your path, while a boy in the Borough told me it was unlucky to walk in the cat's path. I was told in Blackheath that there was a way of avoiding the bad luck. If you wore a hat you turned it round three times, you spat and said, "Toy, toy, toy," then the bad luck was removed. Also in Blackheath I was told that tri-coloured cats were an insurance against fires. (enquiries 1982–84).

Printed versions Kellett, "we all know that to see a black cat is very lucky" (?early noting), p. 38; Knapps, bad luck to have one cross your path, p. 239; Opies, *LLS*, pp. 213–214; Radfords, pp. 85–88.

10.C.32   Dogs

> "If you've got a dog and you've done something wrong you say, 'Touch my dog so that I can go out.'"

> (i.e. the child hopes that the "bad luck" of being told to stay indoors as a punishment may be counteracted by touching the dog).

Barnsbury 1983.

Printed version cf. Opies, *LLS*, p. 208.

10.C.33 Dogs' dung

A. "If you tread in dogs' shit, you christen your shoe."
Kentish Town 1983.

B. Good luck if you tread in dogs' muck.
Borough 1983.

Printed versions Kellett (?early noting), p. 83; Opies, *LLS*, p. 215.

10.C.34 Horse manure

Unlucky to go near horse manure.
Borough 1983.

10.C.35 Horseshoes

"If you have a horseshoe it's good luck, but you mustn't hang it upside down."
Hampstead, Kensington 1984.

Printed versions Nicholson (see below); Radfords, pp. 198–199.

Early noting "A horse-shoe, it is said, means 'luck.'" Nicholson, 1897, p. 65.

10.C.36 Cows

"It's unlucky when cows are lying down, because it's going to rain."

Hampstead, 1984.

Printed version Radfords, pp. 89–90.

10.C.37 Dead frog

Lucky to pick up a dead frog.
Borough 1983.

Birds

10.C.38 Crows

"If you see six crows together, that's supposed to be bad luck."
Stoke Newington 1983.

See also **10.A.4** (blackbirds/ ?black birds), and **10.B.3** (magpies).

Printed versions Halliwell (see below); Opies, *LLS, one* is unlucky, p. 214; Radfords, *four* are unlucky, p. 120.

Early noting One's unlucky,/Two's lucky;/Three is health,/Four is wealth;/Five is sickness,/And six is death! Halliwell, *PRNT*, 1849, from Essex, p. 171.

10.C.39 Feathers

Lucky to find a feather.
Blackheath 1983.

Printed version Opies, *LLS*, p. 224.

10.C.40   Bird droppings

"It's lucky if you're walking along and a bird drops something on your head."

Hampstead 1984.

Printed versions Kellett (?early noting), p. 83; Opies, *LLS*, p. 213.

10.C.41   Dead bird

"If you see a dead bird, cross your heart!"

Borough 1983.

Printed version Opies, *LLS*, p. 225.

Spiders and Insects

10.C.42   A.   "A spider in your house means money soon."
Earlsfield 1982.

B.   "A spider on your clothes means you'll get new ones."
Earlsfield 1982.

C.   "If a spider drops on your head you'll soon get a present."
Earlsfield 1982.

D.   "If you tread on a spider it will rain soon."
Earlsfield 1982.

Printed versions Knapps, D, p. 241; Leach and Fried, several similar beliefs, p. 1074; Opies, *LLS*, a number of similar beliefs, pp. 219–220; Radfords, D, p. 317; A and B, p. 318; Ritchie, *GC*, D, p. 12.

10.C.43 IF YOU WANT TO LIVE AND THRIVE

If you want to live and thrive,
Let a spider run alive.

Earlsfield 1982; Barnsbury 1983.

Printed versions Kellett (?early noting), p. 38; Morrison, p. 126; Northall (see below); Opies, *LLS*, p. 220; Radfords, p. 317.

Early noting If you wish to live and thrive,/Let a spider run alive. Northall, 1892, p. 281.

10.C.44 Cobwebs

"To cure asthma you get cobwebs, roll them into a ball in the palm of your hand and swallow them."

Earlsfield 1982.

Printed versions Leach and Fried, cobweb *and* spider swallowed, remedy for unspecified complaint, p. 1074; Radfords, p. 108.

10.C.45 Ladybirds

Though hardly a superstition, there is a common belief that the number of dots on a ladybird's back indicates its age in years!

See also **10.B.2**.

Trees and plants

10.C.46   Christmas tree

> "Once we burnt a Christmas tree, and the day after, my grandfather died. I think this is because of bad luck!"

Finsbury 1983.

Printed version cf. Radfords, holly, ivy, bay, rosemary, p. 99.

10.C.47   Leaves

A. "If you catch a leaf from the tree, you'll have good luck for the rest of the day."

B. "Catch a leaf, put it in your pocket and save it for a rainy day."

Blackheath 1983.

C. "If you catch leaves you'll get seven years' good luck."

Finsbury 1983.

Printed versions Opies, *LLS*, p. 217; Radfords, p. 216.

10.C.48   Dandelions

A. "You get a dandelion head [in seed] and hold it in your hand and make a wish. If you blow it off to some land it makes your wish come true. If you make your wish and blow it away and then someone touches it, then your wish doesn't come true."

Shepherds Bush 1983. Similar: Hampstead 1984.

Printed version Knapps, p. 240.

B. "If you pick a dandelion and the juice goes on you it means you're going to wet yourself in the night."

Finsbury 1983.

C. "If you pick a dandelion they say you wet the bed."

Borough 1983. Similarly: Dalston, Kentish Town, Shepherds Bush, 1983.

See also **10.A.2**.

Printed version Leach and Fried, p. 296.

10.C.49 Daisies

Good luck to make a daisy chain.

Borough 1983.

See also **10.A.3**.

10.C.50 Four-leaf clover

Good luck to find a four-leaf clover.

Borough 1983.

Printed versions Knapps, p. 239; Morrison, like Northall, below, p. 25; p. 51; Northall (see below); Opies, *LLS*, pp. 222, 223; Radfords, p. 107.

Early noting Find even-ash or four-leaved clover,/An' you'll see your true love before the day's over, Northall, 1892, p. 108.

Stars

10.C.51   Shooting star

"If you see a shooting star you get good luck."

Kentish Town 1983.

Printed versions Knapps, p. 240; Radfords, p. 322.

10.D SAYINGS AND RHYMES

These are an important part of English language and culture. Traditional proverbs and sayings are a vital aspect of the linguistic heritage, but they were not widely known by children in Inner London schools during the survey. My experiences both as a class teacher and a researcher support this contention. A few sayings are in general use: FINDERS, KEEPERS (**10.D.1**), used to justify the right to possession of anything found where the owner is not known, is universal. The only other widespread examples are the rhymes for asking pardon following a belch (**10.D.4**), and for making up after a quarrel (**10.D.5**).

10.D.1 FINDERS, KEEPERS

    A.   Finders, keepers,
          Losers, weepers.

Clapham 1974; Battersea, Earlsfield, Streatham 1982; Borough, Cubitt Town, Dalston, Dulwich, Finsbury 1983; Hampstead 1984.

    B.   Finders, keepers,
          Dustmen, sweepers.

Dalston 1983.

    C.   Old Mrs. Peepses
          Loses, weepses.

Mile End 1968.

Printed versions Halliwell (see below); Northall (see below); *ODEP* (see below); Opies, *LLS*, pp. 136–137; Stork, 4; Todd, 4; Withers, *RIMP*, p. 174.

Early notings Losers seekers, finders keepers, *ODEP*, earliest citation from 1824. No halfers,/ Findee, keepee;/Lossee, seekee, Halliwell, *PRNT*, 1849, p. 257. Northall, 1892, several, including one like Halliwell's, pp. 335–336.

10.D.2 IF YOU SMASH CHINA

If you smash china
You're in for a shiner. ("shiner" is slang for black eye).

Kentish Town 1983.

10.D.3 SEE NO EVIL

See no evil, hear no evil.

Cubitt Town 1983.

10.D.4 PARDON ME FOR BEING RUDE

These follow a belch

A. Pardon me for being rude,
    It was not me, it was my food.
    Instead of staying down below
    It just popped up to say hallo.

Dalston 1983.

B. Pardon me for being rude,
    It was not me, it was my food.

It just popped up to say hallo,
And now it's gone back down below.

Greenwich 1982; Barnsbury, Blackheath, Cubitt Town, Dalston, Finsbury, Shepherds Bush 1983.

These additions follow the above in these versions:

C. If I had not let it pass
It would come out of my arse.

Brixton 1982.

D. It went down my throat and round my heart
Out of my arse and made me fart.

Mile End 1983.

E. If it had gone past my heart
It would have turned into a fart.

Kensington 1984.

Printed version Rutherford, p. 46.

10.D.5 MAKE UP, MAKE UP

These follow the ending of a quarrel

A. Make up, make up,
Never do it again,
Otherwise you'll get the cane.
Punch and Judy got the cane,
Make up, make up,
Never do it again.

West Norwood 1973; Earlsfield 1982; Barnsbury, Brockley, Deptford, Dulwich, Mile End, Stoke Newington 1983; Hampstead 1984.

B. Make friends, make friends,
    Never, never break friends,
    If you do you'll catch the 'flu,
    And that will be the end of you.

Finsbury 1983; Kensington 1984 (accompanied by shaking the little finger).

C. Make up, make up,
    Never, never break up,
    If we do,
    We'll stick our head in glue.

"You shake a little finger and say, '1, 2, 3, sorry!'"

Hampstead 1984.

D. Make it up, make it up,
    Before you wake the baby up.

Cubitt Town 1983.

E. Make it up, make it up,
    Hit the old man's coconut. (Chinese coconut)

Cubitt Town, Kentish Town 1983.

"Some people get their two little fingers and put 'em together and say, 'Make up, make up, never do it again' or they shake hands."

Printed versions Opies, *LLS*, elements of A and B, pp. 324–325; Whelan (see below).

Early noting Make it up, make it up, never do it again. If you do you'll get the cane. Whelan, 1920s, 111.

10.D.6 This follows an answer to a question

   A.   A silly question gets a silly answer.
   B.   Ask a silly question and get a silly answer.

Blackheath, Stoke Newington 1983.

Printed version Opies, *LLS*, p. 43.

10.D.7 This might be said during a quarrel or argument

I believe in Jesus, but not in you.

Deptford 1983.

10.D.8

A penny for your thoughts.

Dulwich 1983.

10.E   SEASONAL LORE

This section indicates an apparent decline in the seasonal traditions of childhood. Only in the celebrations themselves does there appear to be any development, as for example in the importation of the American custom of going round from house to house giving the choice of "trick or treat" at Halloween (**10.E.5**). The University Boat Race, which once led to the division of children into partisans for Oxford or Cambridge, passes now without notice. Neither university meant anything to the children, but the race was preceded by the wearing of light or dark blue favours and, among the boys at any rate, by partisan games and fights which sometimes went beyond the "pretend" stage. No. **10.E.3** I CALL (_____) IN, collected in 1966 as a skipping rhyme, contained the lines "Oxford the winner,/Cambridge the sinner" and must have marked the dying gasp of this rhyme among children in Inner London.

The celebration of November 5th has been in decline in its traditional form and there are mixed feelings about this. Fireworks in the hands of children have led to serious injuries and have frightened many timid people. The collections of "pennies for the guy" used to accompany the display of an effigy which often involved a certain amount of ingenuity, or children dressed and made up to be guys. Nowadays this has been replaced by a mere pair of trousers and shirt, stuffed with paper and topped by a crude mask. Sometimes the request for money is unaccompanied by any effigy. The little "grottoes" which once marked the Feast of St. James the Great (July 25th), consisting of an attractive arrangement of shells, pictures, ornaments, flowers etc., had mostly disappeared by the end of the 1940s. They also were accompanied by a request for "a penny for the grotter" and the effort nearly always deserved a reward. The collection of money at Christmas time by carol singing usually means a few lines of "Good King Wenceslas" and a giggle, before the doorbell is rung and the request made. The CHRISTMAS IS COMING rhyme (**10.E.7**) is subject to widely differing expectations of cash, but where it is used it is a mere begging device.

February 14th, St. Valentine's Day

10.E.1 CAROLINE, CAROLINE

> Caroline, Caroline,
> Will you be my Valentine?
>
> Shepherds Bush 1983.

10.E.2 IF YOU WILL BOWL

> If you will bowl and never bat,
> Share your sweets and hold my wrap,
> ....
> And you will be my Valentine.
>
> Shepherds Bush 1983.

See also "Roses are red, violets are blue" rhymes in **12.C.1**.

University Boat Race

The partisanship and the accompanying rhymes associated with the Boat Race seemed to have vanished in the London schools by the time of the survey. However, in 1966 I collected this rhyme:

10.E.3   I CALL (_____) IN

SKIPPING RHYME

I call (_____) in,
One, two, three,
Up and down the riverside,
You shall see,
Oxford and Cambridge,
Having a cup of tea,
Oxford the winner,
Cambridge the sinner,
O-U-T spells out.

Mile End 1966.

Printed version Opies, *LLS*, p. 350.

Shrove Tuesday, April Fools' Day, Good Friday, Easter, May Day

I did not come across any rhymes or routines associated with these occasions in Inner London. The custom of playing tricks on each other and on adults is still carried out on April 1st, and in some homes the searching for eggs left by Easter bunnies still continues, however.

End of Term

See **8.A.1** and **8.A.2**.

October 31st (Halloween)

Here are some customs and superstitions associated with Halloween, all from one school in Shepherds Bush (1983):

10.E.4   A.   "When you look in a mirror while you comb your hair and eat an apple, you can see your future husband or boyfriend's face in the mirror."

B.   "If you drink cider you won't be frightened of witches."

C.   "Beautiful ladies who are scared of witches will get some salt, throw it in a keyhole and frighten off the witches."

D.   "You make a hole in the bottom of the shell of a boiled egg. If you don't the witches may sink the sailors in their ships."

E.   "You put a candle inside a pumpkin. It scares off the witches because of the face cut in it."

Printed versions Nicholson (see below); Radfords, A, p. 233; D, p. 150; salt as a charm against witches (cf. C), p. 298.

Early noting turnip lanterns, Nicholson, 1897, p. 91.

"Trick or treat"

10.E.5   A.   "If they don't give us a treat we play a trick on them like painting their windows white, or something like that." girl, Finsbury 1983.

B. "On Halloween you go round people's houses and knock on the door and say, 'Trick or treat?' If they say 'Trick' then you throw a tomato or something in their face. If they say 'Treat', they give you some money or sweets, or anything they like." boy, Dulwich 1983.

C. "On Halloween you go out trick or treating. You knock on a door and say, 'Trick or treat?' If they don't give you something you do something wrong to them, like you throw a banger. It might smash their window or something and then they have to give you money." girl, Shepherds Bush 1983.

This custom seems to be an importation from the USA and apparently had not yet penetrated the blocks of flats and estates of much of Inner London at the time I was collecting information. However, see Nicholson and Kellett, below.

Printed versions Beck, 70–88; Knapps, pp. 221–222.

Early notings Nicholson (1897, pp. 92–94) refers to children playing practical jokes on Halloween, e.g. blowing smoke through keyholes, stopping chimneys, window-tapping, sham window-smashing, carrying away ploughs, etc., and leading horses astray. There was once a strong tradition in the North of England of playing practical jokes on what was called "Mischievous Night", or "Mischief Night", 4th November: cf. Kellett for memories of this custom in the 1920s in Leeds, e.g. "tying door snecks together", smearing door handles with grease, and letting off home-made explosives, pp. 88–89.

November 5th (Bonfire Night)

10.E.6 In many areas of Inner London children still make an effigy (usually with the minimum of invention or care) and ask people for "A penny for the guy" for several weeks before November

5th. Many community or municipal events are replacing much of the individual firework and bonfire celebration. Rhymes like "Remember, remember, the 5th of November" and "Guy, guy, stick him in the eye", have evidently disappeared from Inner London.

Printed version Opies, *LLS*, pp. 280–283.

Christmas

10.E.7   CHRISTMAS IS COMING

>Christmas is coming,
>The goose is getting fat,
>Please put a tenner
>In the old man's hat.
>If you haven't got a tenner,
>A fiver will do.
>If you haven't got a fiver
>God bless you.

Mile End 1968 (penny and ha'penny); Blackheath, Deptford (shilling and sixpence), Shepherds Bush 1983.

See also **8.D.29**.

Printed versions Gullen, p. 81; Opies, *LLS*, p. 284; Ritchie, *SS*, Please to help the guisers, p. 116; Todd, 6.

SECTION 11

JUST FOR FUN

Introduction

The following section contains examples of wordplay, songs, rhymes, and jokes whose purpose is to entertain. Some are picked up, some are made up and then passed on. Their dissemination depends on their appeal, and sometimes this appeal is not limited to the world of children. The humour and wit will also attract many adults; much of it is initiated by adults so there is a two-way process. Sometimes, on the other hand, to more sophisticated ears the humour is difficult to appreciate, and occasionally some aspects of it may leave a nasty taste in the mouth. Where the humour is at the expense of another child I have included the wordplay or rhyme in the section on teasing and taunting.

The entertainment can be social, in the form of songs which may accompany school outings, wet playtimes or in the gatherings of children's organisations. In the main, however, the retailing of rhyme or joke is likely to take place among a small group of friends, or perhaps just between a couple of children walking to school or going home, at school meals, waiting in class lines, or whispered behind a hand to relieve a boring lesson or assembly. The material may be very old and the listener may giggle politely, although he or she has heard it many times before. It may be part of the latest fashion or craze. Occasionally it is made up on the spur of the moment and examples may range from inspired wit to utter banality. Just as girls come into their own with singing games and with skipping, ball bouncing, and hand clapping rhymes, the leading role in the entertainment field, both in creativity and in the amassing of repertoires, tends to fall to the boys. This is not the case in all schools. It will certainly be less in those where children's play and friendship circles are more integrated on a gender basis. I may well have failed to note that a particular rhyme in the following sections is in use for other purposes besides being "just for fun". If so, no doubt other researchers will be able to put me right.

11.A NONSENSE RHYMES AND WORDPLAY

It is difficult to make up nonsense which is entertaining, and there have been few successful practitioners of the art: Edward Lear and Lewis Carroll in the nineteenth century and perhaps Spike Milligan in the twentieth. Thus it is not surprising that there are few examples in the field of children's lore and of these they are nearly all well established. **11.A.1** ONE BRIGHT MORNING IN THE MIDDLE OF THE NIGHT may have links with a fifteenth century poem, according to the Opies.[1] This rhyme is well established in Inner London. **11.A.3** I WENT TO THE PICTURES TOMORROW and **11.A.4** LABELS AND JELLYSPOONS were at least sixty years old at the time of collection.

Other rhymes involving wordplay, though not necessarily in the class of humorous nonsense, may depend on punning, alliteration, onomatopoeia, or mild "daring". Unusual or repetitive sounds, metaphor, imagery, and rhyme are all factors which may appeal. Few of the examples here have a long tradition, with the exception of **11.A.7** LONG-LEGGED ITALY, which certainly dates from at least the late nineteenth century. However, I have not been able to trace an early printed version.

NOTES

1. Opies (*LLS*, 1959), a nonsense rhyme found in a minstrel's pocket book, p. 26.

Nonsense Rhymes

11.A.1 ONE BRIGHT MORNING IN THE MIDDLE OF THE NIGHT

One bright morning in the middle of the night,
Two dead men got up to fight,
Back to back they faced each other,
Drew their swords and shot each other.
A deaf policeman heard the noise,
And came and arrested the two dead boys,
Gave them a feast and sent them to jail,
A blind, deaf and dumb man told me the tale.

Blackheath, Dalston 1983; Kensington 1984. Part: Mile End 1968; Battersea, Greenwich 1982; Borough 1983.

Printed versions Abrahams, p. 146; Kellett, p. 95 (and see below); Kelsey, *K1*, 48; Knapps, pp. 97–98; Opies, *ISE*, p. 63, *LLS*, pp. 25–26; Rodger, p. 18; Shaw, 1970, p. 57; Solomons, pp. 101, 102; Turner, p. 100; Withers, *RIMP*, p. 185.

Early notings The Opies (*LLS*, 1959, p. 26) give a Middle English poem c1480 on a similar theme. One fine day in the middle of the night,/Two dead men got up to fight,/A blind man was there to see fair play,/A deaf and dumb man to shout hurray./A scabie eyed donkey came scampering by,/Kicked the blind man in the eye,/Knocked him through a nine inch wall/Into a dry ditch and drowned them all, Kellett, 1920s, pp. 45–46.

11.A.2 ONE BRIGHT MORNING WHEN THE MOON WAS HIGH

> One bright morning when the moon was high,
> The Thames caught fire and the river ran away.
> A man with no legs ran to tell the fire brigade;
> A deaf man heard it.
> A blind man saw it.
> The fire brigade was pulled by six dead horses
> Who ran over a dead cat and half killed it.
> This story was told by a knight,
> Sitting on the corner of a round table,
> Eating vinegar off a plate with a fork.
>
> Mile End 1968; Walworth 1982.

Printed version Sutton-Smith, p. 103.

11.A.3 I WENT TO THE PICTURES TOMORROW

> A. I went to the pictures tomorrow,
>   I got a front seat at the back,
>   I fell from the floor to the balcony,
>   And I broke a front bone in my back.
>   A lady she gave me some chocolate,
>   I ate it and gave it her back.
>   That's the last time I went to the pictures
>   And the first time I'll ever go back.
>
> Mile End 1968; Walworth 1982; Dalston 1983.

Printed versions Kellett (?early noting), p. 44; Opies, *LLS*, p. 25; Rosen and Steele [p. 3]; Shaw, 1970, p. 56; Turner, p. 94.

> B. Lovely weather we're having tomorrow!
>
> Streatham 1982.

11.A.4 LABELS AND JELLYSPOONS

A. Labels and jellyspoons,
I come before you to stand behind you,
To tell you that on Thursday next,
Good Friday,
There'll be a mothers' meeting
Especially for fathers.
No fee, pay at the door,
Take the seats provided
And sit on the floor.
First programme on the item
Will be a female man,
Sitting on the four corners of the round table.
You thank I.

Finsbury 1983.

B. Lords, ladies and jellyfish,
I've come before you to stand behind you,
To tell you something I know nothing about.
On this Good Friday which is really Thursday,
There's a mothers' meeting for fathers only.
Bring your chairs and sit on the floor.
Admission free so pay at the door.

Mile End 1968; Kensington 1984.

Printed versions Fowke, p. 128; Kirshenblatt-Gimblett, pp. 100, 103–104, 108–109; Kelsey, *K1*, 48; Knapps, p. 98; Opies, *LLS*, p. 25; Rosen and Steele, [p. 24]; cf. Solomons, p. 102; Turner, p. 95; Withers, *RIMP*, p. 199.

Printed versions of other nonsense rhymes Barltrop and Wolveridge, p. 67; Cole, pp. 50, 70; Fowke, p. 267; Kirshenblatt-Gimblett, p. 93; Opies, *LLS*, pp. 24–26; Shaw, 1970, pp. 56–57, fragment, p. 113; Turner,

p. 94; Withers, *CO*, Yesterday upon the stair/I saw a man who wasn't there …, [p. 39].

Miscellaneous Wordplay

11.A.5 'TWAS IN A RESTAURANT THEY MET

'Twas in a restaurant they met,
 Romeo and Juliet.
They had no money to pay the debt,
So Rome owed what Julie ate.

Blackheath 1983; Hampstead 1984.

11.A.6 WOULDN'T IT, WOULDN'T IT?

Wouldn't it, wouldn't it,
Wouldn't it be funny,
If a lady had a wooden tit,
Wouldn't it be funny?

Brockley 1983.

11.A.7 LONG-LEGGED ITALY

Long-legged Italy,
Kicked poor little Sicily,
Into the middle of
The Mediterranean Sea.
Austria was Hungary,
Took a bit of Turkey,
Fried it in Japan,
And ate it off China.

Hampstead 1984.

Printed versions Brady, p. 58; cf. Kelsey, *K1*, 47; Opies, *LLS*, p. 29; Shaw, 1970, p. 12; Sluckin, p. 27.

Early noting A correspondent from Tonbridge provided this version, c1905: Austria's Hungary,/ Wants a bit of Turkey/Dipped in Greece,/Up comes Italy,/Kicks poor Sicily/Into the Mediterranean Sea.

11.A.8   FIRE! FIRE!

> "Fire! Fire!" says Mrs. McGuire.
> "Where? Where?" says Mrs. O'Hare.
> "Down Town," says Mrs. Brown.

> Mile End 1983.

Printed versions Abrahams, "Usually an entertainment rhyme", p. 50; Botkin (see below); Wood, *FAFR*, p. 107.

Early noting "Fire, fire!"/Said Mrs. McGuire./"Where, where?"/Said Mrs. Ware./"Down town!"/ Said Mrs. Brown./"Oh, Lord save us!"/Said Mrs. Davis, Botkin, *TAF*, 1944, p. 790.

11.A.9   A KING'S A RULER

> A king's a ruler,
> A ruler's a foot,
> A foot makes a smell,
> A smell makes stink.

Brixton 1982; Cubitt Town, Dalston 1983.

11.A.10 BLOODY'S IN THE BIBLE

Bloody's in the Bible,
Bloody's in the book,
If you don't believe it,
Have a bloody look.

Cubitt Town 1983.

11.A.11 A PEANUT SAT ON A RAILWAY TRACK

A peanut sat on a railway track,
Its heart was all of a flutter,
Along came a train, the 9.15,
Toot! Toot! Peanut butter.

Hampstead 1984.

Printed versions Sutton-Smith, counting-out rhyme, p. 72; Turner, p. 101.

11.A.12 OOEY GOOEY WAS A WORM

Ooey gooey was a worm,
A clever worm was he,
He was on the train track,
But the train he didn't see.
Ooey gooey!

Blackheath 1983.

Printed version Turner, p. 101.

Verses **11.A.11** and **11.A.12** are examples of what Robert Louis Stevenson is said to have termed "grues": "shocking quatrains of a gruesome nature". Cf. Leach and Fried, pp. 466–467: Little Willie on the track/

Didn't hear the engine's squeal:/Now the engine's coming back,/ Scraping Willie off the wheel.

11.B TONGUE TWISTERS etc.

Tongue twisters have a long tradition. **11.B.1** PETER PIPER in various versions has long been acknowledged as a nursery rhyme and was included in Halliwell's collection (1842, p. 104). The Opies (*LLS*, 1959) state that it is of eighteenth century origin.[1] **11.B.20** FUZZY WUZZY WAS A BEAR, **11.B.22** THE RAGGED RASCAL RAN, **11.B.23** I SAW ESAU, and **11.B.25** MOSES SUPPOSES have all amused young people for at least four generations and have been included in many anthologies of verse for children. **11.B.3** SHE SELLS SEASHELLS became a popular First World War song. There is no demarcation line between examples like I SAW ESAU and instances of wordplay already referred to in the previous section.

NOTES

1. Opies (*LLS*, 1959), Dr. Samuel Arnold, *Juvenile Amusements* (1797), p. 30, n.1.

11.B.1 PETER PIPER

    A. Peter Piper picked a peck of pickled pepper.
         If Peter Piper picked a peck of pickled pepper,
         Where's the peck of pickled pepper Peter Piper picked?

Blackheath 1983; <u>Hampstead</u>, Kensington <u>1984</u>. Fragments: Streatham 1982; Battersea, Brockley, Finsbury, Kentish Town 1983.

    B. Peter picked a packet of prawn pasta,
         A peck of pickled pepper,
         And a piano player.

Blackheath 1983.

Printed versions Briggs, p. 184; Cansler, 2; Halliwell (see below); Lang (see below); Leach and Fried, p. 1119; MacBain (see below); Opies, *ODNR*, p. 347; Turner, p. 81; Withers, *RIMP*, p. 79.

Early notings Peter Piper picked a peck of pickled pepper;/A peck of pickled pepper Peter Piper picked;/If Peter Piper picked a peck of pickled pepper,/Where is the peck of pickled pepper Peter Piper picked? Halliwell, *NRE*, 1842, p. 104. In *NRE*, 1844, p. 86, Halliwell added the following before the rhyme: [Sometimes 'off a pewter plate' is added at the end of each line.]. Lang, 1897, p. 146; MacBain, 1933, p. 167.

11.B.2 BETTY BOTTER

A. Betty Botter bought some butter,
    But she said, "The butter's bitter,
    If I put it in my batter,
    It will make my batter bitter."
    But she put it in her batter,
    And it made her batter bitter.

Greenwich 1982; Cubitt Town 1983.

B. Betty bought a bit of butter,
    But the butter Betty bought was bitter,
    So Betty bought a better bit of butter,
    Than the butter Betty bought before.

Brixton 1982; Blackheath, Stoke Newington 1983; Hampstead 1984.

Printed versions Turner, fragment, p. 79; Wood, *FAFR*, p. 50.

11.B.3 SHE SELLS SEASHELLS

A. She sells seashells on the seashore,
    How many seashells does she sell on the seashore?

Finsbury 1983. First line only: Streatham 1982; Kentish Town 1983; Kensington 1984.

Printed versions Briggs, p. 197; Leach and Fried, p. 1118; Rodger, p. 40; Turner, p. 81; Withers, *RIMP*, p. 78.

    B.   Seashells, cockle shells (repeated quickly).

Mile End 1983.

See also **6.A.53B** and **9.A.9C**.

Printed version cf. Shaw, Egg–shells–she–saw, 1970, p. 64.

11.B.4 IF YOU NOTICE THIS NOTICE

    A.   If you notice this notice,
           You'll notice the notice
           Is not worth noticing.

Streatham 1982; <u>Cubitt Town</u>, Kentish Town <u>1983</u>; Earlsfield, Kensington 1984.

    B.   If you did not notice that this notice
           Is not worth noticing,
           You don't notice anything.

Streatham 1982.

11.B.5 RED LORRY etc.

    A.   Red lorry, yellow lorry (repeated, getting faster).

Streatham 1982; Shepherds Bush 1982–84; <u>Blackheath</u>, Finsbury, Kentish Town <u>1983</u>; Hampstead 1984.

    B.   Red leather, yellow leather.

Blackheath, <u>Dulwich</u>, Mile End <u>1983</u>.

C.   Red welly, yellow welly.

Brockley 1983.

D.   Long distance lorry worry.

Blackheath 1983.

11.B.6   WHETHER THE WEATHER

Whether the weather be cold,
Or whether the weather be hot,
Weather the weather,
Whatever the weather,
Whether we like it or not.

Earlsfield 1982.

11.B.7   THE BIG BLACK BUG

The big black bug
Bit the big black bear,
Made the big black bear
Bleed blood.

Walworth 1982.

Printed versions Leach and Fried, p. 1119; Turner, p. 79; Withers, *RIMP*, p. 77.

11.B.8   PINK PANTHER

Pink panther picked a perfect posy of pansies.

Kentish Town 1983.

11.B.9 SMELLY SOCKS

Smelly socks stink,
So sink them in the sea.

Stoke Newington 1983.

11.B.10 HOW MANY FEATHERS?

How many feathers on a thrush's throat?
Three thousand, three hundred and three,
That's how many there be.

Borough 1983.

11.B.11 OLIVER OGLETHORPE

Oliver Oglethorpe ogled an owl and an oyster,
If Oliver Oglethorpe ogled an owl and an oyster,
Where is the owl and the oyster Oliver Oglethorpe ogled?

Dulwich 1983.

11.B.12 ONCE UPON A BARREN MOOR

Once upon a barren moor,
There dwelt a bear, also a boar.
The bear thought the bear a bore;
The bear could not bear the boar.
At last the bear could bear no more,
And left the boar upon the moor.

Hampstead 1984.

11.B.13 SIX SICK SHEIKHS

Six sick sheikhs,
Sitting stitching sheets.

Dulwich 1983.

Printed version cf. Leach and Fried, The sixth sheik's sixth sheep's sick, p. 1118.

11.B.14 I'M NOT A PHEASANT PLUCKER

I'm not a pheasant plucker,
I'm a pheasant plucker's son.
I'm only plucking pheasants
Till the pheasant plucker comes.

Kentish Town 1983.

Nos. **11.B.13** and **11.B.14** above encourage unsuspecting children to repeat them in the hope they will be caught out using a "swearword". Cf. Shaw, "Show me Sally sitting in her china shop", 1970, p. 20. See also **11.G.7**.

11.B.15 IN HEREFORDSHIRE

In Herefordshire, Hertford and Hampshire,
Hurricanes hardly ever happen.

Borough 1983.

A similar version of the above was popularised in the 1938 film version of *Pygmalion*, for which George Bernard Shaw wrote the screenplay, and later in the musical, *My Fair Lady*, first produced in London in 1958.

11.B.16 CRUSHED BISCUITS

> Crushed biscuits, crushed biscuits,
> Mixed biscuits, mixed biscuits.

Hampstead 1984.

Printed version Withers, *RIMP*, p. 78.

11.B.17 FRIED FISH

> You can have fresh fried fish.

Dulwich 1983.

Printed version Withers, *RIMP*, p. 77.

11.B.18 IF YOUR SHORTS GET SHORTER

> If your shorts get shorter,
> How short will they get?

Cubitt Town 1983.

11.B.19 THE SUPER STEAMSHIP

> A.   The super steamship (was) sunk in the sea.

Borough 1983.

> B.   The super steamship sank in the sink.

Dulwich 1983.

11.B.20 FUZZY WUZZY WAS A BEAR

Fuzzy Wuzzy was a bear,
Fuzzy Wuzzy had no hair
Fuzzy Wuzzy wasn't fuzzy,
Was he?

Blackheath 1983.

Printed versions Fowke, p. 126; Turner, p. 90; Wood, *FAFR*, p. 4.

11.B.21 ALGY MET A BEAR

Algy met a bear,
The bear ate Algy,
The bear was bulgy,
The bulge was Algy.

Blackheath 1983; <u>Hampstead 1984</u>.

Printed versions Gadsby and Harrop, No. 1; Kirshenblatt-Gimblett, p. 109; Withers, *RIMP*, p. 183.

11.B.22 THE RAGGED RASCAL RAN

The ragged rascal ran round the rugged rock,
The ragged rascal ran round the rugged rock,
How many times did the ragged rascal run round the rugged rock?

Finsbury 1983.

Printed versions Botkin (see below); Briggs, p. 197; Gullen, p. 21; Leach and Fried, p. 1118; MacBain (see below); Opies, *LLS*, pp. 68, 77; Turner, p. 79; Withers, *RIMP*, p. 78.

Early notings MacBain, 1933, p. 158; Botkin, *TAF*, 1944, p. 775.

11.B.23 I SAW ESAU

> I saw Esau kissing Kate,
> I saw Esau, he saw me,
> That's how I saw Esau.

Greenwich 1982.

See also **9.A.9**.

Printed versions Abrahams, p. 89; Brady, p. 76; Cansler, 2; Opies, *ISE*, pp. 16, 77; *LLS*, p. 13; Turner, p. 80.

11.B.24 I WAS HERE

> I was here,
> Here I was.
> Was I here?
> Yes, I was.

Greenwich 1982; Blackheath 1983.

11.B.25 MOSES SUPPOSES

> Moses supposes his toesies are roses,
> But Moses supposes erroneously,
> For nobody's toesies are posies of roses,
> As Moses supposes his toesies to be.

Kentish Town, Shepherds Bush (fragment) 1983.

Printed version Opies, *ISE*, p. 60.

11.B.26 ALL I WANT IS A PROPER CUP OF COFFEE

All I want is a proper cup of coffee
Made in a proper coffee pot.
I may be off my dot,
But I want a proper coffee
In a proper coffee pot.
Tin coffee pot, iron coffee pot,
Are no use to me.
If I can't have a proper cup of coffee
In a proper coffee pot,
I'll have a cup of tea.

Shepherds Bush 1983.

Printed versions Botkin (see below); Turner, fragment, p. 81.

Early noting Botkin, *TAF*, 1944, fragment, p. 775.

Printed versions of other tongue twisters etc. Abrahams, passim; Botkin, *TAF*, pp. 774–775; Brady, passim; Chambers, 1842, p. 61; Fowke, p. 128; Halliwell, "charms … for the hiccup", 1842, p. 104; Kirshenblatt-Gimblett, pp. 97, 103; Leach and Fried, pp. 117–119; MacBain, p. 63; Opies, *LLS*, pp. 30–31; Rodger, pp. 39–40; Turner, Puzzles and Practical Jokes, pp. 79–81.

11.C RIDDLES

Riddles played an important part in the mythology and legend of the ancient world. A collection of a hundred riddles was written in Old English as early as the eighth century, and others were recorded by churchmen in Latin. Many British ballads and their derivatives are centred on the vital importance of giving the correct answer to a riddle. Examples include "Captain Wedderburn's Courtship" and "King John and the Abbot of Canterbury". Sometimes the song just consists of a series of riddles with the answers, as in "I Gave My Love a Cherry", and "The Weaver's Bonny". Nowadays the riddle seems to have become the almost exclusive province of children, apart from certain obscene varieties which form part of the "dirty joke" repertoire. Some may consider that the riddle is a way to being "one-up" on another child, albeit in a rather restrained way compared with the verbal tricks and catching out illustrated in Section **9.A**. Wolfenstein says that "The desperate concern with being smart is partly gratified and partly mitigated in the joking riddle. It is the hearer who cannot answer ... [it is] not the child who tells it who is stupid." (1954, 1978, p. 157). However, I do not think that this is an important motive in the retailing of riddles.

A new kind of riddle may appear and be taken up by adults for a short time. Soon, however, it loses its novelty value and dies out. It is then left to children to maintain and develop. Examples are the "knock-knock" riddles which date from the 1920s. More recently there were the extravagant "elephant" and "black" riddles which probably originated with adults before children took them over. Old riddles do not have much appeal to children of the age group that I am concerned with. I came across one very old riddle (**11.C.1**), but the child who gave it to me may have got it from a book. The old "simple" type of riddle is despised by this age group, and I did not come across "When is a door not a door?" or "Why did the jam roll?", though some of these survive, such as **11.C.8** "How do you make a sausage roll?" and **11.C.9** "What has a tongue but cannot speak?".

The Opies include a number of riddles in their nursery rhyme collections[1] but only two or three of these were current in Inner London families at the time of my collection. The much parodied "Humpty Dumpty" rhyme can hardly be considered any longer as a riddle; the egg figure in picture form always accompanies the rhyme in children's books. No doubt children pick up their riddles from various sources: friends, family, comics, books, and the media. Most of the riddles of the traditional kind were just "once only" notings. However, the riddle: **11.C.6** "Why did the child take its pencil to bed?" appeared in schools in three different areas in the survey.

Certain themes appear frequently: traffic and policemen, football, and animals, for instance. Sometimes a particular riddle will inspire others of a similar kind such as the three riddles dealing with racing (**11.C.84–11.C.86**). The old riddle: **11.C.36** "What's black and white and red all over?" has inspired a contemporary version (**11.C.37**). The old traditional riddle: **11.C.38** "Why did the chicken cross the road?" has been developed in various directions and I have collected ten variations (**11.C.39–11.C.48**). The original riddle with its banal "let-down" can inspire a witty punning "sick" version: **11.C.43** "Why did the hedgehog cross the road?/To see his flat mate."

The exposure to more sophisticated forms of humour on radio and television has given rise to many kinds of riddle which appeal to the intelligent older child. Younger children may ask riddles without fully appreciating the humour of the answer. The "elephant" type of riddle (**11.C.65–11.C.67**), which began to be current in the 1960s and which became widely popular for a time, depends for its humour on the outrageous or ridiculous nature of the answer. The "vampire", "skeleton" or "ghost" riddles (**11.C.87–11.C.97**) seem to have been a development originating with the children. No doubt the re-showing of films dealing with the Dracula theme and other supernatural manifestations, which many children watch, has had its effect here. I did not come across it until the 1980s, so it may have been a recent development. The American television soap opera *Dallas* gave rise to a number of riddles and jokes which may ultimately be ephemeral (Nos. **11.C.119** and **11.C.120**).

In *Alice in Wonderland*, Lewis Carroll's Alice is asked by the Mad Hatter, "Why is a raven like a writing-desk?" but cannot supply an answer. This once widely used type of opening question appears to have disappeared from children's lore in Inner London, but the opposite kind that asks "What's the difference between …?" has been a popular form of riddle, the answer usually depending on a reversal of the punning words, as in **11.C.103**. I did not come across the other kind where just the initial consonantal sounds are exchanged. These riddles were very popular in the early twentieth century, but none came my way during the study. An example I remember went like this: "What is the difference between a constipated owl and a poor marksman?/ One is a hooter who never shits and the other is a shooter who never hits."

Two other riddle beginnings have developed in the last few years. One is the question "What's the definition of …?" (**11.C.110–**

11.C.112). Examples of these were current in the 1960s, and an example I noted in 1968 appeared during my researches in 1983: **11.C.111** "What's the definition of agony?". The other beginning is "What do you get if you cross …?" (**11.C.70–11.C.74**). The cross is usually suggested between widely dissimilar things such as a hedgehog and a giraffe (**11.C.70**), a kangaroo and a sheep (**11.C.71**), or a fish and an elephant (**11.C.73**). The answer will be of a ridiculous nature but may be very funny.

Riddles **11.C.131–11.C.135** are also products of the 1960s. As with riddles **11.C.121–11.C.130**, their unpleasantness usually outweighs any humour they possess, or so it appears to many adult minds. Children, however, see them differently. They have in any case a desire to be outrageous and to shock. Children in Inner London will often go to great lengths to avoid insulting references to Black people. However, they had no inhibitions when it came to their repertoire of Irish jokes and riddles which insult Irish people and help to perpetuate the "Paddy" stereotype.

NOTES

1. Opies (*ONRB*, 1955), pp. 147–154; (*PBNR*, 1963), pp. 27, 72, 75, 108–109, 112, 159, 160, 178, 182.

Traditional

11.C.1   Q.   I saw a man walking across a bridge. He took off his hat and drew off his gloves.
Who was he?
A.   Andrew.

Earlsfield 1982.

A very old riddle.

Printed versions Lang (see below); MacBain (see below).

Early notings As I was going o'er Westminster bridge,/I met with a Westminster scholar;/He pulled off his cap, *an' drew* off his glove,/And wished me a very good morrow./What is his name? Lang, 1897, p. 132. MacBain, 1933, as Lang, p. 249.

11.C.2 Q. What is it that ten thousand men can't hold?
A. Their breath.

Blackheath 1983.

11.C.3 Q. What is lighter than a feather, but ten men can't pick it up?
A. A bubble.

Blackheath 1983.

11.C.4 Q. Where is Solomon's temple?
A. Near the top of his head.

Blackheath 1983.

11.C.5 Q. What can go round the world yet stay in a corner?
A. A postage stamp.

Blackheath 1983.

11.C.6 Q. Why did the child take its pencil to bed?
A. Because it wanted to draw the curtains in the morning.

Blackheath, Kentish Town 1983; Hampstead 1984.

11.C.7 Q. Why did the orange stop?
A. Because it ran out of juice.

Brockley, Dulwich 1983.

11.C.8   Q.   How do you make a sausage roll?
A.   Push it down a steep hill.

Brockley 1983.

11.C.9   Q.   What has a tongue but cannot speak?
A.   A shoe.

Hampstead 1984.

11.C.10   Q.   Why did the boy close his eyes in front of a mirror?
A.   He wanted to see what he looked like when he was asleep.

Borough 1983.

11.C.11   Q.   Why are flowers lazy?
A.   Because they're in their beds all day.

Dulwich 1983.

11.C.12   Q.   What bow's impossible to tie?
A.   A rainbow.

Dulwich 1983.

11.C.13   Q.   What's the fastest thing in the world?
A.   Milk, because it's pasteurised [past your eyes] before you can see it.

Dulwich 1983.

11.C.14   Q.   What's the longest word in the English dictionary?
A.   Smiles, because there's a mile between the first and last letters.

Dulwich 1983.

11.C.15   Q.   What's worse than raining cats and dogs?
A.   Hailing taxis.

Dulwich 1983.

11.C.16   Q.   Why did the man throw the butter out of the window?
A.   Because he wanted to see the butterfly.

Dulwich 1983.

11.C.17   Q.   What did the old chimney say to the young chimney?
A.   Smoke. (You're too young to smoke).

Dulwich, Kentish Town 1983.

Printed version   Knapps, p. 105.

11.C.18   Q.   What did the big telephone say to the little telephone?
A.   You're too young to be engaged.

Kentish Town 1983.

11.C.19   Q.   What is an erupting volcano?
A.   A mountain with hiccups.

Dulwich 1983.

11.C.20   Q.   What did the hat say to the scarf?
A.   I'll go on ahead and you hang around.

Finsbury 1983.

11.C.21   Q.   Why did a scientist take a ruler to bed?
A.   To see how long he slept.

Cubitt Town 1983.

Printed version   Wolfenstein, p. 122.

11.C.22 Q. Why did the old man put wheels on his rocking chair?
A. Because he wanted to rock and roll.

Shepherds Bush 1983.

11.C.23 Q. Why didn't the bombs fall out when they pressed the button?
A. Because they were flying upside down.

Hampstead 1984.

11.C.24 Q. What do you get if you dial 98765432101234567890?
A. A sore finger.

Hampstead 1984.

11.C.25 Q. What has legs but cannot walk?
A. A chair.

Hampstead 1984.

Printed version Wolfenstein, p. 110.

11.C.26 Q. What has a blind eye at night and an open eye in the morning?
A. A window.

Hampstead 1984.

11.C.27 Q. Why does a golfer keep a spare pair of trousers with him?
A. Because he might get a hole in one.

Cubitt Town, Stoke Newington 1983.

11.C.28 Q. Why did the fireman bring a ladder to school?
A. He wanted to be top of the class.

Borough 1983.

11.C.29 Q. What is a road hog?
A. A pig-headed driver.

Borough 1983.

11.C.30 Q. What would happen if the population of the Isle of Wight lay flat across the Mediterranean Sea?
A. They would drown.

Blackheath 1983.

11.C.31 a. Do you go to bed with Tony Hart?
b. No, of course not.
a. Yes you do. (touching in turn: toe, knee and heart)

Brockley 1983.

11.C.32 a. Do you go to bed with Tony Chestnut?
b. No, of course not.
a. Yes you do. (touching in turn: toe, knee, chest and head)

Brockley 1983.

Printed version Turner, Have you got Tony Chestnut on you? p. 79.

11.C.33 Q. What letters scare a burglar?
A. I C U.

Dulwich 1983.

Printed version Opies, *LLS*, p. 80.

11.C.34 Q. How does a burglar get into a house?
A. In-tru-der window.

Dulwich 1983.

11.C.35 Q. How do you make antifreeze?
A. Steal her nightie.

Hampstead 1984.

The old:

11.C.36 Q. What's black and white and red all over?
A. A newspaper.

Stoke Newington 1983.

Printed versions Knapps, p. 108; Wolfenstein, p. 105.

The new:

11.C.37 Q. What's black and white and red all over?
A. A shy zebra.

Dalston 1983.

Printed version Knapps, p. 108.

An old theme and new variations:

11.C.38 Q. Why did the chicken cross the road?
A. To get to the other side.

Mile End 1983.

Printed versions Knapps, p. 105; Wolfenstein, p. 109.

11.C.39   Q. Why did the chicken sit on the toilet?
A. For a foul reason.

Blackheath 1983.

11.C.40   a. Why did the chicken cross the road?
He wanted to get the one hundred pounds on the other side.
b. I don't get that.
a. I know, neither did he.

Deptford, Finsbury 1983.

11.C.41   Q. Why did the chicken cross the road and come back to the side he started from?
A. Because his braces were caught on the lamp-post.

Finsbury 1983.

11.C.42   Q. Why didn't the chicken cross the road?
A. Because he was chicken.

Finsbury 1983.

11.C.43   Q. Why did the hedgehog cross the road?
A. To see his flat mate.

Blackheath, Finsbury 1983.

11.C.44   Q. Why did the dinosaur cross the road?
A. Because chickens weren't around then.

Finsbury 1983.

11.C.45   Q. Why did the one-handed man cross the road?
A. To get to the secondhand shop.

Mile End 1983.

11.C.46 Q. Why did the frog cross the road?
A. Because it wanted to Kermit* [commit] suicide.

Blackheath 1983.

* Kermit is the name of a frog puppet on the children's television series *The Muppet Show*, created by the American puppeteer Jim Henson, which ran from 1976 to 1981.

See also **11.C.121**, **11.C.122**, and **11.I.50**.

11.C.47 Q. Why did the elephant cross the road?
A. Because it was the chicken's day off.

Blackheath, Shepherds Bush 1983.

11.C.48 Q. Why did the monkey cross the road?
A. Because it was the chicken's day off.

Deptford 1983.

Same for "horse".

Cubitt Town 1983.

Football

11.C.49 Q. Why can't a car play football?
A. Because it's only got one boot.

Blackheath, Deptford 1983.

11.C.50 Q. Why did Manchester United go to America?
A. To Dodge City.

Mile End 1968.

11.C.51 Q. Where do spiders play football?
A. In the webley.

Mile End 1983.

11.C.52 Q. Why were ants playing football in a saucer?
A. They were practising for the cup.

Mile End 1983.

Animals, Plants, and Insects

11.C.53 Q. What sends an animal to sleep?
A. A bulldozer.

Deptford 1983.

11.C.54 Q. What is the wettest animal in the world?
A. A reindeer.

Mile End 1983.

11.C.55 Q. What goes bark, bark, bark, tick, tick, tick?
A. A watch dog.

Stoke Newington 1983.

11.C.56 Q. What do you get if you give a cow money?
A. Rich milk.

Dalston 1983.

11.C.57 Q. Why is the letter V like an angry bull?
A. Because it comes after U.

Mile End 1983.

11.C.58 Q. How do you stop a mole from digging the garden?
A. Hide the spade.

Cubitt Town 1983.

11.C.59 Q. Why did the squirrel scream?
A. Someone pinched his nuts.

Brockley 1983.

11.C.60 Q. What's the best way to catch a squirrel?
A. Climb a tree and act like a nut.

Brockley 1983.

11.C.61 Q. Why don't men play cards in the jungle?
A. Because there are too many cheetahs.

Dalston 1983.

11.C.62 Q. Why did the monkey invite the gorilla for tea?
A. So he could put the toast under the griller.

Finsbury 1983.

11.C.63 Q. What's grey, got four legs and a trunk?
A. A mouse going on holiday.

Mile End 1968; Borough 1983.

The same principle:

11.C.64 Q. What's green and hairy and lies in a deckchair?
A. A gooseberry on holiday.

Deptford 1983.

11.C.65 Q. How can you tell when there's an elephant in your fridge?
A. By the footprints in the butter.

Brockley 1983.

Printed version Knapps, "bear", p. 108.

11.C.66 Q. There were two elephants in a caravan. What were they playing?
A. Squash.

Stoke Newington 1983.

11.C.67 Q. Why is an elephant large, hairy, wrinkled and grey?
A. If it were small, white, hairless and smooth it would be an aspirin.

Stoke Newington 1983.

11.C.68 Q. What goes, "Ninety nine, bonk"?
A. A centipede with a wooden leg.

Blackheath, Stoke Newington 1983.

11.C.69 a. What's black and yellow and has ten legs?
b. I don't know, what is it?
a. I don't know, that's why I'm asking you.

Brockley 1983.

Crossings

11.C.70 Q. What do you get if you cross a hedgehog with a giraffe?
A. A twenty foot toothbrush.

Blackheath, Cubitt Town 1983.

11.C.71 Q. What do you get if you cross a kangaroo with a sheep?
A. A woolly jumper.

Blackheath, Cubitt Town 1983.

11.C.72 Q. What do you get if you cross a parrot with a centipede?
A. A walkie-talkie.

Cubitt Town 1983.

11.C.73 Q. What do you get if you cross a fish with an elephant?
A. A pair of swimming trunks.

Cubitt Town 1983.

11.C.74 a. What do you get if you cross a lion with an elephant?
b. I don't know.
a. Neither do I.

Dulwich 1983.

Printed version cf. Knapps, What do you get when you cross a rhino with an elephant?/The 'ell if I know, p. 110.

Tarzan

11.C.75 Q. What did Tarzan say when he saw the elephants coming over the hill?
A. Here are the elephants coming over the hill.

Stoke Newington 1983; Hampstead 1984.

Q. What did Jane say?
A. Here come the grapes. You see she was colour blind.

Stoke Newington 1983.

11.C.76 Q. Where does Tarzan buy his clothes?
A. From a jungle sale.

Mile End 1983.

Police

11.C.77 Q. What does a policeman have for breakfast?
A. A traffic jam.

Hampstead 1984.

11.C.78 Q. What would you do if coppers were all around you?
A. I'd pick 'em up and put 'em in my pocket.

Dalston 1983.

11.C.79 Q. What did the traffic lights say to the policeman?
A. Turn around while I'm changing.

Dulwich, Finsbury 1983.

Clocks

11.C.80 Q. Why did the boy throw his clock out of the window?
A. He wanted to see time fly.

Dalston 1983.

Printed version Wolfenstein, p. 116.

11.C.81 Q. What did the thief say to the clockmaker?
A. I'm sorry to steal your valuable time.

Borough 1983.

11.C.82 Q. Why are clocks shy?
A. Because they've always got their hands over their faces.

Dulwich 1983.

11.C.83 Q. Why did the man strike the clock?
A. He was trying to kill time.

Dulwich 1983.

Racing

11.C.84 Q. How do you start a pudding race?
A. Say go (sago).

Brockley, Finsbury 1983.

11.C.85 Q. How do you start a jelly race?
A. Get set.

Mile End 1983.

11.C.86 Q. How do you start a flea race?
A. One, two, flea.

Mile End 1983.

Vampires, Skeletons, and Ghosts

11.C.87 Q. What does a vampire doctor ask for?
A. Can I look at your neck and have a sample?

Borough 1983.

11.C.88 Q. What do they call Dracula?
A. A pain in the neck.

Dulwich 1983.

11.C.89 Q. Why did Dracula never get married?
A. His girlfriend said he was a pain in the neck.

Borough 1983.

11.C.90 Q. What did one skeleton say to the other?
            A. I've got a bone to pick with you.

Dulwich 1983.

11.C.91 Q. What do you do if you see a skeleton running down the road?
            A. Jump out of your skin and join him.

Stoke Newington 1982–84.

11.C.92 Q. Why did the skeleton jump off the cliff?
            A. He had no guts.

Cubitt Town 1983.

11.C.93 Q. Why did the skeleton not go to the party?
            A. He had no body to go with.

Cubitt Town, Dalston 1983.

11.C.94 Q. What do ghosts eat for breakfast?
            A. Dreaded wheat.*

Dulwich 1983.

* Referring to the breakfast cereal, Shredded Wheat. See also **11.C.127**.

Q. What do they eat for dinner?
A. Goulash.

Dulwich 1983.

Q. What do they eat for supper?
A. Spookghetti.

Dulwich 1983.

11.C.95   Q. What did the ghost say to the man in the pub?
   A. Do you serve spirits?

   Dalston 1983.

11.C.96   Q. What did the mother spook say to the baby spook?
   A. Don't spook until you're spooken to.

   Dulwich 1983.

11.C.97   Q. What do shortsighted ghosts wear?
   A. Spooktacles.

   Dulwich 1983.

Crumbs, crummy

11.C.98   Q. What did the driver say when he ran over his packet of biscuits?
   A. Oh crumbs!

   Brockley, Deptford, Finsbury 1983.

11.C.99   Q. What did the biscuit say when he was trodden on?
   A. Oh crumbs!

   Brockley, Finsbury, Shepherds Bush 1983.

11.C.100   Q. Why did the boy put bread in his comic?
   A. He liked crummy jokes.

   Mile End 1983.

Hippies

11.C.101   Q.   What happened when a hippy put a bomb in the fridge?
A.   It blew his cool.

Blackheath 1983.

11.C.102   Q.   What are hippies for?
A.   To keep your leggies on.

Blackheath 1983.

What's the difference?

11.C.103   Q.   What's the difference between a jeweller and a jailer?
A.   A jeweller sells watches. A jailer watches cells.

Borough 1983.

Printed version   Opies, *LLS*, p. 79.

11.C.104   Q.   What's the difference between a sigh, a car, and a monkey?
A.   A sigh is "Oh dear!", a car is too dear, and the monkey is you dear.

Dulwich 1983.

Printed version   Opies, *LLS*, p. 80.

11.C.105   a.   What's the difference between a rhinoceros and a tea bag?
b.   I don't know.
a.   I wouldn't send you shopping.

Dulwich 1983.

11.C.106 Q. What's the difference between an elephant and a mouse?
A. The elephant makes bigger holes in the floorboards.

Mile End 1968.

Noises

11.C.107 Q. What did the Pink Panther say when he trod on an ant?
A. Dedant, dedant, dedant, dedant*… (dead ant)

Mile End 1983.

* The answer here is sung to the opening bars of the theme music written by Henry Mancini for the *Pink Panther* series of films starring Peter Sellars, beginning in 1963, and later used for a popular children's cartoon series of the same name.

11.C.108 Q. What noise does a cat make on a motorway?
A. Meeeeeeeeee ouuuuuuuuuuuu*

Barnsbury 1983.

*Imitating the sound of a vehicle approaching and then receding into the distance.

11.C.109 Q. What did the policeman say when he saw his mum?
A. Meee maaaa, meee maaaa. …*

Mile End 1983.

* Chanted to sound like a police car siren.

Definitions

11.C.110 Q. What's the definition of impossible?
A. An elephant hanging over the side of a cliff with its tail tied to a daisy.

Mile End 1968.

11.C.111 Q. What's the definition of agony?
A. Standing outside a toilet with a bent penny.

Mile End 1968; Finsbury 1983.

11.C.112 Q. What's the definition of pain?
A. A one-armed man hanging from a cliff with itchy balls.

Finsbury 1983.

Inspired by television and film

11.C.113 a. Can you tell Stork from butter?*
b. No, can you?
a. Yes.
b. How?
a. Well stork's got longer legs than butter.

Mile End 1968.

* This slogan comes from a television advertising campaign for Stork margarine in 1978.

11.C.114 Q. Why do prostitutes like Martini?
A. Any time, any place, anywhere.*

Brixton 1982.

* The answer was an advertising slogan for "Martini", a brand of Italian vermouth, in the 1970s.

11.C.115   Q.   What's blue and sulks in the corner?
A.   The incredible sulk.*

Deptford 1983.

* The reference is to *The Incredible Hulk*, an American television series aired in Britain from 1978 to 1982.

11.C.116   a.   Did you know there's only twenty-four letters in the alphabet?
b.   No. How is that?
a.   E.T.'s gone home.*

Blackheath 1983.

* The film *E.T. The Extra-Terrestrial* was released by Universal Pictures in 1982. Having crashed to Earth, all the eponymous alien wants to do is "go home", hence the answer above. See also **11.C.117**, **11.C.118**, **11.C.120**, **11.I.52**, and **11.I.53**.

11.C.117   a.   What does E.T. stand for?
b.   Extra-terrestrial.
a.   No, because he wants to.

Cubitt Town 1983.

See note to **11.C.116** above.

11.C.118   Q.   E.T. died. Why was that?
A.   He got his telephone bill.*

Finsbury 1983.

* See note to **11.C.116** above. On several occasions during the film, E.T. announces his intention to "phone home".

11.C.119 a. Do you know there are only twenty-four letters in the American alphabet?
              b. No. How's that?
              a. They don't like J.R.*

Blackheath 1983.

* The television soap opera *Dallas* was first aired in 1978. The series revolved around the wealthy Ewing family, notably the greedy, scheming "J. R." Ewing, who was universally disliked. See also **11.C.120** and **11.I.51**.

11.C.120 a. How many letters are there in the alphabet?
              b. Twenty-six.
              a. No. Nineteen. J.R. got shot, Jacqueline got D.K., E.T. went home and the angels sang No-ell.

Blackheath, Dulwich, Finsbury, Kentish Town 1983.

Printed version cf. Opies, *LLS*, p. 70.

See also notes to **11.C.116**, **11.C.119**, and **11.I.51–11.I.53**.

"Sick" humour

11.C.121 Q. What's green and smells of bacon?
              A. Kermit's hand.*

* As **11.C.46**, **11.C.122**, and **11.I.50**, this refers to Kermit the Frog (and Miss Piggy) in the television series *The Muppet Show*.

11.C.122 Q. What becomes green and red in a liquidiser?
              A. A frog (Kermit the frog*) in a liquidiser.

Borough, Brockley, Shepherds Bush 1983.

* As **11.C.46, 11.C.121,** and **11.I.50,** this refers to Kermit the Frog from *The Muppet Show.*

11.C.123 Q. What goes "Ha ha! Bonk!"?
             A. A man laughing his head off.

Stoke Newington 1983.

11.C.124 a. What did the boy put his hand up for?
              b. To go to the toilet.
              a. No, to pick his nose.

Shepherds Bush

11.C.125 Q. What's the worst thing you can buy secondhand?
              A. Loo paper.

Finsbury 1983.

11.C.126 Q. What's old, wrinkled and belongs to grandpa?
              A. Grandma.

Brockley, Shepherds Bush 1983.

11.C.127 Q. What happens when a bird gets caught in a propeller?
              A. Shredded tweet.*

Mile End 1984.

* Referring to the breakfast cereal, Shredded Wheat. See also **11.C.94.**

11.C.128 Q. What is red and has difficulty in turning corners?
              A. A baby with a javelin through its head.

Blackheath 1983.

11.C.129 Q. What's brown and knocks on windows?
              A. A baby in a microwave oven.

Blackheath 1983.

11.C.130 Q. What's white and knocks on windows?
A. A baby trying to get his friend out of a microwave oven.

Blackheath 1983.

Irishman

11.C.131 Q. How do you brainwash an Irishman?
A. Put water down his wellies.

Blackheath 1983.

11.C.132 Q. Why did the Irishman drive his lorry off the cliff?
A. Because he wanted to test his air brakes.

Cubitt Town 1983.

Printed version Wolfenstein, p. 126.

11.C.133 Q. How do you recognise an Irishman in Holland?
A. He's the only one with wooden wellies.

Blackheath 1983.

11.C.134 Q. How do you confuse an Irishman?
A. Put him in a round room and say, "The whisky is in the corner."

Blackheath 1983.

Printed version cf. Knapps, p. 205.

11.C.135 Q. How do you recognise an Irishman in an oil rig?
A. He's the only one throwing bread to the helicopters.

Blackheath 1983.

11.D KNOCK-KNOCK RIDDLES

This particular kind of riddling question with a joking answer is extremely popular among children, and is a revival of a procedure which goes back at least to the 1920s.[1] There does not seem to be a continuing tradition to bridge the half century, but its popularity is shown by the sixty-six examples collected during my researches, 1982–84. I recall "knock-knock" exchanges when I was a schoolboy, but can only remember and recognise **11.D.27** "Isabel/Is a bell necessary on a bicycle?" and **11.D.52** "Boo/Boo who?/Don't cry". I am sure there are many more with a long life, even if a part of that life was spent in hibernation. In the limited collecting restricted to two or three schools which I undertook in the 1960s, I did not come across the formula, but it may well have thrived elsewhere. I have no means of knowing.

Most of the knock-knock rhymes go through the set formula:

> Knock-Knock!
> Who's there?
> Alison/Alice.
> Alison/Alice who?
> Alison to/Alice on the radio every night. (**11.D.4**)

or

> Knock-Knock!
> Who's there?
> Cook.
> Cook who?
> That's the first one I've heard this year. (**11.D.14**)

The last line either comments on the second question or continues it to make an irrelevant phrase, statement or question which may or may not be funny, as **11.D.20** "Egbert who?/Egg but no bacon". Only a few seem to be of a risqué character (e.g. **11.D.39**, **11.D.40**), and this is in marked contrast to the general run of entertainment jokes and rhymes.

There are a number of knock-knock riddles which differ from the normal formula illustrated above. Nine different ones which have no connection with each other and are of limited spread are **11.D.51–11.D.59**.

Longer exchanges are a feature of two very widespread and popular types. In one of these the response is repeated several times, until irritation is only narrowly averted by a change in the reply (**11.D.60, 11.D.61**). The second type plays on the "Will you remember me?" theme (**11.D.62**), and was apparently equally popular in the American Middle West (Cansler, 1968, 6–7). The play on the word "who" in connection with the character Doctor Who, from the many television series of that name, was obviously too good to miss, and variations on this theme are widespread (**11.D.63–11.D.65**). One example, **11.D.66,** uses the rock group "The Who" instead of the television science fiction character.

NOTES

1. Ritchie (*SS*, 1964), pp. 31–32. The initial form of words is found in a children's game in the late nineteenth century (Northall, 1892, pp. 407–408).

Traditional Formula

11.D.1 Knock, knock!
Who's there?
Abie.
Abie who?
A bee stung me.

Borough 1983.

11.D.2 Knock, knock!
Who's there?
Alaska.
Alaska who?
Alaska no questions and tell no lies.

Dulwich 1983.

11.D.3   Knock, knock!
Who's there?
Ali.
Ali who?
A little boy who can't reach the bell.

Barnsbury 1983.

See also **11.D.19** and **11.D.35**.

11.D.4   Knock, knock!
Who's there?
Alison/Alice.
Alison/Alice who?
Alison to/Alice on to the radio every night.

Blackheath, Mile End 1983.

11.D.5   Knock, knock!
Who's there?
Amos.
Amos who?
A mosquito.

Streatham 1982; Blackheath, Dulwich 1983; Hampstead 1984.

11.D.6   Knock, knock!
Who's there?
Andy.
Andy who?
And he bit me again.

Dulwich 1983.

11.D.7   Knock, knock!
Who's there?
Anna.

Anna who?
Another mosquito.

Streatham 1982; Dulwich, Finsbury, Stoke Newington 1983.

11.D.8   Knock, knock!
Who's there?
Anna.
Anna who?
Anna happy New Year.

Finsbury 1983.

11.D.9   Knock, knock!
Who's there?
Arthur.
Arthur who?
Arthur any more biscuits in the tin?

Deptford, Dulwich, Shepherds Bush 1983.

11.D.10   Knock, knock!
Who's there?
Arthur.
Arthur who?
Arthur crown/Arthur sandwich.

Dalston, Deptford 1983.

11.D.11   Knock, knock!
Who's there?
Cargo.
Cargo who?
Car go beep!

Dulwich 1983.

11.D.12   Knock, knock!
Who's there?

Chester.
Chester who?
Chester minute and I'll tell you.

Mile End 1983.

11.D.13 Knock, knock!
Who's there?
Colin.
Colin who?
Colin all cars.

Deptford 1983.

11.D.14 Knock, knock!
Who's there?
Cook.
Cook who?
That's the first one I've heard this year.

Blackheath 1983.

11.D.15 Knock, knock!
Who's there?
Cow.
Cow who?
Cows go moo! Not who.

Mile End 1983.

11.D.16 Knock, knock!
Who's there?
Dishes.
Dishes who?
Dishes the police.

Shepherds Bush 1983.

11.D.17   Knock, knock!
Who's there?
Dishwasher.
Dishwasher who?
Dishwasher (This was the) way I used to talk with my teeth out.

Finsbury 1983.

11.D.18   Knock, knock!
Who's there?
Eamonn.
Eamonn who?
Eamonn (ham and) eggs are waiting for you on the table.

Blackheath 1983.

11.D.19   Knock, knock!
Who's there?
Eamonn.
Eamonn who?
Eamonn (a man) who can't reach the doorbell.

Shepherds Bush 1983.

See also **11.D.3** and **11.D.35**.

11.D.20   Knock, knock!
Who's there?
Egbert.
Egbert who?
Egbert no bacon.

Dalston, Deptford, Dulwich, Finsbury 1983.

11.D.21   Knock, knock!
Who's there?
Hatch.

Hatch who?
Oh I didn't know you'd got a cold.

Streatham 1982; Blackheath, Stoke Newington 1983.

See also **11.D.59**.

11.D.22   Knock, knock!
Who's there?
Honda.
Honda who?
Your hondawear's sticking out.

Dulwich 1983.

11.D.23   Knock, knock!
Who's there?
Howard.
Howard who?
How would you like to be stuck out in the cold/to open the door?

Cubitt Town, Finsbury 1983.

11.D.24   Knock, knock!
Who's there?
Ida.
Ida who?
Ida Clare war.

Dulwich 1983.

11.D.25   Knock, knock!
Who's there?
Irene.
Irene who?
Irene (I ring) on the bell but it doesn't work.

Blackheath 1983.

11.D.26 Knock, knock!
Who's there?
Irish stew.
Irish stew, who?
Irish stew (I arrest you) in the name of the law.

Brixton 1982; Brockley, Dulwich 1983.

11.D.27 Knock, knock!
Who's there?
Isabel.
Isabel who?
Is a bell necessary on a bicycle?

Finsbury 1983.

11.D.28 Knock, knock!
Who's there?
Isabel.
Isabel who?
Is a bell better than a knocker?

Dalston 1983.

11.D.29 Knock, knock!
Who's there?
Ivor.
Ivor who?
Ivor good mind not to tell you.

Streatham 1982; Cubitt Town 1983.

11.D.30 Knock, knock!
Who's there?
Ivor.
Ivor who?
Ivor sore hand through knocking at your door.

Blackheath 1983.

11.D.31   Knock, knock!
Who's there?
Justin.
Justin who?
Justin time for the party.

Barnsbury, Dulwich 1983.

11.D.32   Knock, knock!
Who's there?
Letter.
Letter who?
Letter me in, it's cold out here.

Stoke Newington 1983.

11.D.33   Knock, knock!
Who's there?
Lettuce.
Lettuce who?
Let us in and you'll find out (I live here).

Blackheath, Shepherds Bush 1983; Kensington 1984.

11.D.34   Knock, knock!
Who's there?
Lettuce.
Lettuce who?
Lettuce off.

Hampstead 1984.

11.D.35   Knock, knock!
Who's there?
Little old lady.
Little old lady who?
Little old lady who can't reach the doorbell.

Blackheath, Dulwich 1983.

See also **11.D.3** and **11.D.19**.

11.D.36　Knock, knock!
Who's there?
Luke.
Luke who?
Luke through the keyhole and you'll see.

Blackheath, Dalston, Dulwich 1983.

11.D.37　Knock, knock!
Who's there?
Martini.
Martini who?
Martini (my teeny) finger got stuck in the doorbell.

Blackheath 1983.

11.D.38　Knock, knock!
Who's there?
Mister.
Mister who?
Mister at the bus stop.

Dalston 1983.

11.D.39　Knock, knock!
Who's there?
Nicholas.
Nicholas who?
Nicholas (knickerless) girls shouldn't climb trees.

Kentish Town 1983.

11.D.40　Knock, knock!
Who's there?
Peter.

Peter who?
Peter night (pee tonight) before you go to bed.

Kensington 1984.

11.D.41   Knock, knock!
Who's there?
Police.
Police who?
Police (please) let us in (may I come in).

Cubitt Town, Dulwich 1983.

11.D.42   Knock, knock!
Who's there?
Scott.
Scott who?
Scott (it's got) nothing to do with you.

Brockley 1983.

11.D.43   Knock, knock!
Who's there?
Scott.
Scott who?
Scott a lotta bottle*.

Dulwich 1983.

* This was a reference to an advertising campaign by the Milk Marketing Board in 1982, encouraging people to drink milk, using the jingle "Milk has gotta lotta bottle".

11.D.44   Knock, knock!
Who's there?
Tina.
Tina who?
Tina baked beans.

Shepherds Bush 1983.

11.D.45   Knock, knock!
Who's there?
Urie.
Urie who?
You remember when we met last.

Deptford 1983.

11.D.46   Knock, knock!
Who's there?
William.
William who?
Will you mind your own business.

Cubitt Town 1983.

11.D.47   Knock, knock!
Who's there?
Wooden.
Wooden who?
Wooden who (wouldn't you) like to know.

Cubitt Town 1983.

11.D.48   Knock, knock!
Who's there?
Yamaha.
Yamaha who?
Yamaha (your mama) wants you.

Dulwich 1983.

11.D.49   Knock, knock!
Who's there?
You.
You who?
You called?

Blackheath 1983.

11.D.50   Knock, knock!
Who's there?
Zebra.
Zebra who?
Ze bra is too big for me.

Kensington 1984.

Variations on the traditional form

11.D.51   Knock, knock!
Who's there?
Arthur.
Arthur who?
I forgot.

Dalston, Deptford 1983.

11.D.52   Knock, knock!
Who's there?
Boo.
Boo who?
Don't cry, it's only a joke (only me).

Blackheath, Dalston, Finsbury, Hampstead, Shepherds Bush, Stoke Newington 1983; Kensington 1984.

11.D.53   Knock, knock!
Who's there?
The invisible man.
Tell him I can't see him.

Hampstead 1984.

11.D.54   Knock, knock!
Who's there?
I've forgotten.

> Forgotten who?
> I've forgotten too.
>
> Blackheath 1983.

11.D.55
> Knock, knock!
> Who's there?
> Little old lady.
> Little old lady who?
> I never knew you could yodel.
>
> Blackheath 1983.

Possibly inspired by the novelty yodelling song "Cinderella Rockefella" written by Mason Williams and Nancy Ames and released by Esther and Abi Ofarim in 1968, which contains the line "You're the lady, the lady who …".

11.D.56
> Knock, knock!
> Who's there?
> Me.
> Me who?
> You've forgotten me.
>
> Blackheath 1983.

11.D.57
> Knock, knock!
> Who's there?
> Open the door and find out.
>
> Shepherds Bush 1983.

11.D.58
> Knock, knock!
> Who's there?
> Owl.
> Owl who?
> Hallo!
>
> Shepherds Bush 1983.

11.D.59   Knock, knock!
Who's there?
Tish.
Tish who?
You've caught it.

Brockley 1983.

See also **11.D.21**.

11.D.60   Knock, knock!
Who's there?
Banana.
Banana who?
Banana.
Banana who?
Banana.
Banana who?
Orange,
Orange who?
Orange (Aren't) you glad I didn't say banana.

Hampstead 1984.

11.D.61   Knock, knock!
Who's there?
Grandma.
Grandma who?
Grandma.
Grandma who?
Grandma.
Grandma who?
Aunt.
Aunt who?
Aunt you glad I got rid of those grannies?

Streatham 1982; Blackheath, Borough, Cubitt Town, Dulwich 1983; Hampstead 1984.

11.D.62   Will you remember me in a couple of weeks' time?
Yes.
Will you remember me in a couple of months' time?
Of course.
Will you remember me in a couple of years' time?
Definitely.
Knock, knock!
Who's there?
See, you've already forgotten me.

Greenwich 1982; Blackheath, Deptford, Dulwich, Mile End, Shepherds Bush, Stoke Newington 1983; Hampstead 1984.

Printed version   Cansler, 6–7.

Variations on the* Doctor Who *theme (a British science fiction television series)

11.D.63   Knock, knock!
Who's there?
Doctor.
Doctor who?
You said it/guessed it.

Borough, Dalston, Deptford, Dulwich, Mile End, Shepherds Bush 1983; Hampstead 1984.

11.D.64   Knock, knock!
Who's there?
Doctor.
Doctor who?
How did you know I was out here?

Barnsbury, Stoke Newington 1983.

11.D.65   Knock, knock!
Who's there?

I love Doctor.
I love Doctor who?
I know you do. (Do you?)

Kentish Town, Mile End 1983.

Reference to "The Who" rock group:

11.D.66   Knock, knock!
Who's there?
The Who.
The who?
You just said it.

Borough 1983.

Printed versions of knock knock riddles Botkin (see below); Northall (see below); Ritchie (*SS*, pp. 31–32) says "'Knock Knock' reached its peak of popularity" in the 1920s, and quotes two examples.

Early notings cf. 1. Knock! knock! 2. Who's there? 1. Buff. 2. What says Buff? 1. Buff says Buff to all his men/And I say Buff to you again. … Northall, 1892, pp. 407–408. This rhyme accompanied a game where the players had to make each other smile by reciting the rhyme, at which they had a pay a forfeit, Botkin, *TAF*, 1944, pp. 474–475.

11.E VERBAL EXCHANGE JOKES

I have used the term "verbal exchange" for the kind of joke which is in the form of a brief dialogue of two or three lines, usually falling into a set formula such as: doctor-patient, teacher-pupil, waiter-customer, parent-child. There are a few miscellaneous ones and some "sick" examples which, like the sick riddles and sick jokes, are probably leftovers from the 1960s. Of these categories, by far the largest number I have collected belong to the doctor-patient exchange (thirty-five examples) and the waiter-customer exchange (twenty-seven examples). I do not know when this form of humour became widely popular. One or two examples are quite old and some seem to have been adapted from old jokes and limericks, like the variations on "There's a fly in my soup" (**11.E.60–11.E.72**). This kind of joke is often featured in children's comic papers and books, but this does not explain why so many were current at the time of my study.

Some of the jokes are not particularly funny and are obviously ephemeral. Others, however, show wit and sophisticated punning. Some depend on their absurdity for their humour. In the doctor-patient jokes, which do not rely on punning, the humour arises from the complaint of the patient being taken absolutely literally by the doctor. The patient who says everyone ignores him is ignored (**11.E.6**). The doctor says, "One at a time" to the patient who thinks there are two of him (**11.E.8**). In some examples the patient is the one to interpret his complaint literally. He claims he is seeing double and asks which couch to sit on when he is offered one (**11.E.1**). The patient who thinks he is a dog says he is not allowed on furniture when asked to sit down (**11.E.21**). In the whole group the patient only holds his own in seven verbal exchanges out of the thirty-four. In the teacher-pupil exchanges the pupil has the best of it every time, as one would expect. In the waiter-customer jokes, the waiter is able to "put down" the customer in every example except four (**11.E.47, 11.E.48, 11.E.54** and **11.E.59**).

Doctor-patient

11.E.1 Doctor, doctor, I keep seeing double.
Well sit down on the couch.
Which one?

Mile End, Stoke Newington 1983.

11.E.2 Doctor, doctor, my hair keeps falling out. Can you give me something to keep it in?
Here's a plastic bag.

Mile End 1983.

11.E.3 Doctor, doctor, there's something wrong with my willy. It's shaped like a rocket.
What does your wife think?
She's over the moon with it.

Brockley 1983.

11.E.4 Doctor, doctor, I think I've lost my memory.
When did it happen?
When did what happen?

Brockley 1983.

11.E.5 Doctor, doctor, I cannot get to sleep.
Go to the end of your bed. You'll soon drop off.

Kentish Town 1983; Hampstead 1984.

11.E.6 Doctor, doctor, everybody keeps ignoring me.
Next please. (Who said that?)

Cubitt Town, Dalston, Finsbury, Stoke Newington 1983.

11.E.7 Doctor, doctor, everyone says I'm invisible.
Who said that? (Next please.)

Deptford 1983; Hampstead 1984.

11.E.8 Doctor, doctor, I keep on thinking there's two of me.
One at a time please.

Deptford 1983.

11.E.9 I keep seeing spots before my eyes.
Have you seen a doctor?
No, only spots.

Hampstead 1984.

11.E.10 Doctor, doctor, every time I drink a cup of tea I get a stabbing pain in my eye.
Why don't you try taking the spoon out?

Hampstead 1984.

11.E.11 Everyone thinks I'm a liar.
Do you expect me to believe that?

Stoke Newington 1983.

11.E.12 Doctor, doctor, I've been trying to think of a word for two weeks.
How about "fortnight"?

Mile End 1983.

11.E.13 Doctor, doctor, how many minutes have I got to live?
Three.
What can you do for me?
I'll boil an egg.

Mile End, Shepherds Bush 1983.

11.E.14 Doctor, doctor, I'm going to die in fifty-nine seconds.
Wait a minute.

Deptford, Mile End, Shepherds Bush 1983; Hampstead, Kensington 1984.

11.E.15 Doctor, doctor, can you help me out?
Which way did you come in?

Mile End 1983.

11.E.16 Doctor, doctor, I feel like a snooker ball.
There's a queue outside. (Wait at the end of the queue).

Barnsbury, Borough 1983.

11.E.17 Doctor, doctor, I feel like a pair of curtains.
Pull yourself together, man.

Barnsbury, Cubitt Town, Dalston, Kentish Town, Shepherds Bush, Stoke Newington 1983.

11.E.18 Doctor, doctor, I feel like a window.
Where's your pain?

Dalston, Mile End 1983.

11.E.19 Doctor, doctor, I feel like a crossword.
I haven't got a clue.

Shepherds Bush 1983.

11.E.20 Doctor, doctor, I feel like a camel.
Don't get the hump.

Deptford 1983.

11.E.21 Doctor, doctor, I keep thinking I'm a dog.
Sit on the couch.
I'm not allowed on furniture.

Stoke Newington 1983.

11.E.22 Doctor, doctor, I feel like a trashcan.
Don't talk rubbish.

Dalston, Mile End, Shepherds Bush 1983; Hampstead 1984.

11.E.23 Doctor, doctor, I feel like a bird.
I'll tweet* you later.

Mile End, Stoke Newington 1983.

* This is a pun on "treat", and predates the use now associated with social media by some twenty-five years.

11.E.24 Doctor, doctor, I feel like an apple.
Sit down, I won't bite you.

Shepherds Bush 1983.

11.E.25 Doctor, doctor, I feel like a pack of cards.
Don't worry, I'll deal with you later.

Barnsbury, Dalston, Finsbury, Kentish Town, Mile End, Shepherds Bush 1983.

11.E.26 Doctor, doctor, I feel like a goat.
How long has this been going on?
Since I was a kid.

Mile End 1983.

11.E.27 Doctor, doctor, I feel like an ice cream.
You don't look like one.

Deptford 1983.

11.E.28 Doctor, doctor, I feel like a pound note.
Go to the shops, the change will do you good.

Hampstead 1984.

11.E.29 Doctor, my daughter's just swallowed half a crown.
Take her home, put her to bed and wait for some change.

Mile End 1968.

11.E.30 Doctor, doctor, I feel like a bridge.
What's come over you?
Two lorries, a bus and three cars.

Barnsbury, Cubitt Town, Dalston, Finsbury, Kentish Town, Mile End, Stoke Newington 1983; Hampstead 1984.

11.E.31 Doctor, doctor, I keep thinking I'm a pen.
I'll give you an injection. (Patient runs out)
That's the trouble with pens; they keep running out.

Stoke Newington 1983.

11.E.32 Doctor, doctor, my son's just swallowed a pen.
Well use a pencil till I get there.

Stoke Newington

11.E.33 Doctor, doctor, my wife thinks she's a television set.
All right I'll try to cure her.
I don't want you to cure her. I just want you to tune her to Channel 4.

Mile End 1983.

11.E.34 Doctor, what's the time?
Tampax two.
Durex pect me to believe that?

Barnsbury 1983.

11.E.35 Why are you creeping by the medicine chest?
I don't want to wake the sleeping pills.

Mile End 1983.

Printed version Wolfenstein, p. 105.

Teacher/pupil etc.

11.E.36 Why weren't you here at ten past nine?
Why, what happened?

Blackheath 1983.

11.E.37 Why are you crawling into school a quarter of an hour late?
Well you tell me not to walk in a quarter of an hour late.

Blackheath 1983.

11.E.38 I'm going to be a policeman and follow my father's footsteps.
But your father's not a policeman.
No, he's a burglar.

Kentish Town 1983.

11.E.39 I don't want to do my homework.
No one's died yet from doing it.
Why should I be the first?

Blackheath 1983.

11.E.40 Your brother's just swallowed half a crown.
It's all right, it was his dinner money.

Mile End 1968.

11.E.41 Can I go to the loo?
Tell me the alphabet first.
A, B, … Z (leaving out P)
You've left out P.
Well it's running down my leg.

Blackheath, Mile End 1983.

11.E.42 Would you punish me for something I haven't done?
No, of course not.
Miss, I ain't done my homework.

Stoke Newington 1983.

Domestic etc.

11.E.43 What's on telly tonight?
Same as usual: a goldfish bowl and a vase of flowers.

Blackheath 1983.

11.E.44 I think Jesus is in our bathroom.
Why?
'Cause every morning Dad says, "Jesus Christ, haven't you finished yet?"

Blackheath 1983.

11.E.45 Have you got a light, Mac?
No, I've only got a dark one.

Kentish Town 1983.

Waiter/customer

11.E.46 Waiter, this soup tastes revolting; get the manager.
Are you sure the manager will eat it?

Blackheath 1983.

11.E.47 Waiter, you must have very clean kitchens.
O thank you, sir. Why?
Because everything tastes of soap.

Blackheath 1983; Kensington 1984.

11.E.48 I think you've got a lot of food on the menu.
O yes, thank you, sir.
Would you wipe it off, please.

Blackheath 1983.

11.E.49   Is there soup on the menu?
No, it was wiped off.

Hampstead 1984.

11.E.50   Waiter, this soup isn't fit for a pig.
All right, I'll get you some that is.

Mile End 1983.

11.E.51   Waiter, I've been waiting for the turtle soup for ages.
You know how slow turtles are, sir.

Mile End 1983.

11.E.52   Waiter, there's a film on my soup.
Well what more do you expect for 25p, Star Wars*?

Finsbury 1983.

* A reference to the film *Star Wars*, written and directed by George Lucas and released in 1977.

11.E.53   Waiter, this egg is strong.
Don't worry, there's weak tea in a minute.

Dalston 1983.

11.E.54   Can I have a crocodile sandwich? And make it snappy.

Kensington 1984.

11.E.55   Waiter, this coffee tastes like mud.
It would sir, it was ground this morning.

Kensington 1984.

Frog theme

11.E.56 Waiter, do you serve frogs?
We serve everybody.

Cubitt Town 1983.

11.E.57 Waiter, there's a frog in my soup.
Tell him to hop it.

Shepherds Bush 1983.

11.E.58 Waiter, have you got frogs' legs?
I don't walk that way, do I?

Blackheath 1983.

11.E.59 Waiter, have you got frogs' legs?
Yes, sir.
Well leap over that counter and get me some ham.

Blackheath 1983.

Insect theme

11.E.60 Waiter, there's a fly in my soup.
Shh! The others will want one too.

Streatham 1982; Barnsbury, Cubitt Town 1983; Hampstead 1984.

11.E.61 Waiter, there's a fly in my soup.
He needs a wash after rolling in the fish paste.

Streatham 1982.

11.E.62 Waiter, there's a fly in my soup.
Oh that will be an extra 5p, please.

Streatham 1982.

11.E.63 Waiter, there's a fly in my soup.
Don't worry, the spider in the bread will catch it.

Streatham 1982; Barnsbury, Dulwich, Mile End 1983.

11.E.64 Waiter, there's a fly in my soup.
Oh yes, the wasps are on strike.

Barnsbury 1983.

11.E.65 Waiter, there's a fly swimming in my soup.
(Waiter removes it)
Sorry, it only likes puddles.

Kensington 1984.

11.E.66 There's a tiny (giant) fly in my soup.
Shall I get you a bigger (smaller) one?

Hampstead 1984.

11.E.67 Waiter, there's a fly in my soup. What's it doing there?
It looks like the breast stroke (crawl, back stroke).

Streatham 1982; Barnsbury, Blackheath, Dulwich, Finsbury, Mile End, Shepherds Bush 1983; Hampstead 1984.

11.E.68 Waiter, there's a fly in my soup.
Hang on a minute, I'll call the R.S.P.C.A.

Hampstead 1984.

11.E.69 Waiter, there's a dead fly in my soup.
It's the hot soup that kills them.

Barnsbury 1983.

11.E.70 Waiter, there's a dead fly in my soup.
Oh! and he was so young.

Hampstead 1984.

11.E.71 Waiter, there are lots of flies in my soup.
Take out the ones you don't fancy and eat the rest.

Dulwich 1983.

11.E.72 Waiter, there's a bee in my soup.
Oh, it must be the fly's day off today.

Barnsbury 1983.

Puns

11.E.73 Lift boy: What floor?
Passenger: Tenth floor, boy.
Lift boy: Tenth floor, boy!
Passenger: How dare you call me boy.
Lift boy: Well I brought you up, didn't I?

Dulwich 1983.

11.E.74 Messy pile of sick: Why are you so tidy?
Tidy pile of sick: I was well brought up.

Kensington 1984.

11.E.75 Released prisoner: I'm free! I'm free!
Boy: So what, I'm four! I'm four!

Dulwich 1983.

11.E.76 First man in aeroplane: If we fly upside down, will we fall out?
Second man in aeroplane: No, we'll still be friends.

Cubitt Town 1983.

11.E.77 (A lady driver on the M1 was seen to be knitting by a policeman. He stopped her).

Pull over!
No, a pair of socks.

Cubitt Town 1983.

Mum(my), Mum(my)

11.E.78   Mummy, Mummy, a man's just fallen off the cliff.
Have you told your Dad about this?
It was him.

Hampstead 1984.

11.E.79   Mummy, Mummy, why is Daddy walking round in circles?
Shut up and nail his other foot to the floor.

Blackheath 1983.

11.E.80   Mummy, Mummy, why is Daddy running away?
Shut up and keep firing.

Blackheath 1983.

11.E.81   Mummy, Mummy, can I play with Grandad?
No, you've already dug him up three times today.

Blackheath 1983.

11.E.82   Mummy, Mummy, what are we having for dinner?
Shut up and get back in the oven.

Mile End 1968.

11.E.83   Mum, Mum, I don't want to go to Australia.
Shut up and keep on digging.

Blackheath 1983.

11.F FUNNY BOOK TITLES AND EPITAPHS

Imaginary book titles give an opportunity for wordplay which does not require a lot of skill, but which can often produce something which is quite funny. A child may notice that a particular word or phrase sounds like a first name, and this may suggest a surname which does not have to be an accepted one. The child may then find a possible title to fit the name of the imaginary author. A really humorous combination of title and author may be a joint effort of more than one child. An imaginative child can grasp the comic possibilities very quickly. Examples of the wittier kind are: **11.F.21** "A Russian Flea by Ivan Ellofanitch" and **11.F.32** "Rusty Bedsprings by I. P. Nightly". I remember sessions in my schooldays when we would exchange a few of these titles and try to make some new ones up. The only one I can still recall from those far off days was typical but not very funny. It was "Short Skirts by Seymour Legs". None of those I collected during my researches evoked any memories. Though the examples may or may not be of recent creation, this kind of humour does have some tradition behind it. Epitaphs are rarer and are probably gathered from books.

Book Titles

11.F.1 How to Get Money by Robin Banks.
Dulwich 1983.

11.F.2 Gone for a Break by T. N. Biscuit.
Stoke Newington 1983.

11.F.3 Somebody Help Me by N. E. Body.
Dulwich 1983.

11.F.4 Dog's Dinner by Norah Bone.
Dulwich 1983.

11.F.5 Let X Equal Y by Algie Bra.
Dulwich 1983.

11.F.6 In the Forest by Teresa Brown.
Dulwich 1983.

11.F.7 The Countryside by Teresa Brown.
Dulwich 1983.

11.F.8 On a Saddle for Fifty Years by Major Bumsore.
Hampstead 1984.

11.F.9 Riding Round the World by Major Bumsore.
Kensington 1984.

11.F.10 Round the World on a Bicycle by Major Bumsore.
Blackheath 1983.

11.F.11 Country Walk by Miss D. Buss.
Blackheath 1983.

11.F.12 Learn to Swim by I. Cant.
Blackheath 1983.

11.F.13 I Can't Move by Andy Capp (handicap).
Blackheath 1983.

11.F.14 Vegetables by Norah Carrot.
Dulwich 1983.

11.F.15 Naughty Boys by Ben Dover. Hampstead 1984.

11.F.16 Schoolboy Troubles by Ben Dover. Blackheath 1983.

11.F.17 Falling Down a Cliff by Eileen Dover. Hampstead 1984.

11.F.18 How I Fell off a Cliff by Eileen Dover. Blackheath 1983.

11.F.19 The Edge of a Cliff by Eileen Dover. Blackheath 1983.

11.F.20 The Edge of a Cliff by Willy Dropp. Blackheath 1983.

11.F.21 A Russian Flea by Ivan Ellofanitch. Finsbury 1983.

11.F.22 How to Make a Cake by Henry Ettit. Dulwich 1983.

11.F.23 Good Jockey by Billy Felloff. Greenwich 1982.

11.F.24 The Edge of a Cliff by Hugo First. Dulwich 1983.

11.F.25　The Haunted House by Hugo First.
　　　　　Blackheath, Stoke Newington 1983; Kensington 1984.

11.F.26　Electric Sword by Andy Gadgit.
　　　　　Blackheath 1983.

11.F.27　Going to School by Ivor Grudge.
　　　　　Dulwich 1983.

11.F.28　Falling Knickers by Lucy Lastic.
　　　　　Blackheath 1983.

11.F.29　Clearing the Plate by Henrietta Lott.
　　　　　Hampstead 1984.

11.F.30　Parachute Jumping by Willy Makit.
　　　　　Stoke Newington 1983.

11.F.31　The Army by Reggie Mental.
　　　　　Dulwich 1983.

11.F.32　Rusty Bedsprings by I. P. Nightly.
　　　　　Blackheath 1983; Kensington 1984.

11.F.33　The Army by Millie Tary.
　　　　　Dulwich 1983.

11.F.34　The Jockey by Willy Winn.
　　　　　Dulwich 1983.

11.F.35 Running for a Bus by Betty Woant.

Hampstead 1984.

11.F.36 Chinese Golf by Ho Lin Wun.

Stoke Newington 1983.

Printed source (other examples) Lowenstein, p. 13.

Epitaphs

11.F.37 She's happy and I'm contented.

Finsbury 1983.

11.F.38 She's at rest and so am I.

Finsbury 1983.

11.F.39 Always let your wind go free,/'Cause the wind it was the death of me.

Finsbury 1983.

11.G PUZZLES

There is little to say about these few examples. They were not a common form of entertainment in junior schools, and only **11.G.2** and **11.G.5** were in general use and might be considered traditional. Mnemonics are rare. No. **11.G.7**, where a child is induced to draw lines which make the word "shit", is not really a puzzle nor a genuine example of catching out. It was probably a bit of ephemera, the use of the word "shit" making it worthwhile to a few children who do not have a developed sense of humour.

11.G.1   F U N E X?   (Have you any eggs?)
             S V F X   (Yes, we have eggs.)
             F U N E T?   (Have you any tea?)
             S V F T   (Yes, we have tea.)
             F U N E M?   (Have you any ham?)
             S V F M   (Yes, we have ham.)

Earlsfield 1982.

11.G.2   Y Y U R   (Too wise you are,)
             Y Y U B   (Too wise you be,)
             I C U R   (I see you are)
             Y Y 4 Me   (Too wise for me.)

Streatham 1982; Blackheath, <u>Finsbury 1983</u>.

Printed versions Kellett (?early noting), p. 108; Knapps, p. 155; Northall (see below); Sutton-Smith, p. 102; Turner, p. 119.

Early noting beginning of a rhyme, every other line consisting of letters standing for words: I.C.U.R.,/Good Monsieur Carr, about to fall. ... Said to be from 1614–19. Northall, 1892, p. 542.

11.G.3   M T G G   (Empty gee-gee – A horse without a rider.)

Finsbury 1983.

Printed version Opies, *LLS*, p. 70.

11.G.4   I 8 0 4 I O 0   (I ate nothing for I owe nothing.)

Stoke Newington 1983.

11.G.5   1 1 was a racehorse   (One-one was a racehorse,)
             2 2 was 1 2   (Two-two was one too,)
             1 1 1 1 race   (One-one won one race,)
             2 2 1 1 2   (Two-two won one too.)

Kensington 1984.

Printed version Turner, p. 117.

Other similar printed puzzles Knapps, Autographs section, p. 155; Turner, Autograph Album section, p. 119; Withers, *RIMP*, Autograph Album section, p. 163.

Mnemonic

11.G.6   Mrs. M, Mrs. I, Mrs. S S I,
Mrs. S S I, Mrs. P P I.

Kentish Town 1983.

Printed version Turner, p. 80.

11.G.7   Draw an S; that's a snake:
Draw four little lines
Cross the bridge
It starts to rain
Put umbrella up.

Barnsbury 1983.

This rhyme is a means of inducing a child to write the word "shit". Cf. Tongue twisters **11.B.13** and **11.B.14** above.

11.H LIMERICKS

According to Legman in his two volume collection of limericks (*TL*, 1976, pp. xii-xiii), this verse form has roots dating back to the fourteenth century. Examples of limericks were appearing in children's books by the 1820s. One example apparently inspired Edward Lear whose *Book of Nonsense* appeared in 1846. By the 1880s this genre had become known as the limerick. The rhyming and metrical pattern is much older, however, and echoes can be found, for example, in three of Shakespeare's plays: Iago's song in *Othello*, Act II, Scene 3, ll. 72–76, one of Ophelia's songs in *Hamlet*, Act IV, Scene 5, ll. 59–66, and Edgar's verse in *King Lear*, Act III, Scene 4, ll. 123–127.

There will usually be one or two children in a class of older juniors who will have a limited repertoire of limericks they have memorised, either aurally from someone else or from the printed page. These may include variations of very well known examples like **11.H.1** "There was a young gardener of Leeds" and **11.H.2** "There was a young man from Bengal". The Lear limericks do not take their fancy, but Spike Milligan's writings may do so. Some of his verse may now have entered the tradition. I collected one of his limericks: "There was a young sergeant called Edsir" (**11.H.9**)[1] in 1984. Of the thirty-three limericks I collected, only ten similar examples are to be found in the extensive Legman collection.[2] Considering the large proportion of children's jokes which have a bawdy theme, and the preponderance of such themes among adult limericks, it is perhaps a matter of surprise that of the thirty-three limericks presented here, only five had a bawdy or obscene character. Even where there were both bawdy and non-bawdy versions of the same limerick, it was the non-bawdy versions that I usually came across.

Some of the children's limericks make use of the Lear device of having the last line virtually a repeat of the first (**11.H.24**, **11.H.27**, **11.H.28**). As a class teacher who encouraged a lot of verse making with junior age children, I found that even clever upper age junior school children found it very difficult to scan accurately while at the same time maintaining a rhyme structure which made sense. When they attempt to construct limericks or even easier verse forms their efforts are not likely to be very successful without adult aid. A number of examples I collected reveal these difficulties (**11.H.18**, **11.H.20**, **11.H.24**, **11.H.31–11.H.33**). They have weaknesses in either rhyme or metre. These may represent attempts to make up new limericks or they may be misheard or half-forgotten verses which needed completion.

NOTES

1. Milligan, S. (1959, 1968). *Silly Verse for Kids.* London: Dennis Dobson; rpt. London: Puffin.

2. Legman (*TL*, 1976), pp. 5, 9, 21, 39, 119, 143, 156, 233, 240, 327.

11.H.1   There was a young gardener of Leeds,
Who swallowed a packet of seeds.
In less than an hour,
His face was a-flower,
And his head was a garden of weeds.

    Blackheath, Borough, Mile End, Stoke Newington 1983; Hampstead, Kensington 1984.

This well-known limerick exists in both "decent" and "indecent" versions.

Printed version Legman, *TL*, p. 39.

11.H.2   There was a young man from Bengal
Who went to a fancy dress ball.
He said he would risk it, (He went just for fun,)
And went as a biscuit, (Dressed up as a bun)
But a dog ate him up in the hall.

    Blackheath, Dulwich, Mile End 1983.

See note to **11.H.1** above.

Printed version Legman, *TL*, p. 119.

11.H.3   There was a young lady of Lynn,
Who was most uncommonly thin,
But when she essayed
To drink lemonade,
She slipped through the straw and fell in.

    Hampstead 1984.

Most versions of this well-known limerick are very similar.

There are many limericks using the rhyme basis "Ealing" or "Darjeeling". The following two are typical, and are of long standing:

11.H.4 There was a man from Darjeeling,
Who travelled from London to Ealing.
It said on the door,
"Don't spit on the floor"
So he carefully spat on the ceiling.

Walworth 1982; Dalston 1983.

Printed version Legman, *TL*, p. 143.

11.H.5 There was an old woman from Ealing,
Who had a peculiar feeling.
She lay on the mat,
And opened her prat,
And peed all over the ceiling.

Mile End 1983.

Printed version Legman, *TL*, p. 156.

11.H.6 A diner while dining at Crewe,
Found a large mouse in his stew.
Said the waiter, "Don't shout
And wave it about,
The others will all want one too."

Mile End 1983; Hampstead 1984.

Printed version Legman, *TL*, p. 5.

11.H.7 There was a young lady of Tottenham,
She'd no manners or she had forgotten 'em.

At tea at the vicar's
She tore off her knickers,
And explained that she felt very 'ot in 'em.

Dalston 1983.

Printed version Legman, *TL*, p. 327.

11.H.8   There was a young lady of Ryde,
Who ate some green apples and died.
The apples fermented
Inside the lamented,
And made cider inside her inside.

Hampstead 1984.

11.H.9   There was a young sergeant called Edsir,
When wanted was always in bed, sir.
One morning at one
They fired the gun,
And Edsir, in bed, sir, was dead, sir.

Mile End 1984.

This is one of Spike Milligan's limericks, published in his *Silly Verse for Kids* (see Notes above).

11.H.10   There was an old man from Brazil,
Who swallowed a gunpowder pill.
His heart it expired,
His bum it backfired,
And his balls flew over the hill.

Walworth 1982; Mile End 1983; <u>Kensington 1984</u>.

Printed version Legman, *TL*, p. 233.

11.H.11   Sir Humphrey de Willoughby Cox,
          Delighted in hunting the fox,
          But the hounds at the meet,
          Could scent only feet,
          Because of his smelly old socks.

          Borough 1983.

11.H.12   There was an old man from Dundee,
          Who climbed a very tall tree.
          He felt such a clown
          When he couldn't get down,
          He's been there since 1903.

          Stoke Newington 1982–84.

11.H.13   There was an old lady of Crete,
          Who smelt from her head to her feet.
          When she brought in a tray,
          We all fainted away,
          And then beat a hasty retreat.

          Hampstead 1984.

11.H.14   There was a young man from Dumbarton,
          Who thought he could run like a Spartan.
          On the thirty ninth lap,
          His braces went snap,
          And his face turned a red Scottish tartan.

          Blackheath 1983.

11.H.15   There was an old lady of Spain,
          Who cocked up her leg on a train.
          The train went fast
          It tickled her arse,

And she never went there again.
(That poor old lady from Spain).

<u>Cubitt Town</u>, Dulwich <u>1983</u>.

Printed version Legman, *TL*, p. 21.

11.H.16 There was an old lady from Spain,
Who couldn't go out in the rain,
'Cause she'd lent her umbrella,
To Queen Isabella,
So never could go out again.

Dulwich 1983.

11.H.17 There was a young lady from Wales,
Whose grandmother reared baby snails.
She collected a lot,
Put them all in a pot,
And stirred them with a dog's tail.

Borough 1983.

11.H.18 There was a young man called Bloggs,
Who regularly went for odd jobs.
He called his dog Rover,
Who then tripped him over,
And he landed upside down in the bog.

Borough 1983.

11.H.19 A girl who weighed many an ounce,
Used language I dare not pronounce,
When a fellow unkind,
Pulled her chair from behind,
Just to see whether she'd bounce.

Mile End 1983.

11.H.20 A gorilla who drove off in a car,
He didn't get very far.
His tyres went flat,
He just missed a cat,
And he ended up behind bars.

Dalston 1983.

11.H.21 There was a young lady from Gloucester,
Whose parents thought they had lost her.
From the fridge came a sound,
And there she was found,
The problem was how to defrost her.

Dulwich 1983.

Printed version Legman, *TL*, p. 9.

11.H.22 There was a young lady from Spa,
Who was drinking a cup of black cha.
She said, "Oh my God!"
'Cause a little black dog,
Had just weed on her brand new car.

Dulwich 1983.

11.H.23 There was an old man from Fife,
Who cooked all the food for his wife.
One day in the custard,
He put in some mustard,
And that was the end of her life.

Kensington 1984.

11.H.24 There was an old person of Fife,
Who decided he hated his wife.
One day he threw her out,

But received back a clout,
That silly old person of Fife.

Kensington 1984.

11.H.25 There was an old man from Havana,
Who wanted to play the pianna.
His fingers slipped
And opened his zip,
And out came a hairy banana.

Battersea 1982; Barnsbury 1983.

Printed version Legman, *TL*, p. 240.

11.H.26 There was a man from outer space,
Who said, "I'm from a superior race.
I am superior,
While you're all inferior,"
Then he tripped and fell flat on his face.

Streatham 1982.

11.H.27 A grubby young schoolboy of Kent,
Didn't know what cleanliness meant.
He bathed in his vest,
And neglected the rest,
That dirty old schoolboy of Kent.

Streatham 1982.

11.H.28 There was a young man named Flop,
Who liked lemon, orange and pop.
When he did burp,
He fell in the dirt,
And that was the end of young Flop.

Dulwich 1983.

11.H.29   There was a young twin called Hannah,
         Who got caught in a flood in Savannah.
         As she floated away,
         Her sister, they say,
         Accompanied her on the pianna.

         Dulwich 1983.

11.H.30   There was a small fishy called Pinkie,
         Who went for a swim in the sinkie.
         When out came the plug,
         He whispered, "Glug! Glug!
         I'll be out to sea in a winkie."

         Kensington 1984.

11.H.31   There was a young man named Babitts,
         Who ate hundreds of rabbits.
         When he'd eaten eighteen,
         He turned perfectly green,
         And then he relinquished those habits.

         Kensington 1984.

11.H.32   There was a cannibal called Ned,
         Who used to eat onions in bed.
         His mother said, "Sonny,
         It's not very funny,
         Why don't you eat people instead?"

         Streatham 1982.

11.H.33   There was a young man called Glosp,
         Who got stung in the eye by a wasp.
         When asked if it hurt,
         He said, "No, not a bit,
         It can do it again it if wants."

         Blackheath 1983.

Printed versions of other limericks Lowenstein, pp. 41, 42.

11.I RHYMES FOR FUN

There are many different kinds of rhymes which are passed around by children "just for fun". They may be traditional like **11.I.1** ONE, TWO, THREE, MOTHER CAUGHT A FLEA, based on an early counting-out rhyme. They may be based on characters from films or television like the "Batman" rhymes (**11.I.2**, **11.I.3**), while some are enjoyed for their wordplay (**11.I.6**, **11.I.7**). Bawdy examples range from the mildly to the grossly indecent. They can be brief like **11.I.20** DIANA DORS, or consist of a number of verses with a refrain, probably adapted from songs (**11.I.30**, **11.I.31**, **11.I.41**). A number, if not all, of the rhymes in the section devoted to parodies could be equally included in this section. One of the variations on the "Mary had a little lamb" theme (**8.D.36G**) uses the same device as a version of **11.I.24C** I HAD A LITTLE BROTHER. The end of the line is expected to be a word of a risqué character which, however, starts a new line of an innocuous kind.

The many "Fatty and Skinny" rhymes (**11.I.23**), which may perhaps have developed from the older "Punch and Judy" ones (**11.I.22**), could be found in almost every Inner London school. The two-line versions are easy enough to make up almost on the spur of the moment, though as most of them are based on breaking wind, one might think the possibilities were rather limited. Some of the lines in versions of **11.J.17** MY OLD MAN'S A DUSTMAN are interchangeable with those in some "Fatty and Skinny" rhymes.

Versions of I HAD A LITTLE BROTHER (**11.I.24A** and **11.I.24B**) include a sequence similar to one in a Gomme singing game: "All the Boys in Our Town" (Gomme, 1894, p. 4). This mentions a doctor, a cat, and a lady with a white straw hat. In contemporary versions these have been changed to a doctor, a nurse, and a lady with an alligator purse. These lines are equally in use in the USA where one presumes alligator purses were more common than in Britain. Once the nurse had been introduced it was necessary to introduce another character to rhyme with "nurse" and retain the metre.

The many bawdy rhymes range from the crudest of efforts like **11.I.21A** and **11.I.21B** to the humour of **11.I.13** MY FRIEND BILLY. Of the fifty-eight rhymes contained in this section there are seven which deal with breaking wind (**11.I.3**, **11.I.9**, **11.I.18**, **11.I.19**, **11.I.23**, **11.I.29A**,

11.I.42), ten that refer to defecation/urination (**11.I.12**, **11.I.21**, **11.I.23g**, **11.I.27**, **11.I.38**, **11.I.39**, **11.I.41**, **11.I.43**, **11.I.45**, **11.I.49b**), eight mentioning nudity or the genitals (**11.I.11**, **11.I.13**, **11.I.15**, **11.I.21**, **11.I.32**, **11.I.37**, **11.I.40**, **11.I.48b**), and four dealing with sexual practices (**11.I.29b**, **11.I.30**, **11.I.31**, **11.I.50**). This is probably about the balance of humorous material in the age group we are dealing with.

Films and television have inspired, in addition to the Batman and Diana Dors rhymes already referred to, one about Donald Duck (**11.I.43b**) and six based on other characters. I have included two rhymes about the Beatles dating from the 1960s (**11.I.56**, **11.I.57**). These are interesting in that the group inspired a number of rhymes, songs, parodies and riddles in that decade. However, when the group split up and were absent from media attention they rapidly disappeared from children's lore and did not seem to leave any trace behind, except in parodies such as **8.D.4d**. Apart from a remnant of the once extensive group of rhymes about Hitler (**11.I.32**) I have only come across one rhyme with any political reference in the form of a variation of a school rhyme: **11.I.58** BUILD A BONFIRE. Two rhymes probably have their origins in Ghana and the Caribbean respectively (**11.I.47** and **11.I.48b**).

11.I.1   ONE, TWO, THREE, MOTHER CAUGHT A FLEA

SOMETIMES USED FOR SKIPPING, BALL BOUNCING, OR AS A COUNTING-OUT RHYME:

One, two, three,
Mother caught a flea,
Put it in the teapot,
And made a cup of tea.
The flea jumped out,
Mother gave a shout,
And down comes Father,
With his shirt hanging out.

Mile End 1968; Barnsbury, Blackheath, Brockley, Shepherds Bush 1983; <u>Kensington 1984</u>.

Printed versions Abrahams, quoting Douglas, p. 36; another version, p. 153; Abrahams and Rankin, p. 182; Bolton (see below); Brady, p. 59; Cole, p. 38; Daiken, *OGS*, p. 32; Douglas (see below); Gregor (see below); Gullen, ball bouncing, p. 34; Holbrook, p. 122; Kellett, pp. 95–96; MacBain (see below); McMorland, p. 31; Nelson, ball bouncing, p. 67; Nicholson (see below); Opies, *LLS*, p. 19, *CGSP*, Oh dear me ..., counting-out rhyme, p. 38; Ritchie, *GC*, p. 44; Rodger, p. 17; Shaw, 1970, pp. 4, 71; Sutton-Smith, pp. 97, 98, 99; Turner, p. 100; Withers, *CO*, [p. 2], *RIMP*, p. 117, both like Bolton's, below; Wood (see below).

Early notings One, two, three,/Nanny caught a flea;/The flea died; and Nanny cried:/Out goes she! **Variations:–** For Nanny, "Granny;" also, "Mother." Line 4. —O-U-T spells out/And in again. Also: Eins, zwei, drei,/Mother caught a fly,/The fly died and mother cried,/Eins, zwei, drei, Bolton, 1888, p. 92. One, two, three,/Granny caught a flee [sic],/Flee died,/Granny cried,/Out goes she. (Granton), Gregor, 1891, p. 30. One, two, three;/Mother caught a flea./Flea died: mother cried!/Out goes she (or he), Nicholson, 1897, p. 307. O dear me, mother caught a flea,/Put it in the tea-pot and made a cup of tea— Douglas, 1916, p. 91, 1931, p. 52. MacBain, 1933, counting-out rhyme, like Bolton, p. 174. Cf. One, two, three,/Towser caught a flea, Wood, *AMG*, 1940, p. 83.

The following two rhymes refer to the character Batman (and his assistant, Robin) who first appeared in 1939 in American children's comics and later in popular television series and films.

11.I.2 BATMAN

> nnnnnnnnnnnn* Batman
> Swinging on an elastic band,
> Landed in a pot of jam,
> Along came a spider man,
> Thought he was a bogeyman,
> Ate him.

Walworth 1979; <u>Greenwich 1982</u>; Borough, Brockley 1983.

* The "nnnnn…" imitates the first notes of the television *Batman* theme tune.

11.I.3 RUNNING DOWN THE HIGHWAY

    A. Running down the highway,
         In a Batmobile,
         Robin done a fart,
          And paralysed the wheel.
         Batman couldn't stand it,
         The engine fell apart,
         All because of Robin,
         And his supersonic fart.

Brockley, Marylebone 1967; Mile End 1968; Battersea 1982; Borough, Dalston, <u>Kentish Town 1983</u>.

Printed versions Knapps, p. 212; Richards and Stubbs, p. 155.

    B. Batman and Robin in a Batmobile,
         Robin did a fart and Batman flew away.

Mile End 1983.

    C. Going down the highway,
         Doing ninety-four,
         (_____) did a fart,
         And blew us out the door.
         (_____) couldn't take it,
         The engine fell apart
         Just because of (_____'s)
         Supersonic fart.

Streatham 1982; <u>Stoke Newington 1983</u>.

See also **11.J.17D**.

Printed versions Lowenstein, p. 20; Turner, Driving up the highway doing 44, p. 88.

11.I.4 SHOCKING

> Oh how shocking!
> A flea ran up my stocking,
> It bit my bum and made me run,
> Oh how shocking!

Dalston 1983.

Printed versions cf. Hepburn and Roberts, 302; Lowenstein, [p. iii]; Opies, *LLS*, p. 95; Turner, p. 103.

11.I.5 NOBODY LOVES ME

> A. Nobody loves me, nobody cares,
>   I think I'm going to eat some worms,
>   Short ones, fat ones,
>   Juicy big fuzzy ones,
>   I think I'm going to eat some worms.

Kensington 1984.

> B. Everybody hates me,
>   Nobody likes me,
>   Going down the garden to eat worms,
>   Big ones, fat ones,
>   Juicy big and hairy ones,
>   See how they squiggle and squirm.
>   Tear their heads off,
>   Squeeze all the juice out,
>   Throw all the skins away.
>   Everybody hates me,

> Nobody likes me,
> I think I'm going to eat some worms.

Streatham 1982; <u>Finsbury 1983</u>.

Typically sung at Scout and Guide camps.

Printed versions Fowke, p. 94; Knapps, p. 182; Opies, *LLS*, p. 175; Turner, p. 89.

Early noting A version of A. was told to me by my mother c1925.

11.I.6 WHERE YOU GOING, BOB?

> Where you going, Bob?
> To the shops, Bob.
> What for, Bob?
> Cigarettes, Bob.
> Want one?
> No, Bob.
> I got a cold, Bob.
> How, Bob?
> I don't know, Bob.

Brixton 1982.

See also **7.7, 8.A.4**, and **11.I.7**.

Printed versions Abrahams, p. 207; Brady, p. 52; cf. Kirshenblatt-Gimblett, p. 109; Rutherford, p. 126.

11.I.7 HERE'S YOUR BUS, SIR

> Here's your bus, sir.
> O.K., Goodbye sir.
> Where, sir?

> There, sir.
> Here, sir,
> Bye bye, sir.

Brixton 1982.

See also **7.7**, **8.A.4**, and **11.I.6**.

11.I.8 WAY DOWN SOUTH

> Way down South where bananas grow,
> The grasshopper stepped on an elephant's toe.
> The elephant said with tears in his eyes,
> "Pick on somebody your own size."

Blackheath 1983.

Printed versions Abrahams, p. 203; Cole, p. 22; Fowke, p. 126; Turner, Down in Africa where the peanuts grow, autograph album rhyme, p. 113.

11.I.9 WE'RE IN THE AIR FORCE

> We're in the Air Force now,
> We went to milk a cow,
> The cow blew off and we flew off,
> And now we're in the Air Force.

Barnsbury 1983.

Printed versions Lowenstein, p. 25; Turner, pp. 92–93.

11.I.10 TIDDLY WINKS OLD MAN

> Tiddly Winks old man,
> Suck a lemon if you can.

If you can't suck a lemon,
Suck an old tin can.

Walworth 1979; Brixton 1982.

Tune "Sailors' Hornpipe".

Printed versions cf. Cray, *BB*, p. 119; cf. Lowenstein, p. 43; Shaw, 1970, p. 61; Turner, p. 106.

11.I.11 THERE'S A PLACE IN FRANCE

There's a place in France,
Where the naked ladies dance,
There's a hole in the wall,
Where the men can see them all.

Hampstead 1984.

Tune (for this and **11.I.12**): "Little Egypt's Dance", otherwise known as "The Snake Charmer Song", written by Sol Bloom for the Chicago World's Columbian Exposition of 1893 for an exotic dancer nicknamed "Little Egypt" to dance to.

Printed versions Boyes, mentioned, 36; Cansler, 7; Cosbey, p. 91; Knapps, p. 185; cf. Lowenstein, p. 42; cf. Shaw, 1970, p. 11; Turner, p. 105.

11.I.12 THERE'S A MAN IN SPAIN

There's a man in Spain,
Who put rhubarb down the drain.
You can hear his mother crowing
When the toilet starts a-growing.
Well he makes a stink,

With some business down the sink.
He says, "Mum you shouldn't spoil it,
For the whole world is my toilet."
Tum te tum poo poo
Tum te tum tee poo de poo.

Hampstead 1984.

Tune "Little Egypt's Dance", as for **11.I.11** above.

11.I.13 MY FRIEND BILLY

My friend Billy
Had a ten foot willy.
He showed it to the girl next door.
She thought it was a snake
And hit it with a rake,
And now it's only five feet four.

Walworth 1982; Brockley 1983; Kensington 1984.

Printed versions Hubbard, mentioned, 262; Lowenstein, Nicker nicker nicker, p. 33; Rutherford, p. 120; Turner, Old King Cole had a forty-foot pole, p. 99.

11.I.14 THERE WAS A LITTLE MAN

There was a little man,
And he had a little gun.
And over ditches he did run.
A bellyful of fat
And a big tall hat,
And a pancake tied to his bum, bum, bum.

Dalston 1983.

See also **6.A.36E**.

Printed versions Brady, p. 74; Fowke, p. 126; Gaskell (see below); Halliwell (see below); Rutherford, p. 125; Shaw, 1970, pp. 19–20, 49–50, 110–111.

Early notings Probably derived from the nursery rhyme with the same first two lines: There was a little man,/And he had a little gun,/And his bullets were made of lead, lead, lead./He went to a brook,/And fired at a duck,/And shot him through the head, head, head. Halliwell, *NRE*, 1842, p. 35. There was a little man/He had a little gun/An' o'er yon field he run, run, run,/He'd a white sthraw hat/A bally full o' fat/An' a pancake stitched to his bum bum bum. Gaskell, c1913, p. 8.

11.I.15 I WISH I WAS A LITTLE WORM

I wish I was a little worm,
With hairs around my willy (tummy),
I'd climb into my honeypot,
And make my willy (tummy) gummy.

Borough 1983.

11.I.16 THERE'S A WORM AT THE BOTTOM OF THE GARDEN

There's a worm at the bottom of the garden,
And his name is Wiggly Worm,
There's a worm at the bottom of the garden,
And he wiggles his way through.
He wiggles all night,
And he wiggles all day,
He wiggles all the time away.

There's a worm at the bottom of the garden,
And his name is Wiggly Worm.

Mile End 1983.

This rhyme is known to have been taught in British nursery and primary schools in the 1970s and in elementary schools in Australia and the USA.

11.I.17 I'M TAKING HOME A LITTLE BUMBLE BEE

I'm taking home a little bumble bee,
Won't my mother be proud of me.
Oo ah! It stung me!
Won't my mother be proud of me!

Squashing up the little bumble bee,
Won't my mother be proud of me.
Oo ah! There's blood on me!
Won't my mother be proud of me.

I'm picking up the little bumble bee,
Won't my mother be proud of me.
Oo ah! No salt!

Finsbury 1983; Dalston 1983 (fragment).

Printed version Fowke, p. 135.

11.I.18 BEANS, BEANS

SOMETIMES A COUNTING-OUT RHYME:

A. Beans, beans,
    Good for your heart,
    The more you eat,

> The more you fart,
> The more you fart,
> The better you feel
> So let's have beans
> For every meal.

Greenwich, Walworth 1982; Barnsbury, <u>Blackheath</u>, Borough, Dalston, Kentish Town, Mile End <u>1983</u>.

> B. Beans, beans,
>   Good for your heart,
>   The more you eat,
>   The more you fart,
>   The more you fart,
>   The more you eat,
>   The more you sit,
>   On the toilet seat.

Shepherds Bush, <u>Stoke Newington 1983</u>; Hampstead, Kensington 1984.

Printed version Knapps, p. 215.

11.I.19 THERE'S A LITTLE BREATH

> There is a little breath of air,
> That starts around the heart,
> The time it gets to open air,
> It's usually called a fart.
> A fart is very useful,
> It gives your body ease
> It warms your little panties,
> And kills off all the fleas.

Finsbury 1983.

11.I.20 DIANA DORS

Diana Dors lost her drawers,
In the British Home Stores.

Marylebone 1967.

See also **4.54B**.

Printed version Opies, *LLS*, p. 108.

11.I.21 IN 1966

A. In 1966,
The people pulled down their knicks.
They licked their bum,
And said, "Yum-yum,
It tastes like [pick and mix]."

<u>Battersea</u>, Greenwich <u>1982</u>; Hampstead 1984.

B. In 1974,
The monkeys had a war,
They lost their guns,
And used their bums,
In 1974.

Hampstead 1984.

See also **8.C.1**.

Printed versions cf. Abrahams, Nineteen hundred forty-two, p. 140; cf. Cansler, several topical rhymes, 10; Gaskell (see below); cf. Knapps, p. 184; Opies, *LLS*, two versions similar to B, pp. 102, 103; Turner, two versions similar to B, p. 97.

Early noting cf. In eighteen-ninety-two/Ah went to Karsley school./ They gan me a book/An' Ah took my hook/In eighteen-ninety-two, Gaskell, c1913, p. 9.

11.I.22 PUNCH AND JUDY

> A. Punch and Judy had a race,
> All around a pillowcase,
> Punch said it wasn't fair,
> 'Cause he lost his underwear.

Mile End 1968.

Printed versions Brady, p. 10; cf. Northall (see below); Opies, *LLS*, p. 60; Talley (see below).

Early notings "'Olly an' Ivoy wun runnin' a race,/'Olly gid Ivoy a smack o' the face;/Ivoy run home to tell her mother,/Ivoy run a'ter 'er an' gid her another." Said to be from Shropshire, Northall, 1892, p. 311. Cf. Buck an' Berry run a race, Talley, 1922, p. 172.

> B. Punch and Judy fought for a pie,
> Punch gave Judy a knock in the eye,
> Says Punch to Judy, "Do you want any more?"
> Says Punch and Judy, "My eye's sore."

Mile End 1968.

Printed versions Briggs, p. 43; Halliwell (see below); Lang (see below); Opies, *ODNR*, pp. 354–355.

Early notings Punch and July/Fought for a pie;/Punch gave Judy/A knock of the eye.//Says Punch to Judy,/Will you have any more?/Says Judy to Punch,/My eye's too sore, Halliwell, *NRE*, 1844, p. 37; Punch and Judy fought for a pie;/Punch gave Judy/A sad blow on the eye, Halliwell, *NRE*, 1870, p. 14. Lang, 1897, p. 71.

See also "Fatty and Skinny" rhymes below.

11.1.23 FATTY AND SKINNY

A. Fatty and Skinny ran a race,
   Running round the pillowcase.
   Fatty said it wasn't fair,
   'Cause he lost his underwear.

Mile End 1968.

Printed versions Turner, p. 89; Withers, *RIMP*, p. 34.

B. Fatty and Skinny went to bed,
   Fatty rolled over and Skinny was dead.

Deptford 1983.

Printed version Cosbey, p. 72; Rosen and Steele, front cover.

C. Fatty and Skinny were in bed,
   Fatty blew off, Skinny flew off.

Cubitt Town, Deptford, 1983.

D. Fatty and Skinny were in bed,
   Fatty blew off and Skinny was dead.

Walworth 1982; Cubitt Town, Dalston, Deptford, Dulwich, Kentish Town, Shepherds Bush 1983.

Printed version Knapps, p. 213.

E. Fatty and Skinny in a bath,
   Fatty blew off and Skinny laughed.

Brixton, Walworth 1982; Kentish Town 1983; Hampstead 1984.

Printed versions Rutherford, p. 90; Turner, p. 89.

> F. Fatty and Skinny in the bath,
> Fatty blew off,
> Skinny took off,
> To see the man in the moon.

Brockley 1983.

> G. Fatty and Skinny went up in a rocket,
> Fatty came down with shit in his pocket.

Battersea, Walworth 1982; Cubitt Town, Dalston 1983; Hampstead 1984.

> H. Fatty and Skinny were playing cricket,
> Fatty blew off and broke the wicket.

Battersea 1982.

> I. Fatty and Skinny went out (swimming) one day,
> Fatty blew a fart and blew Skinny away.

Shepherds Bush 1983.

> J. Fatty and Skinny were in the shower,
> Fatty blew off and broke all the power.

Battersea 1982.

See "Punch and Judy" rhymes, **11.I.22A** and **11.I.22B** above; see also **11.J.17B**.

Other printed versions Cosbey, p. 72; Knapps, p. 213; Lowenstein, p. 19; Rutherford, pp. 89, 96; Sutton-Smith, p. 96; Turner, pp. 89–90; Withers, *RIMP*, p. 120.

11.I.24 I HAD A LITTLE BROTHER

A. I had a little brother,
    His name was Tiny Tim,
    I put him in the bathtub,
    To teach him how to swim.
    He drank up all the water,
    He ate up all the soap,
    He died last night,
    With a bubble in his throat.
    In came the doctor,
    In came the nurse,
    In came the lady
    With the alligator purse.
    "Dead," said the doctor,
    "Dead," said the nurse,
    "Dead," said the lady
    With the alligator purse.
    Out went the doctor,
    Out went the nurse,
    Out went the lady
    With the alligator purse.

Hampstead 1972; Streatham 1982; Barnsbury, <u>Finsbury 1983</u>.

B. Susie had a baby,
    Its name was Tiny Tim,
    She put it in the bathtub,
    And taught it how to swim.
    It drank up all the water,
    And swallowed all the soap,
    It tried to eat the bathtub,
    But it wouldn't fit down its throat.
    Susie called the doctor,
    Susie called the nurse,
    Susie called the lady
    With the alligator purse.

> "Measles," said the doctor,
> "Mumps," said the nurse,
> "Chicken pox," said the lady
> With the alligator purse.

Finsbury 1983.

See also **5.9**.

Printed versions Abrahams, skipping rhyme, pp. 79–80, 126; Botkin (see below); Cosbey, p. 75; Douglas (see below); Evans, *JRR*, a version of ll. 9–16 of both A. and B, p. 3; Fowke, p. 50; Gomme (see below); Jorgensen, I had a little sister, her name was Suzy Q, *LL*, 111–112; Kenney, Miss Lucy had a Baby, p. 29; Knapps, p. 113; Mills and Bishop (see below); Nelson, Miss Lucy had a baby, p. 66; Opies, *SG*, The Johnsons had a baby, etc., pp. 472–473; Rosen and Steele, [p. 25]; Shaw, 1970, pp. 109–110; Smith, *BBHG*, singing game, pp. 41–42; Solomons, pp. 57–58; Withers, *RIMP*, p. 30; Wood, *FAFR*, I had a little dog, his name was Tim, p. 35.

Early notings Up came the doctor, up came the cat,/Up came the devil with a white straw hat./Down went the doctor, down went the cat,/Down went the devil with a white straw hat, Gomme, 1894, p. 4, "All the boys in our town". Douglas has a version of "All the boys in our town" ending "Up goes the doctor, up goes the cat,/Up goes a little boy in a white straw hat", 1916, pp. 59–60, 1931, p. 32. Mills and Bishop, 1937, 32. Botkin, *TAF*, 1944: Virginia had a baby, p. 794, I had a little brother, as Mills and Bishop, p. 797.

The "doctor, nurse, lady with alligator purse" sequence also occurs in the rhyme "Mother, Mother, I feel ill (sick)", though I did not come across this rhyme or any variants of it in London schools. The following early noting is interesting (it was current c1930 in South London):

> C. Lulu had a baby,
> She called him Sunny Jim,

> She put him in a bathtub,
> To see if he could swim.
> He swam to the bottom,
> He swam to the top,
> Lulu got excited
> And caught it by its
> Cocktails and whisky,
> Sell them by the glass,
> If you don't like it,
> Stick it up your
> Ask no questions,
> Tell no lies,
> Ever seen a copper
> Doing up his
> Flies are a nuisance,
> Bugs are worse,
> That's the end of
> A Chinese verse.

Mile End 1966, 1968.

See also **8.D.36G** for a similar ending, and **8.D.14B**, **9.A.3** and **12.C.2** for similar wordplay.

Printed versions Kellett (see below); Kelsey, *K1*, 48; Opies (see below).

Early notings Lulu had a baby, she called it Sunny Jim,/She took it to the bathroom to see if it could swim./It swam to the bottom, it swam to the top,/Lulu got excited and grabbed it by the—/Cocktails, ginger ale, two and six a glass … Bawdy verse of the 1920s, Opies, *SG*, 1985, p. 473. Lulu had a baby, she called it Sonny Jim,/She took it to the bathroom to see if it could swim./It swam to the bottom, it swam to the top,/And Lulu got excited and grabbed it by the/Cockles and mussels two and six a pound,/If you don't like them stick 'em up your/Ask no questions tell no lies,/Have you seen a choirboy buttoning up his/Flies are a nuisance, pests are even worse,/This is the end of my naughty little verse, Kellett, 1920s, p. 27.

Other printed versions (like lines 13–17 of Version C): Barltrop and Wolveridge, p. 66; Boyes, Helen had a steamboat, 34; Cosbey, Mary had a steamboat, p. 80; Fowke, Helen had a steamboat, p. 146; Kellett, 1920s, Rule Brittania [sic] two monkies [sic] up a stick, p. 37, and The higher up the mountain ..., p. 94; Kelsey, *K1*, 48; Knapps, p. 183; cf. Lowenstein, pp. 31, 40; Opies, *LLS*, lines 9–12, p. 94; Shaw, fragment, 1970, p. 46.

11.I.25 JOHNNY WENT TO CHURCH

Johnny went to church one day,
Climbed upon the steeple,
Took his shoes and socks off,
And threw them at the people.

Walworth 1982.

11.I.26 WENT A-WALKING

Went a-walking through the London zoo,
Saw a lion, a monkey and a kangaroo,
Tried to stare at the big brown bear,
The bear fell dead, Coo, what a scare!

Brockley 1967.

11.I.27 LITTLE DROPS OF WATER

Little drops of water,
Upon the toilet floor,
It uses lots of elbow grease,
Which makes the muscles sore,
So please remember well,
Before the water flows,

Please adjust your distance,
According to your hose.

Finsbury 1983.

11.I.28 LITTLE FREDDIE FROGGIE

Little Freddie Froggie,
With a great big hop,
Jumped into the water,
With a great big plop.

Dulwich 1983.

11.I.29 TEN, TWENTY, THIRTY, FORTY, FIFTY OR MORE

A. Ten, twenty, thirty, forty, fifty or more,
 (_____) done a fart in the grocery store,
 Waving and trying to hold their breath,
 (_____) did another, and killed the rest.

Stoke Newington, Streatham 1983.

Printed version Knapps, about Snoopy, p. 213 (see note after version B. below).

B. Ten, twenty, thirty, forty, fifty or more,
 (_____) kissed (_____) on the kitchen floor,
 He kissed her once, he kissed her twice,
 He pulled down her knickers,
 And he (she) said, "That's nice!"

Battersea, Streatham, 1982; <u>Dalston</u>, Deptford, Dulwich, Stoke Newington <u>1983</u>.

The first line is the same as that of the chorus of a pop song "Snoopy vs. The Red Baron" written by Richard L. Holler and Phil Gernhard in 1967 and released by an American band called The Royal Guardsmen. Snoopy is the dog in the *Peanuts* cartoons by Charles Schultz.

11.I.30 I GOT OFF THE BUS

> I got off the bus like a good girl should,
> He followed me like I knew he would,
> 'Cause a girl's a girl, a boy's a boy,
> That's what he done to me.
>
> I walked up the stairs like a good girl should,
> He followed me like I knew he would,
> 'Cause a girl's a girl, a boy's a boy,
> That's what he done to me.
>
> I got undressed like a good girl should,
> He done it too like I knew he would, etc.
>
> I put on my nightdress like a good girl should,
> He took it off like I knew he would, etc.
>
> I got into bed like a good girl should,
> He got in too like I knew he would, etc.
>
> I opened my legs like a good girl should,
> He popped it in like I knew he would, etc.
>
> Kentish Town 1983.

Printed version Ritchie, *GC*, pp. 99–100.

11.I.31 JERRY AND JENNIFER WENT DOWN TO THE DAIRY

Jerry and Jennifer went down to the dairy,
Boomper-de-boom, Boomper-de-boom.
Jerry pulled out his hairy canary,
Boomper-de-boom, Boomper-de-boom.
Jennifer said, "Oh what a whopper!"
Boomper-de-boom, Boomper-de-boom.
Jerry said, "Let's do it proper."
Boomper-de-boom, Boomper-de-boom.
One month later all went well,
Boomper-de-boom, Boomper-de-boom.
Four months later, belly swell,
Boomper-de-boom, Boomper-de-boom.
Nine months later, belly went pop,
Boomper-de-boom, Boomper-de-boom.
Out jumped a baby with a ten foot cock.
Boomper-de-boom, Boomper-de-boom.

Finsbury 1983; Hampstead 1984.

Printed version Turner, p. 106.

11.I.32 HITLER HAS ONLY GOT ONE BALL

Hitler has only got one ball,
The other is in the Albert Hall.
His brother, the dirty bugger,
Cut it off when he was small.

Finsbury 1983; Kensington 1984.

Tune "Colonel Bogey", a march tune written in 1914 by Lieutenant F. J. Ricketts.

Printed versions cf. Lowenstein, p. 21; Turner, p. 91.

Other parodies sung to this tune Ritchie, *SS*, p. 25 (popular during WWI); Turner, p. 87.

11.I.33 WHO'S THAT?

> Who's that?
> Uncle Dave, having a bathe,
> Who's that?
> Auntie Mabel under the table.
> Who's that?
> Uncle Billy being silly,
> Who's that?
> Miss Chat with her cat.
> Who's that?
> Baby Joe licking his toe.
> Who's that?
> Uncle John singing a song.
> Who's that?
> Auntie Clare in a chair.
> and so on

Dalston 1983.

11.I.34 I'M EDUCATED MARMALADE

> I'm educated Marmalade*,
> They kicked me from the Boys' Brigade,
> The worst mistake they ever made,
> Was me, Marmalade.

Brockley 1984.

* *Educating Marmalade* was a children's television series about "the worst girl in the world" screened by Thames Television in 1981–82.

11.I.35 LULU WAS A ZULU

> Lulu was a Zulu,
> And a pretty brown girl was she,
> And all the time she walked along,
> Her little bangles bangles went ding-dong,
> Dingle-dangle, ingle-angle,
> That's the music of her bangle.
>
> Walworth 1974.

A song called "My Lulu is Half-Zulu" was performed in music halls in the late nineteenth century.

11.I.36 PICK IT, LICK IT

> Nose picking:
>
> Pick it,
> Lick it,
> Roll it,
> And flick it.
>
> Kentish Town 1983.

Printed version Rosen and Steele, [p. 9].

11.I.37 OLD MOTHER JELLY BELLY

> Old Mother Jelly Belly lived at number nine,
> With hairs on her belly as thick as twine,
> Sitting on the grass with a carrot up her arse,
> And her old fanny winking at the moon.
>
> Deptford 1983.

11.I.38 THERE'S SOMETHING IN MY NAPPY

There's something in my nappy,
It's making me unhappy,
It's big and brown,
I can't sit down.

<u>Hampstead</u>, Kensington <u>1984</u>.

Tune "I Came, I Saw, I Conga'd", written by James Cavanaugh, John Redmond and Frank Weldon in 1940 and performed by Edmundo Ros and His Orchestra.

See also **9.C.24**, **9.C.27,** and **12.A.10** for similar uses of the rhythmic formula of "I Came, I Saw, I Conga'd".

11.I.39 HARK HARK, THE GUNS ARE ROLLING

Hark, Hark! The guns are rolling,
It must be the beans I had this morning,
Quick to the lavatory door,
It's too late, it's on the floor.

Walworth 1982.

11.I.40 OLLY, OLLY, OLLY

Olly, olly, olly!
My balls on a trolley,
Your tits tied up with string,
Sitting on the grass,
Your finger up your arse,
Ting-a-ling-a-ling-a-ling-a-ling.

Battersea, Brixton 1982; Dalston, Kentish Town 1983.

Printed version cf. Shaw, Does yer mother ride a bike, 1970, p. 54.

11.1.41 DIARRHOEA

>Diarrhoea! Diarrhoea!
>Some people think it funny,
>But it's brown, thick and runny,
>Diarrhoea! Diarrhoea!
>
>Diarrhoea! Diarrhoea!
>No pain, no strain,
>Just trickles down the drain,
>Diarrhoea! Diarrhoea!
>
>Diarrhoea! Diarrhoea!
>Just open up your knees,
>And give a little squeeze,
>Diarrhoea! Diarrhoea!
>
>Diarrhoea! Diarrhoea!
>It feels like rum,
>When it trickles down your bum,
>Diarrhoea! Diarrhoea!
>
>Diarrhoea! Diarrhoea!
>People laugh,
>When you do it in the bath,
>Diarrhoea! Diarrhoea!

Streatham 1982; Finsbury, Kentish Town, Mile End 1983; Kensington 1984.

11.1.42 AUNTIE MARY HAD A CANARY

>Auntie Mary had a canary,
>Up the leg of her drawers,

> When she farted it departed
> Flying round her drawers.

Hampstead 1984.

Tune "Cock of the North" (traditional).

Printed versions Kellett (see below); cf. Lowenstein, p. 12; Montgomeries, *SNR*, Barnum an Bayley/Had a canary,/Whustled "The Cock o the North"./It whustled for ooers,/An frichtened the Booers,/An they a fell intae the Forth …, pp. 95–96; Ritchie, *SS*, p. 15; Rutherford, p. 108; Turner, p. 85.

Early notings Chase me Charley, chase me Charley/I've lost the leg of me drawers,/If you find them/starch and iron them,/Send them on to the Boers, one of several versions dating from the Boer War (1899–1902), Kellett, pp. 70–71. Another of these versions has the chorus: Singing chase me Jimmy/I've lost my shimmy/And half a leg of me drawers/Auntie Mary, Auntie Mary/Will you lend me yours?

11.I.43 PATSY BOOP DONE A POOP

> A. Patsy Boop* done a poop,
> Behind the kitchen door,
> Along came a cat, licked it all up,
> And said, " I want some more."

Greenwich 1982.

* Probably from Betty Boop, an animated cartoon character created by Max Fleischer, first appearing in the film *Dizzy Dishes* in 1930.

> B. Donald Duck* done some muck,
> Behind the kitchen door,
> Daisy Duck picked it up,

>   And Donald done some more.
>
> Streatham 1982.

* The Disney cartoon character created in 1934.

Printed versions Lowenstein, p. 14, version D; Ritchie, *GC*, "Captain Cook", p. 49; Turner, twelve versions beginning "Captain Cook", one beginning "Captain Drake", pp. 64–65; one version beginning "Mr. Magoo", p. 96.

11.I.44 THERE'S A COP, COP, COPPER

> There's a cop, cop, copper on the corner of the street,
> All dressed up in navy blue,
> If it wasn't for the law,
> I'd sock him on the jaw
> And he wouldn't be a copper any more.

Tune chorus of the song "Tramp! Tramp! Tramp! (The Prisoner's Hope)", written during the American Civil War by George F. Root.

11.I.45 THERE HE SAT

> There he sat in his vapour,
> Someone picked the toilet paper.
> "What shall I do with this little plum?"
> So out of the window went his bum.
> There came a prince galloping by,
> Wallopy, dollopy, straight in the eye.

Walworth 1982.

11.I.46 THERE WAS AN OLD MAN

There was an old man who lived in a pram,
He covered the pram with lots of jam,
His mother came out and gave him a clout,
And that was the end of Robinson Jam.

Brockley 1967.

Printed versions Brady, p. 73; Ritchie, *GC*, There was a wee man, pp. 35–36.

11.I.47 MA-MA-MARMALADE

Ma-ma-marmalade,
Toff-ee cake,
Mama give me pizza,
Pizza, Betty Lanka.

girl, 10, Shepherds Bush 1983, from Accra, Ghana.

11.I.48 I WAS WALKING IN THE JUNGLE

A. I was walking in the jungle on Saturday night,
    I heard a big noise and it gave me a fright,
    I looked around and who did I see?
    Someone in the garden in the apple tree.

Streatham 1982.

B. I was walking down the jungle with a stick in my hand,
    Says, "Excuse me lady, I'm a jungle man."
    I look in the treetop, what did I see?
    I saw a green-eyed boogy looking at me.
    I pick up a rock, I hit him in the cock,

> We run ten times around the block.

Brixton 1982.

From a Jamaican dialect speaker.

Printed version Knapps, pp. 189–190.

11.I.49 IT'S RAINING, IT'S POURING

> A. It's raining, it's pouring,
> The old man's snoring.
> He went to bed and bumped his head,
> And couldn't get up in the morning.

Mile End 1968; Deptford, Finsbury 1983.

Printed versions Briggs, p. 75; Fowke, p. 94; Hubbard, mentioned, 262; Knapps, p 241; Morrison, p. 147; Opies, *ISE*, p. 16, *ONRB*, p. 75, *LLS*, p. 218; Sutton-Smith, p. 99; Turner, p. 94.

> B. It's raining, it's pouring,
> The old man's snoring.
> He went to bed and bumped his head,
> And couldn't shit in the morning.
> The doctor came and pulled the chain,
> And out came a choo choo train (aeroplane).

Streatham 1982.

Printed version McMorland, p. 25.

The Muppets

The children's television series *The Muppet Show*, created by the American puppeteer Jim Henson, ran on British television from 1976 to 1981. Kermit is the name of a frog puppet on the show.

11.I.50 KERMIT THE FROG

    A. Kermit the Frog
        Got smacked in the gob,
        For messing about with Miss Piggy,
        He stuck it up once,
        He stuck it up twice,
        And now he's got a sore willy.

Barnsbury 1983.

Tune "Messing About on the River", written by Tony Hatch and Les Reed and first made popular by Josh MacRae in 1962.

Printed version Wilson, 980.

    B. Kermit the Frog,
        Got kicked in the gob,
        For playing about with Miss Piggy,
        He undone her zip and out popped her tits
        And so did Kermit's green willy.

Greenwich, Streatham, Walworth 1982; Barnsbury, Blackheath, <u>Brockley</u>, Dulwich <u>1983</u>.

See also **11.C.46**, **11.C.121**, and **11.C.122**.

Dallas

The television soap opera *Dallas* was first aired in 1978. For another song based on *Dallas*, sung to the tune of "Land of Hope and Glory", see Hubbard, 261.

11.I.51 I'M ONLY A POOR LITTLE EWING

> I'm only a poor little Ewing,
> J.R. keeps on picking on me,
> Sue Ellen's a drunk,
> Her baby's a punk,
> And Bobby lives under the sea.

> Barnsbury, Dulwich, Kentish Town, Mile End, Stoke Newington 1983; Kensington 1984.

> Variations: Sue Ellen is drunk/Sue Ellen's a junk.
> Bobby comes out of the sea/gets back to the sea.

Printed version Opies, *SG*, p. 445.

See also **11.C.119** and **11.C.120**.

E.T.

The film *E.T. The Extra-Terrestrial* was released by Universal Pictures in 1982. See also **11.C.116 – 11.C.118** and **11.C.120**.

11.I.52 THERE CAME FROM MARS, E.T.

> There came from Mars, E.T.
> Who took a fancy to P.G.*
> Drinking all day,
> He just flew away,
> Did poor old little E.T.

> Kensington 1984.

* P.G. Tips, a well-known brand of tea in the UK.

11.I.53 CAN YOU SEE YOUR DAD?

>Can you see your dad,
>Riding a bike in the sky?
>He looks like E.T.
>And he's going to die.

>Borough 1983.

The Smurfs

Originally an animated cartoon by Belgian cartoonist "Peyo", screened on British television from 1981.

11.I.54 WHERE ARE YOU ALL COMING FROM?

>Where are you all coming from?
>We come from Smurfland where we belong.
>Do you pick your toes in bed?
>No, we pick our nose instead.
>Do you wipe it on the sheet?
>No, we think it's nice to eat.

>Brockley 1983.

11.I.55 NOBODY WOULD LISTEN

>Nobody would listen to the Smurfs in prison,
>So they jumped over a wall.
>A policeman who'd taught them,
>He chased and caught them,
>This is what he asked them all:
>Where are you coming from?
>We're from Dartmoor on the run.
>What were you in Dartmoor for?

We borrowed the safe from the bank next door.
How did you plan out your route?
We followed the arrows on our suit.

Streatham 1982.

The Beatles

The famous English rock band founded in 1962.

11.I.56 BEATLES, BEATLES, EVERYWHERE

Beatles, Beatles everywhere,
Combing out their golden hair,
John, Paul, George and Ringo,
Anyone want a game of Bingo?

Putney 1967.

11.I.57 WE LOVE YOU BEATLES

We love you, Beatles, oh yes we do,
We love your E boots, your haircut too,
When you're not near us, we're blue,
Oh Beatles, we love you!

We love you Paul, oh yes we do,
We love your nice blue eyes, your hair too,
When you're not near us, we're blue,
Oh Paul, we love you!

We love you John, oh yes we do,
We love your kinky boots, your black hair too,
When you're not near us, we're blue,
Oh John, we love you!

We love you George, oh yes we do,
We love your eyes so blue, your suit too,
When you're not near us, we're blue,
Oh George, we love you!

We love you Ringo, oh yes we do,
We love your nose, your suit too,
When you're not near us, we're blue,
Oh Ringo, we love you!

We love you Beatles, oh yes we do.
 etc.

Scream!

Mile End 1966.

Political

11.I.58 BUILD A BONFIRE

Build a bonfire, build a bonfire,
Put the Argies on the top,
Galtieri in the middle,
And burn the bloody lot.

Blackheath 1983.

See also **8.A.3** and **12.A.12**.

11.J SONGS

Songs (as distinct from rhymes with tunes) are not transmitted on a one-to-one or small group basis. They depend on social situations such as outings, school journeys, coach trips, wet playtimes and dinnertimes, or unusual classroom situations. Many of these songs belong to the meetings, camps, and other activities of Cubs, Brownies, and other children's organisations. Well-known songs of this type are **11.J.2** THE ANIMAL FAIR, **11.J.3** MICHAEL FINNEGAN, **11.J.4** SHE'LL BE COMING ROUND THE MOUNTAIN, **11.J.5** WE ARE RED MEN TALL AND QUAINT, **11.J.6** TEN GREEN BOTTLES, **11.J.7** THREE LITTLE ANGELS, **11.J.8** YOU'LL NEVER GET TO HEAVEN, and **11.J.9** ONE MAN WENT TO MOW. More recent songs from the same sources include: **11.J.10** FOUND A PEANUT and **11.J.11** THE ADMIRAL WAS THE FIRST TO JUMP.

Cockney music hall choruses are not widely known by Inner London children, though individuals have given me authentic versions of "My old man said follow the van" and "Boiled beef and carrots". More widely known in parodied versions are **8.D.19** TA RA RA BOOM DE AY and **8.D.22** DAISY, DAISY. Cockney street songs which are part of the children's tradition are represented in this section by **11.J.16** MY HUSBAND WAS A LAVATORY CLEANER and **11.J.17** MY OLD MAN'S A DUSTMAN which is widespread in all parts of Inner London, not just in Cockney speaking areas. It has very many versions, including some with Fatty and Skinny insertions (**11.J.17B**).

During the Second World War a song was popular in the forces and elsewhere which began: "This is number one, and we've only just begun" and it had a chorus "Roll me over, lay me down and do it again". An almost identical version is **11.J.18A**; **11.J.18B** is on similar lines. It might have owed its origin to the old folksong "Gently Johnny my Jingalo", which begins "I put my hand all on her toe" (Reeves, 1958, pp. 113–114). Other adult party and student songs on similar lines include the one known as "How Ashamed I Was", and "Oh, Sir Jasper". Though several schools gave me versions of "This is Number One", I do not know under what circumstances it is likely to be sung communally. I would be interested to learn what led this song, which apparently died out among adults in the late 1940s, to be taken up and altered by schoolchildren in the 1980s. **11.I.30** I GOT OFF THE BUS and **11.I.31** JERRY AND JENNIFER WENT DOWN TO THE DAIRY have some similarity. They are both sexually explicit but the second one is much cruder.

Judging by other material which children volunteered to me when I was a serving class teacher in the 1960s and 1970s, I do not think shyness or modesty on their part would have come between me and the song if it had been known by them. On the other hand the much greater degree of sexual frankness in the succeeding twenty years means that explicit sexual material is exchanged and understood by almost all children at an earlier age. Children are far less inhibited when it comes to reciting this kind of song in mixed groups than they were a generation ago. Older friends and/or relations may have sung the song and it would be picked up by more receptive children. More widespread than the above group of songs in Inner London is **11.J.21** WHAT DO YOU DO?, made up to fit Percy Grainger's tune "Country Gardens". This song dealing with defecation probably appeals to a wider age group than the sexually explicit songs. An interesting find was a variation of the First World War song **11.J.15** VICTORIOUS from just one school.

11.J.1   BANANAS IN PYJAMAS

> Bananas in pyjamas are coming down the stairs,
> Bananas in pyjamas are chasing Teddy bears,
> Bananas in pyjamas are coming down in pairs.
> Because on Thursdays they all choose,
> To catch them unawares.

> Greenwich 1982; <u>Mile End</u>, Shepherds Bush, Stoke Newington <u>1983</u>.

This is a version of a song by Carey Blyton written in 1967, published in *Bananas in Pyjamas: A Book of Nonsense* (1972). London: Faber and Faber.

Printed version See also Harrop, Blakeley, and Gadsby, p. 20.

11.J.2   THE ANIMAL FAIR

> We went to the animal fair,
> The birds and the beasts were there,
> The big baboon by the light of the moon,

Was combing his auburn hair;
The monkey fell out of his bunk,
And slid down the elephant's trunk
The elephant sneezed and fell on his knees,
And that was the end of the monkey, monkey …

Brockley 1983; Kensington 1984.

Typically sung at Scout and Guide camps.

Printed versions Abrahams, pp. 95–96; Douglas (see below); Harrop, Friend, and Gadsby, p. 11; Nelson, pp. 14–15; Opies, *LLS*, p. 38; Talley (see below); Withers, *RIMP*, p. 36; *Woodcraft Folk Song Book*, p. 41.

Early notings I went to the animal show, and what do you think I saw there?/The Elephant sneezed and fell on his knees,/And what became of the monkey— (Keep saying monkey untill [sic] out), skipping rhyme, Douglas, 1916, p. 77, 1931, p. 43; Talley, 1922, pp. 159–160.

11.J.3 MICHAEL FINNEGAN

There was an old man named Michael Finnegan,
He grew whiskers on his chinegan,
The wind came out and blew them inegan,
Poor old Michael Finnegan, begin again.

Repeat as often as wanted.

Shepherds Bush 1983; Kensington 1984.

Printed versions Abrahams, I know a man …, p. 83; Opies, *LLS*, p. 31; Shaw, 1970, referred to, p. 29; Sutton Smith, Little Michael Finnigan, p. 99; Withers, *RIMP*, p. 68; Wood (see below).

Early notings First documented in *The Hackney Scout Song Book* (1921). London: Stacy and Son. Wood, *AMG*, 1940, p. 71.

11.J.4 SHE'LL BE COMING ROUND THE MOUNTAIN

> She'll be coming round the mountain when she comes,
> She'll be coming round the mountain when she comes,
> She'll be coming round the mountain,
> Coming round the mountain,
> She'll be coming round the mountain when she comes.
>
> She'll be wearing silky pyjamas when she comes, etc.
>
> She'll be riding on six white horses, etc.
>
> She'd love to sleep with granpa, etc.
>
> Walworth 1984; Dalston 1983.

Printed versions Rohrbough (see below); Whyton, p. 43; and many versions in young people's song books.

Early notings She'll be comin' round the mountain …/She'll be drivin' six white horses …/She'll be loaded with bright angels …/She will neither rock nor totter …/She will run so level and steady …/ She will take us to the portals …/Oh, we'll all go to meet her …/We will kill the old red rooster …/We'll have chicken-pie and dumplin' … Rohrbough, *SSG*, 1938, p. 7, *HPPB*, 1940, p. 39.

11.J.5 WE ARE RED MEN TALL AND QUAINT

> We are red men tall and quaint,
> In our feathers and red paint,
> Pow wow! Pow wow!
> We're the men of the old Dun Cow. How!
>
>> All of us are red men,
>> Feathers in our head men,
>> Down among the dead men
>> Pow wow! Pow wow!

We can fight with sticks and stones
Bows and arrows, bricks and bones,
Pow wow! Pow wow!
We're the men of the old Dun Cow. How!
    All of us ... etc.

We come home from a distant shore,
Greeted by a long-nosed squaw,
Pow wow! Pow wow!
We're the men of the old Dun Cow. How!
    All of us ... etc.

Dulwich 1983; <u>Hampstead 1984</u>.

Typically sung at Scout and Guide camps.

11.J.6   TEN GREEN BOTTLES

There were ten green bottles hanging on the wall,
Ten green bottles hanging on the wall,
And if one green bottle should accidentally fall,
There'd be nine green bottles hanging on the wall.

There were nine green bottles hanging on the wall, etc.

Reducing to 9, 8, 7, 6, 5, 4, 3, 2, 1 and finally "no green bottles hanging on the wall."

Cubitt Town, <u>Kentish Town 1983</u>.

See also **8.D.11**.

Printed versions Abrahams, Ten black bottles, p. 189; Gullen, p. 129; Kirshenblatt-Gimblett, p. 90; Montgomerie, p. 66; and versions in children's song books, etc.

11.J.7 THREE LITTLE ANGELS

A. Three little angels all dressed in white,
Trying to get to heaven at the end of a kite,
But the kite string broke,
Down they all fell,
Instead of going to heaven,
They all went down to

Two little angels, all dressed in white,
Trying to get to heaven at the end of a kite,
But the kite string broke,
Down they all fell,
Instead of going to heaven,
They all went down to

One little angel all dressed in white,
Trying to get to heaven at the end of a kite,
But the kite string broke,
And down he fell,
Instead of going to heaven,
He went down to (hell!)

West Norwood 1970.

B. Three little devils all dressed in red,
Trying to get to heaven at the end of a bed,
But the bedpost broke
Down they all fell,
Instead of going to heaven,
They all went back to …

Similarly for two devils and one devil.

Typically sung at Scout and Guide camps.

Printed versions Abrahams, Three little Negroes, p. 193; Knapps, Three little Negroes, p. 195; Talley (see below); Withers, *RIMP*, p. 188.

Early noting cf. Two liddle Nigger boys as black as tar,/Tryin' to go to Heaben on a railroad chyar./Off fall Nigger boys on a cross-tie!/Dey's gwineter git to Heaben shore bye-an'-bye, Talley, 1922, p. 188.

11.J.8   YOU'LL NEVER GET TO HEAVEN

You'll never get to heaven in an old Ford car,
'Cause an old Ford car won't go that far.

> I ain't gonna rieve my Lord no more
> I ain't gonna rieve my Lord no more,
> I ain't gonna rieve my Lord no more
> I ain't gonna rieve.

You'll never get to heaven in a sardine tin,
'Cause a sardine tin is much too thin.
> I ain't gonna rieve … etc.

You'll never get to heaven in a jumbo jet,
'Cause the Lord ain't built no runways yet.
> I ain't gonna rieve … etc.

You'll never get to heaven on roller skates,
'Cause you'll roll right past them pearly gates.
> I ain't gonna rieve … etc.

If I get there before you do,
I'll dig a hole and laugh at you.
> I ain't gonna rieve … etc.

Dalston 1983.

Other verses:

You'll never get to heaven in a Playtex bra,
'Cause a Playtex bra don't stretch that far.

You'll never get to heaven in a biscuit tin
'Cause the Lord don't let no crummy ones in.

You'll never get to heaven with a bottle of gin,
'Cause the Lord don't let no spirits in.

You'll never get to heaven on a plate of glass
'Cause the glass might break and cut your finger (arse).

Brockley 1983.

You'll never get to heaven on a Cub Scout's knee,
'Cause a Cub Scout's knee's too knob-ber-lee.

Dulwich 1983.

You'll never get to heaven in a ping pong ball,
'Cause a ping pong ball won't hold us all.

You'll never get to heaven with a fat Boy Scout
'Cause the pearly gates, they ain't that stout.

You'll never get to heaven in a limousine
'Cause the Lord ain't got no gasoline.

You'll never get to heaven in a Boy Scout's arms,
'Cause the Lord don't care for masculine charms.

Brockley 1967.

This has been sung in various versions in youth organisations (including Scouts and Cub Scouts as some verses indicate) for singsongs, campfires etc. I remember it from c1930. Only the Dalston version included the chorus but the child had misheard the word "grieve" and gave me "rieve".

Printed versions cf. Ritchie, *SS*, The Salvation Army began to sin/So they went up to Heaven in a corn-beef tin:/… p. 108; cf. Shaw, Boy Scout's Trumpet Call: And you won't go to heaven when you die, Mary Ann,/…, 1970, p. 121; Sutton-Smith (see below); Turner, You can't go to heaven in a Berlei bra, p. 108.

Early noting Sutton-Smith notes the taunting endured by the newly formed Salvation Army in the 1890s, when gangs of boys would follow the Salvation Army band with kerosene tins, squeakers and comb-and-paper, singing such verses as "Oh, you must be a lover of the Lord, of the Lord,/Or you won't go to heaven when you die, when you die./Oh, you must wear a collar and a tie, and a tie,/Or you won't go to heaven when you die."

11.J.9   ONE MAN WENT TO MOW

>One man went to mow,
>Went to mow a meadow,
>One man and his dog, Spot, Spot,
>Bottle of pop, packet of biscuits (sausage roll),
>Old Man Riley had a cow,
>Didn't know how to milk it, milk it.
>
>Two men went to mow,
>Went to mow a meadow,
>Two men, one man and his dog, Spot, Spot,
>Bottle of pop, packet of biscuits,
>Old Man Riley had a cow,
>Didn't know how to milk it, milk it.
>
>Three men went to mow, etc. and so on ad infinitum.
>
>Marylebone 1967; <u>Finsbury 1983</u>.

This song had been around for more than sixty years at the time of my collecting, but without the additions at the end.

Printed versions Sims, One Cub Went to Camp, pp. 43–44.

11.J.10 FOUND A PEANUT

A. Found a peanut,
Found a peanut,
Found a peanut,
Yesterday,
Found a peanut,
Found a peanut,
Found a peanut
Yesterday.

> It was mouldy, etc., as above.
>
> So I ate it, etc.
>
> Got the tummyache, etc.
>
> Went to the doctor, etc.
>
> He cut me open, etc.
>
> He left his scissors in, etc.
>
> So I died, etc.
>
> Went to heaven, etc.
>
> Found a job, etc.
>
> Selling peanuts, etc.
>
> Found a peanut, etc., and so on.

Finsbury 1983.

Tune "Oh My Darling, Clementine", an American folk ballad, usually credited to Percy Montrose (1884).

B. Found a peanut,
Found a peanut,

Found a peanut,
Last night,
Last night I found a peanut,
Found a peanut,
Last night.

Cracked it open, etc.

It was mouldy, etc.

Ate it anyway, etc.

Had a tummy ache, etc.

Went to the hospital, etc.

Had an operation, etc.

Died anyway, etc.

Went to heaven, etc.

They didn't want me, etc.

Went to other place, etc.

Guess what I found there? etc.

Found a peanut, etc. and so on.

Hampstead 1984.

Typically sung at Scout and Guide camps.

Printed versions Fowke, p. 138; Lowenstein, p. 19; Sims, pp. 58–59; Turner, p. 90.

11.J.11 THE ADMIRAL WAS THE FIRST TO JUMP

The admiral was the first to jump, the last to hit the ground,
The admiral was the first to jump, the last to hit the ground,
The admiral was the first to jump, the last to hit the ground,
And he ain't going to jump no more.

Glory, glory, what a helluva way to die,
Glory, glory, what a helluva way to die,
Glory, glory, what a helluva way to die,
And he ain't going to jump no more.

He landed on the runway like a lump of strawberry jam (three times)
And he ain't going to jump no more.
Glory, glory etc.

They scooped him off the runway with a shovel and a pick (three times)
And he ain't going to jump no more.
Glory, glory etc.

They put him in a matchbox and they sent him home to mum. (three times)
And he ain't going to jump no more.
Glory, glory, etc.

They put him on the mantelpiece for everyone to see. (three times)
And he ain't going to jump no more.
Glory, glory, etc.

Blackheath 1983.

One version of a song typically sung at Scout and Guide camps. A version I came across in 1967 in Palmers Green began: "Young (_____ _____) forgot his parachute". Otherwise it was the same.

Tune "John Brown's Body", an American marching song from Civil War times.

Printed version cf. Lowenstein, He fell from forty thousand feet without a parachute, p. 21.

11.J.12 DOWN BY THE BAY

Down by the bay,
Down by the bay,
Where the watermelons grow,
Where the watermelons grow,
Back to my home,
Back to my home,
I dare not go,
I dare not go,
For if I do,
For if I do,
My mother would say:
My mother would say:

Have you seen a flower,
Have you seen a flower,
Taking a shower?
Taking a shower?
    Down by the bay,
    Down by the bay etc.

Have you seen a cow?
Have you seen a cow?
Pushing a plough?
Pushing a plough?
    Down by the bay,
    Down by the bay etc.

Other verses: Have you seen a pig wearing a wig?
                 Have you seen a dog sitting in a bog?
                 Have you seen a mouse building a house?

and so on extemporised.

Dalston 1983.

Typically sung at Scout and Guide camps.

11.J.13   MY AUNT, GREELY GREELY GREET

> My aunt, Greely Greely Greet
> Had that puss, vida vida voos,
> And that puss, veela veela voos,
> Had a tail.
> And that tail, veela veela vale,
> Had a curl, veela veela vurl,
> And that curl, veela veela vurl,
> And that curl, veela veela vurl,
> Had a tip.
> And my aunt etc.
>   (repeated ad lib)

Dalston 1983.

A camp song typically sung at Brownie meetings.

11.J.14   THERE IT WAS I MET MY SUSIE

PLAY-PARTY GAME in the USA.

> There it was I met my Susie,
> There it was I met my Susie,
> There it was I met my Susie,
> Way down yonder in the ba-ba patch (paw-paw patch)
>
>> Picking up ba-bas, putting them in your basket,
>> Picking up ba-bas, putting them in your basket,
>> Picking up ba-bas, putting them in your basket,
>> Way down yonder in the ba-ba patch.

There it was I married Susie (three times)
Way down yonder in the ba-ba patch.
    Picking up ba-bas etc.

There it was we brought up children (three times)
Way down yonder in the ba-ba patch.
    Picking up ba-bas etc.

There it was I buried Susie (three times)
Way down yonder in the ba-ba patch.
    Picking up ba-bas etc.

There it was her ghost goes walking (three times)
Way down yonder in the ba-ba patch.
    Picking up ba-bas etc.

Mile End 1967.

Printed versions Botkin (see below); Poston, pp. 48–49; Rohrbough (see below).

Early notings cf. Paw Paw Patch, Rohrbough, *PPG*, 1930, p. 24. Cf. Pawpaw Land, Botkin, *APPS*, 1937, pp. 289–290. Rohrbough, *HPPB*, 1940, p. 24.

11.J.15 VICTORIOUS

Victorious! Victorious!
One bottle of beer between the four of us.
Glory be to God that there ain't no more of us,
'Cause one of us would have to drink the blooming lot.
Bottle and all, cork and all, label and all,
Start again.

Earlsfield 1982.

This is the chorus to a traditional drinking song, "The Goddamned Dutch", also called "The Souse Family" and "Drunk Last Night", which seems to have first appeared in print in *Immortalia: An Anthology of American Ballads, Sailors' Songs, Cowboy Songs, College Songs, Parodies, Limericks, and other humorous verses and doggerel*, a book published in New York by a "Gentleman About Town" in 1927. One version was used in the musical satire *Oh What a Lovely War*, about World War I, brought to the London stage in 1963 by Joan Littlewood.

Early noting cf. Shaw, 1970, a verse from the 1920s, p. 38.

11.J.16   MY HUSBAND WAS A LAVATORY CLEANER

A. My husband was a lavatory cleaner,
He works for a bit by bit.
But when he comes home in the morning
He smells like a lump of shit.

Some say that he died of pneumonia,
Some say that he died of the 'flu,
But I know what my husband died of,
He died of the smell of the poo.

Borough 1983.

B. My daddy's a lavatory cleaner,
He works very hard for his bit (I said bit!)
And when he comes home in the evening,
He brings all the smell of the shit.

Mile End 1966.

Tune "My Bonny Lies Over the Ocean", a traditional Scottish folksong. Kellett's version (see below) was sung to the same tune.

Printed versions Gaskell (see below); Kellett, My father's a lavatory cleaner, p. 26. Kellett asserts that the rhyme is a parody of the chorus from a song called "Sweet Violets", written in 1882 by Joseph Emmet: Sweet Violets/Sweeter than the roses/Covered all over from head to toe/Covered all over with sweet violets.

Early noting My father is a muckman,/He empties the middens at night,/And when he comes home in the morning/He's covered all over with shight, Gaskell, c1913, p. 10.

Recording MacColl and Behan, *Streets of Song*.

11.J.17   MY OLD MAN'S A DUSTMAN

Originally a British army song, the words were rewritten by Lonnie Donegan, Peter Buchanan, and Beverley Thorn in 1960 and set to a traditional tune.

> A. My old man's a dustman,
> He wears a dustman's hat,
> He wears gor blimey trousers,
> And he lives in a council flat.
> He looks a proper 'nana,
> In his hob-nailed boots,
> He has no time to pull 'em up,
> And he calls them daisy roots.

Mile End 1968, 1982; Blackheath, Brockley, Cubitt Town, Kentish Town 1982; <u>Deptford 1983</u>*.

* This is the longest example of this version I have come across.

> B. My old man's a dustman,
> He wears a dustman's hat,
> He bought a thousand tickets (He bought a football ticket)
> To watch a football match.
> Now Fatty passed to Skinny,

> Skinny passed it back,
> Fatty took a rotten shot,
> And knocked the goalie flat.
> Where was the goalie
> When the ball was in the net?
> Halfway up to heaven
> In a supersonic jet,
> Singing: Rule Britannia!
> Marmalade and jam,
> We throw sausages
> At our old man.

Mile End 1966; Battersea, Streatham 1982; <u>Borough</u>, Brockley <u>1983</u>; Hampstead 1984.

Alternatively: the goalie was "Halfway up the goalpost with his knickers round his neck". (Hampstead and Streatham).

In the Battersea version: They laid him on a stretcher,
> They laid him on the bed,
> They rubbed his belly with a lump of jelly,
> And found out he was dead.

Printed versions Opies, *LLS*, a version from Enfield, with an ending similar to that of the Battersea version above, pp. 353–354; Ritchie, *SS*, My old man's a scaffie, p. 127; Rosen and Steele, like version B, [p. 9], Battersea ending, [p. 10].

For other Fatty and Skinny rhymes see **11.I.23A–J**.

> C. My old man's a dustman,
> He wears a dustman's hat,
> He killed five thousand Germans,
> And what do you think of that?
> One lay here, one lay there,
> One lay round the corner,

> One had a bayonet up his arse,
> Crying out for water,
> Water, water, came at last,
> "I don't want your water,
> You can stick it up your arse."

Mile End 1968, 1983.

This may be the oldest tradition. I remember (c1930) a rhyme set to the same tune which began: "My old man's a soldier,/He fought at the battle of Mons,/He killed five thousand Germans/With half a dozen bombs."

> D. My old man's a dustman,
> He wears a dustman's hat,
> He farted through the keyhole
> And paralysed the cat.
> The chairs couldn't stand it,
> The table fell apart,
> And all because of my old man's
> Supersonic fart.

Streatham 1982; <u>Dalston 1983</u>.

See also **11.I.3A**.

> E. My uncle's a dustman,
> He works in a dustman's hat,
> He farted through the keyhole,
> And paralysed the cat.
> The cat ran up the chimney,
> He couldn't stand the smell,
> He caught his arse on a six-inch nail,
> And shouted, "Bloody hell."

Brockley 1983.

This song/rhyme seems to be almost universal in Inner London in one or other of its versions, and sometimes two or three of them are known in the same school.

Printed versions Ritchie, *GC*, My wee man's a miner, p. 89; Rutherford, p. 97; Shaw, 1970, My old man's a trimmer, p. 100.

11.J.18   THIS IS NUMBER ONE

A. This is number one, and the story's just begun,

> Roll me over, lay me down and do it again,
> I like the feeling,
> Roll me over, in the clover,
> Roll me over, lay me down and do it again.

And this is number two, and I'm telling it to you,
> Roll me over, etc.

And this is number three and he's got me on his knee,
> Roll me over, etc.

And this is number four and he's got me on the floor,
> Roll me over, etc.

And this is number five and he's got me on the side,
> Roll me over, etc.

And this is number six and he's pulling down my knicks,
> Roll me over, etc.

And this is number seven and it feels like we're in heaven,
> Roll me over, etc.

And this is number eight and the doctor's at the gate,
> Roll me over, etc.

And this is number nine and the twins are doing fine,
   Roll me over, etc.

And this is number ten and he wants to do it again,
   Roll me over, etc.

Kentish Town 1983.

Tune "Roll Me Over in the Clover", a song popular during the Second World War whose lyrics are very similar to the version here.

Printed versions Cray, *BB*, pp. 117, 231–233; Shaw, mentioned, 1969, p. 64, 1970, p. 113; Sluckin, p. 28.

B. Number one, the story's just begun,
   Singing oo-a-dary-dary, dum-dary-dee.

   Number two and I'm doing it to you,
   Singing oo-a-dary-dary, dum-dary-doo.

   Number three and I've got her on my knee,
   Singing oo-a-dary-dary, dum-dary-doo.

   Number four and I've got her on the floor,
   Singing oo-a-dary-dary, dum-dary-doo.

   Number five and her legs are open wide,
   Singing oo-a-dary-dary, dum-dary-doo.

   Number six and I'm pulling down her knicks,
   Singing oo-a-dary-dary, dum-dary-doo.

   Number seven and she's going up to heaven,
   Singing oo-a-dary-dary, dum-dary-doo.

> Number eight and the doctor's at the gate,
> Singing oo-a-dary-dary, dum-dary-doo.
>
> Number nine and the twins are doing fine,
> Singing oo-a-dary-dary, dum-dary-doo.
>
> Number ten and I'm doing it again,
> Singing oo-a-dary-dary, dum-dary-doo.

<u>Greenwich 1982</u>; Mile End 1983.

Tune more or less as in version A.

11.J.19   TEA FOR ONE

> Tea for one, the story's just begun,
> Tea for two, I'm telling it to you,
> Tea for three, he's got me on his knee,
> Tea for four, he's got me on the floor,
> Tea for five, he's pulling down his flies,
> Tea for six, he's pulling down my knicks,
> Tea for seven, he's mmmmmmm me up to heaven,
> Tea for eight, the doctor's at the gate,
> Tea for nine, the twins are doing fine,
> Tea for ten, I'll tell you it again.

Brixton 1982.

Tune taken from part of the song "Tea for Two", written in 1925 by Vincent Youmans and Irving Caesar and featured in the musical *No, No, Nanette*.

Printed versions cf. Lowenstein, p. 15; Rutherford, p. 124.

11.J.20 BELL BOTTOMED TROUSERS

A. Bell-bottomed trousers,
    Suit of navy blue,
    She loves a sailor,
    I love him too.
    When we're together,
    All our dreams come true,
    With his bell-bottomed trousers,
    Suit of navy blue.

Hampstead 1984.

B. L button trousers,
    Shirt of navy blue,
    I love a sailor,
    He loves me too,
    When I get married,
    I shall say to you,
    "Bell-bottomed trousers,
    Shirt of navy blue."

Song is then repeated, using "la, la, la …" instead of words.

Deptford 1983.

Tune originally a bawdy sea shanty with the chorus: Bell bottom trousers,/Coat of navy-blue./Let him climb the rigging/Like his daddy used to do. This song was also made popular in a version written by Moe Jaffe, recorded by Guy Lombardo and his Royal Canadians in 1945, with the chorus: With his bell bottom trousers, coat of navy blue/She loves her sailor and he loves her too.

Printed versions Cray, *BB*, pp. 32–33; Kellett (see below); Shaw, 1970, p. 117.

Early noting A pair of bell-bottom trousers,/A suit of navy-blue/And he will climb the rigging/Like I climbed you, part of a longer rhyme, Kellett, 1920s, p. 51.

11.J.21   WHAT DO YOU DO?

> A. What do you do when you need to go to loo (do a poo)
> In an English country – garden?
> You pull down your pants and suffocate (paralyse) the ants,
> In an English country – garden.
>
> You pull down (pick off) a leaf,
> And wipe your underneath,
> In an English country – garden.
> That's what you do when you need to go to loo
> In an English country – garden.

Greenwich 1982 (first part only); Blackheath, Brockley, Dalston, Kentish Town 1983.

Alternative second verse:

> B. You sit on the grass,
> And wipe your dirty arse
> In an English country – garden.
> Then you get a spade and cover what you've made
> In an English country – garden.

Finsbury, Mile End 1983.

Tune "Country Gardens" by Percy Grainger, adapted from an Oxfordshire Morris tune. The tune was collected by Cecil Sharp and published as "Handkerchief Dance" in *Morris Dance Tunes* (1907) by Sharp and Herbert C. Macilwaine (London: Novello). The melody was first published in 1728 as part of a work called *The Quaker's Opera* by Thomas Walker, itself an imitation of John Gay's *Beggar's Opera*.

11.K JOKES

In this section I have included a number of short pithy jokes, some of which are quite witty. Most of them came from a relatively small number of boys in a few schools. Though some of them seem to be of an adult character, a few obviously fall into the category of children's humour. As I only collected these examples on one occasion, and they rarely appear in print, as far as I can ascertain, it is not possible to draw any conclusions about them. When one considers the longer jokes of a narrative character which are passed around by the children of the age group we are considering, most of them have characteristics which indicate that they are essentially children's lore. Like children's riddles and the verbal exchange type of mini-joke, they rely heavily on wordplay rather than on comic situations for their humorous effect. They can get very involved, taking a long time to get to the point. The listener has to suspend any visualisation of real life situations, and this is particularly the case with stories dealing with sex like **11.K.36** and **11.K.38**. They often share a set formula, like the "Englishman, Scotsman and Irishman" type jokes (**11..K.25–11.K.33**). Joke **11.K.22** about three boys and a policeman relies for its humour on the boys having impossible names; similarly with **11.K.38**, which is widespread on both sides of the Atlantic. I have witnessed children convulsed with laughter at this kind of joke. Misunderstandings based on possible names might amuse adults, but the use of inconceivable names is not likely to do so.

Many children's "funny stories" appear to many adults to be remarkably unfunny. Wolfenstein says this is "… partly because of differences in technical expertise, partly because the adult and the child rarely find themselves in the same emotional situation at the same time" (1954, pp. 213–214). The persistence of some types of jokes over many years, and their wide distribution, show that they obviously fulfil a need. They certainly strike a chord and evoke a response from children of widely differing social backgrounds and intellectual levels, but who nevertheless share common emotional experiences arising from the particular stage in their physical and emotional development.

Most children do not seem to make a sharp distinction between jokes which their elders, whether parents or teachers, might accept, and those which might be condemned as "dirty". In this respect, probably many adults forget their own childhood experiences. It is likely that jokes dealing explicitly with sex appear in a child's repertoire at an earlier age nowadays, but those dealing with urination, defecation, and passing wind still form the major proportion of what the children themselves refer to as "rude" jokes. Wolfenstein suggests that these jokes are a way of gratifying the child's impulses (1954, p. 161):

> … the child must find ways to gratify his impulses while disclaiming responsibility for them. Thus he proceeds from naughty acts to stories in which such acts are committed by others. Later these acts, even when attributed to fictitious characters, must be excused as comic mistakes. In addition, authority figures are made responsible for them.

At the time this collection was made, however, there was a much greater exchange of all forms of verbal lore, especially of the entertainment kind, between boys and girls than there was in the days of segregated playgrounds, and greater reticence among adults and the media about sexual matters. No embarrassment was expressed in either the telling or hearing of jokes of a bawdy character in mixed groups of boys and girls, once they realised that this material would not be revealed to any adults in authority. Negative reactions were only expressed to a few really unpleasant jokes. These might include some "sick" or racist jokes, as well as very explicit jokes about defecation. I believe the racist jokes are no more than a reflection of adult attitudes, rather than coming from the children themselves. As noted earlier, children of junior school age usually avoid references to specific racial and national groups when there are children of these specific groups in the school who are likely to be offended. When there were children from ethnic minorities present in the group, other children would react with acute embarrassment if someone told a racist joke, and the child responsible was usually apologetic. It would be surprising if the cheap "Paddy" stereotype indulged in by some adult "comedians" did not find reflection in children's jokes and riddles. Children are slower to realise when those of Irish extraction might be present and be upset.

Humorous injunctions and observations

11.K.1 We don't swim in your toilets, so don't pee in our pool.

Finsbury 1983.

11.K.2 We don't sleep in your ashtrays, so don't smoke in our beds.

Finsbury 1983.

11.K.3 Save water, bath with a friend; save fuel, get cremated with a friend.

Finsbury 1983.

11.K.4 Make cash in your spare time, blackmail your friend.

Finsbury 1983.

11.K.5 Jesus saves, but Brennan scores on the rebound.

Finsbury 1983.

11.K.6 Jesus saves, but he doesn't have my telephone bill.

Finsbury 1983.

11.K.7 Hotel notice: Please wash your hands after using this towel.

Blackheath 1983.

Brief jokes

11.K.8 There were three nuns talking. One said, "I drink." The second one said, "I'm married." The third one said, "I gossip."

Streatham 1982.

11.K.9 When God finished making us he put us in the oven. When he'd finished he pressed each one and said, "You're done," and so on. That's why we've all got belly buttons.

Blackheath 1983.

11.K.10 A male centipede passed a female centipede. The male centipede said, "What a nice pair of legs, pair of legs, pair of legs …"

Blackheath 1983.

11.K.11 A boy called his dog "Sandwich", because he was half bred.

Blackheath 1983.

11.K.12 Channel 4 won't be on the air this week. The viewer has gone on holiday.

Mile End 1983.

11.K.13 I haven't eaten for three days: yesterday, today and tomorrow.

Streatham 1982.

11.K.14 Virginity is like a balloon: one prick and it's gone.

Finsbury 1983.

11.K.15 An Englishman said, "I like English women." A Frenchman said, "I like French women." A bear said, "I like bare women."

Streatham 1982.

11.K.16 In a survey, twenty-three percent of men said they like women with thin legs, seventeen percent said they like women with fat legs. The rest said they liked them in between.

Finsbury 1983.

11.K.17 Dan Dare* got lost in the jungle. He said to himself, "Everybody knows me." He said to a person he saw in a tree, "Hallo up there." The one in the tree replied, "Hallo down dere."

Mile End 1983.

* Dan Dare was a heroic character created by Frank Hampson and featuring in a British comic, the *Eagle*.

11.K.18 A dog was barking loudly at a postman. An old lady said, "You know the saying, 'A barking dog never bites'." The postman said, "I know the old saying, you know the old saying, but does the dog know it?"

Hampstead 1984.

11.K.19 The thunder god, Thor, was riding on his favourite horse to a village. When he got there he shouted out, "I'm Thor." The horse said, "Well you forgot the thaddle, thilly."

Blackheath 1983.

11.K.20 Two giants were walking along the road. One pulled some sweets from his pocket. The other said, "Chocolates?" "No, small geezers",* the first one replied.

Streatham 1982

* Reference to "Maltesers", a form of chocolate sweet, and specifically to the television advertisement containing the dialogue: "Chocolates?" "Maltesers – the chocolates with the less fattening centre".

11.K.21 A man has been blind from birth. Every time he walks down the street, people start laughing. He says, "I fail to see what is funny."

Longer jokes; funny stories

11.K.22 There were three boys, one called Trouble, one called Mind Your Own Business and one called Manners. One day Trouble got lost so Mind Your Own Business and Manners went to the police station. Mind Your Own Business said to Manners, "You wait outside and I will go in and tell the policeman." He went in and he said, "My friend's lost." The policeman said, "What's your name?" "Mind Your Own Business," the boy replied. "Where's your manners?" said the policeman. "He's outside on the doorstep." "Are you looking for trouble?" "Yes, have you seen him?"

Printed version Wolfenstein, p. 87.

11.K.23 A teddy bear was working on a construction site. He was hacking away at the side of a mountain. The foreman said, "Lunch break." They all walked off and ate their lunches. When the teddy bear went back to the place where he was working he found that someone had taken his pick. He went to the foreman and said, "Hey foreman, someone's taken my pick." The foreman sang: "Today's the day the teddy bears have their pick nicked."*

Blackheath 1983.

* The reference is to the line "Today's the day the teddy bears have their picnic" from "Teddy Bears' Picnic", written in 1907 by John Walter Bratton.

11.K.24 A lion came up to a giraffe. He said, "Who is the king of the jungle?" "You are, master," said the giraffe. Then he came to a crocodile and said, "Who is the king of the jungle?" The crocodile said, "You are, master." Then he came to an elephant and said, "Who is the king of the jungle?" The elephant kicked him to the other side of the forest and stamped on him. The lion said, "You don't need to go mad, just because you know the answer."

Blackheath 1983.

Most children's jokes seem to fit into set formulas. One of the most common and persistent is to start the story with something like, "There was an Englishman, a Scotsman and an Irishman …" The tradition for this kind of beginning is fairly old. I recall exchanging such jokes as a schoolboy some fifty-five years before this study was undertaken. A few of these jokes are mildly indecent. Several had an unpleasant chauvinist or racist slant when I was collecting examples in 1982–84, mostly directed at the Irish. The selection here is fairly representative.

11.K.25 There was an Englishman, an Irishman and a Chinese man. They had all come out of prison and were on top of a big mountain. The Englishman said, "I can see England." The Irishman said, "I can see Ireland." The Chinese man had a big Chinese vase. He threw it and said, "I can see China."

Deptford 1983.

11.K.26 There was an Englishman, an Irishman and a Scotsman and three lovely ladies. They each loved a lady. The first lady said to the Irishman, "If you want to marry me, jump off the cliff," and the Irishman did. The second lady said, "If you wish to marry me, jump off the cliff," so the Scotsman did. The third lady said, "If you want to marry me, jump off the cliff," and the Englishman said, "Ladies first."

Finsbury 1983.

11.K.27 An Englishman, Irishman and Scotsman were squabbling over a bar of chocolate. The Irishman said, "The person who dreams the best dream tonight shall have the chocolate." The Englishman dreamt that he had lots of ladies for himself. The

Irishman dreamt he had lots of beer and cigars. The Scotsman dreamt that the chocolate was melting, so he went and ate it.

Finsbury 1983.

A variation of this story with a different setting came from Blackheath (1983).

11.K.28 There was an Irishman, a Scotsman and a *Sun* reader. They agreed to enter a competition as to who could manage to have the least sex. The Irishman won a Rolls Royce. The Scotsman won a Mercedes. The *Sun* reader won a Mini. The others laughed at him. He went off very upset but came back laughing. They said, "Why are you laughing, you only got a Mini?" The *Sun* reader said, "But I've just seen the vicar with a moped."

Finsbury 1983.

11.K.29 An Englishman, Irishman and Scotsman are in the desert. The Englishman finds a bottle. He rubs the bottle and a genie appears. The genie says, "I am the genie of the bottle. You may have two wishes." The Englishman says, "I'd like to be in England and have a thousand bottles of whisky." He disappears and starts drinking. The Scotsman rubs the bottle and wishes to go back to Scotland and have six thousand haggises. The Irishman when it's his turn, says, "I'd like to have a bottle of Guinness which refills again when it is drunk." He gets the bottle and starts drinking and says, "I'll have another one of them."

Blackheath 1983.

A variation of this story from Finsbury (1983) begins in the same way. When it comes to the wishes the Englishman wishes to be back home with lots of money. The Scotsman wishes the same. The Irishman, when it is his turn, says, "I'm lonely. I wish I could have my friends back."

11.K.30 An Englishman, a Scotsman and an Irishman all went into a haunted house. They had been warned there was a ghost there. They heard a noise from a wardrobe. The Englishman went to the window and said, "God save me." He jumped out and landed in a haystack. The Scotsman did the same and also landed in the haystack. The Irishman said, "God shave me," and landed in a barber's.

Brockley 1983.

11.K.31 An Englishman, a Scotsman and an Irishman were just about to be killed by a firing squad. The Englishman shouted, "Volcano!" They all ducked and he got away. The Scotsman shouted, "Flood!" and they ran, so he got away. The Irishman, when it came to his turn, shouted, "Fire!" They all fired.

11.K.32 An Englishman, a Scotsman and an Irishman were on a cliff. If they jumped and said something in the air they would land in it. The Englishman jumped off and said, "Gold." He landed in a pile of gold. The Scotsman shouted, "Silver," and landed in a pile of silver. The Irishman tripped as he jumped and said, "Shit!" He landed in a pile of shit.

Mile End 1983.

11.K.33 An Englishman, a Scotsman and an Irishman all loved a woman who lived in a block of high rise flats. She said, "Whoever catches this clock can marry me." She threw the clock down and the Englishman and Scotsman went running down as fast as they could. The Irishman walked down. He went into a Wimpy bar and had something to eat. Then he had a drink in a pub. He went back to the block and caught the clock. The others said, "How did you do it?" The Irishman said, "The clock was an hour slow."

Dulwich 1983.

A similar story was given me at a school in Blackheath (1983).

Junior school children tell many jokes ranging from the mildly indecent to the obscene. Usually the "fun" consists of elaborate play on words. These are representative:

11.K.34 One man said, "I've got a motor bike that will do eighty miles an hour, lick that." A second man said, "I've got a motor bike that does a hundred and twenty miles an hour, lick that." A third man said, "I've got a dog with a dirty behind, lick that."

Mile End 1983.

A story with a similar ending but with the formula: "There was an Englishman, an American and an Irishman …" was collected in Blackheath (1983).

11.K.35 A man went with an unattractive prostitute because she was cheap. They went up to her flat. She said, "Wait a minute, I've got to take my leg off." She took it off and they were just about to start when she said, "I've got to take my false arm off." They got into bed and she said, "I must take my false eye out." The man said, "This is it, I'm going." As he passed her window she shouted, "I thought you wanted a bit of tit." He said, "Throw it down then."

Finsbury 1983.

11.K.36 A boy asked his mother if he could get in the shower with her. She said he could and he said, "What are those two things there?" She said, "They are my traffic lights." Then he said, "What is the hairy thing?" She said, "That's my tunnel." When his dad was in the shower he asked if he could share it and his father said he could. He said, "What's that long thing?" His father said, "That's my lorry." That night he asked his parents if he could get into bed with them and they said he could. In the middle of the night he shouted, "Mum, put your traffic lights on, there's a lorry coming through your tunnel."

Dulwich 1983.

I came across several variations of this story.

Printed versions Knapps, pp. 185–186; Legman, *RDJ*, p. 52.

11.K.37 A girl who has been told never to let a man see her underpants is offered a pound by a man if she will climb up a ladder. She does so and gets the money. She goes home and tells her mother, who scolds her, "He saw your underpants." "Oh no," says the girl, "I fooled him. I didn't wear any."

This story was collected from several schools.

Printed version Wolfenstein, p. 172.

11.K.38 A boy is called Johnny Fuckerada. He is indulging in sexual intercourse (versions differ widely as to with whom). His name is called by one of his parents, using his full name. He says, "I am fucking her as hard as I can."

Versions of this story were given me by children in several schools.

Printed versions Legman, "A current American story", p. 106; Wolfenstein, pp. 85–86.

SECTION 12

MISCELLANY

Introduction

The items in this final section have nothing in common, but they do not seem to belong to any other category. Football rhymes are overwhelmingly, though not completely, the province of boys, as the album rhymes and Valentine messages are for girls. The examples of so-called "backslang" were only volunteered by girls. The rhymes for little children are of course universal. The remaining categories illustrate various other forms of children's lore.

12.A FOOTBALL RHYMES AND CHANTS

Rutherford's collection from North East England includes a number of football rhymes and chants from a school in Chester le Street, which is roughly midway between Newcastle upon Tyne and Sunderland (Rutherford, 1971, pp. 93–100). The rhymes mainly praise one of the teams from these two places, and disparage the other. There does not seem to be the same local football team loyalty in the Inner London schools from which I collected the material in this section. Rhymes were collected from schools in North, North West, West, South West, South East, and Central London, but the partisanship is not localised. Tottenham Hotspur is referred to in twelve rhymes. Of these, six schools gave wholly favouring rhymes, one gave a wholly unfavouring rhyme, and four gave both favouring and unfavouring rhymes. Neither the partisanship nor the lack of support was confined to the Tottenham area, but was spread widely within the capital.

Other London teams referred to are Fulham (one school favouring); Arsenal (three schools favouring and two opposing); Millwall (one school favouring); Chelsea (one school opposing); Queen's Park Rangers (two schools opposing); West Ham (two schools opposing); and Charlton (one school favouring). Of teams outside London, Liverpool had three schools favouring and two opposing; Manchester United and Nottingham Forest had one favouring rhyme each; Ipswich had two opposing rhymes, and "City", probably Manchester City, had one opposing rhyme, **12.A.22**. It is likely that most of the rhymes are shared with adult partisans, but others appear to be inventions by the children. No. **12.A.11** SPURS ARE ON THEIR WAY TO WEMBLEY came into the pop charts for a brief period.

12.A.1   Dennis Winter, Dennis Winter
Snowy Lane, Snowy Lane,
Pickapocka Nory, Pickapocka Nory,
Dennis North, Dennis North.

Brockley 1983.

Tune "Frère Jacques" (traditional).

12.A.2   Fulham, Fulham, Fulham …

Kensington 1984.

Tune "The Stars and Stripes Forever", a march composed by John Philip Sousa in 1896.

12.A.3 Glory, Glory, Man United
Glory, Glory, Man United,
Glory, Glory, Man United,
When the boys go marching in.

Kensington 1984.

Tune "Glory, glory, halleluia", the chorus to "Battle Hymn of the Republic" written by Julia Ward Howe in 1861.

See also **8.A.9**, which is sung to the same tune.

12.A.4 We hate Tottenham Hotspur
We hate Arsenal too,
But Liverpool are the greatest
'Cause we love you.

Finsbury, 1983; same idea, different teams: Shepherds Bush 1983.

Tune "Land of Hope and Glory", the trio theme from Elgar's *Pomp and Circumstance March No. 1*.

12.A.5 is sung to the same tune.

12.A.5 Ipswich Town are rubbish
Liverpool are the best,
No one can beat them (Tottenham can't beat them),
Nor can the rest.

Battersea 1982; Stoke Newington 1983.

Tune "Land of Hope and Glory" – see note to **12.A.4** above.

12.A.6   White Hart Lane is falling down
Falling down, falling down,
White Hart Lane is falling down,
Poor old Tottenham.

Cubitt Town 1983.

Tune "London Bridge is Falling Down" (traditional).

12.A.7   Stand up, stand up for Jesus
Ye soldiers of the cross,
Lift up his royal banner,
And Tottenham won the toss …

Brockley 1967.

Tune "Stand Up, Stand Up for Jesus", a hymn tune written by George Webb in 1830, words by George Duffield, Jr., 1858.

12.A.8   When the reds go marching in
When the reds go marching in,
I want to be among that number,
When the reds go marching in.

Marylebone 1967; Kentish Town 1983.

Tune "When the Saints Go Marching In", the American gospel song.

Printed version Kellett, whites, p. 81.

12.A.9   We're forever blowing bubbles
Pretty bubbles in the air.
They fly so high and reach the sky,
And like our dreams they fade and die. (And like West Ham)
Tottenham always running,

So are Ipswich too,
You can see our flags flying,
… (unfinished)

<u>Battersea 1982</u>; Stoke Newington 1983.

Tune "I'm Forever Blowing Bubbles", written by John Kellette in 1918 with lyrics by James Kendis, James Brockman and Nat Vincent, for the Broadway musical *The Passing Show of 1918*.

12.A.10   When _____ comes to Wembley
His knees are going all trembly,
Come on you Spurs,
Come on you Spurs,
But when it comes to grumble,
They get their clothes from jumble,
Come on you Spurs,
Come on you Spurs.

<u>Brockley</u>, Kentish Town, Mile End <u>1983</u>.

Tune "I Came, I Saw, I Conga'd", written by James Cavanaugh, John Redmond and Frank Weldon in 1940 and performed by Edmundo Ros and His Orchestra.

See also **9.C.24, 9.C.27,** and **11.I.38** for similar uses of the rhythmic formula of "I Came, I Saw, I Conga'd".

12.A.11   Spurs are on their way to Wembley
Tottenham's going to do it again,
They've got Tottenham (They're going to shake 'em up),
The boys got Nottenham (sic) (They're going to win the cup),
They're all going to White Hart Lane (going back to White Hart Lane).

<u>Brockley</u>, Finsbury, Mile End <u>1983</u>.

The original inspiration for this rhyme seems to have come from the pop song "Ossie's Dream (Spurs Are On Their Way to Wembley)", written and recorded by Chas 'n' Dave, 1981. "Ossie" refers to the Spurs midfielder Osvaldo Ardiles. I found several versions in schools.

12.A.12   Build a bonfire, build a bonfire
Put Liverpool on the top,
Put Ipswich in the middle,
And burn the bloody lot.

Battersea 1982.

Tune "Oh My Darling, Clementine", an American folk ballad, usually credited to Percy Montrose (1884).

See also **8.A.3** and **11.I.58**.

12.A.13   Liverpool fell down the drain
Arsenal came and pulled the chain,
Ee i addi o, Liverpool won again.

Battersea 1982; Shepherds Bush 1983 (different teams).

12.A.14   I like Nottingham Forest
I like Charlton too,
I like Tottenham Hotspur,
But I hate you.

Streatham 1982.

12.A.15   Can you hear the Gunners sing? (Arsenal)
Oh no!
Can you hear the Gunners sing?
Oh no!

Can you hear the Gunners sing?
I can't hear a bloody thing.

Blackheath 1983.

12.A.16 He shot, he missed
He must be bloody pissed.
Oh no!

Finsbury 1983.

12.A.17 Tottenham, Tottenham
No one can stop them,
We are going to do 'em,
Like we did last year.
Tottenham, Tottenham,
No one can stop them,
We're going to do it again,
We're not giving up,
We're going to win the cup,
Back up to White Hart Lane.

<u>Hampstead 1984</u>. Shorter versions: Deptford, Shepherds Bush 1983.

Versions of the pop song "Tottenham, Tottenham" written by Chas 'n' Dave and recorded in 1982.

12.A.18 Play on Millwall
Can't play football,
Oh yes they can,
We beat West Ham.
What was the score?
It was 6 – 4.

Brockley 1967.

Tune "Westminster Quarters", melody by William Crotch, 1794, later adopted for the clock tower at the Houses of Parliament.

Early noting correspondent (Thornton Heath), memory of London SE17, 1930s (skipping).

Recording BBC 16076 (78) (1951, Sidbury, Devon).

12.A.19 We have joy, we have fun
Getting Liverpool on the run,
But the sun gets too hot,
And it turns them into snot.

   Battersea 1982.

This echoes the chorus of a pop song, "Seasons in the Sun" sung by Terry Jacks in 1974: "We had joy, we had fun,/We had seasons in the sun/But the hills that we climbed/Were just seasons out of time." etc.

12.A.20 Swinging McClintock
Swinging McClintock ..., etc.

   Marylebone 1967.

12.A.21 Why are we waiting?
We are suffocating,
Why are we waiting?
Oh why? Oh why?

   Blackheath 1983.

12.A.22 Hurray we are the Michaelson boys
Hurray we are the Michaelson boys,
And if you are a City fan,

Surrender all your dough,
And we will follow the Spurs.

Mile End 1968.

12.A.23   Q.P.R
Quarter pound of rubbish.

Borough, Shepherds Bush 1983.

12.A.24   A.   Chelsea are magic!
Watch them disappear from the First Division.

Streatham 1982.

B.   Liverpool magic, Arsenal tragic!

Shepherds Bush 1983.

Other football rhymes from printed sources Brady, pp. 176–177; Kellett, pp. 79–82; MacBain, p. 55; Opies, *LLS*, pp. 350–353; Ritchie, *SS*, pp. 121–132; Rosen and Steele, [pp. 9–10]; Rutherford, pp. 94–100.

12.B RHYMES AND SONGS FOR BABIES AND TODDLERS

I would not have heard these rhymes, with the possible exception of **12.B.13** ONE, TWO, THREE, FOUR, FIVE/Once I caught a fish alive, if I had not specifically asked the children to give me examples of rhymes and songs that they might recite to, or with, little children, particularly at home. Ten- and eleven-year-old children had not outgrown all these rhymes – indeed some were in use for counting out etc. – but they needed encouragement to recite them without embarrassment. Where the rhymes have the status of nursery rhymes and appear as such in printed collections, the versions do not depart very much, if at all, from those in standard collections. The versions of **12.B.4** THIS LITTLE PIGGY, for example, are mostly fairly standard, the variations usually dealing with the last little piggy.

12.B.1 HUSH LITTLE BABY

>Hush little baby don't say a word,
>Mother's going to buy you a mocking-bird.
>If that mocking-bird won't sing,
>Mother's going to buy you a diamond ring.
>If that ring should turn to brass,
>Mother's going to buy you a looking-glass.
>If that looking-glass gets broke,
>Mother's going to buy you a billy goat.
>If that billy goat runs away,
>Mother's going to buy you another today.
>
>Shepherds Bush 1983.

Printed versions Abrahams, Mother, mother, have you heard? p. 125; Briggs, p. 89; Fowke, Momma, momma, have you heard? p. 90; Fulton and Smith, Hambone, Hambone have you heard? Papa's gonna buy you a mocking bird …, pp. 44–45; Wood (see below).

Early noting Hush my baby, don't say a word,/Daddy'll buy you a mocking bird./When that mocking bird won't sing,/Daddy'll buy you a diamond ring./When that diamond ring turns to brass,/Daddy'll buy you a looking glass./When that looking glass gets broke,/Daddy'll buy you a billy goat./When that billy goat gets bony,/Daddy'll buy you a shetland [sic] pony./When that pony runs away,/Ta-ra-ra-ra-boom-de-ay, Wood, *AMG*, 1940, pp. 63–65.

12.B.2 OPEN YOUR MOUTH

    A. Open your mouth and shut your eyes,
         And God will bring you a big surprise.

Kensington 1984.

Printed versions Brady, p. 22; Fowke, p. 124; Withers, *RIMP*, p. 126.

    B. Bozy, Bozy aeroplane,
         Now open your mouth.

Mile End 1983.

12.B.3 ROUND AND ROUND THE GARDEN

    Round and round the garden, (corner,)
    Like a teddy bear,
    One step, two steps,
    Tickle you under there.

Brixton 1982; Barnsbury, Cubitt Town, Kentish Town, Mile End, Stoke Newington 1983; Hampstead 1984.

Printed versions Boyce and Bartlett (see below); Brady, p. 6; Cosbey, p. 8; Fowke, Round about, round about/Ran a wee mouse, p. 102; Gullen, Round and round ran a wee hare, p. 43; Montgomerie, p. 19; Opies, *ODNR*, p. 184; Ritchie, *GC*, p. 7; Taylors, pp. 4–6; Turner, p. 60.

Early noting Walking round the garden, Boyce and Bartlett, 1941, p. 24.

12.B.4 THIS LITTLE PIGGY

    A. This little piggy went to market,
         This little piggy stayed at home,

This little pig had roast beef,
This little piggy had none
This little piggy went "Wee wee wee I'll tell my mum when I get home."

Mile End 1983.

B. One little piggy went to market,
One little piggy stayed at home,
One little piggy had roast beef,
One little piggy had none,
One little piggy went Weeeeeeee, all the way home
And tickle you under there.

Finsbury 1983.

Other versions: Dalston, Shepherds Bush, Stoke Newington 1983; Hampstead 1984.

Printed versions Botkin (see below); Boyce and Bartlett (see below); Brady, p. 7; Fowke, p. 100; Gullen, p. 8; Halliwell (see below); Kings (see below); Leach and Fried, p. 804; Montgomerie, p. 15; Northall (see below); Opies, *ODNR*, pp. 349–350, *PBNR*, pp. 124, 200; Ritchie, *GC*, p. 7; Sutton-Smith, p. 134; Taylors, pp. 14-17; Withers, *RIMP*, p. 109; Wood, *FAFR*, p. 40.

Early notings 1. This little pig went to market;/2. This little pig staid at home;/3. This little pig had a bit of bread and butter;/4. This little pig had none;/5. This little pig said, Wee, wee, wee!/I can't find my way home, Halliwell, *NRE*, 1842, p. 119; slightly different versions in the 1846 (p. 109) and 5th (p. 68) edns. This pig went to market,/Squeak, mouse, mouse, mousey;/Shoe, shoe, shoe the wild colt,/And here's my own doll dowsy, Halliwell, *PRNT*, 1849, p. 102. Halliwell states that this was a rhyme used by "English nurses … when a child's shoe is tight, and they pat the foot to induce him to allow it to be tried on". This differs from all the other sources noted above, which are rhymes accompanying a toe-counting game. Northall (1892, p. 415) reproduces Halliwell's

PRNT rhyme together with Halliwell's original explanatory comment, almost verbatim, although unattributed; he quotes several other versions of the rhyme and indicates their geographical distribution on p. 420. This little pig went to market,/This little pig stayed at home,/This little pig got sugar and bread,/And this little pig got none,/And this little pig went winky-wanky all the way home, Kings 2, 1930, p. 36. Boyce and Bartlett, 1941, p. 57; Botkin, *TAF*, 1944, p. 783.

12.B.5 TWO LITTLE BLACKBIRDS

Two little blackbirds sat upon a wall,
One named Peter, one named Paul,
Fly away Peter, fly away Paul,
Come back Peter, come back Paul.

Kentish Town 1983; Hampstead 1984 (finger play).

Printed versions Abrahams, Two little dicky birds, p. 198; Beckwith (see below); Boyce and Bartlett (see below); Brady, p. 81; Cosbey, p. 93; Daiken, *CGTY*, Two little dickie-birds, p. 116, Two little birdeens, p. 122; Fowke, p. 103; Gullen, p. 10; Halliwell (see below); Lang (see below); MacBain (see below); McMorland, Two little dicky birds, p. 36; Montgomerie, p. 52; Northall (see below); Opies, *ODNR*, Two little dicky birds, and There were two blackbirds, p. 147, *ONRB*, Two little dicky birds, p. 9, *CGSP*, Two little dicky birds, p. 196; Ritchie, *GC*, p. 7; Smith, *TGH*, p. 17; Sutton-Smith, p. 133; Taylors, There were two blackbirds, pp. 20–22; Turner, Two little dicky birds, p. 40; Withers, *RIMP*, There were two blackbirds, p. 107.

Early notings There were two black-birds,/Sitting on a hill,/The one nam'd Jack,/The other nam'd Jill;/Fly away Jack!/Fly away Jill!/Come again Jack!/Come again Jill! Halliwell, 1842, p. 110. Two little blackbirds sat upon a wall,/One named Peter, one named Paul;/Fly away Peter, Fly away Paul,/ Come again Peter,/Come again Paul. And: There were two blackbirds sitting on a hill,/The one named Jack, the other named Jill, etc., Northall, 1892, p. 419. Lang, 1897, as Halliwell, p. 188. Beckwith, *FGJ*, 1922, p. 12; MacBain, 1933, pp. 2, 4. Two little dicky birds, Boyce and Bartlett, 1941, p. 50.

Recording BBC 16076 (78) (1951, Sidbury, Devon) (skipping).

12.B.6 IPSY WIPSY SPIDER

FINGER PLAY:

Ipsy wipsy spider, climbing up the spout, (or "Incy wincy spider,")
Down came the rain and washed the spider out,
Out came the sun and dried up all the rain,
Ipsy wipsy spider climbed up the spout again.

Cubitt Town, Dalston, Kentish Town, Stoke Newington 1983; Kensington 1984.

Printed versions Boyce and Bartlett (see below); Fowke, p. 103; Montgomerie, p. 52; Opies, *LLS*, p. 38; Ritchie, *GC*, p. 6; Smith, *TGH*, pp. 20–21; Taylors, pp. 32–34; Turner, pp. 57–58; Wood, *FAFR*, A little sparrow built his nest, up in a waterspout, p. 58.

Early noting Insey Winsey Spider, Boyce and Bartlett, 1941, p. 50.

12.B.7 HERE'S THE CHURCH

Here's the church and here's the steeple,
Open up and here are the people.
Here's the parson running upstairs,
Here he is saying his prayers.

Dalston, Finsbury, Kentish Town, Shepherds Bush 1983.

Printed versions Botkin (see below); Boyce and Bartlett (see below); Daiken, *CGTY*, p. 142; Fowke, p. 103; Gullen, p. 5; Leach and Fried, p. 804; McMorland, p. 38; Montgomerie, p 58; Newell (see below); Northall (see below); Opies, *ODNR*, p. 125; *ONRB*, p. 8; Ritchie, *GC*, p. 6; Rodger, p. 7; Smith, *TGH*, p. 23; Sutton Smith, p. 133; Taylors, p. 10; Turner, p. 56; Withers, *RIMP*, p. 108; Wood (see below).

Early notings Lock the hands, the fingers of the right hand between those of the left, knuckles upward, saying— "Here's the church; here's the steeple (*elevating the little fingers*),/Here's the priests (*elevating thumbs*); here's the people" (*elevating all the fingers*), Northall, 1892, p. 417. Newell, 1903, p. 138; Wood, *AMG*, 1940, p. 107; Boyce and Bartlett, 1941, p. 49; Botkin, *TAF*, 1944, p. 789.

12.B.8 WEE WILLY WINKLE

Wee Willy Winkle runs through the town
Upstairs and downstairs in his nightgown,
Looking through the windows, looking through the lock,
Saying, "Are the children still in bed? It's past eight o'clock."

Brockley 1967; Shepherds Bush 1983.

Printed versions Gullen, p. 61; Lang (see below); MacBain (see below); Montgomeries, *SNR*, pp. 130–131, *HBSNR*, p. 103; Opies, *ODNR*, pp. 424–425; *ONRB*, p. 36; Rosen and Steele, a parody, [pp. 19–20].

Early notings Wee Willie Winkie runs through the town,/Upstairs and downstairs in his nightgown,/ Rapping at the window, crying through the lock,/"Are the children in their beds, for now it's eight o'clock?" Lang, 1897, p. 119; MacBain, 1933, p. 153.

12.B.9 WHAT ARE LITTLE GIRLS MADE OF?

What are little girls made of?
Sugar and spice and all things nice.
What are little boys made of?
Slugs and snails and puppy dogs' tails.
What are old women made of?
Moans and groans an' aching bones.

Battersea 1982.

Printed versions Briggs, p. 59; Cosbey, Sugar and spice and everything nice, pp. 89–90; Graves (see below); Halliwell (see below); Lang (see below); MacBain (see below); Northall (see below); Opies, *ODNR*, What are little boys made of, pp. 100–101; *ONRB*, p. 69; Sutton-Smith, Little boys are made of slugs and snails, p. 100; Withers, *RIMP*, Girls are dandy, p. 11.

Early notings What are little boys made of, made of,/What are little boys made of?/Snaps and snails, and puppy-dog's tails;/And that's what little boys are made of, made of.//What are little girls made of, made of,/What are little girls made of?/Sugar and spice, and all that's nice;/And that's what little girls are made of, made of, Halliwell, *NRE*, 1844, p. 191, 1846, p. 119. What are boys made of? (*repeat*),/ Liver and lights and hearts and pipes,/And that's what boys are made of.//What are girls made of? (*repeat*),/Sugar and spice and all things nice,/And that's what girls are made of. What are old women made of? (repeat),/Bushes and thorns and old cows' horns,/And that's what old women are made of, Northall, 1892, pp. 315–316. Lang, 1897, p. 265; Graves, 1927, pp. 20–21; MacBain, 1933, p. 37.

12.B.10 DOWN IN THE STATION

Down in the station early in the morning,
All the little puffer trains all in a row,

Out came the driver, turned a little handle,
Uff, Uff, Uff, off we go.

Mile End 1968.

Printed versions Abrahams, p. 40; Montgomerie, p. 80; Withers, *RIMP*, Early in the morning, let's go to the country, p. 13.

12.B.11 FIVE LITTLE MONKEYS

Five little monkeys went up ashore,
One went a-sailing and then there were four.

Four little monkeys climbed up a tree,
One slipped and tumbled down and then there were three.

Three little monkeys found a pot of glue,
One got stuck in it and then there were two.

Two little monkeys found a currant bun,
One ran away with it and then there was one.

One little monkey cried all afternoon,
So they put him in an aeroplane and sent him to the moon.

Mile End 1983.

Printed version cf. Abrahams, Two little monkeys/Jumping on the bed,/One fell off/And broke his head … p. 198.

Printed versions of other reducing rhymes cf. Abrahams, One little, two little, three little Indians, p. 148; Botkin, John Brown had a little Indian, *APPS*, 1937, pp. 218–220; Gullen, Ten little chickadees, p. 129, Ten little nigger boys, p. 130; MacBain, 1933, Ten little Nigger Boys going out to dine …, pp. 141–142, Old Joe Badger had a little Indian …, pp. 143–144; Montgomerie, Ten little chickadees, pp. 62–63, Ten little Injuns, pp. 64–65; Opies, *ODNR*, Ten little nigger boys, p. 327, Ten little Injuns, p. 328; Rutherford, Four little boys went to school one day, pp. 111–112; Smith, *TGH*, pp. 10, 42–43, 48–49, 52–53.

12.B.12 FIVE LITTLE DUCKLINGS

Five little ducklings went out one day,
Over the hills and far away,
Mother duck said, Quack! Quack! Quack!
And only four little ducks came waddling back.

Four little ducklings went out one day,
Over the hills and far away,
Mother duck said, Quack! Quack! Quack!
And only three little ducks came waddling back.

Three little ducklings went out one day,
Over the hills and far away,
Mother duck said, Quack! Quack! Quack!
And only two little ducks came waddling back.

Two little ducklings went out one day,
Over the hills and far away,
Mother duck said, Quack! Quack! Quack!
And only one little duck came waddling back.

One little duckling went out one day,
Over the hills and far away,
Mother duck said, Quack! Quack! Quack!
But no little ducks came waddling back.

No little ducklings went out one day,
Over the hills and far away,

Mother duck said Quack! Quack! Quack!
And five little ducklings came waddling back.

Mile End 1983.

Printed versions cf. Fowke, Six little ducks, pp. 104–105; Smith, *TGH*, pp. 18–19; cf. Wood, *FAFR*, Five little chickadees, p. 38.

12.B.13 ONE, TWO, THREE, FOUR, FIVE

ALSO USED AS A COUNTING-OUT AND BALL BOUNCING RHYME:

A. One, two, three, four, five,
    Once I caught a fish alive.
    Why did you let it go?
    Because it bit my finger so.
    Which finger did it bite?
    The little finger on the right.

Barnsbury, Battersea, Brixton, Dalston, Mile End, Shepherds Bush, Streatham 1983.

B. One, two, three, four, five,
    If you want to stay alive,
    Six, seven, eight, nine, ten,
    Never go to the lions' den.

Mile End 1968.

Printed versions Abrahams, pp. 150–151; Abrahams and Rankin, pp. 175–176; Bolton (see below); Boyce and Bartlett (see below); Briggs, p. 149; Coffin and Cohen, ... I caught a hen alive, counting-out, p. 190; Douglas (see below); Fowke, p. 109; Gullen, p. 34; Halliwell (see below); Montgomerie, p. 67; Opies, *ODNR*, pp. 334–335, *ONRB*, p. 112; Ritchie, *GC*, p. 6; Rodger p. 20; Turner, p. 15; Withers, *CO*, pp. 5, 7, *RIMP*, p. 86; Wood, *FAFR*, p. 109.

Early notings 1, 2, 3, 4, 5!/I caught a hare alive;/6, 7, 8, 9, 10,/I let her go again, Halliwell, *NRE*, 1842, p. 131. The sequence also appears in a rhyme beginning "See saw, sacradown", 1842, p. 124. Several versions in Bolton, 1888, p. 93. Douglas, 1916, p. 63, 1931, p. 34; Boyce and Bartlett, 1941, p. 20.

12.B.14 ALL I WANT FOR CHRISTMAS

> All I want for Christmas is my two front teeth,
> My two front teeth, my two front teeth,
> All I want for Christmas is my two front teeth,
> And that is all I want.

<u>Barnsbury</u>, Shepherds Bush <u>1983</u>.

Based on the chorus of a humorous song written by Don Gardner for Christmas 1946.

12.B.15 I'M A LITTLE TEAPOT

ACTION SONG:

> A. I'm a little teapot, straight and stout,
>   Here's my handle, here's my spout.
>   When the tea is ready, hear me shout,
>   Pick me up and pour me out.

Brixton 1982.

Printed versions Fowke, p. 106; Harrop, Friend, and Gadsby, p. 33; Taylors, p. 38; Wood, *FAFR*, p. 104.

> B. I'm a little teapot, short and stout,
>   Here's my handle, here's my spout.
>   Oh dear! I'm a china vase!

Blackheath 1983.

12.B.16 THIS OLD MAN

This old man, he played one,
He played nick nack on my bum,

> Nick nack paddy whack,
> Give a dog a bone,
> This old man came rolling home.

This old man he played two,
He played nick nack on my shoe,
> Nick nack paddy whack, etc.

This old man, he played three,
He played nick nack on my knee,
> Nick nack paddy whack, etc.

Brixton, Earlsfield 1982.

Printed versions Abrahams, My old man number one, quoting Withers, p. 137; Baring Gould and Sharp (see below); Daiken, *CGTY*, Nick nack Paddy Whack, singing rhyme, p. 36, This old man, he played one, finger game, p. 144; Harrop, Friend, and Gadsby, p. 39; Kidson (see below); Montgomerie, pp. 31–32; Sims, pp. 54–55; Smith, *TGH*, pp. 43–45; Withers, *RIMP*, My old man number one, pp. 72–73.

Early notings This old man, he played one,/He played nick nack on my drum;/Nick nack paddy whack, give a dog a bone,/This old man came rolling home, Baring Gould and Sharp, 1906, pp. 94–95. I am Jack Jinkle, Kidson, 1916, pp. 106–107.

12.C WRITINGS FOR ALBUMS, etc.

Album writing was not common among junior school children during my survey, and belonged to a slightly older age group. However, the rhymes in this section do not belong to the usual oral repertoire. They are likely to be written down, even though most of them were given to me orally when I asked for them. They tend to be of a benign character. The ones which are less kind are presented in Section **9.C** Taunts and Epithets.

12.C.1 ROSES ARE RED

    A. Roses are red,
         Violets are blue,
         I've never met no one
         As nice as you.

Walworth 1982.

    B. Roses are red,
         Violets are blue,
         Sugar is sweet,
         And so are you.

Greenwich 1982; Mile End, Stoke Newington 1983; Kensington 1984.

    C. Roses are red,
         Violets are blue,
         I love you Mummy,
         And Dad too.

Barnsbury 1983.

    D. Roses are red,
         Violets are blue,
         Kiss me do, (Best of luck)
         I love you.

Barnsbury 1983.

    E. Roses are red,
         Violets are blue,

>   'Cause I really, really
>   Yes I do, love you.

Shepherds Bush 1983.

F. Roses are red,
    Violets are blue,
    Your eyes are sweet,
    And so are you.

Stoke Newington 1983.

G. Roses are red,
    Violets are blue,
    Bees make sweet honey,
    Especially for you.

Mile End 1983.

See also **5.21**, **8.D.44**, **9.C.1c**, **9.C.13**, **9.C.21**, and **9.C.31d** ("Roses are red" rhymes).

Printed versions Abrahams, p. 171; Briggs, p. 22; Halliwell (see below); Hepburn and Roberts, 302–303; Hughes and Bontemps, p. 332; Kellett, pp. 110–111; MacBain (see below); Northall (see below); Opies, *ODNR*, p. 375, *ONRB*, p. 60, *LLS*, p. 237; Petershams, p. 41; Ritchie, *SS*, pp. 49, 50, 110; Turner, pp. 74–75, 118; Withers, *RIMP*, p. 157.

Early notings Roses are red, diddle, diddle,/Lavender's blue,/If you will have me, diddle diddle,/I will have you, plus three further verses, quoted from *Gammer Gurton's Garland* (1783) by Northall, 1892, pp. 545–546. The rose is red, the violet's blue,/The honey's sweet, and so are you./ … Halliwell, *NRE*, 1842, p. 150. The rose is red,/The violet's blue;/Pinks are sweet,/And so are you! Halliwell, *PRNT*, 1849, p. 239. The rose is red, the violet's blue,/The gilly-flower sweet, and so are you;/These are the words you bade me say/For a pair of new gloves on Easter day, Halliwell, *PRNT*, 1849, p. 250. MacBain, 1933, p. 310.

12.C.2 I LOVE YOU HIGH, I LOVE YOU MIGHTY

> I love you high, I love you mighty,
> I wish that my pyjamas were next to your nightie.
> Now don't you blush,
> Don't you go red,
> I mean on the clothesline and not in bed.
>
> Kensington 1984.

See also **8.D.14B**, **9.A.3** and **11.I.24C** for similar wordplay.

Printed versions Hepburn and Roberts, 304; Knapps, p. 183; Lowenstein, p. 23; Shaw, 1970, p. 109; Turner, p. 114 (and see below).

Early notings Turner (1969, p. 114) cites a version of the above from New South Wales in 1935, and also: Oi sweet mama, oi sweet mama,/I'd like to see your nightie next to my pajama./Now don't get excited, now don't get red, I mean on the clothes line and not in bed, Turner (1969, p. 114), quoting Rolland, F. "Street Songs of Children". *New Masses* 27 (1938, May 10) (New York).

12.C.3 IF I WAS A CABBAGE

> A. If I was a cabbage,
> I'd break myself in two,
> I'd throw away the leaves
> And give my heart to you.
>
> Kensington 1984.
>
> B. My life is like a cabbage,
> Often split in two,

> The leaves I give to others
> But the heart I give to you.

Earlsfield 1982.

Printed versions Kellett, p. 106; Opies, *LLS*, p. 237.

12.C.4 WHEN YOU'RE OLD

> When you're old and your face goes purple,
> Don't forget the girl who wrote in the circle.

Blackheath 1983.

12.C.5 TWO IN A HAMMOCK

> Two in a hammock attempted a kiss,
> They both fell out and landed like **this**.

Earlsfield 1982.

Printed versions cf. Fowke, skipping, p. 58; Hepburn and Roberts, 303; Turner, p. 119.

12.C.6 TWO LITTLE CARS

> Two little cars,
> Two little kisses,
> Two weeks later,
> Mr. and Mrs.

Earlsfield 1982.

Printed versions Fowke, skipping, p. 58; Hepburn and Roberts, 303; cf. Ritchie, *SS*, I love your hugs/I love your kisses:/I hope some day/We'll be Mr and Mrs., p. 50; Turner, p. 119.

Signature

12.C.7 I'M A LITTLE CHINA GIRL

    A. I'm a little China girl
          I live in China town,
          And when I write my name,
          I write it upside down.

    B. I'm a little China girl,
          Dressed in blue,
          Just like you.

"When people ask you to write your signature, you do this. Then you sign your name but upside down." girl, 11, Kensington 1984.

Writing on Envelope or Notepaper

12.C.8   "If you fancy a boy a bit and you write to him, you put on the envelope: S-W-A-L-K (Sealed with a loving kiss)."

Printed version Hepburn and Roberts, 302.

12.C.9   "You can write T-L-E (true love for ever) or do it like this:"

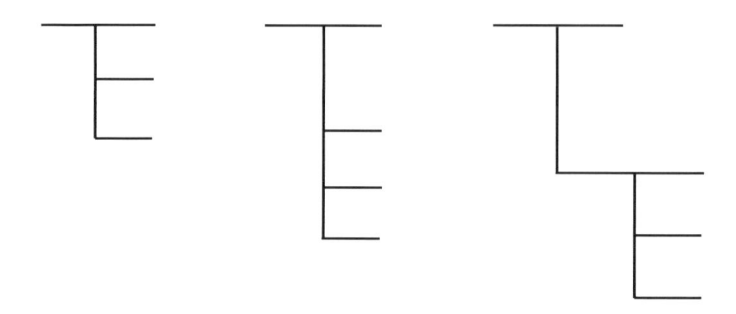

```
 ___              ___              ___
|                    |                    |
|___             |                    |___
|                    |___             ___
|                    |                    |
|___             |___             |___
                                        |
                                        |___
```

girl, 11, EC1 1983.

12.D BEING FIRST IN LINE, etc.

Versions of the rhyme **12.D.1** FIRST THE WORST were in general use in the upper junior age group. The children might use it when competing to be the first to sit down in the classroom, to be first in lining up or for getting dressed at the end of a physical education lesson. It may perhaps be derived from the rhyme beginning "Go to bed first", noted by Halliwell in 1844, though it has lost some of the poetry of that rhyme. Remnants still remain in version A with: "Fourth a golden eagle's nest,/Fifth the one with the treasure chest."

12.D.1 FIRST THE WORST

    A. First the worst,
        Second the best,
        Third the one with the hairy chest,
        Fourth a golden eagle's nest,
        Fifth the one with the treasure chest.

Dalston (part), Finsbury, Kentish Town 1983; Hampstead 1984.

    B. First the worst,
        Second the best,
        Third the one with the hairy chest,
        Fourth the king,
        Fifth the queen,
        Sixth the royal washing machine.

Shepherds Bush 1983; Kensington 1984.

    C. First the worst,
        Second the best,
        Third the one with the hairy chest,
        Fourth the one that can't get dressed.

Dulwich, Finsbury 1983 (after swimming).

D. First the worst,
   Second the best,
   Third the one with the hairy chest,
   Fourth the one with the smelly vest.

Earlsfield 1982.

E. First the worst,
   Second the best,
   Third the one with the hairy chest,
   Fourth's all right,
   Fifth's outside.

Brockley 1983.

F. First the worst,
   Second's the best,
   Third's doctor,
   Fourth's the one that picks his nose,
   Fifth's the one that eats it.

Deptford 1983.

Many "last one's", e.g.: The last one to sit down stinks/is a wanker/is a woolly back, etc.

Printed versions Botkin (see below); Halliwell (see below); Northall (see below); Opies, *CGSP*, p. 185; cf. Turner, Last, last, lucky last,/Find a penny in the grass, p. 73; Withers, *RIMP*, p. 169.

Early noting cf. GO to bed first, a golden purse;/Go to bed second, a golden pheasant;/Go to bed third, a golden bird! Halliwell, *NRE*, 1844, p. 44. First the best, Second the same,/Last the worst in all the game, Northall, 1892, p. 359. Also, "a fragment from Oswestry": First, for the golden purse,/Second, for the same,/Third,/Fourth, for the sugar loaf,/Fifth,/Seven, for the key of Heaven,/Last, for the bag of brass, p. 358, recited in association with running a race, Northall (p. 338) also notes:

"Schoolboys have several kinds of divination verses on going to bed, now repeated 'more in mock than mark,' but no doubt originating in serious belief—'Go to bed first, a golden purse;/... second, ... pheasant;/... third, ... bird' ", Botkin, *TAF*, 1944, p. 778.

12.E FOR MARCHING

Not much marching was done by children at school during the time the survey was undertaken. Marching was part of physical education in my schooldays in the 1920s, and is still used in some children's uniformed organisations. In the old "drill" lesson, a muttered rhyme often punctuated the teacher's instructions to keep in step.

12.E.1 LEFT, LEFT

> Left, left, left and right,
> My boots are busted,
> My knickers are tight,
> My balls are banging,
> My hands are right.

Printed versions based on "Left, left, I had a good job and I left" (a World War I marching chant) and all the following are versions of this rhyme: Opies, *LLS*, p. 39; Richards and Stubbs, p. 53; Ritchie, *SS*, p. 25; Shaw, 1970, p. 2; Turner, p. 92; Withers, *RIMP*, p. 133.

Early noting Nettleingham, F. T. (2nd Lt, RFC). (1917). *Tommy's Tunes*. London: Erskine MacDonald.

12.F STARTING STORIES

These rhymes were not much in use when I was collecting, but probably had a new lease of life from the BBC television programme *Jackanory* which was broadcast for many years from 1965.

12.F.1 TELL ME A STORY

    A. Tell me a story
         About Jackanory,
         Now my story's begun.
         Tell me another,
         About his brother,
         Now my story's done.

Mile End 1968.

    B. Rosy, Rosy,
         Tell me a story.

Stoke Newington 1983.

Printed versions Botkin (see below); Brady, I'll tell you a story/About Johnny Magory, p. 9; Briggs, Jack a Nory, p. 176; Fowke, I'll tell you a story about Mother Magory/of Rig-a ma-rory, p. 126; Graves (see below); Gullen, p. 122; Halliwell (see below); Lowenstein, p. 24; Northall (see below); Opies, *ODNR*, p. 233 (and see below); Ritchie, *GC*, Johnny Nory, p. 3; a different version, p. 4; Rodger, p. 3; Shaw, 1970, Shall I begin it? p. 1, That's all that's in it, p. 121; Turner, p. 92.

Early notings I'll tell you a Story, of Jacky Nory, Will you have it now or anon? I will tell you another, of Jack and his Brother, And my Story's done, Opies, *ODNR*, p. 233, quoting Baldwin, R. *The Top Book of All, for Little Masters and Misses* (c1760), and several further early versions. I'll tell you a story,/About Jack a Nory;/And now my story's begun:/I'll tell you another/About Jack his brother,/And now my story's done, Halliwell, *NRE*, 1842, p. 24. I'll tell you a tale./Shall I begin it?/There's nothing in it, Northall, 1892, p. 339. Lang, 1897, p. 58. I'll tell you a story of Jock o' Binnorie, Graves, 1927, p. 16. I'll tell you a story/About old Mother Morey, Botkin, *TAF*, 1944, p. 786, … About Jack a Nory, p. 787.

12.G EVERLASTING STORIES

These examples are interesting survivals, not in general use. There are of course everlasting songs like "The Bear Went Over the Mountain" and **11.J.3** MICHAEL FINNEGAN in use still perhaps among Cub Scouts and Brownies.

12.G.1 It was a dark and stormy night. The wind howled. The captain said, "Hal, tell me a story." This is the story Hal told: "It was a dark and stormy night …"

Shepherds Bush 1983.

Printed versions Opies, *LLS*, p. 31; Shaw, 1970, p. 58; Withers, *RIMP*, p. 131.

Early noting I remember the following from c1930: It was a dark and stormy night/And the rain came down in torrents./The sailor said he'd tell a tale/And this is how it follows: It was a dark and stormy night …

12.G.2 There were two men behind a rock. One man said to the other: "Tell me a story," so he began. "There were two men …"

Kensington 1984.

12.G.3 a. There were two cows in a field, one called Pansy and one called "Tell me again." Pansy went to the dairy, who do you think was left?
 b. Tell me again.
 a. There were two cows …

12.H SO-CALLED "BACKSLANG"

The six examples given here are not, of course, genuine backslang which, as the Opies point out, "consists of saying each word backwards" (*LLS*, 1959, pp. 320–321). However, the rapid rendering of language with apparently simple changes and additions can be completely incomprehensible to those who do not share the secret. A girl (Hampstead 1984) gave me example **12.H.4**. She put on an air of mystery and told me that she could not give me the key to what it meant and that it was much too difficult to explain. In fact, one of my informants told me what they did to the words, but they usually gave me a translation from which, in the light of the examples given by the Opies (*LLS*, 1959, pp. 320–321), it was a simple matter to see how the "language" was made up. All the examples were given to me by girls. One or two boys attempted to give me examples but were unable to sustain them.

I did not come across any examples of genuine backslang where the order of the letters is reversed. Here are examples of what the Opies (*LLS*, 1959, p. 321) call "pig Latin" as well as "Arague Language"; I also collected "arag language" and similar "avag" and "ivag" "languages". There are also "languages" made with "p" and "gv" sounds. I presume in other schools there are variants.

12.H.1 Pig Latin

The first single (or double) consonant is transferred to the end of the word and the sound "ay" is added:

    A.   Let's   go   to   the   shop.
                         becomes:
        Etslay   ogay   ootay   hetay   hopsay.

In this example (Stoke Newington 1983) only a single consonant is moved. If the double consonant was moved it would be:

    B.   Etslay   ogay   ootay   ethay   opshay

For ease of speaking, an additional "e" may be sounded as in this example (Hampstead 1984):

C. I   like   you   and   you   like   me
                    becomes:
    Iay   ikelay   oojay   anday   oojay   ikelay eema

    (ikelay pronounced eye-ke-lay)

Printed versions Botkin (see below); Brady, "fancy endings": If-ika you-ika can-ika swim-ika/Li-ika my-ika son-ika John-ika/I-ika will-ika give-ika you-ika/Bob-ika (*or* shilling), pp. 172–173; Chambers (see below); Gaskell (see below); Gregor (see below); Opies, *LLS*, p. 321.

Early notings I wad gie my ten owsen that my wife was as fair as yon swan/That is fleeing owre yon mill-dam. It is necessary in the above case to add *co* to each syllable, Chambers, 1842, p. 61. In the following formula the syllable *ca* must be added to the end of each word. I wad gee a' my livin'/That my wife were as fite an as fair/As the swans that flee o'er the mill-dam, (Portsoy), Gregor, 1891, p. 32. Cf. Balloo katto adonoy alloway-ay/You mellakalloy-oy/Ashade bokay/Balloo kallay, nonsense rhyme, Gaskell, c1913, p. 11. "Hog Latin": Igry knowgry somegry thinggry yougry don'tgry knowgry, Botkin, *TAF*, 1944, pp. 776–777.

12.H.2 "Arag" or "Arague" "language"

"Arag" is inserted between the initial single (or double) consonant and the rest of the syllable. If there is no consonant at the start of the word then "rag" is inserted. This example was found in The Borough (1983):

    Can   you   un-   der-   stand   me?
    Caragan   youragoo   uragun   darager   staragans maragee?

    I   hope   you   can   be-   cause
    Irag   haragope   youragoo caragan   baragee   caragause

I	want	to	talk	to		you.
Irag	waragant	tooragoo	taragalk	tooragoo		youragoo.

Printed version Opies, *LLS*, pp. 320, 321.

12.H.3 "Avag language"

A.	Do	you	un-	der	stand	me?
	Davagoo	youvagoo	uvagun	davager	stavergand	mavagee?

Barnsbury 1983.

B.	My	name	is	Em	il	y
	Mavagy	navagame	avagis	Avagem	avagil	avagee

Hampstead 1984.

12.H.4 "Ivag language" is similar:

Ip	dip	dog		shit.
Ivagip	divagip	divagog		shivagit.

Who	stepped	in	it?
Hivagoo	stivagooed	ivagin	ivagit?

Hampstead 1984.

12.H.5 "P" language

A "p" sound is inserted before each vowel sound. Sometimes an indefinite "e" sound is put in between syllables or before an initial vowel.

I	want	to	go	shopping	tomorrow.
(e)Pi	wpont	tpoe	gpo	shpopperping	tpoom(e)por(e)poe.

Stoke Newington 1983.

12.H.6 "Gv" language

As above but "gv" is inserted:

What	is	your	name	please?
Wgvot	igvis	ygvor	ngvame	plgvease?

Stoke Newington 1983.

Children in one school gave me an example which I was unable to decipher, but my informant might have got his translation wrong!

12.I RHYMING SLANG

Rhyming slang is rarely found as a living part of the language of children in this age group in Inner London, but I was able to record the following examples during the survey.

12.I.1
Apples and pears	stairs
Around the houses	trousers
Daisy roots	boots
Holler boys holler	collar
Rory O'More	door
Trouble and strife	wife
Whistle and flute	suit

Barnsbury, Cubitt Town 1983.

12.I.2
Currant bun	son
Jam jar	car
Uncle Ned	bed

Cubitt Town 1983

12.1.3 I suppose   nose
Mince pies   eyes
Plates of meat   feet

Dulwich 1983.

Printed versions Opies, *LLS*, p. 320.

BIBLIOGRAPHY

With acronym or abbreviated designation where more than one work cited per author

Name of publication	Acronym or abbreviation used in the text
Abrahams, R. D. (Ed.). (1969). *Jump-rope rhymes: A dictionary*. Publications of the American Folklore Society, Bibliographical and Special Series, Vol. 20. Austin, TX and London: University of Texas Press.	
Abrahams, R. D., and Rankin, L. (Eds.). (1980). *Counting out rhymes: A dictionary.* Publications of the American Folklore Society, Bibliographical and Special Series, Vol. 31. Austin, TX and London: University of Texas Press.	
Ballads and Songs. (1965). 3 children's songs. Unsigned. (4), Salford, [8–9].	

Name of publication	Acronym or abbreviation used in the text
Baring Gould, S., and Sharp, C. J. (1906). *English folk songs for schools*. London: Curwen.	
Barltrop, R., and Wolveridge, J. (1980). *The muvver tongue*. London: Journeyman Press.	
Beck, E. (1983, July). Children's Halloween customs in Sheffield. *Lore and Language*, 3(9), 70–88.	
Beckwith, M. W. (1928). *Jamaica folk-lore*. New York, NY: American Folk-Lore Society.	JFL
Beckwith, M. W., and Roberts, H. H. (1922). *Folk games of Jamaica*. Publications of the Folk-Lore Foundation, No. 1. Poughkeepsie, NY: Vassar College.	FGJ
Bett, H. M. A. (1924). *Nursery rhymes and tales: Their origin and history*. London: Methuen.	NRT
Bett, H. M. A. (1929). *The games of children: Their origin and history*. London: Methuen.	TGC
Bluebells my cockle shells. See Cumnock Academy.	
Bolton, H. C. (1888, 1969). *The counting-out rhymes of children*. London: Elliot Stock; rpt. Detroit, MI: Singing Tree Press.	
Botkin, B. A. (1937, 1963). *The American play party song*. Lincoln, NE: University of Nebraska [privately printed]; rpt. New York, NY: Frederick Ungar Publishing.	APPS
Botkin, B. A. (Ed.). (1944). *A treasury of American folklore: Stories, ballads, and traditions of the people*. New York, NY: Crown.	TAF
Boyce, E. R., and Bartlett, K. (1941). *Number rhymes and finger plays*. London: Pitman.	
Boyes, G. (1984). Children's clapping rhymes from Newfoundland and Sheffield. *Folk Song Research*, 3(3), 33–42.	
Brady, E. (1975). *All in! All in!* Dublin: Comhairle Bhéaloideas Eireann.	

Name of publication	Acronym or abbreviation used in the text
Brewster, P. G. (1939, September). Rope-skipping, counting-out, and other rhymes of children. *Southern Folklore Quarterly*, *3*(2), 173–178.	RCORC
Brewster, P. G. (1953). *American nonsinging games.* Norman, OK: University of Oklahoma Press.	ANG
Briggs, R. (1973). *The Mother Goose treasury.* Harmondsworth: Puffin Books.	
Browne, J. P. (1974, July). The songs that we sung in the days when we were young ... *Folk Review*, *3*(9), 17–19.	
Cansler, L. D. (1968). Midwestern and British children's lore compared. *Western Folklore*, *27*(1), 1–18.	
Chambers, R. (1826). *The popular rhymes of Scotland.* Edinburgh: William Hunter/Charles Smith; London: James Duncan. 2nd ed., Edinburgh: W. and R. Chambers (1842); *Popular Rhymes of Scotland*, 3rd ed., Edinburgh: W. and R. Chambers (1847); new ed., London and Edinburgh: W. and R. Chambers (1870); rpt. Detroit, MI: Singing Tree Press (1969). https://archive.org/details/popularrhymesofs00chamrich	
Chase, R. (Coll. and Ed.). (1938). *Old songs and singing games.* Chapel Hill, NC: University of North Carolina Press.	OSASG
Chase, R. (Comp.). (1956). *American folk tales and songs.* New York, NY: New American Library.	AFTS
Chase, R. (1967). *Singing games and playparty games*, New York, NY: Dover. (Rpt. of *Hullabaloo and other singing folk games.* Boston, MA: Houghton Mifflin, 1949).	SGPPG
Children's games and sports. (1973). *Encyclopedia Britannica* (14th ed.) 5. Chicago, IL: Cox.	
Coffin, T., and Cohen, H. (1966). *Folklore in America.* Garden City, NY: Doubleday.	

Name of publication	Acronym or abbreviation used in the text
Cole, W. (Ed.). (1966). *Oh, what nonsense!* London: Methuen.	
Cosbey, R. C. (1980). *All in together, girls: Skipping songs from Regina, Saskatchewan.* Occasional Paper 2. Regina: University of Regina, Canadian Plains Research Center.	
Cray, E. (Comp. and Ed.). (1969). *The erotic muse.* New York: Oak Publications. 2nd ed., Urbana, IL: University of Illinois Press (1992); also published under title *Bawdy ballads*, London: Blond (1970).	*BB*
Cumnock Academy. (1961). *Bluebells my cockle shells.* Kilmarnock: Cumnock Academy.	
Daiken, L. (1949). *Children's games throughout the year.* London: Batsford.	*CGTY*
Daiken, L. (1954). *Teaching through play: A teacher's handbook on games.* London: Pitman.	*TTP*
Daiken, L. (1963). *Out goes she: Dublin street rhymes.* Dublin: Dolmen Press.	*OGS*
Dennison, D. (1957, August). Old singing games. *The Dalesman, 19*(5), 292–295.	
Douglas, N. (1916). *London street games.* London: The St. Catherine Press. 2nd ed., London: Chatto and Windus (1931); rpt. Detroit, MI: Singing Tree Press (1968); rpt. New York, NY: Johnson Reprint (1969).	
Eckenstein, L. (1906). *Comparative studies in nursery rhymes.* London: Duckworth.	
Elder, J. D. (1965). *Song games from Trinidad and Tobago.* Boston, MA: Publications of the American Folklore Society, Bibliographical and Special Series, Vol. 16.	
Ellis, V. (1979, July). The games we played. *London Lore, 1*(4), 38–40.	

Name of publication	Acronym or abbreviation used in the text
Encyclopedia Britannica, see Children's games and sports; Folk rhymes.	
Evans, P. (Comp.). (1954). *Jump rope rhymes.* San Francisco, CA: The Porpoise Bookshop.	*JRR*
Evans, P. (1956). *Who's it?* San Francisco, CA: The Porpoise Bookshop.	*WI*
Farjeon, E. (1956). *Grannie Gray, children's plays and games.* London: Oxford University Press.	
Foakes, G. (1974). *My part of the river.* London: Shepheard-Walwyn.	
Folk Rhymes. (1973). *Encyclopedia Britannica* (14th ed.), 5. Chicago, IL: Cox.	
Ford, R. (1904). *Children's rhymes, children's games, children's songs, children's stories: A book for bairns and big folk.* Paisley: Alexander Gardner.	
Fowke, E. (1969). *Sally go round the Sun.* Toronto: McClelland and Stewart.	
Fulton, E., and Smith, P. (1978). *Let's slice the ice: African American children's ring games and chants.* St. Louis, MO: MMB Music.	
Gadsby, D., and Harrop, B. (1982). *Flying a round: 88 rounds and partner songs.* London: A. and C. Black.	
Gainer, D. H. (1980, Summer and Fall). Eeny meeny miney mo: violence and other elements in children's rhymes. *Southwest Folklore, 4*(3 and 4), 44–50.	
Gallagher, J. (1969). *The Festival book of singing games.* Accompanying booklet to *Children's singing games*, Impact Record No. IMP-A 101: Impact Records.	
Gardner, E. E. (1918, October-December). Some counting-out rhymes in Michigan. *Journal of American Folklore, 31*(122), 531.	

Name of publication	Acronym or abbreviation used in the text
Gaskell, A. (1963). *Those were the days: The games and jingles played and sung by the children of a Lancashire village, fifty and more years ago.* Manchester: Swinton and Pendlebury Public Libraries.	
Gillington, A. E. (Ed.). (1909). *Old Hampshire singing games and trilling the rope rhymes.* London: Curwen.	OHSG
Gillington, A. E. (Ed.). (1909). *Old Isle of Wight singing games.* London: Curwen.	OIWSG
Gillington, A. E. (Ed.). (1909). *Old Surrey singing games and skipping-rope rhymes.* London: Curwen.	OSSG
Gillington, A. E. (Ed.). (1913). *Old Dorset singing games.* London: Curwen.	ODSG
Gomme, A. B. (1894 and 1898). *The traditional games of England, Scotland and Ireland*, Vols. I and II. London: David Nutt; rpt. New York, NY: Dover Publications (1964); one vol. ed. with introduction by Fr. Damian Webb, London: Thames and Hudson (1984).	
Graves, R. (1927). *The less familiar nursery rhymes.* London: Ernest Benn.	
Gregor, W. (1891, 1973). *Counting out rhymes of children.* London: David Nutt; rpt. Darby, PA: Norwood.	
Gullen, F. D. (1950). *Traditional number rhymes and games.* Publications of the Scottish Council for Research in Education, Vol. 32. London: University of London Press.	
Halliwell, J. O. (1842). *The nursery rhymes of England, collected principally from oral tradition.* London: The Percy Society; 2nd ed., London: John Russell Smith (1843); 3rd ed., London: John Russell Smith (1844); 4th ed., London: John Russell Smith (1846); 6th ed., London: John Russell Smith (1853); new ed., London and Edinburgh: W. and R. Chambers (1870); rpt. London: The Bodley Head (1970).	NRE

Name of publication	Acronym or abbreviation used in the text
Halliwell, J. O. (1849, 1970). *Popular rhymes and nursery tales*. London: John Russell Smith; new ed., *Popular rhymes and nursery tales of England*. London: The Bodley Head.	PRNT
Halliwell, J. O. (Coll.). (n.d., c1870). *Nursery rhymes and nursery tales of England*. London: Frederick Warne/New York, NY: Scribner, Welford, and Armstrong.	NRNTE
Harrop, B., Blakeley, P., and Gadsby, D. (1975). *Apusskidu: Songs for children*. London: A. and C. Black.	
Harrop, B., Friend, L., and Gadsby, D. (1976). *Okki-tokki-unga: Action songs for children*. London: A. and C. Black.	
Harrowven, J. (1977). *Origins of rhymes, songs and sayings*. London: Kaye and Ward.	
Hepburn, A., and Roberts, A. (1978, February 9). Roses are red, violets are blue. *New Society*, 302–304.	
Hewins, A. (Ed.). (1981). *The Dillen, memories of a man of Stratford-upon-Avon*. London: Elm Tree/Hamish Hamilton.	
Holbrook, D. (1957). *Children's games*. Bedford: Gordon Fraser.	
Hopkin, J. B. (1984, January). Jamaican children's songs. *Ethnomusicology*, 28(1), 1–36.	
Hubbard, J. A. (1982). Children's traditional games from Birdsedge: Clapping songs and their notation. *Folk Music Journal*, 4(3), 246–264.	
Hughes, J. L. and Bontemps, A. (Eds.). (1958). *The book of Negro folklore*. New York, NY: Dodd, Mead.	
Jorgensen, M. G. (1980, Summer and Fall). An analysis of boy-girl relationships portrayed in contemporary jump rope and handclapping rhymes. *Southwest Folklore*, 4(3 and 4), 63–71.	SWF

Name of publication	Acronym or abbreviation used in the text
Jorgensen., M. G. (1982, June). A comparison of U.S. and British children's play rhymes. *London Lore*, *1*(9), 111–114.	LL
Keeping, C. (Ed.). (1975). *Cockney ding dong*. Harmondsworth: Kestrel Books; London: EMI Music Publishing.	
Kellett, R. (1966). Heritage of the streets: a collection of children's songs, games and jingles. Unpublished ms deposited in the Vaughan Williams Memorial Library, English Folk Dance and Song Society, treated in the notes in the present collection as a printed source.	
Kelsey, N. G. N. (1979, July). Tradition & innovation in playground games & songs. *London Lore*, *1*(4), 40–49.	*K1*
Kelsey, N. G. N. (1981). When they were young girls: A singing game through the century. *Folklore*, *92*(1), 104–109.	*K2*
Kelsey, N. G. N. (1985). The lady on the mountain: A century of play rhyme tradition. *Lore and Language*, *4*(1), 78–85.	*K3*
Kenney, M. (Coll.). (1975). *Circle round the zero, play chants & singing games of city children*. St. Louis, MO: Magnamusic-Baton.	
Kidson, F. (Ed.), and Moffat, A. (pianoforte accompaniments). (1916). *100 singing games: Old, new, and adapted*. London: Bayley and Ferguson.	
King, M., and King, R. (Eds.). (1926). *Street games of North Shields children*. First Series. Tynemouth: Priory Press.	Kings 1
King, M., and King, R. (Eds.). (1930). *Street games of North Shields children*. Second Series. Tynemouth: Priory Press.	Kings 2

Name of publication	Acronym or abbreviation used in the text
Kirshenblatt-Gimblett, B. (Ed.). (1976). *Speech play.* Philadelphia, PA: University of Pennsylvania Press.	
Knapp, M., and Knapp, H. (1976). *One potato, two potato … : The folklore of American children.* New York, NY: Norton.	
Lang, A. (Ed.). (1897). *The nursery rhyme book.* London: Frederick Warne.	
Leach, M., and Fried, J. (Eds.). (1949–1950). *Funk and Wagnalls standard dictionary of folklore, mythology and legend.* New York, NY: Funk and Wagnalls.	
Legman G. (1968, 1969). *Rationale of the dirty joke: An analysis of sexual humor.* New York, NY: Grove; rpt. London: Cape.	RDJ
Legman, G. (Ed.). (1976). *The limerick: 1700 examples, with notes, variants and index.* 2 vols. New York, NY: Bell Publishing; St. Albans: Panther.	TL
Lowenstein, W. (1974). *Shocking, shocking, shocking: The improper play rhymes of Australian children.* Australian Folklore Occasional Paper No. 5. Prahran, Victoria, Australia: Fish and Chip Press; rpt. Kuranda, Queensland, Rams Skull Press (1986, 1988, 1989).	
Lyons, A. (1979, July). Favourite games. *London Lore,* *1*(4), 49–51.	
MacBain, J. M. (Coll.). (1933). *The London treasury of nursery rhymes.* London: University of London Press.	
McMorland, A. (1978). *The funny family: Songs, rhymes and games for children.* London: Ward Lock Educational.	
Mills, D., and Bishop, M. (1937, November 13). Songs of innocence. *The New Yorker, 13*(39), 32–42.	

Name of publication	Acronym or abbreviation used in the text
Montgomerie, N. (Comp.). (1966). *This little pig went to market: Play rhymes for infants and young children.* London: The Bodley Head.	
Montgomerie, N., and Montgomerie, W. (Eds.). (1946). *Scottish nursery rhymes.* London: Hogarth Press.	*SNR*
Montgomerie, N., and Montgomerie, W. (Eds.). (1948). *Sandy Candy and other Scottish nursery rhymes.* London: Hogarth Press.	*SC*
Montgomerie, N., and Montgomerie, W. (Eds.). (1964). *The Hogarth book of Scottish nursery rhymes.* London: Hogarth Press.	*HBSNR*
Morrison, L. (Comp.). (1958). *Touch blue.* New York, NY: Thomas Crowell.	
Muir, W. (1965). *Living with ballads.* London: Hogarth Press; New York, NY: Oxford University Press.	
Nelson, E. L. (1976). *Musical games for children of all ages.* New York, NY: Sterling; London: Oak Tree Press.	
Newell, W. W. (1883, 1903, 1963). *Games and songs of American children.* New York, NY: Harper; 2nd ed. New York, NY: Harper; rpt. of 2nd ed., with a new introduction and index by C. Withers, New York, NY: Dover.	
Nicholson, E. W. B. (Coll. and Ed.). (1897, 1975). *Golspie: Contributions to its folklore.* London: David Nutt; rpt. Norwood, PA: Norwood Editions.	
Northall, G. F. (1892, 1968). *English folk-rhymes: A collection of traditional verses relating to places and persons, customs, superstitions, etc.* London: Kegan Paul, Trench, Trübner; rpt. Detroit, MI: Singing Tree Press.	
Opie, I., and Opie, P. (1947). *I saw Esau: Traditional rhymes of youth.* London: Williams and Norgate.	*ISE*

Name of publication	Acronym or abbreviation used in the text
Opie, I., and Opie, P. (1951). *The Oxford dictionary of nursery rhymes*. Oxford: Clarendon Press.	ODNR
Opie, I., and Opie, P. (1955). *The Oxford nursery rhyme book*. Oxford: Clarendon Press.	ONRB
Opie, I., and Opie, P. (1959). *The lore and language of schoolchildren*. Oxford: Clarendon Press.	LLS
Opie, I., and Opie, P. (1963). *The Puffin book of nursery rhymes*. Harmondsworth: Penguin.	PBNR
Opie, I., and Opie, P. (1969). *Children's games in street and playground*. Oxford: Clarendon Press.	CGSP
Opie, I., and Opie, P. (1985). *The singing game*. Oxford: Oxford University Press.	SG
Oxford dictionary of English proverbs, The. (1935, 1970). W. G. Smith (Comp.). 3rd ed. Oxford: Clarendon Press; revised F. P. Wilson, Oxford: Clarendon Press.	ODEP
Parry-Jones, D. (1964). *Welsh children's games and pastimes*. Denbigh: Gee.	
Petersham, M., and Petersham, M. (1945). *The rooster crows: A book of American rhymes and jingles*. New York, NY: Macmillan.	
Plunket, E. M. (1886). *Merrie games in rhyme from ye olden time*. London: Wells Gardner.	
Poston, E. (1961). *The children's song book*. London: Bodley Head.	
Radford, E., and Radford, M. A. (1948, 1961). *Encyclopaedia of superstitions*. London: Hutchinson; revised ed., C. Hole (Ed.). London: Hutchinson.	
Reeves, J. (1958). *The idiom of the people: English traditional verse*. London: Heinemann.	
Richards, S., and Stubbs, T. (1979). *The English folksinger*. Glasgow and London: Collins.	

Name of publication	Acronym or abbreviation used in the text
Ritchie, J. T. R. (1964). *The singing street*. Edinburgh and London: Oliver and Boyd.	SS
Ritchie, J. T. R. (1965). *Golden city*. Edinburgh and London: Oliver and Boyd.	GC
Robertson, E. (1971). *Let us play*. Port-of-Spain, Trinidad: Columbus.	
Rodger, J. C. (1958). *Lang strang*. Forfar: Forfar Press.	
Rohrbough, L. (1930). *Play party games*. Delaware, OH: Cooperative Recreation Service.	PPG
Rohrbough, L. (1938). *Southern singing games*. Delaware, OH: Cooperative Recreation Service.	SSG
Rohrbough, L. (1940). *Handy play party book*. Delaware, OH: Cooperative Recreation Service.	HPPB
Rosen, M., and Steele, S. (Eds.). (1982). *Inky pinky ponky*. London: Granada.	
Roud, S. (1984, May). Random notes from an Andover playground. *Downs Miscellany*, 2(1), 21–32.	DM1
Roud, S. (1985, May). Random notes from an Andover playground, Part 2: Elastics. *Downs Miscellany*, 3(1), 10–15.	DM2
Rutherford, F. (1971). *All the way to Pennywell: Children's rhymes of the North East*. Durham: University of Durham Institute of Education.	
Searle, M. V. (1972, Winter). London singing games. *English Dance and Song*, 34(10), 132–133.	
Shaw, F. (1969, 1970). *You know me Anty Nelly? Liverpool children's rhymes*. Liverpool: Gear Press; new revised and enlarged ed., London: Wolfe.	
Sims, B. J. (1972). *Cub Scout songs: A collection of folk songs and others complete with guitar chords*. Glasgow: Brown, Son and Ferguson.	

Name of publication	Acronym or abbreviation used in the text
Sluckin, A. (1981). *Growing up in the playground: The social development of children.* London: Routledge and Kegan Paul.	
Smith, G. (1973, January). Query. *Lore and Language,* [*1*]8, 28–29.	*L&L*
Smith, M. (1979). *Ten galloping horses: Action songs and number rhymes.* London: Frederick Warne.	*TGH*
Smith, R. A. (1982, 1983). *Blue Bell Hill games.* Harmondsworth: Kestrel Books; rpt. Harmondsworth: Puffin.	*BBHG*
Solomon, J., and Solomon, O. (Eds.). (1980). *Zackary Zan: Childhood folklore.* Tuscaloosa, AL: University of Alabama Press.	
Spin. (1973). Kids' stuff. Unsigned article. *9*(4), 4–5 and 22.	
Starn, D. (1978). When I was a child. In *Writing* (pp. 97–100). London: Federation of Worker Writers and Community Publishers.	
Stork, F. C. (1969, July). Childlore in Sheffield. *Lore and Language,* [*1*](1): 3–5.	
Strutt, J. (1801, 1830). *The sports and pastimes of the people of England.* London: John White; new indexed ed., London: William Reeves.	
Sutton-Smith, B. (1959). *The games of New Zealand children.* Berkeley and Los Angeles, CA: University of California Press.	
Swift, E. (1949, June). Singing games of Leicestershire and Rutland. *Leicestershire and Rutland Magazine, 1*(3), 145–152.	
Talley, T. W. (1922). *Negro folk rhymes, wise and otherwise.* New York, NY: Macmillan.	

Name of publication	Acronym or abbreviation used in the text
Taylor, D., and Taylor, J. (1976). *Finger rhymes.* Loughborough: Ladybird Books.	
Thornhill, S. E. (Coll.). (1911). *London Bridge and other old singing games.* London: Curwen.	
Todd, L. (1973, January). Childhood in County Tyrone. *Lore and Language,* [*1*](8), 1–12.	
Turner, I. (1969, 1972). *Cinderella dressed in yella.* Melbourne: Heinemann Educational; rpt. New York, NY: Taplinger.	
Turner, I., Factor, J., and Lowenstein, W. (Comps. and Eds.). (1978). *Cinderella dressed in yella.* 2nd ed., Richmond, Victoria, Australia: Heinemann.	
Uttley, A. (1948). *Carts and candlesticks.* London: Faber.	
Wade, B. (1982, August 6). Skipping the words. *Times Educational Supplement,* p. 14.	Wade 1
Wade, B. (1982). "That's not a book". *Children's Literature in Education, 18*(1), 32–38.	Wade 2
Webb, D. (1969, May 8). Singing games. *The Listener,* 637–640.	
Whelan, Mrs. P. (1982, June). My childhood in Poplar. *London Lore, 1*(9), 106–111.	
Whyton, W. (Comp.). (1964). *100 children's songs: A collection of popular nursery rhymes and songs for the younger generation.* London and New York, NY: Essex Music.	
Wilson, G. (1979, December 21–28). Suzie, the highly inventive schoolgirl. *New Statesman,* pp. 980–981, and letter in reply, *New Statesman,* 1980, January 4.	

Name of publication	Acronym or abbreviation used in the text
Wilson, M., and Gallagher, J. (1969). *The Festival book of singing games*. Accompanying booklet to *Children's singing games*. Impact record No. IMP-A 10. London: Topic Records.	
Withers, C. A. (Coll.). (1946, 1970). *Counting out*. New York, NY: Oxford University Press; rpt. in facsimile as *Counting out rhymes*. New York, NY: Dover.	*CO*
Withers, C. A. (1948). *A rocket in my pocket: The rhymes and chants of young Americans*. New York, NY: Holt.	*RIMP*
Wolfenstein, M. (1954, 1978). *Children's humor: A psychological analysis*. Glencoe, IL: The Free Press; rpt. Bloomington, IN and London: Indiana University Press.	
Wood, R. (1940). *The American Mother Goose*. Philadelphia, PA and New York, NY: Lippincott.	*AMG*
Wood, R. (1952). *Fun in American folk rhymes*. Philadelphia, PA and New York, NY: Lippincott.	*FAFR*
Woodcraft folk song book. (n.d.). London: The Woodcraft Folk.	
Worstell, E. V. (1961). *Jump the rope jingles*. New York, NY: Macmillan.	

KEY TO ACRONYMS AND ABBREVIATIONS DESIGNATING PUBLICATIONS CITED

Acronyms and abbreviated designations are used for ease of reference when more than one work by the same author(s) is cited, or where several authors share the same surname.

AFTS	Chase, R. (Comp.). (1956). *American folk tales and songs*. New York, NY: New American Library.
AMG	Wood, R. (1940). *The American Mother Goose*. Philadelphia, PA and New York, NY: Lippincott.
ANG	Brewster, P. G. (1953). *American nonsinging games*. Norman, OK: University of Oklahoma Press.
APPS	Botkin, B. A. (1937, 1963). *The American play party song*. Lincoln, NE: University of Nebraska [privately printed]; rpt. New York, NY: Frederick Ungar Publishing.
BB	Cray, E. (Comp. and Ed.). (1970). *Bawdy ballads*. London: Blond.

BBHG   Smith, R. A. (1982, 1983). *Blue Bell Hill games.* Harmondsworth: Kestrel Books; rpt. Harmondsworth: Puffin.

CGSP   Opie, I., and Opie, P. (1969). *Children's games in street and playground.* Oxford: Clarendon Press.

CGTY   Daiken, L. (1949). *Children's games throughout the year.* London: Batsford.

CO   Withers, C. A. (Coll.). (1946, 1970). *Counting out.* New York, NY: Oxford University Press; rpt. in facsimile as *Counting out rhymes.* New York, NY: Dover.

DM1   Roud, S. (1984, May). Random notes from an Andover playground. *Downs Miscellany, 2*(1), 21–32.

DM2   Roud, S. (1985, May). Random notes from an Andover playground, Part 2: Elastics. *Downs Miscellany, 3*(1), 10–15.

FAFR   Wood, R. (1952). *Fun in American folk rhymes.* Philadelphia, PA and New York, NY: Lippincott.

FGJ   Beckwith, M. W., and Roberts, H. H. (1922). *Folk games of Jamaica.* Publications of the Folk-Lore Foundation, No. 1. Poughkeepsie, NY: Vassar College.

GC   Ritchie, J. T. R. (1965). *Golden city.* Edinburgh and London: Oliver and Boyd.

HBSNR Montgomerie, N., and Montgomerie, W. (Eds.). (1964). *The Hogarth book of Scottish nursery rhymes.* London: Hogarth Press.

HPPB   Rohrbough, L. (1940). *Handy play party book.* Delaware, OH: Cooperative Recreation Service.

ISE   Opie, I., and Opie, P. (1947). *I saw Esau: Traditional rhymes of youth.* London: Williams and Norgate.

JFL   Beckwith, M. W. (1928). *Jamaica folk-lore.* New York, NY: American Folk-Lore Society.

JRR   Evans, P. (Comp.). (1954). *Jump rope rhymes.* San Francisco, CA: The Porpoise Bookshop.

K1   Kelsey, N. G. N. (1979, July). Tradition & innovation in playground games & songs. *London Lore, 1*(4), 40–49.

K2   Kelsey, N. G. N. (1981). When they were young girls: A singing game through the century. *Folklore, 92*(1), 104–109.
K3   Kelsey, N. G. N. (1985). The lady on the mountain: A century of play rhyme tradition. *Lore and Language, 4*(1), 78–85.
Kings 1   King, M., and King, R. (Eds.). (1926). *Street games of North Shields children*. First Series. Tynemouth: Priory Press.
Kings 2   King, M., and King, R. (Eds.). (1930). *Street games of North Shields children*. Second Series. Tynemouth: Priory Press.
L&L   Smith, G. (1973, January). Query. *Lore and Language,* [*1*]8, 28–29.
LL   Jorgensen., M. G. (1982, June). A comparison of U.S. and British children's play rhymes. *London Lore, 1*(9), 111–114.
LLS   Opie, I., and Opie, P. (1959). *The lore and language of schoolchildren*. Oxford: Clarendon Press.
NRE   Halliwell, J. O. (1842). *The nursery rhymes of England, collected principally from oral tradition*. London: The Percy Society; 2nd ed., London: John Russell Smith (1843); 3rd ed., London: John Russell Smith (1844); 4th ed., London: John Russell Smith (1846); new ed., London and Edinburgh: W. and R. Chambers (1870), rpt. London: The Bodley Head (1970).
NRNTE   Halliwell, J. O. (Coll.). (n.d., c1870). *Nursery rhymes and nursery tales of England*. London: Frederick Warne/New York, NY: Scribner, Welford, and Armstrong.
NRT   Bett, H. M. A. (1924). *Nursery rhymes and tales: Their origin and history*. London: Methuen.
ODEP   *Oxford dictionary of English proverbs, The.* (1935, 1970). W. G. Smith (Comp.). 3rd ed. Oxford: Clarendon Press; revised F. P. Wilson, Oxford: Clarendon Press.
ODNR   Opie, I., and Opie, P. (1951). *The Oxford dictionary of nursery rhymes*. Oxford: Clarendon Press.
ODSG   Gillington, A. E. (Ed.). (1913). *Old Dorset singing games*. London: Curwen.

OGS   Daiken, L. (1963). *Out goes she: Dublin street rhymes.* Dublin: Dolmen Press.

OHSG   Gillington, A. E. (Ed.). (1909). *Old Hampshire singing games and trilling the rope rhymes.* London: Curwen.

OIWSG   Gillington, A. E. (Ed.). (1909). *Old Isle of Wight singing games.* London: Curwen.

ONRB   Opie, I., and Opie, P. (1955). *The Oxford nursery rhyme book.* Oxford: Clarendon Press.

OSASG   Chase, R. (Coll. and Ed.). (1938). *Old songs and singing games.* Chapel Hill, NC: University of North Carolina Press.

OSSG   Gillington, A. E. (Ed.). (1909). *Old Surrey singing games and skipping-rope rhymes.* London: Curwen.

PBNR   Opie, I., and Opie, P. (1963). *The Puffin book of nursery rhymes.* Harmondsworth: Penguin.

PPG   Rohrbough, L. (1930). *Play party games.* Delaware, OH: Cooperative Recreation Service.

PRNT   Halliwell, J. O. (1849, 1970). *Popular rhymes and nursery tales.* London: John Russell Smith; new ed., *Popular rhymes and nursery tales of England.* London: The Bodley Head.

RCORC   Brewster, P. G. (1939, September). Rope-skipping, counting-out, and other rhymes of children. *Southern Folklore Quarterly, 3*(2), 173–178.

RDJ   Legman G. (1968, 1969). *Rationale of the dirty joke: An analysis of sexual humor.* New York, NY: Grove; rpt. London: Cape.

RIMP   Withers, C. A. (1948). *A rocket in my pocket: The rhymes and chants of young Americans.* New York, NY: Holt.

SC   Montgomerie, N., and Montgomerie, W. (Eds.). (1948). *Sandy Candy and other Scottish nursery rhymes.* London: Hogarth Press.

SG   Opie, I., and Opie, P. (1985). *The singing game.* Oxford: Oxford University Press.

SGPPG   Chase, R. (1967). *Singing games and playparty games*, New York, NY: Dover. (Rpt. of *Hullabaloo and other singing folk games.* Boston, MA: Houghton Mifflin, 1949).

SNR	Montgomerie, N., and Montgomerie, W. (Eds.). (1946). *Scottish nursery rhymes*. London: Hogarth Press.
SS	Ritchie, J. T. R. (1964). *The singing street*. Edinburgh and London: Oliver and Boyd.
SSG	Rohrbough, L. (1938). *Southern singing games*. Delaware, OH: Cooperative Recreation Service.
SWF	Jorgensen, M. G. (1980, Summer and Fall). An analysis of boy-girl relationships portrayed in contemporary jump rope and handclapping rhymes. *Southwest Folklore, 4*(3 and 4), 63–71.
TAF	Botkin, B. A. (Ed.). (1944). *A treasury of American folklore: Stories, ballads, and traditions of the people*. New York, NY: Crown.
TGC	Bett, H. M. A. (1929). *The games of children: Their origin and history*. London: Methuen.
TGH	Smith, M. (1979). *Ten galloping horses: Action songs and number rhymes*. London: Frederick Warne.
TL	Legman, G. (Ed.). (1976). *The limerick: 1700 examples, with notes, variants and index*. 2 vols. New York, NY: Bell Publishing; St. Albans: Panther.
TTP	Daiken, L. (1954). *Teaching through play: A teacher's handbook on games*. London: Pitman.
Wade 1	Wade, B. (1982, August 6). Skipping the words. *Times Educational Supplement*, p. 14.
Wade 2	Wade, B. (1982). "That's not a book". *Children's Literature in Education, 18*(1), 32–38.
WI	Evans, P. (1956). *Who's it?* San Francisco, CA: The Porpoise Bookshop.

DISCOGRAPHY

RECORDINGS CITED

BBC 3539 (78). (1941). Yorkshire.
BBC 6669 (78). (1941). Bristol.
BBC 13869 (78). (1949). Edinburgh.
BBC 16074 (78). (1951). Sidbury, Devon.
BBC 16075 (78). (1951). Sidbury, Devon.
BBC 16076 (78). (1951). Sidbury, Devon.
BBC 19003 (78). (1953). Kentish Town.
BBC 19004 (78). (1953). Kentish Town.
BBC 19005 (78). (1953). Kentish Town.
BBC 19926 (78). (1953). Edinburgh.
BBC 19927 (78). (1953). Edinburgh.
BBC 20536 (78). (1952). Northamptonshire.
Hammond, D. (1974). *Green peas and barley, O: Children's street songs and rhymes from Belfast*. St. Mary's Primary School, Belfast. Belfast: L.B.J. Recordings.

MacColl, E., and Behan, D. (1959). *Streets of song: Childhood memories of city streets from Glasgow, Salford and Dublin*. London: Topic Records, TOPIC 12–T–41. Re–released (1964) as *The singing streets: Childhood memories of Ireland and Scotland*. New York, NY: Folkways Records, FW08501.

MacColl, E., and Seeger, P. (1962). *The Elliotts of Birtley*. New York, NY: Folkways Records, FG3565.

Ring games, line games and play party songs of Alabama. New York, NY: Folkways Records, FP704.

Ritchie, J. *Jean Ritchie sings children's songs and games from the Southern Mountains*. New York, NY: Folkways, FC754.

Wales, T. *Folk songs and ballads of Sussex*. New York, NY: Folkways Records, FG3515.

Webb, D. (1983). *Children's singing games*. [Singing games from England, Wales, Southern Ireland, and Scotland]. Saydisc Traditional Series, LP, SDL 338, Mono (also on cassette).

Wilson, M., and Gallagher, J. (1969). *Children's singing games*. [Sung by children of Redriff Primary School, Bermondsey]. Impact Record, IMP–A 101.

SELECTED FURTHER READING

A listing of some significant pre-1986 works not consulted by Nigel Kelsey, and works published after the present collection was completed in 1986.

Arleo, A. (1990, December; 1991, September). The international diffusion of the jump-rope game "Elastics". *Australian Children's Folklore Newsletter*, (19), 5–9; *Australian Children's Folklore Newsletter*, (20/21), 16–21.

Arleo, A. (1991, Fall). Strategy in counting-out, Saint-Nazaire, France. *Children's Folklore Review*, *14*(1), 25–29.

Avedon, E. M., and Sutton-Smith, B. (1971). *The study of games*. New York, NY: John Wiley.

Bauer, L., and Bauer, W. (2003). *Playground talk*. Wellington: Victoria University, School of Linguistics and Applied Language Studies.

Beckwith, I., and Shirley, B. (1975, November). Truce terms: a Lincolnshire survey. *Local Historian*, *11*(8), 441–444.

Beresin, A. R. (2010). *Recess battles: Play, fighting, and storytelling*. Jackson, MI: University Press of Mississippi.

Bishop, J. C., and Curtis, M. (Eds.). (2001). *Play today in the primary school playground: Life, learning and creativity*. Buckingham and Philadelphia, PA: Open University Press.

Boyes, G. (1995). The legacy of the work of Iona and Peter Opie: The lore and language of today's children. In R. Beard (Ed.), *Rhyme, reading and writing* (pp. 131–146). London: Hodder and Stoughton Educational

Brain, J. (1984). *Children's games*. London: Bethnal Green Museum of Childhood.

Brewer, S. (2008). *Classic playground games from hopscotch to Simon says*. Barnsley: Pen and Sword Books.

Brewster, P. G. (1952, 1976). Children's games and rhymes. In N. I. White (Gen. Ed.), *The Frank C. Brown collection of North Carolina folklore*, Vol. 1 (pp. 29–219). Durham, NC: Duke University Press; rpt. New York, NY: Arno Press.

Bronner, S. J. (1988). *American children's folklore*, Little Rock, AR: August House.

Burn, A., and Richards, C. (Eds.). (2014). *Children's games in the New Media Age: Childlore, media and the playground*. Farnham, Surrey, and Burlington, VT: Ashgate.

Chudacoff, H. P. (2007). *Children at play: An American history*. New York, NY: New York University Press.

Curtis, M. (1997). Transatlantic patterns of transmission in children's oral tradition. *Lore and Language*, 15(1–2), 141–160.

Curtis, M. (2004). A sailor went to sea: Theme and variations. *Folk Music Journal*, 8(4), 421–437.

Curtis, M. (2010). The multicultural playground. In S. Roud (Ed.), *The lore of the playground: One hundred years of children's games, rhymes and traditions* (pp. 393–409). London: Random House.

Dargan, A., and Zeitlin, S. (1990). *City play*. New Brunswick, NJ: Rutgers University Press.

Darian-Smith, K., and Factor, J. (Eds.). (2005). *Child's play: Dorothy Howard and the folklore of Australian children*. Melbourne: Museum Victoria.

Darian-Smith, K., and Pascoe, C. (Eds.). (2013). *Children, childhood and cultural heritage*. Abingdon and New York, NY: Routledge.

Factor, J. (1983). *Far out, Brussel sprout!* Melbourne: Oxford University Press.
Factor, J. (1985). *All right, Vegemite!* Melbourne: Oxford University Press.
Factor, J. (1987). *Unreal, banana peel!* Melbourne: Oxford University Press.
Factor, J. (1988). *Captain Cook chased a chook: Children's folklore in Australia.* Ringwood, Victoria: Penguin.
Factor, J. (1989). *Real keen baked bean!* Sydney: Hodder and Stoughton.
Factor, J. (1992). *Roll over, Pavlova!* Sydney: Hodder and Stoughton.
Factor, J. (1996). *Kidspeak: A dictionary of Australian children's words, expressions and games.* Melbourne: Melbourne University Press.
Factor, J. (2005). *Okey dokey, karaoke.* Melbourne: Brolly Books.
Ford, R. (1894, 1913). *Ballads of bairnhood.* Paisley: Alexander Gardner; rpt. Paisley: Alexander Gardner.
Fowke, E. (1988). *Red rover, red rover: Children's games played in Canada.* Toronto: Doubleday Canada.
Fraser, A. S. (Coll. and Ed.). (1975). *Dae ye min' langsyne? A pot-pourri of games, rhymes, and ploys of Scottish childhood.* London: Routledge and Kegan Paul.
Gomme, Lady A. B. (Coll.). (1900). *Old English singing games.* London: George Allen.
Gomme, Lady A. B., and Sharp, C. J. (Colls. and Eds.). (1909–1912). *Children's singing games.* London and New York, NY: Novello.
Gomme, Sir L., and Gomme, Lady A. B. (1916). *British folk-lore, folksongs, and singing games.* London: David Nutt.
Green, J., and Widdowson, J. D. A. (2003). *Traditional English language genres: Continuity and change, 1950–2000.* Sheffield: National Centre for English Cultural Tradition. http://collections.mun.ca/cdm/ref/collection/folklore/id/2028
Grider, S. A. (Ed.). (1980, July). Children's folklore. *Western Folklore, 39*(3), 159–265.
Hastings, S. E., Jr. (1990). *Miss Mary Mac all dressed in black: Tongue twisters, jump-rope rhymes and other children's lore from New England.* Little Rock, AR: August House.
Herron, R. E., and Sutton-Smith, B. (Eds.). (1971). *Child's play.* New York: Wiley.

Hinkson, K. (1991). *Victorian singing games.* London: Folklore Society (reprints articles from the *Monthly Packet*, 1896–1897).

Jekyll, W. (1907). *Jamaican song and story: Annancy stories, digging sings, ring tunes, and dancing tunes.* London: David Nutt, for the Folk-Lore Society.

Jorgensen, M. (1983). Anti-school parodies as speech play and social protest. In F. E. Manning (Ed.), *The world of play: Proceedings of the Annual Meeting of the Association for the Anthropological Study of Play.* West Point, NY: Leisure Press.

Kane, A. (1983). *Songs and sayings of an Ulster childhood.* E. Fowke (Ed.). Toronto: McClelland and Stewart.

Lanclos, D. M. (2003). *At play in Belfast: Children's folklore and identities in Northern Ireland.* New Brunswick, NJ: Rutgers University Press.

Leyden, M. (1993). *Boys and girls come out to play: A collection of Irish singing games.* Belfast: Appletree Press.

Liben, M. (1984). *New York street games.* New York, NY: Schacken.

Logue, C. (Comp.). (1986, 1987). *The children's book of children's rhymes.* London: Batsford; rpt. London: Piccolo Books.

Lomax, A., Elder, J. D., and Hawes, B. L. (1997). *Brown girl in the ring: An anthology of song games from the eastern Caribbean.* New York, NY: Pantheon Books.

Maclagan, R. C. (1901). *The games and diversions of Argyleshire.* London: David Nutt, for the Folk-Lore Society.

Macnab, I. (1932). *Nicht at Eenie: The bairns' Parnassus.* Warlingham, Surrey: Samson Press.

McCosh, S. (1976, 1979). *Children's humour: A joke for every occasion.* London: Hanau Publications; rpt. London and New York, NY: Granada.

McDowell, J. H. (1979). *Children's riddling.* Bloomington, IN: Indiana University Press.

McVicar, E. (2007). *Doh ray me, when Ah wis wee: Scots children's songs and rhymes.* Edinburgh: Birlinn.

McVicar, E. (2011). *ABC, my grannie caught a flea: Scots children's songs and rhymes.* Edinburgh: Birlinn.

Marsh, J., and Bishop, J. C. (2013). *Changing play: Play, media and commercial culture from the 1950s to the present day.* New York, NY: Open University Press, McGraw-Hill Education.

Marsh, K. (2008). *The musical playground: Global tradition and change in children's songs and games*. Oxford: Oxford University Press.

Mechling, J. (1986). Children's folklore. In E. Oring (Ed.). *Folk groups and folklore genres: An introduction* (pp. 91–120). Logan, UT: Utah State University Press.

Milberg, A. (1976). *Street games*. New York, NY: McGraw-Hill.

Newton, D. (1951–52, Winter). Children's games. *Far and Wide*, the magazine of the Guest Keen and Nettlefields group of companies. (19), 32–36.

Opie, I. (1993). *The people in the playground*, Oxford: Oxford University Press.

Opie, I., and Opie, P. (1997). *Children's games with things*. Oxford: Oxford University Press.

Pascoe, C. (2011). *Spaces imagined, places remembered: Childhood in 1950s Australia*. Newcastle: Cambridge Scholars.

Peirce, M. K. (Comp.). (1983). *Keep the kettle boiling: Rhymes from a Belfast childhood*. Belfast: Appletree.

Roud, S. (2008). *Monday's child is fair of face: … And other traditional beliefs about babies and motherhood*. London: Random House.

Roud, S. (2010). *The lore of the playground: One hundred years of children's games, rhymes and traditions*. London: Random House.

Skolnik, P. (1974). *Jump rope*. New York, NY: Workman.

Sluckin, A. (1979, January). Order and disorder in the playground. *Lore and Language*, 2(10), 1–9.

Struthers, C. (1912). *Number plays and games for infants: Stepping stones to visual and observational arithmetic*. London: Pitman.

Sutton-Smith, B. (1972). *The folk games of children*. Austin, TX: University of Texas Press.

Sutton-Smith, B. (1981). *A history of children's play: The New Zealand playground 1840–1950*. Philadelphia, PA: University of Pennsylvania Press.

Sutton-Smith, B., Mechling, J., Johnson, T. W., and McMahon, F. R. (Eds.). (1995). *Children's folklore: A source book*. New York, NY: Garland Publishing.

Symonds, J. (1996). *Playground games*. London: Dorling Kindersley.

Teece, A. (1985). "Just for fun": children's playground songs from Derbyshire. *Lore and Language*, 4(2), 68–83.

Thorne, B. (1993). *Gender play: Girls and boys in school*. New Brunswick, NJ: Rutgers University Press.

Tucker, E. (2008). *Children's folklore: A handbook*. Westport, CT: Greenwood Press.

Van Peer, W. (1988). Counting out: Form and function of children's counting-out rhymes. In M. Modare, T. Phillips, and A. Wilkinson (Eds.), *Oracy Matters*. Milton Keynes: Open University Press.

Virtanen, L. (1978). *Children's lore*. Helsinki: Suomalaisen Kirjallisuuden Seura.

Wales, T. (1983). *Long summer days: Games and pastimes of Sussex children*. Horsham: Field and Furrow Books.

Willett, R., Richards, C., Marsh, J., Burn, A., and Bishop, J. C. (2013). *Children, media and playground cultures: Ethnographic studies of school playtimes*. Studies in Childhood and Youth series. Basingstoke: Palgrave Macmillan.

Withers, C. A. (1947). *Ready or not, here I come*. New York, NY: Grosset and Dunlap.

Withers, C. A. (1974). *A treasury of games, riddles, mystery stunts, tricks, tongue twisters, rhymes, chants, singing*. New York, NY: Grosset and Dunlap.

Woolley, H., with Armitage, M., Bishop, J. C., Curtis, M., and Ginsborg, J. (2005). *Inclusion of disabled children in primary school playgrounds*. London: National Children's Bureau for the Joseph Rowntree Foundation.

Journals etc.

Australian Children's Folklore Newsletter (archive copies)
http://museumvictoria.com.au/.../australian-childrens-folklore-index-issues...
Children's Folklore eNewsletter (American Folklore Society)
https://www.afsnet.org/?Children
Children's Folklore Review (American Folklore Society)
http://www.afsnet.org/?page=CFR
International Journal of Play (Taylor and Francis Online)

http://www.tandfonline.com/loi/rijp20#.VhVgZaRlV0I
Lore and Learning (Newsletter of the Folklore Society Education Group): 1 (1993, November); 2 (1994, July); 3 (1996, March).
Play and Folklore
http://museumvictoria.com.au/about/books-and-journals/journals/play-and-folklore/

Recordings

Clancy Children. (1997). *So early in the morning: Irish children's songs, rhymes and games.* Tradition CD TCD 1053.
Lomax, A. (1997). *Caribbean voyage: brown girl in the ring.* Rounder 1716.

Online

Australian Children's Folklore Collection in Museums Victoria Collections:
https://collections.museumvictoria.com.au/articles/24/
Children's Playground Games and Songs in the New Media Age, part of the Beyond Text programme:
https://www.bl.uk/projects/childrens-playground-games
https://www.bl.uk/playtimes
http://projects.beyondtext.ac.uk/playgroundgames/
KidsPlayBook:
http://www.kidsplaybook.com/
Malarkey Playwork:
https://www.malarkeyplaywork.com.au/
New Zealand Playground Language Project, Victoria University of Wellington, 1999–2001:
http://www.victoria.ac.nz/lals/research/projects/language-in-the-playground-project
Playing the Archive:
https://playingthearchive.net/about/

INDEX[1]

NUMBERS AND SYMBOLS
1 1 was a racehorse **11.G.5**

A
A boy stood on a burning deck **8.D.31B**
A boy stood on the burning deck **8.D.31C**
A diner while dining at Crewe **11.H.6**
A duke came a-riding, a-riding, a-riding **4.1B**
A gipsy came a-riding, a-riding **4.1A**
A girl who weighed many an ounce **11.H.19**
A gorilla who drove off in a car **11.H.20**
A grubby young schoolboy of Kent **11.H.27**
A kick up the bum **9.B.7G**
A king's a ruler **11.A.9**
A peanut sat on a railway track **11.A.11**
A penny for the guy **10.E.6**
A penny for your thoughts **10.D.8**
A pinch and a punch **9.B.7A-C**
A poke in the eye for being so sly **9.B.7D**
A punch in the eye for being so sly **9.B.7D**
A sailor went to Hawaii **5.1B**
A sailor went to sea, sea, sea **5.1A**
A ship sails from China with a cargo of tea **4.44A**
A silly question gets a silly answer **10.D.6A**
Adam and Eve and Pinch-me **9.B.12A**
AGROE **3.A.12**

---

[1] Note: The index comprises a listing of the first lines of rhymes, songs, and sayings, except in the case of games, the names of which are presented in full capitals.

© The Author(s) 2019
Games, Rhymes, and Wordplay of London Children,
https://doi.org/10.1007/978-3-030-02910-4

A-hunting we shall go **4.12**
(_____) ain't no good **9.C.22**
… Air I chickali, chickali air I **5.10F**
Ala ala ming mong **2.17**
Algy met a bear **11.B.21**
Alice in Wonderland **6.A.22**, **7.2**
All Clear is a shampoo **8.D.47**
All I want for Christmas **12.B.14**
All I want is a proper cup of coffee **11.B.26**
All in together **6.A.45A**
All in together, girls **6.A.45B**
All join in **9.C.46D**
… All right (_____) I'll tell your mother **6.A.55B**
All the girls in our town lead a happy life **6.A.54**
All the monkeys in the zoo **2.29**
ALLIGATOR, ALLIGATOR **3.A.33**
ALPHABET **7.36C**
Ambulance **10.C.22**
AMERICAN FOOTBALL **3.H.14**
(_____) and (_____) in a tree **9.C.54B**
(_____) and (_____) sitting in a tree **9.C.54A**
Apple crumble, apple tart **6.A.58B**
Apple tart makes you fart **8.B.4**
Apples **10.A.8**
Arag language **12.H.2**
Arague language **12.H.2**
ARCHIBALD, BALD, BALD **7.46**
Are you ready for a fight? **4.21**
Are you scared of squirrels? **9.A.18**
ARM RELIEF **3.A.19**
ARMIES **3.L.1**
As I was walking down Inky-pinky Lane **2.26**
Ask a silly question and get a silly answer **10.D.6B**

Ask no questions, tell no lies **9.D.34**
At dinner time … **9.A.19**
Aunt Mildred's crooked **4.64**
Auntie Mary had a canary **11.I.42**
Avag language **12.H.3**

B

Baa baa, white sheep **8.D.37**
BABY IF YOU LOVE ME, SMILE **3.N.3**
BAD EGGS **3.A.8**
Baldy **9.C.4E**
BALL IN THE STOCKING **3.C.4**
BALLIE **3.A.6**
Bananas in pyjamas are coming down the stairs **11.J.1**
BARLEY **3.H.10**
BASKETBALL **3.I.9**
Batman and Robin in a Batmobile **11.I.3B**
Beans, beans **11.I.18A**, **11.I.18B**
Beatles, Beatles everywhere **11.I.56**
Beauty! Beauty! **9.D.25**
Beefy **9.C.10A**
Begin: B.B.C. 1, B.B.C. 2. **4.67B**
Bell-bottomed trousers **11.J.20A**
Bell horses, bell horses **3.B.v**, **3.B.vi**
Betty Botter bought some butter **11.B.2A**
Betty bought a bit of butter **11.B.2B**
Big Ben strikes one, tick-tock, two tick-tock **6.A.16**
Big Ben strikes ten **2.10**
BINGO **4.5**
Bird, dead **10.C.41**
Bird droppings **10.C.40**
BISCUIT **4.61**
Black cat sat on the mat **7.1**

BLACK MAGIC **3.A.17**
BLACK POISON **3.A.17**
Blackbirds **10.A.4**
BLIND MAN'S BUFF **3.A.27**
Blinds **10.C.13**
Bloody's in the Bible **11.A.10**
BLUE PETER **3.A.30**
Bluebells, cockle shells **6.A.53A**, **6.A.53C-F**
BOMBS **3.B.13**
Bonfire Night **10.E.6**
BOO **3.D.6**
Booby one, booby two **4.67A**
BOOK TITLES **11.F1-11.F.36**
BOOTS **3.G.5**
BOOTS AND SHOES **3.B.17**
Boy Scout, walk out **2.43**
Boys are fantastic, girls are elastic **9.C.46B**
BOX HAD **3.A.22**
BOXES **3.A.22**
Bozy, Bozy aeroplane **12.B.2B**
Break my cross **10.B.5H**
Break my cross and hope to die **10.B.4E**
BRITISH BULLDOG **3.A.28**
(_____) broke an egg **9.E.6B**
Broken glass **10.C.8A**
Broken plate **10.C.8B**
Brown girl in the ring **4.24**
Brownies' honour **10.B.5E**
BUBBLE AND SQUEAK **3.N.2**
BUCKAMAROO **3.L.3**
Build a bonfire, build a bonfire **11.I.58, 12.A.12**
BULLDOG **3.A.28**
BULLDOG (SUBJECTS) **3.A.29**
Bum, tit, bum, tit **9.C.18**

Bumper car, bumper car **6.A.32C, 6.A.32E**
BUNDLE **3.G.2**
… Burglar in the house, burglar in the house **6.A.39C**
Bus tickets **10.A.9**
Buttercups **10.A.1**
BUZZ **3.A.21**

C

Can you hear the Gunners sing? **12.A.15**
Can you see your dad **11.I.53**
Caroline, Caroline **10.E.1**
Carrot top **9.C.4A**
CAT AND MOUSE **3.A.26**
CAT'S CRADLE **3.K.2**
Cat's got the measles **4.52A, 4.52B**
Cats **10.C.31**
Cemetery **10.C.24**
CHAIN HE **3.A.15**
CHAMP **3.I.11**
Change keys with your next door neighbour **6.A.2**
CHARLIE **3.A.24**
Charlie Chaplin went to France **6.A.52**
Charlie got drunk on a bottle of gin **4.60A**
Chelsea are magic! **12.A.24A**
Cherry stones **10.A.6**
CHINESE FOOTBALL **3.H.11**
CHINESE HANDBALL **3.I.1**
Chinese, Japanese **4.69**
CHINESE MUDDLE **3.E.2**
CHINESE STINGER **3.A.6**
CHINESE WHISPERS **3.N.1**

Ching Chong, Chinaman, tried to milk a cow **2.56**
Chocolate biscuit in the tin **2.50**
Chocolate biscuits down the lane **6.A.28**
Christmas **10.E.7**
Christmas is coming **8.D.29**, **10.E.7**
Christmas tree **10.C.46**
Cinderella, Arabella **6.A.27A**
Cinderella dressed in red **6.A.27C**
Cinderella, dressed in yella **2.59**, **4.63A**, **4.63B**, **6.A.27A**, **6.A.27B**
Cissy **9.C.40B**
Clever clocks **9.C.30A**
Coal **10.C.15**
Cobwebs **10.C.44**
COCOA **3.B.12**
Coconut, caramel, cherries and chocolate **4.68**
Coins **10.C.10**, **10.C.11**
Colour **10.C.28**
COLOURS **3.A.32**
COLOURS (JUMPING ROPE) **3.C.1**
COLOURS (RACING) **3.B.4**, **3.B.5**
Come all ye faithful **8.A.19**
Come to our school, come to our school **8.A.3**
CONCENTRATION **3.N.10**
Concrete chips, concrete chips **8.B.2B**
CONKERS **3.F.5**
Constantinople is a very long word. Now spell it. **9.A.10**
Copy cat, copy cat **9.C.35A–C**
Counting **10.A.5**

(_____, _____), covered in snot **9.C.15**
Cowboy Joe from Mexico **2.48**, **6.A.29**
Cows **10.C.36**
Crackerjack, crackerjack, Boompity boom **4.55**
CRICKET **3.J.5**
CROCODILE, CROCODILE **3.A.33**
Cross my heart and hope to die **10.B.4C**
Cross my heart, hope to die **10.B.4A**, **10.B.4B**
Crows **10.C.38**
Crushed biscuits, crushed biscuits **11.B.16**
Cry, Baby Bunting **9.C.37**
Cubs' honour **10.B.5E**
Cucumber, my Lord, cucumber **8.D.24**
CUPPIE **3.H.6**
… Custard by the side, custard by the side **6.A.39B**
(_____, _____), custard pie **9.C.48D**

D

Daddy, Mummy, Uncle Dick **7.3**
Daisies **10.A.3**, **10.C.49**
Daisy, Daisy **8.D.22A**
Daisy, Daisy, give me your answer, do **8.D.22B**
Dan, Dan, the lavatory man **9.C.19C**
Dandelions **10.A.2**, **10.C.48**
Dash, dash, dash **7.18**
Dasha marmalade **7.5**
DAYS OF THE WEEK **3.B.1B**

Dennis Winter, Dennis Winter **12.A.1**
Diana Dors lost her drawers **11.I.20**
Diarrhoea! Diarrhoea! **11.I.41**
(_____) did a whiffy **9.E.6A**
Did you clean your shoes last night? **2.38A–C**
Did you wash your shoes this morning **2.38D**
DIGS **3.G.4**
DING DONG THE BELLS **3.M.2**
Dip, dip, ana ma da **2.36**
Dip, dip, do a skip **6.A.21**
Dirty shoes, dirty socks **2.40**
Do me a favour **9.B.13**
Do you know about the man going round saying, "No." **9.A.12**
Do you want a sweet? **9.D.13**
Do you want to come to my party? **9.B.11**
Do you want to photograph me? **9.D.14**
DOCTOR, DOCTOR, **3.E.2**
Doctor, Doctor, how do you do? **6.A.9**
Doctor Foster went to Gloucester **2.57**
Doctor Knickerbocker, Knickerbocker number nine **4.60B**
Dogs **10.C.32**
Dogs' dung **10.C.33**
Dogs go Woof! Woof! **9.B.15**
Donald Duck done some muck **11.I.43B**
Donald Duck washing up **7.8**
DONKEY **3.I.4**

Donna, donna, donna – a biscuit **4.61C**
Don't go to Granny's any more, more, more **7.4**
Don't mess with the best **9.B.28**
Don't touch the Oxfam **9.D.15**
Don't walk on the cracks … **9.B.25**
Down by the bay **11.J.12**
Down by the crossings of the green cross code **4.14D**
Down by the river where nobody knows **4.14E**
Down in the jungle where nobody knows **4.14B**
Down in the station early in the morning **12.B.10**
Down in the valley where nobody knows **4.14C**
Down in the valley where the green grass grows **4.14A**
Down to Mississippi **6.A.42A**
Down to Mississippi with the girls in blue **6.A.42C**
Draw an S; that's a snake **11.G.7**
Drip, drop, dropping in the sea **6.A.60A**
Drip, drop, drops in the sea **6.A.60B**
Dubba, dubba, doo **2.34B**
Dunce, dunce, double D **9.C.32**
D'you want a cigarette, sir? **7.7**

E

Each, peach, pear, plum **2.44**, **7.9**
Easie peasie **2.15**
Eeny deeny dip **2.16**
Eeny meeny macker acker **2.13**
Eeny meeny miny mo **2.14**

Eever, weever, chimney sweeper **6.A.3A**
Eggs a penny each **6.A.4**
Eggs, butter, sugar, tea **2.6A**, **2.6B**
Eh? **9.D.3**
Elephant ears **9.C.3B**
Engine, engine, number nine **2.4B**
England, Ireland, Scotland, Wales **6.B.1**
EPITAPHS **11.F.37-11.F.39**
EVERLASTING STORIES **12.G**
Everybody gather round **4.41**
Everybody hates me **11.I.5B**
Everywhere we go **8.C.4B**
Eye, eye, ackers **9.C.46C**
Eyes, nose, mouth and chin **4.66B**

F

F.A. Cup handles **9.C.3A**
F U N E X ? **11.G.1**
Fair Rosie was a sweet princess **4.17**
Fairy cake and bumble bee **2.6C**
FAME **4.47**
FAMILY BULLDOG **3.A.28**
FAMILY HAD **3.A.14**
FAMILY HE **3.A.14**
FAMILY TREE **3.A.19**
Far away in Germany, a long way off **6.A.24**
Father Christmas came last night **6.A.36F**
Father Christmas, Father Christmas **8.D.28**
Fatso **9.C.10B**
Fatty **9.C.10C**
Fatty and Skinny in a bath **11.I.23E**
Fatty and Skinny in the bath **11.I.23F**
Fatty and Skinny ran a race **11.I.23A**
Fatty and Skinny went out (swimming) one day **11.I.23I**
Fatty and Skinny went to bed **11.I.23B**
Fatty and Skinny went up in a rocket **11.I.23G**
Fatty and Skinny were in bed **11.I.23C**, **11.I.23D**
Fatty and Skinny were in the shower **11.I.23J**
Fatty and Skinny were playing cricket **11.I.23H**
Fear **10.C.29**
Feathers **10.C.39**
FEET OFF LONDON **3.A.13**
Fight the good fight with all thy might **8.D.7**
FINALS **3.H.1**
… find a 5p piece, **10.C.11C**
Find a penny, pick it up **10.C.10B**
Finders, keepers **10.D.1A**, **10.D.1B**
Fingers **10.A.12**, **10.C.2**
Fire, Fire! says Mrs. McGuire **11.A.8**
FIRECRACKER **4.55**
First a wish **10.A.5B**
First the worst **12.D.1A-F**
Fish and chips and vinegar, vinegar, vinegar **6.A.17**
FISH IN THE NET **3.A.15**
Five little ducklings went out one day **12.B.12**
Five little monkeys went up ashore **12.B.11**
Flower **10.A.3F**
Food **10.C.5**
FOOTBALL **3.H.16**
Football **10.C.25**
Football rhymes **12.A**
FOOTBALL ROUNDERS **3.H.13**

FOOTSIE **3.B.8**
FORTY FORTY **3.D.2**
Found a peanut **11.J.10**
Four eyes **9.C.5c**, **9.D.7**
Four eyes, goggle eyes **9.C.5b**
Four-leaf clover **10.C.50**
FOUR SQUARE **3.I.11**
FOX AND HOUNDS **3.A.23**
FOXIE, FOXIE, 1, 2, 3 **3.D.4**
FRENCH AND ENGLISH **3.A.10**
FRENCH HAD **3.A.15**
Friday the 13th **10.C.26**
Frog, dead **10.C.37**
From here to there is an inch **9.B.2**
Fudge, fudge, call the judge **7.11**
Fulham, Fulham, Fulham **12.A.2**
Funeral **10.C.23b**
Funeral hearse **10.C.23a**
Fuzzy Wuzzy was a bear **11.B.20**

G

Georgie Porgie, pudden' and pie **9.C.48c**
Georgie Porgie, pudding and pie **9.C.10d**, **9.C.48a**, **9.C.48b**
Get the keys and lock her up **4.7c**
GHOSTS **3.A.16**
Ginger **9.C.4b**
Ginger nut **9.C.4c**
Gipsy, gipsy lived in a tent **7.10**
Girls are fantastic, boys are elastic **9.C.46a**
Give a thing, take a thing **9.C.42a**, **9.C.42b**
Give me an S **8.C.5**
Give us an S **8.C.5**
Glory, glory, halleluia **8.A.9a-e**, **12.A.3**

Glory, glory, Man United **12.A.3**
Go up the first flight of stairs **9.A.24a**
GOBS **3.K.1**
God made the sea **9.C.11**
God's honour **10.B.5f**, **10.B.5h**
(_____) goes to Mothercare **9.C.27b**
(_____) goes to Tesco's **9.C.27a**
Goggle eyes **9.C.5c**
Goggles for girls **9.C.5a**
Going down the highway **11.I.3c**
Good King Wenceslas looked out **8.D.1a**, **8.D.1b**
Goofy **9.C.2a**
(_____, _____) got false teeth **9.C.2c**
GRANDMOTHER **3.B.6**
Grandmother Gray, may I go out to play? **4.22c**
Granny in the kitchen **6.A.43b**
Granny put her knickers aside **6.B.3**
Graveyard **10.C.24**
Green gravel, green gravel **6.A.56**
Grow up, grow up **9.C.39**
Gv language **12.H.6**

H

H-E-L-P, H-E-L-P ... **6.A.15**
HAD **3.A.1**
(_____ _____) had a fright **7.22b**
HAD ON THE LINE **3.A.2**
Half a pound of nuts and bolts **8.D.38**
... Haila, chicka lom pom Suzianna **5.10d**
Halloween **10.E.4**
Ham, bacon, pork chop **2.54**
HANDBALL **3.I.7**

HANDSTANDS **3.C.6**
HANGMAN **3.O.2**
Happy birthday to you **8.D.10**, **9.C.49A-F**
Hares **10.B.7A**
Hark, Hark! The guns are rolling **11.I.39**
Hark the hairy angels sing **8.D.2A**
Hark the jelly babies sing **8.D.2B**
Have you ever, ever, ever **5.2**
HE **3.A.1**
HE BALL **3.A.4**
He loves me **10.A.3B**
He loves me, yes **10.A.3C**
HE ON LINES **3.A.2**
HE ON THE LINE **3.A.2**
He shot, he missed **12.A.16**
Head, shoulders, knees and toes, knees and toes **4.42**
HEADS AND VOLLEYS **3.H.8**
HEAVERS **3.F.3**
Heel and toe **4.31**
… Henry Hall at the stable **7.9B**
Here comes Mrs. Macaroni **4.26**
Here comes Mrs. Molly around the ring **4.38**
Here comes the bride **8.D.8A-E**
Here we go loobee-loo **4.3**
Here's a little French girl, E-I-E-I-O **6.A.46**
Here's a tree, here's a bush **9.B.6**
Here's the church and here's the steeple **12.B.7**
Here's your bus, sir **11.I.7**
Hey diddle diddle **8.D.40**
Hey! you up there **9.C.4F**
Hey, you're a dirty kangaroo **9.C.20**
Hi ho! Hi ho! **8.A.5A**, **8.A.5B**
HIDE AND SEEK **3.D.1**

High, low, dolly, pepper **6.A.19A**
High, low, slow, dolly, rocker, pepper … **6.A.19C**
High, low, swinging, dolly **6.A.19B**
His hand was round her shoulder **9.A.2**
HIT AND RUN **3.A.5**
Hit me. What did I say? **9.B.3**
Hitler has only got one ball **11.I.32**
Hitler in his submarine **8.D.18A**
Ho! Ho! Ho! He! He! He! **8.A.16**
Hobbit **9.C.7A**
HOCKEY **3.J.4**
HOLD OUT YOUR HAND **9.B.22A-D**
HOPSCOTCH **3.K.4**
Horse manure **10.C.34**
Horseshoes **10.C.35**
Horsy, horsy in the stable **2.46**
HOT CHOCOLATE **3.B.9**
HOT POTATO **3.N.7**
How many blackbirds in a tree? **10.A.4A**
How many feathers on a thrush's throat? **11.B.10**
Humpty Dumpty fell on the grass **8.D.39D**
Humpty Dumpty sat on a wall **8.D.39A-C**
Hurray we are the Michaelson boys **12.A.22**
Hush little baby don't say a word **12.B.1**

I 8 0 4 I O 0 **11.G.4**
I am a Girl Guide, dressed in blue **6.A.26B**

I am a pretty little Dutch girl **5.4A**, **5.4B**
I believe in Jesus, but not in you **10.D.7**
I bet I can make you say "black" **9.A.4A**, **9.A.4B**
I call (_____) in **10.E.3**
I can do the can-can **4.46**
I can prove you're a Red Indian **9.A.16**
I Draw a Snake **3.D.i**
I get up **9.A.22**
I got off the bus like a good girl should **11.I.30**
I had a little brother **5.9A**, **11.I.24A**
I had an old stocking **8.D.14C**
I had the German measles **5.7A**
I had the scarlet fever **5.7B**
I have a black cat and I gave him a pat **8.D.41**
I know a boy who's double jointed **6.A.55A**
I know a girl who's sly and deceitful **9.C.23**
I know what you're going to say **9.A.11**
I like coffee **6.A.31A**, **6.A.31B**, **6.A.31D**
I like Nottingham Forest **12.A.14**
I lost my arm in the army **7.19**
I love you high, I love you mighty **12.C.2**
I saw a bee upon the wall **2.52B**
I saw a fly passing by **2.52A**
I saw a signorina going to the fair **4.25B**
I saw Esau kissing Kate **11.B.23**
I saw Esau sitting on a seesaw **9.A.9A**

I saw my boyfriend walking down the street **5.22**
I sent a letter to my love **4.15**
I swear on my granny's life **10.B.5C**
I swear on my mother's deathbed **10.B.5B**
I swear on my mother's life **10.B.5A**, **10.B.5H**
I swear on the Holy Bible **10.B.5D**
I thought ... **9.D.5B**
I was going through the traffic lights **4.25C**
I was here **11.B.24**
I was walking down the jungle with a stick in my hand **11.I.48B**
I was walking in the jungle on Saturday night **11.I.48A**
I went down the lane to get a penny whistle **6.A.48**
I went down the road **9.A.24C**
I went to a Chinese restaurant **5.10A**
I went to California, far, far away **4.25A**
I went to the funfair **9.A.25B**
I went to the library **9.A.24B**
I went to the park **9.A.20**
I went to the pictures tomorrow **11.A.3A**
I went to the shop **9.A.23**
I went up one stair **9.A.21**
I wish I was a little worm **11.I.15**
I wish tonight was Saturday night **6.A.5**
Ibble obble, black bobble **2.1A**, **2.1B**
ICE AND WATER **3.A.25**
Icklety, picklety, my black hen **2.23**
Icky ocky, horse's cocky **2.1C**
If all the boys lived overseas **9.C.52**

If all the boys lived over the hills **9.C.52**
If I had not let it pass **10.D.4c**
If I had the wings of a sparrow **8.D.15**
If I tell a lie **10.B.4f**
If I'm a chicken you're a duck **9.D.6**
If I was a cabbage **12.C.3a**
If it had gone past my heart **10.D.4e**
… If not now, then later on **7.14b**
If you did not notice that this notice **11.B.4b**
If you don't step on the cracks **10.C.18c**
If you ever, *see* a bunny **9.B.23a**
If you go down in the woods today **8.D.21a**
If you go down to the woods today **8.D.21b**
If you go to school dinners **8.B.1b**
If you notice this notice **11.B.4a**
If you smash china **10.D.2**
If you stay to school dinners **8.B.1a**
If you step on a crack **10.C.17a**
If you step on a line **10.C.17c**
If you tread on a nick **10.C.17b**
If you walk on a line **10.C.18a**
If you want to live and thrive **10.C.43**
If you wear blue **9.C.29b**
If you will bowl and never bat **10.E.2**
If your shorts get shorter **11.B.18**
I'm a bald-headed chicken with a feather in my hair **4.32c**
I'm a bald-headed chicken with a feather in my head **4.32g**
I'm a ballet chicken and I got no sense **4.32f**
I'm a Girl Guide, dressed in blue **6.A.26a**
I'm a little bubble car **6.A.32a**, **6.A.32b**
I'm a little bumper car **6.A.32a**, **6.A.32d**, **6.A.32f**
I'm a little China girl **12.C.7a**, **12.C.7b**
I'm a little Dutch girl, Dutch girl, Dutch girl **4.30a**, **4.30b**
I'm a little teapot, short and stout **12.B.15b**
I'm a little teapot, straight and stout **12.B.15a**
I'm a locked-up chicken, I'm a locked-up hen **4.32a**
I'm a London girl **4.40a**
I'm a one-legged chicken and I got no sense **4.32e**
I'm a sailor young and gay **4.62**
I'm a stuffed-up chicken and a knock-kneed hen **4.32d**
I'm a Texas girl **4.40b**
I'm educated Marmalade **11.I.34**
I'm not a pheasant plucker **11.B.14**
I'm only a poor little Ewing **11.I.51**
I'm Popeye the sailor man **7.13a**, **7.13c**, **7.13f**
I'm Popeye the sailor man, Whoo ooh! **7.13b**
I'm Shirley Temple **4.56a**, **4.56b**, **4.56d**
I'm sorry you missed the wrong turning **9.C.31a**
I'm taking home a little bumble bee **11.I.17**
I'm telling on you **9.B.14**
I'm the king of the swingers too **4.50**
Im pim, septipim **2.22**

Im pom pay, polonay, polonesky **5.6A**
Im stim, stammer bommer **2.21**
In 1966 **11.I.21A**
In 1974 **11.I.21B**
In a cottage in a wood **4.37**
In a dark, dark street **9.A.1A**
In and out the dusting bluebells **4.18B**
In and out the dusty bluebells **4.18A**
In Herefordshire, Hertford and Hampshire **11.B.15**
In prison you get coffee **7.20**
In the dark, dark world **9.A.1B**
Incy wincy spider, climbing up the spout **12.B.6**
Indian giver **9.C.43**
Ingle, spingle, spangle, One, two, three **6.A.1**
Injections **10.B.11**
Inky, pinky, perky, plum **2.19**
Inky, pinky, ponky **2.20**
Into the centre and nod your head **4.28A**
Ip, dip, ana ma da **2.36**
Ip, dip, dogs' shit **2.33**
Ip, dip, doo **2.34A**, **2.35**
Ip, dip, sky blue **2.30B**, **2.31**, **2.32**
Ip, dip, threepenny bit **2.30A**
Ipper dipper dation **2.5A**, **2.5B**
Ipswich Town are rubbish **12.A.5**
Ipsy wipsy spider, climbing up the spout **12.B.6**
(_____) is a nutter **9.C.24**
(_____) is crooked, (_____) is bent **9.C.25**
IT **3.A.1**
It's raining, it's pouring **11.I.49A**, **11.I.49B**

It went down my throat and round my heart **10.D.4D**
Ivag language **12.H.4**
I've been to Harlem **5.20**, **6.A.51**
I've got a daughter **4.39**

J

Jack and Jill went up the hill **8.D.42**
JACKS **3.K.1**
Jam tart, marmalade tart **6.A.58C**
Jelly on the plate, jelly on the plate **6.A.39**
Jenny got the measles, the measles, the measles **2.53**
Jerry and Jennifer went down to the dairy **11.I.31**
Jesus Christ, superstar **8.D.20A**, **8.D.20B**
Jimmy got drunk on a bottle of gin **4.60A**
Jingle bells, jingle bells **8.D.30A-C**
Jingle, jangle, centre spangle **6.B.2**
Jink, jink, pom, pink **2.18**
Jinx **10.B.12**
JOEY BEACON **3.A.20**
Johnny broke a bottle **5.11A**
Johnny went over the ocean **5.11B**
Johnny went riding **7.47**
Johnny went to church one day **11.I.25**
JOKES **11.K.1-38**
JOKES, VERBAL EXCHANGE **11.E.1-11.E.83**
JUMPING A SWINGING ROPE **3.C.2**
Just one cornetto **8.D.46**

K

K.P. penny a packet **7.21**
KARATE **3.F.13**
KARIMPA **3.D.3**
Keep the kettle boiling **6.A.6**
Keep your sunny side up, up **4.49A, 4.49B**
Kermit the Frog **11.I.50A, 11.I.50B**
Kick-me, Punch-me and Slap-me **9.B.12B**
KILLER SLAPSIES **3.F.10**
KING BALL **3.I.11**
KING OF THE CASTLE **3.F.6**
KING'S KEYS **3.N.13**
KING'S SQUARE **3.I.11**
KISS CHASE **3.D.7**
Knives **10.C.7**
Knobbly knees **9.C.8A**
KNOCK DOWN GINGER **3.M.1**
KNOCK KNOCK RIDDLES **11.D**
KNOCKOUT **3.H.1**
KNUCKLES **3.F.7**

L

L button trousers **11.J.20B**
Labels and jellyspoons **11.A.4A**
LADDERS **3.N.16**
Ladders **10.C.16**
Ladybird, ladybird, fly away **10.B.2D-G**
Ladybird, ladybird, fly away home **10.B.2A-C**
Ladybirds **10.C.45**
Land of soap and bubbles **8.D.12**
Lanky **9.C.6A**
Lanky legs **9.C.8B**
LEAP FROGS **3.C.5**
Leaves **10.C.47**
Left, left, left and right **12.E.1**
Legs **10.A.13, 10.C.3**
LETTERS **3.B.2**
Liar, liar, your pants on fire **9.C.34C**
Liar, liar, your tongue's on fire **9.C.34C**
(_____) likes coffee **6.A.31C**
LIMERICKS **11.H.1-11.H.33**
LINE HAD **3.A.2**
Little boys and their silly toys! **9.C.38**
Little drops of water **11.I.27**
Little Freddie Froggie **11.I.28**
Little Miss Muffet sat on a tuffet **8.D.34A, 8.D.34B**
Little Nell **6.A.7B**
Little nigger pulled a trigger **7.24B**
Liverpool fell down the drain **12.A.13**
Liverpool magic, Arsenal tragic! **12.A.24B**
Lofty **9.C.6B**
London Bridge is falling down **4.7A, 4.7B**
London County Council, L.C.C. **2.51**
Long distance lorry worry **11.B.5D**
Long legged Italy **11.A.7**
LONG SAUSAGE **3.A.15**
Look up, look down **9.D.24**
Look who's coming down the street **6.A.57**
Lords, ladies and jellyfish **11.A.4B**
Lou, Lou, skip to my Lou **4.23**
Lovely weather we're having tomorrow! **11.A.3B**
Love me, love me not **10.A.3D**
Lulu had a baby **11.I.24C**
Lulu was a Zulu **11.I.35**

M

M T G G **11.G.3**
Mack, Mack, Mack **5.15**
MAD BULLDOG **3.A.28**
MAD FOOTBALL **3.H.9**
Made you look, made you stare **9.D.23**A-C
Mademoiselle **6.A.7**A
Mademosel from Armenteers **4.28**B
Magpie, magpie, flutter and flee **10.B.3**
Magpies **10.A.4**
Make friends, make friends **10.D.5**B
Make it up, make it up **10.D.5**D, **10.D.5**E
Make up, make up **10.D.5**A, **10.D.5**C
Ma-ma-marmalade **11.I.47**
Manners, pianners, tables and chairs **9.D.16**
MARBLES **3.K.3**
Mario se fera **5.3**
Mary ate jam, Mary ate jelly **9.A.3**
Mary had a little dog **8.D.36**H
Mary had a little lamb **8.D.36**A-G
Mary, Mary, quite contrary **8.D.35**
Mary Morgan played the organ **7.41**
MATILDA **4.48**
Matthew, Mark, Luke and John **7.14**A
MEGGY PEGGY **3.B.11**
MERCY **3.F.8**
Mickey Mouse in his house **2.45**
Mickey Mouse is dead **6.A.49**
Milk, milk, lemonade **4.66**A
Milly Molly Mandy **5.19**
Mirrors **10.C.9**
MONDAY, TUESDAY **3.A.34**
Moses supposes his toesies are roses **11.B.25**
Mother calls me Archie **7.46**
MOTHER, MAY I? **3.B.1**
Mother's in the kitchen **6.A.43**A, **6.A.43**C
MR. TANGLE **3.E.2**
Mrs. Brown went to town **8.D.27**D
Mrs. M, Mrs. I, Mrs. S S I **11.G.6**
Mrs. Minny wore her pinny **7.15**
Mrs. Mop has a shop **2.25**
Mrs. Mop owned a shop **2.25**, **7.39**
Mrs. One goes in, Mrs. Two goes in **6.A.45**C
Mrs. Polly had a dolly **7.16**
Mrs. Rumble, apple crumble **7.17**
Mrs. Squirrel up the tree **6.A.13**
Mrs. White had a fright **7.22**A
My Aunt Daisy drives me crazy **6.A.8**A
My aunt, Greely Greely Greet **11.J.13**
My best colour's green, 'cause I love the Queen **10.C.28**
My boyfriend gave me an apple **5.5**A
My boyfriend gave me apples **5.5**B
My daddy's a lavatory cleaner **11.J.16**B
My dad's a banker **9.B.24**
My friend Billy **11.I.13**
My husband was a lavatory cleaner **11.J.16**A
My life is like a cabbage **12.C.3b**
My mama told me, comma, comma, full stop **5.14**
My mother is a baker, yum yum **5.16**B
My mother is a baker, yum yummy, yum yummy! **5.16**A

My mother said I never should **6.A.37A**, **6.A.37B**
My mum and your mum **2.11**
My mum's a secretary **7.23**
My name is (_____) and I've got freckles on my face **9.B.29**
My name is Chinky China **9.C.55**
My name is Dinah Dors **4.53B**
… My name is Elvis Presley **5.10C**, **5.10E**
My name is Sexy Sue **4.54A**
My name is Shirley Temple **4.56C**
My old man's a dustman **11.J.17A-D**
My ship sailed to China with a cargo of tea **4.44B**
My teacher's got a bunion **8.A.12**
My uncle's a dustman **11.J.17E**

N

Name play, Appearance or personality **9.E.5**
Name play, Rhymes **9.E.6**, **9.E.7**
Nelson, Nelson, lost one eye **6.A.30**
NETBALL **3.I.9**
New spelling **9.E.1**
Nicknames, Appearance or personality **9.E.5A**, **9.E.5B**
NICKNAMES FOR SCHOOL FOOD **8.B.6A-E**
Nicknames, Other first names **9.E.4**
Nicknames, Other surnames **9.E.3**
Nicknames, Rhyming **9.E.2**
Nigger, nigger, pull the trigger **7.24A**
nnnnnnnnnnnn Batman **11.I.2**
No more school tomorrow, no more school today **8.A.2C**
No wonder (_____)'s that thick **9.C.31C**
Nobody loves me, nobody cares **11.I.5A**
Nobody would listen to the Smurfs in prison **11.I.55**
Noddy has a little car **2.47**
NORTH, EAST, SOUTH, WEST **3.L.5**
Nose **10.A.14**
Not last night but the night before **6.A.36A-E**
NOUGHTS AND CROSSES **3.O.1**
November 5th **10.E.6**
Nullifying promises **10.B.6**
Number one, suck your thumb **6.A.34**
Number one, the story's just begun **11.J.18B**
Numbers **10.C.27**
Nuts **10.A.10**

O

O cha cha wa wa – a biscuit **4.61**
Oaths **10.B.4**
ODD PRANKS **3.M.3**
OFF GROUND TOUCH **3.A.13**
Oh dear what can the matter be? **8.D.9A**, **8.D.9B**
Oh how shocking! **11.I.4**
Oh Semina, Semina **4.57D**
Oi, you in the red **9.C.29A**
Old King Cole was a merry old soul **8.D.43**
Old Macdonald had a farm **8.D.23**
Old Mother Hubbard **6.A.44**
Old Mother Jelly Belly lived at number nine **11.I.37**
Old Mrs. Peepses **10.D.1C**

INDEX **825**

Oliver Oglethorpe ogled an owl and an oyster **11.B.11**
Oliver, Oliver, Oliver Twist **7.25A**
Oliver Twist, Oliver Twist **7.25B**
Olly, olly, olly! **11.I.40**
Om pom vee, diddlee, diddle ishu **5.6B**
On a mountain stands a lady **6.A.59**
ON IT ON THE LINE **3.A.2**
ON IT ON THE LINE (WITH BALL) **3.A.3**
ON MY HOLIDAY **3.N.6**
On top of a sandpit **8.A.7**
On top [of] Old Smoky **8.D.14B**
On top of spaghetti **8.D.14A**
Once upon a barren moor **11.B.12**
Once you give you can't have back **9.C.42D**
One banana, two banana, three banana, four **2.12C**
One bright morning in the middle of the night **11.A.1**
One bright morning when the moon was high **11.A.2**
One day he gave me peaches **5.5C**
One for sorrow **10.A.4A**
One for the ice cream **10.A.4B**
ONE HE ALL HE **3.A.14**
One little piggy went to market **12.B.4B**
One man went to mow **11.J.9**
One more day at school **8.A.2A**, **8.A.2B**
One potato, two potato **2.12A**, **2.12B**
One to get ready **3.B.i**, **3.B.ii**
One, two, buckle my shoe **7.29**
One, two, three **11.I.1**
One, two, three a-lairy **7.26A**, **7.26B**

One, two, three and upsie **7.35**
One, two, three, Auntie Lulu **6.A.8B**
One, two, three, four **8.A.6**
ONE, TWO, THREE, FOUR, FIVE **3.A.9**
One, two, three, four, five **12.B.13A**, **12.B.13B**
One, two, three, four, five, six, seven **2.2**
ONE, TWO, THREE (THUMB WRESTLING) **3.F.9**
One, two, three together **5.8**
One's a wish **10.A.5A**
Only the crumbliest flakiest chocolate **8.D.45**
Onward Christian soldiers **8.D.6A**, **8.D.6B**
… Oo ee ah ha ha **5.10B**
Ooey gooey was a worm **11.A.12**
Open your mouth and shut your eyes **12.B.2A**
Orange balls, orange balls **4.33**
Oranges and lemons **4.20**
Oranges, lemons, two for a penny **7.12**
Our school dinners, our school dinners **8.B.2A**
Out in Arizona where the cowboys are **4.58**
Over the garden wall **7.27**
Over the moon and under the moon **6.A.10**
Over the moon and under the stars **6.A.10**
Over Scotland Yard **7.34C**
Oxfam **9.C.28B**
OXO **3.K.4A-D**

P

P.K. penny a packet **7.21**
P language **12.H.5**
Palm of the hand **10.A.11**
Pardon me for being rude **10.D.4A**, **10.D.4B**
PASS THE LEMON **3.N.7**
PAT BALL **3.I.10**
Patsy Boop done a poop **11.I.43A**
Paving stones **10.C.17**, **10.C.18**
PEEP BEHIND THE CURTAIN **3.B.6**
Pepsi Cola, Pepsi Cola, up **6.A.35**
Peter, Peter, pumpkin eater **6.A.3B**
Peter picked a packet of prawn pasta **11.B.1B**
Peter Piper picked a peck of pickled pepper **11.B.1A**
Pick it **11.I.36**
Pig Latin **12.H.1A-C**
PIGGY-BACK FIGHTS **3.F.1**
PIGGY BEHIND THE CURTAIN **3.B.6**
PIGGY IN THE MIDDLE **3.I.6**
Pinch and a punch, join in the ring **9.B.7F**
Pinch, punch, first day of the month **9.B.7E**
Pink panther picked a perfect posy of pansies **11.B.8**
Pinocchio **9.C.1A**
Pins **10.C.10**
Plainsie, Billy Balloo **7.34D**
Plainsie, clapsie **7.33**
Plainsie Jim, swallowed a pin **7.31**
Plainsie Mrs. Brown **7.34B**
Plainsie to America **7.32**
Play on Millwall **12.A.18**
Please keep off the grass, sir **8.A.4**
Please Miss **7.37A**, **7.37B**
Please Mother, may I go out to play? **4.22**
PLEASE MR. CROCODILE/MR. BUMBLEBEE **3.A.33**
Please Nanny Granny may we go out to play? **4.22B**
Please, please!/Bread and cheese **9.D.28**
Plum stones **10.A.6**
POISON **3.A.17**
POISON FINGER **3.A.17**
Policeman, policeman, Hullo! Hullo! **8.A.13E**
Polish it **9.B.23B**
POLO **3.B.12**
Poor Jenny is a-weeping **4.16**
POOR PUSSY **3.N.5**
POP GOES THE WEASEL **4.65**
Popeye the sailor man **7.13D**, **7.13E**
Pounds, shillings and pence **8.A.8**
Pratty Annie, Pratty Annie **9.C.17**
PRETEND FIGHTING/WARS/FIGHTS **3.F.11**
Prince Charming, Prince Charming **8.A.17**
Punch and Judy fought for a pie **11.I.22B**
Punch and Judy had a race **11.I.22A**
PUSHING OFF THE BENCHES **3.F.2**
PUZZLES **11.G.1-11.G.7**

Q

Q.P.R. **12.A.23**
Quee-ee-nie, Quee-ee-nie, Quee-ee-nie-I **4.9B**
Queenie, Queenie Caroline **7.38**

Queenie, Queenie, who's got the ball? **4.9A**
QUESTIONS **3.N.9**

R
Rabbits **10.B.7**
Racial epithets **9.C.47**
Racing car number nine **2.4A, 6.A.33**
Rain, rain, go away **10.B.1A-D**
Reading, Writing, Arithmetic **8.A.11**
Ready **3.B.iii, 3.B.iv**
Red and yellow custard **8.B.3B**
RED, GOLD AND GREEN **2.60, 3.B.10**
Red leather, yellow leather **11.B.5B**
Red lorry, yellow lorry **11.B.5A**
RED RIVER **9.B.21**
Red Rose, picked her nose **6.A.14**
RED ROVER **3.F.4**
Red welly, yellow welly **11.B.5C**
RELEASE **3.A.19**
Rhyming nicknames **9.E.2**
Rhyming slang **12.I**
RIDDLES **11.C**
Rin-Tin-Tin swallowed a pin **7.30**
Ring a ring a roses **4.13**
Robin Hood and all his men **8.D.16**
Robin Hood, Robin Hood, riding through the trees **8.D.17**
ROLLER COASTER **3.E.1**
Roses are red **5.21, 8.D.44A-C, 9.C.1C, 9.C.13A-C, 9.C.21A-I, 9.C.31D, 12.C.1A-G**
Rosy apple, lemon tart **6.A.58A**
Rosy, Rosy **12.F.1B**
Rosy, Rosy, how do you do? **2.49**
ROTTEN EGG **3.A.7**

Round and round the apple pie **2.8**
Round and round the bushes **2.7B**
Round and round the butter dish **2.7A**
Round and round the corner **12.B.3**
Round and round the garden **12.B.3**
ROUNDERS **3.J.1**
Row, row gently down the stream **8.A.14**
Row, row, row your boat **4.8**
Royal Mail, one, two, three **9.B.9**
RUGBY **3.H.15**
Rule Britannia **7.48**
RUN OUTS **3.D.8**
Running down the highway **11.I.3A**

S
S-W-A-L-K **12.C.8**
Sabrina, Sabrina **4.57A, 4.57C**
Sal-o-me, Sal-o-me **4.57B**
Salt **10.C.6**
Salt, vinegar, mustard, pepper **6.A.18**
Sam, Sam, dirty old man **9.C.19A**
Sam, Sam, the dirty man **9.C.19B**
SARDINES **3.D.9, 3.I.5**
SAUSAGES **3.N.4**
Scaredy cat, scaredy cat **9.C.36A, 9.C.36B**
SCATTIE **3.A.28**
SCHOOL HUMOUR **8.A.20A, 8.A.20B**
SCHOOL MEALS HUMOUR **8.B.5A-E**
SEA AND FISHES **3.N.15**
SEA, SKY, EARTH **3.B.16**
Sealing bargains **10.B.8**

Seashells, cockle shells **6.A.53B**, **9.A.9C**, **11B.3B**
See a pin and pick it up **10.C.10A**
See my finger, see my thumb **9.B.5**
See no evil, hear no evil **10.D.3**
See-saw, see-saw, sitting on a see-saw **9.A.9B**
See, see my baby **5.17B**, **5.17D**
See, see my brownie **5.17**
See, see my mama **5.17C**
See, see my playmate **5.17A**
See this wet, see this dry **10.B.4D**
Seven little girls, sitting in the back row **4.59**
SEVENSIES **3.C.3**, **7.36A**
Shamerla, my darling **4.61**
… she did **9.D.8**
She'll be coming round the mountain when she comes **11.J.4**
She loves me **10.A.3A**
She sells seashells on the seashore **11.B.3A**
She wears red feathers and a hula-hula skirt **4.34**
SHEEP AND WOLVES **3.A.31**
SHIPS, SHARKS AND TORPEDOES **3.B.14**
SHIP, SHORE, DECK **3.B.15**
Shirley Temple is a star **7.42**
Shoes **10.C.4**
Shooting star **10.C.51**
Show off, show off **9.C.45**
Shut up! **9.D.4A-D**
Silence in the courtyard **9.D.17B**
Silence in the gallery **9.D.17A**
SIMPLE SIMON SAYS **3.N.14**
Sir Humphrey de Willoughby Cox **11.H.11**

Six sick sheikhs **11.B.13**
Skinamalinky long legs **6.A.12**
Skip a Lulu, skip a Lulu **6.A.25**
SKIP TO MY LOU **4.23**
SKITTLEBALL **3.J.2**
Slap, slap, heavily on thigh **8.D.3**
SLAPSIES **3.F.10**
SMACK RACE **3.A.11**
Smart moccasins **9.C.30C**
Smarty boots **9.C.30B**
SMASH **3.H.2**
Smelly socks stink **11.B.9**
Smith's Crisps are the best **6.A.11**
Snot and bogey custard pie **8.B.3A**
So? **9.D.1**
So call in my (_____ _____) **6.A.61A**
So come in (_____ _____, _____ _____, _____ _____) **6.A.61B**
Sorry, it's against my religion **9.D.12**
SPACE INVADERS **3.H.12**, **3.O.3**
SPAM **3.G.3**
Spiders **10.C.42**, **10.C.43**
Spurs are on their way to Wembley **12.A.11**
SQUASH **3.H.2**
Staircases **10.C.12**
STALKY **3.N.13**
Stand up, stand up for Jesus **12.A.7**
Stare, stare; over there **9.D.22**
STATUES **3.B.7**
Step back Charlie, Charlie, Charlie **4.53B**
Stick a needle in my heart **10.B.5G**
Sticks and stones can't break my bones **9.B.8**
Sticks and stones will break my bones **9.D.33**
STICKY TOFFEE **3.A.15**

STING BALL **3.A.6**
STING UPS **3.A.6**
STINGIE **3.A.6**
STOOLBALL **3.J.3**
STUCK IN THE MUD **3.A.19**
SUBJECTS **3.A.8**
Susie had a baby **5.9B, 11.I.24B**
Sussed out? **9.D.27**
Swinging McClintock **12.A.20**
Swopsie, swopsie **9.C.42C**

T

T-L-E (true love forever) **12.C.9**
Ta ra ra boom de ay **8.D.19A**
TAG **3.A.1**
Talking to me or chewing a brick **9.B.1**
TALLEST BUILDING **3.L.2**
Tap out a boy's (girl's) name **9.B.27**
Tarzan in the jungle **2.9A**
Taxi **10.C.19**
Tea for one, the story's just begun **11.J.19**
Teacher, teacher, don't be dumb **8.A.13A-C**
Teacher, teacher, Humpty Dumpty **8.A.13D**
Teacher, teacher, it's not fair **8.A.18**
Teacher's kind, teacher's gentle **8.A.15**
Teacher's pet, teacher's pet **9.C.41A**
Teddy Bear, Teddy Bear, turn around **6.A.40**
Teddy Bear, Teddy Bear, turn right round **6.A.40**
Teeth **10.C.1**
Telecom van **10.C.21**
Tell me a story **12.F.1A**

Tell tale tit **9.C.33A, 9.C.33B**
Ten sticks of dynamite hanging on the wall **8.D.11A, 8.D.11B**
Ten, twenty, thirty, forty, fifty or more **11.I.29A, 11.I.29B**
TENNIS **3.J.6**
TENNIS SQUASH **3.I.2**
TENSIES **7.36B**
That's my name, don't wear it out **9.D.11**
(_____ the _____) **9.C.16**
The admiral was the first to jump, the last to hit the ground **11.J.11**
The big black bug **11.B.7**
The big ship sails on the Allee-allee-o **4.19B**
The big ship sails too slow, too slow **4.19C**
The boy stood on the burning deck **8.D.31A**
The farmer's in his den **4.10A, 4.10B**
The good ship sails on the Allee-allee-o **4.19A**
The grand old Duke of York **4.11**
The grass is green **2.28**
THE HOKEY POKEY **4.4**
The last one to say "frazzles" did it **9.D.18D**
The one who denied it, supplied it **9.D.18B**
The one who smelt it, dealt it **9.D.18A**
The ragged rascal ran round the rugged rock **11.B.22**
The rain makes all things beautiful **9.C.12**
THE RED BRIDGE **9.B.21**

… The rolling pin was made of glass **6.A.36B**
The second sign of madness is hairs on the palm of your hand **9.B.17**
The super steamship sank in the sink **11.B.19B**
The super steamship (was) sunk in the sea **1.B.19A**
The Tunnel of Death **3.A.8.i**
The Tunnel of Love **3.A.8.i**
The yellow rose of Texas **8.D.26**
There came from Mars, E.T. **11.I.52**
There came three dukes a-riding **4.1C**
There he sat in his vapour **11.I.45**
There is a little breath of air **11.I.19**
There it was I met my Susie **11.J.14**
There was a cannibal called Ned **11.H.32**
There was a dead frog in the road **9.A.25A**
There was a girl called (____) **9.E.6C**
There was a girl from Italy **4.45**
There was a little man **11.I.14**
There was a man from Darjeeling **11.H.4**
There was a man from outer space **11.H.26**
There was a man who had a dog **4.5**
There was a small fishy called Pinkie **11.H.30**
There was a young gardener of Leeds **11.H.1**
There was a young lady from Gloucester **11.H.21**
There was a young lady from Spa **11.H.22**
There was a young lady from Wales **11.H.17**
There was a young lady of Lynn **11.H.3**
There was a young lady of Ryde **11.H.8**
There was a young lady of Tottenham **11.H.7**
There was a young man called Bloggs **11.H.18**
There was a young man called Glosp **11.H.33**
There was a young man from Bengal **11.H.2**
There was a young man from Dumbarton **11.H.14**
There was a young man named Babitts **11.H.31**
There was a young man named Flop **11.H.28**
There was a young sergeant called Edsir **11.H.9**
There was a young twin called Hannah **11.H.29**
There was an old lady from Spain **11.H.16**
There was an old lady of Crete **11.H.13**
There was an old lady of ninety two **8.D.18B**
There was an old lady of Spain **11.H.15**
There was an old man from Brazil **11.H.10**
There was an old man from Dundee **11.H.12**
There was an old man from Fife **11.H.23**

There was an old man from Havana **11.H.25**
There was an old man named Michael Finnegan **11.J.3**
There was an old man who lived in a pram **11.I.46**
There was an old person of Fife **11.H.24**
There was an old woman from Ealing **11.H.5**
There was an old woman who lived in a shoe **8.D.33**
There was (_____) standing in the snow **9.C.26**
There were ten green bottles hanging on the wall **11.J.6**
There were ten in a bed **4.27**
There were two horses in a field … **9.A.17**
There's a boat leaving for Calais today **9.C.53**
There's a cop, cop, copper on the corner of the street **11.I.44**
There's a hole in your back … **9.B.26**
There's a jungle in his hair **9.C.4D**
There's a knock-kneed (bow-legged) chicken and a back-boned hen **4.32B**
There's a man in Spain **11.I.12**
There's a monkey in the grass **2.27B**
There's a party on the hill **2.24**
There's a place in France **11.I.11**
There's a soldier on the grass **2.27A**
There's a tiny house **4.43**
There's a worm at the bottom of the garden **11.I.16**
There's someone under the bed **6.A.38**
There's something in my nappy **11.I.38**
Thin as a lamp-post **9.C.9**
This is number one, and the story's just begun **11.J.18A**
This little piggy went to market **12.B.4A**
This old man, he played one **12.B.16**
This way Valerie, that way Valerie **4.53A**
THREE AND IN **3.H.5**
THREE BAD EGGS **3.A.8**
Three little angels all dressed in white **11.J.7A**
Three little devils all dressed in red **11.J.7B**
Three, six, nine, the goose drank wine **5.13**
THREE, TWO, ONE **3.H.3**
Three white horses in a stable **6.A.47**
THUMB BALL **3.H.8**
Tiddly Winks old man **11.I.10**
TIN CAN TOLLY **3.D.5**
Ting-ling-ling **8.A.10**
Tinker, tailor, soldier, sailor **10.A.6A**, **10.A.6B**
Titch **9.C.7B**
Too much Guantanabeera **8.D.25**
Tottenham, Tottenham **12.A.17**
Touch black **9.C.42E**
Touching wood **10.B.10**
Tra la la boom de ay **8.D.19B**
Treading on holes in pavements **10.C.18D**
Treading on lines unlucky **10.C.18E**
TREASURE HUNT **3.L.4**
Trick or treat **10.E.5**
Truck **10.C.20**

TRUE DARE, DOUBLE DARE, LOVE, KISS OR PROMISE **3.L.6**
Tulips in the garden **9.C.51**
Tuppence on the water **2.3**
… Turn my back to the fairy queen **6.A.26D**
… Turn right round to the L.C.C. **6.A.26E**
Turn the dirty dish cloth **2.41**
'Twas in a restaurant they met **11.A.5**
Twinkle, twinkle, little star **8.D.32**
… Twist right round to the fairy queen **6.A.26C**
Two, four, six and a quarter **8.C.7**
Two, four, six, eight **8.C.6a**, **8.C.6B**
Two in a hammock attempted a kiss **12.C.5**
Two little blackbirds sat upon a wall **12.B.5**
Two little cars **12.C.6**
Two little men in a flying saucer **6.A.50**
Two little sausages, frying in the pan **6.A.23**
TWO TOUCH FOOTBALL **3.H.7**

U

Umbrellas **10.C.14**
Under and over, Casanova **6.A.20**
Under the apple tree **7.40**
Under the brown bush **5.11C**, **5.12**
Underneath the spreading chestnut tree **4.51**
University Boat Race **10.E.3**
Up in Aberdeen **7.6**
Up in the North, a long way off **6.A.24**
Up to Mississippi **6.A.42B**
Upsie Mrs. Dee **7.34A**

V

Valentine's Day **10.E.1**, **10.E.2**
Victorious! Victorious! **11.J.15**
VINEGAR, MUSTARD, PEPPER **3.B.3**
VOLLEYBALL **3.I.8**
Vote, vote, vote, for (_____ _____) **6.A.41A**
Vote, vote, vote, for little (_____) **6.A.41B-D**

W

Walk on the lines **10.C.18B**
Walking through the jungle **2.9B**
WALL/SQUARE/BASE **3.I.3**
Wash the dishes, dry the dishes **2.42**
Wash those dirty faces **4.48**
WATER FIGHTING **3.F.12**
Way down South where bananas grow **11.I.8**
We are red men tall and quaint **11.J.5**
We are the boys in red and white **8.C.2**
We are the Deptford girls **4.35**
We are the (nickname for school) **8.C.4A**
We break up, we break down **8.A.1A**, **8.A.1B**
We hate (name of another school) **8.C.8**
We hate Tottenham Hotspur **12.A.4**

We have joy, we have fun **12.A.19**
We love you, Beatles, oh yes we do **11.I.57**
We three kings of Leicester Square **8.D.4A**
We three kings of Orient are **8.D.4B-D**
We went to the animal fair **11.J.2**
We won the war in 1984 **8.C.1**
Weakling **9.C.40A**
Wee Willy Winkle runs through the town **12.B.8**
WEMBLEY **3.H.4**
Went a-walking through the London zoo **11.I.26**
We're all marching for the army **8.C.3**
We're forever blowing bubbles **12.A.9**
We're in the Air Force now **11.I.9**
What? **9.D.2**
What are little girls made of? **12.B.9**
What are you doing? **9.D.26**
What are you looking at? **9.D.20A**, **9.D.20B**
What can you do, Punchinello, little fellow? **4.29**
What do you do when you need to do a poo **11.J.21A**
What do you do when you need to go to loo **11.J.21A**
What hand do you use to wipe your bum with? **9.A.15**
What is the difference between a weasel, a stoat and a monkey? **9.A.8**
What's frozen water? **9.A.13**
What's the time? **9.D.29A-D**, **9.D.30A**, **9.D.30B**

WHAT'S THE TIME, MR. CLOCK? **3.A.18**
WHAT'S THE TIME, MR. CROCODILE? **3.A.18**
WHAT'S THE TIME, MR. WOLF? **3.A.18**
What's the worst thing you can get in a second-hand shop? **9.A.14**
What's your favourite animal? **9.A.6**
What's your name? **9.A.5**, **9.D.31A**, **9.D.31B**
When (_____) comes to Wembley **12.A.10**
When (girl's name) was younger **9.C.50**
When grandmama met grandpapa **4.36**
When I was one I sucked my thumb **7.45A**, **7.45C**, **7.45D**
When I was one I'd just begun **7.45B**
When I went up in a yellow balloon **7.28**
When Mary was a baby, a baby, a baby **4.2B**
When Susie was a baby **4.2A**
When the reds go marching in **12.A.8**
When the war was over **7.44**
When you're old and your face goes purple **12.C.4**
Where are you all coming from? **11.I.54**
Where do you live? **9.D.32A**, **9.D.32B**
Where is it? **9.B.27**
Where you going, Bob? **11.I.6**
Where's the chocolate? **9.A.7**
Whether the weather be cold **11.B.6**

While shepherds cooked their supper by night **8.D.5c**
While shepherds washed their socks by night **8.D.5a**
While shepherds watched their flocks by night **8.D.5b**
Whistle while we work **8.D.13b**
Whistle while you work **8.D.13a**
White Hart Lane is falling down **12.A.6**
White rabbits **10.B.7a**, **10.B.7b**
Who do you think you're looking at? **9.D.21**
Who has stole my watch and chain? **4.6**
Who let Polly out of prison? **9.D.18c**
Who stole the apples from the greengrocer's shop? **5.18b**
Who stole the bread from the baker's shop? **5.18b**
Who stole the cookies from the cookery stall? **5.18a**
Who stole the cookies from the cookie jar? **5.18c**
Who stole the cookies from the Kookaburra shop? **5.18a**
Who's a posh boy? **9.C.28a**
Who's a posh girl? **9.C.28a**
Who's she, the cat's mother? **9.D.8**
Who's that? **11.I.33**
Whose shoes are the cleanest? **2.37**
Why are we waiting? **12.A.21**
WINK **3.N.11**
WINK MURDER **3.N.12**
WINKING MURDER **3.N.12**
Winnie the witch fell down the ditch **7.43**

Wishes **10.C.30**
Wood **10.A.7**
Wouldn't it, wouldn't it **11.A.6**

Y

Y Y U R **11.G.2**
Yankee Doodle rode to town **8.D.27b**
Yankee Doodle stayed at home **8.D.27c**
Yankee Doodle went to town **8.D.27a**
YES HARRY **3.N.8**
You can have fresh fried fish **11.B.17**
You can't put your muck in my dustbin **2.55**
You can't stand it with (_____) **9.C.10e**
You cow! **9.D.9a**
You go to Mothercare **9.C.27b**
You go to Tesco's **9.C.27a**
You have your hand in a sort of tube shape ... **9.B.19**
You know what thought did? **9.D.5a**
You liar, you liar **9.C.34a**, **9.C.34b**
You look like a pig's backside **9.C.14a**
You look like a pig's rear end **9.C.14b**
You pig! **9.D.9b**
You put the hand of a person, palm upwards ... **9.B.20**
You put your fist on the palm of your hand ... **9.B.18**
You put your right arm in **4.4**
You said the rhyme, so you did the crime **9.D.19**
You think you're cool **9.C.44b**

You think you're fly **9.C.44A**
You were made with two bricks short **9.C.31B**
You'd better not … **9.B.10**
You'll never get to heaven in an old Ford car **11.J.8**
You're an Indian giver! **9.C.43**
You're chicken **9.D.6**
You're flash **9.C.44C**
You're teacher's pet … **9.C.41B**
Your money or your life **9.B.4**
Your nose is so long … **9.C.1B**
Your shoelace is undone **9.B.16**
Your shoes need cleaning **2.39**
Your teeth are like stars … **9.C.2B**
You've got sawdust in your head **9.D.10**
Yum, yum, bubblegum **2.58**

Z
ZOMBIE **3.G.1**

FSC
www.fsc.org
MIX
Papier aus ver-
antwortungsvollen
Quellen
Paper from
responsible sources
FSC® C141904

**Druck:
Customized Business Services GmbH
im Auftrag der KNV-Gruppe
Ferdinand-Jühlke-Str. 7
99095 Erfurt**